Global Business Today

Titles in International Business and Economics

Appleyard and Field,
International Economics,
Second Edition, 1995

Ball and McCulloch,
International Business:
Introduction and Essentials,
Sixth Edition, 1996

Bartlett and Ghoshal,
Transnational Management: Text Cases and
Readings in Cross-Border Management,
Second Edition, 1995

Beamish, Killing, Lecraw, and Crookell,
International Management: Text and Cases,
Third Edition, 1997

Bornstein,
Comparative Economic Systems:
Models and Cases,
Seventh Edition, 1993

Cateora,
International Marketing,
Ninth Edition, 1996

Grosse and Kujawa,
International Business:
Theory and Managerial Applications,
Third Edition, 1995

Lindert and Pugel,
International Economics,
Tenth Edition, 1996

Mueller, Gernon, and Meek,
Accounting: An International Perspective,
Fourth Edition, 1997

Robock and Simmonds,
International Business and the
Multinational Enterprise,
Fourth Edition, 1989

Hill,
International Business:
Competing in the Global Marketplace,
Second Edition, 1997

Hodgetts and Luthaus,
International Management,
Third Edition, 1997

Global Business Today

Charles W. L. Hill
University of Washington

**Irwin
McGraw-Hill**

Boston, Massachusetts   Burr Ridge, Illinois   Dubuque, Iowa
Madison, Wisconsin   New York, New York   San Francisco, California   St. Louis, Missouri

Irwin/McGraw-Hill

*A Division of The **McGraw·Hill** Companies*

GLOBAL BUSINESS TODAY

This book is printed on acid-free paper.

1 2 3 4 5 6 7 8 9 0 VNH/VNH 9 0 9 8 7

ISBN 0-256-21431-X

Vice president and Editorial director: *Michael W. Junior*
Publisher: *Craig S. Beytien*
Sponsoring editor: *Patrice Schmitt*
Senior developmental editor: *Laura Hurst Spell*
Editorial assistant: *Matt McGuire*
Marketing manager: *Kenyetta Giles*
Project manager: *Jim Labeots*
Production supervisor: *Lori Koetters*
Senior designer: *Crispin Prebys*
Photo research coordinator: *Sharon Miller*
Compositor: *York Graphic Services, Inc.*
Typeface: *10/12 New Aster*
Printer: *Von Hoffman Press, Inc.*

Library of Congress Cataloging-In-Publication Data
Hill, Charles W. L.
  Global business today / Charles W. L. Hill.—1st ed.
    p. cm.
  Includes bibliographical references and index.
  ISBN 0-256-21431-X
  1. International business enterprises—Management.
2. International trade. 3. Investments, Foreign. 4. Capital market. I. Title.
  HD62.4.H548 1998
  658'.049—dc21   97-11584

INTERNATIONAL EDITION
Copyright ©1998. Exclusive rights by The McGraw-Hill Companies, Inc. for manufacture and export. This book cannot be re-exported from the country to which it is consigned by McGraw-Hill.
The International edition is not available in North America.

When ordering the title, use ISBN 0-07-115325-X.

http://www.mhhe.com

**For June and Mike Hill,
my parents**

About the Author

Charles W. L. Hill is the Hughes M. Blake Professor of International Business at the School of Business, University of Washington. Professor Hill received his Ph.D. in industrial organization economics in 1983 from the University of Manchester's Institute of Science and Technology (UMIST) in Britain. In addition to the University of Washington, he has served on the faculties of UMIST, Texas A&M University, and Michigan State University.

Professor Hill has published over 40 articles in peer-reviewed academic journals. He has also published two college textbooks, one on strategic management and the other on international business. Professor Hill serves on the editorial boards of several academic journals and previously served as consulting editor at the *Academy of Management Review*.

Professor Hill teaches in the MBA and executive MBA programs at the University of Washington and has received awards for teaching excellence in both programs. He has also taught on several customized executive programs.

Preface

Global Business Today is intended for the first international business course at the undergraduate level. My goals in writing this book have been to produce a work that (1) is comprehensive and up-to-date, (2) goes beyond the uncritical presentation and shallow explanation of the body of knowledge, (3) maintains a tight integrated flow between chapters, (4) focuses on managerial implications, and (5) makes important theories accessible and interesting to students.

COMPREHENSIVE AND UP-TO-DATE

To be comprehensive, an international business textbook must:

- Introduce students to the process of globalization and the implications of globalization for business firms and their managers.
- Explain how and why the world's countries differ.
- Present a thorough review of the economies and policies of international trade and investment.
- Examine the different strategies that businesses can adopt to compete in the global mar-

ketplace and enter specific foreign markets.

- Explore the role played by marketing, operations, and human resource management within an international business.

This textbook does all of these things. Comprehensiveness and relevance also require coverage of major theories. Although many international business texts do a reasonable job of reviewing long-established theories, they tend to ignore or gloss over important newer works such as:

- The new trade theory and strategic trade policy.
- Michael Porter's theory of the competitive advantage of nations.
- Robert Reich's work on national competitive advantage.
- The new growth theory championed by Paul Romer and Gene Grossman.
- The work of Douglass North and others on national institutional structures and the protection of property rights.
- The market imperfections approach to foreign direct investment that has grown out of Ronald Coase and Oliver Williamson's work on transaction cost economics.

- Bartlett and Ghoshal's research on the transnational corporation.
- The writings of C. K. Prahalad and Gary Hamel on core competencies, global competition, and global strategic alliances.

The failure of many books to discuss such work is a serious deficiency considering how influential these theories have become, not just in academic circles, but also in the world at large. A major proponent of strategic trade policy, Laura Tyson, served for a time as chairperson of President Clinton's Council of Economic Advisors. Robert Reich served as Secretary of Labor in the Clinton administration. Ronald Coase won the 1992 Nobel Prize in economics, giving the market imperfections approach new respectability. Two years later, Douglass North won the Nobel Prize in economics for his work showing how a nation's economic history influences its contemporary institutions and property rights regime. The work of Bartlett, Ghoshal, Hamel, and Prahalad is having an important impact on business practices.

I have incorporated all relevant state-of-the-art work at the appropriate points in this book. For example, in Chapter 2, "Country Differences in Political Economy," reference is made to the new growth and the work of North and others on national institutional structures and property rights. In Chapter 4, "International Trade Theory," in addition to such standard theories as the theory of comparative advantage and the Heckscher-Ohlin theory, there is detailed discussion of the new trade theory and Porter's theory of national competitive advantage. In Chapter 5, "The Global Trading System," the pros and cons of strategic trade policy are discussed. In Chapter 6, "Foreign Direct Investment," the market imperfections approach is reviewed. Chapter 10, which deals with the strategy of global business, draws extensively on the work of Bartlett, Ghoshal, Hamel, and Prahalad.

In addition to the inclusion of leading edge theory, in light of the fast changing nature of the global economy and global trading system every effort is being made to ensure that this book is up-to-date as possible when it goes to press. A significant amount has happened in the world since the early 1990s, all of which is discussed in the text. In 1994 the Uruguay Round of GATT negotiations was successfully concluded and the World Trade Organization was established. Since then, the WTO has emerged as a major

player in the global trading system. For example, in 1997 it brokered a landmark deal to remove barriers to cross-border trade and investment in the global telecommunications industry, and it now looks like the WTO may broker the same kind of deal in the financial services industry. The European Union continues to move forward with its post 1992 agenda to achieve a closer economic and monetary union, including plans to establish a common currency by 1999. The North American Free Trade Agreement passed into law in 1994, and Chile has indicated its desire to become the next member of the free trade area. The Asian Pacific Economic Cooperation forum (APEC) has recently emerged as the kernel of a possible future Asia Pacific free trade area. The former communist states of Eastern Europe and Asia continue down the road to economic and political reform. As they do, so the euphoric mood that followed the collapse of communism in 1989 has been slowly replaced with a growing sense of realism about the hard path ahead for many of these countries. The global money market continues its meteoric growth. By 1996 over $1.2 trillion per day was flowing across national borders. The size of such flows fueled concern about the ability of short term speculative shifts in global capital markets to destabilize the world

economy. These fears were fanned by the well publicized financial problems of a number of organizations that traded derivations through the medium of a global money market, such as Baring's Bank. The world wide web has emerged from nowhere to become the backbone of an emerging global network for electronic commerce. The world economy has become more global. Several Asian Pacific economies, including most notably China, are growing their economies at a rapid rate. New multinationals are emerging from developing nations in addition to the world's established industrial powers. And increasingly, the globalization of the world economy is impacting on a wide range of firms of all sizes, from the very large to the very small. Reflecting this rapid pace change, in this book I have tried to ensure that all material and statistics are as up to date as possible as of 1997.

BEYOND UNCRITICAL PRESENTATION AND SHALLOW EXPLANATION

Many issues in global business are complex and thus necessitate considerations of pros and cons. To demonstrate this to students, I have adopted a critical approach that presents the arguments for and against economic theories, government policies, business strategies, and so on.

Related to this, I have attempted to explain the complexities of the many theories and phenomena unique to global business so that the student might fully comprehend the statements of a theory or the reasons that a phenomenon is the way it is. These theories and phenomena are typically explained in more depth in this book than they are in competing textbooks. The rationale being that a shallow explanation is little better than no explanation. In the world of global business, a little knowledge is indeed a dangerous thing.

INTEGRATED PROGRESSION OF TOPICS

Many textbooks lack a tight integrated flow of topics from chapter to chapter. In this book students are told in Chapter 1 how the various sections of the book relate to each other. Integration has been achieved by organizing the material so that each chapter builds on the material of the previous one in a logical fashion.

Chapter 1 is principally concerned with a discussion of the causes of consequences of the globalization of the world economy. The last section of this chapter asks "what does the shift towards a global economy mean for managers within an international business?" Much of the rest of the

book is devoted to answering this question. Chapters 2 and 3 explore how countries differ from each other with regard to their political, economic, legal, and cultural institutions. This is followed by a block of four chapters (Chapters 4 to 7) that look at the international trade and investment environment within which international businesses must operate. After this section, there are two chapters (Chapters 8 and 9) that review the international monetary system. These chapters focus on the nature of the foreign exchange market and the emerging global monetary system. The book closes with a group of five chapters (Chapters 10 to 14) that explore in detail the strategies and operating policies of international businesses. By the time the student has completed this book, they should have a good grasp of the issues that managers working within international businesses have to grapple with on a daily basis, and they should be familiar with the range of strategies and operating policies that managers can adopt in order to compete more effectively in today's rapidly emerging global economy.

Throughout the book, the relationship of new material to topics discussed in earlier chapters is pointed out to the students to reinforce their understanding of how the material comprises an integrated whole. Each chapter also contains sever-

al structural features designed to help students. A set of **objectives** at the start of the chapter provides an overview of the chapter's contents and of the concepts and skills students will be expected to learn. An end-of-chapter summary is then linked to these learning objectives, assuring continuity in the learning process. Throughout the chapter **key terms** and definitions are highlighted in the margins, followed by a list of the key terms with page references at the chapter's end. In addition to the closing case and discussion questions mentioned above, the end matter of the chapter also includes two other features which help students go beyond simple memorization of text concepts: a set of **critical thinking questions** and an **Internet Exercise**. These exercises encourage students to go on-line to learn more about topics and organizations covered in the text and can also give students a chance to develop teamwork skills when they work together on these assignments.

FOCUS ON MANAGERIAL IMPLICATIONS

Many international business textbooks fail to discuss the implications of the various topics contained within for the actual practice of international business. This does not serve the needs of business school students, many of whom will soon be employed by business enterprises that have to compete in the global marketplace. Accordingly, the usefulness of this book's material in the practice of international business management is discussed explicitly. At the end of Chapters 2 through 9, where the focus is on the environment of international business as opposed to particular firms, there is a section entitled *Implications for Business*. In this section, the managerial implications of the material discussed in the chapter are clearly explained. For example, Chapter 4 "International Trade Theory," ends with a detailed discussion of the implications of various trade theories for international business management.

In addition, each chapter begins with a case that illustrates the relevance of chapter material for the practice of international business. Chapter 2, "Country Differences in Political Economy," for example, opens with a case that describes the problems that General Electric has had in trying to establish profitable operations in Hungary. As the case makes clear, these problems are rooted in the political economy of Hungary, and in General Electric's initial failure to fully appreciate the impact that political economy has on business operations. I have also added a closing case to each chapter. These cases are also designed to illustrate the relevance of chapter material for the practice of international business. The closing case to Chapter 2, for example, describes how the political economy of Russia has adversely impacted on the operations of a General Motors dealership established by United States investors in Moscow. Each closing case is followed by a list of discussion questions, which facilitates the use of these cases as a vehicle for in-class case discussion and analysis. Another tool that I have used to focus on managerial implications is the inclusion of *management focus* boxes. There is a management focus box in each chapter. Like the opening case, the purpose of these boxes is to illustrate the relevance of chapter material for the practice of international business. The management focus box in Chapter 2, for example, looks at Microsoft's battle against software piracy in China. This box fits in well with a section of the chapter that looks at the protection of intellectual property rights in different countries.

ACCESSIBLE AND INTERESTING

The global business arena is fascinating and exciting, and I have tried to communicate my enthusiasm for it to the student. Learning is easier, better, and more enjoyable if the subject matter is communicated in an interesting, informative, and accessible manner. I believe that with the right approach, even complex abstract ideas and theories can be made accessible and interesting to a wide range of students with differing abilities and backgrounds. The vast majority of people, I submit, are smart enough to grasp the basic principles that underlie the global trade and investment system, the global monetary system, and international business management. The task confronting a textbook author is to package complex ideas in such a way that they are accessible to as wide an audience as possible.

One technique I have used to achieve this is to weave interesting anecdotes into the narrative of the text—stories that illustrate theory. The opening cases and management focus boxes are also used to make theory discussed in the text both accessible and interesting. The opening cases and boxes are not free floating. I continually refer to and utilize opening cases and boxed material in the main body of the text.

SUPPORT MATERIALS

Instructors Manual/Test Bank: Bruce Barringer (University of Central Florida)

Study Guide: Douglas Copeland (Johnson County Community College)

Internet Exercises: Susan Sebok (South Suburban Community College)

Entrepreneurial Profiles: Helena Czepiec (California State Polytechnic University—Pomona)

ACKNOWLEDGMENTS

Numerous people deserve to be thanked for their assistance in preparing this book. First, thank you to all the people at Irwin/McGraw-Hill who have worked with me on this project:

Craig Beytien, Publisher
Patrice Schmitt, Sponsoring Editor
Laura Hurst Spell, Development Editor
Matthew McGuire, Editorial Assistant
Crispin Prebys, Designer
Jim Labeots, Project Manager
Sharon Miller, Photo Research
Lori Koetters, Production Supervisor
Kenyetta Giles, Marketing Manager

Second, my thanks go to the reviewers and focus group participants, whose excellent feedback helped to shape the form and content of the book:

Hal Babson, Columbus State Community College
Michael Cicero, Highline College
Doug Copeland, Johnson County Community College
Fred Ellis, Richland Community College
Jim Fatina, Harper College
Thomas Fletcher Grooms, Northwood University
Marty Hanson, Black Hawk College
Neila A. Holland, Richland College
John Kapoor, College of DuPage
Robert Redich, Lincoln Land Community College

And last but no means least, I would like to thank my wife, Alexandra, and my daughters, Elizabeth, Charlotte, and Michelle for their support and tolerance of the hours I spend in front of a computer screen working on manuscripts.

Brief Contents

Contents

Chapter 1
The Emerging Global Economy

©PhotoDisc

Citicorp—Building a Global Growth Company

With 1996 revenues of $21.5 billion and net income of $3.8 billion, Citicorp is frequently described in the business press as the second largest bank in America. This description, however, is misleading for Citicorp is far more than an "American bank." According to the company's longtime chief executive officer (CEO), John Reed, Citicorp is a "global growth company" that already generates more than half of its revenues outside of North America and looks set to expand this propor-

Learning Objectives:

1 Understand what is meant by the term *globalization*.

2 Be familiar with the main causes of globalization.

3 Understand why globalization is now proceeding at a rapid rate.

4 Appreciate how changing international trade patterns, foreign direct investment flows, differences in economic growth rates among countries, and the rise of new multinational corporations are all changing the nature of the world economy.

5 Have a good grasp of the main arguments in the debate over the impact of globalization on job security, income levels, labor and environmental policies, and national sovereignty.

6 Appreciate that globalization is giving rise to numerous opportunities and challenges that business managers must confront.

tion significantly over the next few years. Reed is on a quest to establish "Citicorp" as a global brand, in effect positioning the bank as the Coca-Cola or McDonald's of financial services.

Citicorp has two main legs to its business, its corporate banking activities and its consumer banking activities. The corporate banking side of Citicorp focuses on providing a wide range of financial services to 20,000 corporations in 75 emerging economies and 22 developed economies. This business, which has always had an international focus, generated revenues of $7.1 billion in 1996, over half of which came from activities in the world's emerging economies. What has captured the attention of many observers, however, has been the rapid growth of Citicorp's global consumer banking business. The consumer banking business focuses on providing basic financial services to individuals, including checking accounts, credit cards, and personal loans. In 1996 this business served 50 million consumers in 56 countries through a global network of 1,200 retail branches and generated revenues of $13.4 billion. According to John Reed, this is just the beginning.

The basic belief that underpins Citicorp's consumer banking strategy is that people everywhere have the same financial needs—needs that broaden as they pass through various life stages and levels of affluence. At the outset customers need the basics—a checking account, a credit card, and perhaps a loan for college.

As they mature financially customers add a mortgage, car loan, and investments. As they accumulate wealth, portfolio management and estate planning become priorities. Citicorp aims to provide these services to customers around the globe in a standardized fashion, in much the same way as McDonald's provides the same basic menu of fast food to consumers everywhere.

Citicorp believes that global demographic, economic, and political forces strongly favor such a strategy. In the developed world, aging populations are buying more financial services. In the rapidly growing economies of many developing nations, Citicorp is targeting the emerging middle classes, whose needs for consumer banking services are rising with their affluence. This world view got Citicorp into many developing economies years ahead of its slowly awakening rivals. As a result, Citicorp is today the largest credit card issuer in Asia and Latin America, with 7 million cards issued in Asia and 9 million in Latin America. As for po-

litical forces, a worldwide movement toward greater deregulation of financial services has allowed Citicorp to set up consumer banking operations in countries that only a decade ago did not allow foreign banks into their markets. Examples in the fast-growing Asian region include India, Indonesia, Japan, Taiwan, Vietnam, and the biggest potential prize of all, China.

A key element of Citicorp's global strategy for its consumer bank is the standardization of operations around the globe. This has found its most visible expression in the so-called model branch. Originally designed in Chile and refined in Athens, the idea is to give Citicorp's mobile customers the same retail experience everywhere in the world, from the greeter by the door to the standard blue sign overhead to the ATM machine to the gilded doorway through which the retail-elite "Citi-Gold" customers pass to meet with their "personal financial executives." By the end of 1996 this model branch was in place at 555 of Citicorp's

1,200 retail locations and it was being rapidly introduced elsewhere.

Another element of standardization, less obvious to customers, is Citicorp's emphasis on the uniformity of a range of back office systems across its branches, including the systems to manage checking and savings accounts, mutual fund investments, and so on. According to Citicorp, this emphasis on uniformity makes it much easier for Citicorp to roll out branches in a new market. Citicorp has also taken advantage of its global reach to centralize certain aspects of its operations to cut costs through economies of scale. Take Citicorp's fast-growing European credit card business as an example. All credit cards are manufactured in Nevada. Printing and mailing are done in the Netherlands, and data processing in South Dakota. Within each country, credit card operations are limited to marketing people and two staff units, customer service and collections.[1]

Introduction

A fundamental shift is occurring in the world economy. We are moving progressively away from a world in which national economies are relatively isolated from each other by barriers to cross-border trade and investment, by distance, time zones, and language, and by national differences in government regulation, culture, and business systems, and toward a world in which national economies are merging into one huge interdependent global economic system. Commonly referred to as **globalization**, the trend toward a more integrated global economic system has been in place for many years. However, the rate at which this shift is occurring has been accelerating recently, and it looks set to continue to do so during the early years of the next millennium.

globalization The trend toward a more integrated global economic system.

The rapidly emerging global economy raises a multitude of issues for businesses both large and small. It creates all sorts of opportunities for businesses to expand their revenues, drive down their costs, and boost their profits. At the same time, it creates challenges and threats that yesterday's business managers did not have to deal with. For example, managers now routinely have to decide how best to expand into a foreign market. Should they export to that market from their home base; should they invest in productive facilities in that market, producing locally in order to sell locally; or should they produce in some third country where the cost of production is favorable and export from that base to other foreign markets and, perhaps, to their home market? Managers have to decide whether and how to customize their product offerings, marketing policies, human resource practices, and business strategies in order to deal with national differences in culture, language, business practices, and government regulation. And managers have to decide how best to deal with the threat posed by efficient foreign competitors entering their home market.

The opening case on Citicorp provides us with one illustration of how a company is positioning itself to take advantage of this new reality. The case describes how Citicorp is trying to build a global brand in the consumer banking business. A decade ago the strategy now being pursued by Citicorp would not have been possible. At that time, government regulations throughout much of the world limited the ability of a bank to enter a foreign market and set up retail branches. But a tide of deregulation is now sweeping the world, and Citicorp has capitalized on this opportunity by establishing a retail banking presence in a large number of developed and emerging economies.

Against the background of rapid globalization, the goal of this book is to explain how and why globalization is occurring and to explore the impact globalization has on the business firm and its management. In this introductory chapter we discuss what we mean by globalization, review the main drivers of globalization, look at the changing profile of firms that do business outside their national borders, highlight concerns raised by critics of globalization, and explore what globalization holds for managers within an international business.

What Is Globalization?

As used in this book, *globalization* refers to the shift toward a more integrated and interdependent world economy. Globalization has two main components—the globalization of markets and the globalization of production.

The Globalization of Markets

The **globalization of markets** refers to the fact that in many industries historically distinct and separate national markets are merging into one huge global marketplace. It has been argued that the tastes and preferences of consumers in different nations are converging on some global norm, thereby helping to create a global market.[2] The global acceptance of consumer products such as Citicorp credit cards, Coca-Cola, Levi's jeans, the music of Madonna or Nirvana, MTV, Sony Walkmans, and McDonald's hamburgers are all frequently held up as prototypical examples of this trend. Indeed, firms such as Citicorp, Coca-Cola, McDonald's, and Levi Strauss are more than just benefactors of this trend; they are also facilitators of it. By offering a standardized product worldwide, they are helping to *create* a global market.

globalization of markets
The merging of historically distinct and separate national markets into one huge global marketplace.

A company does not have to be the size of these multinational giants to facilitate and benefit from the globalization of markets. For example, the accompanying "Management Focus" describes how a small British enterprise with annual sales of £10 million ($16 million) is trying to capitalize on the Japanese love of high-fat foreign food and build a global market for the traditional British fare of fish 'n' chips.

Despite the global prevalence of Citicorp credit cards, Coca-Cola, Levi blue jeans, McDonald's hamburgers, and (perhaps one day) Harry Ramsden's fish 'n' chips, national markets are not disappearing. As we shall see in later chapters, very significant differences in consumer tastes and preferences among national markets still remain in many industries. Particularly in the case of many consumer products, these differences frequently require that marketing strategies and product features be customized to local conditions.

The most global of markets are not markets for consumer products—where national differences in tastes and preferences are still often important enough to act as a brake on globalization—but markets for industrial goods and materials that serve a universal need the world over. These include the markets for commodities such as aluminum, oil, and wheat; the markets for industrial products such as microprocessors, memory devices, and commercial jet aircraft; and the markets for financial assets from U.S. Treasury bills to Eurobonds and futures on the Nikkei Index or the Mexican peso.

An important feature of many global markets—whether they be in consumer, industrial, material, or financial industries—is that the same firms frequently confront each other as competitors in nation after nation. Coca-Cola's rivalry with Pepsi is a global one, as are the rivalries between Ford and Toyota, Boeing and Airbus, Caterpillar and Komatsu, and Nintendo and Sega. In keeping with the global nature of this rivalry, if one firm moves into a nation that is currently unserved by its rivals, those rivals are sure to follow lest their competitor gain an advantage.[4] Before long this process results in the same group of firms confronting each other worldwide. Since these firms bring with them many of the assets that have served them well in other national markets—including their products, operating strategies, marketing strategies, and brand names—the process creates a certain degree of homogeneity across markets; diversity is replaced by greater uniformity. As the process of rivals following rivals around the world unfolds, these multinational enterprises emerge as an important driver of the convergence of different national markets into a single, and increasingly homogeneous, global marketplace. Due to such developments, in an increasing number of industries it is no longer meaningful to talk about "the German market," "the American market," "the Brazilian market," or "the Japanese market"; for many firms there is only the global market.

The Globalization of Production

globalization of production The sourcing of goods and services from different locations around the globe to take advantage of national differences in the cost and quality of factors of production.

The **globalization of production** refers to the tendency among many firms to source goods and services from different locations around the globe in an attempt to take advantage of national differences in the cost and quality of factors of production (such as labor, energy, land, and capital). By doing so, companies hope to lower their overall cost structure and/or improve the quality or functionality of their product, thereby allowing them to compete more effectively against their rivals. Consider the Boeing Company's latest com-

Getting the World **Hooked** on **Fish and Chips**

Courtesy Harry Ramsden's, plc

Deep-fried fish and chips is perennially popular food in England. Harry Ramsden's, whose first fish and chip shop was located in Guiseley, Yorkshire, has long been considered one of the premium fish and chip "shops" in England, and it is one of the few to open up at multiple locations. In 1994 the company had eight branches in Britain, with four more scheduled for opening, and one in Dublin. Its busiest United Kingdom location, the resort town of Blackpool, generates annual sales of £1.5 million ($2.3 million). Harry Ramsden's managers, however, are not satisfied with this success; they want to turn Harry Ramsden's into a global enterprise.

To this end, in 1992 the company opened its first international operation in Hong Kong. According to finance director Richard Taylor, "We marketed the product as Britain's fast food, and it's proved extremely successful." Indeed, within two years the Hong Kong venture was already generating annual sales equivalent to the company's Blackpool operations. Moreover, while half of the initial clientele in Hong Kong were British expatriates, now more than 80 percent are ethnic Chinese. Harry Ramsden's seems to be well on the way to changing the tastes and preferences of Hong Kong Chinese.

Emboldened by this success, Harry Ramsden's has plans to open additional branches in Singapore and Melbourne, Australia, but its biggest target market is Japan. To get a feel for the market, in the spring of 1994 Harry Ramsden's set up a temporary store in Tokyo's Yoyagi Park. The shop, which served more than 500 portions of fish and chips covered in salt and vinegar, was an experiment to see whether the Japanese would take to the product. Despite the traditional aversion of Japanese consumers to greasy food, apparently they did. According to Katie Garritt, who cooked the fish and chips over the 12 days the shop was open: "Sometimes one member of the family would try it, and then all the others would buy portions." Now Harry Ramsden's is looking for a Japanese partner to establish a joint venture in Japan, and it hopes to open its first stores in 1995.

As for the future, according to Richard Taylor, "We want Harry Ramsden's to become a global brand. In the short term the greatest returns will be in the U.K. But it would be a mistake to saturate the U.K. and then turn to the rest of the world. We'd probably come a cropper when we internationalized. We need experience now."[3]

mercial jet airliner, the 777. The 777 contains 132,500 major component parts that are produced around the world by 545 different suppliers. Eight Japanese suppliers make parts for the fuselage, doors, and wings; a supplier in Singapore makes the doors for the nose landing gear; three suppliers in Italy manufacture wing flaps; and so on.[5] Part of Boeing's rationale for outsourcing so much production to foreign suppliers is that these various suppliers are the best in the world at performing their particular activity. (Boeing also outsources some production to foreign countries to increase the chance that it will win significant orders from airliners based in that country.) The result of having a *global web* of suppliers is a better final product, which enhances the chances of Boeing winning a greater share of aircraft orders than its global rival, Airbus.

The global dispersal of productive activities is not limited to giants like Boeing. Many much smaller firms are also getting into the act. Consider Swan Optical, a U.S.-based manufacturer and distributor of eyewear. With sales revenues between $20 and $30 million, Swan is hardly a giant, yet Swan manufactures its eyewear in low-cost factories in Hong Kong and China that it jointly owns with a Hong Kong-based partner. Swan also has a minority stake in eyewear design houses in Japan, France, and Italy. Swan Optical has dispersed its manufacturing and design processes to different locations around the world to take advantage of the favorable skill base and cost structure found in foreign countries. Foreign investments in Hong Kong and then China have helped Swan to lower its cost structure, while investments in Japan, France, and Italy have helped it to produce designer eyewear for which it can charge a premium price. By dispersing its manufacturing and design activities, Swan has established a competitive advantage for itself in the global marketplace for eyewear, just as Boeing has tried to do by dispersing some of its activities to other countries.[6]

Robert Reich, the secretary of labor in the first Clinton administration, has argued that as a consequence of the trend exemplified by Boeing and Swan Optical, in many industries it is becoming irrelevant to talk about American products, Japanese products, German products, or Korean products. Increasingly, according to Reich, the outsourcing of different productive activities to different suppliers results in the creation of "global products."[7]

In sum, we are traveling down the road toward a future characterized by the globalization of markets, production, ownership, and management. Modern firms are important actors in this drama, fostering by their actions increased globalization. These firms, however, are merely responding in an efficient manner to changing conditions in their operating environment—as well they should. In the next section, we look at the main drivers of globalization.

Drivers of Globalization

Two macro factors seem to underlie the trend toward greater globalization. The first is the decline in barriers to the free flow of goods, services, and capital that has occurred since the end of World War II. The second factor is technological change, particularly the dramatic developments that have occurred in recent years in communications, information processing, and transportation technologies.

Declining Trade and Investment Barriers

During the 1920s and 30s many nation-states erected formidable barriers to international trade and foreign direct investment. **International trade** occurs when a firm exports goods or services to consumers in another country. **Foreign direct investment** occurs when a firm invests resources in business activities outside its home country. Many of the barriers to international trade took the form of high tariffs on imports of manufactured goods. The typical aim of such tariffs was to protect domestic industries from "foreign competition." One of their consequences, however, was "beggar thy neighbor" retaliatory trade policies with countries progressively raising trade barriers against each other. Ultimately, this depressed world demand and contributed to the Great Depression of the 1930s.

Having learned from this experience, after World War II, the advanced industrial nations of the West—under U.S. leadership—committed themselves to removing barriers to the free flow of goods, services, and capital between nations.[8] The goal of removing these barriers was enshrined in the treaty known as the **General Agreement on Tariffs and Trade** (GATT). Under the umbrella of GATT, there have been eight rounds of negotiations among member states, which now number over 120, designed to lower barriers to the free flow of goods and services. The most recent round of negotiations—known as the Uruguay Round—was completed in December 1993. The Uruguay Round further reduced trade barriers; for the first time extended GATT to cover services as well as manufactured goods; provided enhanced protection for patents, trademarks, and copyrights; and established a **World Trade Organization** (WTO) to police the international trading system.[9] Table 1.1 summarizes the impact of GATT agreements on average tariff rates for manufactured goods. As can be seen, average tariff rates have fallen significantly since 1950 and under the Uruguay agreement, they will approach 3.9 percent by 2000.

In addition to lowering trade barriers, many countries have also been progressively removing restrictions on barriers to foreign direct investment.

international trade The exporting of goods or services to consumers in another country.

foreign direct investment The investing of resources in business activities outside a firm's home country.

General Agreement on Tariffs and Trade Treaty designed to remove barriers to the free flow of goods, services, and capital between nations; often referred to as GATT.

World Trade Organization Agency established at the Uruguay Round in 1993 to police the international trading system.

9

Chapter 1 The Emerging Global Economy

TABLE 1.1

Average Tariff Rates on Manufactured Products % of Value

	1913	1950	1990	2000*
France	21%	18%	5.9%	3.9%
Germany	20	26	5.9	3.9
Italy	18	25	5.9	3.9
Japan	30	—	5.3	3.9
Holland	5	11	5.9	3.9
Sweden	20	9	4.4	3.9
Britain	—	23	5.9	3.9
United States	44	14	4.8	3.9

*Rates for 2000 based on full implementation of Uruguay agreement.

Source: "Who Wants to Be a Giant?" *The Economist: A Survey of the Multinationals*, June 24, 1995, pp. 3–4.

During 1991 alone, for example, 34 countries, rich and poor, made 82 changes to their laws governing investment by foreign businesses in their economies. All but two of those changes made the laws less restrictive, thereby encouraging both outward investment by domestic firms and inward investment by foreign firms.[10] Citicorp, whose story was reviewed in the opening case, has been a beneficiary of these trends. Citicorp's ability to establish a retail branch presence in foreign markets has been significantly enhanced as a result of declining barriers to foreign direct investment.

These trends facilitate both the globalization of markets and the globalization of production. Increasingly, the lowering of barriers to international trade enables firms to view the world, rather than a single country, as their market. The lowering of trade *and* investment barriers also allows firms to base individual production activities at the optimal location for that activity, serving the world market from that location. Thus, a firm might design a product in one country, produce component parts in two other countries, assemble the product in yet another country, and then export the finished product around the world.

There is plenty of evidence that the lowering of trade barriers has facilitated the globalization of production. According to data from the World Trade Organization, the volume of world trade has grown faster than the volume of world output since the 1950s.[11] Between 1950 and 1994 the volume of world merchandised trade grew at slightly more than 6 percent a year, while the volume of world output has grown at around 4 percent a year. Put differently, by 1995 world output was 6 times as large as it was in 1950, while world trade was 15 times larger, both in real terms (a 6 percent annual growth rate means that the volume of world trade doubles every 12 years, on average).[12] Moreover, the excess of world trade growth over world output appears to have accelerated in recent years. Figure 1.1 gives data for 1984 to 1995. In every year except 1985, world trade grew significantly faster than world output. In 1995 the volume of world trade surged by 9.5 percent, while the volume of world output increased by 3.5 percent.

The data summarized in Figure 1.1 imply two things. First, more firms are doing what Boeing does with the 777 and dispersing different parts of their overall production process to different locations around the globe to drive down production costs and increase product quality. Second, the economies of the world's nation-states are becoming more closely intertwined. As trade expands, so nations are becoming increasingly dependent on each other for important goods and services.

The evidence also suggests that foreign direct investment (FDI) is playing an increasing role in the global economy as firms ranging in size from Boeing to Swan Optical and Harry Ramsden's increase their cross-border investments. Between 1985 and 1995 the total annual flow of FDI from all countries increased nearly sixfold to $315 billion, a growth rate that was more than twice as fast as the growth rate in world trade.[13] The major investors have been U.S., Japanese, and Western European companies investing in Europe, Asia (particularly China), and the United States. For example, Japanese auto companies have been investing rapidly in Asian, European, and U.S. auto assembly operations.

Finally, the globalization of markets and production, and the resulting growth of world trade, foreign direct investment, and imports, all imply that firms around the globe are finding their home markets under attack from foreign competitors. This is true in Japan where Kodak has taken market share

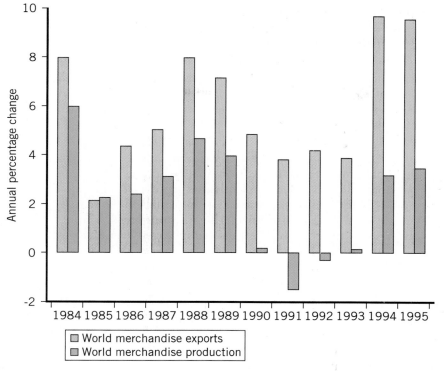

FIGURE 1.1

The Growth of World Trade and Output, 1984–1995
Source: World Trade Organization, *International Trade Trends and Statistics,* 1996

in the film industry away from Fuji in recent years, in the United States where Japanese automobile firms have taken market share away from General Motors, Ford, and Chrysler, and in Western Europe where the once-dominant Dutch company Philips has seen its market share in the consumer electronics industry taken by Japan's JVC, Matsushita, and Sony. The bottom line is that the growing integration of the world economy into a single, huge marketplace is increasing the intensity of competition in a wide range of manufacturing and service industries.

Having said all this, it would be a mistake to take declining trade barriers for granted. As we shall see in the following chapters, demands for "protection" from foreign competitors are still often heard in the United States and elsewhere. Although a return to the "beggar thy neighbor" trade policies of the 1920s and 30s is unlikely, it is not clear whether the political majority in the industrialized world favors further reductions in trade barriers. If trade barriers decline no further, at least for the time being, a temporary limit may have been reached in the globalization of both markets and production.

The Role of Technological Change

While the lowering of trade barriers made globalization of markets and production a theoretical possibility, technological change made it a tangible reality. Since the end of World War II, there have been major advances in communications, information processing, and transportation technology including, most recently, the explosive emergence of the Internet and World Wide Web. In the words of Renato Ruggiero, director general of the World Trade Organization,

> Telecommunications is creating a global audience. Transport is creating a global village. From Buenos Aires to Boston to Beijing, ordinary people are watching MTV, they're wearing Levi's jeans, and they're listening to Sony Walkmans as they commute to work.[14]

MICROPROCESSORS AND TELECOMMUNICATIONS   Perhaps the single most important innovation has been the development of the microprocessor, which enabled the explosive growth of high-power, low-cost computing, vastly increasing the amount of information that can be processed by individuals and firms. Moreover, the microprocessor underlies many recent advances in telecommunications technology. Over the past 30 years, global communications have been revolutionized by developments in satellite, optical fiber, and wireless technology, and now the Internet and the World Wide Web. All these technologies rely on the microprocessor to encode, transmit, and decode the vast amount of information that flows along these electronic highways. Moreover, the cost of microprocessors continues to fall, while their power increases (a phenomenon known as **Moore's Law**, which predicts that the power of microprocessor technology doubles and its cost of production falls in half every 18 months).[15] As this happens, the cost of global communications plummets, which lowers the cost of coordinating and controlling a global organization. For example, between 1973 and 1993 the cost of a three-minute phone call from London to New York fell from $13.73 to $1.78.[16] Recent estimates suggest that the cost of servicing a long-distance call will fall to 5 cents per minute by 2000, down from 20 cents per minute in 1995.[17]

THE INTERNET AND WORLD WIDE WEB   The phenomenal recent growth of the Internet and the associated World Wide Web (which utilizes the Internet to communicate between World Wide Web sites) is the latest expression of this development. In 1990 fewer than 1 million users were connected to the Internet. By mid-1995 the Internet had about 40 million users, connecting more than 40,000 individual networks within organizations and almost 5 million host computers. By the year 2000 there may be well over 100 million users of the Internet. As of 1995 over half of all U.S. publicly traded companies with sales in excess of $1.5 billion had a presence on the Internet, and new commercial sites were being added at a rate of over 100 percent annually.[18]

The Internet and World Wide Web (WWW) promise to develop into the information backbone of tomorrow's global economy. By the year 2000 it is likely that not only will voice, data, and real-time video communication such as videoconferencing be transmitted through the WWW, but also a vast array of commercial transactions may be executed via the WWW. Included in these will be many cross-border transactions. For example, an individual in India that wishes to purchase some software from Microsoft in the United States may be able to do this by going to Microsoft's home page on the Web and purchasing the software using a credit card. The software will then be downloaded in a matter of minutes directly onto her computer via the Internet.

Moore's Law
Prediction that the power of microprocessor technology doubles and its cost of production falls in half every 18 months.

1500-1840

Best average speed of horse-drawn coaches
and sailing ships, 10 mph.

1850-1930

Steam locomotives average 65 mph.
Steamships average 36 mph.

1950s

Propeller aircraft
300-400 mph.

1960s

Jet passenger aircraft,
500-700 mph.

FIGURE 1.2

The Shrinking Globe
Source: P. Dicken, *Global Shift* (New York: Guilford Press, 1992), p. 104

More generally, across a whole range of markets, the WWW holds out the promise of bringing together buyers and sellers who are scattered around the globe.

For illustration, imagine a construction company in Brazil that wishes to purchase a bulldozer. Using a WWW search engine (for example, Yahoo!—the address is www.yahoo.com) the purchasing manager of the Brazilian firm can quickly identify every firm in the world that manufactures bulldozers. He may find that firms in Japan, South Korea, Germany, Sweden, China, and the United States are all in this business. He will be able to quickly visit their WWW sites and download information on product specifications and prices. He may find two products he likes—one produced by a German firm and the other by a Chinese firm. He may then be able to talk directly to salespeople at these firms using a real-time videoconferencing link. On the basis of these discussions and the ensuing negotiations—all of which will be conducted via videoconferencing and in English (the probable business language of the 21st century)—he may decide to purchase the bulldozer from the Chinese firm. The transaction may then be executed over the WWW—with both payment and documentation required for exporting from China to Brazil transmitted over the Web.

This example is hardly far-fetched; the required technology already exists and is being used by many organizations. The important point to understand is that the WWW will do two things: it will further lower the costs of global communications, and it will facilitate the creation of a truly global electronic marketplace for all kinds of goods and services, such as the software and bulldozers used in the above examples. By doing these things, the WWW makes it much easier for firms of all sizes to enter the global marketplace.

TRANSPORTATION TECHNOLOGY In addition to these developments, several major innovations in transportation technology have occurred since World War II. In economic terms, the most important are probably development of commercial jet aircraft and superfreighters and the introduction of containerization, which greatly simplifies trans-shipment from one mode of transport to another. Most significant, the advent of commercial jet travel, by reducing the time needed to get from one location to another, has effectively shrunk the globe (see Figure 1.2). As a consequence of jet travel, New York is now "closer" to Tokyo than it was to Philadelphia in the Colonial era.

IMPLICATIONS FOR THE GLOBALIZATION OF PRODUCTION

As a result of the technological innovations discussed above, the real costs of information processing and communication have fallen dramatically in the last two decades. Making it possible for a firm to manage a globally dispersed production system has facilitated the globalization of production. Indeed, a worldwide communications network has become essential for many international businesses. For example, Texas Instruments (TI), the U.S. electronics firm, has approximately 50 plants in some 19 countries. A satellite-based communications system allows TI to coordinate, on a global scale, its production planning, cost accounting, financial planning, marketing, customer service, and personnel management. The system consists of more than 300 remote job-entry terminals, 8,000 inquiry terminals, and 140 mainframe computers. The system enables managers of TI's worldwide operations to send vast amounts of information to each other instantaneously and to effect tight coordination between the firm's different plants and activities.[19]

A similar example is that of another U.S. electronics firm, Hewlett-Packard, which uses satellite communications and information processing technologies to link its worldwide operations. Hewlett-Packard has new-product development teams composed of individuals based in different countries (e.g., Japan, the United States, Great Britain, and Germany). When developing new products, these individuals use videoconferencing technologies to "meet" on a weekly basis. They also communicate with each other daily via telephone, electronic mail, and fax. Communication technologies have enabled Hewlett-Packard to increase the integration of its globally dispersed operations and to reduce the time needed for developing new products.[20]

In addition to communications and information processing technology, the development of commercial jet aircraft has helped knit together the worldwide operations of many international businesses. Using jet travel, an American manager need spend a day at most traveling to her firm's European or Asian operations. This enables her to oversee a globally dispersed production system.

IMPLICATIONS FOR THE GLOBALIZATION OF MARKETS

In addition to the globalization of production, technological innovations have also facilitated the globalization of markets. As noted above, low-cost global communications networks are helping to create electronic global marketplaces. In addition, low-cost jet travel has resulted in the mass movement of people between countries. This has reduced the cultural distance between countries and is bringing about some convergence of consumer tastes and preferences. At the same time, global communications networks and global media are creating a worldwide culture. U.S. television networks such as CNN, MTV, and HBO are now received in many countries around the world, and Hollywood films are shown the world over. In any society the media are the primary conveyors of culture; as global media develop, we must expect the evolution of something akin to a global culture. A logical result of this evolution is the emergence of global markets for consumer products. Indeed, the first signs that this is occurring are already apparent. It is now as easy to find a McDonald's restaurant in Tokyo as it is in New York, to buy a Sony Walkman in Rio as it is in Berlin, and to buy Levi's jeans in Paris as it is in San Francisco.

On the other hand, we must be careful not to overemphasize this trend. While modern communications and transport technologies are ushering in the "global village," very significant differences remain between countries in culture, consumer preferences, and how business is conducted. A firm that ignores differences between countries does so at its peril. We will stress this point repeatedly throughout this book and elaborate on it in later chapters.

The Changing Demographics of the Global Economy

Hand in hand with the trend toward globalization has been a fairly dramatic change in the demographics of the global economy over the past 30 years. As late as the 1960s four stylized facts described the demographics of the global economy. The first was U.S. dominance in the world economy and world trade. The second was U.S. dominance in the world foreign direct investment picture. Related to this, the third fact was the dominance of large, multinational U.S. firms on the international business scene. The fourth was that roughly half of the globe—the centrally planned economies of the Communist world—was off-limits to Western international businesses. As will be explained below, all four of these facts either have changed or are now changing rapidly.

The Changing World Output and World Trade Picture

In the early 1960s the United States was still by far the world's dominant industrial power. In 1963, for example, the United States accounted for 40.3 percent of world manufacturing output. By 1995 the United States accounted for only 21.9 percent (see Table 1.2). This decline in the U.S. position was not

TABLE 1.2

The Changing Pattern of World Output and Trade

Country	Share of World Output in 1963	Share of World Output in 1995	Share of World Exports in 1995
United States	40.3%	21.9%	12.2%
Japan	5.5	8.2	9.4
Germany*	9.7	4.3	10.1
France	6.3	3.5	5.6
United Kingdom	6.5	3.4	4.9
Italy	3.4	3.2	4.5
Canada	3.0	2.1	3.9

*1963 figure for Germany refers to the former West Germany.

Source: Export data from World Trade Organization, *International Trade Trends and Statistics, 1996*. WTO, Geneva. World output data from *CIA Factbook*, 1996 (1995 world output figures are estimates).

an absolute decline, since the U.S. economy grew at a relatively robust average annual rate of 2.8 percent in the 1963–95 period. Rather, it was a relative decline, reflecting the faster economic growth of several other economies, most notably that of Japan. As can be seen from Table 1.2, between 1963 and 1995, Japan's share of world manufacturing output increased from 5.5 percent to 8.2 percent. Other countries that markedly increased their share of world output included China, South Korea, and Taiwan.

By the end of the 1980s the U.S. position as the world's leading exporter was threatened. Over the past 30 years U.S. dominance in export markets has waned as Japan, Germany, and a number of newly industrialized countries such as South Korea and Taiwan have taken a larger share of world exports. During the 1960s the United States routinely accounted for 20 percent of world exports of manufactured goods. Table 1.2 also reports manufacturing exports as a percentage of the world total in 1995. As can be seen, the U.S. share of world exports of manufactured goods had slipped to 12.2 percent by 1995. Despite the fall, the United States still remained the world's largest exporter, followed closely by Germany and Japan.

Given the rapid economic growth rates now being experienced by countries such as China, Thailand, and Indonesia, further *relative* decline in the U.S. share of world output and world exports seems likely. By itself, however, this is not necessarily bad. The relative decline of the United States reflects the growing industrialization of the world economy, as opposed to any absolute decline in the health of the U.S. economy.

If we look 20 years into the future, most forecasts now predict a rapid rise in the share of world output accounted for by developing nations such as China, India, Indonesia, Thailand, and South Korea, and a commensurate decline in the share enjoyed by rich industrialized countries such as Britain, Japan, and the United States. The World Bank, for example, forecasts that the world's developing nations will grow their economic output by 4.8 percent annually between 1994 and 2003, while the rich industrialized states will enjoy an annual average growth rate of 2.7 percent.[21] Moreover, the World Bank sees even higher growth rates being attained by the developing nations of East and South Asia. East Asia, which includes China and South Korea, is expected to increase economic output at an annual rate of 7.6 percent between 1994 and 2003, while the forecasted growth rate for South Asia, which includes India, is 5.3 percent annually.

If these growth rates are attained and sustained over the next quarter of a century, then we will witness a dramatic shift in the economic geography of the world. World Bank forecasts suggest that by 2020 the Chinese economy could be 40 percent larger than that of the United States, while the economy of India will be larger than that of Germany. Figure 1.3 illustrates the likely share of world output produced by today's rich industrialized and developing nations by 2020 if current World Bank forecasts hold true. Today's developing nations may account for over 60 percent of world economic activity by 2020, while today's rich nations, which currently account for over 55 percent of world economic activity, may account for only about 38 percent by 2020.[22] For international businesses the implications of this changing economic geography are clear; many of tomorrow's economic opportunities may be found in the developing nations of the world, and many of tomorrow's most capable competitors will probably also emerge from these regions.

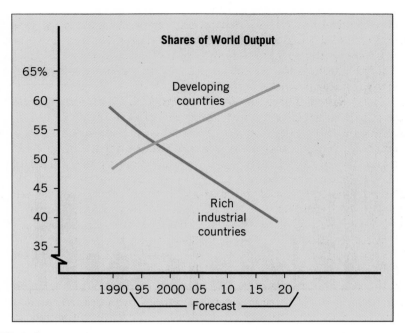

FIGURE 1.3

The Changing Nature of Global Output
Source: World Bank data.

The Changing Foreign Direct Investment Picture

Reflecting the dominance of the United States in the global economy, U.S. firms accounted for 66.3 percent of worldwide foreign direct investment flows in the 1960s. British firms were second, accounting for 10.5 percent, while Japanese firms were a distant eighth, with only 2 percent. The dominance of U.S. firms was so great that European books were written about the economic threat posed to Europe by U.S. corporations.[23] Several European governments, most notably that of France, talked of limiting inward investment by U.S. firms in their economies.

However, as the barriers to the free flow of goods, services, and capital fell, and as other countries increased their shares of world output, non-U.S. firms increasingly began to invest across national borders. This foreign direct investment by non-U.S. firms was motivated by the desire to disperse production activities to optimal locations and to build a direct presence in major foreign markets. Thus, for example, during the 1970s and 80s European and Japanese firms began to shift labor-intensive manufacturing operations from their home markets to developing nations where labor costs were lower. Many Japanese firms also have invested in North America and Europe as a hedge against unfavorable currency movements and the possible imposition of trade barriers. For example, Toyota, the Japanese automobile company, rapidly increased its investment in automobile production facilities in the United States and Britain during the

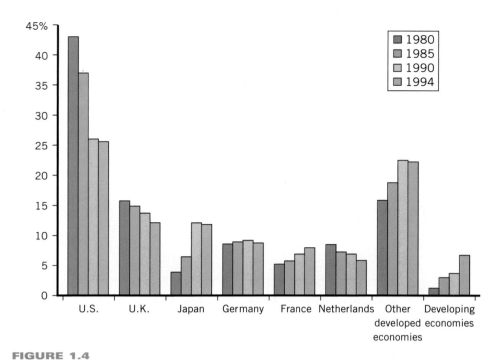

FIGURE 1.4

Percentage Share of Total FDI Stock 1980–1994
Source: United Nations World Investment Report, 1996.

late 1980s and early 1990s. These investments were driven by Toyota's belief that an increasingly strong Japanese yen would price Japanese automobile exports out of foreign markets, so production in the most important foreign markets, as opposed to exports from Japan, made sense. Toyota also undertook these investments to head off growing political pressures in the United States and Europe to restrict Japanese automobile exports into those markets.

One consequence of these developments is mapped out in Figure 1.4, which shows how the stock of foreign direct investment accounted for by the world's six most important national sources of such investment—the United States, Britain, Japan, Germany, France, and the Netherlands—changed between 1980 and 1994. (The **stock of foreign direct investment** refers to the total cumulative value of foreign investments.) Also shown in Figure 1.4 is the stock accounted for by firms from other developed nations and firms from developing economies. As can be seen, the share of the total stock accounted for by U.S. firms declined substantially from around 44 percent in 1980 to 25 percent in 1994. Meanwhile, the share accounted for by Japan, France, other developed nations, and the world's developing nations all increased markedly. The rise in the share of developing nations reflects a small but growing trend for firms from these countries, such as South Korea, to invest outside their borders (see the "Country Focus" on the emergence of South Korean multinationals).

Figure 1.5 illustrates another important trend: the increasing tendency for cross-border investments to be directed at developing rather than rich industrialized nations. Figure 1.5 details recent changes in the annual inflows of foreign direct investment (the **flow of foreign direct investment** refers to amounts invested across national borders each year). What stands out in Figure 1.5 is the increase in the share of foreign direct investment inflows accounted for by

stock of foreign direct investment The total cumulative value of foreign investments in a country.

flow of foreign direct investment The amount of money invested across national borders.

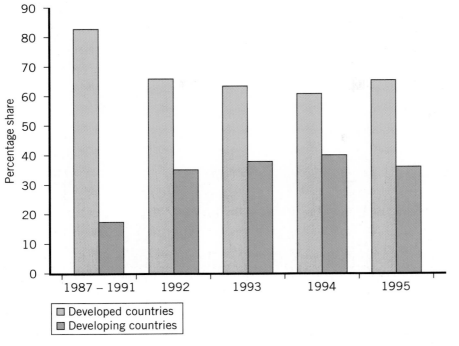

FIGURE 1.5

FDI Inflows into Developed and Developing Nations
Source: United Nations. World Investment Report, 1996.

developing countries during the 1990s, and the commensurate decline in the share of inflows directed at developing nations. Among developing nations, China has received the greatest volume of inward FDI in recent years. China took in $38 billion of the total $100 billion in foreign direct investment that went to developing nations in 1995. Other developing nations receiving a large amount of FDI in 1995 included Indonesia, Malaysia, the Philippines, Thailand, which collectively accounted for $14 billion of inward FDI, and Mexico, which received $7 billion of FDI in 1995. At the other end of the spectrum, the small-est 100 recipient countries accounted for just 1 percent of all FDI inflows.[24] In other words, foreign investment into developing nations is focused on a rela-tively small number of countries that are currently experiencing rapid indus-trialization and economic growth. Businesses investing in these nations are po-sitioning themselves to be active participants in those areas of the world that are expected to grow most rapidly over the next quarter of a century.

The Changing Nature of the Multinational Enterprise

A **multinational enterprise** is any business that has productive activities in two or more countries. Since the 1960s, there have been two notable trends in the demographics of the multinational enterprise. The first has been the rise of non-U.S. multinationals, particularly Japanese multinationals. The second is the growth of mini-multinationals.

multinational enterprise
Any business that has
productive activities in
two or more countries.

TABLE 1.3

The National Composition of the Largest Multinationals

	Of the Top 260 in 1973	Of the Top 500 in 1994
United States	126 (48.5%)	151 (30.2%)
Japan	9 (3.5%)	149 (29.8%)
Britain	49 (18.8%)	33 (6.6%)
France	19 (7.3%)	40 (8.0%)
Germany	21 (8.1%)	44 (8.8%)
Switzerland	8 (3.1%)	14 (2.8%)

Source: Figures for 1973 from Hood and Young, *The Economics of the Multinational Enterprise* (New York: Longman, 1979). Figures for 1994 from "The Global 500," *Fortune*, August 7, 1995, pp. 130–31.

NON-U.S. MULTINATIONALS   In the 1960s global business activity was dominated by large U.S. multinational corporations. With U.S. firms accounting for approximately two-thirds of foreign direct investment during the 1960s, one would expect most multinationals to be U.S. enterprises. According to the data presented in Table 1.3, in 1973, 48.5 percent of the world's 260 largest multinationals were U.S. firms. The second-largest source country was Great Britain, with 18.8 percent of the largest multinationals. Japan accounted for only 3.5 percent of the world's largest multinationals at the time. The large number of U.S. multinationals reflected U.S. economic dominance in the three decades after World War II, while the large number of British multinationals reflected that country's industrial dominance in the early decades of the 20th century.

By 1994, however, things had shifted significantly. In that year U.S. firms accounted for 30.2 percent of the world's 500 largest multinationals, followed closely by Japan with 29.8 percent. Germany was a distant third with 8.8 percent. Although the two sets of figures in Table 1.3 are not strictly comparable (the 1973 figures are based on the largest 260 firms, whereas the 1994 figures are based on the largest 500), they illustrate the trend very well. The globalization of the world economy, together with Japan's rise to the top rank of economic powers, has resulted in a relative decline in the dominance of U.S. (and, to a lesser extent, British) firms in the global marketplace. Table 1.4 adds some detail to this picture by listing the largest 25 multinational corporations ranked by foreign assets in 1994. Seven of the top 25 are U.S. enterprises; seven are Japanese; five are either U.K. companies or jointly incorporated in the United Kingdom and the Netherlands; and the remainder are accounted for by France, Switzerland, Germany, and the Netherlands.

Looking to the future, we can reasonably expect the growth of new multinational enterprises from the world's developing nations. As the accompanying "Country Focus" clearly demonstrates, there is already a strong tendency for South Korean firms to start investing outside their national borders. The South Koreans may soon be followed by firms from countries such as Mexico, China, Russia, and Brazil.

THE RISE OF MINI-MULTINATIONALS   Another trend in international business has been the growth of medium-sized and small multinationals (mini-multinationals). When people think of international businesses they tend

TABLE 1.4

The Top 25 Multinational Businesses in 1994 (ranked by foreign assets)

Ranking	Company	Home Country	Industry	Assets (in billions)		Sales (in billions)		Number of Employees	
				Foreign	Total	Foreign	Total	Foreign	Total
1	Royal Dutch Shell	Netherlands/United Kingdom	Petroleum refining	$69.4	$100.8	$45.5	$95.2	85,000	117,000
2	Exxon	United States	Petroleum refining	47.4	84.1	87.7	111.2	57,000	91,000
3	IBM	United States	Computers	44.1	81.1	37.0	64.1	130,655	256,207
4	General Motors	United States	Motor vehicles and parts	36.9	167.4	28.6	133.6	270,000	756,000
5	General Electric	United States	Electronics	31.6	251.5	11.2	60.5	59,000	222,000
6	Toyota	Japan	Motor vehicles and parts	...	97.6	41.1	94.6	23,824	110,534
7	Ford	United States	Motor vehicles and parts	30.9	198.9	36.0	108.5	180,904	332,700
8	Hitachi	Japan	Electronics	...	86.7	16.5	71.8	...	330,637
9	Sony	Japan	Electronics	...	41.5	26.3	36.3	70,000	130,000
10	Mitsubishi	Japan	Trading	...	85.2	65.3	168.4	...	157,900
11	Nestlé	Switzerland	Food	24.8	30.6	38.4	39.2	203,100	209,800
12	Mobil	United States	Petroleum refining	23.1	40.7	42.5	63.5	28,600	61,900
13	Nissan Motor	Japan	Motor vehicles and parts	...	68.3	24.2	56.5	34,464	143,916
14	Matsushita Electric	Japan	Electronics	22.5	77.2	31.7	64.3	98,639	254,059
15	Elf Aquitaine	France	Petroleum refining	22.4	45.5	14.9	35.5	44,603	94,253
16	Asea Brown Boveri	Switzerland	Electrical equipment	21.5	24.9	24.7	28.3	...	206,490
17	Philips Electronics	Netherlands	Electronics	...	23.8	26.6	30.3	200,000	244,400
18	British Petroleum	United Kingdom	Petroleum	19.0	28.1	39.2	52.4	62,600	84,500
19	Hanson	United Kingdom	Building materials	19.0	37.9	7.6	15.4	53,000	71,000
20	Siemens	Germany	Electronics	...	58.4	13.8	50.0	153,000	403,800
21	Unilever	Netherlands/United Kingdom	Food	18.0	24.7	16.1	40.0	187,000	294,000
22	Mitsui	Japan	Trading	...	72.5	49.8	172.9	11,528	
23	Alcatel Alsthom	France	Electronics	...	44.2	5.0	26.5	115,500	196,500
24	Du Pont	United States	Chemicals	16.4	37.1	16.8	37.1	36,400	114,000
25	B.A.T. Industries	United Kingdom	Tobacco	15.7	50.5	25.3	33.2	175,500	190,308

South Korea's New Multinationals

In the forefront of South Korea's emergence as a modern industrial economy over the past 25 years have been the diversified business groups known as the *chaebol*. Samsung, the largest of the *chaebol*, had 1994 revenues of $63 billion and is involved in a wide range of industries including electronics (it is the world's largest manufacturer of memory chips for computers), automobiles, shipbuilding, aerospace, and machinery. Samsung is closely followed in size by three other major *chaebol*, Hyundai, LG (formally Lucky Goldstar), and Daewoo. Together with six smaller *chaebol*, these large, diversified industrial groups collectively account for about one-quarter of South Korea's gross national product.

Historically, South Korea's *chaebol* took advantage of low labor costs to export a wide range of goods to industrialized countries. In recent years, however, the costs of both land and labor in South Korea have risen sharply, nullifying important sources of the *chaebol's* competitive advantage in the global economy. A recent analysis of national competitiveness by the Swiss-based International Institute of Management Development ranked South Korea 24th out of 41 developed and developing nations, just behind Thailand and Chile, and just ahead of Spain and Mexico. (The three top countries were the United States, Singapore, and Japan.)

Unlike Japanese enterprises, with which the South Koreans are so often compared, many of the *chaebol* suffer from relatively poor product quality and inferior product design. Thus, they have been unable to respond to higher costs by moving their exported products upmarket and raising prices. Rather, in an attempt to maintain their competitive position, the *chaebol* have responded to rising costs at home by expanding overseas, establishing factories in countries where direct labor costs are lower and employee productivity is higher than in South Korea. Daewoo, for example, has found that the average $1,300 monthly wage at its video recorder plant in Kumi, South Korea, is now higher than the $1,200 it pays at a similar factory in Antrim, Northern Ireland, while the output per em-

to think of firms such as Exxon, General Motors, Ford, Fuji, Kodak, Matsushita, Procter & Gamble, Sony, and Unilever—large, complex multinational corporations with operations that span the globe. Although most international trade and investment are still conducted by large firms, many medium-sized and small businesses are increasingly involved in international trade and investment. We have already discussed two examples in this chapter—Swan Optical and Harry Ramsden's. For another example, consider Lubricating Systems, Inc., of Kent, Washington. Lubricating Systems, which manufactures lubricating fluids for machine tools, employs 25 people and generates sales of $6.5 million. Hardly a large, complex multinational, yet more than $2 million of the company's sales are generated by exports to a score of countries from Japan to Israel and the United Arab Emirates. Moreover, Lubricating Systems is now setting up a joint venture with a German company to serve the European market.[26] Also consider Lixi, Inc., a small U.S. manufacturer of industrial X-ray equipment; 70 percent of Lixi's $4.5 million in revenues came from ployee is 20 percent higher at the Irish plant.

Another reason for foreign investment by the *chaebol* has been to acquire foreign-owned entities that have the quality, design, engineering know-how, or market presence that the *chaebol* lack. For example, in early 1995 Samsung acquired 40 percent of AST, one of the largest manufacturers of personal computers in the United States, for $378 million. Similarly, Hyundai Electronics Industries, a subsidiary of Hyundai, the second largest *chaebol*, recently acquired U.S. computer diskmaker Maxtor for $165 million and a semiconductor division of AT&T for $340 million. Daewoo, meanwhile, has been acquiring automobile plants in Eastern Europe, Vietnam, and Brazil as part of its strategy to become a major supplier of automobiles to developing nations and to use that low-cost base to export to the developed world.

A third rationale for foreign expansion by South Korea's *chaebol* has been to placate foreign governments that have expressed concerns about the rising tide of Korean imports into their economies. This has been particularly notable in Western Europe, where a succession of lawsuits has been filed with the European Commission claiming that Korean firms have been dumping products in the European market—selling the products at a price below their cost of production—in an attempt to gain market share and drive European firms out of business. Korean firms are increasingly trying to sidestep such charges by setting up production facilities in Europe. For example, a recent complaint against Samsung and Hyundai by European manufacturers of earthmoving equipment triggered both *chaebol* to invest in facilities to manufacture the equipment in Europe.

Spurred on by such forces, foreign direct investment by South Korea's *chaebol* has accelerated rapidly in recent years. In 1985 South Korean firms invested a little over $300 million in foreign establishments. By 1990 the figure had risen to $1.5 billion, and by 1994 the figure was $3.5 billion. Since 1985, about 50 percent of this investment has been directed at other Asian countries, 30 percent at North America, and 15 percent at Europe.

It seems unlikely that this trend will slow down anytime soon. Recent revisions in South Korea's foreign exchange regulations have made it easier for the *chaebol* to take money out of the country and invest it elsewhere, which has helped facilitate the migration of production out of Korea. Moreover, all of the big four *chaebol* have announced aggressive plans to invest in foreign productive capacity. Samsung plans to establish electronics facilities in China and Mexico; Hyundai plans to invest $4 billion in foreign automobile, telecommunications, and semiconductor facilities; Daewoo is investing heavily in automobile and electronics plants in developing nations; and LG has announced plans to set up petrochemical and electronics plants in developing countries. It seems highly probable, therefore, that the Korean multinational corporation is here to stay.[25]

exports to Japan in 1991.[27] Or take G. W. Barth, a manufacturer of cocoa-bean roasting machinery based in Ludwigsburg, Germany. Employing just 65 people, this small company has captured 70 percent of the global market for cocoa-bean roasting machines.[28] The point is, international business is conducted not just by large firms but also by medium-sized and small enterprises.

The Changing World Order

Between 1989 and 1991 a series of remarkable democratic revolutions swept the Communist world. For reasons that are explored in more detail in Chapter 2, in country after country throughout Eastern Europe and eventually in the Soviet Union itself, Communist governments collapsed like the shells of rotten eggs. The Soviet Union is now history, having been replaced by 15 independent republics. Czechoslovakia has divided itself into two states, while Yugoslavia has dissolved into a bloody civil war among its five successor states.

Many of the former Communist nations of Europe and Asia seem to share a commitment to democratic politics and free market economics. If this continues, the opportunities for international businesses may be enormous. For about half a century these countries were essentially closed to Western international businesses. Now they present a host of export and investment opportunities. Just how this will play itself out over the next 10 to 20 years is difficult to say. The economies of most of the former Communist states are in very poor condition, and their continued commitment to democracy and free market economics cannot be taken for granted. Indeed, disturbing signs of growing unrest and totalitarian tendencies are seen in many Eastern European states. Thus, the risks involved in doing business in such countries are very high, but then again, so may be the returns.

In addition to these changes, more quiet revolutions have been occurring in China and Latin America. Their implications for international businesses may be just as profound as the collapse of Communism in Eastern Europe. China suppressed its own prodemocracy movement in the bloody Tiananmen Square massacre of 1989. Despite this, China seems to be moving progressively toward greater free market reforms. The southern Chinese province of Guangong, where these reforms have been pushed the furthest, now has the fastest growing economy in the world.[29] If what is now occurring in southern China continues, and particularly if it spreads throughout the country, China may move from Third World to industrial superpower status even more rapidly than Japan did. If China's gross domestic product (GDP) per capita grows by an average of 6 percent to 7 percent, which is slower than the 8 percent growth rate achieved during the last decade, then by 2020 this nation of 1.5 billion people could boast an average income per capita of about $13,000, roughly equivalent to that of Spain today. The potential consequences for Western international business are enormous. On the one hand, with 1.2 billion people, China represents a huge and largely untapped market. Reflecting this, between 1983 and 1995 annual foreign direct investment in China increased from less than $2 billion to over $38 billion. On the other hand, China's new firms are already proving to be very capable competitors, and they might take global market share away from Western and Japanese enterprises. Thus, the changes in China are creating both opportunities and threats for established international businesses.

As for Latin America, here too both democracy and free market reforms seem to have taken hold. For decades most Latin American countries were ruled by dictators, many of whom seemed to view Western international businesses as instruments of imperialist domination. Accordingly, they restricted direct investment by foreign firms. In addition, the poorly managed economies of Latin America were characterized by low growth, high debt, and hyperinflation—all of which discouraged investment by international businesses. Now all of this seems to be changing. Throughout most of Latin America, debt and inflation are down, governments are selling state-owned enterprises to private investors, foreign investment is welcomed, and the region's economies are growing rapidly. These changes have increased the attractiveness of Latin America both as a market for exports and as a site for foreign direct investment. At the same time, given the long history of economic mismanagement in Latin America, there is no guarantee that these favorable trends will continue. As in the case of Eastern Europe, substantial opportunities are accompanied by substantial risks.

The Globalization Debate: Prosperity or Impoverishment?

Is the shift toward a more integrated and interdependent global economy a good thing? Many influential economists, politicians, and business leaders seem to think so. They argue that falling barriers to international trade and investment are the twin engines that are driving the global economy toward ever greater prosperity. They argue that increased international trade and cross-border investment will result in lower prices for goods and services. They believe that globalization stimulates economic growth, raises the incomes of consumers, and helps to create jobs in all countries that choose to participate in the global trading system.

The arguments of those who support globalization are covered in detail in Chapters 4, 5, 6, and 7. As we shall see in these chapters, there are good theoretical reasons for believing that declining barriers to international trade and investment do stimulate economic growth, create jobs, and raise income levels. Moreover, as described in Chapters 5 through 7, considerable empirical evidence lends support to the predictions of this theory. However, despite the existence of a compelling body of theory and evidence, the process of globalization has its critics.[30] We would be remiss if we did not mention their concerns. Here we briefly review the main themes of the debate. In later chapters we shall elaborate on many of the points mentioned below.

Globalization, Jobs, and Incomes

One frequently voiced concern is that far from creating jobs, removing barriers to international trade actually destroys manufacturing jobs in wealthy advanced economies such as the United States. The basic thrust of the critics' argument is that falling trade barriers allow firms to move their manufacturing activities offshore to countries where wage rates are much lower.[31] Bartlett and Steele, two journalists for the *Philadelphia Inquirer* who have gained notoriety for their attacks on free trade, cite the case of Harwood Industries, a U.S. clothing manufacturer that closed its U.S. operations, where it paid workers $9 per hour, and shifted manufacturing to Honduras, where textile workers receive 48 cents per hour.[32] Because of moves like this, argue Bartlett and Steele, the wage rates of poorer Americans have fallen significantly over the last quarter of a century.

Supporters of globalization reply that critics such as Bartlett and Steele miss the essential point about free trade—the benefits outweigh the costs.[33] They argue that free trade results in countries specializing in the production of those goods and services that they can produce most efficiently, while importing goods that they cannot produce as efficiently from other countries. When a country embraces free trade there is always some dislocation—lost textile jobs at Harwood Industries, for example—but the whole economy is better off as a result. According to this view, it makes little sense for the United States to produce textiles at home when they can be produced at a lower cost in Honduras or China (which, unlike Honduras, is a major source of U.S. textile imports). Importing textiles from China leads to lower prices for clothes in the United States, which enables U.S. consumers to spend more of their money on other items. At the same time, the increased income generated in China from textile exports increases income levels in that country, which helps the Chinese to purchase more products produced in the United States, such as Boeing jets, Intel-based computers, Microsoft software, and Motorola cellular telephones. In this manner, supporters of globalization argue that free trade benefits all countries that adhere to a free trade regime.

Supporters of globalization do concede that the wage rate enjoyed by unskilled workers in many advanced economies has declined in recent years. For example, data from the Organization of Economic Cooperation and Development suggest that since 1980 the lowest 10 percent of American workers have seen a drop in their real wages (adjusted for inflation) of about 20 percent, while the top 10 percent have enjoyed a real pay increase of about 10 percent.[34] Similar trends can be seen in many other countries. However, while critics of globalization argue that the decline in unskilled wage rates is due to the migration of low-wage manufacturing jobs offshore, and a corresponding reduction in demand for unskilled workers, supporters of globalization see a more complex picture. They maintain that the declining real wage rates of unskilled workers owes far more to a technology-induced shift within advanced economies away from jobs where the only qualification was a willingness to turn up for work every day and toward jobs that require employees to possess significant education and skills. They point out that within many advanced economies there is a shortage of highly skilled workers and an excess supply of unskilled workers. Thus, growing income inequality is a result of the wages for skilled workers being bid up by the labor market and the wages for unskilled workers being discounted. If one agrees with this logic, a solution to the problem of declining incomes is to be found not in limiting free trade and globalization, but in increasing society's investment in education to reduce the supply of unskilled workers.[35]

Globalization, Labor Policies, and the Environment

A second source of concern is that free trade encourages firms from advanced nations to move manufacturing facilities offshore to less developed countries that lack adequate regulations to protect labor and the environment from abuse by the unscrupulous.[36] Critics argue that adhering to labor and environmental regulations significantly increases the costs of manufacturing enterprises and puts them at a competitive disadvantage in the global marketplace vis-à-vis firms based in developing nations that do not have to comply with such regulations. Firms deal with this cost disadvantage, so the theory goes, by moving their production facilities to nations that do not have such burdensome regulations or fail to enforce the regulations they do have. If this is the case, one might expect free trade to lead to an increase in pollution and result in firms from advanced nations exploiting the labor of less developed nations.[37] This argument was used repeatedly by those who opposed the 1994 formation of the North American Free Trade Agreement (NAFTA) among Canada, Mexico, and the United States. The vision they painted was one of U.S. manufacturing firms moving to Mexico in droves so that they would be free to pollute the environment, employ child labor, and ignore workplace safety and health issues, all in the name of higher profits.[38]

Supporters of free trade and greater globalization express serious doubts about this scenario. They point out that tougher environmental regulations and stricter labor standards go hand in hand with economic progress. In general, as countries get richer, they enact tougher environmental and labor regulations. Since free trade enables developing countries to increase their economic growth rates and become richer, this should be correlated with the introduction of tougher environmental and labor laws. In this view, the critics of free trade have got it backward—free trade does not lead to more pollution and labor exploitation; it leads to less! Moreover, supporters of free trade point out that it is possible to tie free trade agreements to the implementation of tougher environmental and labor laws in less developed countries. NAFTA, for example, was passed only after side agreements had been negotiated that committed Mexico to tougher enforcement of environmental protection regulations. Thus, supporters of free trade argue that factories based in Mexico are now cleaner than they would have been without the passage of NAFTA.[39]

Free trade supporters also argue that business firms are not the amoral organizations that critics suggest. While there may be a few rotten apples, the vast majority of business enterprises are staffed by managers who are committed to behave in an ethical manner and would be unlikely to move production offshore just so they could pump more pollution into the atmosphere or exploit labor. Furthermore, the relationship among pollution, labor exploitation, and production costs may not be that suggested by critics. In general, a well-treated labor force is a productive work force, and it is productivity rather than base wage rates that often has the greatest influence on costs. Given this, in the vast majority of cases, the vision of greedy managers who shift production to low-wage companies in order to "exploit" their labor force may be misplaced.

Globalization and National Sovereignty

A final concern voiced by critics of globalization is that in today's increasingly interdependent global economy, economic power is shifting away from national governments and toward supranational organizations such as the World Trade Organization (WTO), the European Union, and the United Nations. As perceived by critics, the problem is that unelected bureaucrats are now sometimes able to impose policies on the democratically elected governments of nation-states, thereby undermining the sovereignty of those states. In this manner, claim critics, the ability of the nation-state to control its own destiny is being limited.[40]

The World Trade Organization is a favorite target of those who attack the world's headlong rush toward a global economy. The WTO was founded in 1994 to police the world trading system established by the General Agreement on Tariffs and Trade (GATT). The WTO arbitrates trade disputes between the 120 or so nation-states that have signed the GATT. The WTO arbitration panel can issue a ruling instructing a member state to change trade policies that violate GATT regulations. If the violator refuses to comply with the ruling, the WTO allows other states to impose appropriate trade sanctions on the transgressor. As a result, according to one prominent critic, the U.S. environmentalist and consumer rights advocate Ralph Nader:

Under the new system, many decisions that affect billions of people are no longer made by local or national governments but instead, if challenged by any WTO member nation, would be deferred to a group of unelected bureaucrats sitting behind closed doors in Geneva (which is where the headquarters of the WTO are located). The bureaucrats can decide whether or not people in California can prevent the destruction of the last virgin forests or determine if carcinogenic pesticides can be banned from their foods; or whether European countries have the right to ban dangerous biotech hormones in meat . . . At risk is the very basis of democracy and accountable decision making.[41]

In contrast to Nader's inflammatory rhetoric, many economists and politicians maintain that the power of supranational organizations such as the WTO is limited to what nation-states collectively agree to grant. They argue that bodies such as the United Nations and the WTO exist to serve the collective interests of member states, not to subvert those interests. Moreover, supporters of supranational organizations point out that in reality, the power of these bodies rests largely on their ability to *persuade* member states to follow a certain course of action. If these bodies fail to serve the collective interests of member states, those states will withdraw their support, and the supranational organization will quickly collapse. In this view, then, real power still resides with individual nation-states, not supranational organizations.

Managing in the Global Marketplace

international business Any business that engages in international trade or investment.

Much of this book is concerned with the challenges of managing an international business. An **international business** is any firm that engages in international trade or investment. A firm does not have to become a multinational enterprise, investing directly in operations in other countries, to engage in international business. All a firm has to do is start to export products or import products from other countries. As the world shifts toward a truly integrated global economy, more firms, both large and small, are becoming international businesses. What does this shift toward a global economy mean for managers within an international business?

As their organizations increasingly engage in cross-border trade and investment, managers need to recognize that the task of managing an international business differs from that of managing a purely domestic business in many ways. At the most fundamental level, the differences arise from the simple fact that countries are different. Countries differ in their cultures, political systems, economic systems, legal systems, and levels of economic development. Despite all the talk about the emerging global village, and despite the trends toward globalization of markets and production, as we shall see in this book many of these differences are very profound and enduring.

Differences between countries require that an international business vary its practices country by country. Marketing a product in Brazil may require a different approach from marketing the product in Germany; managing U.S. workers might require different skills than managing Japanese workers; maintaining close relations with a particular level of government may be very important in Mexico and irrelevant in Great Britain; the business strategy pursued in Canada might not work in South Korea; and so on. Managers in an international business must not only be sensitive to these differences,

Procter & Gamble
in Japan

Procter & Gamble entered the Japanese market in 1972, was the first company to introduce disposable diapers in Japan, and soon commanded an 80 percent share of the market. This had all the makings of a great success story; except that by 1985 P&G's share of the diaper market had slipped to 8 percent, the company had failed repeatedly to establish a strong position in the Japanese laundry detergent and personal care product markets, and its Japanese subsidiary was reportedly losing $40 million per year. The central problem: P&G had simply transferred its marketing strategies and products wholesale to Japan, without customizing them to account for local cultural differences. The American managers who headed

P&G's Japanese subsidiary failed to appreciate that what worked in America would not work in Japan.

When it launched its bath soap in Japan, P&G used TV advertising that showed a Japanese woman relaxing in a luxurious bath of soap bubbles while her husband walked in and asked her about the soap. This same advertisement had worked well in the United States and Europe, but in Japan, where it was culturally frowned upon for a man to walk in on a woman having a bath, even if she is his wife, it was a huge flop.

P&G's Japanese competitors soon took advantage of P&G's cultural myopia. In the diaper market, for example, Kao took market share from P&G by developing a line of trim-fit diapers

that were more in tune with the tastes of Japanese consumers. The company was quickly rewarded with a 30 percent share of the market, all taken at P&G's expense.

Realizing that a lack of international business literacy among many of the Americans that worked in its Japanese operation had contributed toward the debacle in that country, P&G in recent years has started to appoint local nationals to key management positions in many foreign subsidiaries.[42]

but they must also adopt the appropriate policies and strategies for coping with them. Much of this book is devoted to explaining the sources of these differences and the methods for coping with them successfully. The accompanying "Management Focus," which reviews Procter & Gamble's experience in Japan, shows what happens when managers don't take country differences into account.

Another way in which international business differs from domestic business is the greater complexity of managing an international business. In addition to addressing the problems that arise from the differences between countries, a manager in an international business is confronted with a range of other issues that the manager in a domestic business never faces. An international business must decide where in the world to site its production activities in order to minimize costs and to maximize value added. Then it must decide how best to coordinate and control its globally dispersed production activities (which, as we shall see later in the book, is not a trivial problem). An international business also must decide which foreign markets to enter and which to avoid. Moreover, it must choose the appropriate mode for entering a particular foreign country. Is it best to export its product to the foreign country? Should the firm allow a local firm to produce its product under license in that country? Should the firm enter into a joint venture with a local firm to produce its product in that country? Or should the firm set up a wholly owned subsidiary to serve the market in that country? As we shall see, the choice of entry mode is critical because it has major implications for the long-term health of the firm.

Another way international business is different from domestic business is that the conduct of business involves transactions across national borders. Because it is involved in international trade and investment, an international business must operate within the framework of the international trading and investment system. To do so successfully, it must understand the rules governing this framework. Managers in an international business must also deal with government restrictions on international trade and investment. They must find ways to work within the limits imposed by specific governmental interventions. As this book explains, despite the fact that many governments are nominally committed to free trade, substantial interventions are used to regulate cross-border trade and investment. Managers within international businesses must develop strategies and policies for dealing with such interventions.

Moreover, cross-border transactions also require that money be converted from the firm's home currency into a foreign currency and vice versa. Since currency exchange rates are not stable over time but vary in response to changing economic conditions, an international business must develop policies for dealing with exchange rate movements. A firm that adopts a wrong policy can lose large amounts of money, whereas a firm that adopts the right policy can increase the profitability of its international transactions.

In sum, managing an international business is different from managing a purely domestic business for at least four reasons: (1) countries are different; (2) the range of problems confronted by a manager in an international business is wider and the problems themselves more complex than those confronted by a manager in a domestic business; (3) an international business must find ways to work within the limits imposed by government intervention in the international trade and investment system; and (4) international transactions involve converting money into different currencies.

In this book we examine all these issues in depth, paying close attention to the different strategies and policies that managers pursue in order to deal with the various challenges created when a firm becomes an international business. Chapters 2 and 3 explore how countries differ from each other with regard to their political, economic, legal, and cultural institutions. Chapters 4 to 7 look at the international trade and investment environment within which international businesses must operate. Chapters 8 and 9 review the international monetary system. These chapters focus on the nature of the foreign exchange market and the emerging global monetary system. Chapters 10 to 13 explore in detail the strategies and operating policies of international businesses. By the time you have completed this book, you should have a good grasp of the issues that managers working within international business have to grapple with on a daily basis, and you should be familiar with the range of strategies and operating policies that managers can adopt in order to compete more effectively in today's rapidly emerging global economy.

Key Terms

Summary

This chapter sets the scene for the rest of the book. We have seen how the world economy is becoming more global. We have reviewed the main drivers of globalization and argued that they seem to be thrusting nation-states toward a more tightly integrated global economy. We have looked at how the nature of international business is changing in response to the changing global economy. We have discussed some of the concerns raised by rapid globalization, and we have reviewed some implications of rapid globalization for individual managers. These major points were made in the chapter:

1 Over the past two decades we have witnessed the globalization of markets and production.

2 The globalization of markets implies that national markets are merging into one huge marketplace. However, it is important not to push this view too far.

3 The globalization of production implies that firms are basing individual productive activities at the optimal world locations for the particular activities. As a consequence, it is increasingly irrelevant to talk about "American" products, "Japanese" products, or "German" products, since these are being replaced by "global" products.

4 Two factors seem to underlie the trend toward globalization: declining trade barriers and changes in communication, information, and transportation technologies.

5 Since the end of World War II there has been a significant lowering of barriers to the free flow of goods, services, and capital. More than anything else, this has facilitated the trend toward the globalization of production and has enabled firms to view the world as a single market.

6 As a consequence of the globalization of production and markets, in the last decade, world trade has grown faster than world output, foreign direct investment has surged, imports have penetrated more deeply into the world's industrial nations, and competitive pressures have increased in industry after industry.

7 The development of the microprocessor and related developments in communications and information processing technology have helped firms to link their worldwide operations into sophisticated information networks. Jet air travel, by shrinking travel time, has also helped to link the worldwide operations of international businesses. These changes have enabled firms to achieve tight coordination of their worldwide operations and to view the world as a single market.

8 Over the last three decades a number of dramatic changes have occurred in the nature of international business. In the 1960s, the U.S. economy was dominant in the world, U.S. firms accounted for most of the foreign direct investment in the world economy, U.S. firms dominated the list of large multinationals, and roughly half the world—the centrally planned economies of the Communist world—was closed to Western businesses.

9 By the mid-1990s, the U.S. share of world output had been cut in half, with major shares of world output being accounted for by Western European and Southeast Asian economies. The U.S. share of worldwide foreign direct investment had also fallen, by about two-thirds. Moreover, U.S. multinationals were now facing competition from a large number of Japanese and European multinationals. In addition, the emergence of mini-multinationals was noted.

10 The most dramatic environmental trend has been the collapse of Communist power in Eastern Europe, which has created enormous long-run opportunities for international businesses. In addition, the move toward free market economies in China and Latin America is creating opportunities (and threats) for Western international businesses.

11 The benefits and costs of the emerging global economy are being hotly debated among businesspeople, economists, and politicians. The debate focuses on the impact of globalization on jobs, wages, the environment, working conditions, and national sovereignty.

12 Managing an international business is different from managing a domestic business for at least four reasons: (i) countries are different; (ii) the range of problems confronted by a manager in an international business is wider and the problems themselves more complex than those confronted by a manager in a domestic business; (iii) managers in an international business must find ways to work within the limits imposed by governments' intervention in the international trade and investment system; and (iv) international transactions involve converting money into different currencies.

Critical Thinking and Discussion Questions

1 Describe the shifts in the world economy over the last 30 years. What are the implications of these shifts for international businesses based in
- Britain?
- North America?
- Hong Kong?

2 "The study of international business is fine if you are going to work in a large multinational enterprise, but it has no relevance for individuals who are going to work in small firms." Critically evaluate this statement.

3 How have changes in technology contributed to the globalization of markets and of production? Would the globalization of production and markets have been possible without these technological changes?

4 How might the Internet and the associated World Wide Web impact international business activity and the globalization of the world economy?

5 If current trends continue, China may emerge as the world's largest economy by 2020.

Discuss the possible implications of such a development for
- The world trading system.
- The world monetary system.
- The business strategy of today's European and U.S.-based global corporations.

6 "Ultimately, the study of international business is no different from the study of domestic business. Thus, there is no point in having a separate course on international business." Evaluate this statement.

Internet Exercise

Rapid globalization parallels the rapid growth of the Internet, and several of the corporations featured in this chapter demonstrate their worldwide operations on the World Wide Web. For example, Citibank explains how it serves international customers on its Citibank Around the World page (http://www.citibank.com/world/)

and how users can create a pocket guide customized to a particular country as part of its global services (http://www.citibank.com/global/country.html).

Procter & Gamble gives a comprehensive history of the corporation on its site, starting with its origins in 1837. The years 1980–1996 are proclaimed "A

Global Company," and details are given of P&G's globalization efforts to serve more than five billion consumers worldwide (http://www.pg.com/docCareers/orientation/legacy/1980.html).

At the Ford Around the World site (http://www.ford.com/corporate-info/international/), the Ford Motor Company describes its manufacturing facilities and vehicle sales around the world. The Ford WorldWide Connection site (http://www.ford.com/global/) allows users to choose from more than 70 countries, from Africa to Yemen, to obtain information about the corporation's presence in that area of the world. Ford's market efforts are detailed at its Worldwide Direct Market Operations page (http://www.ford.com/corporate-info/international/WEOinfo.html).

The @Toyota page provides links to various Toyota activities in the United States (http://www.toyota.com/inside_toyota/), and related sites detail the corporation's operations in Japan (http://www.toyota.com/japan/), Australia (http://www.toyota.com.au/), and Belgium (http://www.toyota.be).

Global Surfing

Explore the Citibank sites. Describe the financial products and services available in various countries. Create a Customized Pocket Guide for two countries and describe the services Citibank provides in each. Jump to Procter & Gamble's site and describe how the corporation's growth since 1980 parallels the Growth of World Trade and Output in Figure 1.1. What products has P&G developed and acquired to expand its global presence? What are Ford's worldwide initiatives and joint ventures? Choose two countries from Ford's WorldWide Connection and compare and contrast Ford's presence in each country. What are Ford's export activities? How do Ford's worldwide operations compare and contrast with Toyota's? Describe the similarities and differences in Toyota's globalization activities in the United States, Japan, Australia, and Belgium. How might these corporations' sites impact their international business activities and globalization efforts?

Kodak versus Fuji in 1995

Eastman Kodak first started selling photographic equipment in Japan in 1889, and by the 1930s, it had a dominant position in the Japanese market. Then came World War II and the subsequent occupation of Japan. In the aftermath of the war, U.S. occupation forces persuaded most U.S. companies, including Kodak, to leave Japan to give the war-torn local industry a chance to recover. Kodak reluctantly handed over the marketing of its products to Japanese distributors. Effectively priced out of the market by tariff barriers, Kodak saw its share slip to a miserable 5 percent over the next 35 years, while Fuji gained a 70 percent share of the market. During this period Kodak limited much of its activities in Japan to the sale of technology. To quote Albert Sieg, who headed Kodak's Japanese operations from 1984 until the early 1990s, "Like most American companies [in the 1950s and 1960s] we were content to sell technology to the Japanese to make money. And we did. We sold technology to Fuji Photo Film and Konica and anybody that came to our door. That was the way we decided to make money in Japan. It was also a judgment—obviously not right—that we didn't need to worry about the Japanese as a competitor."

This situation persisted until the early 1980s when Fuji launched an aggressive export drive, attacking Kodak in the North American and European markets where for decades Kodak had enjoyed a lucrative dominance in color film. Fuji's onslaught squeezed Kodak's margins, took market share, and forced the company to slash costs. With their backs to the wall, Kodak's top executives admitted to themselves that their company faced a global challenge from Fuji that would only grow. Deciding that a good offense is the best defense, in 1984 Kodak set out to invade its rival's home market. Over the next six years, Kodak spent an estimated $500 million in Japan. At a time when Fuji was committed to heavy spending on promotion abroad, Kodak outspent Fuji in Japan by a ratio of more than 3 to 1. It erected mammoth $1 million neon signs as landmarks in many of Japan's big cities. It sponsored sumo wrestling, judo, and tennis tournaments and even the Japanese team at the 1988 Seoul Olympics, a neat reversal of Fuji's 1984 coup when it won the race to become the official sponsor of the Los Angeles Olympics.

Kodak realized that to make any headway in Japan, it had to control its own distribution and marketing channels. Rather than go it alone, Kodak established a joint venture with its distributor, Nagase Sangyo, an Osaka-based trading company specializing in chemicals. Kodak also realized that it would not succeed in Japan unless it thought and acted just like a Japanese company. Today, apart from a small unit that liaises with Kodak's headquarters in Rochester, New York, all of Kodak's employees in Japan are Japanese, complete with a Japanese boss and Japanese management. There are only 30 foreigners among Kodak's 4,500 employees in Japan. So thoroughly Japanese has Kodak become that it even has its own *keiretsu* (family of suppliers with cross-holdings in each other).

All this activity has brought success. Between 1984 and 1990, Kodak's sales in Japan soared six-fold to an estimated $1.3 billion. Kodak's share of sales to amateur photographers has grown by a steady 1 percent each year for the past six years. Kodak now has a 15 percent share of that market and may overtake second-place Konica within the next few years. Kodak's success has been even more impressive in Tokyo, where it now has 35 percent of the amateur market. In addition, Kodak now has 85 percent of the market for medical X-ray film and photographic supplies to the graphic arts and publishing industries. Perhaps the most important effect of Kodak's Japanese thrust, however, is that Fuji's margins in Japan have been squeezed. Kodak has put Fuji on the defensive, forcing it to divert resources from overseas to defend itself at home. By 1990, some of Fuji's best executives had been pulled back to Tokyo.

All this success, however, was apparently not enough for Kodak. In May 1995 Kodak filed a petition with the U.S. Trade Office that accused the Japanese government and Fuji of "unfair trading practices." According to the petition, the Japanese government helped to create a "profit sanctuary" for Fuji in Japan by systematically denying Kodak access to Japanese distribution channels for consumer film and paper. In Japan—unlike in the United States—film manufacturers do not sell directly to retailers and photofinishers; in between stand distributors. Kodak claims that Fuji has effectively shut Kodak products out of four distributors that have a 70 percent share of the photo distribution market. Fuji has an equity position in two of the distributors, gives large year-end rebates and cash payments to all four distributors as a reward for their loyalty to Fuji, and owns stakes in the banks that finance them. Kodak also claims that Fuji uses similar tactics to control 430 wholesale photofinishing labs in Japan to which it is the exclusive supplier. Moreover, Kodak's petition claims that the Japanese government has actively encouraged these practices.

Fuji has not taken these charges lying down. In a 585-page document called "Rewriting History," Fuji states bluntly that Kodak's charges are a clear case of the pot calling the kettle black. Fuji claims that Kodak has locked up chunks of the U.S. market through exclusive dealing arrangements with retailers won by up-front payments and rebates. Among other charges, Fuji's document claims that Kodak has an exclusive agreement with Eckerd Corp., the fourth largest photo retailer in the United States; that Kodak paid rebates of $2.7 million per year to the Army and Air Force Exchange Services for an exclusive arrangement; and that Kodak offered Genovese Drug Stores Inc., a 144-store chain based in New York, $40,000 plus rebates if the company promised to carry only Kodak film. Kodak has responded that while it does offer incentives, "Retailers are free to carry other brands if they wish. These relationships are completely voluntary."

This trade dispute may take several years to resolve. There are signs that the U.S. government is taking a go-slow approach to pushing Kodak's case while it works with the Japanese government on issues that it sees as more pressing, such as opening the Japanese market to imports of U.S. automobiles. In the meantime, Kodak has further intensified its war with Fuji. In August 1995 Kodak announced that under a co-branding agreement with a group of Japanese retailers, it will sell its film in Japan for half of the prevailing retail price. In September 1995 Kodak began to sell film to Niho Ryutsu Sangyo Co., a group of Japanese retailers with about 800 sales outlets. The film carries both the Kodak name and a Japanese name. Analysts doubt that Fuji will cut prices in Japan to meet Kodak's challenge, since that would decimate profits in its home market.[43]

Case Discussion Questions

1 How has Kodak helped to create a competitor in Fuji Photo Film?

2 What critical catalyst led Kodak to start taking the Japanese market seriously?

3 What have been the keys to Kodak's post-1984 success in Japan?

4 From the evidence given in the case, do you think that Kodak's charges of unfair trading practices against Fuji are valid, or are they simply a case of the pot calling the kettle black?

Suddenly Lynda

Three years ago, at only 22, Lynda Luna's life took an unexpected turn. She and her fiancé sold all their possessions in California and moved to the Philippines to get married and to run his family's international trading company. Once there, however, Lynda decided to break the engagement. Overnight, she found herself in a foreign country with no family and only a few friends made through her now ex-fiancé. Although Lynda was born in the Philippines, she emigrated to the United States when she was ten-years-old. When she ended the engagement, she determined not to return home without proving to her parents and to herself that she could make it on her own. Her biggest concern was that she had disappointed her family.

Lynda decided to go after her dream. Instead of operating a his and hers business, it would now be hers alone. Lynda had some previous experience in international trade. While still in the United States, she and her fiancé ran RITZ International Trading on a part-time basis. They imported Filipino products such as baskets. She handled the paperwork while he handled the sales and vendors. "R was the initial of his first name, I stood for international, and T for trading," Lynda explained. "The Z was added for class."

Through a Filipino friend, she met the owner of a chain of cellular phone stores. He was very interested in obtaining products

Lynda Luna

from the United States, where the market was saturated and prices were cheaper. She believed she could handle the job. For three months, Lynda worked at his retail store and visited service providers to acquaint herself with the products and the industry. She then returned to California and began supplying him with cellular phones and beepers.

Now, as the 25-year-old general manager of RITZ International Trading, she has been shipping product to the Philippines for over two years. She retained the RITZ name in the amicable split. "Why waste a perfectly good name and logo?" Lynda reasoned. She uses the general manager title because it conveys that she oversees everything.

"It has never been easier to start your own international business if you are resourceful," Lynda believes, "because of the plenitude of resources provided by chambers of commerce, the

Small Business Administration, the internet, and the library."

Working as a reseller, Lynda locates the best suppliers. If the order is not too large, she packages the products herself. Otherwise she arranges for packaging through the supplier. She also arranges for a freight forwarder to ship the product.

Lynda has now developed a network of some twenty retailers and distributors in California from whom she buys, and two in Hong Kong. She made her original contacts with the United States suppliers at the annual Consumer Electronics Trade Show in Las Vegas. She obtained additional suppliers from directories published by the United States Department of Commerce, and from listings in trade journals. She found her Hong Kong suppliers from the recommendations of friends.

When she needs to place an order, Lynda makes her decision based on "the three Ps": product, price, and promptness. The supplier must have the right product available in the right quantities. They must return her calls promptly and they should offer her a good price. Even if all the elements are present Lynda will test a new supplier with a small order before risking a large one.

Lynda has had very good experience with her suppliers. "Since many typically do not sell in such large volumes, they really try to provide me with good service," says Lynda. "However, it is very important to meet with the suppliers in person and to establish relationships."

According to Lynda there are differences when dealing with suppliers from the United States versus those in Hong Kong. Americans are satisfied if you visit them once or twice a year and telephone contact may be adequate. Those in Hong Kong not only want you to visit and take them out to dinner, but to bring a present as well. "Anything from ties to jewelry to shoes is acceptable as long as it has a designer label." Lynda visits her suppliers in Hong Kong at least once a year, armed with gifts.

Proper packaging is critical. She must meet the buyer's specifications precisely. Otherwise there may be problems with breakage or even entry into the Philippines. Lynda has selected her freight forwarders both in the United States and Hong Kong based on the recommendations of friends. She has received very good service from her freight forwarders, which is essential when speed is critical. Since the product life cycle of cellular phones is short, the retailer in the Philippines commands his best price when demand is high but supplies are limited. Typically the elapsed time between the placement and delivery of the buyer's order is only a week.

Lynda manages to run RITZ part-time while attending university. "In reality when you have your own business, especially an international one, you are always on call," Lynda says. Her bedroom is her office, and the fax machine is next to her bed.

Over the last two years, Lynda estimates that she has filled six

to seven orders ranging from 5,000 to 10,000 units each. So far the volume has been steady. Lynda predicts that the cellular telephone market is on the verge of accelerating: it is difficult to get a landline in the Philippines, per capita income is increasing, and the affluent are very concerned with conspicuous consumption.

Statistics bear out Lynda's observations. According to an industry analysis, "The mobile wireless segment is the most dynamic in terms of growth, competition, and technology. The number of subscribers grew from 200,000 to over 500,000 over 1995 and is expected to increase to 1,000,000 by the end of 1996." Increased demand is due to increased commercial activity as well as increased population growth, which is among the highest in Asia.

Lynda was able to start her international business with very little capital by insisting on a "cash in advance" policy. When her client in the Philippines sends his purchase order, he wires her bank the payment. She keeps her overhead low by working out of her home. She combines her trips to the Philippines and to Hong Kong with visits to her friends.

Lynda is not too concerned that her client in the Philippines will start dealing directly with her United States suppliers as long as she continues to provide efficient, reliable service. However, she still takes care to guard the identity of her suppliers. She also has visited her client in the Philippines five times in the last two years to cement their relationship. "In the Philippines, personal relations are more impor-

tant than business relations," Lynda says.

Nor does she fear that her United States suppliers will bypass her and begin selling in the Philippines. According to Lynda, it is difficult to penetrate the Filipino market without personal contacts. "Unlike in the United States, the government in the Philippines provides little help to prospective entrepreneurs and little information on potential buyers."

Nonetheless conducting business in the Philippines and in Hong Kong presents its own set of challenges especially if you are young and female. Lynda recommends that as a woman you be straightforward and never flirtatious. She dresses very conservatively. She says that she never brings up her age and if asked just jokes that she has stopped counting. Fortunately Lynda can joke fluently in three Filipino dialects.

For the time being, Lynda intends to keep reselling cell phones and pagers but is always on the look out for new products. Long term after graduation, Lynda plans to operate her own international trading or export management company. Certainly these goals are well within her reach having demonstrated the ability to make it on her own.

Helena Czepiec
California State Polytechnic University, Pomona

Chapter 2
National Differences in Political Economy

©PhotoDisc

Opening Case

General
Electric in
Hungary

In the heady days of late 1989 when Communist regimes were disintegrating across Eastern Europe, the General Electric Company (GE) launched a major expansion in Hungary with the $150 million acquisition of a 51 percent interest in Tungsram. A manufacturer of lighting products, Tungsram was widely regarded as one of Hungary's industrial gems. GE was attracted to Tungsram by Hungary's low wage rates and by the possibility of using the company to export lighting products to Western

Learning Objectives:

1 Understand how the political systems of countries differ.

2 Understand how the economic systems of countries differ.

3 Understand how the legal systems of countries differ.

4 Understand how political, economic, and legal systems collectively influence a country's ability to achieve meaningful economic progress.

5 Be familiar with the main changes that are currently reshaping the political, economic, and legal systems of many nation-states.

6 Appreciate how a country's political, economic, and legal systems influence the benefits, costs, and risks associated with doing business in that country.

7 Be conversant with the ethical issues that can arise when doing business in a nation whose political and legal system are not supportive of basic human rights.

Europe. Moreover, like many other Western companies, GE believed that Hungary's shift from a totalitarian Communist country with a state-owned-and-planned economic system to a politically democratic country with a largely free market economic system would create enormous long-run business opportunities.

At the time, many observers believed that General Electric would show other Western companies how to turn enterprises once run by Communist party hacks into capitalist moneymak-

ers. GE promptly transferred some of its best management talent to Tungsram and waited for the miracle to happen. It's still waiting! As losses mounted General Electric faced the reality of what happens when grand expectations collide with the grim realities of an embedded culture of waste, inefficiency, and indifference about customers and quality.

The American managers complained that the Hungarians were lackadaisical; the Hungarians thought the Americans pushy.

The company's aggressive management system depends on communication between workers and managers; the old Communist system had forbidden this, and changing attitudes at Tungsram proved difficult. The Americans wanted strong sales and marketing functions that would pamper customers; used to life in a centrally planned economy, the Hungarians believed that these things took care of themselves. Hungarians expected GE to deliver Western-style wages, but GE came to Hungary to take advantage of the country's low wages.

In retrospect, GE managers admit they underestimated how long it would take to turn Tungsram around—and how much it would cost. As Charles Pipper, Tungsram's American general manager, said, "Human engineering was much more difficult than product engineering." GE now believes that it has turned the corner. However, getting to this point has meant laying off half of Tungsram's 20,000 employees, including two out of every three managers. It has also meant an additional $400 million investment in new plant and equipment and in retraining the employees and managers who remained.[1]

Introduction

As noted in Chapter 1, international business is much more complicated than domestic business because countries differ in many ways. Different countries have different political systems, economic systems, and legal systems. Cultural practices can vary dramatically from country to country, as can the education and skill level of the population, while different countries are at different stages of economic development. All these differences have major implications for the practice of international business. They have a profound impact on the benefits, costs, and risks associated with doing business in different countries; on the way operations in different countries should be managed; and on the strategy that international firms should pursue in different countries. The international manager who has no awareness of or appreciation for these differences is like a fool walking in front of a buffalo stampede—he or she is likely to get trampled quickly. This chapter and the next will help develop an awareness of and appreciation for the significance of country differences in political systems, economic systems, legal systems, and national culture.

The opening case illustrates some problems created by country differences in political systems, economic systems, and culture. The culture of Hungarian society has been shaped by over 40 years of Communist rule. Although both the Communist government and the centrally planned economic system it fostered collapsed in 1989, its influence is still felt through its more enduring impact on attitudes toward work, business efficiency, and customer service. Like many other Western companies, General Electric did not fully appreciate how enduring the impact of such attitudes would be and how difficult these attitudes would make it to transform an enterprise such as Tungsram into a Western-style business operation. Although General Electric's managers now believe they have turned an important corner at Tungsram, the economic cost to GE of getting to this point has been far higher than originally anticipated.

In this chapter we focus our attention on how the political, economic, and legal systems of countries differ. Collectively we refer to these systems as constituting the **political economy** of a country. The political, economic, and legal systems of a country are not independent of each other. As we shall see, they interact and influence each other, and in doing so they affect the level of economic well-being in a country. In addition to reviewing these systems, in this chapter we explore how differences in political economy influence the benefits, costs, and risks associated with doing business in different countries, and how they impact management practice and strategy. In the next chapter we will look at how differences in culture influence the practice of

political economy

Political, economic, and legal systems of a country.

international business. Keep in mind, however, that the political ec
and culture of a nation are not independent of each other. Thus, the
case tells us that the political and economic institutions that e
Hungary during 40-plus years of Communist rule have cast a lor
over the culture that exists in Hungary today.

Political Systems

The economic and legal systems of a country are often shaped by
system.[2] As such, it is important that we understand the nature of dni
political systems before discussing the nature of different economic and legal
systems. By **political system** we mean the system of government in a nation.
Political systems can be assessed according to two *related* dimensions. The
first is the degree to which they emphasize collectivism as opposed to individualism. The second dimension is the degree to which they are democratic
or totalitarian. These dimensions are interrelated; systems that emphasize
collectivism tend to be totalitarian, while systems that place a high value on
individualism tend to be democratic. However, there is a gray area in the middle. It is possible to have democratic societies that emphasize a mix of collectivism and individualism. Similarly, it is possible to have totalitarian societies that are not collectivist.

Collectivism and Individualism

The term **collectivism** refers to a system that stresses the primacy of collective goals over individual goals.[3] When collectivism is emphasized, the needs
of society as a whole are generally viewed as being more important than individual freedoms. In such circumstances, an individual's right to do something may be restricted because it runs counter to "the good of society" or
"the common good." Advocacy of collectivism can be traced to the ancient
Greek philosopher Plato (427–347 BC), who in *The Republic* argued that individual rights should be sacrificed for the good of the majority and that property should be owned in common. In modern times the collectivist mantle has
been picked up by socialists.

collectivism
Political system
that stresses the
primacy of col-
lective goals over
individual goals.

SOCIALISM Socialists trace their intellectual roots to Karl Marx
(1818–1883). Marx's basic argument is that in a capitalist society where individual freedoms are not restricted, the few benefit at the expense of the many.
While successful capitalists are able to accumulate considerable wealth, Marx
postulated that the wages earned by the majority of workers in a capitalist society would be forced down to subsistence levels. Marx argued that capitalists
expropriate for their own use the value created by workers, while paying workers only subsistence wages in return. Put another way, according to Marx, the
pay of workers does not reflect the full value of their labor. To correct this perceived wrong, Marx advocated state ownership of the basic means of production, distribution, and exchange (i.e., businesses). His logic was that if the
state owned the means of production, the state could ensure that workers were
fully compensated for their labor. Thus, the idea is to manage state-owned enterprise to benefit society as a whole, rather than individual capitalists.[4]

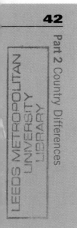

Social Democrats
Followers of socialist ideology who commit themselves to achieving socialism through democratic means.

In the early 20th century the socialist ideology split into two broad camps. On the one hand there were the **Communists** who believed that socialism could be achieved only through violent revolution and totalitarian dictatorship. On the other hand, there were the **Social Democrats** who committed themselves to achieving socialism by democratic means, and who turned their back on violent revolution and dictatorship. Both versions of socialism have waxed and waned during the 20th century.

The Communist version of socialism reached its high point in the late 1970s, when the majority of the world's population lived in Communist states. The countries under Communist rule at that time included the former Soviet Union; its Eastern European client nations (e.g., Poland, Czechoslovakia, Hungary); China; the Southeast Asian nations of Cambodia, Laos, and Vietnam; various African nations (e.g., Angola, Mozambique); and the Latin American nations of Cuba and Nicaragua. By the mid-1990s, however, Communism was in retreat worldwide. The Soviet Union had collapsed and had been replaced by a collection of 15 republics, most of which were at least nominally structured as democracies. Communism was swept out of Eastern Europe by the largely bloodless revolutions of 1989. Many believe it is now only a matter of time before Communism collapses in China, the last major Communist power left. Indeed, although China is still nominally a Communist state, and while substantial limits to individual political freedom exist, in the economic sphere the country has recently moved significantly away from strict adherence to Communist ideology.[5]

Social democracy also seems to have passed its high-water mark, although the ideology may prove to be more enduring than Communism. Social democracy has had perhaps its greatest influence in a number of democratic Western nations, including Australia, Britain, France, Germany, Norway, Spain, and Sweden, where Social Democratic parties have from time to time held political power. Other countries where social democracy has had an important influence include India and Brazil. Consistent with their Marxists roots, many Social Democratic governments have nationalized private companies in certain industries, transforming them into state-owned enterprises to be run for the "public good rather than private profit." In Britain, for example, by the end of the 1970s, state-owned companies had a monopoly in the telecommunications, electricity, gas, coal, railway, and shipbuilding industries, as well as having substantial interests in the oil, airline, auto, and steel industries.

However, experience has demonstrated that far from being in the public interest, state ownership of the means of production often runs counter to the public interest. In many countries state-owned companies have performed poorly. Protected from significant competition by their monopoly position and guaranteed government financial support, many state-owned companies became increasingly inefficient. In the end, individuals found themselves having to pay for the luxury of state ownership through higher prices and higher taxes. In a number of Western democracies, one consequence has been that many Social Democratic parties were voted out of office in the late 1970s and early 1980s. They were succeeded by political parties, such as Britain's Conservative Party and Germany's Christian Democratic Party, that were more committed to free market economics. These parties have spent most of the last decade selling state-owned enterprises to private investors (a process referred to as privatization). Thus, in Britain, the Conservative government of Margaret Thatcher sold the state's interests in telecommunications, electricity, gas, shipbuilding, oil, airlines, autos, and steel to private investors.

Moreover, even those Social Democratic parties that do remain in power now seem to be committed to greater private ownership.

INDIVIDUALISM Individualism is the opposite of collectivism. In a political sense, **individualism** refers to a philosophy that an individual should have freedom in his or her economic and political pursuits. In contrast to collectivism, individualism stresses that the interests of the individual should take precedence over the interests of the state. Like collectivism, individualism can be traced to an ancient Greek philosopher, in this case Plato's disciple Aristotle (384–322 BC). In contrast to Plato, Aristotle argued that individual diversity and private ownership are desirable. In a passage that might have been taken from a speech by Margaret Thatcher or Ronald Reagan, he argued that private property is more productive than communal property and will thus make for progress. According to Aristotle, communal property receives little care, whereas property that is owned by an individual will receive the greatest care and therefore be most productive.

After sinking into oblivion for the best part of two millennia, individualism was reborn as an influential political philosophy in the Protestant trading nations of England and the Netherlands during the 16th century. The philosophy was refined in the work of a number of British philosophers, including David Hume (1711–1776), Adam Smith (1723–1790), and John Stuart Mill (1806–1873). The philosophy of individualism exercised a profound influence on those in the American colonies who sought independence from Britain. Indeed, individualism underlies the ideas expressed in the Declaration of Independence. In more recent years the philosophy has been championed by several Nobel Prize-winning economists, including Milton Friedman, Friedrich von Hayek, and James Buchanan.

Individualism is built on two central tenets. The first is an emphasis on the importance of guaranteeing individual freedom and self-expression. As John Stuart Mill put it,

> The sole end for which mankind are warranted, individually or collectively, in interfering with the liberty of action of any of their number is self-protection . . . The only purpose for which power can be rightfully exercised over any member of a civilized community, against his will, is to prevent harm to others. His own good, either physical or moral, is not a sufficient warrant . . . The only part of the conduct of any one, for which he is amenable to society, is that which concerns others. In the part which merely concerns himself, his independence is, of right, absolute. Over himself, over his own body and mind, the individual is sovereign.[6]

The second tenet of individualism is that the welfare of society is best served by letting people pursue their own economic self-interest, as opposed to having some collective body (such as government) try to dictate what is in society's best interest. Or as Adam Smith put it in a famous passage from *The Wealth of Nations*, an individual who intends his own gain is

> led by an invisible hand to promote an end which was no part of his intention. Nor is it always worse for the society that it was no part of it. By pursuing his own interest he frequently promotes that of the society more effectually than when he really intends to promote it. I have never known much good done by those who effect to trade for the public good.[7]

individualism Political philosophy that an individual should have freedom over his or her economic and political pursuits.

The central message of individualism, therefore, is that individual economic and political freedoms are the ground rules on which a society should be based. This puts individualism in direct conflict with collectivism. Collectivism asserts the primacy of the collective over the individual, while individualism asserts just the opposite. This underlying ideological conflict has shaped much of the recent history of the world. The Cold War, for example, was essentially a war between collectivism, championed by the now-defunct Soviet Union, and individualism, championed by the United States.

In practical terms, individualism translates into an advocacy for democratic political systems and free market economics. Viewed this way, we can see that since the late 1980s the waning of collectivism has been matched by the ascendancy of individualism. A wave of democratic ideals and free market economics is currently sweeping away socialism and communism worldwide. The changes of the last few years go beyond the revolutions in Eastern Europe and the former Soviet Union to include a move toward greater individualism in Latin America and in some of the social democratic states of the West (e.g., Britain and Sweden). This is not to claim that individualism has finally won a long battle with collectivism; it has not. But as a guiding political philosophy, there is no doubt that individualism is currently on the ascendancy. This represents good news for international business, since the pro-business and pro-free trade values of individualism create a favorable environment within which international business can thrive.

Democracy and Totalitarianism

democracy
Political system in which government is by the people, exercised either directly or through elected representatives.

totalitarianism Form of government in which one person or political party exercises absolute control over all spheres of human life and in which opposing political parties are prohibited.

representative democracy Political system in which citizens periodically elect individuals to represent them.

Democracy and totalitarianism are at different ends of a political dimension. **Democracy** refers to a political system in which government is by the people, exercised either directly or through elected representatives. **Totalitarianism** is a form of government in which one person or political party exercises absolute control over all spheres of human life, and opposing political parties are prohibited. The democratic–totalitarian dimension is not independent of the collectivism–individualism dimension. Democracy and individualism go hand in hand, as do the communist version of collectivism and totalitarianism. However, gray areas exist; it is possible to have a democratic state where collective values predominate, and it is possible to have a totalitarian state that is hostile to collectivism and in which some degree of individualism, particularly in the economic sphere, is encouraged. For example, Chile in the 1980s was ruled by a totalitarian military dictatorship that encouraged economic freedom but not political freedom.

DEMOCRACY The pure form of democracy, as originally practiced by several city-states in ancient Greece, is based on a belief that citizens should be directly involved in decision making. In complex advanced societies with populations in the tens or hundreds of millions, this is impractical. Most modern democratic states practice what is commonly referred to as **representative democracy**. In a representative democracy, citizens periodically elect individuals to represent them. These elected representatives then form a government, whose function is to make decisions on behalf of the electorate. A representative democracy rests on the assumption that if elected representatives fail to perform this job adequately, they can and will be voted down at the next election.

To guarantee that elected representatives can be held accountable for their actions by the electorate, an ideal representative democracy has a number of safeguards that are typically enshrined in constitutional law. These include

- An individual's right to freedom of expression, opinion, and organization.
- A free media.
- Regular elections in which all eligible citizens are allowed to vote.
- Universal adult suffrage.
- Limited terms for elected representatives.
- A fair court system that is independent from the political system.
- A nonpolitical state bureaucracy.
- A nonpolitical police force and armed services.
- A relatively free access to state information.[8]

TOTALITARIANISM In a totalitarian country all the constitutional guarantees on which representative democracies are built, such as an individual's right to freedom of expression and organization, a free media, and regular elections, are denied to the citizens. In most totalitarian states, political repression is widespread and those who question the right of the rulers to rule find themselves imprisoned, or worse.

Map 2.1 reports data on the extent of totalitarianism in the world. This map charts political freedom in 1994, on a scale from 1 for the highest degree of political freedom to 7 for the lowest. Among the criteria for a high rating are recent free and fair elections, a parliament with effective power, a significant opposition, and recent shifts in power through election. Factors contributing to a low rating (i.e., to totalitarianism) include military or foreign control, the denial of self-determination to major population groups, a lack of decentralized political power, and an absence of democratic elections.

There are four major forms of totalitarianism in the world today. Until recently the most widespread was **communist totalitarianism**. As discussed earlier, communism is a version of collectivism that advocates that socialism can be achieved only through totalitarian dictatorship. Communism, however, is in decline worldwide, and many of the old Communist dictatorships have collapsed since 1989. The major exceptions to this trend (so far) are China, Vietnam, Laos, North Korea, and Cuba, although all these states show clear signs that the Communist party's monopoly on political power is under attack.

A second form of totalitarianism might be labeled **theocratic totalitarianism**. Theocratic totalitarianism is found in states where political power is monopolized by a party, group, or individual that governs according to religious principles. The most common form of theocratic totalitarianism is that based on Islam. It is exemplified by states such as Iran and Saudi Arabia. In these states not only is freedom of political expression restricted, but so is freedom of religious expression, while the laws of the state are based on Islamic principles.

A third form of totalitarianism might be referred to as **tribal totalitarianism**. Tribal totalitarianism is found mainly in African countries such as Zimbabwe, Tanzania, Uganda, and Kenya. The borders of most African states reflect the administrative boundaries drawn by the old European colonial powers, rather than tribal realities. Consequently, the typical African country

communist totalitarianism Form of totalitarianism that advocates achieving socialism through totalitarian dictatorship.

theocratic totalitarianism Form of totalitarianism in which political power is monopolized by a party, group, or individual that governs according to religious principles.

tribal totalitarianism Form of totalitarianism found mainly in Africa in which a political party that represents the interests of a particular tribe monopolizes power.

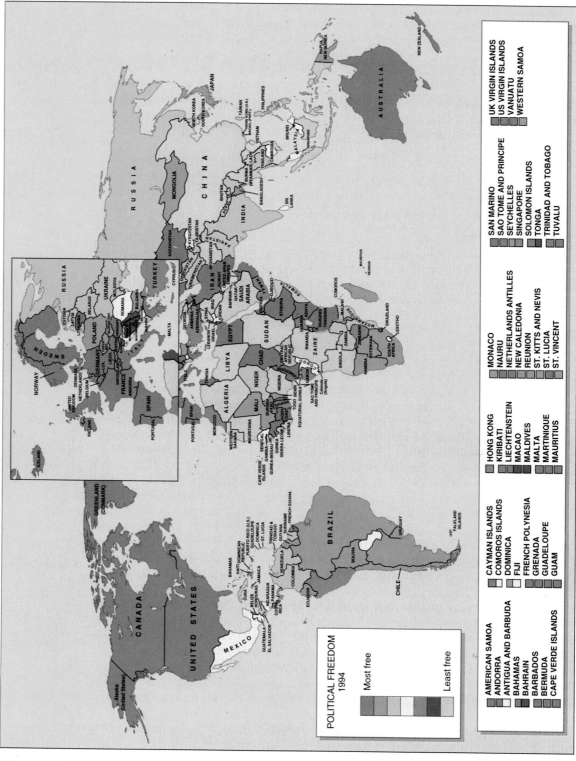

MAP 2.1

Political Freedom in 1994

Source: Map data from *Freedom Review* 26, no. 1 (January–February), pp.15–17.

contains a number of different tribes. Tribal totalitarianism occurs when a political party that represents the interests of a particular tribe (and not always the majority tribe) monopolizes power. Such one-party states are found throughout Africa.

A fourth major form of totalitarianism might be described as **right-wing totalitarianism**. Right-wing totalitarianism generally permits individual economic freedom, but restricts individual political freedom on the grounds that it would lead to a rise of communism. One of the common features of most right-wing dictatorships is an overt hostility to socialist or communist ideas. Many right-wing totalitarian governments are backed by the military, and in some cases the government is made up of military officers. Until the early 1980s right-wing dictatorships, many of which were military dictatorships, were common throughout Latin American. They were also found in several Asian countries, particularly South Korea, Taiwan, Singapore, Indonesia, and the Philippines. Since the early 1980s, however, this form of government has been in retreat. The majority of Latin American countries are now genuine multiparty democracies, while significant political freedoms have been granted to the political opposition in countries such as South Korea, Taiwan, and the Philippines.

right-wing totalitarianism Form of totalitarianism in which individual economic freedom is allowed but individual political freedom is restricted in the belief that it could lead to communism.

Economic Systems

It should be clear from the previous section that there is a connection between political ideology and economic systems. In countries where individual goals are given primacy over collective goals, we are more likely to find free market economic systems. In contrast, in countries where collective goals are given preeminence, the state may have taken control over many enterprises, while markets in such countries are likely to be restricted rather than free. More specifically, we can identify three broad types of economic system—a market economy, a command economy, and a mixed economy.

Market Economy

In a pure **market economy** the goods and services that a country produces, and the quantity in which they are produced, is not planned by anyone. Rather, it is determined by the interaction of supply and demand and signaled to producers through the price system. If demand for a product exceeds supply, prices will rise, signaling producers to produce more. If supply exceeds demand, prices will fall, signaling producers to produce less. In this system consumers are sovereign. It is the purchasing patterns of consumers, as signaled to producers through the mechanism of the price system, that determines what is produced and in what quantity.

For a market to work in this manner, there must be no restrictions on supply. A restriction on supply occurs when a market is monopolized by a single firm. In such circumstances, rather than increasing output in response to increased demand, a monopolist might restrict output and let prices rise. This allows the monopolist to take a greater profit margin on each unit it sells. Although this is good for the monopolist, it is bad for the consumer, who has to pay higher prices. Moreover, it is probably bad for the welfare of society.

market economy Economic system in which the interaction of supply and demand determines the quantity in which goods and services are produced.

Since, by definition, a monopolist has no competitors, it has no incentive to search for ways to lower its production costs. Rather, it can simply pass on cost increases to consumers in the form of higher prices. The net result is that the monopolist is likely to become increasingly inefficient, producing high-priced, low-quality goods, while society suffers as a consequence.

Given the dangers inherent in monopoly, the role of government in a market economy is to encourage vigorous competition between producers. Governments do this by outlawing monopolies and restrictive business practices designed to monopolize a market (U.S. antitrust laws serve this function). The institution of private ownership also encourages vigorous competition and economic efficiency. Private ownership ensures that entrepreneurs have a right to the profits generated by their own efforts. This gives entrepreneurs an incentive to search for better ways of serving consumer needs, whether that be through introducing new products, by developing more efficient production processes, by providing better marketing and aftersales service, or simply through managing their businesses more efficiently than their competitors. In turn, the constant improvement in product and process that results from such an incentive has been argued to have a major positive impact on economic growth and development.[9]

Command Economy

command economy Economic system in which the goods and services produced, the quantity in which they are produced, and the prices at which they are sold are all planned by the government.

In a pure **command economy** the goods and services that a country produces, the quantity in which they are produced, and the prices at which they are sold are all *planned* by the government. Consistent with the collectivist ideology, the objective of a command economy is for government to allocate resources for "the good of society." In addition, in a *pure* command economy all businesses are state owned, the rationale being that the government can then direct them to make investments that are in the best interests of the nation as a whole, rather than in the interests of private individuals.

Command economies are typically found in communist countries where collectivist goals are given priority over individual goals. However, a good deal of government planning, mixed with some state ownership, has also been undertaken in a number of democratic nations by socialist-inclined governments. France and India, in particular, have both experimented with extensive government planning and state ownership, although in both countries government planning has recently fallen into disfavor.

While the objective of a command economy is to mobilize economic resources for the public good, in practice just the opposite seems to have occurred. In a command economy, state-owned enterprises have little incentive to control costs and be efficient, since they cannot go out of business. Moreover, the abolition of private ownership means there is no incentive for individuals to look for better ways of serving consumer needs; hence, there is a general absence of dynamism and innovation in command economies. Instead of growing and becoming more prosperous, they tend to be characterized by economic stagnation.

Mixed Economy

Between market economies and command economies can be found mixed economies. In a mixed economy certain sectors of the economy are left to private ownership and free market mechanisms, while in other sectors there is significant state ownership and government planning. Mixed economies are relatively common among the states of Western Europe, although they are becoming less so. France, Italy, and Sweden can all be classified as mixed economies. In these countries the government intervenes in those sectors where it believes private ownership is not in the best interests of society. For example, Britain and Sweden both have extensive state-owned health systems that provide free universal health care to all citizens (it is paid for through higher taxes). In both countries it is felt that government has a moral obligation to provide for the health of its citizens. One consequence is that private ownership of health care operations is very restricted in both countries.

In mixed economies governments also tend to take into state ownership troubled firms whose continued operation is thought to be vital to national interests. The French automobile company, Renault, was state owned until recently. The government took over the company when it ran into serious financial problems. The French government reasoned that the social costs of the unemployment that might result if Renault collapsed were unacceptable, so it nationalized the company to save it from bankruptcy. Renault's competitors weren't thrilled by this move, since they had to compete with a company whose costs were subsidized by the state.

Legal System

The **legal system** of a country refers to the rules, or laws, that regulate behavior, along with the processes by which the laws of a country are enforced and through which redress for grievances is obtained. The legal system of a country is of immense importance to international business. A country's laws regulate business practice, define the manner in which business transactions are to be executed, and set down the rights and obligations of those involved in business transactions. The legal environments of different countries can and do differ in significant ways. As we shall see, differences in legal systems can have an important impact on the attractiveness of a country as an investment site and/or market.

Like the economic system of a country, the legal system is influenced by the prevailing political system. It is the country's government that defines the legal framework within which firms do business—and often the laws that regulate business in a country are a reflection of the rulers' dominant political ideology. For example, collectivist-inclined totalitarian states tend to enact laws that severely restrict private enterprise, while the laws enacted by governments in democratic states where individualism is the dominant political philosophy tend to be pro-private enterprise and pro-consumer.

The variation in the structure of law between countries is a massive topic that warrants its own textbook. Here we do not attempt to give a full description of the variations in legal systems. Rather, we will focus on three issues that illustrate how legal systems can vary between countries—and how such variations can affect the practice of international business. First we look at the laws governing property rights with particular reference to patents, copyrights, and trademarks. Second, we look at laws covering product safety and product liability. Third, we look at country differences in contract law.

legal system The rules, or laws, that regulate behavior and the processes by which the laws of a country are enforced and through which redress of grievances is obtained.

Property Rights

In a legal sense the term *property* refers to a resource over which an individual or business holds a legal title; that is, a resource that they own. **Property rights** refer to the bundle of legal rights over the *use* to which a resource is put and over the *use* made of any income that may be derived from that resource.[10] Countries differ significantly in the extent to which their legal system protects property rights. Although almost all countries have laws on their books that protect property rights, in many countries these laws are not well enforced by the authorities and property rights are routinely violated. There are two ways in which property rights can be violated—through private action and through public action.

PRIVATE ACTION Private action refers to theft, piracy, blackmail, and the like by private individuals or groups. While theft occurs in all countries, in some countries a weak legal system allows for a much higher level of criminal action than in others. An example much in the news recently is Russia, where the chaotic legal system of the post-Communist era, coupled with a weak police force and judicial system, offers both domestic and foreign businesses scant protection from blackmail by the "Russian Mafia." Indeed, often in Russia successful business owners must pay "protection money" to the Mafia or face violent retribution, including bombings and assassinations (more than 500 businessmen were murdered in 1994).[11]

Of course, Russia is not alone in having Mafia problems. The Mafia has a long history in the United States. Similarly, in Japan the local version of the Mafia, known as the *yakuza*, runs protection rackets, particularly in the food and entertainment industries.[12] However, there is an enormous difference between the large magnitude of such activity in Russia and its limited impact in Japan and the United States. This difference arises because the legal enforcement apparatus, such as the police and court system, is so weak in Russia. Many other countries have problems similar to or even greater in magnitude than those currently being experienced by Russia. In Somalia during 1993–94, for example, the breakdown of law and order was so complete that even United Nations food relief convoys proceeding to famine areas under armed guard were held up by bandits.

PUBLIC ACTION Public action to violate property rights occurs when public officials, such as politicians and government bureaucrats, extort income or resources from property holders. This can be done through a number of mechanisms, including levying excessive taxation, requiring expensive licenses or permits from property holders, taking assets into state ownership without compensating the owners (as occurred to the assets of numerous U.S. firms in Iran after the 1979 Iranian revolution), or by demanding bribes from businesses in return for the rights to operate in a country, industry, or location. For example, the government of the late Ferdinand Marcos in the Philippines was famous for demanding bribes from foreign businesses wishing to operate in that country.[13]

Another example of such activity surfaced in mid-February 1994. The British paper *The Sunday Times* ran an article that alleged a £1 billion ($1.6 billion) sale of defense equipment by British companies to Malaysia was secured only after bribes had been paid to Malaysian government officials and

version n.翻译；说法
/'və:ʃən/

murder n.谋杀，凶杀
/'mə:də/ v.谋杀；糟蹋
损毁

spinster
spinter

after the British Overseas Development Administration (ODA) had agreed to approve a £234 million grant to the Malaysian government for a hydroelectric dam of (according to *The Sunday Times*) dubious economic value. The clear implication was that U.K. officials, in their enthusiasm to see British companies win a large defense contract, had yielded to pressures from "corrupt" Malaysian officials for bribes—both personal and in the form of the £234 million development grant.[14]

The Protection of Intellectual Property

Intellectual property refers to property, such as computer software, a screenplay, a music score, or the chemical formula for a new drug, that is the product of intellectual activity. It is possible to establish ownership rights over intellectual property through patents, copyrights, and trademarks. A **patent** grants the inventor of a new product or process exclusive rights to the manufacture, use, or sale of that invention. **Copyrights** are the exclusive legal rights of authors, composers, playwrights, artists, and publishers to publish and dispose of their work as they see fit. **Trademarks** are designs and names, often officially registered, by which merchants or manufacturers designate and differentiate their products (e.g., Christian Dior clothes).

The philosophy behind intellectual property laws is to reward the originator of a new invention, book, musical record, clothes design, restaurant chain, and the like for his or her idea and effort. As such, the laws are a very important stimulus to innovation and creative work. They provide an incentive for people to search for novel ways of doing things and they reward creativity. For example, consider innovation in the pharmaceutical industry. A patent will grant the inventor of a new drug a 17-year monopoly in production of that drug. This gives pharmaceutical firms an incentive to undertake the expensive, difficult, and time-consuming basic research required to generate new drugs (on average it costs $100 million in research and development [R&D] and takes 12 years to get a new drug on the market). Without the guarantees provided by patents, it is unlikely that companies would commit themselves to extensive basic research.[15]

The protection of intellectual property rights differs greatly from country to country. While many countries have stringent intellectual property regulations on their books, the *enforcement* of these regulations has often been lax. This has been the case even among countries that have signed important international agreements to protect intellectual property, such as the **Paris Convention for the Protection of Industrial Property**, which 96 countries are party to. Weak enforcement encourages the piracy of intellectual property. China and Thailand have recently been among the worst offenders in Asia. For example, in China local bookstores commonly maintain a section that is off-limits to foreigners; it ostensibly is reserved for sensitive political literature, but it more often displays illegally copied textbooks. Pirated computer software is also widely available in China. Similarly, the streets of Bangkok, the capital of Thailand, are lined with stands selling pirated copies of Rolex watches, Levi blue jeans, videotapes, and computer software.

Estimates suggest that Asian violations of intellectual property rights cost U.S. computer software companies $6 billion annually and U.S. pharmaceutical companies at least $500 million annually.[16] Moreover, according to the Business Software Alliance, the software industry's trade group, in 1995

intellectual property Property, such as computer software, screenplays, musical scores, or chemical formulas for new drugs, that is the product of intellectual activity.

patent Document giving the inventor of a new product or process exclusive rights to the manufacture, use, or sale of that invention.

copyrights Exclusive legal rights of authors, composers, playwrights, artists, and publishers to publish and dispose of their work as they see fit.

trademarks Designs and names, often officially registered, by which merchants or manufacturers designate and differentiate their products.

Paris Convention for the Protection of Industrial Property International agreement signed by 96 countries to protect intellectual property rights.

piracy cost the global software industry $15.2 billion in lost revenues.[17] China emerges as the biggest single offender. The U.S. Department of Commerce estimates that during 1994 some 98 percent of computer software in use in China was pirated, as were 90 percent of all CD music recordings. In total, the Department of Commerce estimates that business worth $3 billion to U.S. corporations is lost to piracy in China.[18]

International businesses have a number of possible responses to such violations. Firms can lobby their respective governments to push for international agreements to ensure that intellectual property rights are protected in law, and that the law is enforced. An example of such lobbying is given in the "Management Focus" on page 54, which looks at how Microsoft prompted the U.S. government to start insisting that other countries abide by stricter intellectual property laws.

Partly as a result of such actions, international laws are currently being strengthened. As we shall see in Chapter 5, the most recent world trade agreement, which was signed in 1994 by 117 countries, for the first time extends the scope of the General Agreement on Tariffs and Trade (GATT) to cover intellectual property. Under the new agreement, as of 1995 a council of the newly created World Trade Organization (WTO) oversees the enforcement of much stricter intellectual property regulations. These regulations oblige WTO members to grant and enforce patents lasting at least 20 years and copyrights lasting 50 years. Rich countries must comply with the rules within a year. Poor countries, in which such protection has generally been much weaker, have 5 years' grace, and the very poorest have 10 years.[19] (For further details, see Chapter 5.)

One problem with these new regulations, however, is that the world's biggest violator—China—is not yet a member of the WTO and is not obliged to adhere to the agreement. However, after pressure from the U.S. government, which included the threat of substantial trade sanctions, in 1996 the Chinese government agreed to enforce its existing intellectual property rights regulations (in China, as in many countries, the problem is not a lack of laws; the problem is that the existing laws are not enforced). During 1996 Chinese officials closed down 19 counterfeit CD-ROM factories with a capacity of 30 to 50 million units a year. Still, according to the Business Software Alliance, a further 21 counterfeit CD-ROM factories were still operating in China as of late 1996.[20]

In addition to lobbying their governments, firms may want to stay out of countries where intellectual property laws are lax rather than risk having their ideas stolen by local entrepreneurs (such reasoning partly underlay decisions by Coca-Cola and IBM to pull out of India in the early 1970s). Firms also need to be alert to ensure that pirated copies of their products produced in countries where intellectual property laws are lax do not turn up in their home market or in third countries. The U.S. computer software giant Microsoft, for example, recently discovered that pirated Microsoft software, produced illegally in Thailand, was being sold worldwide as the real thing (including in the United States). In addition, Microsoft has encountered significant problems with pirated software in China, the details of which are discussed in the next "Management Focus."

Product Safety and Product Liability

Product safety laws set certain safety standards to which a product must adhere. Product liability involves holding a firm and its officers responsible when a product causes injury, death, or damage. Product liability can be much greater if a product does not conform to required safety standards. There are both civil and criminal product liability laws. Civil laws call for payment and money damages. Criminal liability laws result in fines or imprisonment. Both civil and criminal liability laws are probably more extensive in the United States than in any other country; although many other Western nations also have comprehensive liability laws. Liability laws are typically least extensive in less developed nations.

A boom in product liability suits and awards in the United States has resulted in a dramatic increase in the cost of liability insurance. In turn, many business executives argue that the high costs of liability insurance in the United States are making American businesses less competitive in the global marketplace. This view was supported by the Bush administration. For example, former Vice President Dan Quayle once argued that the United States has too many lawyers and that product liability awards are too large. According to Quayle, the result is that product liability insurance rates are typically much lower overseas, thereby giving foreign firms a competitive advantage. Quayle does have a point; American tort costs amount to about 2.4 percent of gross domestic product (GDP), three times as much as in any other industrialized country. So the costs of lawsuits do seem to put America at a competitive disadvantage.[22]

The competitiveness issue apart, country differences in product safety and liability laws raise an important ethical issue for firms doing business abroad. Specifically, when the product safety laws are tougher in a firm's home country than in a foreign country, and/or when liability laws are more lax, should a firm doing business in that foreign country adhere to the more relaxed local standards, or should it adhere to the standards of its home country? While the ethical thing to do is undoubtedly to adhere to home country standards, firms have been known to take advantage of lax safety and liability laws to do business in a manner that would not be allowed back home.

Contract Law

A contract is a document that specifies the conditions under which an exchange is to occur, and details the rights and obligations of the parties to a contract. Many business transactions are regulated by some form of contract. Contract law is the body of law that governs contract enforcement. The parties to an agreement normally resort to contract law when one party believes the other has violated either the letter or the spirit of an agreement.

Contract law can differ significantly among countries, and as such it affects the kind of contracts that an international business will want to use to safeguard its position should a contract dispute arise. The main differences can be traced to differences in legal tradition. There are two main legal traditions found in the world today—the **common law system** and the **civil law system**. The common law system evolved in England over hundreds of years. It is now found in most of Britain's former colonies, including the United States. Common law is based on tradition, precedent, and custom. When law courts interpret common law, they do so with regard to these characteristics. Civil law is based on a very detailed set of laws that are organized into codes. Among other things, these codes define the laws that govern business transactions. When law courts interpret civil law, they do so with regard to these codes. Over 80 countries, including Germany, France, Japan, and Russia, operate with a civil law system. Since

common law system Legal system based on tradition, precedent, and custom that evolved in England over hundreds of years and is now found in Britain's former colonies, including the United States.

civil law system Legal system based on a detailed set of laws, organized into codes, that is used in more than 80 countries, including Germany, France, Japan, and Russia.

Microsoft Battles Software Piracy in China

Microsoft, the world's biggest personal computer software company, developed MS-DOS and then Windows, respectively the operating system and graphical user interface that now reside on over 90 percent of the world's personal computers. In addition, Microsoft has a slew of best-selling applications software, including its word processing program (Microsoft Word), spreadsheet program (Excel), and presentation program (Power Point). An integral part of Microsoft's international strategy has been expansion into mainland China, where there were an estimated 2.2 million

personal computers in use in 1994, a number that is expected to grow by at least 1 million per year through the rest of the decade. Moreover, with a population of 1.5 billion, China represents a potentially huge market for Microsoft.

Microsoft's initial goal is to build up Chinese sales from nothing in 1994 to $100 million by 2000. However, the company has to overcome a very serious obstacle before it can achieve this goal—software piracy. Over 95 percent of the software used in China in 1995 was pirated. Microsoft is a prime target of this activity. Most Microsoft products used in China are illegal copies made and then sold with no payment being made to Microsoft. For example, Microsoft executives

in China recently came across a pirated CD-ROM set containing nearly every top-selling program that Microsoft had ever written. China's government is believed to be one of the worst offenders. Microsoft's lawyers complain that Beijing doesn't yet budget for software purchases, forcing its cash-strapped bureaucracy to find cheap software solutions. Thus, Microsoft claims, much of the government ends up using pirated software.

To make matters worse, China is becoming a mass exporter of counterfeit software. Just a few blocks from Microsoft's Hong Kong office is a tiny shop that offers CD-ROMs, each crammed with dozens of computer programs that collectively are worth about $20,000. The asking price

common law tends to be relatively ill-specified, contracts drafted under a common law framework tend to be very detailed with all contingencies spelled out. In civil law systems, however, contracts tend to be much shorter and less specific, since many of the issues typically covered in a common law contract are already covered in a civil code.

The Determinants of Economic Development

One reason for looking at the different political, economic, and legal systems in the world is that collectively these different systems can have a profound impact on the level of a country's economic development, and hence on the is about 500 Hong Kong dollars, or $52! The Hong Kong customs recently seized a shipment of 2,200 such CDs en route from China to Belgium.

Microsoft officials are quick to point out the problem arises because the Chinese judicial authorities do not enforce their own laws. Microsoft found this out in 1993 when it first tried to use China's judicial system to sue software pirates. Microsoft pressed officials in China's southern province of Guangdong to raid a manufacturer who was producing counterfeit holograms that Microsoft used to authenticate its software manuals. The Chinese authorities prosecuted the counterfeit manufacturer, acknowledged that a copyright violation had occurred, but awarded Microsoft only $2,600 and fined the pirate company $3,000! Microsoft is appealing the verdict and is requesting $20 million in damages.

Another Microsoft response to the problem has been to reduce the price on its software to compete with pirated versions. In October 1994 Microsoft reduced the price on its Chinese software by as much as 200 percent. However, this action may have little impact, for the programs are still priced at $100 to $200, compared to a price of about $20 for an illegal copy of the same software.

Yet another tactic adopted by the company has been to lobby the U.S. government to pressure Chinese authorities to start enforcing their own laws. As part of its lobbying effort, Microsoft has engaged in its own version of "guerrilla warfare," digging through trash bins, paying locals to spy, even posing as money-grubbing businessmen to collect evidence of piracy, which is then passed on to U.S. trade officials. The tactic has worked because the U.S. government currently has some leverage over China. China wishes to join the new World Trade Organization and views U.S. support as crucial. The United States has said it will not support Chinese membership unless China starts enforcing its intellectual property laws. This demand was backed up by a threat to impose tariffs of $1.08 billion on Chinese exports unless China agreed to stricter enforcement. After a tense period during which both countries were at loggerheads, the Chinese backed down and acquiesced to U.S. demands in February 1995. The Chinese government agreed to start enforcing its intellectual property rights laws, to crack down on factories that the U.S. identified as pirating U.S. goods, to respect U.S. trademarks, including Microsoft's, and to instruct Chinese government ministries to stop using pirated software.

Whether this agreement will make a difference remains to be seen. Microsoft, however, is taking no chances. The company announced it would work with the Chinese Ministry of Electronics to develop a Chinese version of the Windows® 95 operating system. Microsoft's logic is that the best way to stop the Chinese government from using pirated software is to go into business together. Once the Chinese have a stake in maximizing sales of legitimate Microsoft products, the company reckons the government will also have a strong incentive to crack down on sales of counterfeit software.[21]

attractiveness of a country as a possible market and/or production location for a firm. Here we look first at how countries differ in their level of development. Then we look at how political economy impacts on economic progress.

Differences in Economic Development

Different countries have dramatically different levels of economic development. One common measure of economic development is a country's gross domestic product (GDP) per head of population. GDP is often regarded as a yardstick for the economic activity of a country; it measures the total value of the goods and services produced annually. Map 2.2 (page 58) summarizes the GDP per head of the world's nations in 1994. As can be seen, countries

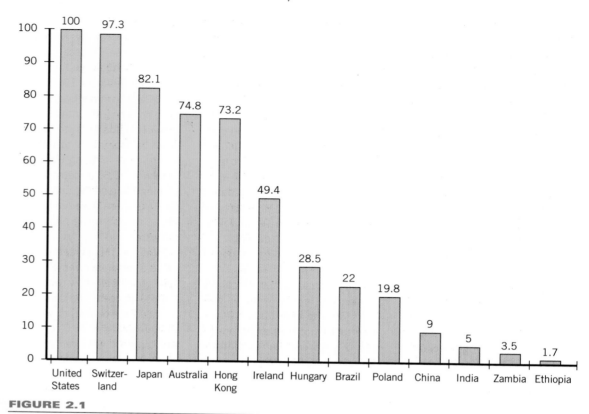

FIGURE 2.1

PPP Index for Selected Countries
Source: United Nations.

such as Japan, Sweden, Switzerland, and the United States are among the richest on this measure, while the large countries of China and India are among the poorest. Japan, for example, had a 1993 GDP per head of $28,217, whereas China achieved only $379 and India $307. The world's poorest country, the Sudan, had a GDP per head of only $55, while the world's richest, Switzerland, came in at $36,231.[23]

However, GDP per head figures can be misleading since they don't consider differences in the cost of living. For example, although the 1993 GDP per head of Switzerland at $36,231 exceeded that of the United States, which was $23,119, the higher cost of living in Switzerland meant that American citizens could actually afford more goods and services than Swiss citizens. To account for differences in the cost of living, the United Nations has calculated a purchasing power parity index (PPP). This adjusts GDP per head for the cost of living. This index allows for a more direct comparison of living standards in different countries. The index is set equal to 100 for the country in which PPP is the highest (which happens to be the United States). The PPP index for a selection of countries is summarized in Figure 2.1.

As can be seen, there are striking differences in the standard of living in different countries. Figure 2.1 suggests that the average Indian citizen can afford to consume only 5 percent of the goods and services consumed by the average U.S. citizen. Given this, one might conclude that despite having a population of close to 900 million, India is unlikely to be a very lucrative market for the consumer products produced by many Western international businesses. However, this is not quite the correct conclusion to draw, for India has a fairly wealthy middle class, despite its large number of very poor people.

A problem with the data presented in both Map 2.2 and Figure 2.1 is that they give a static picture of development. They tell us, for example, that China is much poorer than the United States, but they do not tell us if China is closing the gap. To assess this, we have to look at the economic growth rates achieved by different countries. Figure 2.2 summarizes the rate of growth in GDP achieved by a number of countries between 1985 and 1993. Although countries such as China and India are currently very poor, their economies are growing more rapidly than those of many of the advanced nations of the West. Thus, in time they may become advanced nations themselves and become huge markets for the products of international businesses. Given their future potential, international businesses may want to get a foothold in these markets now. Even though their current contribution to an international firm's revenues might be small, their future contributions could be much larger. But Figure 2.2 also tells us that the economies of the former Communist states of Russia and Hungary have shrunk substantially over the 1985–93 time period.

A number of other indicators can also be used to get a feeling for the level of a country's economic development, and for its likely future growth rate. These include literacy rates, the number of people per doctor, infant mortality rates, life expectancy, calorie (food) consumption per head, car ownership per 1,000 people, and education spending as a percentage of GDP. In an attempt to assess the impact of such factors on the quality of life in a country, the United Nations has developed a **Human Development Index**. This index is based on three measures: life expectancy, literacy rates, and whether average incomes, based on PPP estimates, are sufficient to meet the basic needs of life in a country (adequate food, shelter, and health care). The Human Development Index is scaled from 0 to 100. Countries scoring less than 50 are classified as having low human development (the quality of life is poor), those scoring from 50 to 80 are classified as having medium human development, while those countries that score above 80 are classified as having high human development. Table 2.1 (page 60) summarizes the scores received by a select group of countries. Table 2.1 also gives population figures and average annual population growth rates for 1996. The disturbing fact revealed by Table 2.1 is that some of the world's poorest countries, as measured by the Human Development Index, are not only heavily populated, but also have rapidly expanding populations. (For example, if India's population growth rate of 1.64 percent is maintained, the country's population will double in just over 44 years). Thus, their situation may deteriorate rather than improve over the next few decades. If this occurs, the implications for the rest of the world could be profound and may include widespread famine and war. In such circumstances, the underdevelopment of the Third World may hold back the continuing economic growth of the world's advanced industrialized nations.

Human Development Index United Nations-developed index based on life expectancy, literacy rates, and whether average incomes are sufficient to meet the basic needs of life in a country.

Political Economy and Economic Progress

What is the relationship between political economy and economic progress? This question has been the subject of a vigorous debate among academics and policy makers for some time. Despite the long debate, this remains a question for which it is impossible to give an unambiguous answer. However, it is

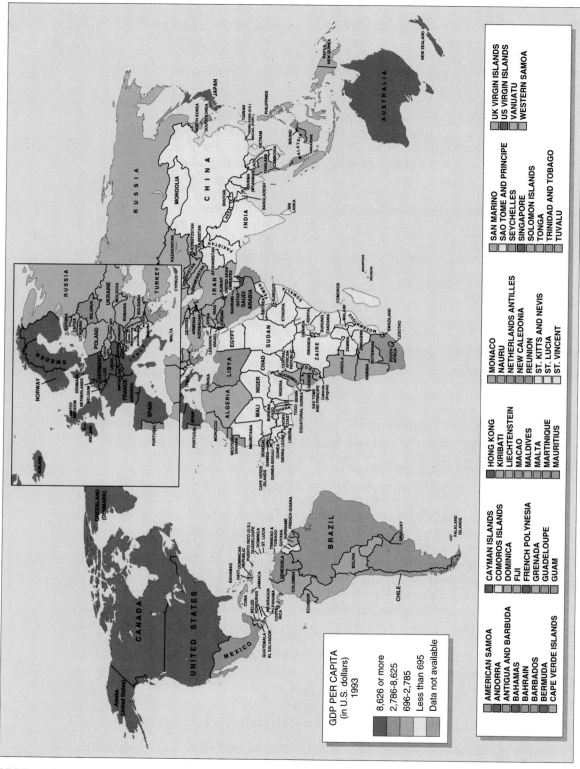

MAP 2.2

GDP per Head, 1994

Source: Map data from World Bank, *World Development Report,* 1994.

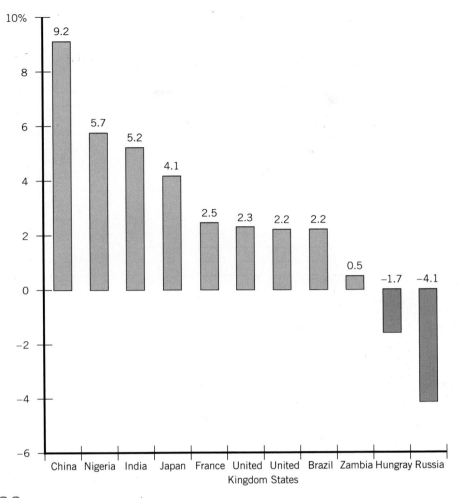

FIGURE 2.2

Average Annual Percentage Change in Real GDP for Select Countries, 1985–93
Source: *1997 CIA Fact Book.*

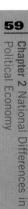
possible to untangle the main threads of the academic arguments and make a few broad generalizations as to the nature of the relationship between political economy and economic progress.

INNOVATION IS THE ENGINE OF GROWTH There is general agreement that innovation is the engine of long-run economic growth.[24] Those who make this argument define **innovation** broadly to include not just new products, but also new processes, new organizations, new management practices, and new strategies. Thus, the Toys R Us strategy of establishing large warehouse-type toy stores and then engaging in heavy advertising and price discounting to sell the merchandise can be classified as an innovation because Toys R Us was the first company to pursue this particular strategy. So one can conclude that if a country's economy is to sustain long-run economic growth, the business environment within that country must be conducive to the production of innovations.

innovation Process through which people create new products, new processes, new organizations, new management practices, and new strategies.

TABLE 2.1

Human Development Index and Population Statistics

Country	Human Development Index	Population (millions)	Annual Percentage Population Growth Rate
Japan	98	124.3	0.4
United States	98	255.4	0.9
Canada	98	27.9	1.4
Britain	96	57.7	0.3
Germany	96	80.5	0.6
Hungary	89	10.2	-0.6
Mexico	81	85.0	1.8
Malaysia	79	18.6	2.5
Brazil	73	153.8	1.8
Thailand	72	58.0	1.7
China	57	1,166.1	1.5
Indonesia	52	185.3	1.8
India	31	883.5	2.1
Pakistan	31	119.3	3.1
Nigeria	25	101.9	2.9
Bangladesh	19	112.8	2.2

Source: Human Development Index from World Bank, *World Development Report 1996*. Population and population growth data from *1997 CIA Fact Book*. CIA data are all 1996 estimates.

INNOVATION REQUIRES A MARKET ECONOMY This leads logically to a further question: what is required for the business environment of a country to be conducive to innovation? One factor is the advantages of a market economy.[25] It has been argued that the economic freedom associated with a market economy creates greater incentives for innovation than either a planned or mixed economy. In a market economy any individual who has an innovative idea is free to try to make money out of that idea by starting a business (by engaging in entrepreneurial activity). Similarly, existing businesses are free to improve their operations through innovation. To the extent that they are successful, both individual entrepreneurs and established businesses can reap rewards in the form of high profits. Thus, in market economies there are enormous incentives to try to develop innovations.

In contrast, in a planned economy the state owns all means of production. Consequently there is no opportunity for entrepreneurial individuals to try to develop valuable new innovations, since it is the state, rather than the individual, that captures all the gains. The lack of economic freedom and incentives for innovation was probably one main factor in the economic stagnation of so many former Communists states, which led ultimately to their collapse at the end of the 1980s. Similar stagnation occurred in many mixed economies in those sectors where the state had a monopoly (such as health care and telecommunications in Britain). In turn, this stagnation provided the impetus for the widespread privatization of state-owned enterprises that began in many mixed economies during the mid-1980s and that is still occurring today (**privatization** refers to the process of selling state-owned enterprises to private investors).

A recent study of 102 countries over a 20-year period provides compelling evidence that there is a strong relationship between economic freedom (as

privatization Process of selling state-owned enterprises to private investors.

provided by a market economy) and economic growth.[26] This study found that the more economic freedom a country had between 1975 and 1995, the more economic growth it achieved and the richer its citizens became. The 6 countries that had persistently high ratings of economic freedom during the 1975–95 period (Hong Kong, Switzerland, Singapore, the United States, Canada, and Germany) were also all in the top 10 in terms of economic growth rates. In contrast, no country with a persistently low rating achieved a respectable growth rate. Indeed, average annual GDP *fell* at an annual rate of 0.6 percent in the 16 countries for which the index of economic freedom declined the most during the 1975–95 period.

INNOVATION REQUIRES STRONG PROPERTY RIGHTS

Strong legal protection of property rights is another requirement for a business environment conducive to innovation and economic growth.[27] Both individuals and businesses must be given the opportunity to profit from innovative ideas. Without strong property rights protection, businesses and individuals run the risk that the profits from their innovative efforts will be expropriated, either by criminal elements or by the state itself. The state can expropriate the profits from innovation through legal means such as excessive taxation or through illegal means such as demands from state bureaucrats for kickbacks in return for granting an individual or firm a license to do business in a certain area. According to the Nobel Prize-winning economist Douglass North, throughout history many governments have displayed a tendency toward such behavior. When property rights are not adequately enforced, the incentives for innovation and entrepreneurial activity are reduced—since the profits from such activity are "stolen"—and hence the rate of economic growth is reduced.

THE REQUIRED POLITICAL SYSTEM

There is a great deal of debate as to the kind of political system that best achieves a functioning market economy with strong protection for property rights.[28] We in the West tend to associate a representative democracy with a market economic system, strong property rights protection, and economic progress. Building on this, we tend to argue that democracy is good for growth.[29] However, there are examples of totalitarian regimes that have fostered a market economy and strong property rights protection and experienced rapid economic growth. The examples include four of the fastest-growing economies of the past 30 years—South Korea, Taiwan, Singapore, and Hong Kong—all of which have grown faster than the Western democracies. All these economies had one thing in common for at least the first period of their economic takeoff—undemocratic governments! At the same time, there are examples of countries with stable democratic governments, such as India, where economic growth has remained very sluggish for long periods (although things are now changing in India).

Commenting on this issue in 1992, Lee Kuan Yew, Singapore's leader for many years, told an audience, "I do not believe that democracy necessarily leads to development. I believe that a country needs to develop discipline more than democracy. The exuberance of democracy leads to undisciplined and disorderly conduct which is inimical to development."[30] Others have argued that many of the current problems in Eastern Europe and the states of the former Soviet Union are due to the fact that democracy arrived before economic reform, making it more difficult for elected governments to introduce the policies that, while painful in the short run, were needed to promote rapid economic growth. It has become something of a cliché to argue that Russia got its political and economic reforms the wrong way around, unlike China, which maintains a totalitarian government but has moved rapidly toward a market economy.

However, those who argue for the value of a totalitarian regime miss an important point—if dictators made countries rich, then much of Africa, Asia, and Latin America should have been growing rapidly for the past 40 years, and this has not been the case. Only a certain kind of totalitarian regime is capable of promoting economic growth. It must be a dictatorship that is committed to a free market system and strong protection of property rights. Moreover, there is no guarantee that a dictatorship will continue to pursue such progressive policies. Dictators are rarely so benevolent; many are tempted to use the apparatus of the state to further their own private ends, in which cases property rights are often violated and economic growth stalls. Given this, it seems likely that democratic regimes are far more conducive to long-term economic growth than a dictatorship, even one of the benevolent kind. Only in a well-functioning mature democracy are property rights truly secure.[31]

ECONOMIC PROGRESS BEGETS DEMOCRACY While it is possible to argue that democracy is not a necessary precondition for the establishment of a free market economy in which property rights are protected, it seems evident that subsequent economic growth leads to establishment of democratic regimes. Several of the fastest-growing Asian economies have recently adopted more democratic governments, including South Korea and Taiwan. Thus, while democracy may not always be the cause of initial economic progress, it seems to be one of the consequences of that progress.

A strong belief that economic progress leads to the adoption of a democratic regime underlies the fairly permissive attitude that many Western governments have adopted toward human rights in China. Although China has a totalitarian government in which human rights are abused, many Western countries have been hesitant to criticize the country too much for fear that this might hurt the country's march toward a free market system. The belief is that once China has a free market system, democracy will follow. Whether this optimistic vision comes to pass remains to be seen. Nevertheless, such a vision was an important factor in the U.S. government's 1995 decision to grant China most-favored-nation trading status (which makes it easier for Chinese firms to sell products in the United States) despite reports of widespread human rights abuses in China.

States in Transition

Since the late 1980s there have been major changes in the political economy of many of the world's nation-states. Two trends have been evident. First, during the late 1980s and early 1990s, a wave of democratic revolutions swept the world. In country after country totalitarian governments collapsed, to be replaced by democratically elected governments that were typically more committed to free market capitalism than their predecessors had been. The change was most dramatic in Eastern Europe, where the collapse of

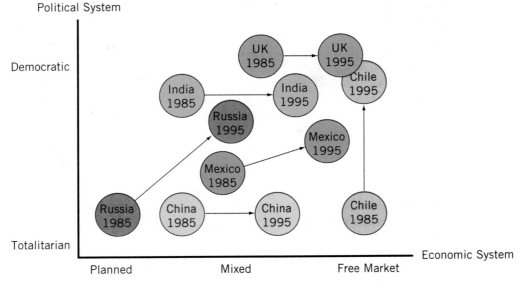

FIGURE 2.3

Changing Political Economy, 1985–95

Communism brought an end to the Cold War and led to the breakup of the Soviet Union, but similar changes were occurring throughout the world during the same period. Across much of Asia, Latin America, and Africa there was a shift toward greater democracy. Second, there has been a strong move away from centrally planned and mixed economies and toward more of a free market economic model.

Figure 2.3 illustrates some shifts in political economy that occurred during the 1985–96 period. While changes were widespread and while there was a general shift toward democratic political institutions and a free market system, there was a major difference in the degree of change from country to country. Russia has undergone a marked change, with major shifts in both its political and economic system. The same is true of most other Eastern European states in the post-Communist era (e.g., the Czech Republic, Poland, Hungary). In contrast, countries such as India and the United Kingdom, which already had democratic political institutions and a mixed economy in place, have undergone a less dramatic shift toward a more free market system. Below we briefly review some of these changes and draw out the implications for business.

Eastern Europe and the Former Soviet Union

Following the end of World War II, Soviet-backed Communist governments took power in eight Eastern European states: Poland, Czechoslovakia, Hungary, Romania, Bulgaria, Albania, Yugoslavia, and East Germany. This set the scene for 40 years of ideological conflict between the Communist bloc, dominated by the Soviet Union, and the democratic West. The conflict began to thaw in 1985 when Mikhail Gorbachev became general secretary of the Soviet Communist party and began his program of *perestroika*. By that time the gulf between the vibrant and wealthy economies of the West and the stagnating economies of the Communist East had become so immense that even the most hard-line Communist ideologue had to have noticed. With the tacit support of Gorbachev, several of the Communist regimes of Eastern Europe began to loosen their repressive economic and political systems in an attempt to revive their stalled economies. What they discovered, however, was that once the genie of freedom had been let out of the bottle, it could not easily be put back. During 1989, Communist government after Communist government fell.

The biggest change occurred in 1991 in the Soviet Union. By 1991 the USSR had already moved significantly down the road toward political freedom—but not economic freedom. Faced with the breakup of the USSR into quasi-independent and democratically inclined states, the old Communist hard-liners attempted to remove Mikhail Gorbachev from power. The coup d'état attempt collapsed when it became apparent that much of the military was not going to back the coup plotters. The end result was that the Communist party was outlawed and the reform movement gained strength. As a result, on January 1, 1992, the Union of Soviet Socialist Republics passed into history, to be replaced by 15 independent republics, 11 of which elected to remain associated as a Commonwealth of Independent States.

The post-Communist history of this region has not been easy. The move toward greater political and economic freedom has often been accompanied by economic and political chaos.[32] Most of these countries began to liberalize their economies in the heady days of the early 1990s. They dismantled decades of price controls, allowed widespread private ownership of businesses, and permitted much greater competition. Most also planned to sell state-owned enterprises to private investors. However, given the vast number of such enterprises and how inefficient many were, and hence how unappealing to private investors, most privatization efforts moved forward slowly. In this new environment many inefficient state-owned enterprises found that without a guaranteed market they could not survive. The newly democratic governments often continued to support these loss-making enterprises in an attempt to stave off massive unemployment. The resulting subsidies to state-owned enterprises led to ballooning budget deficits that were typically financed by printing money. The tendency of governments in these countries to print money, along with the lack of price controls, also often led to hyperinflation. In 1993 the inflation rate was 21 percent in Hungary, 38 percent in Poland, 841 percent in Russia, and a staggering 10,000 percent in the Ukraine.[33]

Another consequence of the shift toward a market economy was collapsing output as inefficient state-owned enterprises failed to find buyers for their goods. As Figure 2.4 illustrates, real gross domestic product (GDP) fell dramatically in many post-Communist states in the 1990–94 period. However, the corner has been turned in a number of countries. Poland, the Czech Republic, and Hungary now all boast growing economies and relatively low inflation. On the other hand, countries such as Russia and the Ukraine still grapple with major economic problems.

A recent study by the World Bank suggests the post-Communist states that have been most successful at transforming their economies were those that followed an economic policy best described as "shock therapy." In these coun-

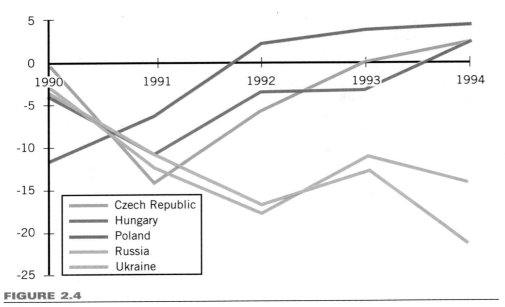

FIGURE 2.4

Real Percentage GDP Growth for 1990–94 in Five Post-Communist States
Source: M. Wolf and C. Freeland, "The Long Day's Journey to Market," *Financial Times*, March 7, 1995, p. 15.

tries, which include the Czech Republic, Hungary, and Poland, prices and trade were liberated quickly, inflation was held in check by tight monetary policy, and the privatization of state-owned industries was implemented quickly. Among the 26 economies of Eastern Europe and the former Soviet Union, the World Bank found a strong positive correlation between the imposition of such "shock therapy" and subsequent economic growth. Speedy reformers suffered smaller falls in output and returned to growth more quickly than those such as Russia and the Ukraine that moved more slowly.[34]

Western Europe

Although most of Western Europe has enjoyed stable democratic government for some time, there has been a major ideological shift in recent years. For most of the post-WWII period, social democratic ideology, with its emphasis on state involvement in certain sectors of the economy, was adhered to throughout Western Europe. In many Western European nations basic industries such as telecommunications, energy production, airlines, and railroads were often state owned, while many other sectors of the economy faced heavy state regulation. Starting with Margaret Thatcher's Conservative government in Britain during the early 1980s, governments have moved progressively away from this mixed economy model. State-owned industries have been **privatized** (sold to private investors) and restrictive regulations have been lifted, allowing for much greater competition in industries formerly dominated by state-owned monopolies. For example, the privatization of the formerly state-owned British telephone company, British Telecom (BT), in the mid-1980s was followed by deregulation of the British telecommunications industry, which allowed other companies to compete with the formerly state-owned company.

privatized Sold to private investors.

The trend toward privatization and deregulation is still going on. In France the government is implementing a program that calls for the privatization of 21 state-owned enterprises between 1994 and 2000, including some of France's most powerful industrial groups such as oil giant Elf-Aquitaine, Renault, and Union des Assurances de Paris, an insurance company. In Germany the government is pressing ahead slowly but steadily with its privatization plans, including Deutsche Telekom, the German telecommunications monopoly. Italy has plans to privatize 18 state-owned enterprises.[35]

Asia

During the 1980s and early 1990s significant changes were also occurring in Asia. A shift toward greater political democracy occurred in the Philippines, Thailand, Taiwan, and South Korea. In Vietnam the ruling Communist party removed many price controls and began to shift toward a market economy. In North Korea, still one of the most repressive of all Communist regimes, signs of a thaw in relations with its longtime capitalist enemy South Korea could be seen. In India, a democratic country since 1947 but one with a long history of government involvement in economic activity and a mixed economy, the government of P.V. Narasimha Rao embarked on an aggressive reform program aimed at moving the Indian economy sharply in the direction of the free market model. The "Country Focus" on page 68 profiles these changes in detail.

Notwithstanding what is now occurring in India, perhaps the most momentous changes in Asia are those taking place in China. In 1979 the Communist government of China started to shift the Chinese economy from a pure command economy to a mixed economy. The government began by permitting private ownership of farmland and allowing free markets for farm products. The growth rate of farmers' output quadrupled, from 2 percent a year in 1958–78 to 8 percent a year in 1979–84. In 1984 the reforms were extended to the cities. Private ownership was allowed in a number of industries; the number of products allocated through central planning was reduced from 250 to 20; and free markets were allowed to function in a wide range of industries. Perhaps the most important reform at this time, however, was creation of a number of special economic zones in which free markets were allowed to operate without any restrictions, private ownership was allowed, and foreign companies were permitted to invest. Three of the original four economic zones were set up in the Southern province of Guangdong (next to Hong Kong). Since then, Guangdong has become the fastest-growing region in the world, with growth rates of over 20 percent per year during the late 1980s and early 1990s, while China's economy as a whole has been growing at over 10 percent per year during the 1990s. Clearly, the shift toward free market economics, by creating incentives for entrepreneurial activity, is sending China down a road that has already been taken by many of its Asian neighbors, such as Japan, Taiwan, and South Korea.[37]

As with much of Eastern Europe, in 1989 China was also swept by a wave of protests in favor of greater political democracy. Unlike Eastern Europe, however, in China the democracy movement was violently suppressed by the brutal 1989 massacre in Tiananmen Square. This was initially accompanied by a scaling back of China's pro-market reforms. Fortunately, the scaling back seems to have been temporary. China now seems to be back on the road to economic reform and many longtime observers believe political reform will follow within a decade.[38]

Latin America

Latin America, too, shifted toward greater democracy and a greater commitment to free market economics during the late 1980s and early 1990s. At the beginning of the 1980s, almost all the countries of Latin America were run by dictatorships, most of them military (although Communists held sway in Nicaragua and Cuba). By the early 1990s almost all the countries were run by democratic governments (although in 1992 Peru's democratically elected president suspended many democratic institutions, and in Cuba Communists still ruled).

Under their dictatorships, Latin American countries for decades erected high barriers to imports and foreign direct investment. The belief was that allowing free trade and investment would result in Latin American economies becoming dominated by Western—particularly U.S.—multinational firms. Thus, in the interest of preserving their "national sovereignty," many Latin countries severely restricted trade and investment. At the same time, in several countries socialist-inclined governments took major corporations into state ownership. However, these policies failed to deliver economic growth and seemed to have had the opposite effect.

The tide began to turn in Chile in the 1970s when that country, under the government of an unsavory military dictatorship, shifted sharply in the direction of a free market economy. The largest shift, however, occurred in 1989 when Mexico, then run by the civilian government of President Salinas, moved toward a more free market economy. Under Salinas the Mexican government privatized many state-owned enterprises, repealed many of the laws that limited foreign direct investment, cut import tariffs to world levels, and in 1994 brought Mexico into the North American Free Trade Agreement (NAFTA) with the United States and Canada (discussed in Chapter 7). A host of other countries are now following Mexico's lead, including, most notably, the two Latin American giants of Argentina and Brazil.

Africa

Africa also is moving toward more democratic modes of government and free market economics. Most African countries gained their independence from colonial powers, particularly Britain, France, and Portugal, in the 1950s and 1960s. Although there were originally high hopes that the newly independent nations of Africa would become Western-style democracies, this did not happen. Instead, most rapidly became one-party states ruled by authoritarian leaders. Moreover, most of these leaders adhered to socialist theories and applied them to the running of their countries. One result was 30 years of economic mismanagement during which the African continent stagnated.

Today both socialism and totalitarianism are in a slow retreat across Africa. Since the late 1980s some 30 African countries have abandoned their experiments with socialism and moved toward a market economy. Similarly, de-

The Changing Political Economy of India

After gaining independence from Britain in 1947, India adopted a democratic system of government. However, the economic system that developed in India was a mixed economy characterized by a heavy dose of state enterprise and planning. This system placed major constraints around the growth of the private sector. Private companies could expand only with government permission. Under this system, derisively dubbed the "License Raj," private companies often had to wait months for government approval of routine business activities, such as expanding production or hiring a new director. It could take years to get permission to diversify into a new product. Moreover, much of heavy industry, such as autos, chemicals, and steel production, was reserved for state-owned enter-

prises. The development of a healthy private sector was also stunted by the imposition of production quotas and high tariffs on imports. Access to foreign exchange was limited, investment by foreign firms was restricted, there were strict controls on land use, and prices were routinely managed by the government, as opposed to being determined by market forces.

By the early 1990s it was clear that after 40 years of near stagnation, this economic system was incapable of delivering the kind of dramatic economic progress that many Southeastern Asian nations had started to enjoy. By 1994 India had an economy that was still smaller than Belgium's, despite having a population of 950 million. Its GDP per head was a paltry $310 and less than half the population could read. Only 6 million had access to telephones, and only 14 percent had access to clean sanitation. The World Bank estimated that some 40 percent of the world's desperately poor lived in India, and only 2.3 percent of

the population had a household income in excess of $2,484.

In 1991 the lack of progress led the government of Prime Minister P.V. Narasimha Rao to embark on an ambitious economic reform program. Much of the industrial licensing system was dismantled and several areas once closed to the private sector were opened, including electricity generation, parts of the oil industry, steelmaking, air transport, and some areas of the telecommunications industry. Foreign investment, formerly allowed in only grudgingly and subject to arbitrary ceilings, was suddenly welcomed. Approval is now automatic for foreign equity stakes of up to 51 percent in an Indian enterprise, and 100 percent foreign ownership is now allowed under certain circumstances. Raw materials and many industrial goods can now be freely imported, and the maximum tariff that can be levied on imports has been reduced from 400 percent to 65 percent. The top rate of income tax has also been reduced, and corporate tax has come down from 57.5 percent to 46 percent.

mocratic regimes are now gaining a foothold in Africa. During 1994 South Africa, Malawi, and Mozambique all held their first democratic elections, and 1996 saw the advent of democratic elections in Sierra Leone and Uganda. Nevertheless, even optimistic observers note that most African countries have a long way to go. Rigged elections, one-party states, and military governments are still common across the continent.

During the 1970s and 1980s the economies of most African states contracted sharply. According to a recent World Bank report, even if African countries now achieve a 3 percent annual growth rate in GDP, it will take 40

Judged by some measures, the response has been impressive. The economy has been expanding at an annual rate of just under 4 percent since 1992, exports have begun to grow at a respectable pace (they were up by 20 percent between 1993 and 1994), and corporate profits jumped 102 percent during 1994. Delivery trucks loaded with once-banned foreign products, such as Ruffles potato chips and Nestlé Crunch bars, rumble over India's pot-holed highways. Advertisements for AT&T's communications solutions are to be seen on New Delhi streets, signs of an upcoming liberalization of the telecom-munications industry. Moreover, foreign investment, which is a good indicator of the perceptions that foreign companies have about the health of the India economy, surged from $150 million in 1991 to $700 million in 1994.

However, India is still some way off from achieving the kind of free market economic system that can be found in the West. The reform process is being fought by many bureaucrats and politicians. Several Western companies now investing in India have painful memories of the 1970s when India nationalized the assets of foreign companies on terms that were tantamount to confiscation. Such memories are one reason companies such as IBM, Coca-Cola, and Mobil have kept their investments modest. Other foreign companies have made major investment commitments to India only after securing special guarantees. For example, AES Corporation, a power-generating company based in Virginia, recently concluded a deal to build power stations in India, but only after the Indian government agreed to give guarantees that it would pay for power delivered to Indian electric utilities if the utilities defaulted.[36]

years before many return to the level they were at in the early 1970s! The same report notes that foreign investors who might otherwise be attracted by Africa's cheap labor are deterred by the problems of doing business in countries where the rule of law is so weak that even simple contracts can be difficult to enforce and where businesses that do persevere have to bribe many poorly paid bureaucrats who can otherwise make business impossible.[39] The great hope for Africa is that the continent's potential economic powers, which include Nigeria, Kenya, and South Africa, will get their acts together and pull the rest of Africa along with them.

Implications

The geopolitical changes discussed above have several implications for international business. For one thing, the ideological conflict between collectivism and individualism that so defined the 20th century is winding down. The democratic free market ideology of the West has won the Cold War and has never been more widespread than it is in the mid-1990s. Although command economies still remain, and although totalitarian dictatorships can still be found around the world, for now the tide is running in favor of democracy and free markets.

The implications for business are enormous. For almost 50 years, half of the world was off-limits to Western businesses. Now that is changing. Many of the national markets of Eastern Europe, Latin America, Africa, and Asia may still be undeveloped and impoverished, but they are potentially enormous. With a population of 1.2 billion, the Chinese market alone is potentially bigger than that of the United States, the European Union, and Japan combined! Similarly India, with its 930 million people, is a potentially huge future market. In Latin America there are another 400 million potential consumers. It is unlikely that China, Russia, Poland, or any of the other states now moving toward a free market system will attain the living standards of the West soon. Nevertheless, the upside potential is so large that companies need to consider making inroads now.

However, just as the upside potential is large, so are the risks. Take the newly democratic states of Eastern Europe; they all profess a desire to move toward a free market economic system. Yet today, more than five years after the collapse of Communism, not all appear to know what that means. After decades of central planning and tight control over prices, markets are poorly understood, profit is still too often a dirty word, and the laws required to regulate business transactions, which we take for granted in the West, are largely absent. Moreover, faced with economic chaos, there is no guarantee that democracy will thrive. Totalitarian dictatorships could return, although they are unlikely to be of the Communist variety. Put another way, while the long-term potential for economic gain from investment in the world's new market economies is large, the risks associated with any such investment are also substantial. It would be foolish to ignore these.

Implications for Business

The implications of the material discussed in this chapter fall into two broad categories. First, the political, economic, and legal environments of a country clearly influence the *attractiveness* of that country as a market and/or investment site. The benefits, costs, and risks associated with doing business in a country are in part a function of that country's political, economic, and legal systems. Second, the political, economic, and legal systems of a country can raise important *ethical issues* that have implications for the practice of international business. Here we consider each of these issues.

Attractiveness

The overall attractiveness of a country as a market and/or investment site depends on balancing the likely long-term benefits of doing business in that country against the likely costs and risks. Next, we consider the determinants of benefits, costs, and risks.

BENEFITS In the most general sense the long-run monetary benefits of doing business in a country are a function of the size of a market, the present wealth (purchasing power) of consumers in that market, and the likely future wealth of consumers. While some markets are very large when measured by numbers of consumers (e.g., China and India), low living standards may imply limited purchasing power and, therefore, a relatively small market when measured in economic terms. While international businesses need to be aware of this distinction, they also need to keep in mind the likely future prospects of a country. In 1960, for example, South Korea was viewed as just another impoverished Third World nation. By 1988 it was the world's 18th largest economy, measured in terms of GDP. If present trends continue, by the year 2000 it will be one of the 10 largest economies in the world and the fourth largest trading nation after Japan, the United States, and Germany. International firms that recognized South Korea's potential in 1960, and began to do business in that country, may have reaped greater benefits than those that wrote off South Korea as another Third World nation.

By identifying and investing early in a potential future economic star, international firms get a head start in building up brand loyalty and learning about business practices in that country. These will pay back substantial dividends if that country achieves sustained high economic growth rates. In contrast, late entrants may find that they lack the brand loyalty and experience necessary to achieve a significant presence in the market. Put differently, in the language of business strategy, early entrants into potential future economic stars may be able to reap substantial **first-mover advantages**, while late entrants may fall victim to **late-mover disadvantages**.[40] (First-mover advantages are the advantages that accrue to early entrants into a market. Late-mover disadvantages are the handicap that late entrants might suffer.)

Two reasonably good predictors of a country's future economic prospects are its economic system and property rights regime. In this chapter we have seen that countries with free market economies in which property rights are well protected tend to achieve greater economic growth rates than command economies and/or economies where property rights are poorly protected. It follows that a country's economic system and property right regime, when taken together with market size (in terms of population), probably constitute reasonably good indicators of the potential long-run benefits of doing business in a country.[41]

COSTS The costs of doing business in a country are determined by a number of political, economic, and legal factors. With regard to political factors, the costs of doing business in a country can be increased by a need to pay off the politically powerful in order to be allowed by the government to do business in that country. Generally, the need to pay what are essentially bribes is greater in closed totalitarian states than in open democratic societies where politicians are held accountable by the electorate (although this is not a hard and fast distinction). Whether a company should pay bribes in return for market access should be determined on the basis of the legal and ethical implications of such action. We discuss this consideration later.

With regard to economic factors, one of the most important variables is the sophistication of a country's economy. It may be more costly to do business in relatively primitive or undeveloped economies because of the lack of infrastructure and supporting businesses. At the extreme, an international firm may have to provide its own infrastructure and supporting business, which obviously raises costs. For example, when McDonald's decided to open its

first-mover advantages
Advantages that accrue to early entrants into a business market.

late-mover disadvantages
Handicap suffered by late entrants into a business market.

first restaurant in Moscow, it found, much to its initial dismay, that to serve food and drink indistinguishable from that served in McDonald's restaurants elsewhere, it had to vertically integrate backward to supply its own needs. The quality of Russian-grown potatoes and meat was simply too poor. Thus, to protect the quality of its product, McDonald's set up its own dairy farms, cattle ranches, vegetable plots, and food-processing plants within Russia. This raised the costs of doing business in Russia relative to the costs in more sophisticated economies where high-quality inputs could be purchased on the open market.

As for legal factors, it can be more costly to do business in a country where local laws and regulations set strict standards with regard to product safety, safety in the workplace, environmental pollution, and the like (since adhering to such regulations is costly). It can also be more costly to do business in a country such as the United States, where the absence of a cap on damage awards has meant spiraling liability insurance rates. Moreover, it can be more costly to do business in a country that lacks well-established laws for regulating business practice (as is the case in many of the former Communist nations). Without a well-developed body of business contract law, international firms may find that there is no satisfactory way to resolve contract disputes and so they routinely face large losses from contract violations. Similarly, when local laws fail to adequately protect intellectual property, this can lead to the "theft" of an international business's intellectual property, with all that such action means in terms of lost income (see the "Management Focus" on Microsoft).

RISKS As with costs, the risks of doing business in a country are determined by a number of political, economic, and legal factors. On the political front, there is the issue of **political risk**. Political risk has been defined as *the likelihood that political forces will cause drastic changes in a country's business environment that adversely affect the profit and other goals of a particular business enterprise*.[42] So defined, political risk tends to be greater in countries experiencing social unrest and disorder, or in countries where the underlying nature of a society means there is a high likelihood of social unrest. Social unrest typically finds expression in strikes, demonstrations, terrorism, and, perhaps, violent conflict. Such unrest is more likely to be found in countries that contain more than one ethnic nationality, in countries where competing ideologies are battling for political control, and in countries where economic mismanagement has created high inflation and falling living standards (e.g., Russia in the early 1990s).

Social unrest can result in abrupt changes in government and government policy or, in some cases, in protracted civil strife. By its very nature, such strife has negative economic implications that may affect the profit goals of business enterprises. For example, in the aftermath of the 1979 Islamic revolution in Iran, the Iranian assets of numerous U.S. companies were seized by the new Iranian government without compensation. Similarly, today the violent disintegration of the Yugoslavian federation into warring states, including Bosnia, Croatia, and Serbia, has precipitated a collapse in the local economy and, consequently, a collapse in the profitability of investments in those countries.

On the economic front, **economic risks** arise from economic mismanagement by the government of a country. Economic risks can be defined as *the likelihood that economic mismanagement will cause drastic changes in a*

political risk

Likelihood that political forces will cause drastic changes in a country's business environment that adversely affect the profit and other goals of a business enterprise.

economic risk

Likelihood that economic mismanagement will cause drastic changes in a country's business environment that adversely affect the profit and other goals of a business enterprise.

country's business environment that adversely affect the profit and other goals of a particular business enterprise. Of course, economic risks are not independent of political risk. Economic mismanagement may give rise to significant social unrest and hence political risk. Nevertheless, economic risks are worth emphasizing as a separate category, since there is not always a one-to-one relationship between economic mismanagement and social unrest. The most visible indicator of economic mismanagement tends to be a country's inflation rate.

On the legal front, risks arise when a country's legal system fails to provide adequate safeguards in the case of contract violations or to provide for the protection of property rights. When legal safeguards are weak, firms are more likely to break contracts and/or steal intellectual property if they perceive it as being in their interests to do so. Thus, **legal risks** might be defined as *the likelihood that a trading partner will opportunistically break a contract or expropriate property rights*. When legal risks in a country are high, an international business might be hesitant to enter into a long-term contract or joint-venture agreement with a firm in that country. For example, in the 1970s when the Indian government passed a law requiring all foreign investors to enter into joint ventures with Indian companies, U.S. companies such as IBM and Coca-Cola closed their investments in India. They believed the Indian legal system did not provide for adequate protection of intellectual property rights. Thus, a very real danger existed that the Indian partners of IBM and Coca-Cola might expropriate the intellectual property of the American companies, which in the case of both IBM and Coca-Cola amounted to the core of their competitive advantage.

legal risk Likelihood that a trading partner will opportunistically break a contract or expropriate property rights.

OVERALL ATTRACTIVENESS The overall attractiveness of a country as a potential market and/or investment site for an international business depends on balancing the benefits, costs, and risks associated with doing business in that country. The costs and risks associated with doing business in a foreign country are typically lower in economically advanced and politically stable democratic nations, whereas they are greater in less developed and politically unstable nations. The calculus is complicated, however, by the fact that the potential *long-run* benefits bear little relationship to a nation's current stage of economic development or political stability. Rather, they depend on likely future economic growth rates. In turn, among other things, economic growth appears to be a function of a free market system and a country's capacity for growth (which may be greater in less developed nations). This leads one to conclude that, other things being equal, the benefit, cost, risk trade-off is likely to be most favorable in the case of politically stable developing nations that have free market systems. It is likely to be least favorable in the case of politically unstable developing nations that operate with a mixed or command economy.

Ethical Issues

Country differences give rise to some interesting and contentious ethical issues. One major ethical dilemma facing firms from Western democracies is whether they should do business in totalitarian countries that routinely violate the human rights of their citizens (such as China). There are two sides to this issue.

On the one hand, some argue that investing in totalitarian countries provides comfort to dictators and can help prop up repressive regimes that abuse basic human rights. For instance, Human Rights Watch, an organization that promotes the protection of basic human rights around the world, has argued that the progressive trade policies adopted by Western nations toward China have done little to encourage the Chinese to limit human rights abuses.[43] In fact, according to Human Rights Watch, the Chinese government stepped up its repression of political dissidents in 1996 after the Clinton administration removed human rights as a factor in determining China's trade status with the United States. Without investment by Western firms, and the support of Western governments, critics such as Human Rights Watch argue that many repressive regimes would collapse and be replaced by more democratically inclined governments. In recent years, firms that have invested in Chile, China, Iraq, and South Africa have all been the direct targets of such criticisms. The dismantling of the apartheid system in South Africa, which occurred in 1994, has been credited to economic sanctions by Western nations, including a lack of investment by Western firms. This, say those who argue against investment in totalitarian countries, is proof that investment boycotts can work (although decades of U.S.-led investment boycotts against Cuba and Iran, among others, have failed to have a similar impact).

In contrast, there are those who argue that investment by a Western firm, by raising the level of economic development of a totalitarian country, can help change it from within. They note that economic well-being and political freedoms often go hand in hand. Thus, for example, when arguing against attempts to apply trade sanctions to China in the wake of the violent 1989 government crackdown on prodemocracy demonstrators, the Bush administration claimed that U.S. firms should continue to be allowed to invest in mainland China, since greater political freedoms would follow the resulting economic growth. The Clinton administration used similar logic as the basis for its 1996 decision to decouple human rights issues from trade policy considerations.

Since both positions have some merit, it is difficult to arrive at a general statement of what firms should do. Unless mandated by government (as in the case of investment in South Africa), each firm must make its own judgments about the ethical implications of investment in totalitarian states on a case-by-case basis. The more repressive the regime, however, and the less amenable it seems to be to change, the greater the case for not investing.

A second interesting ethical issue is whether an international firm should adhere to the same standards of product safety, work safety, and environmental protection that are required in its home country. This is of particular concern to many firms based in Western nations, where product safety, worker safety, and environmental protection laws are among the toughest in the world. Should Western firms investing in less developed countries adhere to tough Western standards, even though local laws don't require them to do so? Again there is no easy answer. While on the face of it the argument for adhering to Western standards might seem strong, on closer examination the issue becomes more complicated. What if adhering to Western standards would make the foreign investment unprofitable, thereby denying the foreign country much-needed jobs? What then is the ethical thing to do? As with many ethical dilemmas, there is no easy answer. Each case needs to be assessed on its own merits.

A final ethical issue concerns bribes. Should an international business pay bribes to government officials to gain market access to a foreign country? To most Westerners bribery seems to be a corrupt and morally repugnant way of doing business, so the answer might initially be no. Moreover, some countries have laws on their books that prohibit their citizens from paying bribes to foreign government officials in return for economic favors. In the United States, for example, the **Foreign Corrupt Practices Act** of 1977 prohibits U.S. companies from making "corrupt" payments to foreign officials for the purpose of obtaining or retaining business. Many other developed nations, however, lack similar laws. Also, in many parts of the world the simple fact is that payoffs to government officials are part of life. Not investing if bribes are required ignores the fact that such investment can bring substantial benefits to the local populace in terms of income and jobs. Given this, from a purely ethical standpoint perhaps the practice of giving bribes, although a little evil, is the price that must be paid to do a greater good (assuming that the investment creates jobs where none existed before, and assuming that the practice is not illegal). Again, given the complexity of the issue, generalization is difficult. One thing seems certain, however: it is clearly unethical to go around offering bribes.

Foreign Corrupt Practices Act U.S. law enacted in 1977 that prohibits U.S. companies from making "corrupt" payments to foreign officials for the purpose of obtaining or retaining business.

Key Terms

Summary

This chapter has reviewed how the political, economic, and legal systems of different countries vary from one another. We have noted that the potential benefits, costs, and risks of doing business in a country are a function of its political, economic, and legal systems. More specifically:

1 Political systems can be assessed according to two dimensions: the degree to which they emphasize collectivism as opposed to individualism and the degree to which they are democratic or totalitarian.

2 Collectivism is an ideology that views the needs of society as being more important than the needs of individuals. Collectivism translates into an advocacy for state intervention in economic activity and, in the case of communism, a totalitarian dictatorship.

3 Individualism is an ideology that emphasizes the primacy of individuals' freedoms in the political, economic, and cultural realm. Individualism translates into an advocacy for democratic ideals and free market economics.

4 Democracy and totalitarianism are at different ends of a political spectrum. In a representative democracy, citizens periodically elect individuals to represent them and political freedoms are guaranteed by a constitution. In a totalitarian state, political power is monopolized by a party, group, or individual, and basic political freedoms are denied to citizens of the state.

5 There are three broad types of economic system: a market economy, a command economy, and a mixed economy. In a market economy, prices are free of any controls and private ownership is predominant. In a command economy, prices are set by central planners, productive assets are owned by the state, and private ownership is forbidden. A mixed economy has elements of both a market economy and a command economy.

6 Differences in the structure of law between countries can have important implications for the practice of international business. The degree to which property rights are protected can vary dramatically from country to country, as can product safety and product liability legislation and the nature of contract law.

7 The rate of economic progress in a country seems to depend on the extent to which that country has a well-functioning market economy in which property rights are protected.

8 Many countries are now in a state of transition. There is a marked shift away from totalitarian governments and command or mixed economic systems and toward democratic political institutions and free market economic systems.

9 The attractiveness of a country as a market and/or investment site depends on balancing the likely long-run benefits of doing business in that country against the likely costs and risks.

10 The benefits of doing business in a country are a function of the size of the market (population), its present wealth (purchasing power), and its future growth prospects. By investing early in countries that are currently poor but are growing rapidly, firms can gain first-mover advantages that will pay back substantial dividends in the future.

11 The costs of doing business in a country tend to be greater in those countries where political payoffs are required to gain market access, where supporting infrastructure is lacking or underdeveloped, and where adhering to local laws and regulations is costly.

12 The risks of doing business in a country tend to be greater in countries that (i) are politically unstable, (ii) are subject to economic mismanagement, and (iii) have a legal system that fails to provide adequate safeguards in the case of contract violations or property rights.

13 Country differences give rise to several ethical dilemmas. These include (i) should a firm do business in a repressive totalitarian state, (ii) should a firm conform to its home product, workplace, and environmental standards when they are not required by host country laws, and (iii) should a firm pay bribes to government officials in order to gain market access?

Critical Thinking and Discussion Questions

1 Free market economies stimulate greater economic growth, whereas command economies stifle growth! Discuss.

2 A democratic political system is an essential condition for *sustained* economic progress. Discuss.

3 During the late 1980s and early 1990s, China was routinely cited by various international organizations such as Amnesty International and Freedom Watch for major human rights violations, including torture, beatings, imprisonment, and executions of political dissidents. Despite this, in the mid-1990s China was the recipient of record levels of foreign direct investment, mainly from firms based in democratic societies such as the United States, Japan, and Germany. Evaluate this trend from an ethical perspective. If you were the CEO of a firm that had the option of making a potentially very profitable investment in China, what would you do?

4 You are the CEO of a company that has to choose between making a $100 million investment in either Russia or the Czech Republic. Both investments promise the same long-run return, so your choice of which investment to make is driven by considerations of risk. Assess the various risks of doing business in each of these nations. Which investment would you favor and why?

Internet Exercise

Pirated computer software is a major international problem, as you learned in this chapter. According to the Software Publishers Association (http://www.spa.org/), which is an international software trade group serving more than 1,200 members, practically one-half of all business software in the world is pirated (http://www. spa.org/piracy/releases/96pir.htm). The SPA has a variety of publications focusing on international software issues to help corporations compete globally (http://www.spa. org/publications/catalog/pg18.htm).

You read that most software and CDs in China are pirated, but that country is one of many cited for such illegal activity.

The Business Software Alliance (http://www.bsa.org/) has set up worldwide hotlines at its Internet site (http://www.bsa.org/info/hotline.html), and the SPA provides an Internet Piracy Intake Form (http://www.spa.org/piracy/ireport. htm) to enable surfers to report incidents of suspected software violations.

Research the SPA and BSA sites. Describe the similarities and differences in their anti- piracy policies. What international software issues do the SPA publications address? Which countries do the SPA and BSA profile as being major piracy offenders? What programs have these two organizations developed to combat software piracy globally?

Closing Case

Trinity Motors in
Russia

Mark Thimming moved to Moscow in 1992 to run Trinity Motors, a General Motors' dealership owned by private investors from Britain, Russia, and the United States. On Mark Thimming's office wall is a large map of Russia with about 40 major cities highlighted in orange. Ultimately, Mark Thimming hopes to franchise dealerships in each of these cities. So far Trinity sells its North American-made Chevrolets, Pontiacs, and Cadillacs in Moscow, St. Petersburg, and Kiev—but it hasn't been easy going.

Several problems are hurting Trinity's efforts to expand in Russia. The cash-strapped Russian government has tried to raise funds by placing steep duties on all kinds of imports, including the cars Trinity brings in, and by raising taxes across the board. In 1992 duties and value-added taxes amounted to about 25 percent of the value of an imported car; now the figure is closer to 166 percent! The result is a Chevrolet Caprice that retails for $24,000 in the United States but sells for about $58,000 in Moscow. It's hardly surprising then that Trinity's sales have fallen 50 percent from their early 1993 peak.

Russia's gangsterism, too, is taking its toll. One associate of Mark Thimming, Boris Berezovsky, who runs a major Russian car dealer, Logo VAZ, narrowly escaped a recent car bomb attack. Mark won't travel without an armed guard, while his wife and children remain in the United States. Mark Thimming has good reason to be worried. According to a 1994 report prepared for Russian President Boris Yeltsin, the Russian Mafia controlled 70 to 80 percent of all business and banking activity in 1994. Primarily, this control is exercised by demanding the payment of protection money (the Mafia has a much higher collection rate than the official state tax authorities). But in an increasing number of cases, organized crime groups have a minority or even majority ownership stake in businesses.

Mark Thimming fears that his main competitors in the car import business are Russian gangsters who pay bribes to state bureaucrats so they can import Western cars without paying the staggering import duties and taxes that are crippling Trinity Motors. Thimming estimates that about 80 percent of all cars imported into Moscow come via the black or gray markets. To make matters worse, frequently the GM cars imported into Russia by the Mafia aren't those designed for the market. They can't run on the leaded fuel used in Russia, for example, or they lack the special suspension systems required for Russia's rough roads. As a result, Thimming is concerned that GM buyers may end up with an ownership experience that would give them a negative attitude toward the company.

In an ironic twist, however, Thimming reckons that some of his best customers are gangsters. The high retail prices dictated by the steep taxes and import duties mean that the successful members of the criminal underworld are among the few who have enough cash to purchase one of Trinity's imports. When requesting service on their cars, he says, these people "have a tendency to go to their strong suit and show off their guns and ammunition." Trinity tries to cope with the problem by offering good service to all clients. As Thimming's service department manager once told a Mafia member, "There is no use killing me, because no one else could service your car."

Despite all these problems Mark Thimming remains remarkably upbeat. He continues to see great long-run growth prospects in Russia. Trinity Motors is profitable, thanks to its service and parts department, which covers 80 percent of its expenses. Thimming figures that the economy and legal system will have improved enough by 2000 to transform the country into a real growth opportunity for Western businesses. In the meantime Thimming is content to build up Trinity's reputation for excellent products and service. Still, sales remain slack at under 1,000 per year, compared to the 5,000 plus per year that Thimming thinks should be attainable in Moscow alone.[44]

Case Discussion Questions

1 What is the exact nature of the problems encountered by Trinity Motors in Russia? Are these problems due to deficiencies in Russia's political system, economic system, or legal system? What will it take to correct these problems?

2 Until the problems that Trinity is facing are corrected, how should Mark Thimming deal with them?

3 Does it make sense for Trinity to tough it out in Russia until the current problems are resolved?

4 How long do you think it will be before Russia resembles a stable Western democracy?

Chapter 3
Differences in Culture

©PhotoDisc

Opening Case

Euro-Disneyland "Where Are the French?"

Until 1992 Disney had experienced nothing but success in the theme park business. Its first park, Disneyland, opened in Anaheim, California, in 1955. Its theme song, "It's a Small World After All," promoted

an idealized vision of America spiced with reassuring glimpses of exotic cultures all calculated to promote heart-warming feelings about living together as one happy family. There were dark tunnels and bumpy rides to scare the chil-

Learning Objectives:

1 Understand that substantial differences among societies arise from cultural differences.

2 Know what is meant by the term *culture*.

3 Appreciate that culture is different because of differences in social structure, religion, language, education, economic philosophy, and political philosophy.

4 Understand the relationship between culture and the values found in the workplace.

5 Appreciate that culture is not a constant, but changes over time.

6 Appreciate that much of the change in contemporary social culture is being driven by economic advancement, technological change, and globalization.

7 Understand the implications for international business management of differences in culture.

dren a little but none of the terrors of the real world . . . The Disney characters that everyone knew from the cartoons and comic books were on hand to shepherd the guests and to direct them to the Mickey Mouse watches and Little Mermaid records.[1]

The Anaheim park was an instant success.

In the 1970s the triumph was repeated in Florida, and in 1983 Disney proved that the Japanese have a real affinity for Mickey Mouse with the successful opening of Tokyo Disneyland. Having wooed the Japanese, Disney executives in 1986 turned their attention to Paris, the self-proclaimed capital of European high culture and style. "Why did they pick France?" many asked. When word first got out that Disney wanted to build another international theme park, officials from more than 200 locations all over the world descended on Disney with pleas and cash inducements to work the Disney magic in their hometowns. But Paris was chosen because of demographics and subsidies. About 17 million Europeans live less than a two hours' drive from Paris. Another 310 million can fly there in the same time or less. Moreover, the French government was so eager to attract Disney to Paris that it offered the company more than $1 billion in various incentives, all in the expectation that the project would create 30,000 French jobs.

Right from the beginning, cultural gaffes by Disney set the tone for the project. By late

1986 Disney was deep in negotiations with the French government. To the exasperation of the Disney team, headed by Joe Shapiro, the talks were taking far longer than expected. Jean-Rene Bernard, the chief French negotiator, said he was astonished when Mr. Shapiro, his patience ebbing, ran to the door of the room and in a very un-Gallic gesture, began kicking it repeatedly, shouting, "Get me something to break!"

There was also sniping from Parisian intellectuals who attacked the transplantation of Disney's dreamworld as an assault on French culture, "a cultural Chernobyl," one prominent intellectual called it. The minister of culture announced he would boycott the opening, proclaiming it to be an unwelcome symbol of American clichés and a consumer society. Unperturbed, Disney pushed ahead with the planned summer 1992 opening of the $5 billion park. Shortly after Euro-Disneyland opened, French farmers drove their tractors to the entrance and blocked it. This globally televised act of protest was aimed not at Disney, but at the U.S. government, which had been demanding that the French cut their agricultural subsidies. Still, it focused world attention on the loveless marriage of Disneyland and Paris.

Then there were the operational errors. Disney's policy of serving no alcohol in the park, since reversed, caused astonishment in a country where a glass of wine for lunch is expected. Disney thought that Monday would be a light day for visitors and Friday a heavy one, and it allocated staff accordingly, but the reality was the reverse. Another unpleasant surprise was the hotel breakfast debacle. "We were told that Europeans don't take breakfast, so we downsized the restaurants," recalled one Disney executive. "And guess what? Everybody showed up for breakfast. We were trying to serve 2,500 breakfasts in a 350-seat restaurant at some of the hotels. The lines were horrendous. And they didn't just want croissants and coffee. They wanted bacon and eggs." Lunch turned out to be another problem. "Everybody wanted lunch at 12:30. The crowds were huge. Our smiling cast members had to calm down surly patrons and engage in some 'behavior modification' to teach them that they could eat lunch at 11 A.M. or 2 P.M."

There were major staffing problems too. Disney tried to use the same teamwork model that had worked so well in America and Japan, but the model ran into trouble in France. Within the first nine weeks of Euro-Disneyland's operation, roughly 1,000 employees, 10 percent of the total, left. One former employee was a 22-year-old medical student from a nearby town who signed up for a weekend job. After two days of "brainwashing," as he called Disney's training, he left following a dispute with his supervisor over the timing of his lunch hour. Another former employee noted, "I don't think that they realized what Europeans were like . . . that we ask questions and don't think all the same way."

One of the biggest problems, however, was that Europeans just didn't stay as long at the park as Disney expected. While Disney did get close to 1 million visitors a year through the park gates, in line with its plans, most stayed only a day or two. Few stayed the four to five days that Disney had hoped for. It seems that most Europeans regard theme parks as places for day excursions, not extended vacations. This was a big shock for Disney; the company had invested billions in building luxury hotels next to the park—hotels the day-trippers didn't need and that stood half empty most of the time. To make matters worse, the French didn't show up in the expected numbers. In 1994 only 40 percent of the park's visitors were French. One puzzled executive noted that many visitors were Americans living in Europe or, stranger still, Japanese on a European vacation! As a result, by the end of 1994 Euro-Disneyland had cumulative losses of $2 billion.[2]

Introduction

International business is different from domestic business because countries are different. In Chapter 2 we saw how national differences in political, economic, and legal systems influence the benefits, costs, and risks associated with doing business in different countries. In this chapter we will explore how differences in culture both across *and* within countries can affect the practice of international business.

Two themes run through this chapter. One theme is that operating a successful international business requires cross-cultural literacy. By cross-cultural literacy we mean an understanding of how cultural differences both across and within nations can affect how business is practiced. In these days of global communication, rapid transportation, and global markets, when the era of the global village seems just around the corner, it is easy to forget just how different various cultures really are. Yet deep cultural differences remain. The importance of cross-cultural literacy cannot be overemphasized. Without it, managers may make mistakes that jeopardize lucrative opportunities.

The opening case illustrates how a lack of cross-cultural literacy can affect a business venture. Disney has been one of the most successful managers of theme parks in the world, but its Euro-Disney venture has yet to turn a profit. Although a lack of cultural literacy on the part of Disney's American managers isn't the whole explanation for this failure, it didn't help. The tone was set early by Joe Shapiro when he displayed his frustrations with the slow pace of negotiations by kicking the door to the room in the expensive French hotel where Disney and French government officials were negotiating. This inappropriate action was widely reported in the French press as an example of the "cowboy values" of Disney's managers.

Then there was Disney's underestimation of the negative press that would be created by the juxtaposition of Paris and Disney. Disney was focused on demographics and subsidies when choosing a location. As one observer put it, "I think as far as the (Disney) management is concerned, Euro-Disney just happens to be in the middle of Europe, handy for a big population." What Disney's management lost sight of was that Mickey Mouse and Left-Bank intellectuals do not mix very well; and the French take their intellectuals seriously. The characterization of Euro-Disneyland as "a cultural Chernobyl" resonated not just with French intellectuals, but also with many middle-class French, who were the people Disney wanted to attract to its expensive hotels. In retrospect, Paris was not the best location for this theme park; locating it there simply raised a red flag to France's influential intellectuals. Nor did it help that Disney's managers publicly characterized some criticisms as the "ravings of a small cultural elite." While the cultural elite in America may be easily dismissed, the French take their cultural elite more seriously and saw such criticisms as an attack on their national character.

Disney's managers also erred by making assumptions about European cultural habits that were based on simplistic characterizations, such as the assumption that Europeans didn't eat breakfast. Further, after having worked with the clean-cut and service-oriented staff in America and Japan, Disney was caught off-guard by the less enthusiastic and malleable character of many European employees. Nor did Disney's managers appreciate the different attitudes toward vacationing and theme parks that exist in Europe. Disney assumed that Europeans would vacation like Americans and Japanese, that they would be happy to stay for several days at a theme park. But middle-class Europeans try to "get away from it all" on their vacations by going to the beach or the mountains, and Euro-Disneyland lacked that kind of appeal.

A second theme found in this chapter is that a relationship may exist between culture and the costs of doing business in a country or region. It can be argued that the culture of some countries (or regions) supports the capitalist mode of production and lowers the costs of doing business there. Cultural factors can help assist firms based in such countries to achieve a competitive advantage in the world economy. For example, some observers have argued that cultural factors have helped to lower the costs of doing business in Japan.[3] This may have helped some Japanese businesses achieve a competitive advantage in the world economy. By the same token cultural factors can sometimes raise the costs of doing business. For example, until recently firms found it difficult to achieve cooperation between management and labor in Britain, historically a culture that emphasized class conflict. Such conflict was reflected in a high level of industrial disputes. In turn, this raised the costs of doing business in Britain relative to the costs of doing business in countries such as Switzerland, Norway, Germany, or Japan, where class conflict was historically less prevalent.

We open this chapter with a general discussion of what culture actually is. Then we focus on how differences in social structure, religion, language, and education influence the culture of a country. The implications of these differences will be highlighted throughout the chapter and summarized in a section at the end.

What Is Culture?

Scholars have never been able to agree on a simple definition of culture. In the 1870s the anthropologist Edward Tylor defined culture as *that complex whole which includes knowledge, belief, art, morals, law, custom, and other capabilities acquired by man as a member of society*.[4] Since then hundreds of other definitions have been offered. Geert Hofstede, an expert on cross-cultural differences and management, defined culture as *the collective programming of the mind which distinguishes the members of one human group from another . . . Culture, in this sense, includes systems of values; and values are among the building blocks of culture*.[5] Another definition of culture comes from sociologists Zvi Namenwirth and Robert Weber, who see culture as *a system of ideas* and argue that these ideas constitute *a design for living*.[6]

Here we follow both Hofstede and Namenwirth and Weber by viewing **culture** as *a system of values and norms that are shared among a group of people and that when taken together constitute a design for living*. By **values** we mean abstract *ideas* about what a group believes to be good, right, and desirable. Put differently, values are shared assumptions about how things ought to be.[7] By **norms** we mean the social rules and guidelines that prescribe appropriate behavior in particular situations. We shall use the term **society** to refer to a group of people who share a common set of values and norms.

Values and Norms

Values form the bedrock of a culture. They provide the context within which a society's norms are established and justified. They may include a society's attitudes toward such concepts as individual freedom, democracy, truth, justice, honesty, loyalty, social obligations, collective responsibility, the role of women, love, sex, marriage, and so on. Values are not just abstract concepts; they are invested with considerable emotional significance. People argue,

Part 2 Country Differences

culture System of values and norms that are shared among a group of people and that when taken together constitute a design for living.

values Abstract ideas about what a group believes to be good, right, and desirable.

norms Social rules and guidelines that prescribe appropriate behavior in particular situations.

Society Group of people who share a common set of values and norms.

fight, and even die over values such as "freedom." Values may also often be reflected in the political and economic system of a society. As we saw in Chapter 2, democratic free market capitalism is a reflection of a philosophical value system that emphasizes individual freedom.

Norms are the social rules that govern the actions of people toward one another. Norms can be subdivided further into two major categories: folkways and mores. **Folkways** are the routine conventions of everyday life. Generally, folkways are actions of little *moral* significance. Rather, folkways are social conventions concerning things such as what constitutes the appropriate dress code in a particular situation, good social manners, eating with the correct utensils, neighborly behavior, and the like. While folkways define the way people are expected to behave, violating folkways is not normally a serious matter. People who violate folkways may be thought of as eccentric or ill-mannered, but they are not usually considered to be evil or bad. In many countries foreigners may be initially excused for violating folkways.

A good example of folkways concerns attitudes toward time in different countries. In the United States people are very time-conscious. Americans tend to arrive a few minutes early for business appointments. When invited for dinner to someone's home, it is considered polite to arrive on time or just a few minutes late. In other countries the concept of time can be very different. It is not necessarily a breach of etiquette to arrive a little late for a business appointment; it might be considered more impolite to arrive early. As for dinner invitations, arriving on time for a dinner engagement can be very bad manners. In Britain, for example, when someone says, "Come for dinner at 7 P.M." he or she means "come for dinner at 7:30 to 8:00 P.M." The guest who arrives at 7 P.M. is likely to find an unprepared and embarrassed host. Similarly, when an Argentinean says, "Come for dinner anytime after 8 P.M.," he or she means don't come at 8 P.M.—it's far too early!

Mores are norms that are seen as central to the functioning of a society and to its social life. They are much more significant than folkways. Accordingly, violating mores can bring serious retribution. Mores include such factors as indictments against theft, adultery, incest, and cannibalism. In many societies certain mores have been enacted into law. Thus, all advanced societies have laws against theft, incest, and cannibalism. However, there are also many differences among cultures as to what is perceived as mores. In America, for example, drinking alcohol is widely accepted, whereas in Saudi Arabia the consumption of alcohol is viewed as violating important social mores and is punishable by imprisonment (as some Western citizens working in Saudi Arabia have found out).

Culture, Society, and the Nation-State

We have defined a society as a group of people that share a common set of values and norms; that is, a group bound together by a common culture. But there is *not* a strict one-to-one correspondence between a society and a nation-state. Nation-states are political creations. They may contain a single culture or several distinct cultures. For example, during the Gulf War the prevailing view presented to Western audiences was that Iraq was a homogeneous Arab nation. But in the chaos that followed the war, it became apparent that there are several different societies within Iraq, each with its own culture. In the north are the Kurds, who don't view themselves as Arabs and who have their own distinct history and traditions. Then there are two Arab societies, the Shiites in the south and the Sunnis. The Sunnis populate the middle of the country and rule Iraq (the terms *Shiites* and *Sunnis* refer to different sects within the religion of Islam). Moreover, among the southern Sunnis is another distinct society of 500,000 "Marsh Arabs" who live where the Tigris and Euphrates rivers join and pursue a way of life that dates back 5,000 years.[8]

To complicate things further, we can also talk about culture at different levels. It is reasonable to talk about "American society" and "American culture," but at the same time we must recognize that there are several societies within America, each with its own culture. One can talk about African-American culture, Cajun culture, Chinese-American culture, Hispanic culture, Indian culture, Irish-American culture, and Southern culture.

The point is that the relationship between culture and country is often ambiguous. One cannot always characterize a country as having a single homogeneous culture, and even when one can, one must also often recognize that the national culture is a mosaic of subcultures, many of which can be quite distinct.

The Determinants of Culture

The values and norms of a culture do not emerge from nowhere fully formed. They are the evolutionary product of a number of factors at work in a society. These factors include the prevailing political and economic philosophy, the social structure of a society, and the dominant religion, language, and education (see Figure 3.1). We discussed political and economic philosophy at length in Chapter 2. Such philosophy clearly influences the value systems of a society. For example, the values found in the former Soviet Union toward freedom, justice, and individual achievement were clearly different from the values found in the United States, precisely because each society operated according to a different political and economic philosophy. Below we will discuss the influence of social structure, religion, language, and education. Remember that the chain of causation runs both ways. While factors such as social structure and religion clearly influence the values and norms of a society, it is also true that the values and norms of a society can influence social structure and religion.

Social Structure

A society's *social structure* refers to its basic social organization. Although there are many different aspects of social structure, two main dimensions stand out when explaining differences between cultures. The first is the degree to which the basic unit of social organization is the individual, as opposed to the group. Western societies tend to emphasize the primacy of the individual, while groups tend to figure much larger in many other societies. The second dimension is the degree to which a society is stratified into classes or castes. Some societies are characterized by a relatively high degree of social stratification and relatively low mobility between strata (e.g., India), while other societies are characterized by a low degree of social stratification and high mobility between strata (e.g., the United States).

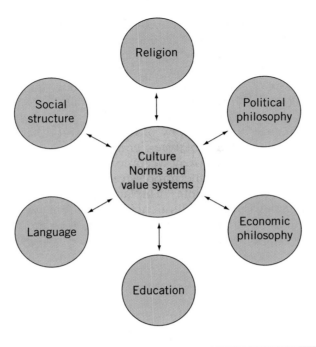

FIGURE 3.1

The Determinants of Culture

Individuals and Groups

A **group** is an association of two or more individuals who have a shared sense of identity and who interact with each other in structured ways on the basis of a common set of expectations about each other's behavior.[9] Human social life is group life. Individuals are involved in families, work groups, social groups, recreational groups, and so on. However, while groups are found in all societies, societies differ according to the degree to which the group is viewed as the primary means of social organization.[10] In some societies individual attributes and achievements are viewed as being more important than group membership, while in other societies the reverse is true.

THE INDIVIDUAL   In Chapter 2 we discussed individualism as a political philosophy. However, individualism is more than just an abstract political philosophy. In many Western societies the individual is the basic building block of social organization. This is reflected not just in the political and economic organization of society, but also in the way people perceive themselves and relate to each other in social and business settings. In the value systems of many Western societies, for example, individual achievement is emphasized. The social standing of an individual is not so much a function of whom they work for as of their individual performance in whatever work setting they choose for themselves.

The emphasis placed on individual performance in many Western societies has both beneficial and harmful aspects. In the United States, for example, the emphasis placed on individual performance finds expression in an admiration of "rugged individualism" and entrepreneurship. One bene-

group Association of two or more individuals who have a shared sense of identity and who interact with each other in structured ways on the basis of a common set of expectations about each other's behavior.

fit of this is the high level of entrepreneurial activity in the United States and other Western societies. New products and new ways of doing business (e.g., personal computers, photocopiers, computer software, biotechnology, supermarkets, and discount retail stores) have repeatedly been created in the United States by entrepreneurial individuals. One can argue that the dynamism of the U.S. economy owes much to the philosophy of individualism.

On the other hand, the philosophy of individualism also finds expression in much managerial mobility between companies, and this is not always good. While moving from company to company may be good for individual managers, who are trying to build impressive résumés, it is not necessarily a good thing for American companies. The lack of loyalty and commitment to an individual company, and the tendency to move on when a better offer comes along, can result in managers who have good general skills but lack the in-depth knowledge, experience, and network of interpersonal contacts that come from years of working within the same company. Company-specific experience, knowledge, and personal contacts are probably all good things, since they may increase the manager's ability to perform his or her job effectively. A manager may draw on past experience, knowledge, and a network of contacts to find solutions to current problems. It follows that American companies may suffer if their managers lack these things.

The emphasis on individualism may make it difficult to build teams within an organization to perform collective tasks. If individuals are always competing with each other on the basis of individual performance, it may prove difficult for them to cooperate. A recent study of U.S. competitiveness by the Massachusetts Institute of Technology concluded that failure to achieve cooperation both within a company (e.g., between functions; between management and labor) and between companies (e.g., between a firm and its suppliers) is hurting U.S. firms in the global economy. Given the emphasis on individualism in the American value system, perhaps this failure is not surprising.[11] The emphasis on individualism, while helping to create a dynamic entrepreneurial economy, may also raise the costs of doing business due to its adverse impact on managerial mobility and cooperation.

There is one positive aspect of high managerial mobility. Moving from firm to firm exposes executives to different ways of doing business. The ability to compare and contrast different business practices helps U.S. executives identify how good practices and techniques developed in one firm might be profitably applied to other firms.

THE GROUP   In contrast to the Western emphasis on the individual, in many other societies the group is the primary unit of social organization. In Japan, for example, the social status of an individual is determined as much by the standing of the group to which he or she belongs as by his or her individual performance.[12] In traditional Japanese society the group was the family or village to which an individual belonged. Today the group is frequently associated with the work team or business organization to which an individual belongs. In a now classic study of Japanese society, Nakane has noted how this expresses itself in everyday life:

> When a Japanese faces the outside (confronts another person) and affixes some position to himself socially he is inclined to give precedence to institution over kind of occupation. Rather than saying, "I am a type setter" or "I am a

filing clerk," he is likely to say, "I am from B Publishing Group" or "I belong to S company."[13]

Nakane observes that the primacy of the group to which an individual belongs often evolves into a deeply emotional attachment in which identification with the group becomes all-important in one's life. A central value of Japanese culture is the importance attached to group membership. This may benefit businesses. Strong identification with the group creates pressures for mutual self-help and collective action. If the worth of an individual is closely linked to the achievements of the group (e.g., firm), as Nakane maintains is the case in Japan, this creates a strong incentive for individual members of the group to work together for the common good. In other words, the failures of cooperation that the MIT study found in many American firms may not be a problem in Japanese firms. Some argue that the competitive advantage of Japanese enterprises in the global economy is based partly on their ability to achieve close cooperation between individuals within a company and between companies. This is expressed in the widespread diffusion of self-managing work teams within Japanese organizations, the close cooperation between different functions within Japanese companies (e.g., between manufacturing, marketing, and R&D), and the cooperation between a company and its suppliers on issues such as design, quality control, and inventory reduction.[14] In all these cases, cooperation is driven by the need to improve the performance of the group (i.e., the business firm) to which individuals belong.

The primacy of the value of group identification in cultures such as Japan can also be expected to discourage managers and workers from moving from company to company. This is the case in Japan, where lifetime employment in a particular company is the norm in certain sectors of the economy (estimates suggest between 20 and 40 percent of all Japanese employees have formal or informal lifetime employment guarantees). Among other things, one result of the lifetime employment system is that managers and workers build up knowledge, experience, and a network of interpersonal business contacts. All these things can help managers perform their jobs more effectively and achieve cooperation with others.

However, the primacy of the group is not always beneficial. Just as U.S. society is characterized by a great deal of dynamism and entrepreneurship, reflecting the primacy of values associated with individualism, so there are those who argue that Japanese society is characterized by a corresponding lack of dynamism and entrepreneurship. Although it is not clear how this will play itself out in the long run, it is possible that, for cultural reasons, the United States may continue to be more successful than Japan at pioneering radically new products and new ways of doing business.

Social Stratification

All societies are stratified on a hierarchical basis into social categories, or **social strata**. These strata are typically defined on the basis of characteristics such as family background, occupation, and income. Individuals are born into a particular stratum. They become a member of the social category to which their parents belong. Individuals born into a stratum toward the top of the social hierarchy tend to have better *life chances* than individuals born

social strata Social categories in a society defined on the basis of characteristics such as family background, occupation, and income.

into a stratum toward the bottom of the hierarchy. They are likely to have a better education, better health, a better standard of living, and better work opportunities. Although all societies are stratified to some degree, societies differ from each other in two related ways that are of interest to us here. First, they differ from each other with regard to the degree of *mobility* between social strata, and second, they differ from each other with regard to the *significance* attached to social strata in business contexts.

SOCIAL MOBILITY   The term **social mobility** refers to the extent to which individuals can move out of the strata into which they are born. Social mobility varies significantly from society to society. The most rigid system of stratification is a caste system. A **caste system** is a *closed system of stratification* in which social position is determined by the family into which a person is born, and change in that position is usually not possible during an individual's lifetime (i.e., social mobility is very limited). Often a caste position carries with it a specific occupation. Members of one caste might be shoemakers, members of another caste might be butchers, and so on. These occupations are embedded in the caste and passed down through the family to succeeding generations. Although the number of societies with caste systems has diminished rapidly during the 20th century, one major example still remains: India. India has four main castes and several thousand subcastes. Even though the caste system was officially abolished in 1949, two years after India became independent, the caste system is still a powerful force in rural Indian society where occupation and marital opportunities are still partly related to caste.

A **class system** is a less rigid form of social stratification in which social mobility is possible. A class system is a form of *open stratification* in which the position a person has by birth can be changed through his or her own achievements and/or luck. Individuals born into a class at the bottom of the hierarchy can work their way upward, while individuals born into a class at the top of the hierarchy can slip down.

While many societies have class systems, social mobility within a class system varies from society to society. One example of a class society with relatively low mobility is Britain.[15] British society is divided into three main classes: the *upper class*, which is made up of individuals whose families have had wealth, prestige, and occasionally power for generations; the *middle class*, whose members are involved in professional, managerial, and clerical occupations; and the *working class*, whose members earn their living from manual occupations. The middle class is further subdivided into the *upper-middle class*, whose members are involved in important managerial occupations and the prestigious professions (e.g., lawyers, accountants, doctors), and the *lower-middle class*, whose members are involved in clerical work (e.g., bank tellers) and the less prestigious professions (e.g., schoolteachers).

The British class system is marked by differences in the life chances of members of different classes. The upper and upper-middle classes typically send their children to a select group of private schools, where they don't mix with lower-class children and where they pick up many of the speech accents and social norms that mark them as being from the higher strata of society. These same private schools often have close ties with the most prestigious universities, such as Oxford and Cambridge. Until recently Oxford and Cambridge reserved a certain number of places for the graduates of these private schools. Having been to a prestigious university, the offspring of the upper and upper-middle classes then have an excellent chance of being offered a prestigious job in companies, banks, brokerage firms, and law firms, which are run by members of the upper and upper-middle classes.

In stark contrast, members of the British working and lower-middle classes typically go to state schools. The majority of them leave school at 16, and those who go on to higher education find it more difficult to get accepted at the best universities. When they do, they will find that their lower-class accent and lack of social skills mark them as being from a lower social stratum. Unless they can change this, it will be more difficult for them to get access to the most prestigious jobs.

As a result of these factors, the class system in Britain tends to perpetuate itself from generation to generation, and mobility is limited. Although upward mobility is possible, it cannot normally be achieved in one generation. While an individual from a working-class background may earn an income that is consistent with membership in the upper-middle class, he or she may not be accepted as a member of the upper-middle class because of accent and background. However, by sending his or her offspring to the "right kind of school," the individual can help his or her children to be accepted.

The class system in the United States is less extreme than in Britain and mobility is much greater. Like Britain, the United States has its own upper, middle, and working classes. However, in the United States class membership is determined mainly by individual economic achievements, as opposed to background and schooling. Thus, an individual can, through economic achievement, move smoothly from the working class to the upper class in his or her lifetime. Indeed, American society respects successful individuals from humble origins, whereas British society regards such individuals as being *nouveau riche* and they are never quite accepted by their economic peers.

SIGNIFICANCE From a business perspective the stratification of a society is significant insofar as it affects the operation of the business organization. In American society, the high degree of social mobility and the extreme emphasis on individualism limits the impact of class background on business operations. The same is true in Japan, where most people perceive themselves to be middle class. In a country such as Britain, however, the relative lack of class mobility and the striking differences between classes has resulted in the emergence of class consciousness. **Class consciousness** refers to a condition where people perceive themselves in terms of their class background, and this shapes their relationships with members of other classes.

This has been played out in British society through the traditional hostility between upper-middle-class managers and their working-class employees. Mutual antagonism and lack of respect have made it difficult to achieve cooperation between management and labor in many British companies. Historically, British industry has been racked by a high level of strikes, many of which have been politically motivated and depicted as "class warfare" between the disadvantaged working classes and the advantaged middle and upper classes. Moreover, politics in Britain tends to follow class lines to a much greater degree than in the United States. The Labor Party represents the interests of the working class, and the Conservative Party represents middle- and upper-class interests.

The antagonistic relationship between management and labor and the resulting lack of cooperation and high level of industrial disruption raise production costs in Britain relative to the costs in countries such as the United

class consciousness
Condition where people perceive themselves in terms of their class background, and this shapes their relationships with members of other classes.

States and Japan where the degree of class-based conflict is significantly lower. This has made it more difficult for companies based in Britain to establish a competitive advantage in the global economy. Britain is not the only society where class-based differences have resulted in industrial disruption and a lack of cooperation. Similar problems have emerged in Italy, Spain, Greece, and Australia. The level of industrial disruption has been significantly higher in all these countries in recent years than in Britain.

Religion

Religion may be defined as a system of shared beliefs and rituals that are concerned with the realm of the sacred.[16] The relationship between religion and society is subtle, complex, and profound. While there are thousands of different religions in the world, five dominate: Christianity, Islam, Hinduism, Buddhism, and Confucianism (see Figure 3.2). We review each, focusing primarily on their business implications. Perhaps the most important implications center on the extent to which different religions shape attitudes toward work and entrepreneurship and the degree to which the religious ethics of a society affect the costs of doing business in a country.

Christianity

Christianity is the most widely practiced religion in the world. About 1 billion people, approximately 20 percent of the world's population, identify themselves as Christians. The vast majority of Christians live in Europe and the Americas, although their numbers are growing rapidly in Africa. Christianity grew out of Judaism. Like Judaism it is a monotheistic religion. (Monotheism is the belief in one god.) A religious division in the 11th century led to the establishment of two major Christian organizations: the Roman Catholic church and the Orthodox church. Today the Roman Catholic church accounts for over half of all Christians, most of whom are found in Southern Europe and Latin America. The Orthodox church, while less influential, is still of major importance in several countries (e.g., Greece and Russia). In the 16th century the Reformation led to a further split with Rome; the result was Protestantism. In turn, the nonconformist nature of Protestantism has facilitated the emergence of numerous denominations under the Protestant umbrella (e.g., Baptist, Methodist, Calvinist).

ECONOMIC IMPLICATIONS OF CHRISTIANITY: THE PROTESTANT WORK ETHIC Some sociologists have argued that of the two main branches of Christianity—Catholicism and Protestantism—the latter has the more important economic implications. In 1904 a German sociologist, Max Weber, made a connection between Protestant ethics and "the spirit of capitalism" that has since become famous.[17] Weber noted that capitalism emerged in Western Europe. Moreover, he noted that in Western Europe:

> Business leaders and owners of capital, as well as the higher grades of skilled labor, and even more the higher technically and commercially trained personnel of modern enterprises, are overwhelmingly Protestant.[18]

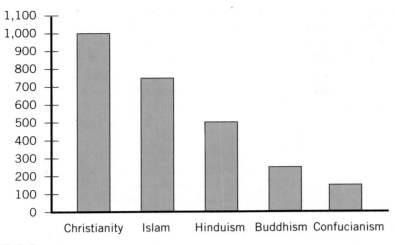

FIGURE 3.2

World's Major Religions (millions of adherents)
Source: *The Economist.* Book of Vital World Statistics. Random House, 1990.

According to Weber, there was a relationship between Protestantism and the emergence of modern capitalism. Weber argued that Protestant ethics emphasize the importance of hard work and wealth creation (for the glory of God) and frugality (abstinence from worldly pleasures). According to Weber, this was just the kind of value system needed to facilitate the development of capitalism. Protestants worked hard and systematically to accumulate wealth. However, their ascetic beliefs suggested that rather than consuming this wealth by indulging in worldly pleasures, they should reinvest it in the expansion of capitalist enterprises. Thus, the combination of hard work and the accumulation of capital that could be used to finance investment and expansion helped paved the way for the development of capitalism in Western Europe and the United States. Weber argued that the Catholic promise of salvation in the next world, rather than this world, did not foster the same kind of work ethic among members of the Catholic religion.

Protestantism may have encouraged the development of capitalism in another way also. By breaking away from the hierarchical domination of religious and social life that characterized the Catholic church for much of its history, Protestantism gave individuals more freedom to develop their own relationship with God. The right to freedom of form of worship was central to the nonconformist nature of early Protestantism. In turn, the emphasis on individual religious freedom may have paved the way for the subsequent emphasis on individual economic and political freedoms and the development of individualism as an economic and political philosophy. As we saw in Chapter 2, such a philosophy forms the bedrock on which entrepreneurial free market capitalism is based.

Islam

With 750 million adherents, Islam is the second largest of the world's major religions. Islam dates to AD 610 when the Prophet Mohammed began spreading the word. Adherents of Islam are referred to as Muslims. Muslims constitute a majority in over 35 countries and inhabit a nearly contiguous stretch of land from the northwest coast of Africa, through the Middle East, to China and Malaysia in the Far East.

Islam has roots in both Judaism and Christianity (Islam views Jesus Christ as one of God's prophets, whereas Christians view Christ as the son of God). Like Christianity and Judaism, Islam is a monotheistic religion. The central principle of Islam is that there is no god but the one true omnipotent God. Other major principles of Islam include (1) honoring and respecting parents, (2) respecting the rights of others, (3) being generous but not a squanderer, (4) avoiding killing except for justifiable causes, (5) not committing adultery, (6) dealing justly and equitably with others, (7) being of pure heart and mind, (8) safeguarding the possessions of orphans, and (9) being humble and unpretentious.[19] There are obvious parallels with many of the central principles of both Judaism and Christianity.

Islam is an all-embracing way of life governing the totality of a Muslim's being. As God's surrogate in this world, a Muslim is circumscribed by religious principles—by a code of conduct for interpersonal relations—in his or her social and economic activities. Religion is paramount in all areas of life. The Muslim lives in a social structure that is shaped by Islamic values and norms of moral conduct. The ritual nature of everyday life in a Muslim country is perhaps one of the most striking things to a Western visitor. Among other things, Muslim ritual requires prayer five times a day (it is not unusual for business meetings to be put on hold while the Muslim participants engage in their daily prayer ritual), requires women to be dressed in a certain manner and subordinate to men, and forbids the consumption of either pig meat or alcohol.

ISLAMIC FUNDAMENTALISM The past two decades have witnessed a surge in Islamic fundamentalism.[20] Although the rise of fundamentalism has no one cause, in part it is a response to the social pressures created in traditional Islamic societies by the move toward modernization and by the influence of Western ideas, such as liberal democracy, materialism, equal rights for women, and by Western attitudes toward sex, marriage, and alcohol. In many Muslim countries modernization has been accompanied by a growing gap between a rich urban minority and an impoverished urban and rural majority. For the impoverished majority, modernization has too often offered little in the way of tangible economic progress, while threatening their traditional value system. Thus, for a Muslim who cherishes his traditions and feels that his identity is jeopardized by the encroachment of alien Western values, Islamic fundamentalism has become a cultural anchor.

Fundamentalists demand a rigid commitment to traditional religious beliefs and rituals. The result has been a marked increase in the use of symbolic gestures that confirm Islamic values. Women are once again wearing floor-length, long-sleeved dresses and covering their hair; religious studies have increased in universities; the publication of religious tracts has increased; and more religious orations are heard in public.[21] Moreover, the sentiments of some fundamentalist groups are increasingly anti-Western. Rightly or wrongly, Western influence is blamed for a whole range of social ills, and the actions of many fundamentalists are directed against Western governments, cultural symbols, businesses, and even individuals.

In several Muslim countries fundamentalists have gained political power and have used this to try to make Islamic law (as set down in the Koran—the bible of Islam) the law of the land. The fundamentalists have been most successful in Iran, where a fundamentalist party has held power since 1979, but they also have a considerable and growing influence in many other countries, such as Algeria, Egypt, Pakistan, and Saudi Arabia. The next "Country Focus" profiles the rise of Islamic fundamentalism in Saudi Arabia.

ECONOMIC IMPLICATIONS OF ISLAM Some explicit economic principles are set down in the Koran.[23] Many of the economic principles of Islam are pro-free enterprise. The Koran speaks approvingly of free enterprise and of earning *legitimate* profit through trade and commerce (the Prophet Mohammed was once a trader). The protection of the right to private property is also embedded within Islam, although Islam asserts that all property is a favor from Allah (God), who created and so owns everything. In this sense, those who hold property are regarded as trustees who are entitled to receive profits from it, rather than owners in the Western sense of the word. Those who hold property are admonished to use it in a righteous, socially beneficial, and prudent manner. This reflects Islam's concern with social justice. Islam is critical of those who earn profit through the exploitation of others. In the Islamic view of the world, humans are part of a collective in which the wealthy and successful have obligations to help the disadvantaged. Put simply, in Muslim countries it is fine to earn a profit, as long as that profit is justly earned and not based on the exploitation of others for one's own advantage. It also helps if those making profits undertake charitable acts to help the poor. Furthermore, Islam stresses the importance of living up to contractual obligations, of keeping one's word, and of abstaining from deception.

In general, fundamentalist critiques apart, Islamic countries are likely to be receptive to international businesses as long as those businesses behave in a manner that is consistent with Islamic ethics. Businesses that are perceived as making an unjust profit through the exploitation of others, by deception, or by breaking contractual obligations are unlikely to be welcomed in an Islamic state. In addition, in Islamic states where fundamentalism is on the rise, it is also likely that hostility to Western-owned business will be increasing.

One economic principle of Islam that has received particular attention is the prohibition of the payment or receipt of interest, which is considered usury. To the devout Muslim, acceptance of interest payments is seen as a very grave sin. Practitioners of the black art of usury are warned on the pain of hellfire to abstain; the giver and the taker are equally damned. This is not just a matter of theology; in several Islamic states it is also becoming a matter of law. In 1992, for example, Pakistan's Federal Shariat Court, the highest Islamic law-making body in the country, pronounced interest to be un-Islamic and therefore illegal and demanded that the government amend all financial laws accordingly.[24]

On the face of it, rigid adherence to this particular Islamic law could ruin a country's financial and banking system, raising the costs of doing business and scaring away international businesses and international investors. To skirt the ban on interest, Islamic banks have been experimenting with a profit-sharing system to replace interest on borrowed money. When an Islamic bank lends money to a business, rather than charging that business interest on the loan, it takes a share in the profits that are derived from the investment. Similarly, when a business (or individual) deposits money at an Islamic bank in a savings account, the deposit is treated as an equity investment in whatever activity the bank uses the capital for. Thus, the depositor receives a share in the profit from the bank's investment (as opposed to interest payments). Some Muslims claim

Islamic Dissent in Saudi Arabia

The desert kingdom of Saudi Arabia is a new nation. This state of 7 million was a loosely governed area inhabited by numerous Bedouin tribes until King Abdel-Aziz unified the country by conquest and intermarriage in 1935. His descendants—the House of Saud—still rule what remains a monarchy with few democratic institutions. The majority of Saudis are Sunnis, although a Shiite minority lives on the eastern coast. Saudi Arabia has long been thought of as a close ally of the West. Western governments have gone out of their way to curry the favor of Saudi Arabia, a cynic might say, because the country sits on top of more than a quarter of the world's oil reserves—oil that the West needs to keep its industrial machinery humming. In the 1970s and early 1980s high oil prices turned Saudi Arabia into one of the richest countries on earth when measured by GDP per capita. This oil wealth supported a spending spree on basic infrastructure that gave the country all the trappings of a modern state. Nevertheless, traditional tribal values remained just below the surface.

The spending spree is now over. The high oil prices that sustained Saudi spending collapsed in 1985 and have yet to recover. Moreover, while Saudi Arabia was on the winning side in the Gulf War, the cost of financing the war drained the Saudi treasury. As a consequence, government spending has been declining sharply since 1991. In 1994 the Saudi government announced that it would cut spending by 20 percent.

As oil revenues and government spending shrank, the Saudis began to experience unemployment and social unrest. This has led Islamic fundamentalists to question the legitimacy of the rule of the House of Saud. The irony of the current Saudi predicament is that the House of Saud has always seen itself as the guardian of traditional Islamic values. The legitimacy of the royal family has been based in part on the backing of the *ulema*, an influential group of Islamic scholars. Moreover, the laws of Saudi Arabia have always been based on Islamic principles. Still, dissident members of the *ulema* have united with hard-line Islamic radicals—a group that includes preachers, professors, students, and marginalized city dwellers—to criticize the ruling family. These radicals tend to be xenophobic, anti-Western, anti-Shiite, and highly critical of the ruling family. Their opposition is based not just on economic problems, but also on a perception that the House of Saud has been corrupted by its wealth and has monopolized political power in

that this is a more efficient system than the Western banking system, since it encourages both long-term savings and long-term investment. However, there is no hard evidence to this effect and many believe that the Islamic banking system is less efficient than a conventional Western banking system.

Hinduism

Hinduism has approximately 500 million adherents, most of whom are to be found on the Indian subcontinent. Hinduism began in the Indus Valley in India over 4,000 years ago, making it the world's oldest major religion. Unlike Christianity and Islam, its founding is not linked to a particular person. Nor

©Photri

the country. Moreover, there is lingering resentment among the radicals of the government's decision to allow 500,000 Western troops onto Saudi soil during the Gulf War. The fact that Saudi Arabia was on the winning side during the war apparently matters less to the fundamentalists than the "dishonor" associated with having to rely on outsiders, and Western ones at that, to protect Saudi sovereignty.

The sermons of radical preachers denounce a Judeo-Christian conspiracy against Islam and criticize Western values and lifestyles. In September 1994 one of the best known radical preachers, Sheik Salman al-Audah, was asked by the government to sign a gag order. He refused, published the order, and was arrested. Hundreds of his followers were also arrested when they protested by taking to the

streets of Buraida, a fundamentalist stronghold. Harassing, arresting, and sometimes torturing its fundamentalist opponents may prove to be a costly error. As the governments of Algeria and Egypt have recently discovered, fundamentalists seem to be able to draw strength from repression.[22]

does it have an officially sanctioned sacred book like the Bible or the Koran. Hindus believe there is a moral force in society that requires the acceptance of certain responsibilities, called *dharma*. Hindus believe in *reincarnation*, rebirth into a different body after death. Hindus also believe in *karma*, the spiritual progression of each person's soul. A person's *karma* is affected by the way he or she lives. The moral state of an individual's *karma* determines the challenges he or she will face in the next life. By perfecting the soul in each new life, Hindus believe that an individual can eventually achieve *nirvana*, a state of complete spiritual perfection that renders reincarnation no longer necessary. Many Hindus believe that the way to achieve nirvana is to lead a severe ascetic lifestyle of material and physical self-denial, devoting life to a spiritual rather than material quest.

Max Weber, who is famous for expounding on the Protestant work ethic, also argued that whatever its spiritual merits, the ascetic principles embedded in Hinduism do not encourage the kind of entrepreneurial activity that we find in Protestantism.[25] According to Weber, traditional Hindu values emphasize that individuals should not be judged by their material achievements, but by their spiritual achievements. Hindus perceive the pursuit of material well-being as making the attainment of *nirvana* more difficult. Given the emphasis on an ascetic lifestyle, Weber thought that devout Hindus would be less likely to engage in entrepreneurial activity than devout Protestants.

Mahatma Gandhi, the famous Indian nationalist and spiritual leader, was certainly the embodiment of Hindu asceticism. It has been argued that the values of Hindu asceticism and self-reliance that Gandhi advocated had a negative impact on the economic development of post-independence India.[26] On the other hand, one must be careful not to read too much into Weber's arguments. Today there are millions of hardworking entrepreneurs in India, where they form the economic backbone of a rapidly growing economy.

Hinduism also supports India's caste system. The concept of mobility between castes within an individual's lifetime makes no sense to Hindus. Hindus see mobility between castes as something that is achieved through spiritual progression and reincarnation. Individuals can be reborn into a higher caste in their next life if they achieve spiritual development in this life. Insofar as the caste system limits the opportunities for otherwise able individuals to adopt positions of responsibility and influence in society, the economic consequences of this religious belief are bound to be negative. For example, within a business organization, the most able individuals may find their route to the higher levels of the organization blocked simply because they come from a lower caste. By the same token, individuals may get promoted to higher positions within a firm as much because of their caste background as because of their ability.

Buddhism

Buddhism was founded in India in the sixth century BC by Siddhartha Gautama, an Indian prince who renounced his wealth to pursue an ascetic lifestyle and spiritual perfection. Siddhartha achieved *nirvana*, but decided to remain on earth to teach his followers how they too could achieve this state of spiritual enlightenment. Siddhartha became known as the Buddha (which means "the awakened one"). Today Buddhism has 250 million followers, most of whom are found in Central and Southeast Asia, China, Korea, and Japan. According to Buddhism, life is composed of suffering. Misery is everywhere and originates in people's desires for pleasure. These desires can be curbed by systematically following the *Noble Eightfold Path*, which emphasizes right seeing, thinking, speech, action, living, effort, mindfulness, and meditation. Unlike Hinduism, Buddhism does not support the caste system. Nor does Buddhism advocate the kind of extreme ascetic behavior that is encouraged by Hinduism. Nevertheless, like Hindus, Buddhists stress the afterlife and spiritual achievement, rather than involvement in this world.

Because Buddhists, like Hindus, stress spiritual achievement rather than involvement in this world, the emphasis on wealth creation that is embedded in Protestantism is not found in Buddhism. Thus, in Buddhist societies we do not see the same kind of cultural stress on entrepreneurial behavior that we see in the Protestant West. On the other hand, unlike Hinduism, the lack of support for the caste system and extreme ascetic behavior in Buddhism suggests that a Buddhist society may represent a more fertile ground for entrepreneurial activity than Hinduism.

Confucianism

Confucianism was founded in the fifth century BC by K'ung-Fu-tzu, more generally known as Confucius. For more than 2,000 years until the 1949 Communist revolution, Confucianism was the official religion of China. While religious observance has been weakened in China since 1949, over 150 million people still follow the teachings of Confucius, mainly in China, Korea, and Japan. Confucianism teaches the importance of attaining personal salvation through right action. Confucianism is built around a comprehensive ethical code that establishes guidelines for relationships with others. The need for high moral and ethical conduct and loyalty to others is central to Confucianism. Unlike other religions, Confucianism is not concerned with the supernatural and has little to say about the concept of an afterlife. This has led many to argue that Confucianism is not a religion, but simply an ethical system. However, Confucianism is treated by many of its adherents as a religion.

ECONOMIC IMPLICATIONS OF CONFUCIANISM There are those who maintain that Confucianism may have economic implications that are as profound as those found in Protestantism, although they are of a different nature.[27] The basic thesis of those who take this position is that the influence of Confucian ethics on the culture of Japan, South Korea, and Taiwan, by lowering the costs of doing business in those countries, may help explain their economic success. In this regard, three values that are central to the Confucian system of ethics are of particular interest: loyalty, reciprocal obligations, and honesty in dealings with others.

In Confucian thought, loyalty to one's superiors is regarded as a sacred duty, an absolute obligation that is necessary for religious salvation. In modern organizations based in Confucian cultures, the bonds of loyalty that bind employees to the heads of their organization can be seen as reducing the conflict between management and labor that we find in class-conscious societies such as Britain. Cooperation between management and labor can be achieved at a lower cost in a culture where the virtue of loyalty is emphasized in the value systems.

It must be realized, however, that in a Confucian culture, loyalty to one's superiors, such as a worker's loyalty to management, is not blind loyalty. The concept of reciprocal obligations also comes into play. Confucian ethics stress that superiors are obliged to reward the loyalty of their subordinates by bestowing blessings on them. If these "blessings" are not forthcoming, then neither will be the loyalty. In Japanese organizations, this Confucian ethic exhibits itself in the concept of lifetime employment. The employees of a Japanese company are loyal to the leaders of the organization, and in return the leaders bestow on them the "blessing" of lifetime employment. The lack of mobility between companies implied by the lifetime employment system suggests that over the years managers and workers build up knowledge, experience, and a network of interpersonal business contacts, which help them perform their jobs more effectively and so improve the economic performance of the company.

A third concept found in Confucian ethics is the importance attached to honesty. Confucian thinkers emphasize that although dishonest behavior may yield short-term benefits for the transgressor, in the long run dishonesty does not pay. The importance attached to honesty has major economic implications. In a society where companies can trust each other not to break contractual obligations, the costs of doing business are lowered. Expensive lawyers are not needed to resolve contract disputes. In addition, in a Confucian society there may be less hesitation to commit substantial resources to cooperative ventures than in a society where honesty is less pervasive. When companies adhere to Confucian ethics, they can trust each other not to violate the terms of cooperative agreements. Thus, the costs of achieving cooperation between companies may be lowered in societies like Japan (relative to societies like the United States where trust is less pervasive).

For example, it has been argued that the close ties between the automobile companies and their component part suppliers in Japan are facilitated by a combination of trust and reciprocal obligations. These close ties allow the auto companies and their suppliers to work together on a whole range of issues, including inventory reduction, quality control, and design. In turn, it is claimed that the competitive advantage of Japanese auto companies can in part be explained by such factors.[28]

Language

One obvious way in which countries differ is language. By language, we mean both the spoken and the unspoken means of communication. Language is one of the defining characteristics of a culture.

Spoken Language

Language does far more than simply enable people to communicate with each other. The nature of a language also structures the way we perceive the world. The language of a society can direct attention to certain features of the world rather than others. The classic illustration of this phenomenon is that whereas the English language has but one word for snow, the language of the Inuit (Eskimos) lacks a general term for it. Instead, because distinguishing different forms of snow is so important in the lives of the Inuit, they have 24 words that describe different types of snow (e.g., powder snow, falling snow, wet snow, drifting snow).[29]

Since language shapes the way people perceive the world, it also helps define culture. In countries with more than one language, one also often finds more than one culture. In Canada, for example, there is an English-speaking culture and a French-speaking culture. Tensions between the two run quite high, with a substantial proportion of the French-speaking minority de-

Language	Percentage of World Population for Whom This Is a First Language
Chinese	20.0
English	6.0
Hindi	4.5
Russian	4.5
Spanish	3.0
Portuguese	2.0
Japanese	2.0
Arabic	2.0
French	1.5
German	1.5
Other	54.0

FIGURE 3.3

Mother Tongues
Source: *The Economist Atlas* (The Economist Books, 1991), London, p. 116.

manding independence from a Canada "dominated by English speakers." The same phenomenon can be observed in many other countries. For example, Belgium is divided into Flemish and French speakers, and tensions between the two groups exist; in Spain a Basque-speaking minority with its own distinctive culture has been agitating for independence from the Spanish-speaking majority for decades; on the Mediterranean island of Cyprus the culturally diverse Greek- and Turkish-speaking populations of the island engaged in open conflict in the 1970s, and the island is now partitioned into two halves. While it does not necessarily follow that language differences create differences in culture and, therefore, separatist pressures (e.g., witness the harmony in Switzerland where four languages are spoken) there certainly seems to be a tendency in this direction.

Chinese is the "mother tongue" of the largest number of people, followed by English and Hindi, which is spoken in India (see Figure 3.3). However, the most widely spoken language in the world is English, followed by French, Spanish, and Chinese (i.e., many people speak English as a second language). English increasingly is becoming the language of international business. When a Japanese and a German businessperson do business together, it is almost certain they will communicate in English. However, while English is widely used, there are still considerable advantages to learning the local language. Most people prefer to converse in their own language and being able to speak the local language can help build rapport, which may be very important for a business deal.

International businesses that do not understand the local language can make some major blunders through improper translation. For example, the Sunbeam Corporation used the English words for its "Mist-Stick" mist-producing hair curling iron when it entered the German market, only to discover after an expensive advertising campaign that *mist* means *excrement* in German. General Motors was troubled by the lack of enthusiasm among Puerto Rican dealers for its newly introduced Chevrolet Nova. When literally translated into Spanish, *Nova* meant "star". However, when spoken it sounded like "no va," which in Spanish means "it doesn't go." General Motors subsequently changed the name of the car to Caribe.[30]

Unspoken Language

Unspoken language refers to nonverbal communication. We all communicate with each other by a host of nonverbal cues. The raising of eyebrows, for example, is a sign of recognition in most cultures, while a smile is a sign of joy. Many nonverbal cues, however, are culturally bound. A failure to understand the nonverbal cues of another culture can lead to a failure of communication. For example, making a circle with the thumb and the forefinger is a friendly gesture in the United States, but it is a vulgar sexual invitation in Greece and Turkey. Similarly, while most Americans and Europeans use the "thumbs-up" gesture to indicate that "it's all right," in Greece the gesture is obscene.

Another aspect of nonverbal communication is personal space, which is the "comfortable" amount of distance between you and someone you are talking to. In the United States, the customary distance adopted by parties in a business discussion is five to eight feet apart. In Latin America it is three to five feet. Consequently, many North Americans unconsciously feel that Latin Americans are "invading their personal space" and can be seen backing away from them during a conversation. In turn, the Latin American may interpret such backing away as aloofness. The result can be a regrettable lack of rapport between two businesspeople from different cultures.

Education

Formal education plays a key role in a society. Formal education is the medium through which individuals learn many of the language, conceptual, and mathematical skills that are indispensable in a modern society. Formal education also supplements the family's role in socializing the young into the values and norms of a society. Values and norms are taught both directly and indirectly. Schools generally teach basic facts about the social and political nature of a society. They also focus on the fundamental obligations of citizenship. Cultural norms are also taught indirectly at school. Respect for others, obedience to authority, honesty, neatness, being on time, and so on, are all part of the "hidden curriculum" of schools. The use of a grading system also teaches children the value of personal achievement and competition.[31]

From an international business perspective, education plays an important role as a determinant of national competitive advantage.[32] The availability of a pool of skilled and educated human resources seems to be a major determinant of the likely economic success of a country. In analyzing the competitive success of Japan since 1945, for example, Michael Porter notes that after the war Japan had almost nothing except for a pool of skilled and educated human resources.

> With a long tradition of respect for education that borders on reverence, Japan possessed a large pool of literate, educated, and increasingly skilled human resources . . . Japan has benefited from a large pool of trained engineers. Japanese universities graduate many more engineers per capita than in the United States . . . A first-rate primary and secondary education system in Japan operates based on high standards and emphasizes math and science. Primary and secondary education is highly competitive . . . Japanese education provides most students all over Japan with a sound education for later education and training. A

Japanese high school graduate knows as much about math as most American college graduates.[33]

Porter's point is that Japan's excellent education system was an important factor explaining the country's post-war economic success. Not only is a good education system a determinant of national competitive advantage, but it is also an important factor guiding the location choices of international businesses. For example, it would make little sense to base production facilities that require highly skilled labor in a country where the education system was so poor that a skilled labor pool wasn't available.

The general education level of a country is also a good index of the kind of products that might sell in a country and of the type of promotional material that should be used. For example, a country such as Pakistan where 73.8 percent of the population is illiterate is unlikely to be a good market for popular books. Promotional materials containing written descriptions of mass-marketed products are unlikely to have an effect in a country where almost three-quarters of the population cannot read. It is far better to use pictorial promotions in such circumstances.

Maps 3.1 and 3.2 provide some important data on education worldwide. Map 3.1 shows the percentage of a country's GDP that is devoted to education. Map 3.2 shows literacy rates. Although there is not a perfect one-to-one correspondence between the percentage of GDP devoted to education and the quality of education, the overall level of spending gives some indication of a country's commitment to education. Note that the United States spends more of its GDP on education than many other advanced industrialized nations, including Germany and Japan. Despite this, the *quality* of U.S. education is often argued to be inferior to that offered in many other industrialized countries.

Culture and the Workplace

For an international business with operations in different countries, a question of considerable importance is *how does a society's culture impact on the values found in the workplace?* The question points to the need to vary management process and practices to take different culturally determined work-related values into account. So for example, if the United States and France have different cultures, and if these cultures result in different work-related values, it might make sense for an international business with operations in both countries to vary its management process and practices to take these differences into account. The opening case illustrates these issues. One reason for the problems at Euro-Disney was that Disney tried to impose American work practices on French employees, who had a different set of work-related values. The result was employee resistance and high turnover, as those who objected to Disney's "brainwashing," as one former employee put it, left the company.

Hofstede's Model

The most famous study of how culture relates to values in the workplace was undertaken by Geert Hofstede.[34] As part of his job as a psychologist working for IBM, from 1967 to 1973, Hofstede collected data on employee attitudes

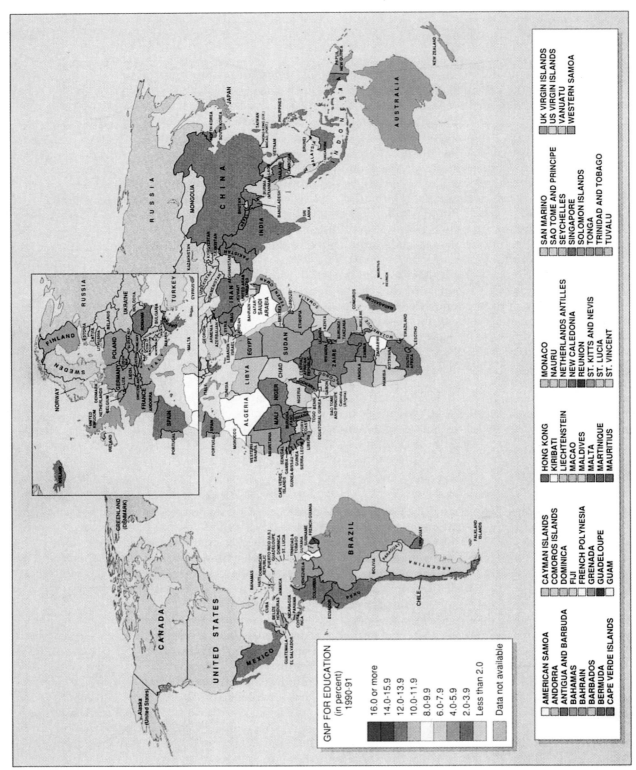

MAP 3.1

Percentage of Gross Domestic Product (GDP) Spent on Education
Source: Map data copyright ©1992 PC Globe, Inc., Tempe, Arizona, USA. All Rights Reserved
Worldwide.

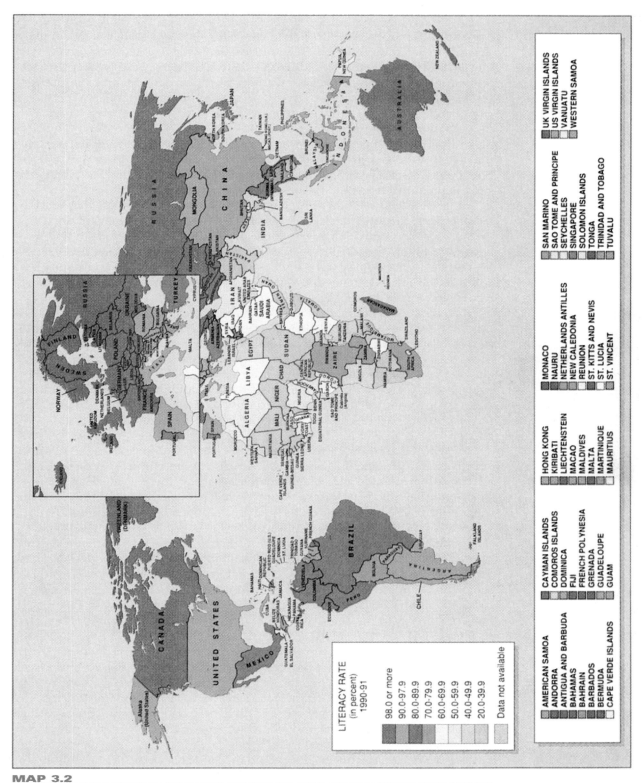

MAP 3.2

Percentage World Literacy Rates

Source: Map data copyright ©1992 PC Globe, Inc., Tempe, Arizona, USA. All Rights Reserved Worldwide.

and values for over 100,000 individuals. This data enabled him to compare dimensions of culture across 40 countries. Hofstede isolated four dimensions that he claimed summarized different cultures. These were power distance, individualism versus collectivism, uncertainty avoidance, and masculinity versus femininity.

Hofstede's *power distance* dimension focused on how a society deals with the fact that people are unequal in physical and intellectual capabilities. According to Hofstede, high power distance cultures were found in countries that let inequalities grow over time into inequalities of power and wealth. Low power distance cultures were found in societies that tried to play down such inequalities as much as possible.

The *individualism versus collectivism* dimension focused on the relationship between the individual and his or her fellows. In individualistic societies, the ties between individuals were loose and individual achievement and freedom were highly valued. In societies where collectivism was emphasized, the ties between individuals were tight. In such societies people were born into collectives, such as extended families, and everyone was supposed to look after the interest of his or her collective.

Hofstede's *uncertainty avoidance* dimension measured the extent to which different cultures socialized their members into accepting ambiguous situations and tolerating uncertainty. Members of high uncertainty avoidance cultures placed a premium on job security, career patterns, retirement benefits, and so on. They also had a strong need for rules and regulations; the manager was expected to issue clear instructions, and subordinates' initiatives were tightly controlled. Lower uncertainty avoidance cultures were characterized by a greater readiness to take risks and less emotional resistance to change.

Hofstede's *masculinity versus femininity* dimension looked at the relationship between gender and work roles. In masculine cultures, sex roles were sharply differentiated and traditional "masculine values," such as achievement and the effective exercise of power, determined cultural ideals. In feminine cultures, sex roles were less sharply distinguished, and little differentiation was made between men and women in the same job.

Hofstede created an index score for each of these four dimensions that ranged from 0 to 100 and scored high for high individualism, high power distance, high uncertainty avoidance, and high masculinity. He averaged the score for all employees from a given country and plotted the resulting score for each country on a series of graphs, two of which are shown in Figures 3.5 and 3.6 (the key to the countries and regions given in these figures is reported in Figure 3.4).

Figure 3.5 plots the power distance index against the individualism dimension (low individualism implies high collectivism). This graph tells us that advanced Western nations such as the United States, Canada, and Britain score high on the individualism scale and low on the power distance scale. At the other extreme are a group of Latin American and Asian countries that emphasize collectivism over individualism and score high on the power distance scale.

Figure 3.6 plots the uncertainty avoidance index against the masculinity index. Again some countries stand out. Japan is highlighted as a country with a culture of strong uncertainty avoidance and high masculinity. This characterization fits the standard stereotype of Japan as a country that is male dominant and where uncertainty avoidance exhibits itself in the institution of life-

ARA	Arab countries (Egypt, Lebanon, Libya, Kuwait, Iraq, Saudi Arabia, United Arab Emirates)		JAM	Jamaica
			JPN	Japan
			KOR	South Korea
ARG	Argentina		MAL	Malaysia
AUL	Australia		MEX	Mexico
AUT	Austria		NET	Netherlands
BEL	Belgium		NOR	Norway
BRA	Brazil		NZL	New Zealand
CAN	Canada		PAK	Pakistan
CHL	Chile		PAN	Panama
COL	Colombia		PER	Peru
COS	Costa Rica		PHI	Philippines
DEN	Denmark		POR	Portugal
EAF	East Africa (Kenya, Ethiopia, Zambia)		SAF	South Africa
			SAL	Salvador
EOA	Ecuador		SIN	Singapore
FIN	Finland		SPA	Spain
FRA	France		SWE	Sweden
GBR	Great Britain		SWI	Switzerland
GER	Germany		TAI	Taiwan
GRE	Greece		THA	Thailand
GUA	Guatemala		TUR	Turkey
HOK	Hong Kong		URU	Uruguay
IDO	Indonesia		USA	United States
IND	India		VEN	Venezuela
IRA	Iran		WAF	West Africa (Nigeria, Ghana, Sierra Leone)
IRE	Ireland			
ISR	Israel		YUG	Yugoslavia
ITA	Italy			

FIGURE 3.4

Key to Countries and Regions in Hofstede's Graphs

Source: G. Hofstede, "The Cultural Relativity of Organizational Practices and Theories," *Journal of International Business Studies* 14 (Fall 1983), pp. 75–89.

time employment. Sweden and Denmark stand out as countries that have both low uncertainty avoidance and low masculinity (high emphasis on "feminine" values).

Evaluating Hofstede's Model

Hofstede's results are interesting for what they tell us in a general way about differences between cultures. Many of Hofstede's findings are consistent with some standard Western stereotypes about cultural differences. For example, the finding that Americans are more individualistic and egalitarian than the Japanese (they have a lower power distance), who in turn are more individualistic and egalitarian than Mexicans, might strike many people as being valid. Similarly, many might agree that Latin countries, such as Italy, Colombia, and Mexico, place a higher emphasis on masculine value—they are machismo cultures—than the Nordic countries of Denmark, Finland, Norway, and Sweden.

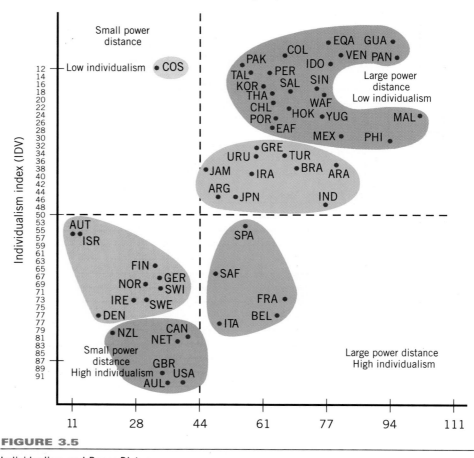

FIGURE 3.5

Individualism and Power Distance
Source: G. Hofstede, "The Cultural Relativity of Organizational Practices and Theories," *Journal of International Business Studies* 14 (Fall 1983), pp. 75–89.

However, one should be careful about reading too much into Hofstede's research. For all of its fame, it is deficient in a number of important respects.[35] First, Hofstede assumes there is a one-to-one correspondence between culture and the nation-state, but as we saw earlier, many countries have more than one culture. Hofstede's results do not capture this distinction. Second, the research may have been culturally bound. The research team was composed of Europeans and Americans. The questions they asked of IBM employees and the analysis they made of the answers may have been shaped by their own cultural biases and concerns. So it is not surprising that Hofstede's results confirm Western stereotypes, since it was Westerners who undertook the research!

Third, Hofstede's subjects worked not only within a single industry, the computer industry, but also within one company, IBM. At the time IBM was renowned for its own strong corporate culture and employee selection procedures. It is possible, therefore, that the values of IBM employees are different in important respects from the values that underlie the cultures from which those employees came. Moreover, certain social classes (such as un-

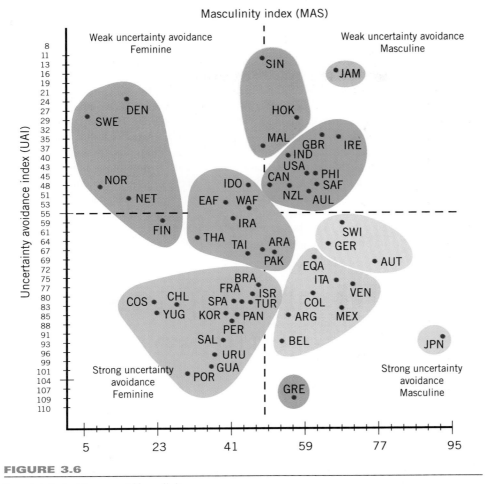

Masculinity index (MAS)

FIGURE 3.6

Uncertainty Avoidance and Masculinity

Source: G. Hofstede, "The Cultural Relativity of Organizational Practices and Theories," *Journal of International Business Studies* 14 (Fall 1983), pp. 75–89.

skilled manual workers) were excluded from Hofstede's sample. A final caution is that Hofstede's work is now beginning to look dated. Cultures do not stand still; they evolve over time, albeit slowly. What was a reasonable characterization in the 1960s and 1970s may not be so reasonable today.

Still, just as it should not be accepted without question, Hofstede's work should not be dismissed lightly either. It represents a reasonable starting point for managers trying to figure out how cultures differ and what that might mean for management practices. At the same time, it is no more than a starting point. Managers should use the results with caution, for they are not necessarily accurate.

Cultural Change

Culture evolves over time, although changes in value systems can be slow and painful for a society. In the 1960s, for example, American values toward the role of women, love, sex, and marriage changed significantly. Much of the so-

Hitachi was founded in 1911 by Namihei Odaira, who named his company after the town in which it was based. By 1965 Hitachi was one of the giants of Japanese industry, with its sales accounting for over 1 percent of Japan's gross domestic product. In many ways, Hitachi was a typical Japanese company. New recruits were lectured on Odaira's reverence for *wa*, or harmony. Managers and workers, dressed in identical uniforms, were tirelessly punctual and trusted each other like brothers. Decision making

public facilities were few, everyone went to the company bathhouse. In the evenings employees saw the same colleagues in the same company bars. Their wives shopped at the company store. The company even provided a wedding hall and funeral parlor.

Today two forces are impacting on Japan's culture—prosperity and globalization. Both are leading to changes at Hitachi. Over the past four decades Japan has become one of the world's richest countries. At Hitachi, prosperity means nobody sleeps two to a

the anchor of social life. Companies such as Hitachi used to provide for all aspects of employees' lives. Now leisure is an opportunity for individualism, not a prop for workplace harmony.

Like many other Japanese companies, Hitachi is now a global enterprise with worldwide operations. Japanese society, too, has become more international in recent years. In this new environment, top management states bluntly that monocultural firms will not survive. In 1991 Hitachi set up a department to educate

Hitachi and Japan's Changing Culture

was characterized by the consensus model, so typical of Japanese corporations, where managers consulted juniors exhaustively before making a decision. And the lifetime employment system was instituted at Hitachi.

According to old Hitachi hands, the harmony and togetherness owed as much to poverty as it did to anything else. Historically, many employees and their families were housed in company dormitories because they could afford nothing else. Younger employees slept two to a room, and all ate their meals communally in the company cafeteria. Because

room in the company dormitory anymore. Since the 1960s employees have been moving "outside the fence," away from the company dormitories. Prosperity has brought more entertainment and leisure options. The company bathhouse has given way to private bathhouses. The choice between a French restaurant and an Indian restaurant divides one employee from the next. Hobbies are more diverse. There are cars, drinking, bonsai gardening, music bands; before it was only drinking in company bars. Employees spend more time with their families; the biological family is replacing the company family as

executives in other cultures. This department deliberately downplays the old notions of harmony and consensus decision making in its programs. Hitachi is also sending increasing numbers of its executives for prolonged postings overseas, and it is starting to bring foreign managers back to Japan. The foreign experience has encouraged senior managers to seek firmer leadership in Japan—to shift away from the old consensus decision-making model—and Hitachi's top executives have encouraged this trend.[38]

---

cial turmoil of that time reflected these changes. Similarly, today the value systems of many ex-Communist states, such as Russia, are undergoing significant changes as those countries move away from values that emphasize collectivism and toward those that emphasize individualism. Social turmoil is an inevitable outcome of this process.

Some claim that a major cultural shift is now occuring in Japan, with a move toward much greater individualism.[36] The model Japanese office worker, or salary man, is pictured as being loyal to his boss and the organization to the point of giving up evenings, weekends, and vacations to serve the organization, which is the collective of which he is a member. However, a new generation of office workers does not seem to fit this model. It is claimed that an individual from the new generation

is more direct than the traditional Japanese. He acts more like a Westerner, a *gaijian*. He does not live for the company and will move on if he gets the offer of a better job. He is not keen on overtime, especially if he has a date with a girl. He has his own plans for his free time, and they may not include drinking or playing golf with the boss.[37]

The "Management Focus" looks at the impact of Japan's changing culture on Hitachi.

The Hitachi example reviewed in the "Management Focus" points to two forces that may result in culture change—economic advancement and globalization. Several studies have suggested that both these forces may be important factors in societal change.[39] For example, there is evidence that economic progress is accompanied by a shift in values away from collectivism and toward individualism.[40] Thus, as Japan has become richer, so the cultural stress placed on collectivism has declined and greater individualism is being witnessed. If the Hitachi example is any guide, one reason for this shift may be that in richer societies there is less need for social and material support structures built on collectives, whether the collective is the extended family or the paternalistic company. People are better able to take care of their own needs. As a result, the importance attached to collectivism declines, while greater economic freedoms lead directly to an increase in opportunities for expressing individualism.

The culture of societies may also change as they become richer because economic progress affects a number of other factors, which impact on culture. For example, increased urbanization and improvements in the quality and availability of education are both a function of economic progress, and both can lead to declining emphasis on the traditional values associated with poor rural societies.

It can be argued that advances in transportation and communications technologies, the dramatic increase in trade in goods and services since WWII, and the rise of global corporations are creating the conditions for the merging of cultures.[41] With McDonald's in China, Levi's in India, Sony Walkmans in South Africa, and MTV everywhere helping to foster a ubiquitous youth culture, one can argue that the conditions have been met for a reduction in cultural variation. At the same time, one must not ignore important countertrends, such as the shift toward Islamic fundamentalism in several Muslim countries, the separatist movement in Quebec, Canada, or the continuing ethnic strains and separatist movements in Russia. Such countertrends are in many ways a reaction to the pressures for cultural convergence that we have been discussing here. In an increasingly homogeneous and materialistic world, some societies are trying to reemphasize their cultural roots and uniqueness.

Implications for Business

International business is different from domestic business because countries and societies are different. In this chapter we have seen just how different societies can be. Societies differ because their culture is different. Their culture is different because of profound differences in social structure, religion, language, education, economic philosophy, and political philosophy. Two important implications for international business flow from these differences. The first is the need to develop cross-cultural literacy. There is a need to appreciate not only that cultural differences exist, but also what such differences mean for the practice of international business. A second implication centers on the connection among culture, the costs of doing business in a country, and national competitive advantage. In this section, we will explore both these issues in greater detail.

Cross-Cultural Literacy

One big danger confronting a company that goes abroad for the first time is the danger of being ill-informed. International businesses that are ill-informed about the practices of another culture are unlikely to succeed. Doing business in different cultures requires adaptation to conform with the value systems and norms of that culture. Adaptation can embrace all aspects of an international firm's operations in a foreign country. How deals are negotiated, the appropriate incentive pay systems for salespeople, the structure of the organization, the name of a product, the tenor of relations between management and labor, the manner in which the product is promoted, and so on, are all sensitive to cultural differences. As we saw in the Euro-Disney case that opened the chapter, what works in one culture might not work in another.

To combat the danger of being ill-informed, international businesses should consider employing local citizens to help them do business in a particular culture. They must also ensure that home country executives are cosmopolitan enough to understand how differences in culture affect the practice of international business. One way to build a cadre of cosmopolitan executives is to transfer executives overseas at regular intervals so they gain exposure to different cultures. Hitachi is now taking this approach as it struggles to transform itself from a Japanese into a global company (see the "Management Focus" for details).

ethnocentric behavior
Acting on the belief in the superiority of one's own ethnic group or culture.

An international business must also be constantly on guard against the dangers of **ethnocentric behavior**. Ethnocentrism is a belief in the superiority of one's own ethnic group or culture. Hand in hand with ethnocentrism goes a disregard or contempt for the culture of other countries. Unfortunately ethnocentrism is all too prevalent—many Americans are guilty of it, as are many French people, Japanese people, British people, and so on. Ugly as it is, ethnocentrism happens to be a fact of life. It is one, however, that the international business must be on continual guard against.

Culture and Competitive Advantage

One theme that continually surfaced in this chapter is the relationship between culture and national competitive advantage. Put simply, the value systems and norms of a country influence the costs of doing business in that country. The costs of doing business in a country influence the ability of firms based in that culture to establish a competitive advantage in the global marketplace. For example, we have seen how attitudes toward cooperation between management and labor, toward work, and toward the payment of interest are influenced by social structure and religion. It can be argued that the class-based conflict between workers and management that we find in British society, insofar as it leads to industrial disruption, raises the costs of doing business in that culture. This factor will tend to work against British firms relative to, say, Japanese firms, where the importance of group identification minimizes conflict between management and labor. Similarly, we have seen how the ascetic "other worldly" ethics of Hinduism may not be as supportive of capitalism as the ethics embedded in Protestantism and Confucianism. We have also alluded to the possibility that the constraints on a country's banking system contained in Islamic laws on interest payments may put enterprises based in Islamic countries at a competitive disadvantage.

Japan presents us with an interesting example of how culture can influence competitive advantage. It can be argued that the culture of modern Japan lowers the costs of doing business in that country, relative to the costs of doing business in most Western nations. The emphasis placed on group affiliation, loyalty, reciprocal obligations, honesty, and education all boost the competitiveness of Japanese companies. The emphasis on group affiliation and loyalty encourages individuals to identify strongly with the companies in which they work. In turn, this tends to foster an ethic of hard work and cooperation between management and labor "for the good of the company." Similarly, the concepts of reciprocal obligations and honesty help foster an atmosphere of trust between companies and their suppliers. This encourages them to enter into long-term relationships with each other to work on factors such as inventory reduction, quality control, and joint design—all of which improve the competitiveness of an organization. This level of cooperation has often been lacking in the West, where the relationship between a company and its suppliers tends to be a short-term one structured around competitive bidding. In addition, the availability of a pool of highly skilled labor, particularly engineers, has undoubtedly helped Japanese enterprises develop a number of cost-reducing process innovations that have boosted their productivity.[42] Thus, cultural factors may help explain the competitive advantage enjoyed by many Japanese businesses in the global marketplace. Indeed, the rise of Japan as an economic superpower during the second half of the 20th century may be in part attributed to the economic consequences of its culture.

For the international business, the connection between culture and competitive advantage is important for two reasons. First, the connection suggests which countries are likely to produce the most viable competitors. For example, it is likely that U.S. enterprises are going to see a continued growth in aggressive, cost-efficient competitors from those Pacific Rim nations where a combination of free market economics, Confucian ideology, group-oriented social structures, and advanced education systems can all be found (e.g., South Korea, Taiwan, Japan, and increasingly China).

Second, the connection between culture and competitive advantage has important implications for the choice of countries in which to locate production facilities and do business. Consider a hypothetical case when a company has to choose between two countries, A and B, for locating a production facility. Both countries are characterized by low labor costs and good access to world markets. Both countries are of roughly the same size (in terms of population) and currently both are at a similar stage of economic development. In country A the education system is undeveloped; the society is characterized by a marked stratification between the upper and lower classes; the dominant religion stresses the importance of reincarnation; and there are three major linguistic groups. In country B the education system is well developed; there is a lack of social stratification; group identification is a value that is stressed by the culture; the dominant religion stresses the virtue of hard work; and there is only one linguistic group. Which country, A or B, makes the better investment site?

Country B does. The culture of country B is supportive of the capitalist mode of production and social harmony, whereas the culture of country A is not. In country A conflict between management and labor, and between different language groups, can be expected to lead to social and industrial disruption, thereby raising the costs of doing business. The lack of a good education system and the dominance of a religion that stresses ascetic behavior as a way of achieving advancement in the next life can also be expected to work against the attainment of business goals.

The same kind of comparison could be made for an international business trying to decide which country to push its products in, A or B. Again, country B would be the logical choice, precisely because cultural factors suggest that in the long run, country B is the nation most likely to achieve the greatest level of economic growth. In comparison, the culture of country A may produce economic stagnation.

Key Terms

Summary

We have looked at the nature of social culture and drawn out some of the implications for business practice. The following points have been made in the chapter:

1 Culture is that complex whole that includes knowledge, belief, art, morals, law, custom, and other capabilities acquired by people as members of society.

2 Values and norms are the central components of a culture. Values are abstract ideals about what a society believes to be good, right, and desirable. Norms are social rules and guidelines that prescribe appropriate behavior in particular situations.

3 Values and norms are influenced by political and economic philosophy, social structure, religion, language, and education.

4 The social structure of a society refers to its basic social organization. There are two main dimensions along which social structures differ: the individual–group dimension and the stratification dimension.

5 In some societies the individual is the basic building block of social organization. In these societies individual achievements are emphasized above all else. In other societies the group is the basic building block of social organization. In these societies group membership and group achievements are emphasized above all else.

6 All societies are stratified into different classes. Class-conscious societies are characterized by low social mobility and a high degree of stratification.

7 Religion may be defined as a system of shared beliefs and rituals that are concerned with the realm of the sacred. The world's major religions are Christianity, Islam, Hinduism, Buddhism, and Confucianism. The value systems of different religions have different implications for business practice.

8 Language is one of the defining characteristics of a culture. It has both a spoken and an unspoken dimension. Countries with more than one spoken language tend to have more than one culture.

9 Formal education is the medium through which individuals learn skills and are socialized into the values and norms of a society. Education plays an important role in the determination of national competitive advantage.

10 Geert Hofstede studied how culture relates to values in the workplace. Hofstede isolated four dimensions that he claimed summarized different cultures: power distance, uncertainty avoidance, individualism versus collectivism, and masculinity versus femininity.

11 Culture is not a constant; it can and does evolve over time. Economic progress and globalization seem to be two important engines of cultural change.

12 One danger confronting a company that goes abroad for the first time is being ill-informed. To develop cross-cultural literacy, international businesses need to employ host country nationals, build a cadre of cosmopolitan executives, and guard against the dangers of ethnocentric behavior.

13 The value systems and norms of a country can affect the costs of doing business in that country.

Critical Thinking and Discussion Questions

1 Outline why the culture of a country influences the costs of doing business in that country. Illustrate your answer with examples.

2 How do you think business practices in an Islamic country are likely to differ from business practices in the United States?

3 What are the implications for international business of differences in the dominant religion of a country?

4 Choose two countries that appear to be culturally diverse. Compare the culture of those countries and then indicate how cultural differences influence (*i*) the costs of doing business in each country, (*ii*) the likely future economic development of that country, and (*iii*) business practices.

Internet Exercise

Understanding the link between culture and the workplace is crucial to success in today's global economy, as you learned in this chapter. Geert Hofstede's research on employee attitudes and values is noted as being a good starting point for managers attempting to appreciate their employees' differences and backgrounds.

Hofstede's studies are cited in the Aviation and Space Research at the Aerospace Crew Research Project site (http://www.psy.utexas.edu/psy/helmreich/ongoing.htm). This project, funded by the Federal Aviation Administration and the National Aeronautics and Space Administration, studies factors that influence flight crew performance. NASA has supported projects studying astronauts' and pilots' national and organizational culture, personality and performance, and measures of individual and team performance. The FAA has supported studies to evaluate cultural issues in air crew performance, human factors in training programs, human factors in air traffic control, and attitudes toward flightdeck automation (http://www.psy.utexas.edu/psy/helmreich/autocult.htm).

The FAA also has funded a study to assess how national and organizational cultures affect Crew Resource Management training (http://www.psy.utexas.edu/psy/helmreich/icaonz96.htm). The researchers conclude that different cultures have different training priorities, so training must be tailored to each organizational and national culture for optimum safety. A second study, Culture in the Cockpit, analyzes cultural similarities and differences in attitudes toward captain and crew command authority, communication, responsibility, and stress (http://www.psy.utexas.edu/psy/helmreich/osuashd.htm). A third study concludes that attitudes toward automation's effect in the cockpit regarding communication, workload, and general preference for automation are affected by the pilot's national culture (http://www.psy.utexas.edu/psy/helmreich/osupjrhd.htm).

Global Surfing

Read the FAA and NASA studies and discuss how Hofstede's research is cited. How do attitudes toward cockpit automation items vary among pilots of different national cultures? How can specialized Crew Resource Management training help prevent human error? How do pilots with different cultures view command structure, information sharing, and organization culture?

Cultural Differences at
ABB

Asea Brown Boveri (ABB) is a quintessential global enterprise. Formed out of the merger of two engineering companies, one Swiss and the other Swedish, ABB has worldwide revenues of over $35 billion, 250,000 employees, and activities in 140 countries. Percy Barnevik, the company's CEO, notes that ABB is a company with no geographical center, no national ax to grind:

> Are we a Swiss company? Our headquarters is in Zurich, but only 100 professionals work at headquarters . . . Are we a Swedish company? I'm the CEO, and I was born and educated in Sweden. But our headquarters is not in Sweden, and only two of the eight members of our board of directors are Swedes. Perhaps we are an American company. We report our financial results in U.S. dollars, and English is ABB's official language. We conduct all high-level meetings in English . . . My point is that ABB is none of these

things—and all of these things. We are not homeless. We are a company with many homes.

In this company with many homes, Barnevik stresses the advantage of building a culturally diverse cadre of global managers. In particular, Barnevik believes that such a management group can improve the quality of managerial decision making.

> If you have 50 business areas and five managers on each business area team, that's 250 people from different parts of the world—people who meet regularly in different places, bring their national perspectives to bear on tough problems, and begin to understand how things are done elsewhere. I experience this every three weeks in our executive committee. When we sit together as Germans, Swiss, Americans, and Swedes, with many of us living, working, and traveling in different places, the insights can be remarkable.

Barnevik also stresses the need to acknowledge cultural differences without becoming paralyzed by them-to work with those differences. Again, Barnevik states the point clearly:

> We've done some surveys (at ABB) . . . and we find interesting differences in perception. For example, a Swede may think a Swiss is not completely frank and open, that he doesn't know exactly where he stands. That is a cultural phenomenon. Swiss culture shuns disagreement. A Swiss might say, "Let's come back to that point later; let me review it with my colleagues." A Swede would prefer to confront the issues directly. How do we undo hundreds of years of upbringing and education? We don't, and we shouldn't try to. But we do need to broaden understanding (of cultural differences).

Thus, Barnevik's argument is that a culturally diverse set of managers can be a source of strength. According to Barnevik, managers should not try to eradicate these differences and establish a uniform managerial culture. Rather, they should seek to understand these cultural differences, to empathize with the views of people from different cultures and to make accommodations for such differences.[43]

Case Discussion Questions

1 How can ABB's culturally diverse management team be a source of competitive strength?

2 What barriers are likely to stand in the way of Percy Barnevik's attempt to make his culturally diverse management

team a source of competitive strength?

3 What do you think that Barnevik means by the need to acknowledge cultural differences without becoming paralyzed by them—to work with those

differences? What does working with cultural differences at a global company such as ABB actually mean?

4 How can ABB increase the cross-cultural literacy of its management cadre?

With a Little Help from My Friends

At 26 with his undergraduate degree in international business nearly complete, Gordon Craig is building his own international business. He has started TA (*Tellurian Armamentaria*) Global, a worldwide commodities distributor. According to Gordon, *tellurian armamentarium* means "supply house for the inhabitants of the earth," which is what he dreams his company will become. Clients from abroad hire him to locate the products they need cheaply and efficiently. He deals primarily in aftermarket automotive performance parts and sound equipment to Japan, Hong Kong, and the Philippines. However, he is now negotiating deals for jet skis and novelty items.

Gordon's quest for an international lifestyle began when he was born in Hong Kong to a Chinese mother and an American father. He has already lived on three continents, having been raised in Australia and moving to the United States ten years ago. Gordon moves easily between the Asian and the Western halves of his heritage.

His business would not be possible without a little help from his friends. Unlike some budding international entrepreneurs, Gordon does not rely on family connections. Instead he depends on an ever-expanding, worldwide network of friends.

Whenever Gordon meets someone new—through his travels, internships, organizations, or the

Gordon Craig

university—he trades business cards. He carefully files each card he receives for future reference. His card collection is an extensive source of prospective customers, distributors and suppliers. It has become one of the most important assets of his business. Yet no one card is more valuable than another. Each represents not only a business contact but also a friend. Gordon advises that it is important to build such friendships and to treat everyone you meet with respect.

His connections multiply when his own cards find their way into the hands of friends of friends. He has more confidence in the contacts which result from such origins. Before he enters an agreement with such a contact he asks his friends for a profile of the prospective client.

He has concentrated on high-performance automotive equip-

ment, ranging from carbon fiber clutches to turbo kits. His strong knowledge and fascination with performance cars dates back to high school. He has developed a comprehensive library of three-ring binders full of product information and industry contacts. Often the key to selecting the right product to export can be found in what you enjoy. It is easier to sell a product that you understand and believe in.

In college he secured an internship with a company that exports automotive performance parts and accessories. He also interned with SEMA (Specialty Equipment Marketing Association) the trade association for the aftermarket automotive performance industry. In these positions he gained even more product knowledge. He also met some individuals who have provided him with the advice necessary for setting up his own business and others who can supply him with the products he needs.

Gordon has been concentrating on customers in the Far East because of his affinity for the Asian culture. "I understand the Asian way of thinking and communicating. I can immerse myself in being Asian." Besides, Gordon speaks fluent Cantonese. Such empathy is key to successfully operating within a foreign culture.

He is working with three Japanese individuals whom he

has not yet met in person. The initial contact was made through a fellow member of the Cal Poly World Traders, a student organization to which he belongs. The contact then recommended Gordon to a friend who in turn recommended him to another friend.

The two companies he is dealing with in the Philippines resulted from referrals from two other friends. He was able to meet them in the Philippines last summer when returning from a study tour of China. To cut down expenses, he was able to stay with friends of his college friends.

His Hong Kong connection was the result of contacts he made while participating in the same summer study tour of China. As part of the study program, he instructed a group of Chinese about U.S. customs, etiquette, and travel. Luckily, the group to whom he had been assigned consisted of high-ranking economic officials, who were impressed with his language skills and his helpfulness.

Gordon started his business with less than $500, and continues to operate with little capital. He works out of his home, where his biggest expense is his telephone bill (about $160 per month). The foreign companies fax Gordon their orders and wire him the money. He then purchases the products and air freights their orders. He keeps no inventory and will not ship an order unless he has been paid. He marks up the orders between 20 to 30 percent.

Gordon devotes three to four hours a day on the enterprise making telephone calls and e-mailing on the computer. He conducts most of his business over the phone or e-mail, both great equalizers when it comes to age and company size. Gordon, who is soft-spoken but articulate, understands the importance of good telephone skills. "I am very comfortable when dealing over the phone. I am assertive but always respectful and down to earth." He also has learned how to

be personable over e-mail. He has found that his Asian clients insist on developing a personal relationship before they engage in a business transaction.

Gordon is now shipping $1,500 to $2,500 worth of merchandise each month. Within the year, he plans to increase that tenfold assuming he can devote himself to the enterprise full-time. Looking to the future, he knows that he will need more capital and more contacts. For example, he maintains the Chinese contacts he made even though the market is still too small and too risky for performance auto parts.

He is investigating other opportunities in Brazil and Egypt. All the while, he continues to give away his business cards to his growing circle of friends.

Helena Czepiec
California State Polytechnic University, Pomona

Chapter 4
International Trade Theory

©PhotoDisc

Opening Case

The Gains from Trade: Ghana and South Korea

In 1970 living standards in Ghana and South Korea were roughly comparable. Ghana's 1970 gross domestic product (GDP) per person was $250, and South Korea's was $260. By 1992 the situation had changed dramatically. South Korea had a GDP per person of $6,790, while Ghana's was only $450, reflecting vastly different economic growth rates. Between 1968 and 1988 the average annual growth rate in Ghana's GDP was 1.5 percent; between 1980 and 1992 it

Learning Objectives:

1 Understand why nations trade with each other.

2 Be conversant with the different theories that have been offered to explain trade flows between nations.

3 Understand why many economists believe that unrestricted (free) trade between nations will raise the economic welfare of all countries that participate in a free trade system.

4 Be familiar with the arguments of those who maintain that govern-

ment can play a proactive role in promoting national competitive advantage in certain industries.

5 Understand the important implications that international trade theory holds for business practice.

was an anemic −0.1 percent. In contrast, South Korea achieved a rate of about 9 percent annually between 1968 and 1992.

What explains the difference between Ghana and South Korea? There is no simple answer, but the attitudes of both countries toward international trade provide part of the explanation. A study by the World Bank suggests that whereas the South Korean government has had a strong pro-trade bias, the actions of the Ghanaian government discour-

aged domestic producers from becoming involved in international trade.

In 1957, Ghana was the first of Great Britain's West African colonies to become independent. Its first president, Kwame Nkrumah, influenced the rest of the continent with his theories of pan-African socialism. For Ghana this meant the imposition of high tariffs on many imports, implementation of an import substitution policy aimed at fostering Ghana's self-sufficiency in certain

manufactured goods, and adoption of policies that discouraged Ghana's enterprises from engaging in exports. The results were an unmitigated disaster that transformed one of Africa's most prosperous nations into one of the world's poorest.

As an illustration of how Ghana's antitrade policies destroyed the Ghanaian economy, consider the Ghanaian government's involvement in the cocoa trade. A combination of favorable climate, good soils, and ready access to world shipping routes has given Ghana an absolute advantage in cocoa production. Quite simply, it is one of the best places in the world to grow cocoa. Ghana was the world's largest producer and exporter of cocoa in 1957. Then the government of the newly independent nation created a state-controlled cocoa marketing board. The board was given the authority to fix prices for cocoa and was designated the sole buyer of all cocoa grown in Ghana. The board held down the prices that it paid farmers for cocoa, while selling the cocoa on the world market at world prices. Thus, it might buy cocoa from farmers at 25 cents a pound and sell it on the world market for 50 cents a pound. In effect, the board was taxing exports by paying farmers considerably less for their cocoa than it was worth on the world market and putting the difference into government coffers. This money was used to fund the government policy of nationalization and industrialization.

Between 1963 and 1979 the price paid by the cocoa marketing board to Ghana's farmers increased by a factor of 6, while the price of consumer goods in Ghana increased by a factor of 22, and the price of cocoa in neighboring countries increased by a factor of 36! In real terms, the Ghanaian farmers were paid less every year for their cocoa by the cocoa marketing board, while the world price increased significantly. Ghana's farmers responded by switching to the production of subsistence foodstuffs that could be sold within Ghana, and the country's production and exports of cocoa plummeted by

more than one-third in seven years. At the same time, the Ghanaian government's attempt to build an industrial base through state-run enterprises failed. The resulting drop in Ghana's export earnings plunged the country into recession, led to a decline in its foreign currency reserves, and severely limited its ability to pay for necessary imports.

Ghana's inward-oriented trade policy resulted in a shift of resources away from the profitable activity of growing cocoa—where it had an absolute advantage in the world economy—and toward growing subsistence foods and manufacturing, where it had no advantage. This inefficient use of the country's resources severely damaged the Ghanaian economy and held back the country's economic development.

In contrast, consider the trade policy adopted by the South Korean government. The World Bank has characterized the trade policy of South Korea as "strongly outward-oriented." Unlike in Ghana, the policies of the South Korean government emphasized low import barriers on manufactured goods (but not on agricultural goods) and the creation of incentives to encourage South Korean firms to export. Beginning in the late 1950s, the South Korean government progressively reduced import tariffs from an average of 60 percent of the price of an imported good to less than 20 percent in the mid-1980s. On most nonagricultural goods, import tariffs were reduced to zero. In addition, the number of imported goods subjected to quotas was reduced from more than 90 percent in

the late 1950s to zero by the early 1980s. Over the same period South Korea progressively reduced the subsidies given to South Korean exporters from an average of 80 percent of their sales price in the late 1950s to an average of less than 20 percent of their sales price in 1965 and down to zero in 1984. With the exception of the agricultural sector (where a strong farm lobby maintained import controls), South Korea moved progressively toward a free trade stance.

South Korea's outward-looking orientation has been rewarded by a dramatic transformation of its economy. Initially, South Korea's resources shifted from agriculture to the manufacture of labor-intensive goods, especially textiles, clothing, and footwear. An abundant supply of cheap but well-educated labor helped form the basis of South Korea's comparative advantage in labor-intensive manufacturing. More recently, as labor costs have risen, the economy has grown in the more capital-intensive manufacturing sectors, especially motor vehicles, aerospace, consumer electronics, and advanced materials. As a result of these developments, South Korea has gone through some dramatic changes. In the late 1950s, 77 percent of the country's employment was in the agricultural sector; today the figure is less than 20 percent. Over the same period the percentage of its GDP accounted for by manufacturing increased from less than 10 percent to more than 30 percent, while the overall GDP grew at an annual rate of more than 9 percent.[1]

Introduction

The opening case illustrates the gains that come from international trade. For a long time the economic policies of the Ghanaian government discouraged trade with other nations. The result was a shift in Ghana's resources away from productive uses (growing cocoa) and toward unproductive uses (subsistence agriculture). The economic policies of the South Korean government encouraged trade with other nations. The result was a shift in South Korea's resources away from uses where it had no comparative advantage in the world economy (agriculture) and toward more productive uses (labor-intensive manufacturing). As a direct result of their policies toward international trade, Ghana's economy declined while South Korea's grew.

This chapter has two goals that are related to the story of Ghana and South Korea. The first goal is to review a number of theories that explain why it is beneficial for a country to engage in international trade. The second goal is to explain the pattern of international trade that we observe in the world economy. We will be primarily concerned with explaining the pattern of exports and imports of products between countries. The pattern of foreign direct investment between countries will be discussed in Chapter 6.

An Overview of Trade Theory

We open this chapter with a discussion of mercantilism. Propagated in the 16th and 17th centuries, mercantilism advocated that countries should simultaneously encourage exports and discourage imports. Although mercantilism is an old and largely discredited doctrine, its echoes remain in modern political debate and in the trade policies of many countries.

Next we will look at Adam Smith's theory of absolute advantage. Proposed in 1776, Smith's theory was the first to explain why unrestricted free trade is beneficial to a country. **Free trade** refers to a situation where a government does not attempt to influence through quotas or duties what its citizens can buy from another country or what they can produce and sell to another country. Smith argued that the invisible hand of the market mechanism, rather than government policy, should determine what a country imports and what it exports. His arguments imply that such a laissez-faire stance toward trade was in the best interests of a country. Building on Smith's work are two additional theories that we shall review. One is the theory of comparative advantage, advanced by the 19th century English economist David Ricardo. This theory is the intellectual basis of the modern argument for unrestricted free trade. In the 20th century Ricardo's work was refined by two Swedish economists, Eli Heckscher and Bertil Ohlin, whose theory is known as the Heckscher-Ohlin theory.

The Benefits of Trade

The great strength of the theories of Smith, Ricardo, and Heckscher-Ohlin is that they identify the specific benefits of international trade. Common sense suggests that some international trade is beneficial. For example, nobody

free trade
Situation where a government does not attempt to influence through quotas or duties what its citizens can buy from another country or what they can produce and sell to another country.

would suggest that Iceland should grow its own oranges. Iceland can benefit from trade by exchanging some of the products it can produce at a low cost (fish) for products it cannot produce (oranges). Thus, by engaging in international trade, Icelanders can add oranges to their diet of fish.

The theories of Smith, Ricardo, and Heckscher-Ohlin go beyond this commonsense notion, however, to show why it is beneficial for a country to engage in international trade *even for products it is able to produce for itself*. This is a difficult concept for people to grasp. For example, many people in the United States believe that American consumers should buy products produced in the United States by American companies whenever possible to help save American jobs from foreign competition. The same kind of nationalistic sentiments can be observed in many other countries. However, the theories of Smith, Ricardo, and Heckscher-Ohlin tell us that a country's economy may gain if its citizens buy certain products from other nations that could be produced at home. The gains arise because international trade allows a country to specialize in the manufacture and export of products that can be produced most efficiently in that country, while importing products that can be produced more efficiently in other countries. So it may make sense for the United States to specialize in the production and export of commercial jet aircraft, since the efficient production of commercial jet aircraft requires resources that are abundant in the United States, such as a highly skilled labor force and cutting-edge technological know-how. On the other hand, it may make sense for the United States to import textiles from India since the efficient production of textiles requires a relatively cheap labor force—and cheap labor is not abundant in the United States.

This economic argument is often difficult for segments of a country's population to accept. With their future threatened by imports, American textile companies and their employees have tried hard to persuade the U.S. government to limit the importation of textiles by demanding quotas and tariffs to restrict imports. Although such import controls may benefit particular groups, such as American textile businesses and their employees, the theories of Smith, Ricardo, and Heckscher-Ohlin suggest that the economy as a whole is hurt by such protectionist action.

The Pattern of International Trade

The theories of Smith, Ricardo, and Heckscher-Ohlin also help to explain the pattern of international trade that we observe in the world economy. Some aspects of the pattern are easy to understand. Climate and natural resources explain why Ghana exports cocoa, Brazil exports coffee, and Saudi Arabia exports oil. But much of the observed pattern of international trade is more difficult to explain. For example, why does Japan export automobiles, consumer electronics, and machine tools? Why does Switzerland export chemicals, watches, and jewelry? David Ricardo's theory of comparative advantage offers an explanation in terms of international differences in labor productivity. The more sophisticated Heckscher-Ohlin theory emphasizes the interplay between the proportions in which the factors of production (such as land, labor, and capital) are available in different countries and the proportions in which they are needed for producing particular goods. This explanation rests on the assumption that different countries have different endowments of the various factors of production. Tests of this theory, however, suggest it is a less powerful explanation of real-world trade patterns than once thought.

One early response to the failure of the Heckscher-Ohlin theory to explain the observed pattern of international trade was the *product life-cycle theory*. Proposed by Raymond Vernon, this theory suggests that early in their life cycle, most new products are produced in and exported from the country in which they were developed. As a new product becomes widely accepted internationally, however, production starts in other countries. As a result, the theory suggests, the product may ultimately be exported back to the country of its original innovation.

In a similar vein, during the 1980s economists such as Paul Krugman of MIT developed what has come to be known as the *new trade theory*. New trade theory stresses that in some cases countries specialize in the production and export of particular products not because of underlying differences in factor endowments but because in certain industries the world market can support only a limited number of firms. (This is argued to be the case for the commercial aircraft industry.) In such industries, firms that enter the market first build a competitive advantage that is difficult to challenge. Thus, the observed pattern of trade between nations may be due in part to the ability of firms within a given nation to capture first-mover advantages. The United States dominates the export of commercial jet aircraft because American firms such as Boeing were first-movers in the world market. Boeing built a competitive advantage that has subsequently been difficult for firms from countries with equally favorable factor endowments to challenge.

In a work related to the new trade theory, Michael Porter of Harvard Business School recently developed a theory that attempts to explain why particular nations achieve international success in particular industries. We shall refer to this theory as the theory of national competitive advantage. Like the new trade theorists, in addition to factor endowments, Porter points out the importance of country factors such as domestic demand and domestic rivalry in explaining a nation's dominance in the production and export of particular products.

Trade Theory and Government Policy

Before discussing these theories in more detail, we must point out that although they all agree that international trade is beneficial to a country, they lack agreement in their recommendations for government policy. Mercantilism makes a crude case for government involvement in promoting exports and limiting imports. The theories of Smith, Ricardo, and Heckscher-Ohlin form part of the case for unrestricted free trade. The argument for unrestricted free trade is that both import controls and export incentives (such as subsidies) are self-defeating and result in wasted resources. On the other hand, both the new trade theory and Porter's theory of national competitive advantage can be interpreted as justifying some limited and selective government intervention to support the development of certain export-oriented industries. We will discuss the pros and cons of this argument, known as strategic trade policy, as well as the pros and cons of the argument for unrestricted free trade, in Chapter 5.

Mercantilism

The first theory of international trade emerged in England in the mid-16th century. Referred to as *mercantilism*, its principal assertion was that gold and silver were the mainstays of national wealth and essential to vigorous commerce. At that time, gold and silver were the currency of trade between countries; a country could earn gold and silver by exporting goods. By the same token, importing goods from other countries would result in an outflow of gold and silver to those countries. The main tenet of **mercantilism** was that it was in a country's best interests to maintain a trade surplus, to export more than it imported. By doing so, a country would accumulate gold and silver and, consequently, increase its national wealth and prestige. As the English mercantilist writer Thomas Mun put it in 1630:

> The ordinary means therefore to increase our wealth and treasure is by foreign trade, wherein we must ever observe this rule: to sell more to strangers yearly than we consume of theirs in value.[2]

mercantilism Theory of international trade that believes it is in a country's best interests to export more than it imports.

Consistent with this belief, the mercantilist doctrine advocated government intervention to achieve a surplus in the balance of trade. The mercantilists saw no virtue in a large volume of trade per se. Rather, they recommended policies to maximize exports and minimize imports. To achieve this, imports were limited by tariffs and quotas, and exports were subsidized.

An inherent inconsistency in the mercantilist doctrine was pointed out by the classical economist David Hume in 1752. According to Hume, if England had a balance-of-trade surplus with France (it exported more than it imported) the resulting inflow of gold and silver would swell the domestic money supply and generate inflation in England. In France, however, the outflow of gold and silver would have the opposite effect. France's money supply would contract, and its prices would fall. This change in relative prices between France and England would encourage the French to buy fewer English goods (because they were becoming more expensive) and the English to buy more French goods (because they were becoming cheaper). The result would be a deterioration in the English balance of trade and an improvement in France's trade balance, until the English surplus was eliminated. Hence, according to Hume, in the long run no country could sustain a surplus on the balance of trade and so accumulate gold and silver as the mercantilists had envisaged.

The flaw with mercantilism was that it viewed trade as a zero-sum game. (A **zero-sum game** is one in which a gain by one country results in a loss by another.) It was left to Adam Smith and David Ricardo to show the short-sightedness of this approach and to demonstrate that trade is a **positive-sum game**, that being a situation in which all countries can benefit, even if some benefit more than others. We shall discuss the views of Smith next. Before doing so, however, we must note that the mercantilist doctrine is by no means dead.[3] For example, Jarl Hagelstam, a director at the Finnish Ministry of Finance, has observed that in most trade negotiations:

> The approach of individual negotiating countries, both industrialized and developing, has been to press for trade liberalization in areas where their own comparative advantages are the strongest and to resist liberalization in areas where they are less competitive and fear that imports would replace domestic production.[4]

zero-sum game Situation in which a gain by one country results in a loss by another.

positive-sum game Situation in which all countries can benefit, even if some benefit more than others.

Hagelstam attributes this strategy by negotiating countries to a neo-mercantilist belief held by the politicians of many nations. This belief equates political power with economic power and economic power with a balance-of-trade surplus. Thus, the trade strategy of many nations is designed to simultaneously boost exports and limit imports. For example, as described in the "Country Focus," many American politicians claim that Japan is a neo-mercantilist nation because its government, while publicly supporting free trade, simultaneously seeks to protect certain segments of its economy from more efficient foreign competition.

Absolute Advantage

In his 1776 landmark book *The Wealth of Nations*, Adam Smith attacked the mercantilist assumption that trade is a zero-sum game. Smith argued that countries differ in their ability to produce goods efficiently. In his time, for example, by virtue of their superior manufacturing processes, the English were the world's most efficient manufacturers of textiles. Due to the combination of favorable climate, good soils, and accumulated expertise, the French had the world's most efficient wine industry. The English had an *absolute advantage* in the production of textiles, while the French had an *absolute advantage* in the production of wine. Thus, a country has an **absolute advantage** in the production of a product when it is more efficient than any other country in producing it.

According to Smith, countries should specialize in the production of goods for which they have an absolute advantage and then trade these goods for the goods produced by other countries. In Smith's time this suggested that the English should specialize in the production of textiles while the French should specialize in the production of wine. England could get all the wine it needed by selling its textiles to France and buying wine in exchange. Similarly, France could get all the textiles it needed by selling wine to England and buying textiles in exchange. Smith's basic argument, therefore, is that a country should never produce goods at home that it can buy at a lower cost from other countries. Moreover, Smith demonstrates that by specializing in the production of goods in which each has an absolute advantage, both countries benefit by engaging in trade.

Consider the effects of trade between Ghana and South Korea. The production of any good (output) requires resources (inputs) such as land, labor, and capital. Assume that Ghana and South Korea both have the same amount of resources and that these resources can be used to produce either rice or cocoa. Assume further that 200 units of resources are available in each country. Imagine that in Ghana it takes 10 resources to produce one ton of cocoa and 20 resources to produce one ton of rice. Thus, Ghana could produce 20 tons of cocoa and no rice, 10 tons of rice and no cocoa, or some combination of rice and cocoa between these two extremes. The different combinations that Ghana could produce are represented by the line GG′ in Figure 4.1. This is referred to as Ghana's production possibility frontier (PPF). Similarly, imagine that in South Korea it takes 40 resources to produce one ton of cocoa and 10 resources to produce one ton of rice. Thus, South Korea could produce 5 tons of cocoa and no rice, 20 tons of rice and no cocoa, or some combination between these two extremes. The different combinations available to South Korea are represented by the line KK′ in Figure 4.1, which is South Korea's PPF. Clearly, Ghana has an absolute advantage in the production of cocoa. (More resources are

absolute advantage Situation in which one country is more efficient at producing a product than any other country.

Is Japan a Neo-Mercantilist Nation?

In the international arena Japan has long been a strong supporter of free trade agreements. However, the U.S. government has repeatedly suggested that the approach taken by the Japanese is a cynical neo-mercantilist one. The Japanese, they say, are happy to sign international agreements that open foreign markets to the products of Japanese companies, but at the same time they protect their home market from foreign competition. As evidence, U.S. officials point to the large trade imbalance between the United States and Japan, which in 1995 ran at over $60 billion (meaning that the United States imported $60 billion more in goods from Japan than it exported to Japan).

The U.S. government recently received support from an unlikely source: three Japanese economists. In a study published in 1994 the three economists cited food products, cosmetics, and chemical production as areas where the Japanese government protected Japanese industry from more efficient foreign competition through a variety of import restrictions, such as quotas (limits) on the amounts of a product that can be imported into Japan. According to the economists, without barriers protecting these areas from foreign competition, imports would have more than doubled and prices in Japan would have fallen substantially.

The study suggested that falling prices would have saved the average Japanese consumer

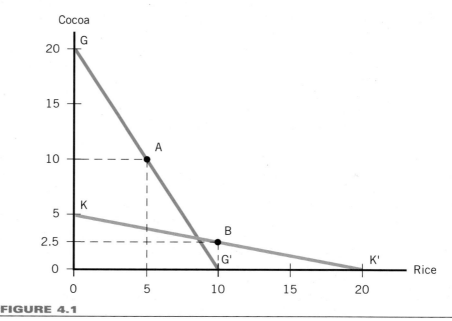

FIGURE 4.1

The Theory of Absolute Advantage

about $890 per year in 1989. At the same time, however, there would have been a fall in Japanese production of more than 20 percent in certain areas, including wheat, oilseeds, leaf tobacco, canned fruit and vegetables, and cosmetics. Trade liberalization would also have resulted in the loss of more than 180,000 Japanese jobs. It would seem, therefore, that Japan's government protects these areas from more efficient foreign competition to save jobs, even though the average Japanese consumer has to pay for this action through higher prices. Protection of the food products area in particular may be motivated by the fact that Japanese farmers, who benefit most from this protection, are a powerful political force in Japan.

The U.S. government claims that another area where Japan has taken a neo-mercantilist stance is in the importation of automobiles and automobile parts. Japan is a major exporter of autos and auto parts to the United States and Europe, but historically it has imported only 3 percent of its autos and 2 percent of its auto components. Other developed countries import between 22 percent and 78 percent of their autos and 16 to 60 percent of their auto parts. According to U.S. trade negotiators, the Japanese government limits imports into Japan by requiring stringent safety inspections on imports that are explicitly designed to raise the costs to foreigners trying to sell in Japan. For example, the U.S. Commerce Department claims that the addition of front brush guards to a recreational vehicle, a safety feature required only in Japan, necessitates a complete re-inspection that costs up to $3,000 per vehicle.

The Japanese government rejects such charges. The Japanese government argues that the main reason U.S. auto companies have not been successful in Japan is that they do not make cars that are suited to the Japanese market. They point out that while 80 percent of the autos sold in the Japanese market have engines smaller than 2,000cc, no U.S. auto company sells cars in Japan in that range. They also point out that imported autos and auto parts are increasing their share of the Japanese market. Between 1990 and 1994, for example, the share of the Japanese market accounted for by imported cars increased from 5.1 percent to 8.1 percent.[5]

needed to produce a ton of cocoa in South Korea than in Ghana.) By the same token, South Korea has an absolute advantage in the production of rice.

Now consider a situation in which neither country trades with any other. Each country devotes half of its resources to the production of rice and half to the production of cocoa. Each country must also consume what it produces. Ghana would be able to produce 10 tons of cocoa and 5 tons of rice (point A in Figure 4.1), while South Korea would be able to produce 10 tons of rice and 2.5 tons of cocoa (point B). Without trade, the combined production of both countries would be 12.5 tons of cocoa (10 tons in Ghana plus 2.5 tons in South Korea) and 15 tons of rice (5 tons in Ghana and 10 tons in South Korea). If each country were to specialize in producing the good for which it had an absolute advantage and then trade with the other for the good it lacks, Ghana could produce 20 tons of cocoa, and South Korea could produce 20 tons of rice. Thus, by specializing, the production of both goods could be increased. Production of cocoa would increase from 12.5 tons to 20 tons, while production of rice would increase from 15 tons to 20 tons. The increase in production that would result from specialization is therefore 7.5 tons of cocoa and 5 tons of rice. These figures are summarized in Table 4.1.

By engaging in trade and swapping one ton of cocoa for one ton of rice, producers in both countries could consume more of both cocoa and rice. Imagine that Ghana and South Korea swap cocoa and rice on a one-to-one basis; that is, the price of one ton of cocoa is equal to the price of one ton of

TABLE 4.1

Absolute Advantage and the Gains from Trade

	Resources Required to Produce 1 Ton of Cocoa and Rice	
	Cocoa	Rice
Ghana	10	20
South Korea	40	10
	Production and Consumption without Trade	
	Cocoa	Rice
Ghana	10.0	5.0
South Korea	2.5	10.0
Total production	12.5	15.0
	Production with Specialization	
	Cocoa	Rice
Ghana	20.0	0.0
South Korea	0.0	20.0
Total production	20.0	20.0
	Consumption after Ghana Trades 6 Tons of Cocoa for 6 Tons of South Korean Rice	
	Cocoa	Rice
Ghana	14.0	6.0
South Korea	6.0	14.0
	Increase in Consumption as a Result of Specialization and Trade	
	Cocoa	Rice
Ghana	4.0	1.0
South Korea	3.5	4.0

rice. If Ghana decided to export 6 tons of cocoa to South Korea and import 6 tons of rice in return, its final consumption after trade would be 14 tons of cocoa and 6 tons of rice. This is 4 tons more cocoa than it could have consumed before specialization and trade and 1 ton more rice. Similarly, South Korea's final consumption after trade would be 6 tons of cocoa and 14 tons of rice. This is 3.5 tons more cocoa than it could have consumed before specialization and trade and 4 tons more rice. Thus, as a result of specialization and trade, output of both cocoa and rice would be increased, and consumers in both nations would be able to consume more. Thus, we can see that trade is a positive-sum game; it produces net gains for all involved.

Comparative Advantage

David Ricardo took Adam Smith's theory one step further by exploring what might happen when one country has an absolute advantage in the production

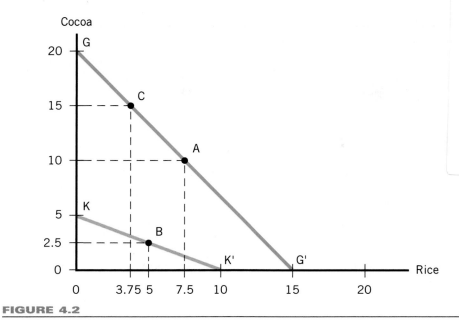

FIGURE 4.2

Theory of Comparative Advantage

of all goods.[6] Smith's theory of absolute advantage suggests that such a country might derive no benefits from international trade. In his 1817 book *Principles of Political Economy*, Ricardo showed that this was not the case. According to Ricardo's theory of **comparative advantage**, it makes sense for a country to specialize in the production of those goods that it produces most efficiently and to buy the goods that it produces less efficiently from other countries, even if this means buying goods from other countries that it could produce more efficiently itself.[7] While this may seem counterintuitive, the logic can be explained with a simple example.

Let us stay with the example of Ghana and South Korea that we used to explain Adam Smith's theory. This time assume that Ghana is more efficient in the production of both cocoa and rice; that is, that Ghana has an absolute advantage in the production of both products. In Ghana it takes 10 resources to produce one ton of cocoa and $13\frac{1}{3}$ resources to produce one ton of rice. Thus, given its 200 units of resources, Ghana can produce 20 tons of cocoa and no rice, 15 tons of rice and no cocoa, or any combination in between on its PPF (the line GG′ in Figure 4.2). In South Korea it takes 40 resources to produce one ton of cocoa and 20 resources to produce one ton of rice. Thus, South Korea can produce 5 tons of cocoa and no rice, 10 tons of rice and no cocoa, or any combination on its PPF (the line KK′ in Figure 4.2). Again assume that without trade, each country uses half of its resources to produce rice and half to produce cocoa. Thus, without trade, Ghana will produce 10 tons of cocoa and 7.5 tons of rice (point A in Figure 4.2), while South Korea will produce 2.5 tons of cocoa and 5 tons of rice (point B in Figure 4.2).

In light of Ghana's absolute advantage in the production of both goods, why should it trade with South Korea? Although Ghana has an absolute advantage in the production of both cocoa and rice, it has a comparative advantage only in the production of cocoa: Ghana can produce 4 times as much cocoa as South Korea, but only 1.5 times as much rice. Ghana is *comparatively* more efficient at producing cocoa than it is at producing rice.

comparative advantage Situation in which a country specializes in producing the goods it produces most efficiently and buys the products it produces less efficiently from other countries, even if it could produce the goods more efficiently itself.

Without trade the combined production of cocoa will be 12.5 tons (10 tons in Ghana and 2.5 in South Korea), and the combined production of rice will also be 12.5 tons (7.5 tons in Ghana and 5 tons in South Korea). Without trade each country must consume what it produces. By engaging in trade, the two countries can increase their combined production of rice and cocoa, and consumers in both nations can consume more of both goods.

The Gains from Trade

Imagine that Ghana exploits its comparative advantage in the production of cocoa to increase its output from 10 tons to 15 tons. This uses up 150 units of resources, leaving the remaining 50 units of resources to use in producing 3.75 tons of rice (point C in Figure 4.2). Meanwhile, South Korea specializes in the production of rice, producing 10 tons. The combined output of both cocoa and rice has now increased. Before specialization, the combined output was 12.5 tons of cocoa and 12.5 tons of rice. Now it is 15 tons of cocoa and 13.75 tons of rice (3.75 tons in Ghana and 10 tons in South Korea). The source of the increase in production is summarized in Table 4.2.

Not only is output higher, but also both countries can now benefit from trade. If Ghana and South Korea swap cocoa and rice on a one-to-one basis, with both countries choosing to exchange four tons of their export for four tons of the import, both countries are able to consume more cocoa and rice than they could before specialization and trade (see Table 4.2). Thus, if Ghana exchanges 4 tons of cocoa with South Korea for 4 tons of rice, it is still left with 11 tons of rice, which is 1 ton more than it had before trade. Moreover, the 4 tons of rice it gets from South Korea in exchange for its 4 tons of cocoa, when added to the 3.75 tons it now produces domestically, leaves it with a total of 7.75 tons of rice, which is .25 of a ton more than it had before trade. Similarly, after swapping 4 tons of rice with Ghana, South Korea still ends up with 6 tons of rice, which is more than it had before trade. In addition, the 4 tons of cocoa it receives in exchange is 1.5 tons more than it produced before trade. Thus, consumption of cocoa and rice can increase in both countries as a result of specialization and trade.

Generalizing from this example, the basic message of the theory of comparative advantage is that *potential world production is greater with unrestricted free trade than it is with restricted trade*. Moreover, Ricardo's theory suggests that consumers in all nations can consume more if there are no restrictions on trade. This occurs even in countries that lack an absolute advantage in the production of any good. To an even greater degree than the theory of absolute advantage, the theory of comparative advantage suggests that trade is a positive-sum game in which all gain. As such, this theory provides a strong rationale for encouraging free trade. Indeed, so powerful is Ricardo's theory that it remains a major intellectual weapon for those who argue for free trade.

Qualifications and Assumptions

Some might object to drawing such a bold conclusion about free trade from such a simple model. There are many unrealistic assumptions inherent in our simple model, including:

1 We have assumed a simple world in which there are only two countries and two goods. In the real world there are many countries and many goods.

TABLE 4.2

Comparative Advantage and the Gains from Trade

	Resources Required to Produce 1 Ton of Cocoa and Rice	
	Cocoa	Rice
Ghana	10	13.33
South Korea	40	20
	Production and Consumption without Trade	
	Cocoa	Rice
Ghana	10.0	7.5
South Korea	2.5	5.0
Total production	12.5	12.5
	Production with Specialization	
	Cocoa	Rice
Ghana	15.0	3.75
South Korea	0.0	10.0
Total production	15.0	13.75
	Consumption after Ghana Trades 4 Tons of Cocoa for 4 Tons of South Korean Rice	
	Cocoa	Rice
Ghana	11.0	7.75
South Korea	4.0	6.0
	Increase in Consumption as a Result of Specialization and Trade	
	Cocoa	Rice
Ghana	1.0	0.25
South Korea	1.5	1.0

2 We have assumed away transportation costs between countries.

3 We have assumed away differences in the price of resources in different countries. We have said nothing about exchange rates, and instead simply assumed that cocoa and rice could be swapped on a one-to-one basis.

4 We have assumed that while resources can move freely from the production of one good to another within a country, they are not free to move internationally. In reality, some resources are somewhat internationally mobile. This is true of capital and, to a lesser extent, labor.

5 We have assumed constant returns to scale; that is, that specialization by Ghana or South Korea has no effect on the amount of resources required to produce one ton of cocoa or rice. In reality, both diminishing and increasing returns to specialization exist. The amount of resources required to produce a good might decrease or increase as a nation specializes in production of that good.

6 We have assumed that each country has a fixed stock of resources and that free trade does not change the efficiency with which a country uses its resources. This static assumption makes no allowances for the dynamic changes in a country's stock of resources and in the efficiency with which the country uses its resources that might result from free trade.

7 We have assumed away the effects of trade on income distribution within a country.

Given these assumptions, the question arises as to whether the conclusion that free trade is mutually beneficial can be extended to the real world of many countries, many goods, positive transportation costs, volatile exchange rates, internationally mobile resources, nonconstant returns to specialization, and dynamic changes. Although a detailed extension of the theory of comparative advantage is beyond the scope of this book, economists have shown that the basic result derived from our simple model can be generalized to a world composed of many countries producing many different goods.[8] Moreover, research data support the basic proposition of the Ricardian model—that countries will export the goods that they are most efficient at producing.[9] However, once all the assumptions are dropped, the case for unrestricted free trade, while still positive, has been argued by some economists associated with the "new trade theory" to lose some of its strength.[10] We return to this issue later in this chapter and in the next.

Trade and Economic Growth

Our simple comparative advantage model assumed that trade does not change a country's stock of resources or the efficiency with which it utilizes those resources. This static assumption makes no allowances for the dynamic changes that might result from trade. If we relax this assumption, it becomes apparent that opening up an economy to trade is likely to generate dynamic gains.[11] These dynamic gains are of two sorts. First, free trade might increase a country's stock of resources as increased supplies of labor and capital from abroad become available for use within the country. This is occurring right now in Eastern Europe, where many Western businesses are investing large amounts of capital in the former Communist bloc countries.

Second, free trade might also increase the efficiency with which a country utilizes its resources. Gains in the efficiency of resource utilization could arise from a number of factors. For example, economies of large-scale production might become available as trade expands the size of the total market available to domestic firms. Trade might make better technology from abroad available to domestic firms. In turn, better technology can increase labor productivity or the productivity of land. (The so-called green revolution had just this effect on agricultural outputs in developing countries.) It is also possible that opening an economy to foreign competition might stimulate domestic producers to look for ways to increase the efficiency of their operations. Again, this phenomenon is arguably occurring currently in the once-protected markets of Eastern Europe, where many former state monopolies are increasing the efficiency of their operations in order to survive in the competitive world market.

Dynamic gains in both the stock of a country's resources and the efficiency with which resources are utilized will cause a country's **PPF** to shift outward.

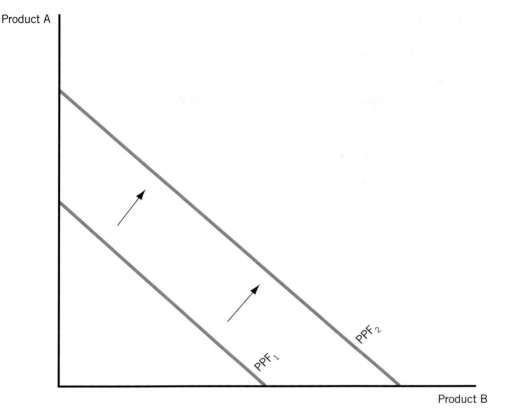

Product A

Product B

FIGURE 4.3

The Influence of Free Trade on the PPF

This is illustrated in Figure 4.3, where the shift from PPF_1 to PPF_2 results from the dynamic gains that arise from free trade. As a consequence of this outward shift, the country in Figure 4.3 can produce more of both goods than it did before introduction of free trade. The theory suggests that opening an economy to free trade not only results in static gains of the type discussed earlier, but also results in dynamic gains that stimulate economic growth. If this is so, the case for free trade becomes stronger, and the World Bank has assembled evidence that suggests a free trade stance does have these beneficial effects on economic growth.[12]

Heckscher-Ohlin Theory

Ricardo's theory stresses that comparative advantage arises from differences in productivity. Thus, whether Ghana is more efficient than South Korea in the production of cocoa depends on how productively it uses its resources. Ricardo particularly stressed labor productivity and argued that differences in labor productivity between nations underlie the notion of comparative advantage. Swedish economists Eli Heckscher (in 1919) and Bertil Ohlin (in 1933) put forward a different explanation of comparative advantage. They argued that comparative advantage arises from differences in national factor endowments.[13] By factor endowments they meant the extent to which a country is endowed with such resources as land, labor, and capital. Different nations have different factor endowments, and different factor endowments explain differences in factor costs. The more abundant a factor, the lower its cost. The Heckscher-Ohlin theory predicts that countries will export those goods that make intensive use of those factors that are locally abundant, while importing goods that make intensive use of factors that are locally scarce. Thus, the Heckscher-Ohlin theory attempts to explain the pattern of international trade that we observe in the world economy. Like Ricardo's theory, the Heckscher-Ohlin theory argues that free trade is beneficial. Unlike Ricardo's theory, however, the Heckscher-Ohlin theory argues that the pattern of international trade is determined by differences in factor endowments, rather than differences in productivity.

The Heckscher-Ohlin theory also has commonsense appeal. For example, the United States has long been a substantial exporter of agricultural goods, reflecting in part its unusual abundance of large tracts of arable land. In contrast, South Korea has excelled in the export of goods produced in labor-intensive manufacturing industries, such as textiles and footwear. This reflects South Korea's relative abundance of low-cost labor. The United States, which lacks abundant low-cost labor, has been a primary importer of these goods. Note that it is relative, not absolute, endowments that are important; a country may have larger absolute amounts of land and labor than another country, but be relatively abundant in one of them.

The Leontief Paradox

The Heckscher-Ohlin theory has been one of the most influential theoretical ideas in international economics. Most economists prefer the Heckscher-Ohlin theory to Ricardo's theory because it makes fewer simplifying assumptions, and it has been subjected to many empirical tests. Beginning with a famous study published in 1953 by Wassily Leontief (winner of the Nobel Prize in Economics in 1973), many of these tests have raised questions about the validity of the Heckscher-Ohlin theory.[14] Using the Heckscher-Ohlin theory, Leontief postulated that since the United States was relatively abundant in capital compared to other nations, the United States would be an exporter of capital-intensive goods and an importer of labor-intensive goods. To his surprise, however, he found that U.S. exports were less capital intensive than U.S. imports. Since this result was at variance with the predictions of the theory, it has become known as the Leontief paradox.

Why do we observe the Leontief paradox? No one is quite sure. One possible explanation is that the United States has a special advantage in producing new products or goods made with innovative technologies. Such products may well be less capital intensive than products whose technology has had time to mature and become suitable for mass production. Thus, the United States may be exporting goods that heavily use skilled labor and innovative entrepreneurship, while importing heavy manufactures that use large amounts of capital. Some more recent empirical studies confirm this.[15] However, recent tests of the Heckscher-Ohlin theory using data for a large number of countries tend to confirm the existence of the Leontief paradox.[16]

This leaves economists with a difficult dilemma. They prefer the Heckscher-Ohlin theory, but it is a relatively poor predictor of real-world international trade patterns. On the other hand, the theory they regard as being too limited, Ricardo's theory of comparative advantage, actually predicts trade patterns with greater accuracy. The best solution to this dilemma may be to return to the Ricardian idea that trade patterns are largely driven by international differences in productivity. Thus, one might argue that the United States exports commercial aircraft and imports automobiles not because its factor endowments are especially suited to aircraft manufacture and not suited to automobile manufacture, but because the United States is more efficient at producing aircraft than automobiles.

The Product Life-Cycle Theory

Raymond Vernon initially proposed the product life-cycle theory in the mid-1960s.[17] Vernon's theory was based on the observation that for most of the 20th century a very large proportion of the world's new products had been developed by U.S. firms and sold first in the U.S. market (e.g., mass-produced automobiles, televisions, instant cameras, photocopiers, personal computers, and semiconductor chips). To explain this, Vernon argued that the wealth and size of the U.S. market gave U.S. firms a strong incentive to develop new consumer products. In addition, the high cost of U.S. labor gave U.S. firms an incentive to develop cost-saving process innovations.

Just because a new product is developed by a U.S. firm and first sold in the U.S. market, it does not follow that the product must be produced in the United States. It could be produced abroad at some low-cost location and then exported back into the United States. However, Vernon argued that most new products were initially produced in America. Apparently, the pioneering firms felt that it was better to keep production facilities close to the market and to the firm's center of decision making, given the uncertainty and risks inherent in new-product introduction. Moreover, the demand for most new products tends to be based on nonprice factors. Consequently, firms can charge relatively high prices for new products, which eliminates the need to look for low-cost production sites in other countries.

Vernon went on to argue that early in the life cycle of a typical new product, while demand is starting to grow rapidly in the United States, demand in other advanced countries is limited to high-income groups. The limited initial demand in other advanced countries does not make it worthwhile for firms in those countries to start producing the new product, but it does necessitate some exports from the United States to those countries.

Over time, however, demand for the new product starts to grow in other advanced countries (e.g., Great Britain, France, Germany, and Japan). As it does, it becomes worthwhile for foreign producers to begin producing for their home markets. In addition, U.S. firms might set up production facilities in those advanced countries where demand is growing. Consequently, production within other advanced countries begins to limit the potential for exports from the United States.

As the market in the United States and other advanced nations matures, the product becomes more standardized, and price becomes the main competitive weapon. As this occurs, cost considerations start to play a greater role in the competitive process. One result is that producers based in advanced countries where labor costs are lower than in the United States (e.g., Italy, Spain) might now be able to export to the United States.

If cost pressures become intense, the process might not stop there. The cycle by which the United States lost its advantage to other advanced countries might be repeated once more as developing countries (e.g., South Korea and Thailand) begin to acquire a production advantage over advanced countries. Thus, the site of global production initially switches from the United States to other advanced nations, and then from those nations to developing countries.

The consequence of these trends for the pattern of world trade is that the United States switches from being an exporter of the product to an importer of the product as production becomes concentrated in lower-cost foreign locations. These dynamics are illustrated in Figure 4.4, which shows the growth of production and consumption over time in the United States, other advanced countries, and developing countries.

Evaluating the Product Life-Cycle Theory

How well does the product life-cycle theory explain international trade patterns? Historically, it is quite accurate. Consider photocopiers; the product was first developed in the early 1960s by Xerox in the United States and sold initially to U.S. users. Originally Xerox exported photocopiers from the United States, primarily to Japan and the advanced countries of Western Europe. As demand began to grow in those countries, Xerox entered into joint ventures to set up production in Japan (Fuji-Xerox) and Great Britain (Rank-Xerox). In addition, once Xerox's patents on the photocopier process expired, other foreign competitors began to enter the market (e.g., Canon in Japan, Olivetti in Italy). As a consequence, exports from the United States declined, and U.S. users began to buy some of their photocopiers from lower-cost foreign sources, particularly from Japan. More recently, Japanese companies have found that their own country is now too expensive for manufacturing photocopiers, so they are switching production to developing countries such as Singapore and Thailand. As a result, initially the United States and now several other advanced countries (e.g., Japan and Great Britain) have switched from being exporters of photocopiers to being importers. This evolution in the pattern of international trade in photocopiers is consistent with the predictions of the product life-cycle theory. The product life-cycle theory clearly does explain the migration of mature industries out of the United States and into low-cost assembly locations.

However, the product life-cycle theory is not without weaknesses. Viewed from an Asian or European perspective, Vernon's argument that most new products are developed and introduced in the United States seems ethnocentric. Although it may be true that during the period of U.S. global dominance (1945–75) most new products were introduced first in the United States, there have always been important exceptions. In recent years these exceptions appear to have become more common. Many new products are now first introduced in Japan (e.g., high-definition television or digital audiotapes). More importantly, with the increased globalization and integration of the world

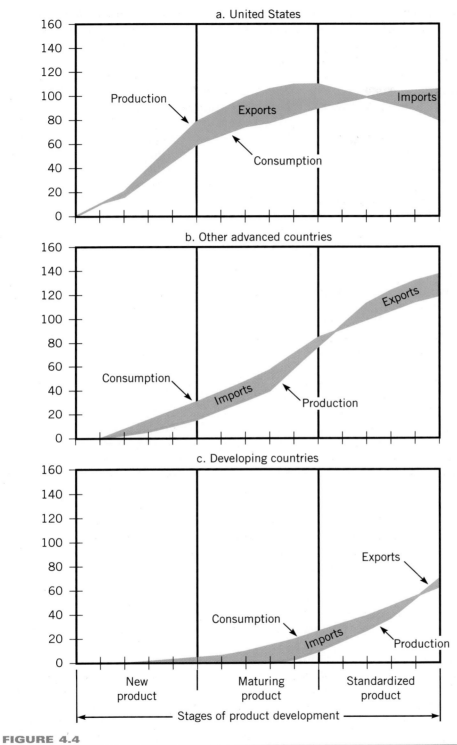

FIGURE 4.4

The Product Life-Cycle Theory

economy that we discussed in Chapter 1, a growing number of new products are now introduced simultaneously in the United States, Japan, and the advanced European nations (e.g., laptop computers, compact disks, and electronic cameras). This may be accompanied by globally dispersed production, with particular components of a new product being produced in those locations around the globe where the mix of factor costs and skills is most favorable (as predicted by the theory of comparative advantage).

Consider laptop computers, which were introduced simultaneously into a number of major national markets by Toshiba. Although various components for Toshiba laptop computers are manufactured in Japan (e.g., display screens, memory chips), other components are manufactured in Singapore and Taiwan, and still others (e.g., hard drives and microprocessors) are manufactured in the United States. All the components are shipped to Singapore for final assembly, and the completed product is then shipped to the major world markets (the United States, Western Europe, and Japan). The pattern of trade associated with this new product is both different from and more complex than the pattern predicted by Vernon's model. Trying to explain this pattern using the product life-cycle theory would be very difficult. The theory of comparative advantage might better explain why certain components are produced in certain locations and why the final product is assembled in Singapore. In short, although Vernon's theory may be useful for explaining the pattern of international trade during the brief period of American global dominance, its relevance in the modern world is limited.

The New Trade Theory

The new trade theory began to emerge in the 1970s. At that time a number of economists were questioning the assumption of diminishing returns to specialization.[18] They argued that in many industries, because of substantial economies of scale, there are increasing returns to specialization. As output expands with specialization, the ability to realize economies of scale increases and so the unit costs of production should decrease. Economies of scale are primarily derived by spreading fixed costs (such as the costs of developing a new product) over a larger output. Consider the commercial jet aircraft industry. The fixed costs of developing a new commercial jet airliner are astronomical. For example, Boeing spent an estimated $5 billion to develop its 777. The company will have to sell at least 350 777s just to recoup these development costs and break even. Thus, due to the high fixed costs of developing a new jet aircraft, the economies of scale in this industry are substantial.

The new trade theorists further argue that due to the presence of substantial scale economies, world demand will support only a few firms in many industries. This is the case in the commercial jet aircraft industry; estimates suggest that, at most, world demand can profitably support only three major manufacturers. For example, the total world demand for 300-seater commercial jet aircraft similar to Boeing's 777 model will probably be only 1,500 aircraft over the 10 years between 1995 and 2005. If we assume that firms must sell at least 500 aircraft to get an acceptable return on their investment (which is reasonable, given the breakeven point of 300 aircraft), we can see that, at most, the world market can profitably support only three firms!

The new trade theorists go on to argue that in those industries where the existence of substantial economies of scale imply that the world market will profitably support only a few firms, countries may export certain products simply because they have a firm that was an early entrant into that industry. Underpinning this argument is the notion of **first-mover advantages**, which are the economic and strategic advantages that accrue to early entrants into an industry.[19] Because they are able to gain economies of scale, early entrants may get a lock on the world market that discourages subsequent entry. In other words, the ability of first-movers to reap economies of scale creates a barrier to entry. In the commercial aircraft industry, for example, the fact that Boeing and Airbus are already in the industry and have the benefits of economies of scale effectively discourages new entries.

This theory has profound implications. The theory suggests that a country may predominate in the export of a good simply because it was lucky enough to have one or more firms among the first to produce that good. This is at variance with the Heckscher-Ohlin theory, which suggests that a country will predominate in the export of a product when it is particularly well endowed with those factors used intensively in its manufacture. Thus, the new trade theorists argue that the United States leads in exports of commercial jet aircraft not because it is better endowed with the factors of production required to manufacture aircraft, but because two of the first movers in the industry, Boeing and McDonnell-Douglas, were U.S. firms. It should be noted, however, that the new trade theory is not at variance with the theory of comparative advantage. Since economies of scale result in an increase in the efficiency of resource utilization, and hence in productivity, the new trade theory identifies an important source of comparative advantage.

How useful is this theory in explaining trade patterns? It is perhaps too early to say; the theory is so new that little supporting empirical work has been done. Consistent with the theory, however, a recent study by Harvard business historian Alfred Chandler suggests that first-mover advantages are an important factor in explaining the dominance of firms from certain nations in certain industries.[20] And it is true that the number of firms is very limited in many global industries. This is the case with the commercial aircraft industry, the chemical industry, the heavy construction-equipment industry, the heavy truck industry, the tire industry, the consumer electronics industry, and the jet engine industry, to name but a few.

Perhaps the most contentious implication of the new trade theory is the argument that it generates for government intervention and strategic trade policy.[21] New trade theorists stress the role of luck, entrepreneurship, and innovation in giving a firm first-mover advantages. According to this argument, the reason Boeing was the first mover in commercial jet aircraft manufacture—rather than firms like Great Britain's DeHavilland and Hawker Siddely, or Holland's Fokker, all of which could have been—was that Boeing was both lucky and innovative. One way Boeing was lucky is that DeHavilland shot itself in the foot when its Comet jet airliner, introduced two years earlier than Boeing's first jet airliner, the 707, was found to be full of serious technological flaws. Had DeHavilland not made some serious technological mistakes, Great Britain might now be the world's leading exporter of commercial jet aircraft!

Boeing's innovativeness was demonstrated by its independent development of the technological know-how required to build a commercial jet airliner. Several new trade theorists have pointed out, however, that Boeing's R&D was largely paid for by the U.S. government; that the 707 was in fact a spinoff

first-mover advantages Economic and strategic advantages that accrue to early entrants into an industry.

from a government-funded military program. Herein lies a rationale for government intervention. Through the sophisticated and judicious use of subsidies, might not a government be able to increase the chances of its domestic firms becoming first movers in newly emerging industries, as the U.S. government apparently did with Boeing? If this is possible, and the new trade theory suggests it might be, then we have an economic rationale for a proactive trade policy that is at variance with the free trade prescriptions of the trade theories we have reviewed so far. We will consider the policy implications of this issue in Chapter 5.

National Competitive Advantage: Porter's Diamond

In 1990 Michael Porter of Harvard Business School published the results of an intensive research effort that attempted to determine why some nations succeed and others fail in international competition.[22] Porter and his team looked at 100 industries in 10 nations. The book that contains the results of this work, *The Competitive Advantage of Nations*, seems destined to become an important contribution. Like the work of the new trade theorists, Porter's work was driven by a belief that the existing theories of international trade told only part of the story. For Porter, the essential task was to explain why a nation achieves international success in a particular industry. Why does Japan do so well in the automobile industry? Why does Switzerland excel in the production and export of precision instruments and pharmaceuticals? Why do Germany and the United States do so well in the chemical industry? These questions cannot be answered easily by the Heckscher-Ohlin theory, and the theory of comparative advantage offers only a partial explanation. The theory of comparative advantage would say that Switzerland excels in the production and export of precision instruments because it uses its resources very productively in these industries. Although this may be correct, this does not explain why Switzerland is more productive in this industry than Great Britain, Germany, or Spain. It is this puzzle that Porter tries to solve.

Porter's thesis is that four broad attributes of a nation shape the environment in which local firms compete, and that these attributes promote or impede the creation of competitive advantage (see Figure 4.5). These attributes are

- Factor endowments—a nation's position in factors of production such as skilled labor or the infrastructure necessary to compete in a given industry.
- Demand conditions—the nature of home demand for the industry's product or service.
- Related and supporting industries—the presence or absence in a nation of supplier industries and related industries that are internationally competitive.
- Firm strategy, structure, and rivalry—the conditions in the nation governing how companies are created, organized, and managed and the nature of domestic rivalry.

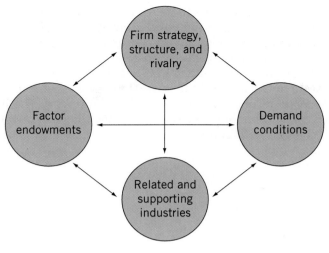

FIGURE 4.5

Determinants of National Competitive Advantage: Porter's Diamond
Source: Adapted from M. E. Porter, "The Competitive Advantage of Nations," *Harvard Business Review*.
March–April 1990, p. 77.

Porter speaks of these four attributes as constituting *the diamond*. He argues that firms are most likely to succeed in industries or industry segments where the diamond is most favorable. He also argues that the diamond is a mutually reinforcing system. The effect of one attribute is contingent on the state of others. For example, Porter argues, favorable demand conditions will not result in competitive advantage unless the state of rivalry is sufficient to cause firms to respond to them.

Porter maintains that two additional variables can influence the national diamond in important ways: chance and government. Chance events, such as major innovations, create discontinuities that can unfreeze or reshape industry structure and provide the opportunity for one nation's firms to supplant another's. Government, by its choice of policies, can detract from or improve national advantage. For example, regulation can alter home demand conditions, antitrust policies can influence the intensity of rivalry within an industry, and government investments in education can change factor endowments.

Factor Endowments

We have seen that factor endowments lie at the center of the Heckscher-Ohlin theory. While Porter does not propose anything radically new, he does analyze the characteristics of factors of production in some detail. He recognizes hierarchies among factors, distinguishing between basic factors (e.g., natural resources, climate, location, and demographics) and advanced factors (e.g., communications infrastructure, sophisticated and skilled labor, research facilities, and technological know-how). He argues that advanced factors are the most significant for competitive advantage. Moreover, unlike basic factors (which are naturally endowed), advanced factors are a product of investment by individuals, companies, and governments. Thus, government investments in basic and higher education, by improving the general skill and knowledge level of the population and by stimulating advanced research at higher education institutions, can upgrade a nation's advanced factors.

The relationship between advanced and basic factors is complex. Basic factors can provide an initial advantage that is subsequently reinforced and extended by investment in advanced factors. Conversely, disadvantages in basic factors can create pressures to invest in advanced factors. The most obvious example of this phenomenon is Japan, a country that lacks arable land and mineral deposits and yet through investment has built a substantial endowment of advanced factors. In particular, Porter notes that Japan's large pool of engineers (reflecting a much higher number of engineering graduates per capita than almost any other nation) has been vital to Japan's success in many manufacturing industries.

Demand Conditions

Porter emphasizes the role home demand plays in providing the impetus for "upgrading" competitive advantage. Firms are typically most sensitive to the needs of their closest customers. Thus, the characteristics of home demand are particularly important in shaping the attributes of domestically made products and in creating pressures for innovation and quality. Porter argues that a nation's firms gain competitive advantage if their domestic consumers are sophisticated and demanding. Sophisticated and demanding consumers pressure local firms to meet high standards of product quality and to produce innovative products. Porter notes that Japan's sophisticated and knowledgeable camera buyers helped stimulate the Japanese camera industry to improve product quality and to introduce innovative models. A similar example can be found in the cellular phone equipment industry, where sophisticated and demanding local customers in Scandinavia helped push Nokia of Finland and Ericsson of Sweden to invest in cellular phone technology long before demand for cellular phones took off in other developed nations. As a result, Nokia and Ericsson, together with Motorola, are today dominant players in the global cellular telephone equipment industry. The case of Nokia is reviewed in more depth in the next "Management Focus."

Related and Supporting Industries

The third broad attribute of national advantage in an industry is the presence in a country of suppliers or related industries that are internationally competitive. The benefits of investments in advanced factors of production by related and supporting industries can spill over into an industry, thereby helping it achieve a strong competitive position internationally. Swedish strength in fabricated steel products (e.g., ball bearings and cutting tools) has drawn on strengths in Sweden's specialty steel industry. Technological leadership in the U.S. semiconductor industry until the mid-1980s provided the basis for U.S. success in personal computers and several other technically advanced electronic products. Similarly, Switzerland's success in pharmaceuticals is closely related to its previous international success in the technologically related dye industry.

One consequence of this process is that successful industries within a country tend to be grouped into "clusters" of related industries. This was one of the most pervasive findings of Porter's study. One such cluster is the German textile and apparel sector, which includes high-quality cotton, wool, synthetic fibers, sewing machine needles, and a wide range of textile machinery.

Firm Strategy, Structure, and Rivalry

The fourth broad attribute of national competitive advantage in Porter's model is the strategy, structure, and rivalry of firms within a nation. Porter makes two important points here. His first is that different nations are characterized by different "management ideologies," which either help them or do not help them to build national competitive advantage. For example, Porter notes the predominance of engineers on the top-management teams of German and Japanese firms. He attributes this to these firms' emphasis on improving manufacturing processes and product design. In contrast, Porter notes a predominance of people with finance backgrounds on the top-management teams of many U.S. firms. He links this to the lack of attention of many U.S. firms to improving manufacturing processes and product design, particularly during the 1970s and 80s. He also argues that the dominance of finance has led to a corresponding overemphasis on maximizing short-term financial returns. According to Porter, one consequence of these different management ideologies has been a relative loss of U.S. competitiveness in those engineering-based industries where manufacturing processes and product design issues are all-important (e.g., the automobile industry).

Porter's second point is that there is a strong association between vigorous domestic rivalry and the creation and persistence of competitive advantage in an industry. Vigorous domestic rivalry induces firms to look for ways to improve efficiency, which in turn makes them better international competitors. Domestic rivalry creates pressures to innovate, to improve quality, to reduce costs, and to invest in upgrading advanced factors. All of this helps to create world-class competitors. As an illustration Porter cites the case of Japan:

> Nowhere is the role of domestic rivalry more evident than in Japan, where it is all-out warfare in which many companies fail to achieve profitability. With goals that stress market share, Japanese companies engage in a continuing struggle to outdo each other. Shares fluctuate markedly. The process is prominently covered in the business press. Elaborate rankings measure which companies are most popular with university graduates. The rate of new product and process development is breathtaking.[23]

A similar point about the stimulating effects of strong domestic competition can be made with regard to the rise of Nokia of Finland to global preeminence in the market for cellular telephone equipment. For details, see the accompanying "Management Focus."

Evaluating Porter's Theory

In sum, Porter's argument is that the degree to which a nation is likely to achieve international success in a certain industry is a function of the combined impact of factor endowments, domestic demand conditions, related and supporting industries, and domestic rivalry. He argues that it usually re-

The Rise of Finland's Nokia

The cellular telephone equipment industry is one of the great growth stories of the 1990s. The number of cellular subscribers has been expanding rapidly. By the end of 1994 there were over 50 million cellular subscribers worldwide, up from under 10 million in 1990. Three firms currently dominate the global market for cellular equipment (e.g., cellular phones, base station equipment, digital switches): Motorola, Nokia, and Ericsson. Of the three, the dramatic rise of Nokia has perhaps been the most surprising. Nokia's roots are in Finland, not normally a country that jumps to mind when one talks about leading-edge technology companies. In the 1980s

Nokia was a rambling Finnish conglomerate with activities that embraced tire manufacturing, paper production, consumer electronics, and telecommunications equipment. Today it is a focused $10 billion telecommunications equipment manufacturer with a global reach second only to that of Motorola, and sales and earnings that are growing in excess of 30 percent annually. How has this former conglomerate emerged to take a global leadership position in cellular equipment? Much of the answer lies in the history, geography, and political economy of Finland and its Nordic neighbors.

The story starts in 1981 when the Nordic nations got together to create the world's first international cellular telephone network. They had good reason to become pioneers. Because of the countries' sparse population and inhos-

pitable cold, it cost far too much to lay a traditional wire-line telephone service. Yet those same features make telecommunications all the more valuable; people driving through the Arctic winter and owners of remote northern houses need a telephone to summon help if things go wrong. As a result, Sweden, Norway, and Finland became the first nations in the world to take cellular telecommunications seriously. They found, for example, that while it cost up to $800 per subscriber to bring a traditional wire-line service to remote locations in the far north, the same locations could be linked by wireless cellular for only $500 per person. As a consequence, by 1994 12 percent of people in Scandinavia owned cellular phones, compared with less than 6 percent in the United States, the world's second most developed market.

quires the presence of all four components (although there are some exceptions) to positively impact competitive performance. Porter also contends that government can influence each of the four components of the diamond either positively or negatively. Factor endowments can be affected by subsidies, policies toward capital markets, policies toward education, and the like. Government can shape domestic demand through local product standards or with regulations that mandate or influence buyer needs. Government policy can influence supporting and related industries through regulation and can influence firm rivalry through such devices as capital market regulation, tax policy, and antitrust laws.

If Porter is correct, we would expect his model to predict the pattern of international trade that we observe in the real world. Countries should be exporting products from those industries where all four components of the diamond are favorable, while importing in those areas where the components are not favorable. Is he correct? We do not know. Porter's theory is so new that it has not yet been subjected to independent empirical testing. There is certainly much about the theory that rings true, but the same can be said for the new trade theory, the theory of comparative advantage, and the Heckscher-

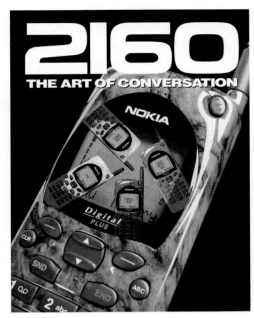

Courtesy Nokia

Nokia, as a longtime telecommunications equipment supplier, was well positioned to take advantage of this development, but other forces at work in Finland also helped Nokia develop its competitive edge. Unlike virtually every other developed nation, Finland has never had a national telephone monopoly. Instead, the country's telephone services have long been provided by about 50 autonomous local telephone companies, whose elected boards set prices by referendum (which naturally means low prices). This army of independent and cost-conscious telephone service providers prevented Nokia from taking anything for granted in its home country. With typical Finnish pragmatism, they have been willing to buy from the lowest-cost supplier, whether that was Nokia, Ericsson, Motorola, or someone else. This situation contrasted sharply with that prevailing in most developed nations until the late 1980s and early 1990s, when domestic telephone monopolies typically purchased equipment from a dominant local supplier or made it themselves. Nokia has responded to this competitive pressure by doing everything possible to drive down its manufacturing costs while still staying at the leading edge of cellular technology.

The consequences of these forces are clear. While Motorola remains the number one firm in cellular equipment, the once obscure Finnish firm Nokia is snapping at its heels. It is Nokia, not Motorola, that is the leader in digital cellular technology, which seems to be the wave of the future. Nokia has the lead because Scandinavia started switching over to digital technology five years before the rest of the world. Moreover, spurred on by its cost-conscious Finnish customers, Nokia now has the lowest cost structure of any cellular phone equipment manufacturer in the world, making it a more profitable enterprise than Motorola. Nokia's operating margins in 1994 were 17.7 percent, compared with 14.4 percent at Motorola.[24]

Ohlin theory. In reality, it may be that each of these theories explains something about the pattern of international trade. After all, in many respects these theories complement each other.

Implications for Business

There are at least three main implications of the material discussed in this chapter for international businesses: location implications, first-mover implications, and policy implications.

Location Implications

One way in which the material discussed in this chapter matters to an international business concerns the link between the theories of international trade and a firm's decision about where to locate its various productive activities. Underlying most of the theories we have discussed is the notion that different countries have particular advantages in different productive activities. Thus, from a profit perspective, it makes sense for a firm to disperse its various productive activities to those countries where, according to the theory of international trade, they can be performed most efficiently. If design can be performed most efficiently in France, that is where design facilities should be located; if the manufacture of basic components can be performed most efficiently in Singapore, that is where they should be manufactured; and if final assembly can be performed most efficiently in China, that is where final assembly should be performed. The end result is a global web of productive activities, with different activities being performed in different locations around the globe depending on considerations of comparative advantage, factor endowments, and the like. If the firm does not do this, it may find itself at a competitive disadvantage.

Consider the production of laptop computers, a process with four major stages: (1) basic research and development of the product design, (2) manufacture of standard electronic components (e.g., memory chips), (3) manufacture of advanced components (e.g., flat-top color display screens and microprocessors), and (4) final assembly. Basic R&D and design require a pool of highly skilled and educated workers with good backgrounds in microelectronics. The two countries with a comparative advantage in basic microelectronics R&D and design are Japan and the United States, so most producers of laptop computers locate their R&D facilities in one, or both, of these countries. (Apple, IBM, Motorola, Texas Instruments, Toshiba, and Sony all have major R&D facilities in both Japan and the United States.)

The manufacture of standard electronic components is a capital-intensive process requiring semiskilled labor, and cost pressures are intense. The best locations for such activities today are places such as Singapore, Taiwan, Malaysia, and South Korea. These countries have pools of relatively skilled, low-cost labor. Thus, many producers of laptop computers have standard components, such as memory chips, produced at these locations.

The manufacture of advanced components such as microprocessors and display screens is a capital-intensive process requiring highly skilled labor, and cost pressures are less intense. Since cost pressures are not so intense at this stage of the process, these components can be—and are—manufactured in countries with high labor costs that also have pools of highly skilled labor (primarily Japan and the United States).

Finally, assembly is a relatively labor-intensive process requiring only low-skilled labor, and cost pressures are intense. As a result, final assembly may be carried out in a country such as Mexico, which has an abundance of low-cost, low-skilled labor.

The end result is that when we look at a laptop computer produced by a U.S. manufacturer, we may find that it was designed in California, its standard components were produced in Taiwan and Singapore, its advanced components were produced in Japan and the United States, its final assembly occurred in Mexico, and the finished product was then sold in the United States or elsewhere in the world. By dispersing production activities to different locations around the globe, the U.S. manufacturer is taking advantage of the difference between countries identified by the various theories of international trade.

First-Mover Implications

The new trade theory suggests the importance to firms of building and exploiting first-mover advantages. According to the new trade theory, firms that establish a first-mover advantage with regard to the production of a particular new product may subsequently dominate global trade in that product. This is particularly true in those industries where the global market can profitably support only a limited number of firms—such as the aerospace market—but early commitments also seem to be important in less concentrated industries such as the market for cellular telephone equipment (again, see the "Management Focus" on Nokia). For the individual firm, the clear message is that it pays to invest substantial financial resources in trying to build a first-mover, or early-mover, advantage, even if that means several years of substantial losses before a new venture becomes profitable. Although the precise details of how to achieve this are beyond the scope of this book, it should be noted that there is a vast literature on strategies for exploiting first-mover advantages.[25] It is often argued that in recent years Japanese firms, rather than their European or North American competitors, seem to have been prepared to undertake the vast investments and bear the years of losses required to build a first-mover advantage. This has certainly been true in the production of liquid crystal display (LCD) screens for laptop computers. While firms such as Toshiba and NEC invested heavily in this technology during the 1980s, many large European and American firms exited the market. As a result, today Japanese firms dominate global trade in LCD screens, even though the technology was invented in the United States.

Policy Implications

The theories of international trade also matter to international businesses because business firms are major players on the international trade scene. Business firms produce exports, and business firms import the products of other countries. Because of their pivotal role in international trade, business firms can and do exert a strong influence on government trade policy. By lobbying government, business firms can help promote free trade, or they can promote trade restrictions. The message for businesses contained in the theories of international trade is that promoting free trade is generally in the best interests of their home country, although it may not always be in the best interest of an individual firm. Many firms do recognize this and do lobby for open markets.

For example, in 1991 when the U.S. government announced its intention to place a tariff on Japanese imports of liquid crystal display (LCD) screens, IBM and Apple Computer protested strongly. Both IBM and Apple pointed out that (1) Japan was the lowest-cost source of LCD screens, (2) they used these screens in their own laptop computers, and (3) the proposed tariff, by increasing the cost of LCD screens, would increase the cost of laptop computers produced by IBM and Apple, thus making them less competitive in the world market. In other words, the tariff, designed to protect U.S. firms, would be self-defeating. In response to these pressures, the U.S. government reversed its posture on this issue.

However, businesses do not always lobby for free trade. In the United States, for example, "voluntary" restrictions on imports of automobiles, machine tools, textiles, and steel are the result of direct pressures by U.S. firms in these industries on the government. The government has responded by getting foreign companies to agree to "voluntary" restrictions on their imports, using the implicit threat of more comprehensive formal trade barriers to get them to adhere to these agreements. As predicted by international trade theory, many of these agreements have been self-defeating. Take the voluntary restriction on machine tool imports agreed to in 1985 as an example. Due to limited import competition from more efficient foreign suppliers, the prices of machine tools in the United States have risen to higher levels than would have prevailed under a free trade scenario. Since machine tools are used throughout the manufacturing industry, the result has been to increase the costs of U.S. manufacturing in general and create a corresponding loss in world market competitiveness. Moreover, shielded from international competition by import barriers, the U.S. machine tool industry has had no incentive to increase its efficiency. Consequently, it has lost many of its export markets to more efficient foreign competitors. Thus, the U.S. machine tool industry is now smaller than it was in 1985. For anyone schooled in international trade theory, none of these events is surprising.[26]

Porter's theory of national competitive advantage also contains important policy implications. Porter's theory suggests that it is in the best interest of a firm to invest in upgrading advanced factors of production; for example, to invest in better training for its employees and to increase its commitment to research and development. It is also in the best interests of business to lobby the government to adopt policies that have a favorable impact on each component of the national "diamond." Thus, according to Porter, businesses should urge government to increase its investment in education, infrastructure, and basic research (since these enhance advanced factors) and to adopt policies that promote strong competition within domestic markets (since this makes firms stronger international competitors, according to Porter's findings).

Key Terms

Summary

This chapter has reviewed a number of theories that explain why it is beneficial for a country to engage in international trade and has explained the pattern of international trade that we observe in the world economy. We have seen how the theories of Smith, Ricardo, and Heckscher-Ohlin all make strong cases for unrestricted free trade. In contrast, the mercantilist doctrine and, to a lesser extent, the new trade theory can be interpreted to support government intervention to promote exports through subsidies and to limit imports through tariffs and quotas.

In explaining the pattern of international trade, the second objective of this chapter, we have seen that with the exception of mercantilism, which is silent on this issue, the different theories offer largely complementary explanations. Although no one theory may explain the apparent pattern of international trade, taken together, the theory of comparative advantage, the Heckscher-Ohlin theory, the product life-cycle theory, the new trade theory, and Porter's theory of national competitive advantage do suggest which factors are important. Comparative advantage tells us that productivity differences are important; Heckscher-Ohlin tells us that factor endowments matter; the product life-cycle theory tells us that where a new product is introduced is important; the new trade theory tells us that increasing returns to specialization and first-mover advantages matter; and Porter tells us that all these factors may be important insofar as they affect the four components of the national diamond.

The following points have been made in this chapter:

1 Mercantilists argued that it was in a country's best interests to run a balance-of-trade surplus. They viewed trade as a zero-sum game, in which one country's gains cause losses for other countries.

2 The theory of absolute advantage suggests that countries differ in their ability to produce goods efficiently. The theory suggests that a country should specialize in producing goods in areas where it has an absolute advantage and import goods in areas where other countries have absolute advantages.

3 The theory of comparative advantage suggests that it makes sense for a country to specialize in producing those goods that it can produce most efficiently while buying from other countries goods that it can produce relatively less efficiently—even if that means buying goods from other countries that it could produce more efficiently itself.

4 The theory of comparative advantage suggests that unrestricted free trade brings about increased world production; that is, that trade is a positive-sum game.

5 The theory of comparative advantage also suggests that opening a country to free trade stimulates economic growth, which in turn creates dynamic gains from trade.

6 The Heckscher-Ohlin theory argues that the pattern of international trade is determined by differences in factor endowments. It predicts that countries will export those goods that make intensive use of locally abundant factors and will import goods that make intensive use of factors that are locally scarce.

7 The product life-cycle theory suggests that trade patterns are influenced by where a new product is introduced. In an increasingly integrated global economy, the product life-cycle theory seems to be less predictive than it was between 1945 and 1975.

8 The new trade theory argues that in those industries where the existence of substantial economies of scale imply that the world market will profitably support only a few firms, countries may predominate in the export of certain products simply because they had a firm that was a first-mover in that industry.

9 Some new trade theorists have promoted the idea of strategic trade policy. The argument is that government, by the sophisticated and judicious use of subsidies, might increase the chances of domestic firms becoming first-movers in newly emerging industries.

10 Porter's theory of national competitive advantage suggests that the pattern of trade is influenced by four attributes of a nation: (*i*) factor endowments, (*ii*) domestic demand conditions, (*iii*) related and supporting industries, and (*iv*) firm strategy, structure, and rivalry.

11 Theories of international trade are important to an individual business firm primarily because they can help the firm decide where to locate its various production activities.

12 Firms involved in international trade can and do exert a strong influence on government policy toward trade. By lobbying government bodies, business firms can help promote free trade or they can promote trade restrictions.

Critical Thinking and Discussion Questions

1 "Mercantilism is a bankrupt theory that has no place in the modern world." Discuss.

2 The "Country Focus" reviews the arguments of those who suggest that Japan is a neo-mercantilist nation. Do you agree with this assessment? Can you think of cases in which your country has taken a neo-mercantilist stance to foreign competition?

3 Using the theory of comparative advantage to support your arguments, outline the case for free trade.

4 Using the new trade theory and Porter's theory of national competitive advantage, outline the case for government policies that would build national competitive advantage in a particular industry. What kind of policies would you recommend that the government adopt? Are these policies at variance with the basic free trade philosophy?

5 You are the CEO of a textile firm that designs and manufactures mass-market clothing products in the United States. Your manufacturing process is labor-intensive and does not require highly skilled employees. Currently you have design facilities in Paris and New York and manufacturing facilities in North Carolina. Drawing on the theory of international trade, decide whether these are optimal locations for these activities.

6 "Policies designed to limit competition from low-cost foreign competitors do not help a country to achieve greater economic growth." Discuss this statement.

Internet Exercise

Many researchers have tested the validity of the Heckscher-Ohlin theory analyzing the pattern of international trade, starting with Wassily Leontief. He is cited in a number of Internet pages, such as The Nobel Prize Internet Archive and Nobel Prize in Economic Sciences Winners (http://nobelprizes.com/nobel/economics/1973a.html). He founded The Institute for Economic Analysis at the Robert F. Wagner Graduate School of Public Service at New York University, which is described as "the principal center for the theoretical extension of input-output economics and its practical application to problems of economic development and environmental degradation" (http://www.nyu.edu/wagner/).

Leontief's theories of the role of automation in society are posted in the World Wide Web. For example, an abstract of his article "Technological Advancement, Employment and the Distribution of Income between Labor and Capital" is available (http://www.smau.it/nobel/nobel94/aleoin94.htm), as are two articles featuring his theories. "The Declining Middle" discusses Leontief's proposal that the increase of automation in the United States has resulted in a loss of wages and consequently a loss of purchasing power. To alleviate this situation by distributing the income and stimulating the economy, Leontief suggests shortening the work week and having the government supple-

ment incomes (http://www.
theatlantic.com/atlantic/election/
connection/ecbig/declkutt.htm).
"Computers are Bad for your
Health" advances Leontief's
theory that automation will
replace workers in factories in
the same manner it has replaced
horses in agriculture (http://
www.winmag.com/library/1995/
1295/12opins.htm#A21).

Global Surfing
Read Leontief's biography at the
Nobel Prize site and examine the
books he has authored. In addition to the Leontief paradox, what
other economic theories has he
advanced? Jump to the New York
University site. What types of
economic theories are explored at
the Institute for Economic
Analysis? In Leontief's
"Technological Advancement"
article, how does he propose
governments adjust their
economies to remain competitive
in international trade? Which
economists' theories regarding
comparative advantages in this
chapter are similar to Leontief's
theories? In "The Declining
Middle" and "Computers are
Bad" articles, how do the authors
apply and expand Leontief's
theories?

Closing Case

The Italian Ceramic Tile Industry

By the early 1990s Italian firms
were by far the world leaders in
the production and export of ceramic roofing and flooring tiles,
accounting for over 30 percent of
world production and 60 percent
of world exports. The rise to
global preeminence of the Italian
tile industry was based on the
superior mechanical and aes-
thetic qualities of Italian tiles.
Italian tile production is concentrated in the Emilia-Romagna region of northern Italy around the
small town of Sassuolo. In the
Sassuolo region there are hundreds of firms involved in the ceramic tile industry and in various
supporting industries such as the
manufacture of glazes, enamels,
and ceramic tile production
equipment. As a result, Sassuolo
boasts the greatest concentration in the world of firms in
the ceramic tile and supporting
industries.

The ceramic tile industry in
Sassuolo grew out of the earthen-
ware and crockery industry, which
could be traced to the 13th century. Demand for ceramic tiles
grew rapidly in Italy in the years
immediately after the second
World War. Reconstruction after
the war created a boom in the
building industry. One reason for
the high domestic demand was
Italy's Mediterranean climate (ceramic floor tiles were cool to the
touch in warm weather). There
was also a tradition in Italy of using natural stone materials for
flooring, as opposed to carpeting
or wood. Because of this tradition, per capita tile consumption
in Italy has long been the highest
in the world. In 1987 it stood at
3.33 square meters per capita,
followed by 2.55 in Spain and
1.81 in Switzerland.

As a result of booming demand, the number of ceramic tile
firms in the Sassuolo region grew
rapidly during the 1950s and
1960s. In 1955 there were 14
tile firms in the region; by 1962
the figure had leaped to 102. In
addition to booming demand, the
low cost of setting up a ceramic
tile business spurred this rapid
growth in the number of enterprises. Rivalry between firms in
the Sassuolo region was intense.
They had to compete vigorously
against each other to get access
to retail outlets. Retailers demanded high quality, low cost,
and aesthetically pleasing tiles.
Firms constantly sought to gain
an edge against each other in
technology, design, and distribution. Innovations were usually
known within a matter of weeks
and quickly copied by rivals.
Firms seeking a leadership position, whether that be in technology, or productive efficiency, or
design, had to constantly improve
their processes and turn over
their product line in order to stay
ahead of rivals.

As the industry grew around
Sassuolo, process technicians
from local tile companies left to

153

start their own process equipment firms. Process equipment in tile making includes kilns for firing the tiles, presses for forming tiles, and glazing machines. By the mid-1980s more than 120 firms in the Sassuolo area were making process equipment for ceramic tile companies. These equipment manufacturers competed fiercely for the business of tile manufacturers. In an attempt to gain business they devoted considerable effort to upgrading the quality of their production equipment and driving down their own manufacturing costs. One result of this competitive process among equipment suppliers was the development of a number of important process innovations that significantly lowered the energy and labor costs of manufacturing ceramic tiles. Advances in kiln technology in particular soon made Sassuolo a leader not just in the tile industry but also in the supporting equipment industry.

By the 1970s the tile industry in Italy was beginning to mature. The long post-WWII boom in domestic demand was losing steam and excess capacity was beginning to develop among Italian tile firms. They responded to this problem by seeking international markets for their products, particularly in North America. In the international market the Sassuolo firms found they had a competitive advantage over their nearest competitors, who were typically from Spain and Germany. This advantage was based on higher productivity, lower costs, better design, and the Italian reputation for style. As a consequence, by the early 1990s Italian firms enjoyed almost twice the global market share of their nearest competitors, the Spanish.[27]

Case Discussion Questions

1 To what extent does the theory of comparative advantage explain the rise of Italian tile firms to global preeminence in the tile industry?

2 To what extent does the Heckscher-Ohlin theory explain the rise of Italian tile firms to global preeminence in the tile industry?

3 Use Michael Porter's diamond to analyze the rise to global preeminence of the Italian tile industry. What does this analysis tell you about how firms gain a competitive advantage in the world economy?

4 Which of the above theories—comparative advantage, Heckscher-Ohlin, or Porter's—gives the best explanation of the rise to global preeminence of the Italian tile industry? Why?

Everything's Coming Up Roses

At 19 Rodrigo de la Cruz was a professional basketball player in Ecuador with dreams of obtaining a basketball scholarship and a college degree at an American university. Although born in the United States, Rodrigo was raised in Ecuador. At 25 his dreams have partially come true. He is completing a bachelor's degree in business at California State Polytechnic University, Pomona, but is financing it with roses, not basketballs. Instead of shooting hoops, he is importing roses. Rodrigo is co-owner of Golden Rose, a wholesale company in Burbank which specializes in roses from Ecuador.

"Ecuador has the most beautiful roses in the world thanks to a perfect combination of temperature, elevation, and hours of daylight," says Rodrigo. "We are the exclusive California distributor of roses from the Rosas del Ecuador Farm which has won the prestigious "Golden Rose Award" for growing the best roses in the world bestowed by the Mehlland House of France. These are the same award-winning roses that are delivered daily to beautify the White House."

Ecuador's export of roses worldwide increased from 9,200 tons in 1994 to 21,945 tons in 1996. The largest market for Ecuadorian roses is the United States with 9,955 tons shipped in 1995 or nine times as many

Rodrigo de la Cruz

as to either of its second largest markets, Holland and Russia.

Rodrigo was introduced to the rose business during Valentine's week, 1993. Monica, then his girlfriend and now his wife, decided it would be more profitable to sell roses than to receive them. Monica asked her father, who owns Rosas del Ecuador, to ship her 100 boxes of roses which she hoped to sell to Los Angeles flower shops. She enlisted Rodrigo and her brother, Jaime Muñoz, to help with the deliveries.

Even with no sales or marketing experience, she sold out very quickly. She benefited from the high season, a quality product, and reasonable prices. Flush with the success of Valentine's week, she decided to continue bringing in roses on a weekly basis. Eventually the trio was able to

set up the business for a few thousand dollars, with their biggest expenses being freight and rent.

Rodrigo and Monica were married five months after their Valentine venture and Rodrigo began working at the business part-time while maintaining a full-time position at Taco Bell. He now works full-time and is responsible for importing the roses, setting the prices, and accounting. His brother-in-law oversees delivery, marketing, and fulfillment. Each still takes turns answering the telephones. Monica still helps with strategic planning and logistics while also raising the couple's two young children.

Despite their delicate nature, roses are a tough business. There are many variables outside of your control. It takes approximately six days from the time the roses are cut in Ecuador to when they arrive at the Golden Rose warehouse. Highly perishable, roses must be sold within two or three days of arrival. Since there are no direct flights from Ecuador to Los Angeles, all shipments first stop in Miami. They must pass through two USDA inspections. According to Rodrigo, "If there is any sign of insects or disease, you are given three choices— all of them at your expense: re-exportation to Ecuador; fumigation, which makes the roses unsaleable; or destruction by the USDA."

It is important to hire a competent broker. Currently, shipments valued over $1,250 or more than 50 boxes require a broker. "Sometimes the broker has earned more than I, but this is necessary because of the distance and the possibility of losing an entire shipment for a variety of reasons," Rodrigo explains.

Competition in the industry is fierce. Rodrigo estimates that there are over 100 flower wholesalers in Los Angeles, 60 of whom import from Ecuador. The competition leads to deep discounting by vendors determined to maintain or acquire market share.

Realizing that the company could not prosper without his total commitment, Rodrigo became full-time two years ago. Rodrigo often works weekends, nights, and even some early mornings. During the busy season like Valentine's he works every day for two weeks straight. He keeps up this schedule while enrolled in three night classes every term.

Success also depends on a dedicated staff. In addition to his brother-in-law, the company has four full time employees—whom Rodrigo treats more like family. He trusts them with access to the facility and gives them as much autonomy as possible in setting up their delivery routes. He also encourages them to learn how the business functions. In response, the workers are very loyal, and willingly work long hours. Rodrigo credits the development of his management skills to his experience at Taco Bell, where he became the firm's youngest assistant manager at 19. Most of his current employees originally worked for him at the fast food restaurant.

Rodrigo has never formally written down his business plan, but he does strictly adhere to a strategy based on quality, knowledge, and service. Rodrigo specializes in high-quality roses. "They are the most beautiful, longest-lasting roses for special customers," he emphasizes. Rodrigo charges a premium price, and would rather destroy his inventory than reduce its price. He sells directly to flower shops, never through the flower market where prices are cut routinely. Rodrigo, now an expert on roses, is quick to educate his clients. Unlike his competitors, he offers free delivery, as well as full refunds if the customers are dissatisfied with the quality or freshness of the roses.

Rodrigo now sells to the three biggest florists in southern California and gets most of his new customers through referrals. He is even planning to open a second warehouse.

As stated on his business card, Rodrigo now competes in the upscale flower arena. Rodrigo, like the Ecuadorian roses he represents, has come up a winner.

Helena Czepiec
California State Polytechnic University, Pomona

Chapter 5
The Global Trading System

©PhotoDisc

Opening Case

Anatomy of a Trade Dispute

The United States and Japan boast one of the largest bilateral trading relationships in the world. It is also a trading relationship that many see as lopsided, with Japan exporting nearly $60 billion more in goods to the United States in 1995 than it imported from the United States. This unbalanced trading relationship gave rise to a 1995 trade dispute between the two countries. The dispute had its roots in a series of talks between Japan and the United States begun in mid-1993. The subject of these talks

Learning Objectives:

1 Be familiar with the various policy instruments that governments use to restrict imports and promote exports.

2 Understand why some governments intervene in international trade to restrict imports and promote exports.

3 Appreciate the position of those who argue that government intervention in international trade can be self-defeating and typically fail to produce the gains that advocates of intervention claim.

4 Be familiar with the evolution, purpose, current status, and future prospects of the global trading system as embodied in the General Agreement on Tariffs and Trade and the World Trade Organization.

5 Understand the important implications for business practice of government intervention in international trade and of the current global trading system.

was Japan's trade imbalance with the United States and steps that might be taken to open the Japanese market to more foreign goods and services. In particular, the Clinton administration believed that various administrative trade barriers worked to exclude foreign companies from competing effectively in Japan's automobile, construction, telecommunications, insurance, and medical equipment industries.

For months the U.S. side had been pushing the Japanese government to agree to set numerical targets for foreign imports. The model was a 1991 agreement between Japan and the United States to increase foreign access to Japan's semiconductor market. That agreement contained an *expectation* that through improved market access, foreign companies would be able to gain 20 percent of the Japanese market for semiconductors by the end of 1992. The U.S. side chose to view the 20 percent figure as a *target*—as opposed to an expectation—and when the 20 percent figure was

reached the Americans concluded that numerical targets work, much to the horror of the Japanese, who had never seen the 20 percent figure as a target. The Japanese resisted the idea of numerical targets for what they saw as a very rational reason; Japan has a free market economy, and in a free market economy the government cannot tell consumers and companies how much of a foreign product to buy. To complicate matters, the government of Morihiro Hosokawa that was then in power was a fragile coalition, and Hosokawa was under strong domestic pressure to stand up to the United States on the issue of numerical targets. The Japanese refused to budge on numerical targets, and on February 11, 1994, the market access talks collapsed.

The American response was swift. On February 15 the U.S. government announced its intent to introduce formal trade sanctions against Japan for protecting its cellular telephone market. The United States stated that within 30 days it would produce a list of Japanese companies that would be punished with trade sanctions unless Japan opened its cellular telephone market. The cellular telephone market was chosen because it was relatively easy to make a case that administrative trade barriers had made it difficult for the U.S. cellular phone company Motorola Inc. to gain market share in Japan. Japan had originally agreed to open a big part of the cellular telephone market to Motorola in 1989. At that time the Japanese cellular phone service company IDO was building a mobile phone system using a rival technology developed by Nippon Telegraph and Telephone (NTT) to serve the highly populated Tokyo-Nagoya corridor. Under pressure from the Japanese government, IDO agreed to build a separate system using Motorola's technology. However, IDO could not easily afford to build two systems, so it concentrated on the one utilizing NTT technology. As of January 1994 it had 400 base stations for the NTT-compatible system compared with 110 for the Motorola system. This meant the NTT phones could be used in 94 percent of the area, compared with 61 percent for the Motorola phones. Given this disparity, it is hardly surprising that more than 310,000 customers chose NTT-compatible phones, and only 10,000 picked the Motorola phones. According to the U.S. government, the resulting lack of sales violated the comparable market access that Japan promised in 1989.

According to many observers, the real agenda of the U.S. government was to create as much uncertainty and anxiety in Japan as possible about Washington's next move. The belief was that uncertainty would drive up the value of the Japanese yen, thereby making Japan's exports more expensive and further hurting Japan's troubled exporting companies—companies that were already mired in their deepest recession since World War II. The net effect, it was hoped, would be to force the Japanese to come back to the bargaining table and make concessions on the key issue of numerical targets.

The U.S. government increased the pressure on Japan in early March when it revived a trade law known as "Super 301" that had lapsed in 1990. Super 301 is a provision in U.S. trade law that allows individuals or the government to retaliate against "unjustifiable, unreasonable, or discriminatory traders abroad." While few believed that the United States would apply Super 301, they saw the revival of this law as another step in the game of piling pressure on the Japanese in an attempt to bring them back to the bargaining table with concessions.

While the Japanese proved unwilling to give ground on the issue of numerical targets, they were willing to make some concessions in an attempt to avoid getting drawn into a trade war. To this extent, the U.S. tactics might be judged to have elicited the desired response. On March 13, 1994, Japan announced it had brokered a deal between Motorola and IDO that would increase Motorola's access to the Japanese market. The deal called for IDO to complete its investment in an additional 159 base stations for the Motorola phone system by autumn 1995. IDO also agreed to reallocate some of its radio frequency used by NTT to Motorola. Further, the Japanese government agreed to monitor IDO's progress in achieving these goals and to provide IDO with low interest rate loans to help it make the accelerated investments.[1]

Introduction

Our review of the classical trade theories of Smith, Ricardo, and Heckscher-Ohlin in Chapter 4 showed us that in a world without trade barriers, trade patterns will be determined by the relative productivity of different factors of production in different countries. Countries will specialize in the production of products that they can produce most efficiently, while importing products that they can produce less efficiently. Chapter 4 also laid out the intellectual case for free trade. Remember, free trade refers to a situation where a government does not attempt to restrict what its citizens can buy from another country or what they can sell to another country. As we saw in Chapter 4, the theories of Smith, Ricardo, and Heckscher-Ohlin predict that the consequences of free trade include both static economic gains (because free trade supports a higher level of domestic consumption and more efficient utilization of resources) and dynamic economic gains (because free trade stimulates economic growth and the creation of wealth).

In this chapter we look at the political reality of international trade. While many nations are nominally committed to free trade, in practice they adopt a neo-mercantilist stance, protecting their home market from foreign competition if possible, while simultaneously trying to gain access to the markets of others for their exports. The opening case illustrates these political realities. The case describes how the lopsided trade imbalance between the United States and Japan has given rise to a long-standing trade dispute between the two countries. In this dispute, the U.S. side claims that the Japanese government is limiting foreign access to the Japanese market, while benefiting from America's low trade barriers. The Japanese government denies that this is the case. Instead the Japanese claim that the U.S. side is making unreasonable demands that cannot be enforced by a government in a country with a free market system. Thus, both sides are implicitly charging that the other is adopting a neo-mercantilist position. Both sides may have a point, which is why this particular trade dispute has been so difficult to resolve. Nevertheless, despite denying the American charges, in 1994 the Japanese government felt pressured enough by the U.S. claims to make it easier for the U.S. firm Motorola to compete in the Japanese market for cellular telephone equipment.

In this chapter we explore the political and economic reasons that governments have for intervening in international trade. When governments intervene, they typically do so by restricting imports of goods and services into the nation while adopting policies that promote exports. Normally their motives for intervention are to protect domestic producers and jobs from foreign competition while increasing the foreign market for the products of domestic producers. We start by describing the range of policy instruments that governments use to intervene in international trade. This is followed by a detailed review of the various political and economic motives that governments have for intervention. In the third section of this chapter we consider how the case for free trade stands up in view of the various justifications given for government intervention in international trade.

Next we look at the emergence of the modern global trading system, which is based on multinational agreements and institutions, particularly the General Agreement on Tariffs and Trade (GATT) and its successor organization, the World Trade Organization (WTO). The GATT was established October 31, 1947, with the purpose of lowering trade barriers between its 23 member states. After eight rounds of negotiations between 1947 and 1994, each of which succeeded in progressively lower barriers to cross-border trade, the GATT was replaced by the WTO on January 1, 1995. With over 126 member states and the power to enforce global trade rules, the WTO has emerged as a central player in the ongoing transformation toward a global economy.

Instruments of Trade Policy

We review six main instruments of trade policy in this section: tariffs, subsidies, import quotas, voluntary export restraints, local content requirements, and administrative policies. Tariffs are the oldest and simplest instrument of trade policy. A fall in tariff barriers since the 1960s has been accompanied by a rise in nontariff barriers such as subsidies, quotas, and voluntary export restraints.

Tariffs

A **tariff** is a tax levied on imports. The oldest form of trade policy, tariffs fall into two categories. **Specific tariffs** are levied as a fixed charge for each unit of a good imported (for example, $3 per barrel of oil). **Ad valorem tariffs** are levied as a proportion of the value of the imported good. An example of an ad valorem tariff is the 25 percent tariff the U.S. government placed on imported light trucks (pickup trucks, four-wheel-drive vehicles, minivans) in the late 1980s.

The effect of a tariff is to raise the cost of imported products relative to domestic products. Thus, the 25 percent tariff on light trucks imported into the United States increased the price of European and Japanese light truck imports relative to U.S.-produced light trucks. The effect of this tariff has been to protect the market share of U.S. auto manufacturers (although a cynic might note that, in practice, all that the tariff did was speed up the plans of European and Japanese automobile companies to build light trucks in the United States). While the principal objective of most tariffs is to protect domestic producers and employees against foreign competition, they also raise revenue for the government. Until the introduction of the income tax, for example, the U.S. government raised most of its revenues from tariffs.

The important thing to understand about a tariff is who suffers and who gains. The government gains, because the tariff increases government revenues. Domestic producers gain, because the tariff affords them some protection against foreign competitors by increasing the cost of imported foreign goods. Consumers lose since they must pay more for certain imports. Whether the gains to the government and domestic producers exceed the loss to consumers depends on various factors such as the amount of the tariff, the importance of the imported good to domestic consumers, the number of jobs saved in the protected industry, and so on.

Although detailed consideration of these issues is beyond the scope of this book, two conclusions can be derived from a more advanced analysis.[2] First, tariffs are unambiguously pro-producer and anti-consumer. While they protect producers from foreign competitors, this restriction of supply also raises domestic prices. Thus, as noted in Chapter 4, a recent study by Japanese economists calculated that in 1989 restrictions on imports of foodstuffs, cosmetics, and chemicals into Japan cost the average Japanese consumer about $890 per year in the form of higher prices.[3] Almost all studies that have looked at the issue have determined that import tariffs impose significant costs on domestic consumers in the form of higher prices.[4] For another example, see the next "Country Focus," which looks at the cost to U.S. consumers of tariffs on imports into the United States.

The United States likes to think of itself as a nation that is committed to unrestricted free trade. In their negotiations with trading partners, such as China, the European Union, and Japan, U.S. trade representatives can often be heard claiming that the U.S. economy is an open one with few import tariffs. However, while it is true that tariffs on the importation of goods into the United States are low when compared to those found in many other industrialized nations, they still exist. A recent study concluded that iffs on economic activity in 21 industries with annual sales of $1 billion or more that the U.S. protected most heavily from foreign competition. The industries included apparel, ceramic tiles, luggage, and sugar. In most of these industries import tariffs had originally been imposed to protect U.S. firms and employees from low-cost foreign competitors. The typical reasoning behind the tariffs was that without such protection, U.S. firms in these industries would go out of business and substantial unemployment of higher prices. Even when the proceeds from the tariffs that accrued to the U.S. Treasury were added into the equation, the total cost to the nation of this protectionism still amounted to $10.2 billion per year, or over $50,000 per job saved.

Moreover, the two economists who undertook the study argued that these figures understated the true cost to the nation. They maintained that by making imports less competitive with American-made

The Costs of
Protectionism in the
United States

©Cameramann International, Ltd.

during the 1980s these tariffs cost U.S. consumers about $32 billion per year.

The study, by Gary Hufbauer and Kim Elliott of the Institute for International Economics, looked at the effect of import tar-

would result. So the tariffs were presented as having positive effects for the U.S. economy, not to mention the U.S. Treasury, which benefited from the associated revenues.

The study found, however, that while these import tariffs saved about 200,000 jobs in the protected industries that would otherwise have been lost to foreign competition, they also cost American consumers about $32 billion per year in the form

products, tariffs allowed domestic producers to charge more than they might otherwise because they did not have to compete with low-priced imports. By dampening competition, even a little, these tariffs removed an incentive for firms in the protected industries to become more efficient, thereby retarding economic progress. Further, the study's authors noted that if the tariffs had not been imposed, some of the $32 billion freed up every year would undoubtedly have been spent on other goods and services, and growth in these areas would have created additional jobs, thereby offsetting the loss of 200,000 jobs in the protected industries.[5]

A second point worth emphasizing is that tariffs reduce the overall efficiency of the world economy. They reduce efficiency because a protective tariff encourages domestic firms to produce products at home that, in theory, could be produced more efficiently abroad. The consequence is an inefficient utilization of resources. For example, tariffs on the importation of rice into South Korea has meant that the land of South Korean rice farmers has been used in an unproductive manner. It would make more sense for the South Koreans to purchase their rice from lower-cost foreign producers and to utilize the land now employed in rice production in some other way, such as growing foodstuffs that cannot be produced more efficiently elsewhere or for residential and industrial purposes.

Subsidies

subsidy Government payment to a domestic producer.

A **subsidy** is a government payment to a domestic producer. Subsidies take many forms, including cash grants, low-interest loans, tax breaks, and government equity participation in domestic firms. By lowering costs, subsidies help domestic producers in two ways: they help them compete against low-cost foreign imports and they help them gain export markets.

According to official national figures, government subsidies to industry in most industrialized countries during the late 1980s amounted to between 2 percent and 3.5 percent of the value of industrial output. (These figures exclude subsidies to agriculture and public services.) The average rate of subsidy in the United States was 0.5 percent; in Japan it was 1 percent; and in Europe it ranged from just below 2 percent in Great Britain and West Germany to as much as 6 to 7 percent in Sweden and Ireland.[6] These figures, however, almost certainly underestimate the true value of subsidies because they are based only on cash grants and ignore other kinds of subsidies (e.g., equity participation or low-interest loans). A more detailed study of subsidies within the European Union (EU) was undertaken by the EU Commission. This study found that subsidies to manufacturing enterprises in 1990 ranged from a low of 2 percent of total valued added in Great Britain to a high of 14.6 percent in Greece. Among the four largest EU countries, Italy was the worst offender; its subsidies are three times those of Great Britain, twice those of Germany, and 1.5 times those of France.[7]

The main gains from subsidies accrue to domestic producers, whose international competitiveness is increased as a result of them. Advocates of strategic trade policy (which as you will recall from Chapter 4 is an outgrowth of the new trade theory) favor the use of subsidies to help domestic firms achieve a dominant position in those industries where economies of scale are important and the world market is not large enough to profitably support more than a few firms (e.g., aerospace, semiconductors). According to this argument, subsidies can help a firm achieve first-mover advantages in an emerging industry (just as U.S. government subsidies, in the form of substantial R&D grants, allegedly helped Boeing). If this is achieved, further gains to the domestic economy arise from the employment and tax revenues generated by a major global company.

On the other hand, subsidies must be paid for. Typically governments pay for subsidies by taxing individuals. Therefore, whether subsidies generate national benefits that exceed their national costs is debatable. Moreover, in practice many subsidies are not that successful at increasing the international competitiveness of domestic producers. Rather, they tend to protect the inefficient, rather than promoting efficiency.

Import Quotas and Voluntary Export Restraints

An **import quota** is a direct restriction on the quantity of some good that may be imported into a country. The restriction is normally enforced by issuing import licenses to a group of individuals or firms. For example, the United States has a quota on cheese imports. The only firms allowed to import cheese are certain trading companies, each of which is allocated the right to import a maximum number of pounds of cheese each year. In some cases the right to sell is given directly to the governments of exporting countries. This is the case for sugar and textile imports in the United States.

import quota Direct restriction on the quantity of some goods that may be imported into a country.

A variant on the import quota is the voluntary export restraint (VER). A **voluntary export restraint** is a quota on trade imposed by the exporting country, typically at the request of the importing country's government. One of the most famous examples is the limitation on auto exports to the United States enforced by Japanese automobile producers in 1981. A response to direct pressure from the U.S. government, this VER limited Japanese imports to no more than 1.68 million vehicles per year. The agreement was revised in 1984 to allow Japanese producers to import 1.85 million vehicles per year. In 1985 the agreement was allowed to lapse, but the Japanese government indicated its intentions to continue to restrict exports to the United States to 1.85 million vehicles per year.[8]

voluntary export restraint Quota on trade imposed by the exporting country, typically at the request of the importing country.

Foreign producers agree to VERs because they fear that if they do not, more damaging punitive tariffs or import quotas might follow. Agreeing to a VER is seen as a way of making the best of a bad situation by appeasing protectionist pressures in a country.

As with tariffs and subsidies, both import quotas and VERs benefit domestic producers by limiting import competition. Quotas do not benefit consumers. An import quota or VER always raises the domestic price of an imported good. Using a quota or VER to limit imports to a low percentage of the market bids up the price for that limited foreign supply. In the case of the automobile industry, for example, the VER increased the price for the limited supply of Japanese imports into the United States. As a result, according to a study by the U.S. Federal Trade Commission, the automobile industry VER cost U.S. consumers about $1 billion per year between 1981 and 1985. That $1 billion per year went to Japanese producers in the form of higher prices.[9]

The 1994 GATT and new WTO rules contain provisions that "gray area measures" such as VERs will be eliminated by member states within four years of the January 1, 1995, establishment of the WTO. Whether this will occur remains to be seen, but there has been a marked absence of new VERs announced since 1994.

Local Content Requirements

A **local content requirement** demands that some specific fraction of a good be produced domestically. The requirement can be expressed either in physical terms (e.g., 75 percent of component parts for this product must be produced locally) or in value terms (e.g., 75 percent of the value of this product must be produced locally). Local content requirements have been widely used by developing countries to shift their manufacturing base from the simple assembly of

local content requirement Government order that some specific fraction of a good be produced domestically.

products whose parts are manufactured elsewhere into the local manufacture of component parts. More recently, the issue of local content has been raised by several developed countries. In the United States, for example, pressure is building to insist that 75 percent of the component parts that go into cars built in the United States by Japanese companies such as Toyota and Honda be manufactured in the United States. Both Toyota and Honda have reacted to such pressures by announcing their intention to buy more American manufactured parts.

For a domestic producer of component parts, local content requirements provide protection in the same way an import quota does: by limiting foreign competition. The aggregate economic effects are also the same; domestic producers benefit, but the restrictions raise the prices of imported components. In turn, higher prices for imported components are passed on to consumers of the final product in the form of higher final prices. So as with all trade policies, local content requirements tend to benefit producers and not consumers.

Administrative Policies

In addition to the formal instruments of trade policy, governments of all types sometimes use a range of informal or administrative policies to restrict imports and boost exports. **Administrative trade policies** are bureaucratic rules that are designed to make it difficult for imports to enter a country. Some would argue that the Japanese are the masters of this kind of trade barrier. In recent years Japan's formal tariff and nontariff barriers have been among the lowest in the world. However, critics charge that their informal administrative barriers to imports more than compensate for this.

One example is that of tulip bulbs; the Netherlands exports tulip bulbs to almost every country in the world except Japan. The reason is that Japanese customs inspectors insist on checking every tulip bulb by cutting it vertically down the middle, and even Japanese ingenuity cannot put them back together! Another example concerns the U.S. express mail operator Federal Express. Federal Express has had a tough time expanding its global express services into Japan, primarily because Japanese customs inspectors insist on opening a large proportion of express packages to check for pornography—a process that can delay an "express" package for days.

It would be wrong to think that Japan is the only country that engages in such policies. France required that all imported videocassette recorders arrive through a small customs entry point that was both remote and poorly staffed. The resulting delays kept Japanese VCRs out of the French market until a VER agreement was negotiated.[10] As with all instruments of trade policy, administrative instruments benefit producers and hurt consumers, who are denied access to possibly superior foreign products.

The Case for Government Intervention

Now that we have reviewed the various instruments of trade policy that governments can use, it is time to take a more detailed look at the case for government intervention in international trade. In general, there are two types of argument for government intervention, political and economic. Political arguments for intervention are concerned with protecting the interests of certain groups within a nation (normally producers), often at the expense of other groups (normally consumers). Economic arguments for intervention are typically concerned with boosting the overall wealth of a nation (to the benefit of all, both producers and consumers).

Political Arguments for Intervention

Political arguments for government intervention cover a range of issues, including protecting jobs, protecting industries deemed important for national security, and retaliating against unfair foreign competition. Political arguments for government intervention are not always based on careful economic reasoning. Thus, they tend to be relatively easy for economists to refute.

PROTECTING JOBS AND INDUSTRIES Perhaps the most common political argument for government intervention is that it is necessary for protecting jobs and industries from foreign competition. The voluntary export restraints (VERs) that offered some protection to the U.S. automobile, machine tool, and steel industries during the 1980s were motivated by such considerations. Similarly, Japan's quotas on rice imports are aimed at protecting jobs in that country's agricultural sector. The same motive was behind establishment of the Common Agricultural Policy (CAP) by the European Union. The CAP was designed to protect the jobs of Europe's politically powerful farmers by restricting imports and guaranteeing prices. However, the higher prices that resulted from the CAP have cost Europe's consumers dearly. This is true of most attempts to protect jobs and industries through government intervention. As we saw earlier in the chapter, all that the VER in the automobile industry succeeded in doing was raising the price of Japanese imports, at a cost of $1 billion per year to U.S. consumers.

In addition to hurting consumers, trade controls may sometimes hurt the producers they are intended to protect. For example, some have argued that a 1980s VER adopted to protect the U.S. machine tool industry from foreign competition was ultimately self-defeating. By limiting Japanese and Taiwanese machine tool imports, the VER raised the prices of machine tools purchased by U.S. manufacturers to levels above those prevailing in the world market. In turn, this raised the capital costs of the U.S. manufacturing industry in general, thereby decreasing its international competitiveness.

NATIONAL SECURITY Countries sometimes argue that it is necessary to protect certain industries because they are important for national security. Defense-related industries often get this kind of attention (e.g., aerospace, advanced electronics, semiconductors, and so on). Although not as common as it used to be, this argument is still made occasionally. Those in favor of protecting the U.S. semiconductor industry from foreign competition, for example, argue that semiconductors are now such important components of defense products that it would be dangerous to rely primarily on foreign producers for them. In 1986 this argument helped persuade the federal government to support Sematech, a consortium of 14 U.S. semiconductor companies that accounts for 90 percent of the U.S. industry's revenues. Sematech's mission is to conduct joint research into manufacturing techniques that can be parceled out to members. The U.S. government provides a $100 million per year subsidy to Sematech.

RETALIATION   Some argue that governments should use the threat to intervene in trade policy as a bargaining tool to help open foreign markets and force trading partners to "play by the rules of the game." Successive U.S. governments have been among those that adopted this "get tough" approach. The opening case illustrates how the U.S. government recently used the threat of imposing trade sanctions on Japanese imports, including punitive tariffs, to pry open the Japanese market for cellular telephone equipment. Similarly, the U.S. government also successfully used the same threat of punitive trade sanctions to get the Chinese government to enforce its intellectual property laws. As you will recall from Chapter 2, lax enforcement of these laws had given rise to massive copyright infringements in China that have been costing U.S. companies such as Microsoft hundreds of millions of dollars per year in lost sales revenues. After the United States threatened to impose 100 percent tariffs on a range of Chinese imports into the United States, and after harsh words between officials from the two countries, the Chinese backed down at the 11th hour and agreed to tighter enforcement of intellectual property regulations.[11]

If it works, such a politically motivated rationale for government intervention may liberalize trade and bring with it resulting economic gains. It is a risky strategy, however; the country that is being pressured may not back down and instead may respond to the punitive tariffs by raising trade barriers of its own. This is exactly what the Chinese government threatened to do when pressured by the United States, although they ultimately did back down. If a government does not back down, however, the results could be higher trade barriers all around and an economic loss to all involved.

Economic Arguments for Intervention

With the development of the new trade theory and strategic trade policy (see Chapter 4), the economic arguments for government intervention have undergone something of a renaissance in recent years. Until the early 1980s, most economists saw little benefit in government intervention and strongly advocated a free trade policy. This position has changed somewhat with the development of strategic trade policy, although as we will see in the next section, there are still strong economic arguments for sticking to a free trade stance.

THE INFANT INDUSTRY ARGUMENT   The infant industry argument is by far the oldest economic argument for government intervention. It was first proposed by Alexander Hamilton in 1792. According to this argument, many developing countries have a potential comparative advantage in manufacturing, but new manufacturing industries there cannot initially compete with well-established industries in developed countries. To allow manufacturing to get a toehold, the argument is that governments should temporarily support new industries (with tariffs, import quotas, and subsidies) until they have grown strong enough to meet international competition.

This argument has had substantial appeal for the governments of developing nations during the past 50 years. Primarily as a result of pressure from the developing world, the infant industry argument was recognized by the GATT as a legitimate reason for protectionism. New WTO rules allow least developed countries to use quantitative import restrictions and export subsidies under certain circumstances to promote infant industries.

Nevertheless, many economists remain very critical of this argument. They make two main points. First, protecting manufacturing from foreign competition does no good unless the protection makes the industry efficient. In case after case, however, protection seems to have done little more than foster the development of inefficient industries that have little hope of ever competing in the world market. Brazil, for example, built up the world's 10th largest auto industry behind tariff barriers and quotas. Once those barriers were removed in the late 1980s, however, foreign imports soared and the industry was forced to face up to the fact that after 30 years of protection, the Brazilian industry was one of the world's most inefficient.[12]

A second point is that the infant industry argument relies on an assumption that firms are unable to make efficient long-term investments by borrowing money from the domestic or international capital market. Consequently, governments have been required to subsidize long-term investments. Given the development of global capital markets over the past 20 years, this assumption no longer looks as valid as it once did (see Chapter 9 for details). Today, if a developing country really does have a potential comparative advantage in a manufacturing industry, firms in that country should be able to borrow money from the capital markets to finance the required investments. Moreover, given financial support, firms based in countries with a potential comparative advantage have an incentive to go through the necessary period of initial losses in order to make long-run gains without requiring government protection. This is what many Taiwanese and South Korean firms did in industries such as textiles, semiconductors, machine tools, steel, and shipping. Thus, given efficient global capital markets, the only industries that would require government protection would be those that are not worthwhile.

STRATEGIC TRADE POLICY The strategic trade policy argument has been proposed by the new trade theorists.[13] We reviewed the basic argument in Chapter 4 when we considered the new trade theory. The new trade theory argues that in industries where the existence of substantial scale economies implies that the world market will profitably support only a few firms, countries may predominate in the export of certain products simply because they had firms that were able to capture first-mover advantages. The dominance of Boeing in the commercial aircraft industry is attributed to such factors.

Against this background, there are two components to the strategic trade policy argument. First, it is argued that a government can help raise national income if it can somehow ensure that the firm or firms to gain first-mover advantages are domestic rather than foreign enterprises. Thus, according to the strategic trade policy argument, a government should use subsidies to support promising firms that are active in newly emerging industries. Advocates of this argument point out that the substantial R&D grants that the U.S. government gave Boeing in the 1950s and 60s probably helped tilt the field of competition in the newly emerging market for jet passenger planes in Boeing's favor. (Boeing's 707 jet airliner was derived from a military plane.) Similar arguments are now made with regard to Japan's dominance in the production of liquid crystal display screens (used in laptop computers).

Although these screens were invented in the United States, the Japanese government, in cooperation with major electronics companies, targeted this industry for research support in the late 1970s and early 80s. The result was that Japanese firms, not U.S. firms, subsequently captured the first-mover advantages in this market.

The second component of the strategic trade policy argument is that it might pay government to intervene in an industry if it helps domestic firms overcome the barriers to entry created by foreign firms that have already reaped first-mover advantages. This catch-up argument underlies government support of Airbus Industrie, Boeing's major competitor. Formed in 1966, Airbus is a consortium of four companies from Great Britain, France, Germany, and Spain. When it began production in the mid-1970s it had less than 5 percent of the world commercial aircraft market. By 1990 it had increased its share to over 30 percent and was beginning to threaten Boeing's dominance. How has Airbus achieved this feat? According to the U.S. government, the answer is a $13.5 billion subsidy from the governments of Great Britain, France, Germany, and Spain.[14] Without this subsidy, Airbus would have never been able to break into the world market. In another example, the rise to dominance of the Japanese semiconductor industry, despite the first-mover advantages enjoyed by U.S. firms, is attributed to intervention by the Japanese government. In this case the government did not subsidize the costs of domestic manufacturers. Rather, it protected the Japanese home market while pursuing policies that ensured Japanese companies got access to the necessary manufacturing and product know-how.

If these arguments are correct, they clearly suggest a rationale for government intervention in international trade. Specifically, governments should target technologies that may be important in the future and use subsidies to support development work aimed at commercializing those technologies. Government should provide export subsidies until the domestic firms have established first-mover advantages in the world market. Government support may also be justified if it can help domestic firms overcome the first-mover advantages enjoyed by foreign competitors and emerge as viable competitors in the world market (as in the Airbus and semiconductor examples). In this case, a combination of home market protection and export-promoting subsidies may be called for.

The Revised Case for Free Trade

As we have just seen, the strategic trade policy arguments of the new trade theorists suggest an economic justification for government intervention in international trade. This justification challenges the rationale for unrestricted free trade found in the work of classic trade theorists such as Adam Smith and David Ricardo. In response to this challenge to economic orthodoxy, a number of economists—including some of those responsible for the development of the new trade theory, such as Paul Krugman of MIT—have been quick to point out that although strategic trade policy looks nice in theory, in practice it may be unworkable. This response to the strategic trade policy argument constitutes the revised case for free trade.[15]

Retaliation and Trade War

Krugman argues that strategic trade policy aimed at establishing domestic firms in a dominant position in a global industry are beggar-thy-neighbor policies that boost national income at the expense of other countries. A country that attempts to use such policies will probably provoke retaliation. In many cases, the resulting trade war between two or more interventionist governments will leave all countries involved worse off than if a hands-off approach had been adopted in the first place. If the U.S. government were to respond to the Airbus subsidy by increasing its own subsidies to Boeing, for example, the result might be that the subsidies would cancel each other out. In the process, both European and U.S. taxpayers would end up supporting an expensive and pointless trade war, and both Europe and the United States would be worse off.

Krugman may be right about the danger of a strategic trade policy leading to a trade war. The problem, however, is how to respond when one's competitors are already being supported by government subsidies; that is, how should Boeing and the United States respond to the subsidization of Airbus? According to Krugman, the answer is probably not to engage in retaliatory action, but to help establish rules of the game that minimize the use of trade-distorting subsidies in the first place. This, of course, is what GATT seeks to do.

Domestic Politics

Governments do not always act in the national interest when they intervene in the economy. Instead they are influenced by politically important interest groups. The European Union's support for the Common Agricultural Policy, which arose because of the political power of French and German farmers, is an example of this. The CAP benefited inefficient farmers and the politicians who relied on the farm vote, but no one else. Thus, a further reason for not embracing strategic trade policy, according to Krugman, is that such a policy is almost certain to be captured by special interest groups within the economy, who will distort it to their own ends. Krugman concludes that with regard to the United States:

> To ask the Commerce Department to ignore special interest politics while formulating detailed policy for many industries is not realistic; to establish a blanket policy of free trade, with exceptions granted only under extreme pressure, may not be the optimal policy according to the theory but may be the best policy that the country is likely to get.[16]

Development of the Global Trading System

We have seen in this chapter and the previous one that there are strong economic arguments for supporting unrestricted free trade. While many governments have recognized the value of these arguments, they have been unwilling to unilaterally lower their trade barriers for fear that other nations might not follow suit. Consider the problem that two neighboring countries, say France and Italy, face when considering whether to lower barriers to trade. In principle, the government of Italy might favor lowering trade barriers, but it might be unwilling to do so for fear that France will not do the same. Instead, the Italians might fear that the French will take advantage of Italy's low barriers to enter the Italian market, while at the same time continuing to shut Italian products out of their market by high trade barriers. The French government might feel that it faces exactly the same dilemma. The essence of the problem is a lack of trust between the governments of France and Italy. Both governments recognize that their respective nations will benefit from lower trade barriers between them, but neither government is willing to lower barriers for fear that the other might not follow.[17]

How is such a deadlock to be resolved? One answer is for both countries to negotiate a set of rules that will govern cross-border trade and lower trade barriers. But who is to monitor the governments to make sure they are not cheating? And who is to impose sanctions on a government that cheats? Both governments could set up an independent body whose function is to act as a referee. This referee could monitor trade between the countries, make sure that no side cheats, and impose sanctions on a country if it does break the rules in the trade game.

While it might sound unlikely that any government would compromise its national sovereignty by submitting to such an arrangement, since World War II an international trading framework has evolved that has exactly these features. For its first 50 years this framework was known as the General Agreement on Tariffs and Trade (GATT). Since 1995 it has been known as the World Trade Organization (WTO). Here we look at the evolution and workings of GATT and the WTO. We begin, however, with a brief discussion of the pre-GATT history of world trade, since this helps set the scene.

From Smith to the Great Depression

As we saw in Chapter 4, the intellectual case for free trade goes back to the late 18th century and the work of Adam Smith and David Ricardo. Free trade as a government policy was first officially embraced by Great Britain in 1846, when the British Parliament repealed the Corn Laws. The Corn Laws placed a high tariff on imports of foreign corn in order to raise government revenues and protect British corn producers. There had been annual motions in Parliament in favor of free trade since the 1820s when David Ricardo was a member of Parliament. However, agricultural protection was withdrawn only as a result of a protracted debate when the effects of a harvest failure in Britain were compounded by the imminent threat of famine in Ireland. Faced with considerable hardship and suffering among the populace, Parliament narrowly reversed its long-held position.

During the next 80 years, Great Britain, as one of the world's dominant trading powers, pushed the case for trade liberalization, but the British government was a voice in the wilderness. Its policy of unilateral free trade was not reciprocated by its major trading partners. Britain was able to maintain this policy for so long because, as the world's largest exporting nation, it had far more to lose from a trade war than did any other country.

By the 1930s, however, the British attempt to stimulate free trade was buried under the economic rubble of the Great Depression. The Great Depression had roots in the failure of the world economy to mount a sustained economic recovery after the end of World War I in 1918. Things got worse in 1929 with the U.S. stock market collapse and the subsequent run on the U.S. banking system. Economic problems were compounded in 1930 when the U.S. Congress passed the Smoot-Hawley Act. Aimed at avoiding rising unemployment by protecting domestic industries and diverting consumer demand away from foreign products, the Smoot-Hawley Act erected an enormous wall of tariffs. Almost every industry was rewarded with its "made-to-order" tariff. A particularly odd aspect of the Smoot-Hawley tariff-raising binge was that the United States was running a balance-of-payment surplus at the time and it was the world's largest creditor nation. The Smoot-Hawley Act hurt employment abroad. Other countries reacted to the U.S. action by raising their own tariff barriers. U.S. exports tumbled in response, and the world slid further into the Great Depression.[18]

1947–79: GATT, Trade Liberalization, and Economic Growth

The economic damage caused by the beggar-thy-neighbor trade policies that the Smoot-Hawley tariffs ushered in profoundly influenced the economic institutions and ideology of the post–World War II world. The United States emerged from the war not only victorious but also economically dominant. After the debacle of the Great Depression, opinion in the U.S. Congress had swung strongly in favor of free trade. As a consequence, under U.S. leadership, GATT was established in 1947. At the time, GATT had 23 member states, mostly advanced industrialized nations.

GATT was a multilateral agreement whose objective was to liberalize trade by eliminating tariffs, subsidies, import quotas, and the like. Between 1947 and 1984 GATT's membership grew from 23 to more than 120 nations. GATT did not attempt to liberalize trade restrictions in one fell swoop; that would have been impossible. Rather, tariff reduction was spread over eight rounds. The last, the Uruguay Round, was launched in 1986 and completed in December 1993. In these rounds mutual tariff reductions were negotiated among all members, who then committed themselves not to raise import tariffs above negotiated rates. GATT regulations were enforced by a mutual monitoring mechanism. If a country believed that one of its trading partners was violating a GATT regulation, it could ask the Geneva-based bureaucracy that administered GATT to investigate. If GATT investigators found the complaints to be valid, member countries could be asked to pressure the offending party to change its policies. In general, such pressure was sufficient to get an offending country to change its policies. If it was not, the offending country could in theory have been expelled from GATT.

In its early years GATT was by most measures very successful. In the United States, for example, the average tariff declined by nearly 92 percent over the 33 years spanning the Geneva Round of 1947 and the Tokyo Round of 1973–79 (see Figure 5.1). Consistent with the theoretical arguments first advanced by Ricardo, the move toward free trade under GATT appeared to stimulate economic growth. From 1953 to 1963 world trade grew at an annual rate of 6.1 percent, and world income grew at an annual rate of 4.3 percent. Performance from 1963 to 1973 was even better; world trade grew at 8.9 percent annually, and world income grew at 5.1 percent.[19]

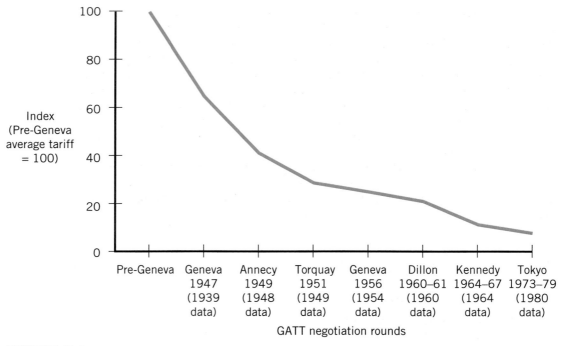

FIGURE 5.1

Average Reductions in U.S. Tariff Rates, 1947–79

Note: Indexes are calculated from percentage reductions in average weighted tariff rates given in Finger, 1979 (Table 1, p. 425), World Bank, 1987 (Table 8.1, p. 136), and World Bank, *World Development Report*, (New York: Oxford University Press, 1994). Weighted average U.S. tariff rate after Tokyo Round was 4.6 percent (World Bank, 1987).

1980–93: Disturbing Trends

During the 1980s and early 1990s the world trading system erected by GATT began to be strained as protectionist pressures arose around the world. There were three main reasons for the rise in protectionist pressures during the 1980s. First, the economic success of Japan strained the world trading system. Japan was in ruins when GATT was created. By the early 1980s, however, it had become the world's second largest economy and its largest exporter. Japan's success in such industries as automobiles and semiconductors by itself might have been enough to strain the world trading system. Things were made worse, however, by the widespread perception in the West that despite low tariff rates and subsidies, Japanese markets were closed to imports and foreign investment by administrative trade barriers.

Second, the world trading system was further strained by the persistent trade deficit in the world's largest economy, the United States. Although the deficit peaked in 1987 at over $170 billion, by the end of 1992 the annual rate was still running at about $80 billion. From a political perspective, the matter was worsened by the fact that in 1992 the United States also ran a $45 billion deficit in its trade with Japan—a country perceived as not playing by the rules. The consequences of the U.S. deficit included painful adjustments in industries such as automobiles, machine tools, semiconductors, steel, and textiles, where domestic producers steadily lost market share to foreign competitors. The resulting unemployment gave rise to renewed protectionist pressures in the U.S. Congress.

A third reason for the trend toward greater protectionism was that many countries found ways to get around GATT regulations. Bilateral voluntary export restraints (VERs) circumvent GATT agreements because neither the importing country nor the exporting country complains to the GATT bureaucracy in Geneva—and without a complaint, the GATT bureaucracy can do nothing. Exporting countries agreed to VERs to avoid more damaging punitive tariffs. One of the best known examples is the VER between Japan and the United States, under which Japanese producers promised to limit their auto imports into the United States as a way of defusing growing trade tensions. According to a World Bank study, 13 percent of the imports of industrialized countries in 1981 were subjected to nontariff trade barriers such as VERs. By 1986 this figure had increased to 16 percent. The most rapid rise was in the United States, where the value of imports affected by nontariff barriers (primarily VERs) increased by 23 percent between 1981 and 1986.[20]

The Uruguay Round and the World Trade Organization

Against the background of rising protectionist pressures, in 1986 GATT members embarked on their eighth round of negotiations to reduce tariffs, the Uruguay Round (so named because they took place in Uruguay). This was the most difficult round of negotiations yet, primarily because it was in many ways also the most ambitious. Until now GATT rules had applied only to trade in manufactured goods and commodities. In the Uruguay Round member countries sought to extend GATT rules to cover trade in services. They also sought to write rules governing the protection of intellectual property, to reduce agricultural subsidies, to curtail the rise of nontariff trade barriers such as VERs, and to strengthen GATT's monitoring and enforcement mechanisms.

The Uruguay Round dragged on for seven years. For a time it looked as if an agreement might not be possible, raising fears that the world might slip into a trade war. The main impediment to an agreement was a long-standing dispute between the United States and the European Union on agricultural subsidies. An agreement had to be reached before December 16, 1993, which was when the "fast-track negotiating authority" granted to U.S. President Bill Clinton by the U.S. Congress would have expired. Had this authority expired, any agreement would have needed approval by the U.S. Congress as a whole, rather than just the president, a much more difficult proposition. An 11th-hour compromise on agricultural subsidies—which reduced the level of subsidies significantly but not by as much as the United States had wanted—saved the day, and an agreement was reached December 15, 1993. The agreement was formally signed by member states at a meeting in Marrakech, Morocco, on April 15, 1994. It went into effect July 1, 1995.

The most important components of the Uruguay Round agreement are detailed in Table 5.1. The Uruguay Round agreement has the following effects:

- Tariffs on industrial goods will be reduced by more than one-third.
- Agricultural subsidies will be substantially reduced.
- GATT fair trade and market access rules will be extended to cover a wide range of services.

TABLE 5.1

Main Features of the Uruguay Round Agreement

Up to 1993	The 1993 Agreement	Main Impact
Industrial Tariffs		
Backbone of previous GATT rounds. Tariffs on industrial goods average 5% in industrialized countries—down from 40% in the late 1940s.	Rich countries will cut tariffs on industrial goods by more than one-third. Tariffs will be scrapped on over 40% of manufactured goods.	Easier access to world markets for exports of industrial goods. Lower prices for consumers.
Agriculture		
High farm subsidies and protected markets in United States and European Community lead to over-production and dumping.	Subsidies and other barriers to trade in agricultural products will be cut over six years. Subsidies cut by 20%. All import barriers will be converted to tariffs and cut by 36%.	Better market opportunities for efficient food producers. Lower prices for consumers. Restraint of farm subsidies war.
Services		
GATT rules do not extend to services. Many countries protect service industries from international competition.	GATT rules on fair trade principles extended to cover many services. Failure to reach agreement on financial services and telecommunications. Special talks will continue.	Increase in trade in services. Further liberalization of trade in services now seems likely.
Intellectual Property		
Standards of protection for patents, copyrights, and trademarks vary widely. Ineffective enforcement of national laws a growing source of trade friction.	Extensive agreements on patents, copyrights, and trademarks. International standards of protection and agreements for effective enforcement all established.	Increased protection and reduction of intellectual property piracy will benefit producers of intellectual property (e.g., computer software firms, performing artists). Will increase technology transfer.
Textiles		
Rich countries have restricted imports of textiles and clothing through bilateral quotas under Multi-Fiber Arrangement (MFA).	MFA quotas progressively dismantled over 10 years and tariffs reduced. Normal GATT rules will apply at end of 10 years.	Increased trade in textiles should benefit developing countries. Reduced prices for consumers worldwide.
GATT Rules		
GATT remains the same as when drafted in 1947, even though many more countries have entered the world trading community and trade patterns have shifted.	Many GATT rules revised and updated. They include codes on customs valuation and import licensing, customs unions and free trade areas, and rules dealing with waivers from GATT regulations.	Greater transparency, security, and predictability in trading policies.
World Trade Organization		
GATT originally envisioned as part of an International Trade Organization. ITO never ratified and GATT applied provisionally.	GATT becomes a permanent world trade body covering goods, services, and intellectual property with a common disputes procedure. WTO to implement results of Uruguay Round.	More effective advocacy and policing of the international trading system.

Source: "The GATT Deal," a special report contained in the *Financial Times*, December 16, 1993, pp. 4–7.

- GATT rules will also now be extended to provide enhanced protection for patents, copyrights, and trademarks (intellectual property).
- Barriers on trade in textiles will be significantly reduced over 10 years.
- GATT rules will be much clearer and stronger.
- World Trade Organization will be created to implement the GATT agreement.

SERVICES AND INTELLECTUAL PROPERTY In the long run the extension of GATT rules to cover services and intellectual property may be particularly significant. Until 1995 GATT rules have applied only to manufactured goods and commodities. In 1994 world trade in services amounted to $1,100 billion out of a total of $5,190 billion.[21] Extending GATT rules to this important trading arena could significantly increase both the total share of world trade accounted for by services and the overall volume of world trade. Moreover, the extension of GATT rules to cover intellectual property will make it much easier for high-technology companies to do business in developing nations where intellectual property rules have historically been poorly enforced (see Chapter 2 for details). High-technology companies will now have a mechanism to force countries to prohibit the piracy of intellectual property.

THE WORLD TRADE ORGANIZATION The clarification and strengthening of GATT rules and the creation of the World Trade Organization hold out the promise of more effective policing and enforcement of GATT rules. This should promote trade and so boost overall economic growth and development. The WTO will act as an umbrella organization that will encompass GATT along with two new sister bodies, one on services and the other on intellectual property. The WTO will take over responsibility for arbitrating trade disputes and monitoring the trade policies of member countries. While the WTO will operate as GATT now does—on the basis of consensus—in the area of dispute settlement, member countries will no longer be able to block adoption of arbitration reports. Arbitration panel reports on trade disputes between member countries will be automatically adopted by the WTO unless there is a consensus to reject them. Countries that have been found by the arbitration panel to violate GATT rules may appeal to a permanent appellate body, but its verdict will be binding. If offenders then fail to comply with the recommendations of the arbitration panel, trading partners will have the right to compensation or, as a last resort, to impose (commensurate) trade sanctions. Every stage of the procedure will be subject to strict time limits. Thus, the WTO will have something that the GATT never had—teeth.[22]

IMPLICATIONS OF THE URUGUAY ROUND Some general implications of the GATT deal are noted in Table 5.1. On balance, the world is better off with a GATT deal than without it. Without the deal there was a very real possibility that the world might have slipped into increasingly dangerous trade wars, which might have triggered a recession. With a GATT deal concluded, the current world trading system looks secure, and there is a good possibility that the world economy will now grow faster than would otherwise have been the case. Estimates as to the overall impact of the GATT agreement, however, are not that dramatic. Three studies undertaken in mid-1993 (before the agreement was finalized) estimated that the deal will add between

$213 billion and $274 billion in 1992 U.S. dollars to aggregate world income by 2002—or about 0.75 percent to 1 percent of gross global income by that time.[23] Others argue that these figures underestimate the potential gain because they do not factor in the gains from the liberalization of trade in services, stronger trade rules, and greater business confidence. Taking such factors into account, it is claimed that due to the GATT agreement global economic output could be as much as 8 percent higher than it would otherwise have been by 2002.[24] Whatever figure is closer to the truth, it is perhaps best to keep in mind what a successful GATT agreement helps avoid: the risk of a trade war that might reduce global economic growth and raise prices for consumers around the globe.

As for the implications for individual firms, here there emerge some clear winners—and some that have not done so well—in the GATT deal. Two big winners in the United States are Caterpillar Inc. and Deere & Co., both manufacturers of heavy construction equipment. The GATT deal eliminates import tariffs on the construction equipment and engines that these companies produce. Caterpillar estimates that the deal will add $125 million to its annual sales of $10 billion and result in another 800 jobs at Caterpillar and a further 1,600 jobs at Caterpillar's suppliers. Other big winners include many small exporters around the world, who will find that they like the simplified import licensing rules and steps for harmonizing customs procedures contained in the GATT deal. These rules promise to simplify the procedures for exporting—procedures that raise exporting costs and are argued to deter many small firms from getting into the export business.

Not everyone is pleased with the deal. While pharmaceutical companies are pleased that tariffs on drugs will be phased out over the next few years, they expressed disappointment that it will take 10 years to phase in patent protection for their products (weak patent protection in many countries has led to local competitors violating patents and copying the successful drugs of multinational pharmaceutical firms). Among the disappointed were financial services companies, particularly big banks. They had hoped the GATT deal would eliminate many of the barriers that prevent them from selling their financial services across borders, but a failure to reach agreement here resulted in financial services being excluded from the deal to extend GATT rules to services. Also disappointed was the Hollywood film and television industry. Hollywood had hoped to use GATT to break down European quotas that limit the number of U.S. movies that can be broadcast on European TV, but opposition from the French government led to this part of the deal being dropped in a last-minute compromise.[25]

WTO: EARLY EXPERIENCE   The first 18 months in the life of the WTO suggest that its policing and enforcement mechanisms are having a positive effect.[26] As of July 31, 1996, 51 trade disputes had been brought to the WTO for arbitration. This compares with 196 cases that were handled by GATT over almost half a century. The fact that countries are using the WTO represents an important vote of confidence in the organization's dispute resolution procedures.

The top four trading nations—the United States, EU, Japan, and Canada—dominated the dispute settlement process, with one or more involved in 43 cases as either a complainant or defendant. But encouraged perhaps by the tougher system, developing countries are also starting to make more use of the settlement procedures. Developing countries had launched 21 complaints by July 1996, including six against the United States and six against the European Union.

The backing of the leading trading powers has been crucial to the WTO's early success. Initially, there were fears that the United States might undermine the system by continuing to rely on unilateral measures when it suited or by refusing to accept WTO verdicts. These fears were enhanced in 1995 when the United States refused to bring a dispute with Japan over trade in autos and auto parts to the WTO (that dispute was settled bilaterally). Since then, however, the United States has emerged as the biggest user of the WTO, bringing 18 complaints on everything from food inspection procedures in South Korea to taxation of foreign film revenues in Turkey.

The United States has also proved willing to accept WTO rulings that go against it. The United States agreed to implement a WTO judgment that called for the country to remove discriminatory antipollution regulations that were applied to gasoline imports. In a dispute with India over textile imports, the United States rescinded quotas before a WTO panel could start work. And in June 1996 the United States preempted the establishment of a WTO panel by revoking punitive tariffs placed on EU food and drink exports that were originally imposed in 1988 in retaliation for the EU's ban on hormone-treated meat (the EU's ban is now the subject of a WTO dispute brought by the United States).

The WTO has been successful in encouraging the settlement of trade disputes before a full investigation has been completed. By June 1996 nine cases had been formally withdrawn, and several others were resolved before a formal ruling by the WTO. Despite its early success, questions still remain as to how effective the WTO's dispute procedures will ultimately be. The first real test of the procedures will arise when the WTO has to arbitrate a politically sensitive case, particularly one that involves the United States, where a significant and vocal minority in Congress argues that the WTO infringes on the national sovereignty of the United States.

The Future of the WTO: Unresolved Issues

The 1994 GATT deal still leaves a lot to be done on the international trade front. Substantial trade barriers still remain in areas such as agriculture, financial services, broadcast entertainment, and telecommunications—although these seem likely to be reduced eventually. Talks on further liberalization of agricultural trade are due to begin in 1999, and a fresh round of talks on services is scheduled for 2000. And there is still a whole range of issues that the WTO has yet to deal with but increasingly will need to. Three of the most important areas for future development are environmentalism, workers' rights, and foreign direct investment.[27]

High on the list of the WTO's future concerns will be the interaction of environmental and trade policies and the issue of how best to promote sustainable development and ecological well-being without resorting to protectionism. The WTO will have to find ways to deal with the increasingly vigorous claims by environmentalists that expanded international trade encourages companies to locate factories in areas where they are freer to pollute and degrade the environment.[28]

Paralleling environmental concerns are concerns that free trade encourages firms to shift their production to countries with low labor rates where workers' rights are routinely violated. The United States has repeatedly and unsuccessfully pressed for discussion of common international standards on workers' rights—an idea strongly opposed by poorer nations that fear that it is just another excuse for protectionism by the rich.

Foreign direct investment emerges as another important area for future WTO-sponsored negotiations (foreign direct investment refers to investment by a firm based in one country in productive facilities in another country). The trade regulations negotiated under successive GATT treaties were never extended to embrace foreign direct investment. Given the globalization of production that we are now witnessing in the world economy, barriers to foreign direct investment seem antiquated. As of 1994 roughly one-third of the volume of world trade flows represented trade that occurred *between* the different subsidiaries of multinational corporations.[29] Automobile companies, for example, will now often manufacture an engine in one country and axles in another and assemble the product in a third. The globalization of production illustrated by such examples suggests that foreign direct investment and global trade are closely linked, with firms establishing subsidiaries in different countries and then engaging in international trade between those subsidiaries. Despite the link between foreign investment and trade flows, barriers to foreign direct investment are still widespread (we will discuss these in detail in the next chapter). Currently many countries limit investment by foreign companies in their economies (e.g., local content requirements, local ownership rules, and even prohibition). Extending the WTO regime to embrace foreign direct investment and remove such limitations is a logical next step, but it will not be easy. Many developing countries are opposed to any such agreement. While they are eager to attract foreign direct investment into their economies, the same countries profess a desire to maintain control over the terms under which foreigners are permitted to invest. A WTO-brokered deal would limit their ability to do this, and so they are likely to oppose it.[30]

Implications for Business

What are the implications of all this for business practice? Why should the international manager care about the political economy of free trade and about the relative merits of arguments for free trade and protectionism? There are two answers. The first concerns the impact of trade barriers on a firm's strategy. The second concerns the role that business firms can play in promoting free trade and/or trade barriers.

Trade Barriers and Firm Strategy

To understand how trade barriers impact a firm's strategy, consider first the material we covered in Chapter 4. Drawing on the theories of international trade, we discussed how it may make sense for the firm to disperse its various production activities to those countries around the globe where they can be performed most efficiently. Thus, it may be best for a firm to design and engineer its product in one country, to manufacture components in another, to perform final assembly operations in yet another country, and then export the finished product to the rest of the world.

Clearly, trade barriers are a constraint on a firm's ability to disperse its productive activities in such a manner. First, and most obviously, tariff barriers raise the cost of exporting products to a country (or of exporting partly finished products between countries). This may put the firm at a competitive disadvantage vis-à-vis indigenous competitors. In response, the firm may then find it economical to locate production facilities in that country so that it can compete on an even footing with indigenous competitors. Second, voluntary export restraints (VERs) may limit a firm's ability to serve a country from locations outside that country. Again, the response by the firm might be to set up production facilities in that country—even though it may result in somewhat higher production costs. Such reasoning was one factor behind the rapid expansion of Japanese automaking capacity in the United States during the 1980s. This followed establishment of a VER between the United States and Japan that limited U.S. imports of Japanese automobiles. For details, see the next "Management Focus," which describes how Toyota responded to protectionist threats by opening car plants in the United States and Europe.

Third, to conform with local content requirements, a firm may have to locate more production activities in a given market than it would otherwise. Again, from the firm's perspective, this might raise costs above the level that could be achieved if each production activity were dispersed to its optimal location. And fourth, even when trade barriers do not exist, the firm may still want to locate some production activities in a given country to reduce the threat of trade barriers being imposed in the future.

All the above effects are likely to raise the firm's costs above the level that could be achieved in a world without trade barriers. The higher costs that result need not translate into a significant competitive disadvantage, however, if the countries imposing trade barriers do so to the imported products of all foreign firms. But when trade barriers are targeted at exports from a particular nation, firms based in that nation may be at a competitive disadvantage vis-à-vis the firms of other nations (VERs are targeted trade barriers). One strategy the firm may adopt to deal with such targeted trade barriers is to move production into the country imposing barriers. Another strategy may be to move production to countries whose exports are not targeted by the specific trade barrier.

Policy Implications

As noted in Chapter 4, business firms are major players on the international trade scene. Because of their pivotal role in international trade, business firms can and do exert a strong influence on government policy toward trade. This influence can encourage protectionism, or it can encourage the government to support the WTO and push for open markets and freer trade among all nations. Moreover, government policies with regard to international trade can have a direct impact on business.

Consistent with strategic trade policy, government intervention in the form of tariffs, quotas, and subsidies can help firms and industries establish a competitive advantage in the world economy. In general, however, the arguments contained in this chapter suggest that a policy of government intervention has the following three drawbacks:

Toyota's Response to Rising Protectionist Pressures in Europe and the United States

In many respects Toyota has been a victim of its own success. Until the 1960s Toyota was viewed as little more than an obscure Japanese automobile company. In 1950 Toyota produced a mere 11,700 vehicles. In 1970 it was producing 1.6 million vehicles, and by 1990 the figure had increased to 4.12 million. In the process, Toyota rose to become the third largest automobile company and the largest automobile exporter in the world. In the view of most analysts, Toyota's dramatic rise was due to the company's world-class manufacturing and design skills. These made Toyota not only the most productive automobile company in the

world, but also the one that consistently produced the highest-quality and best-designed automobiles.

For most of its history Toyota has exported automobiles from its plants in Japan. However, by the early 1980s political pressure and talk of local content requirements in the United States and Europe were forcing an initially reluctant Toyota to rethink its exporting strategy. Toyota had already agreed to "voluntary" export restraints with the United States in 1981. The consequence for Toyota was stagnant export growth between 1981 and 1984. Against this background, in the early 1980s Toyota began to think seriously about setting up manufacturing operations overseas.

Toyota's first overseas operation was a 50/50 joint venture

with General Motors established in February 1983 under the name New United Motor Manufacturing Inc. (NUMMI). NUMMI, which is based in Fremont, California, began producing Chevrolet Nova cars for GM in December 1984. The maximum capacity of the Fremont plant is about 250,000 cars per year.

For Toyota, the joint venture provided a chance to find out whether it could build quality cars in the United States using American workers and American suppliers. It also provided Toyota with experience dealing with an American union (the United Auto Workers Union) and with a means of circumventing "voluntary" import restrictions. By the fall of 1986 the NUMMI plant was running at full capacity and the early indications were that it was

1 Intervention can be self-defeating, since it tends to protect the inefficient rather than help firms become efficient global competitors.

2 Intervention is dangerous, since it may invite retaliation and trigger a trade war.

3 Intervention is unlikely to be well executed, given the opportunity for such a policy to be captured by special interest groups.

Does this mean that business should simply encourage government to adopt a laissez-faire, free trade policy?

Most economists would probably argue that the best interests of international business are served by a free trade stance, but not a laissez-faire stance.

achieving productivity and quality levels close to those achieved at Toyota's major Takaoka plant in Japan.

Encouraged by its success at NUMMI, in December 1985 Toyota announced it would build an automobile manufacturing plant in Georgetown, Kentucky. The plant, which came on stream in May 1988, officially had the capacity to produce 200,000 Toyota Camrys a year. Such was the success of this plant, however, that by early 1990 it was producing the equivalent of 220,000 cars per year. This success was followed by an announcement in December 1990 that Toyota would build a second plant in Georgetown with a capacity to produce a further 200,000 vehicles per year. All told, the two plants and NUMMI now give Toyota the capacity to build 660,000 vehicles per year in North America.

In addition to its North American transplant operations, Toyota moved to set up production facilities in Europe. Here, too, the move was a response to growing protectionist pressures in Europe. Toyota was also anticipating the 1992 lowering of trade barriers among the member states of the European Union (EU). In 1989 the company an-nounced that it would build a plant in England with the capacity to manufacture 200,000 cars per year by 1997. The clear implication was that after 1992, much of the output of this plant would be exported to the rest of the EU. This decision prompted the French Prime Minister to describe Britain as "a Japanese aircraft carrier, sitting off the coast of Europe waiting to attack." Fearing that the EU would limit its expansion, Toyota joined other Japanese automobile companies in agreeing to keep their share of the European auto market to under 11 percent, at least until 2000.

Despite Toyota's apparent commitment to expand its U.S. and European assembly operations, it has not all been smooth sailing. A major problem has been building an overseas supplier network that is comparable to Toyota's Japanese network. For example, in a 1990 meeting of Toyota's North American suppliers' association Toyota executives informed their North American suppliers that the defect ratio for parts produced by 75 North American and European suppliers was 100 times greater than the defect ratio for parts supplied by 147 Japanese suppliers. Moreover, Toyota executives pointed out that parts manufactured by North American and European suppliers tend to be significantly more expensive than comparable parts manufactured in Japan.

Due to these problems, Toyota initially imported many parts from Japan for its European and U.S. assembly operations. However, the general increase in imports of automobile components into the United States from Japan that were the result of this strategy only heightened trade tensions between the two countries. The high volume of such imports has become a major sticking point in trade negotiations between the United States and Japan. In an attempt to diffuse the situation, Toyota is striving to increase the local content of cars assembled in North America and Europe. The company's plan was for 70 percent of the value of Toyota cars assembled in Europe and the United States to be locally produced by January 1996, up from less than 40 percent in 1990. To achieve this, Toyota embarked on an aggressive supplier education drive in both Europe and the United States aimed at familiarizing its local suppliers with Japanese production methods.[31]

Put differently, it is probably in the best long-run interests of the business community to encourage the government to aggressively promote greater free trade by, for example, strengthening the WTO. In general, business has much more to gain from government efforts to open protected markets to imports and foreign direct investment than from government efforts to support certain domestic industries in a manner consistent with the recommendations of strategic trade policy.

This conclusion is reinforced by a phenomenon that we first touched on in Chapter 1: the increasing integration of the world economy and globalization of production that has occurred over the past two decades. We live in a world where many firms of all national origins increasingly depend for their competitive advantage on globally dispersed production systems. Such systems are the result of free trade. Free trade has brought great advantages to firms that have exploited it and to consumers who benefit from the resulting lower prices. Given the danger of retaliatory action, business firms that lobby their governments to engage in protectionism must realize that by doing so they may be denying themselves the opportunity to build a competitive advantage by constructing a globally dispersed production system. And by encouraging their governments to engage in protectionism, their own activities and sales overseas may be jeopardized if other governments retaliate. This is a danger for U.S. firms, which have enormous economic interests abroad. The United States, after all, is still the world's number one exporter.

Key Terms

Summary

The objective of this chapter was to describe how the reality of international trade deviates from the theoretical ideal of unrestricted free trade that we reviewed in Chapter 4. Consistent with this objective, in this chapter we have reviewed the various instruments of trade policy, reviewed the political and economic arguments for government intervention in international trade, reexamined the economic case for free trade in light of the strategic trade policy argument, and looked at the evolution of the world trading framework. The main conclusion reached is that, while a policy of free trade may not always be the theoretically optimal policy (given the arguments of the new trade theorists), in practice it is probably the best policy for a government to pursue. In particular, the long-run interests of business and consumers may be best served by strengthening international institutions such as the WTO. Given the danger that isolated protectionism might escalate into an all-out trade war, business probably has far more to gain from government efforts to open protected markets to imports and foreign direct investment (through the WTO) than from government efforts to protect domestic industries from foreign competition.

In this chapter the following points have been made:

1 The effect of a tariff is to raise the cost of imported products. Gains accrue to the government (from revenues) and to producers (who are protected from foreign competitors). Consumers lose, since they must pay more for imports.

2 By lowering costs, subsidies help domestic producers to compete against low-cost foreign imports and to gain export markets. However, subsidies must be paid for by taxpayers. Moreover, they tend to be captured by special interests that use them to protect the inefficient.

3 An import quota is a direct restriction imposed by an importing country on the quantity of some good that may be imported. A voluntary export restraint (VER) is a quota on trade imposed from the exporting country's side. Both import quotas and VERs benefit domestic producers by limiting import competition, but they result in higher prices, which hurts consumers.

4 A local content requirement is a requirement that some specific fraction of a good be produced domestically. Local content requirements benefit the producers of component parts, but they raise prices of imported components, which hurts consumers.

5 An administrative policy is an informal instrument or bureaucratic rule that can be used to restrict imports and boost exports. Such policies benefit producers but hurt consumers, who are denied access to possibly superior foreign products.

6 There are two types of arguments for government intervention in international trade: political and economic. Political arguments for intervention are concerned with protecting the interests of certain groups, often at the expense of other groups. Economic arguments for intervention are about boosting the overall wealth of a nation.

7 The most common political argument for intervention is that it is necessary to protect jobs. However, political intervention often hurts consumers and that can be self-defeating.

8 Countries sometimes argue that it is important to protect certain industries for reasons of national security.

9 Some argue that government should use the threat to intervene in trade policy as a bargaining tool to open foreign markets. This can be a risky policy; if it fails the result can be higher trade barriers all round.

10 The infant industry argument for government intervention is that to let manufacturing get a toehold, governments should temporarily support new industries. In practice, however, governments often end up protecting the inefficient.

11 Strategic trade policy suggests that with subsidies, government can help domestic firms gain first-mover advantages in global industries where economies of scale are important. Government subsidies may also help domestic firms overcome barriers to entry into such industries.

12 The problems with strategic trade policy are twofold: *(i)* such a policy may well invite retaliation, in which case all will lose, and *(ii)* strategic trade policy may be captured by special interest groups, which will distort it to their own ends.

13 The Smoot-Hawley Act, introduced in 1930, erected an enormous wall of tariffs to U.S. imports. Other countries responded by adopting similar tariffs, and the world slid further into the Great Depression

14 GATT was a product of the post-war free trade movement. GATT was successful in lowering trade barriers on manufactured goods and commodities. The move toward greater free trade under GATT appeared to stimulate economic growth.

15 Completion of the Uruguay Round of GATT talks and establishment of the World Trade Organization have strengthened the world trading system by extending GATT rules to services, increasing protection for intellectual property, reducing agricultural subsidies, and enhancing monitoring and enforcement mechanisms.

16 Trade barriers constrain a firm's ability to disperse its various production activities to optimal locations around the globe. One response to trade barriers is to establish more production activities in the protected country.

17 Business may have more to gain from government efforts to open up protected markets to imports and foreign direct investment than from government efforts to protect domestic industries from foreign competition.

Critical Thinking and Discussion Questions

1 Do you think the U.S. government is correct to use a "get tough" approach in its trade negotiations with Japan (see opening case)? What are the risks of such an approach?

2 Whose interests should be the paramount concern of government trade policy—the interests of producers (businesses and their employees) or those of consumers?

3 Given the arguments relating to the new trade theory and strategic trade policy, what kind of trade policy should business be pressuring government to adopt?

4 You are an employee of a U.S. firm that produces personal computers in Thailand and then exports them to the United States and other countries for sale. The personal computers were originally produced in Thailand to take advantage of relatively low labor costs and a skilled work force. Other possible locations considered at the time were Malaysia and Hong Kong. The U.S. government decides to impose punitive 100 percent ad valorem tariffs on imports of computers from Thailand to punish the country for administrative trade barriers that restrict U.S. exports to Thailand. How do you think your firm should respond? What does this tell you about the use of targeted trade barriers?

Internet Exercise

The development of the global trading system is explored in this chapter, with particular focus on the General Agreements on Tariffs and Trade and the World Trade Organization. Information on these organizations is prevalent on the Internet in both official and unofficial sites. For example, at the World Trade Organization site (http://www.wto.org/), comprehensive details are provided about the objectives, key principles, main functions, structure, and secretariat and budget. Additional information is given on the WTO and international trade. The WTO site also gives links to a description of the Uruguay Round negotiations, the preamble of the Agreement Establishing the WTO, and plurilateral agreements.

At the International Trade Law site (http://itl.irv.uit.no/trade_law/nav/freetrade.html), links are provided for various treaties, and special attention is given to the WTO and GATT.

Researchers and theorists interested in the World Trade Organization are invited to visit the W.T.O. Pages site (http://www.eleves.ens.fr:8080/home/boyd/wto.html) to join in discussions of the organization and to read a variety of articles from around the world.

Global Surfing

Explore the official WTO site and read about the organization's history and organization. What world trading issues are discussed? How are environmental and trade policies analyzed? Jump to the International Trade Law site and follow the links to the various WTO Guides and Summaries. How do these sites address international standards on workers' rights? Which trade disputes are discussed? Finally, go to the W.T.O. Pages site and read the questions posted on the forum pages. What issues from which countries are being probed? Then read some of the articles posted. What topics are analyzed? How do they pertain to developing countries? What do they predict for global trading in the 21st Century?

Closing Case

Malaysia and Britain Enter into a Trade Dispute

In mid-February 1994 the British newspaper *The Sunday Times* ran an article that alleged that a £1 billion ($750 million) sale of defense equipment by British companies to Malaysia was secured only after bribes had been paid to Malaysian government officials and after the British Overseas Development Administration (ODA) had agreed to approve a £234 million grant to the Malaysian government for a hydroelectric dam of (according to *The Sunday Times*) dubious economic value. The clear implication was that U.K. officials, in their enthusiasm to see British companies win a large defense contract, had yielded to pressures from "corrupt" Malaysian officials for bribes—both personal and in the form of the £234 million development grant.[32]

What happened next took everyone by surprise—the Malaysian government promptly announced a ban on the import of all British goods and services into Malaysia and demanded an apology from the British government. Officially the ban applied only to government orders for British goods and services, with the private sector free to buy as it chose. However, British companies with experience in the region were nervous that the private sector would follow the government's lead in shunning British products. At stake was as much as £4 billion in British exports and construction activities in Malaysia and a presence in one of the world's fastest-growing developing economies (Malaysia's economic growth has averaged 8 percent per year since 1989). In announcing the ban, Malaysia's prime minister, Dr. Mahathir Mohamad, noted that the British media portray Malaysians as corrupt because "they are not British and not white" . . . and that "we believe the foreign media must learn the fact that developing countries, including a country led by a brown Moslem, have the ability to manage their own affairs successfully."[33]

The British government responded by stating it could not tell the British press what and what not to publish, to which Dr. Mahathir replied there would be "no contracts for British press freedom to tell lies." At the same time, the British government came under attack from members of Parliament in Britain, who suspected that the government acted unethically and approved the ODA hydroelectric grant in order to help British companies win orders in Malaysia.

Case Discussion Questions

1 What does this case teach us about the relationship between politics and international trade?

2 You are the CEO of a British company that now faces the loss of a lucrative contract in Malaysia because of the dispute. What action should you take?

3 How do you think the British government should respond to the Malaysian action?

From Rings for Your Fingers to Rings for Your Cars

When some exporters consider markets like Central America, they are blinded by obstacles like high unemployment, political instability, and low per capita income. Yanira Gutierrez, a native of Mexico with family ties in Nicaragua, sees only opportunities. For over a year, Yanira has been exporting novelty rings for children, used automobiles, and used auto parts to Nicaragua. Yanira operates her business, Central America Import/Export, part time. She is also busy earning an undergraduate degree in international business and raising a baby.

The key to selling profitably to less-developed markets is first to find a need. Yanira started by selling novelty items because she got a great bargain—70,000 rings for $7,000. The rings were targeted at children and were fairly inexpensive. But despite their low price and her efforts to repackage and better merchandise the items, she still has several thousand in inventory.

She moved to exporting automobiles when a family member in Nicaragua asked her to ship a used car for the family's personal use. As a result, she mastered the ins and outs of buying used cars at auctions and shipping them to Nicaragua. Today she ships about three cars per month. The Nicaraguan market for used

Yanira Gutierrez

autos is relatively small, while the regulations, certifications, and fees are cumbersome. Even though she can sell a used car for double its cost, a car may sit in her driveway for several months while she makes the rounds of regulatory agencies to obtain the necessary clearances. This can leave her profits in park along with her unmoved merchandise. "It is necessary to include the cost of holding the inventory and one's own time when calculating profit," she states.

She expanded into used automobile parts because the market is bigger and less regulated. Nicaraguans are more likely to keep their old cars running than to replace them. They prefer used parts because new ones are too expensive. She learned that even in the United States the cars

bought at auction for resale are typically reconditioned with used parts.

Yanira is determined to be an independent businesswoman. However, she realizes that her success depends on networking and learning from others with more experience. To discover where to obtain merchandise at the best prices, she began working on commission for an entrepreneur who bought close-outs, ranging from toys to office supplies. He bought the items at auctions and resold them domestically. As a result she made her first buy of the novelty rings at an auction with money borrowed from her family with the intention of exporting them to Nicaragua and Mexico.

When looking for sources for used cars, like with the rings, she went to an auction. Since she did not have the necessary credentials, she paid a licensed dealer $100 for each car that he bought for her. She attended the auctions along with him, learned what to look for when buying used cars, and eventually got her own license.

Since her father was in the transportation business in Mexico, Yanira had some familiarity with brakes, auto rings, and carburetors. However, she did not have the necessary contacts to acquire supplies. So she set out to find someone who did, a mechanic who worked in an auto salvage yard. Yanira did hire a mechanic, paying him ten percent of the price of each part he bought. In the end, though, she elected to forge her own loyal network of auto salvage yards. She now relies on her intermediary less and less.

Yanira has structured her business to keep her capital investment at a minimum. She only ships merchandise once she has a firm order accompanied by either cash or a letter of credit. She pays her salesmen in Nicaragua on commission and keeps her advertising to a minimum.

She uses a freight forwarder to ship the products by boat and if necessary to consolidate the shipments. As her sales have increased, she is using full containers and selling any excess space to others interested in transporting small amounts to Nicaragua.

In Nicaragua she has hired family members to sell to mechanics and auto supply stores. She also places display advertisements in the local newspapers. She uses rather small, six-by-six inch display ads which stress low prices. She keeps the style and format consistent to improve her recognition factor.

She prices the auto parts based on cost-plus, adding a 40 percent profit. Her prices are considerably less than her competitors'. To keep them low she only deals in parts for cars four or more years old. Parts for newer cars command a higher tariff than parts for older vehicles.

There are many challenges in operating the business day-to-day. Sometimes she gets orders which she cannot fill in a timely fashion. Even when she ships the order, there is always the possibility of delays in transit. She must be very careful to complete the necessary paperwork accurately to minimize the risk of having the parts reclassified. It is also difficult to supervise and motivate her sales force from such a great distance.

To grow her business, Yanira is continuously on the lookout for other products that are suitable for exporting to an emerging economy. The formula is to find products which are valued by consumers with rising expectations but trailing incomes. The product should be scarce in the country and relatively inexpensive for her to buy. Perhaps some other previously-owned products like personal computers from the United States might hold the key.

Helena Czepiec
California State Polytechnic University, Pomona

Chapter 6
Foreign Direct Investment

©PhotoDisc

Opening Case

Electrolux Invests in Asia and Eastern Europe

With 1994 sales of over $13.5 billion, Electrolux is one of the world's largest manufacturers of household appliances (washing machines, dishwashers, refrigerators, vacuum cleaners, etc.). A Swedish company with a small home market, Electrolux has always had to look to other markets for its growth. By 1994 the company was generating over 85 percent of its sales outside of Sweden. Most of this activity was in Western Europe, where Electrolux held a 25 percent share of the total market for

Learning Objectives:

1 Be familiar with the forces underpinning the rising tide of foreign direct investment in the world economy.

2 Understand why firms often prefer direct investment as a strategy for entering a foreign market over alternatives such as exporting and granting foreign entities the right to produce the firm's product under license.

3 Appreciate why firms based in the same industry often undertake foreign direct investment at the same time.

4 Understand why certain locations are favored as the target of foreign direct investment activity.

5 Appreciate how political ideology influences government policy toward foreign direct investment.

6 Be conversant with the costs and benefits of foreign direct investment to receiving and source countries.

7 Have a good grasp of the different policy instruments that governments can use to restrict and encourage foreign direct investment.

household appliances in 1994, and in North America.

An early 1990s planning review at Electrolux concluded that demand for household appliances was now mature in these regions. Since future growth would be limited to replacement demand and the growth in population, it would be unlikely to exceed 2 to 3 percent annually. Leif Johansson, the CEO of Electrolux, decided the company was too dependent on these mature markets. He reasoned that the company would have to expand aggressively into the emerging markets of Asia and Eastern Europe if it was to maintain its historic growth rate. The company estimated that demand for household appliances in these regions could grow at 20 percent annually for at least the next decade, and probably beyond that. Accordingly, in 1994 he set an ambitious goal for Electrolux: the company would have to double its sales in these emerging markets from the current $1.35 billion, or 10 percent of total 1994 sales, to $2.7 billion by 1997.

As an additional goal he stated that Electrolux should become one of the top three suppliers of household goods in Southeast Asia by the year 2000.

In addition to the obvious growth potential, another consideration for Electrolux was that its main global competitors, General Electric and Whirlpool of the United States and Germany's Bosch-Siemans, had recently announced similar plans. Electrolux believed it had to move quickly or be left out in the race to profit from these emerging markets.

Having committed itself to expansion, the next issue Electrolux had to grapple with was how to achieve its ambitious goals. A combination of cost considerations and import barriers made direct exporting from its Western European and North American plants uneconomical. Instead, different approaches are being adopted for different regions and countries. Acquisitions of going concerns, green-field developments, joint ventures, and enhanced marketing are all being considered. Electrolux says it is prepared to spend $200 million per year to increase its presence in these emerging markets.

Electrolux made its first move into Eastern Europe in 1991 when it acquired Lehel, Hungary's largest manufacturer of household appliances. Electrolux has decided to establish its own operating companies in Russia, Poland, and the Czech Republic. Each of these operating subsidiaries will be a green-field development. In Asia there is a much greater need to adapt to local conditions. Regulations concerning foreign ownership in India and China, for example, virtually compel Electrolux to work through joint ventures with local partners. In China, the world's fastest-growing market, the company already has joint ventures in compressors, vacuum cleaners, and water purification equipment, and it planned to spend $100 million to build another five manufacturing plants in the country by 1997. In Southeast Asia the emphasis is on the marketing of goods imported from China, rather than local production.[1]

Introduction

foreign direct investment
Firm invests directly in new facilities to produce and/or market a product in a foreign country.

multinational enterprise
Company that conducts business in more than one country.

This chapter is concerned with the phenomenon of foreign direct investment (FDI). **Foreign direct investment** occurs when a firm invests directly in new facilities to produce and/or market a product in a foreign country. The 1991 purchase of Hungary's Lehel by Electrolux is an example of FDI, as is the company's decision to invest in joint ventures to manufacture products in China, and the company's investment in production facilities in Russia, Poland, and the Czech Republic (for details, see the opening case). The U.S. Department of Commerce has come up with a more precise definition of FDI: FDI occurs whenever a U.S. citizen, organization, or affiliated group takes an interest of 10 percent or more in a foreign business entity. Once a firm undertakes FDI it becomes a **multinational enterprise** (the meaning of multinational here being "more than one country").

We begin this chapter by looking at the importance of foreign direct investment in the world economy. Next we review the theories that have been used to explain foreign direct investment. The chapter then looks at government policy toward foreign direct investment. As always, the chapter closes with a section on implications for business practice of the material covered in the chapter.

flow of foreign direct investment Amount of FDI undertaken during a given period.

stock of foreign direct investment Total accumulated value of foreign-owned assets at a given time.

Foreign Direct Investment in the World Economy

When discussing foreign direct investment, it is important to distinguish between the *flow* and the *stock* of foreign direct investment. The **flow of foreign direct investment** refers to the amount of FDI undertaken over a given period (normally a year). The **stock of foreign direct investment** refers to the total accumulated value of foreign-owned assets at a given time. We also

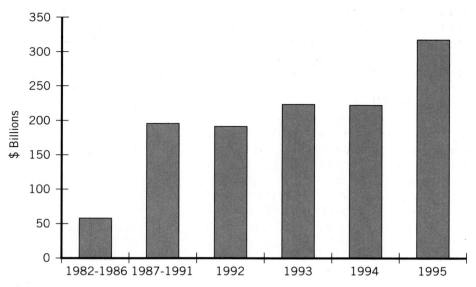

FIGURE 6.1

FDI Outflows, 1982–95 ($ billions)
Source: World Trade Organization, *Trade and Foreign Direct Investment* (Geneva: WTO Secretariat, October 9, 1996), issued as Press Release No. 57, and United Nations Conference on Trade and Development, *World Investment Report, 1996* (New York and Geneva: United Nations, 1996).

talk of **outflows of foreign direct investment**, meaning the flow of FDI out of a country, and **inflows of foreign direct investment**, meaning the flow of FDI into a country.

Several facts characterize foreign direct investment trends over the past 20 years. First, there has been a rapid increase in the total volume of FDI undertaken. Second, there has been a change in the importance of various countries as sources for FDI. In particular, there has been some decline in the *relative* importance of the United States as a source for FDI, while several other countries, most notably Japan, have increased their share of total FDI outflows. Third, there have been notable shifts in the direction of FDI. An increasing share of FDI seems to be directed at the developing nations of Asia and Eastern Europe. The United States has become a major recipient of FDI. Finally, there has been a notable increase in the amount of FDI undertaken by small and medium-sized enterprises.

outflows of foreign direct investment Flow of FDI out of a country.

inflows of foreign direct investment Flow of FDI into a country.

The Growth of Foreign Direct Investment

Over the past 20 years there has been a marked increase in both the *flow* and *stock* of FDI in the world economy. The average yearly *outflow* of FDI increased from about $25 billion in 1975 to a record $315 billion in 1995 (see Figure 6.1).[2] Not only did the flow accelerate during the 1980s, but it also accelerated faster than the growth in world trade. Between 1984 and 1995 the total flow of FDI from all countries increased by more than 700 percent, while world trade grew by 82 percent and world output by 24 percent (see Figure 6.2).[3]

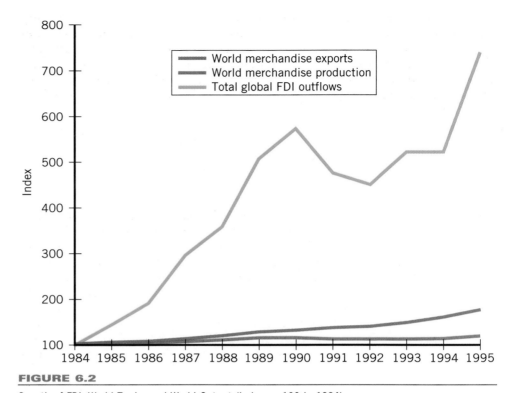

FIGURE 6.2

Growth of FDI, World Trade, and World Output (Index = 100 in 1984)
Source: World Trade Organization, *Trade and Foreign Direct Investment* (Geneva: WTO Secretariat, October 9, 1996), issued as Press Release No. 57, and United Nations Conference on Trade and Development, *World Investment Report, 1996* (New York and Geneva: United Nations, 1996).

There are several reasons FDI is growing more rapidly than world trade and world output. Despite the general decline in trade barriers that we have witnessed over the past 30 years, business firms still fear protectionist pressures. Managers see FDI as a way of circumventing future trade barriers. Thus, much of the investment in the United States by Japanese automobile companies during the 1980s and early 1990s was driven by a desire to reduce exports from Japan, thereby alleviating trade tensions between the two nations.

Second, much of the recent increase in FDI is being driven by the dramatic political and economic changes occurring in many of the world's developing nations. The general shift toward democratic political institutions and free market economics that we discussed in Chapter 2 has encouraged FDI. Across much of Asia, Eastern Europe, and Latin America, increasing economic growth, economic deregulation, privatization programs that are open to foreign investors, and the removal of many restrictions on FDI have all made these countries more attractive to foreign investors. We saw in the opening case how Electrolux has responded to these trends by investing in Eastern Europe and Asia. The acquisition of Lehel of Hungary, for example, was the result of a privatization program that allowed foreign investors to purchase state-owned enterprises.

The globalization of the world economy, a phenomenon that we first discussed in Chapter 1, is also having a positive impact on the volume of FDI. Firms such as Electrolux now see the whole world as their market, and they are undertaking FDI to make sure they have a significant presence in every region of the world. To achieve greater cost economies, many firms are creating a global web of linked production operations, dispersing the responsibility for manufacturing various component parts to factories based in different countries on the basis of a comparison of relative factor costs, and then assembling the final product in major markets. Creating a global web of operations requires substantial FDI.

Changes in the Source of Foreign Direct Investment

Not only has the flow of FDI been accelerating, but its composition has also been changing. For most of the period after World War II, the United States was by far the largest source country for FDI. During the late 1970s the United States was still accounting for about half of all FDI *outflows*, while the second-place United Kingdom accounted for about 18 percent. As a result, by 1980, 178 of the world's largest 382 multinationals were U.S. firms, and 40 of them were British.[4] By 1990, however, the U.S. share of total FDI outflows had slumped to 10.3 percent, pushing the United States into second place behind Japan. While the U.S. share has recently rebounded, reaching 30 percent of total global FDI outflows in 1995, a relative decline in the long-term share of FDI outflows accounted for by the United States is to be expected.[5] This reflects the increasing number of countries that are joining the ranks of developed nations and are becoming major sources for FDI. Despite its declining share, the United States is once again the largest source country for FDI, but by a smaller margin than in the 1960s and 1970s.

One big gainer over most of the past 20 years has been Japan. Japan's share of total FDI outflows increased from 6 percent during the late 1970s to 21 percent in 1990, although it fell back to 10 percent in 1995. As a consequence, Japan's share of the total *stock* of world FDI increased from 0.7 percent in 1960 to 11.7 percent in 1994, while the stock accounted for by the U.S. firms fell from 49.2 percent to 25.7 percent over the same period. Japan's increased share of FDI outflows has been one result of that country's rapid economic progress. However, reflecting Japan's severe economic recession in the early 1990s, Japanese FDI slumped from $48 billion in 1990 to $17.9 billion in 1994, although most observers expect it to increase again once Japan's economy recovers from its recession.[6] Other major source countries for FDI include Germany, France, and the United Kingdom. Among these countries, the share of FDI stock accounted for by the United Kingdom has shrunk, while that of France and Germany has grown.[7]

The Recipients of FDI

Leading recipient economies for FDI inflows between 1985 and 1995 are summarized in Table 6.1. As can be seen, inflows of FDI are heavily concentrated in a small number of host countries, notably the United States, United Kingdom, France, and China, which collectively accounted for 58 percent of total FDI inflows among the top 20 recipient economies from 1985 to 1995. (A **host country** is one that is on the receiving end of foreign direct investment. A **home country** is a source country for FDI.)

host country Country that is on the receiving end of foreign direct investment.

home country Country that is the source of FDI.

TABLE 6.1

Leading Host Countries for FDI Based on Cumulative Inflows, 1985–95

Rank	Country	FDI ($ billion)	FDI per capita ($)	Rank per Capita
1	United States	$477.5	$1,820	13
2	United Kingdom	199.6	3,410	7
3	France	138.0	2,380	10
4	China	130.2	110	20
5	Spain	90.9	2,320	11
6	Belgium-Luxembourg	72.4	6,900	2
7	Netherlands	68.1	4,410	3
8	Australia	62.6	3,470	6
9	Canada	60.9	2,060	12
10	Mexico	44.1	470	17
11	Singapore	40.8	13,650	1
12	Sweden	37.7	4,270	4
13	Italy	36.3	630	16
14	Malaysia	30.7	1,520	14
15	Germany	25.9	320	18
16	Switzerland	25.2	3,580	5
17	Argentina	23.5	680	15
18	Brazil	20.3	130	19
19	Hong Kong	17.9	2,890	9
20	Denmark	15.7	3,000	8

Source: United Nations Conference on Trade and Development and the United Nations.

In terms of absolute dollar amounts, the United States has been by far the largest recipient of FDI. There is a widespread perception that the majority of FDI inflows into the United States during this period were undertaken by Japanese corporations intent on buying up America's industrial base.[8] In reality, however, the leading investors in the United States for much of this period were the British, French, Germans, and Dutch.[9] Although there was a surge in Japanese inward investment, it peaked in 1989 and has declined since.

A number of factors are behind the inflow of FDI into the United States from 1985 to 1995. As the largest and richest consumer market in the world, the United States was clearly attractive to foreign firms. Also, the 1994 expansion of the North American Free Trade Agreement (NAFTA) to include Mexico may have promoted some inward investment from foreign firms eager to share in the gains created by an enlarged market (see Chapter 7 for details of NAFTA). In addition, during this period the value of the dollar fell quite rapidly on foreign exchange markets. At the same time, the value of the Japanese yen and the German mark rose. (For an explanation of this, see

Chapters 8 and 9.) This made it relatively cheap for Japanese and German firms to purchase U.S. assets.[10] It seems likely that this factor lay behind at least some of the continued strength of direct investment in the United States by foreign firms.

The popularity of the United Kingdom as a host country for FDI reflects the fact that many U.S. and Japanese firms see the United Kingdom as a good base for establishing operations to serve the European Union. For example, in recent years the Japanese have invested heavily in automobile production facilities in the United Kingdom, partly to serve the British market and partly with the intention of exporting production from Britain to the rest of Western Europe. The accompanying "Management Focus" profiles the investments made by Nissan in the U.K. since 1984. The United Kingdom's appeal is based on several factors, including a favorable tax regime for foreign investors, relatively low labor costs, and a well-trained and increasingly productive work force. Similar motives underlie the perennial appeal of France as a host economy for FDI.

China rounds out the list of the top four host economies for FDI. Much of the investment into China has been made in the last few years, with over $60 billion being invested in 1994 and 1995 alone. The high level of inward investment in China is a testament to the attractions of a country that is moving rapidly away from a centrally planned system toward a more market-oriented system that contains 1.4 billion people and that has for almost a decade been achieving some of the highest economic growth rates in the world. The major investors in China are U.S., Japanese, and European firms, all of which are hoping to profit from the enormous potential that will be realized if China maintains its current economic trajectory.

Although China is the standout among developing nations, a number of other developing countries have attracted the attention of foreign investors in recent years. These include Mexico, which saw a surge in inward investment associated with the 1994 North American Free Trade Agreement; the dynamic city-state of Singapore, which boasts the highest level of FDI per capita of any country in the world; the fast-growing Southeast Asian economy of Malaysia; and the two largest Latin American economies, Brazil and Argentina. In total, $100 billion was invested by foreign firms in developing economies during 1995, an increase of 15 percent over 1994. For the future, it is reasonable to expect that developing economies of the world will continue to increase their share of total FDI inflows. Vietnam, which is profiled in the "Country Focus" on page 202, is typical of many developing countries that currently do not receive much in the way of FDI but may start to do so if they continue with current economic and political reforms.

FDI by Medium-Sized and Small Firms

FDI used to be associated almost exclusively with multibillion-dollar multinational corporations. Most people probably still think the two are synonymous. In practice, however, the globalization of world markets has been accompanied by the rapid growth of FDI by small and medium-sized firms. FDI by such firms has been driven by a need to stay close to major customers that have gone abroad. Although hard statistics detailing the growth of smaller multinationals are hard to come by, some examples will give a feel for what now seems to be occurring.

Nissan in the United Kingdom

The Nissan Motor Company, Japan's second largest car maker, first began to invest in the United Kingdom in 1984. The investment was originally driven in part by fear that rising protectionist pressures would make it increasingly difficult for Nissan to serve the European market through exports from Japan.

Nissan's plan was to invest in a single country within the European Community (now the European Union) and serve other countries within the European market by exports from that base. After reviewing a number of locations, Nissan decided to build a production plant in Sunderland, in the northeast part of the United Kingdom. In part, Nissan selected the Sunderland location over alternatives in Spain and Belgium because of significant financial incentives, including major tax breaks, being offered by the British government. In addition, a combination of low wage rates and high employee productivity made the U.K. in general, and Sunderland in particular, an at-

tractive location. The incentives offered to Nissan by the British government were felt by many other European governments to be far too generous, and they prompted the French president to characterize Britain as "a Japanese aircraft carrier sitting off the coast of Europe."

When the investment was announced, many critics in Britain believed the plant would be nothing more than a "screwdriver plant" assembling cars from parts and components imported from Japan. Experience, however, has proved the critics to be wrong. When the plant was announced in 1984 the plan was to have 60 percent local (European Union) content by 1990. At the official opening ceremony in September 1986, the president of Nissan announced an acceleration of its U.K. manufacturing program, with local content rising to 60 percent by 1988. This goal was achieved, and local content since has risen to comprise 80 percent of the value of cars rolling off the Sunderland assembly plant. The plant now uses 197 European suppliers accounting for an annual average expenditure of $1,300 million. Two-thirds of these suppliers are located in the

United Kingdom, with other major component suppliers based in Germany, France, and Spain. Thirty of the suppliers are located in the area immediately surrounding the Sunderland plant.

The Nissan plant has produced tangible benefits for the U.K. economy in terms of both exports and jobs. By 1994 Nissan was producing over 250,000 vehicles annually at the Sunderland plant. Over 80 percent of this output was exported to other countries, primarily the European Union nations of Germany, Italy, France, and Spain. In addition, the Nissan plant exported to over 30 other countries, including Japan. The plant is now Britain's largest car exporter. As a consequence of this export-led growth, employment at the Nissan plant has also grown. When it opened in 1986 the plant had 470 employees. By 1994 the number employed had risen to 4,250. Additional jobs have been created in supporting industries, including 3,000 in nearby component suppliers. Nissan estimates that the total permanent employment generated from its Sunderland plant was 8,029 in 1994.[11]

Consider first the experience of Molex, a Chicago-based company with worldwide sales of about $750 million in 1994. Molex makes some 2,500 varieties of connectors used in such applications as linking the wires in an automobile or in the circuit boards of computers and videocassette recorders. The company had little choice but to go abroad because its customers began investing abroad in the early 1970s to take advantage of cheap labor. Molex, which in those days generated revenues of less than $20 million, had to go abroad to keep this business. Today the company's 46 factories in more than 20 countries employ 6,000 foreign workers.

For another example, consider Loctite, a U.S. manufacturer of industrial adhesives that in 1994 generated sales of over $450 million worldwide. Loctite has pushed hard overseas since its founding in the 1950s. Today the company does business in more than 80 countries and has factories in Ireland, Brazil, and Japan (where it dominates the industrial market). Of the 3,000 people in the company worldwide, two-thirds are employed outside of North America.

As an even smaller example, consider Lubricating Systems, Inc., of Kent, Washington. In 1991 this manufacturer of lubricating fluids for machine tools employed 25 people and generated sales of $6.5 million—hardly an industrial giant. Yet more than $2 million of the company's total sales were generated by exports to a score of countries from Japan to Israel and the United Arab Emirates. Moreover, Lubricating Systems is now investing in a joint venture with a German company to serve the European market.[13]

Although large firms still account for the lion's share of FDI, opportunities exist for medium-sized and small firms to profit from investing abroad.

The Theory of Foreign Direct Investment

In this section we review several theories of foreign direct investment. These theories approach the phenomenon of foreign direct investment from three complementary perspectives. One set of theories seeks to explain why a firm will favor direct investment as a means of entering a foreign market when two other alternatives are open to it, exporting and licensing. Another set of theories seeks to explain why firms in the same industry often undertake foreign direct investment at the same time, and why certain locations are favored over others as targets for foreign direct investment. These theories attempt to explain the observed *pattern* of foreign direct investment flows. A third theoretical perspective, known as the **eclectic paradigm**, attempts to combine the two other perspectives into a single holistic explanation of foreign direct investment (the term *eclectic* means picking the best aspects of other theories and combining them into a single explanation).

Why Foreign Direct Investment?

Why do firms go to all of the trouble of establishing operations abroad through foreign direct investment when two alternatives are available to them for exploiting the profit opportunities in a foreign market: exporting and licensing? **Exporting** involves producing goods at home and then shipping them to the receiving country for sale. **Licensing** involves granting a foreign entity (the licensee) the right to produce and sell the firm's product in return for a royalty fee on every unit sold. Why would a firm such as Electrolux choose to invest directly in a factory in Hungary to build home appliances for sale in that country, when it could have exported home appliances to Hungary

eclectic paradigm
Theory of foreign direct investment that combines two other perspectives into a single holistic explanation of FDI.

exporting Producing goods at home and shipping them to the receiving country for sale.

licensing Granting a foreign entity the right to produce and sell a firm's product in return for a royalty fee on every unit sold.

After the fall of Saigon (now Ho Chi Minh City) to the Communist forces of North Vietnam in April 1975, Vietnam effectively closed its doors to foreign investors. But the doors have now opened again. Although the government of Vietnam is still officially Communist, in recent years it has pursued an economic liberalization policy that is similar in many respects to that adopted by another nominally Communist state, China. Market-based reforms

country's infrastructure remains in tatters, the result of war damage and poor upkeep. Still, with a population of over 70 million, economic growth in excess of 8 percent annually during the first half of the 1990s, and a strategic location in the heart of Southeast Asia, Vietnam's long-run prospects are too bright for many foreign investors to ignore.

The result has been a rapid rise in the amount of FDI into Vietnam, particularly in the automobile industry. By early 1995 Ford, Chrysler, Daimler-Benz,

The German company wants to build two production plants, one in the north and one in the south, for a total investment of $70 million. Both plants will come on stream around 2000. They will focus on producing trucks, buses, and some cars. The attraction of Vietnam to foreign investors such as Daimler-Benz is twofold. First, with economic growth expected to average a robust 8 to 10 percent annually for the next decade, both the investors and the Vietnamese government believe that by 2000

FDI in Vietnam's Infant Auto Industry

have been introduced, price controls in many areas have been scrapped; restrictions on foreign direct investment have been loosened; and there is talk of privatizing state-owned enterprises.

Vietnam has a long way to go, however, before it attains the levels of other rapidly developing nations. At $210 per year, its GDP per capita is one of the lowest in the world, and much of the

Toyota, Suzuki, and a consortium of Japanese and Indonesian interests known as VINDACO had all applied to the government for permission to set up production facilities in Vietnam. In total, the planned investment amounts to over $600 million, a large amount for a country as poor as Vietnam.

Typical of the planned investments is that of Daimler-Benz.

incomes will be high enough to justify making and selling cars locally, first in Ho Chi Minh City in the south and then in the north. Daimler-Benz estimates that demand for commercial vehicles will reach 11,000 a year by 2005.

A second reason for investing in Vietnam is that vehicle manufacturers hope to export some of what they produce to other coun-

from one of its Swedish factories, or when it could have allowed a Hungarian firm to build its appliances under license?

The question is an important one given that a cursory examination of the topic suggests that foreign direct investment may be both expensive and risky when compared to exporting and licensing. FDI is expensive because a firm must establish production facilities in a foreign country or acquire a foreign enterprise. FDI is risky because of the problems associated with doing business in a different culture where the "rules of the game" may be very different. Relative to indigenous firms, there is a greater probability that a foreign firm undertaking FDI in a country for the first time will make costly mistakes due to its ignorance. When a firm exports, it need not bear the costs associated with foreign direct investment, and the risks associated with selling tries, particularly members of the Association of South East Asian Nations (ASEAN), an Asian trade bloc that Vietnam joined in July 1994. With low barriers to trade between ASEAN members a possibility in the future, and given its low labor costs, Vietnam could become an export base for the whole region.

However, this investment is not without its problems. The Vietnamese government is insisting that foreign investors in the auto industry ensure that 30 percent of all parts used in vehicles are made locally within 6 to 10 years of establishing an assembly plant. The decision on local content worries many foreign investors. Making auto parts is likely to be tough in a country where even the indigenous bicycle industry has difficulty surviving with outmoded technology. The foreign investors are working hard to persuade some of their component part suppliers to follow them to Vietnam. If successful, the result could be a further surge in inward FDI.[12]

Tony Stone Images, ©Paul Chelsey

abroad can be reduced by using a native sales agent. Similarly, when a firm allows another enterprise to produce its products under license it need not bear the costs or risks of FDI, since these are born by the licensee. So why do so many firms apparently prefer FDI over either exporting or licensing? A deeper examination of the issue reveals that the answer can be found in the limitations of exporting and licensing as means of capitalizing on foreign market opportunities.

LIMITATIONS OF EXPORTING The viability of an exporting strategy is often constrained by transportation costs and trade barriers. When transportation costs are added to production costs, it becomes unprofitable to ship some products over a large distance. This is particularly true of products that have a low value-to-weight ratio and can be produced in almost any location (e.g., cement, soft drinks, etc.). For such products, relative to either FDI or licensing, the attractiveness of exporting decreases. For products with a high value-to-weight ratio, however, transport costs are normally a very minor component of total landed cost (e.g., electronic components, personal computers, medical equipment, computer software, etc.) and have little impact on the relative attractiveness of exporting, licensing, and FDI.

Much foreign direct investment is undertaken as a response to actual or threatened trade barriers such as import tariffs or quotas. By placing tariffs on imported goods, governments can increase the cost of exporting relative to foreign direct investment and licensing. Similarly, by limiting imports through quotas, governments increase the attractiveness of FDI and licensing. For example, the wave of FDI by Japanese auto companies in the United States during the 1980s was partly driven by protectionist threats from Congress and by quotas on the importation of Japanese cars. For Japanese auto companies, these factors decreased the profitability of exporting and increased that of foreign direct investment. Trade barriers do not have to be physically in place for foreign direct investment to be favored over exporting. Often, the desire to reduce the "threat" that trade barriers might be imposed is enough to justify foreign direct investment as an alternative to exporting.

LIMITATIONS OF LICENSING There is a branch of economic theory known as **internalization theory** that seeks to explain why firms often prefer foreign direct investment over licensing as a strategy for entering foreign markets.[14] According to internalization theory, licensing has three major drawbacks as a strategy for exploiting foreign market opportunities. First, *licensing may result in a firm's giving away valuable technological know-how to a potential foreign competitor*. For example, in the 1960s RCA licensed its leading-edge color television technology to a number of Japanese companies, including Matsushita and Sony. At the time RCA saw licensing as a way to earn a good return from its technological know-how in the Japanese market without the costs and risks associated with foreign direct investment. However, Matsushita and Sony quickly assimilated RCA's technology and used it to enter the U.S. market to compete directly against RCA. As a result, RCA is now a minor player in its home market, while Matsushita and Sony have a much bigger market share.

A second problem is that *licensing does not give a firm the tight control over manufacturing, marketing, and strategy in a foreign country that may be required to maximize its profitability*. With licensing, control over manufacturing, marketing, and strategy is granted to a licensee in return for a royalty fee. However, for *both* strategic and operational reasons, a firm may want to retain control over these functions. The rationale for wanting control over the *strategy* of a foreign entity is that a firm might want its foreign subsidiary to price and market very aggressively to keep a foreign competitor in check. Kodak is pursuing this strategy in Japan. The competitive attacks launched by Kodak's Japanese subsidiary are keeping its major global competitor, Fuji, busy defending its competitive position in Japan. Consequently, Fuji has had to pull back from its earlier strategy of attacking Kodak aggressively in the United States. Unlike a wholly owned subsidiary, a licensee would be unlikely to accept such an imposition, since such a strategy implies that the licensee would be allowed to make only a low profit or might have to take a loss.

internalization theory Explains why firms prefer foreign direct investment over licensing when entering foreign markets.

The rationale for wanting control over the *operations* of a foreign entity is that the firm might wish to take advantage of differences in factor costs across countries, producing only part of its final product in a given country while importing other parts from where they can be produced at lower cost. Again, a licensee would be unlikely to accept such an arrangement, since it would limit the licensee's autonomy. Thus, when tight control over a foreign entity is desirable, foreign direct investment is preferable to licensing.

A third problem with licensing arises when the firm's competitive advantage is based not so much on its products as on the management, marketing, and manufacturing capabilities that produce those products. *Such capabilities are often not amenable to licensing.* While a foreign licensee may be able to physically reproduce the firm's product under license, it often may not be able to do so as efficiently as the firm could itself. As a result, the licensee may not be able to fully exploit the profit potential inherent in a foreign market.

Consider Toyota, a company whose competitive advantage in the global auto industry is acknowledged to come from its superior ability to manage the overall process of designing, engineering, manufacturing, and selling automobiles; that is, from its management and organizational capabilities. Toyota is credited with pioneering the development of a new production process, known as lean production, that enables it to produce higher-quality automobiles at a lower cost than its global rivals.[15] Although Toyota has certain products that could be licensed, its real competitive advantage comes from its management and process capabilities. These kinds of skills are difficult to articulate or codify; they cannot be written down in a simple licensing contract. They are organizationwide and they have been developed over years. They are not embodied in any one individual, but instead are widely dispersed throughout the company. Put another way, Toyota's skills are embedded in its organizational culture, and culture is something that cannot be licensed. Thus, if Toyota were to allow a foreign entity to produce its cars under license, it is unlikely the licensee could be as efficient as Toyota. This would limit the foreign entity's ability to fully develop the market potential of that product. Such reasoning underlies Toyota's preference for direct investment in foreign markets, as opposed to allowing foreign automobile companies to produce its cars under license.

ADVANTAGES OF FOREIGN DIRECT INVESTMENT It follows from the above discussion that a firm will favor FDI over exporting as an entry strategy when transportation costs or trade barriers make exporting unattractive. Furthermore, the firm will favor FDI over licensing when it wishes to maintain control over its technological know-how, or over its operations and business strategy, or when the firm's capabilities are simply not amenable to licensing.

The Pattern of Foreign Direct Investment

Firms in the same industry often undertake foreign direct investment at about the same time. Also, firms tend to direct their investment activities toward certain locations. The two theories we consider in this section attempt to explain the patterns that we observe in foreign direct investment flows.

One theory used to explain foreign direct investment patterns is based on the idea that firms follow their domestic competitors overseas. First expounded by F. T. Knickerbocker, this theory has been developed with regard to oligopolistic industries.[16] An **oligopoly** is an industry composed of a limited number of large firms (an industry in which four firms control 80 percent of a domestic market is considered an oligopoly). A critical competitive feature of such industries is interdependence of the major players: what one firm does can have an immediate impact on the major competitors, forcing a response in kind. Thus, if one firm in an oligopoly cuts prices, this can take market share away from its competitors, forcing them to respond with similar price cuts in order to retain their market share.

Such imitative behavior can take many forms in an oligopoly. One firm raises prices, the others follow; someone expands capacity, and the rivals imitate lest they be left at a disadvantage in the future. Building on this, Knickerbocker argued that the same kind of imitative behavior characterizes foreign direct investment. Consider an oligopoly in the United States in which three firms—A, B, and C—dominate the market. Firm A establishes a subsidiary in France. Firms B and C reflect that if this investment is successful, it may knock out their export business to France and give firm A a first-mover advantage. Furthermore, firm A might discover some competitive asset in France that it could repatriate to the United States. Given these possibilities, firms B and C decide to follow firm A and establish operations in France.

There is evidence that imitative behavior does lead to FDI. Several studies of U.S. enterprises suggest that firms based in oliogopolistic industries tend to imitate each other's FDI.[17] The same phenomenon has been observed with regard to Japanese firms.[18] For example, Toyota and Nissan responded to investments by Honda in the United States and Europe by undertaking their own FDI in the United States and Europe. Similarly, in the opening case we saw how Electrolux's expansion into Eastern Europe and Asia was partly driven by the fact that its global competitors, such as Whirlpool and GE, were making similar moves.

THE PRODUCT LIFE CYCLE Raymond Vernon's product life-cycle theory, discussed in Chapter 4, also explains the pattern of FDI over time. Vernon argued that the establishment of facilities abroad to produce a product for consumption in that market or for export to other markets is often undertaken by the same firm or firms that pioneered the product in their home market. Thus, Xerox introduced the photocopier into the U.S. market, and it was Xerox that originally set up production facilities in Japan (Fuji-Xerox) and Great Britain (Rank-Xerox) to serve those markets.

Vernon's view is that firms undertake FDI at particular stages in the life cycle of a product they have pioneered. They invest in other advanced countries when local demand in those countries grows large enough to support local production (as Xerox did). They subsequently shift production to developing countries when product standardization and market saturation give rise to price competition and cost pressures. Investment in developing countries, where labor costs are lower, is seen as the best way to reduce costs.

There is merit to Vernon's theory; firms do invest in a foreign country when demand in that country will support local production, and they do invest in low-cost countries when cost pressures become intense.[19] Vernon's theory fails to explain, however, why it is profitable for a firm to undertake FDI at such times, rather than continuing to export from its home base and rather than licensing a foreign firm to produce its product. Just because demand in a foreign country is large enough to support local production, it does not necessarily follow that local production is the most profitable option. It may still be more profitable to produce at home and export to that country (to realize the scale economies that arise from serving the global market from one location). Alternatively, it may be more profitable for the firm to license a foreign firm to produce its product for sale in that country. The product life-cycle theory ignores these options and, instead, simply argues that once a foreign market is large enough to support local production, FDI will occur. This limits its explanatory power and its usefulness to business because it fails to identify when it is profitable to invest abroad.

The Eclectic Paradigm

The eclectic paradigm has been championed by the British economist John Dunning.[20] Dunning argues that in addition to the various factors discussed above, location-specific advantages are also of considerable importance in explaining both the rationale for and the direction of foreign direct investment. By **location-specific advantages**, Dunning means the advantages that arise from utilizing resource endowments or assets that are tied to a particular foreign location and that a firm finds valuable to combine with its own unique assets (such as the firm's technological, marketing, or management capabilities). Dunning accepts the argument of internalization theory that it is difficult for a firm to license its own unique capabilities and know-how. Therefore, he argues that combining location-specific assets or resource endowments *and* the firm's own unique capabilities often requires foreign direct investment in production facilities.

An obvious example of Dunning's arguments is natural resources, such as oil and other minerals, which are specific to certain locations. Dunning suggests that to exploit such foreign resources a firm must undertake FDI. Clearly this explains the FDI undertaken by many of the world's oil companies, which have to invest where oil is located in order to combine their technological and managerial capabilities with this valuable location-specific resource. Another obvious example is valuable human resources, such as low-cost, high-skilled labor. The cost and skill of labor vary from country to country. Since labor is not internationally mobile, according to Dunning it makes sense for a firm to locate production facilities in those countries where the cost and skills of local labor are most suited to the particular production processes. For example, one reason Electrolux is currently building factories in China is that China has an abundant supply of low-cost but well-educated and skilled labor. Thus, other factors aside, China is a good location for producing household appliances both for the Chinese market and for export elsewhere.

However, Dunning's theory has implications that go beyond basic resources such as minerals and labor. Consider Silicon Valley, which is the world center for the computer and semiconductor industries. Many of the world's major computer and semiconductor companies, such as Apple Computer, Silicon Graphics, and Intel, are located close to each other in the Silicon Valley region of California. As a result, much of the cutting-edge research and product development in computers and semiconductors occurs here. According to Dunning's arguments, knowledge is being generated in Silicon Valley with regard to the design and

location-specific advantages Advantages that arise from using resource endowments or assets that are tied to a particular location and that a firm finds valuable to combine with its own unique assets.

manufacture of computers and semiconductors that is available nowhere else in the world. As it is commercialized, that knowledge diffuses throughout the world, but the leading edge of knowledge generation in the computer and semiconductor industries is to be found in Silicon Valley. In Dunning's language, this means Silicon Valley has a *location-specific advantage* in the generation of knowledge related to the computer and semiconductor industries. In part, this advantage comes from the sheer concentration of intellectual talent in this area, and in part it arises from informal contacts that allow firms to benefit from each other's knowledge-generation activities. Economists refer to such knowledge spillovers as **externalities**, and there is a well-established theory suggesting that firms can benefit from such externalities by locating close to their source.[21]

Given this, it may make sense for foreign computer and semiconductor firms to invest in research and (perhaps) production facilities so that they can benefit from being where the knowledge is generated. Externalities will allow firms based there to learn about and utilize valuable new knowledge before those based elsewhere, thereby giving them a competitive advantage in the global marketplace. European, Japanese, South Korean, and Taiwanese computer and semiconductor firms are investing in the Silicon Valley region, precisely because they wish to benefit from the externalities that arise there.[22] Dunning's theory, therefore, seems to be a useful addition to those outlined above, because it helps explain like no other how location factors affect the direction of FDI.

> **externalities** Knowledge spillovers that occur when companies in the same industry locate in the same area.

Political Ideology and Foreign Direct Investment

Now that we are familiar with the theory of FDI, it is time to focus on government policy toward FDI. Government policy has typically been driven by political ideology. Historically, ideology toward FDI has ranged from a radical stance that is hostile to all FDI to the non-interventionist principle of free market economics. Between these two extremes is an approach that might be called pragmatic nationalism.

The Radical View

The radical view traces its roots to Marxist political and economic theory. Radical writers argue that the multinational enterprise (MNE) is an instrument of imperialist domination. They see MNEs as a tool for exploiting host countries to the exclusive benefit of their capitalist-imperialist home countries. They argue that MNEs extract profits from the host country and take them to their home country, giving nothing of value to the host country in exchange. They note, for example, that key technology is tightly controlled by the MNE, and that important jobs in the foreign subsidiaries of MNEs go to home country nationals rather than to citizens of the host country. Because of this, according to the radical view, FDI by the MNEs of advanced capitalist nations keeps the less developed countries relatively backward and dependent on advanced capitalist nations for investment, jobs, and technology. According to this view, a country should be very reluctant to permit foreign corporations to undertake FDI, since they can never be instruments of economic development, only of economic domination.[23]

From 1945 until the 1980s the radical view was very influential in the world economy. Until the collapse of Communism between 1989 and 1991, the countries of Eastern Europe largely opposed any FDI, as did Communist countries elsewhere. The radical position was also embraced by many socialist countries, particularly in Africa, where one of the first actions of many newly independent states was to nationalize foreign-owned enterprises. The radical position was also embraced by countries whose political ideology was more nationalistic than socialistic. This was true in Iran and India, both of which adopted tough policies restricting FDI and nationalized many foreign-owned enterprises. Iran is a particularly interesting case because its Islamic government, while rejecting Marxist theory, has essentially embraced the radical view that FDI by MNEs is an instrument of imperialism.

By the end of the 1980s, however, the radical position was in retreat almost everywhere. There seem to be three reasons for this:

1 The collapse of Communism in Eastern Europe.

2 The generally abysmal economic performance of those countries that embraced the radical position.

3 The strong economic performance of those developing countries that embraced capitalism rather than radical ideology (e.g., Singapore, Hong Kong, South Korea, and Taiwan).

The Free Market View

The free market view traces its roots to classical economics and the international trade theories of Adam Smith and David Ricardo (see Chapter 4). The free market view argues that international production should be distributed among countries according to the theory of comparative advantage. That is, countries should specialize in the production of those goods and services that they can produce most efficiently. Within this framework, the MNE is seen as an instrument for dispersing the production of goods and services to those locations around the globe where they can be produced most efficiently. Viewed this way, FDI by the MNE is a way to increase the efficiency of the world economy.

The free market view has been embraced in principle by a number of advanced and developing nations, including the United States, Britain, Chile, Switzerland, Singapore, Hong Kong, the Netherlands, and Denmark. And it has been embraced by many of the former Communist countries of Eastern Europe—particularly Poland, the new Czech state, and Hungary—which are aggressively seeking foreign capital and investment. In practice, however, no country has adopted the free market view in its pure form (just as no country has adopted the radical view in its pure form). Countries such as Britain and the United States are among the most open to FDI, but the governments of both have intervened. Britain does so formally by reserving the right to block foreign takeovers of domestic firms if the takeovers are seen as "contrary to national security interests" or if they have the potential for "reducing competition." (This right is rarely exercised.) U.S. controls on FDI are more limited still and largely informal. For political reasons the United States will occasionally restrict U.S. firms from undertaking FDI in certain countries (e.g., Cuba and Iran). In addition, there are limited restrictions on inward FDI. Foreigners are prohibited from purchasing more than 25 percent of any

U.S. airline or from acquiring a controlling interest in a U.S. television broadcast network. Moreover, since 1989 the government has had the right to review foreign investment on the grounds of "national security."

Pragmatic Nationalism

Many countries have adopted neither a radical policy nor a free market policy toward FDI, but instead a policy that can best be described as pragmatic nationalism. The pragmatic nationalist view is that FDI has both benefits and costs. FDI can benefit a host country by bringing capital, skills, technology, and jobs, but those benefits often come at a cost. The profits from a foreign investment go abroad, and a foreign-owned manufacturing plant may import many components from its home country, which has negative implications for the host country's balance-of-payments position.

Recognizing this, countries adopting a pragmatic stance pursue policies designed to maximize the national benefits and minimize the national costs. According to this view, FDI should be allowed only if the benefits outweigh the costs. Japan offers a good example of pragmatic nationalism. Until the 1980s Japan's policy was probably one of the most restrictive among countries adopting a pragmatic nationalist stance. Japan believed that direct entry of foreign (especially U.S.) firms with ample managerial resources could be detrimental to the development and growth of Japan's own industry and technology.[24] This belief led Japan to block the majority of applications by foreign firms to invest in Japan. However, there were always exceptions to this policy. Firms that had important technology were often given permission to undertake FDI if they insisted they would neither license their technology to a Japanese firm nor enter into a joint venture with a Japanese enterprise. IBM and Texas Instruments set up wholly owned subsidiaries in Japan by adopting this negotiating position. From the perspective of the Japanese government, the benefits of FDI in such cases—the stimulus that these firms might impart to the Japanese economy—outweighed the perceived costs.

Another aspect of pragmatic nationalism is the tendency to aggressively court FDI seen to be in the national interest by, for example, offering subsidies to foreign MNEs in the form of tax breaks or grants. As we saw in the "Management Focus," tax breaks were one factor that helped pursuade Nissan to build an assembly plant in the United Kingdom, as opposed to another European Union nation such as Spain or Belgium. The countries of the European Union often seem to be competing with each other to attract U.S. and Japanese FDI by offering large tax breaks and subsidies. Britain has been the most successful at attracting Japanese investment in the automobile industry. In addition to Nissan, Toyota and Honda also now have major assembly plants in Britain. All three now use this country as their base for serving the rest of Europe—with obvious employment and balance-of-payments benefits for Britain.

Shifting Ideology

In recent years the center of gravity on the ideological spectrum has shifted strongly toward the free market view. Although no countries have adopted a *pure* free market policy stance, an increasing number are gravitating toward the free market end of the spectrum and have liberalized their foreign investment regime. This includes many countries that only a few years ago were firmly in the radical camp (e.g., the former Communist countries of Eastern Europe and many of the socialist countries of Africa) and several countries that until recently could best be described as pragmatic nationalists with regard to FDI (e.g., Japan, South Korea, Italy, Spain, and most Latin American countries). One result has been the surge in the volume of FDI worldwide, which as we noted earlier has been growing twice as fast as the growth in world trade. Another result has been a marked increase in the volume of FDI directed at countries that have recently liberalized their FDI regimes, such as China, India, and Vietnam.

Costs and Benefits of FDI to the Nation-State

Many governments can be considered pragmatic nationalists when it comes to FDI. Accordingly, their policy is shaped by a consideration of the costs and benefits of FDI. Here we explore the benefits and costs of FDI, first from the perspective of a host country and then from the perspective of the home country. In the next section we look at the policy instruments governments use to manage FDI.

Host Country Effects: Benefits

Three main benefits of inward FDI for a host country are the resource-transfer effect, the employment effect, and the balance-of-payments effect.

RESOURCE-TRANSFER EFFECTS Foreign direct investment can make a positive contribution to a host economy by supplying capital, technology, and management resources that would otherwise not be available. The provision of these skills by an MNE (through FDI) may boost that country's economic growth rate. The accompanying "Country Focus" describes how the Venezuelan government has been encouraging FDI in its petroleum industry in an attempt to benefit from resource-transfer effects.

The argument with regard to capital is that many MNEs, by virtue of their large size and financial strength, have access to financial resources not available to host country firms. These funds may be available from internal company sources, or, because of their reputation, large MNEs may find it easier to borrow money from capital markets than host country firms would. This was a factor in the Venezuelan government's decision to invite foreign oil companies to enter into joint ventures with PDVSA, the state-owned Venezuelan oil company, to develop Venezuela's oil industry.

As for technology, you will recall from Chapter 2 that technology is a catalyst that can stimulate a country's economic growth and industrialization.[25] Technology can take two forms, both of which are valuable. It can be incorporated in a production process (e.g., the technology for discovering, extracting, and refining oil) or it can be incorporated in a product (e.g., personal computers). However, many countries lack the research and development resources and skills required to develop their own indigenous product and process technology. This is particularly true of the world's less

In 1993 Venezuela announced a plan to invest $45.8 billion in its petroleum industry over the next 10 years. The plan, as outlined by Gustavo Roosen, president of Venezuela's state-owned national oil company, Petroleos de Venezuela SA (PDVSA), assigns a key role to foreign investment in Venezuela's oil and gas sectors for the first time since the country nationalized all private oil vate companies, mainly foreign investors, will supply the remaining $19.4 billion. Groups such as Royal Dutch/Shell, Exxon, Conoco, Mitsubishi, and Total are already planning large joint-venture projects with PDVSA. PDVSA is turning to foreign investors for three reasons. First, it does not have the capital to undertake the investment alone. Second, the company recognizes

The first FDI agreement was signed in 1992 with British Petroleum (BP). BP agreed to invest $60 million by 1995 to develop a marginal oil field that it would then be given the rights to for 20 years. Using a BP study, PDVSA has also identified sectors in eastern Venezuela with strong prospects for large discoveries of crude oil. PDVSA is now looking for foreign partners to develop

Foreign Direct Investment in Venezuela's Petroleum Industry

companies in 1976. PDVSA ranks as one of the world's biggest oil companies; at the end of 1992 it had 63.3 billion barrels of crude oil reserves, one of the largest outside the Middle East. One main thrust of the company's investment program is to develop crude oil production potential of 4 million barrels per day by 2002, up 1.1 million barrels per day from the current capacity.

Of the $48.5 billion in projected capital spending, PDVSA plans to invest $29.1 billion, or 60 percent of the total, and pri-

that it lacks the technological resources and skills of many of the world's major oil companies, particularly in oil exploration, oil field development, and sophisticated refining. PDVSA realizes that if it wants to develop many of Venezuela's oil fields in a timely fashion, it must turn to these foreign companies. Third, PDVSA is hoping to use the joint ventures with foreign oil companies to learn about modern management techniques in the industry, which it can then use to improve the efficiency of its own operations.

these zones. If commercial quantities of oil are discovered, PDVSA will share future production with its partners. Furthermore, together with foreign investors such as Conoco and Total, PDVSA is investing in state of the art refining facilities that can be used to convert heavy crude oil into a lighter weight, high-value crude oil for export. Finally, PDVSA, Shell, Exxon, and Mitsubishi have entered into a $5.6 billion joint venture to produce liquefied natural gas for export.[26]

developed nations. Such countries must rely on advanced industrialized nations for much of the technology required to stimulate economic growth, and FDI can provide it. Thus, as we saw in the "Country Focus" on Venezuela, a lack of relevant technological know-how with regard to the discovery, extraction, and refining of oil was one factor behind the Venezuelan government's decision to invite foreign oil companies into the country.

Foreign management skills provided through FDI may also produce important benefits for the host country. Beneficial spinoff effects arise when local personnel who are trained to occupy managerial, financial, and technical posts in the subsidiary of a foreign MNE subsequently leave the firm and help to establish indigenous firms. Similar benefits may arise if the superior management skills of a foreign MNE stimulate local suppliers, distributors, and competitors to improve their own management skills.

The beneficial effects may be considerably reduced if most management and highly skilled jobs in the subsidiaries of foreign firms are reserved for home country nationals. In such cases, citizens of the host country do not receive the benefits of training by the MNE. This may limit the spinoff effect. Consequently, the percentage of management and skilled jobs that go to citizens of the host country can be a major negotiating point between an MNE and a potential host government. In recent years most MNEs have responded to pressures on this issue by agreeing to reserve a large proportion of management and highly skilled jobs for citizens of the host country.

EMPLOYMENT EFFECTS The beneficial employment effect claimed for FDI is that FDI brings jobs to a host country that would otherwise not be created there. As we saw in the "Management Focus" on Nissan in the United Kingdom, employment effects are both direct and indirect. Direct effects arise when a foreign MNE directly employs a number of host country citizens. Indirect effects arise when jobs are created in local suppliers as a result of the investment and when jobs are created because of the increased spending in the local economy resulting from employees of the MNE. The indirect employment effects are often as large as, if not larger than, the direct effects. In the Nissan case, for example, Nissan's investment created 4,250 direct jobs and at least another 4,000 jobs in support industries in the United Kingdom.

Cynics note that not all the "new jobs" created by FDI represent net additions in employment. In the case of FDI by Japanese auto companies in the United States, for example, some argue that the jobs created by this investment have been more than offset by the jobs lost in U.S.-owned auto companies, which have lost market share to their Japanese competitors. As a consequence of such substitution effects, the net number of new jobs created by FDI may not be as great as initially claimed by an MNE. Not surprisingly, then, the issue of the likely net gain in employment may be a major negotiating point between an MNE and the host government.

BALANCE-OF-PAYMENTS EFFECTS The effect of FDI on a country's balance-of-payments accounts is an important policy issue for most host governments. A country's **balance-of-payments accounts** track both its payments to and its receipts from other countries. Governments normally are concerned when their country is running a deficit on the current account of their balance of payments. The **current account** tracks the export and import of goods and services. A current account deficit, or trade deficit as it is often called, arises when a country is importing more goods and services than it is exporting. Governments typically prefer to see a current account surplus rather than a deficit. The only way in which a current account deficit can be supported in the long run is buy selling assets to foreigners (for a detailed explanation of why this is the case, see Krugman and Obstfeld).[27] For example, the persistent U.S. current account deficit of the 1980s and 1990s

balance-of-payments account Record of a country's payments to and receipts from other countries.

current account Record of a country's export and import of goods and services.

was financed by a steady sale of U.S. assets (stocks, bonds, real estate, and corporations) to foreigners. Since national governments dislike seeing the assets of their country fall into foreign hands, they prefer to run a current account surplus. There are two ways in which FDI can help a country achieve this goal.

First, if the FDI is a substitute for imports of goods or services, it can improve the current account of the host country's balance of payments. Much of the FDI by Japanese automobile companies in the United States and United Kingdom, for example, can be seen as substituting for imports from Japan. Thus, the current account of the U.S. balance of payments has improved somewhat because many Japanese companies are now supplying the U.S. market from production facilities in the United States, as opposed to facilities in Japan. Insofar as this has reduced the need to finance a current account deficit by asset sales to foreigners, the United States has clearly benefited from this.

A second potential benefit arises when the MNE uses a foreign subsidiary to export goods and services to other countries. As outlined in the "Management Focus," one benefit to Britain of Nissan's investment was that Nissan has subsequently exported up to 80 percent of the automobiles assembled at its Sunderland plant—which has had a favorable impact on the current account of Britain's balance of payments.

Host Country Effects: Costs

Three main costs of inward FDI concern host countries: the possible adverse effects of FDI on competition within the host nation, adverse effects on the balance of payments, and the perceived loss of national sovereignty and autonomy.

ADVERSE EFFECTS ON COMPETITION Host governments sometimes worry that the subsidiaries of foreign MNEs operating in their country may have greater economic power than indigenous competitors because they may be part of a larger international organization. As such, the foreign MNE may be able to draw on funds generated elsewhere to subsidize its costs in the host market, which could drive indigenous companies out of business and allow the firm to monopolize the market. Once the market was monopolized, the foreign MNE could raise prices above those that would prevail in competitive markets, with harmful effects on the economic welfare of the host nation. This concern tends to be greater in countries that have few large firms of their own (generally less developed countries). It is a relatively minor concern in most advanced industrialized nations.

Another variant of the competition argument is related to the infant industry concern we discussed in Chapter 5. Import controls may be motivated by a desire to let a local industry develop to a stage where it can compete in world markets. The same logic suggests that FDI should be restricted. If a country with a potential comparative advantage in a particular industry allows FDI in that industry, indigenous firms may never have a chance to develop.

The above arguments are often used by inefficient indigenous competitors when lobbying their government to restrict direct investment by foreign MNEs. Although a host government may state publicly in such cases that its restrictions on inward FDI are designed to protect indigenous competitors from the market power of foreign MNEs, they may have been enacted to protect inefficient but politically powerful indigenous competitors from foreign competition.

ADVERSE EFFECTS ON THE BALANCE OF PAYMENTS The possible adverse effects of FDI on a host country's balance-of-payments position are twofold. First, set against the initial capital inflow that comes with FDI must be the subsequent outflow of capital as the foreign subsidiary repatriates earnings to its parent company. Such outflows show up as a debit on the capital account of the balance of payments (the **capital account** records transactions involving the purchase and sale of assets). Net outflows of capital can lead to a fall in the value of a country's currency on the foreign exchange markets. Since governments often don't like to see this (for reasons that will be explained in Chapter 8), some governments have responded to the danger associated with such outflows by restricting the amount of earnings that can be repatriated to a foreign subsidiary's home country.

A second concern arises when a foreign subsidiary imports a substantial number of its inputs from abroad, which results in a debit on the current account of the host country's balance of payments. One criticism leveled against Japanese-owned auto assembly operations in the United States, for example, is that they import a large number of component parts from Japan. Due to such effects, the favorable impact of this FDI on the current account of the U.S. balance-of-payments position may not be as great as initially supposed. The Japanese auto companies have responded to these criticisms by pledging to purchase 75 percent of their component parts from U.S.-based manufacturers (but not necessarily U.S.-owned manufacturers). In the case of Nissan's investment in the United Kingdom, Nissan responded to concerns about local content by pledging to increase the proportion of local content to 60 percent and by subsequently raising it to over 80 percent.

NATIONAL SOVEREIGNTY AND AUTONOMY Many host governments worry that FDI is accompanied by some loss of economic independence. The concern is that key decisions that can affect the host country's economy will be made by a foreign parent that has no real commitment to the host country, and over which the host country's government has no real control. Twenty years ago this concern was expressed by several European countries that feared that FDI by U.S. MNEs was threatening their national sovereignty. Ironically, the same concerns are now surfacing in the United States with regard to European and Japanese FDI.

The main fear seems to be that if foreigners own assets in the United States, they can somehow "hold the country to economic ransom." Twenty years ago when officials in the French government were making similar complaints about U.S. investments in France, many U.S. politicians dismissed the charge as silly. Now that the shoe is on the other foot, many U.S. politicians no longer think the notion is silly.

However, most economists dismiss such concerns as groundless and irrational. Political scientist Robert Reich recently spoke of such concerns as the product of outmoded thinking because they fail to account for the growing interdependence of the world economy.[28] In a world where firms from all advanced nations are increasingly investing in each other's markets, it is not possible for one country to hold another to "economic ransom" without hurting itself in the process.

capital account Record of transactions involving the purchase and sale of assets.

Home Country Effects: Benefits

Although the costs and benefits of FDI for a host country have received the most attention, there are also costs and benefits to the home (or source) country that warrant attention. Does the U.S. economy benefit or lose from investments by its firms in foreign markets? Does the Japanese economy lose or gain from Nissan's investment in the United Kingdom? Some would argue that FDI is not always in the home country's national interest and should be restricted. Others argue that the benefits far outweigh the costs, and that any restrictions would be contrary to national interests. To understand why people take these positions, let us look at the benefits and costs of FDI to the home (source) country.[29]

The benefits of FDI to the home country arise from three sources. First, the capital account of the home country's balance of payments benefits from the inward flow of foreign earnings. Thus, one benefit to Japan from Nissan's investment in the United Kingdom is the earnings that are subsequently repatriated to Japan. FDI can also benefit the current account of the home country's balance of payments if the foreign subsidiary creates demands for home country exports of capital equipment, intermediate goods, complementary products, and the like.

Second, benefits to the home country from outward FDI arise from employment effects. As with the balance of payments, positive employment effects arise when the foreign subsidiary creates demand for home country exports of capital equipment, intermediate goods, complementary products, and the like. Thus, Nissan's investment in auto assembly operations in the United Kingdom has had a beneficial effect on both the Japanese balance-of-payments position and employment in Japan because Nissan imports some component parts for its U.K.-based auto assembly operations directly from Japan.

Third, benefits arise when the home country MNE learns valuable skills from its exposure to foreign markets that can subsequently be transferred back to the home country. This amounts to a reverse resource-transfer effect. Through its exposure to a foreign market, an MNE can learn about superior management techniques and superior product and process technologies. These resources can then be transferred back to the home country, with a commensurate beneficial effect on the home country's economic growth rate.[30] For example, one purpose behind the investment by General Motors and Ford in Japanese automobile companies (GM owns part of Isuzu, and Ford owns part of Mazda) has been for GM and Ford to learn about those Japanese companies' apparently superior management techniques and production processes. If GM and Ford are successful in transferring this know-how back to their U.S. operations, the result may be a net gain for the U.S. economy.

Home Country Effects: Costs

Against these benefits must be set the apparent costs of FDI for the home (source) country. The most important concerns center around the balance-of-payments and employment effects of outward FDI. The home country's trade position (its current account) may deteriorate if the purpose of the foreign investment is to serve the home market from a low-cost production location. For example, when a U.S. textile company closes its plants in South Carolina and moves production to Central America, as many have, imports into the

216

Part 3 Cross-Border Trade and Investment

United States rise and the trade position deteriorates. The current account of the balance of payments also suffers if the FDI is a substitute for direct exports. Thus, insofar as Toyota's assembly operations in the United States are intended to substitute for direct exports from Japan, the current account position of Japan will deteriorate.

With regard to employment effects, the most serious concerns arise when FDI is seen as a substitute for domestic production. This was the case with Nissan's investment in the United Kingdom. One obvious result of such FDI is reduced home country employment. If the labor market in the home country is already very tight, with little unemployment, this concern may not be that great. However, if the home country is suffering from unemployment, concern about the "export of jobs" may rise to the fore. For example, one objection frequently raised by U.S. labor leaders to the free trade pact among the United States, Mexico, and Canada (see the next chapter) is that the United States will lose hundreds of thousands of jobs as U.S. firms invest in Mexico to take advantage of cheaper labor and then export back to the U.S. market.[31]

International Trade Theory and Offshore Production

When assessing the costs and benefits of FDI to the home country, keep in mind the lessons of international trade theory (see Chapter 4). International trade theory tells us that home country concerns about the negative economic effects of "offshore production" may be misplaced. The term *offshore production* refers to FDI undertaken to serve the home market. By freeing home country resources to concentrate on activities where the home country has a comparative advantage, such FDI may actually stimulate economic growth (and hence employment) in the home country. Also, home country consumers benefit if the price of the particular product falls as a result of the FDI.

If a company were prohibited from making such investments on the grounds of negative employment effects while its international competitors were able to reap the benefits of low-cost production locations, the company would undoubtedly lose market share to its international competitors. Under such a scenario, the adverse long-run economic effects for the domestic economy would probably far outweigh the relatively minor balance-of-payments and employment effects associated with offshore production.

Government Policy Instruments and FDI

We have now reviewed the costs and benefits of FDI from the perspective of both home country and host country. We now need to discuss the policy instruments that governments use to regulate FDI activity by MNEs. Both home (source) countries and host countries have a range of policy instruments that they can use. We will look at each in turn.

Home Country Policies

By their choice of policies, home countries can both encourage and restrict FDI by local firms. We look at policies designed to encourage outward FDI first. These include foreign risk insurance, capital assistance, tax incentives, and political pressure. Then we will look at policies designed to restrict outward FDI.

ENCOURAGING OUTWARD FDI Many investor nations now have government-backed insurance programs to cover major types of foreign investment risk. These programs insure against the risks of expropriation (nationalization), war losses, and the inability to transfer profits back home. Such programs are particularly useful in encouraging firms to invest in politically unstable countries.[32] In addition, several advanced countries also have special funds or banks that make government loans to firms wishing to invest in developing countries. As a further incentive to encourage domestic firms to undertake FDI, many countries have eliminated double taxation of foreign income (i.e., taxation of income in both the host country and the home country). Last, and perhaps most significant, a number of investor countries (particularly the United States) have used their political influence to persuade host countries to relax their restrictions on inbound FDI. For example, in response to direct U.S. pressure, Japan relaxed many of its formal restrictions on inward FDI in the early 1980s. Now, in response to further U.S. pressure, Japan is moving toward relaxing its informal barriers to inward FDI. One beneficiary of this trend is Toys R Us, which, after five years of intensive lobbying by company and U.S. government officials, opened its first retail stores in Japan in December 1991.

RESTRICTING OUTWARD FDI Virtually all investor countries, including the United States, have exercised some control over outward FDI from time to time. One common policy has been to limit capital outflows out of concern for the country's balance of payments. From the early 1960s until 1979, for example, Britain had exchange-control regulations that limited the amount of capital a firm could take out of the country. Although the main intent of such policies was to improve the British balance of payments, an important secondary intent was to make it more difficult for British firms to undertake FDI.

In addition, countries have occasionally manipulated tax rules to try to encourage their firms to invest at home. The objective behind such policies is to create jobs at home rather than in other nations. At one time these policies were also adopted by Britain. The British advanced corporation tax system taxed British companies' foreign earnings at a higher rate than their domestic earnings. This tax code created an incentive for British companies to invest at home.

Finally, countries sometimes prohibit national firms from investing in certain countries for political reasons. Such restrictions can be formal or informal. For example, formal U.S. rules have prohibited U.S. firms from investing in countries such as Cuba, Libya, and Iran, whose political ideology and actions are judged to be contrary to U.S. interests. Similarly, during the 1980s informal pressure was applied to dissuade U.S. firms from investing in South Africa. In this case, the objective was to pressure South Africa to change its apartheid laws, which occurred during the early 1990s. Thus, this policy was successful.

Host Country Policies

Host countries adopt policies designed both to restrict and to encourage inward FDI. As noted earlier in this chapter, political ideology has determined the type and scope of these policies in the past. In the last decade of the 20th century, we seem to be moving quickly away from a situation where many countries adhered to some version of the radical stance and prohibited much FDI and toward a situation where a combination of free market objectives and pragmatic nationalism seems to be taking hold.

ENCOURAGING INWARD FDI It is increasingly common for governments to offer incentives to foreign firms to invest in their countries. Such incentives take many forms, but the most common are tax concessions, low-interest loans, and grants or subsidies. Incentives are motivated by a desire to gain from the resource-transfer and employment effects of FDI. They are also motivated by a desire to capture FDI away from other potential host countries. For example, as we saw in the opening case, the governments of Britain and Spain competed with each other on the size of the incentives they offered Nissan to invest in their respective countries. Britain won this competition, and the size of the tax concessions granted to Nissan was no small factor in the final decision. Not only do countries compete with each other to attract FDI, but regions of countries do as well. In the United States, for example, state governments often compete with each other to attract FDI. It has been estimated that in attempting to persuade Toyota to build its U.S. automobile assembly plants in Kentucky, rather than elsewhere in the United States, the state offered Toyota an incentive package worth $112 million. The package included tax breaks, new state spending on infrastructure, and low-interest loans.[33]

RESTRICTING INWARD FDI Host governments use a wide range of controls to restrict FDI. The two most common, however, are ownership restraints and performance requirements. Ownership restraints can take several forms. In some countries foreign companies are excluded from specific business fields. For example, they are excluded from tobacco and mining in Sweden and from the development of certain natural resources in Brazil, Finland, and Morocco. In other industries, foreign ownership may be permitted, although local ownership of a significant proportion of the subsidiary may be required. For example, foreign ownership is restricted to 25 percent or less of an airline in the United States.

The rationale underlying ownership restraints seems to be twofold. First, foreign firms are often excluded from certain sectors on the grounds of national security or competition. Particularly in less developed countries, the feeling seems to be that local firms might not be able to develop unless foreign competition is restricted by a combination of import tariffs and controls on FDI. This is really a variant of the infant industry argument discussed in Chapter 5.

Second, ownership restraints seem to be based on a belief that local owners can help to maximize the resource-transfer and employment benefits of FDI for the host country. Consistent with this belief, until the early 1980s the Japanese government prohibited most FDI but was prepared to allow joint ventures between Japanese firms and foreign MNEs if the MNE had a particularly valuable technology. The Japanese government clearly felt that such an arrangement would help speed up the subsequent diffusion of the MNE's valuable technology throughout the Japanese economy.

As for performance requirements, these too can take several forms. Performance requirements are controls over the behavior of the local subsidiary of an MNE. The most common performance requirements are related to local content, exports, technology transfer, and local participation in top management. As with certain ownership restrictions, the logic underlying performance requirements is that such rules help to maximize the benefits and minimize the costs of FDI for the host country. Virtually all countries employ some form of performance requirement when it suits their objectives. However, performance requirements tend to be more common in less developed countries than in advanced industrialized nations. For example, one study found that some 30 percent of the affiliates of U.S. MNEs in less developed countries were subject to performance requirements, while only 6 percent of the affiliates in advanced countries were faced with such requirements.[34]

Implications for Business

Several implications for business are inherent in the material discussed in this chapter. We deal first with the implications of the theory of FDI, and then turn our attention to the implications of government policy.

The Theory of FDI

The implications of the theories of FDI for business practice are straightforward. First, the location-specific advantages argument associated with John Dunning helps explain the *direction* of FDI. However, the location-specific advantages argument does not explain *why* firms prefer FDI to licensing or to exporting. In this regard, from both an explanatory and a business perspective, perhaps the most useful theories are those that focus on the limitations of exporting and licensing. These theories are useful because they identify how the relative profitability of foreign direct investment, exporting, and licensing vary with circumstances. The theories suggest that exporting is preferable to licensing and foreign direct investment as long as transport costs are minor and trade barriers are trivial. As transport costs and/or trade barriers increase, exporting becomes unprofitable, and the choice is between FDI and licensing. Since FDI is more costly and more risky than licensing, other things being equal, the theories argue that licensing is preferable to FDI. Other things are seldom equal, however. Although licensing may work, it is not an attractive option when one or more of the following conditions exist:

- The firm has valuable know-how that cannot be adequately protected by a licensing contract.
- The firm needs tight control over a foreign entity in order to maximize its market share and earnings in that country.
- A firm's skills and capabilities are not amenable to licensing.

Figure 6.3 presents these considerations as a decision tree.

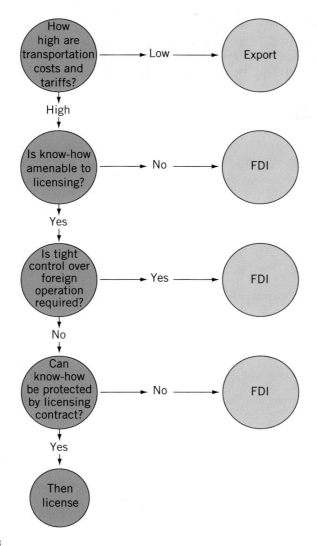

FIGURE 6.3

A Decision Framework

Firms for which licensing is not a good option tend to be clustered in three types of industries:

1 High-technology industries where protecting firm-specific expertise is of paramount importance and licensing is hazardous.

2 Global oligopolies, where competitive interdependence requires that multinational firms maintain tight control over foreign operations so they have the ability to launch coordinated attacks against their global competitors (as Kodak has done with Fuji).

3 Industries where intense cost pressures require that multinational firms maintain tight control over foreign operations (so they can disperse manufacturing to locations around the globe where factor costs are most favorable in order to minimize costs).

Although empirical evidence is limited, the majority of the evidence seems to support these conjectures.[35]

Firms for which licensing is a good option tend to be in industries whose conditions are opposite to those specified above. That is, licensing tends to be more common (and more profitable) in fragmented, low-technology industries in which globally dispersed manufacturing is not an option. A good example is the fast food industry. McDonald's has expanded globally by using a franchising strategy. Franchising is essentially the service industry version of licensing—although it normally involves much longer-term commitments than licensing. With franchising, the firm licenses its brand name to a foreign firm in return for a percentage of the franchisee's profits. The franchising contract specifies the conditions that the franchisee must fulfill if it is to use the franchisor's brand name. Thus, McDonald's allows foreign firms to use its brand name as long as they agree to run their restaurants on exactly the same lines as McDonald's restaurants elsewhere in the world. This strategy makes sense for McDonald's because

- Like many services, fast food cannot be exported.
- Franchising economizes the costs and risks associated with opening foreign markets.
- Unlike technological know-how, brand names are relatively easy to protect using a contract.
- There is no compelling reason for McDonald's to have tight control over franchisees.
- McDonald's know-how, in terms of how to run a fast food restaurant, is amenable to being specified in a written contract (e.g., the contract specifies the details of how to run a McDonald's restaurant).

Finally, it should be noted that the product life-cycle theory and Knickerbocker's theory of FDI tend to be less useful from a business perspective. They are descriptive rather than analytical. They do a good job of describing the historical evolution of FDI, but they do a relatively poor job of identifying the factors that influence the relative profitability of FDI, licensing, and exporting. Indeed, the issue of licensing as an alternative to FDI is ignored by both of these theories.

Government Policy

A host government's attitude toward FDI should be an important variable in decisions about where to locate foreign production facilities and where to make a foreign direct investment. Other things being equal, investing in countries that have permissive policies toward FDI is clearly preferable to investing in countries that restrict FDI.

However, often the issue is not this straightforward. Despite the move toward a free market stance in recent years, many countries still have a rather pragmatic stance toward FDI. In such cases, a firm considering FDI usually must often negotiate the specific terms of the investment with the country's government. Such negotiations center on two broad issues. If the host government is trying to attract FDI, the central issue is likely to be the kind of incentives the host government is prepared to offer to the MNE and what the firm will commit in exchange. If the host government is uncertain about the benefits of FDI and might restrict access, the central issue is likely to be the concessions the firm must make to be allowed to go forward with a proposed investment.

To a large degree, the outcome of any negotiated agreement depends on the relative bargaining power of both parties. Each side's bargaining power depends on three factors:

- The value each side places on what the other has to offer.
- The number of comparable alternatives available to each side.
- Each party's time horizon.

From the perspective of a firm negotiating the terms of an investment with a host government, the firm's bargaining power is high when the host government places a high value on what the firm has to offer, the number of comparable alternatives open to the firm is great, and the firm has a long time in which to complete the negotiations. The converse also holds. The firm's bargaining power is low when the host government places a low value on what the firm has to offer, the number of comparable alternatives open to the firm is small, and the firm has a short time in which to complete the negotiations.[36]

Key Terms

balance-of-payments accounts, p. 214

capital account, p. 215

current account, p. 214

eclectic paradigm, p. 201

exporting, p. 201

externalities, p. 208

flow of foreign direct investment, p. 194

foreign direct investment, p. 194

home country, p. 197

host country, p. 197

inflows of foreign direct investment, p. 195

internalization theory, p. 204

licensing, p. 201

location-specific advantages, p. 207

multinational enterprise, p. 194

oligopoly, p. 206

outflows of foreign direct investment, p. 195

stock of foreign direct investment, p. 194

Summary

The objectives of this chapter were to review theories that attempt to explain the pattern of FDI between countries and to examine governments' influence on firms' decisions to invest in foreign countries. The following points have been made:

1 Any theory seeking to explain FDI must explain why firms go to the trouble of acquiring or establishing operations abroad, when the alternatives of exporting and licensing are available.

2 High transportation costs and/or tariffs imposed on imports help explain why many firms prefer FDI or licensing over exporting.

3 Firms often prefer FDI to licensing when: *(i)* a firm has valuable know-how that cannot be adequately protected by a licensing contract, *(ii)* a firm needs tight control over a foreign entity in order to maximize its market share and earnings in that country, and *(iii)* a firm's skills and capabilities are not amenable to licensing.

4 Knickerbocker's theory suggests that much FDI is explained by imitative behavior by rival firms in an oligopolistic industry.

5 Vernon's product life-cycle theory suggests that firms undertake FDI at particular stages in the life cycle of products they have pioneered. However, Vernon's theory does not address the issue of whether FDI is more efficient than exporting or licensing for expanding abroad.

6 Dunning has argued that location-specific advantages are of considerable importance in explaining the nature and direction of FDI. According to Dunning, firms undertake FDI to exploit resource endowments or assets that are location specific.

7 Political ideology is an important determinant of government policy toward FDI. Ideology ranges from a radical stance that is hostile to FDI to a noninterventionist, free market stance. Between the two extremes is an approach best described as pragmatic nationalism.

8 Benefits of FDI to a host country arise from resource-transfer effects, employment effects, and balance-of-payments effects.

9 The costs of FDI to a host country include adverse effects on competition and balance of payments and a perceived loss of national sovereignty.

10 The benefits of FDI to the home (source) country include improvement in the balance of payments as a result of the inward flow of foreign earnings, positive employment effects when the foreign subsidiary creates demand for home-country exports, and benefits from a reverse resource-transfer effect. A reverse resource-transfer effect arises when the foreign subsidiary learns valuable skills abroad that can be transferred back to the home country.

11 The costs of FDI to the home country include adverse balance-of-payments effects that arise from the initial capital outflow and from the export substitution effects of FDI. Costs also arise when FDI exports jobs abroad.

12 Home countries can adopt policies designed to both encourage and restrict FDI. Host countries try to attract FDI by offering incentives and try to restrict FDI by dictating ownership restraints and requiring that foreign MNEs meet specific performance requirements.

Critical Thinking and Discussion Questions

1 In recent years Japanese FDI in the United States has grown far more rapidly than U.S. FDI in Japan. Why do you think this is the case? What are the implications of this trend?

2 Compare these explanations of FDI: internalization theory, Vernon's product life-cycle theory, and Knickerbocker's theory of FDI. Which theory do you think offers the best explanation of the historical pattern of FDI? Why?

3 You are the international manager of a U.S. business that has just developed a revolutionary new personal computer that can perform the same functions as IBM and Apple computers and their clones but costs only half as much to manufacture. Your CEO has asked you to formulate a recommendation for how to expand into Western Europe. Your options are *(i)* to export from the United States, *(ii)* to license a European firm to manufacture and market the computer in Europe, and *(iii)* to set up a wholly owned subsidiary in Europe. Evaluate the pros and cons of each alternative and suggest a course of action to your CEO.

4 Explain how the political ideology of a host government might influence the process of negotiating access between the host government and a foreign MNE.

5 "Firms should not be investing abroad when there is a need for investment to create jobs at home!" Discuss.

Internet Exercise

The global nature of the Internet encourages discussion and information on foreign direct investment on sites throughout the world. The Paris-based Organisation for Economic Development is an outgrowth of the Organisation for European Economic Co-operation, which was developed to help European countries recover from the devastating effects of World War II. The extensive site (http://www. oecd.org/) describes the origins of the forum, foreign direct investment trends and statistics (http:// cs1-hq.oecd.org/daf/cmis/statist. htm), and country reviews (http:// www.oecd.org/daf/cmis/fdirev.htm).

Both the Centre for Monitoring Indian Economy in Bombay, India (http://www.indianconsulate-sf.org/ fdic.htm) and the Bureau of Economic Analysis, an agency of the Department of Commerce, (http://www.bea.doc.gov/bea/ fdius-d.htm) post major foreign direct investments in the United States and financial and operating data of U.S. affiliates. Also, the Japanese Government's Ministry of International Trade and Industry site (http://www. jef.or.jp/news/inv/measures.html) describes how the Japanese government is attempting to promote foreign direct investment and gives charts and tables detailing foreign direct investment in Japan (http://www.jef. or.jp/news/jp/index.html). Finally, IPAnet includes databases, direc-tories, and details of global investment opportunities (http:// www.ipanet.net/guide.htm).

Global Surfing

How does the Organisation for Economic Development promote economic growth for the member and non-member countries? What trends in foreign direct investment are revealed at this site? Select a country from the list of foreign direct investment review and describe its investment trends. Which countries are increasing their major foreign direct investments, according to the Centre for Monitoring Indian Economy and the BEA? Using the Japanese Government site, describe how Japan has encouraged foreign direct investment in that country. What investment trends are described at that site? Describe how the databases available at the IPAnet site help investors explore the costs and benefits of foreign direct investment. Which sites promote Knickerbocker's, Vernon's, or Dunning's theories?

Closing Case

Conoco's Russian Investment

Since the collapse of Communism and the shift toward a market economy, senior officials of the Russian government have gone out of their way to encourage foreign companies to invest in Russia. Their rationale is fairly obvious—Russia is in desperate need of capital resources to upgrade its crumbling infrastructure, which is suffering from years of neglect and mismanagement. The Russian oil and gas industry is an example. Russia has the largest oil and gas reserves in the world, but increasingly it is finding it difficult to get these reserves out of the ground and to the international market. This is a major problem for a country that is short of export earnings and foreign currency. Between 1990 and 1994 oil and gas production in Russia declined by 40 percent. The problems include leaking pipelines, aging oil wells, a lack of new drilling, and conflict between the various states of the former Soviet Union as to who actually owns much of the oil and gas infrastructure. According to estimates by the World Bank, Russia will need to spend between $40 and $50 billion per year just to maintain oil and gas

production at its current (relatively low) levels. Boosting production back to the levels achieved in the 1980s could require investments of $80 to $100 billion per year—money that Russia just does not have!

Conoco, a subsidiary of Du Pont, is one foreign oil company that has invested in the Russian oil and gas industry. In 1991 Conoco participated in the first U.S.–Russian joint venture to develop a new oil field. The field is in the Arkhangel'sk region, north of the Arctic Circle and 1,000 miles northeast of Moscow. Conoco's joint-venture partner is the Russian geologic enterprise Arkhangelskgeologia, and the joint venture is called Polar Lights. One of Conoco's motives was to use the joint venture as a test case to learn whether the company could successfully do business in Russia.

To its surprise, Conoco found that the technical skills of the Russian workers were excellent. In most instances, they also found that the physical infrastructure was in better condition than they had been led to believe. On the other hand, they have encountered serious logistical, efficiency, and managerial

shortcomings. At the same time, Conoco's management believes that these problems are short-term ones, and that with proper training and tools Russian managers will improve rapidly.

The major problem encountered by Conoco so far has been the generally adverse political and legal climate toward foreign investment. Although Russian law currently allows Western joint ventures to export oil, in practice the ability to export has been significantly reduced by the government's bureaucratic efforts to allocate export licenses. Conoco has not always been able to get export licenses or has been asked to pay unrealistically high prices for the right to export oil from Russia. Another problem concerns the lack of a defined tax code in Russia. Various taxes are being invented by different government entities, which often seem to be working at cross-purposes. Conoco has calculated that if these taxes were actually imposed, they would exceed the total income that investments would generate. To make matters worse, growing disillusionment with the reform process in Russia has led to calls from some quarters for the renationalization of newly privatized assets and for limiting foreign direct investment into key industries, such as oil and gas. Although the current Russian government has worked hard to play down the importance of such calls, there is no doubt that they have spooked several foreign investors.[37]

Case Discussion Questions

1 What are the benefits to the Russian economy from Conoco's investment?

2 What are the risks that Conoco must bear in investing in Russia?

3 Is there any way Conoco can reduce these risks without significantly curtailing its investment in Russia?

Chapter 7

Regional Economic Integration

PhotoEdit, ©Jeff Greenberg

Opening Case

Tales from the New Europe

On January 1, 1993, the 12 member states of the European Union implemented the Single European Act (the European Union, or EU, was expanded from 12 to 15 members on January 1, 1996). This act mandated the removal of all frontier controls between EU countries, thereby abolishing delays and reducing the resources required for complying with trade bureaucracy. The act was the logical cumulation of the 35-year history of this trading bloc, which has progressively reduced barriers to the free flow of

Learning Objectives:

1 Appreciate the different levels of economic integration that are possible between nations.
2 Understand the economic and political arguments for regional economic integration.

3 Understand the economic and political arguments against regional economic integration.
4 Be familiar with the history, current scope, and future prospects of the world's most important regional economic agreements, including the European Union, the North

American Free Trade Agreement, MERCOSUR, and Asian Pacific Economic Cooperation.
5 Understand the implications for business that are inherent in regional economic integration agreements.

goods, services, and factors of production between its member states. With the implementation of the Single European Act, the EU became a single market of 340 million consumers.

For some, the creation of a single market has had a profound impact. Consider Bernard Cornille, a Frenchman who lives in the port of Calais just 20 miles across the English Channel from the British port of Dover. Mr. Cornille was an agent for a French manufacturer of cash machines. Before January 1, 1993,

he made a decent income selling this equipment, enough to live well and employ three assistants. However, in the months after implementation of the Single European Act, he watched demand for these products—and hence his income—plunge as less expensive equipment poured in from Spain and Italy. A desperate Mr. Cornille was forced to lay off his assistants and look for another source of income. He noted that British shoppers were beginning to flood into Calais via ferries to purchase alcohol and

tobacco, which cost half as much in France as in Britain and which the shoppers could now take home in unlimited amounts. So Mr. Cornille turned the garage behind his sales office into a wine cellar and distributed leaflets at the ferry dock with directions to his new "Cash & Carry Wine Store." Now his machine showroom is quiet, but he is making over $2,000 a week from the wine business, more than his previous income.

Barry Cotter has also seen his life take a turn for the better. A beer-bellied English truck driver, Barry Cotter speaks no foreign languages and jokes about "Cloggies" (the Dutch) and "Kermits" (as in "Frogs," or the French). Despite his provincialism, Mr. Cotter can't say enough good things about the new Europe. This Englishman makes his living by driving for a German trucking company, primarily hauling chemicals between Spain and Italy. Before 1993 Mr. Cotter needed 70 forms to cross the frontier between Spain and France. It could take hours, even days, but now he speeds straight through without so much as a glance from the lone guard. With traditional delays vanishing across Europe, he can now cross the Continent in just three days compared to five before 1993. "In this business time is money," he says, "and these days I've got a lot more of both."

Not everyone has had it as easy as Bernard Cornille and Barry Cotter. For many European companies, language, culture, and custom barriers still remain daunting. Take Atag Holdings NV, a Dutch company whose main business is kitchen appliances. Atag thought it was well placed to benefit from the single market, but so far it has found it tough going. Atag's plant is just one mile from the German border and near the center of the EU's population. The company thought it could cater to both the "potato" and "spaghetti" belts—marketers' terms for consumers in Southern and Northern Europe—by producing two main product lines and selling these standardized "Euro-products" to "Euro-consumers." Atag quickly discovered that the "Euro-consumer" is a myth. Consumer preferences vary much more across nations than Atag had thought. Consider ceramic stove tops; Atag planned to market just two varieties throughout the EU but has found it needs 11. Belgians, who cook in huge pots, require extra large burners. Germans like oval pots and burners to fit. The French need small burners and very low temperatures for simmering sauces and broths. Germans like oven knobs on the top; the French want them on the front. Most Germans and French prefer black and white; the British demand a vast range of different colors, including peach, pigeon blue, and mint green. Despite these problems, foreign sales of Atag's kitchen ware has increased from 4 percent of its total revenues in 1985 to 25 percent in 1994. And the company now has a much more realistic assessment of the benefits of a single market among a group of countries whose cultures and traditions still differ in deep and often profound ways. Atag now believes that its range of designs and product quality, rather than the magic bullet of a "Euro-product" designed for a "Euro-consumer," will keep the company competitive.[1]

Introduction

regional economic integration Agreement between countries in a geographic region to reduce tariff and nontariff barriers to the free flow of goods, services, and factors of production between each other.

One notable trend in the global economy in recent years has been the accelerated movement toward regional economic integration. By **regional economic integration** we mean agreements between groups of countries in a geographic region to reduce, and ultimately remove, tariff and nontariff barriers to the free flow of goods, services, and factors of production between each other. According to the World Trade Organization, between 1990 and 1996 the number of regional trade agreements increased from 38 to almost 80 (see Figure 7.1).[2] Consistent with the predictions of international trade theory, and particularly the theory of comparative advantage (see Chapter 4), the belief has been that regional free trade zones will produce nontrivial gains from trade for all member countries. As we saw in Chapter 5, the General Agreement on Tariffs and Trade (GATT) and its successor, the World Trade Organization (WTO), also seek to reduce trade barriers. However, with over 120 member states, the WTO has a worldwide perspective. By entering into regional agreements, groups of countries aim to reduce trade barriers more rapidly than can be achieved under the auspices of the WTO.

Nowhere has the movement toward regional economic integration been more successful than in Europe. As noted in the opening case, on January 1,

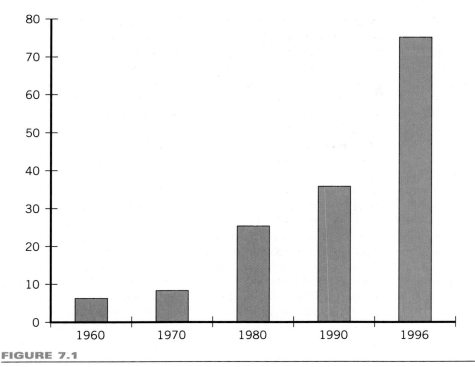

FIGURE 7.1

Number of Regional Integration Agreements
Source: World Trade Organization, Annual Report, (Geneva, 1996)

1993, the European Union effectively became a single market with 340 million consumers. Nor does the EU intend to stop here. Members of the EU have plans to establish a single currency—the euro—by 2002; they are moving toward a closer political union; and they are discussing enlargement of the EU from the current 15 countries to include another 15 Eastern European states. Similar moves toward regional integration are being pursued elsewhere in the world. Canada, Mexico, and the United States recently implemented the North American Free Trade Agreement (NAFTA). This promises to ultimately remove all barriers to the free flow of goods and services among the three countries. In 1991 Argentina, Brazil, Paraguay, and Uruguay agreed to start reducing barriers to trade between themselves. Known as MERCO-SUR, this free trade area is now widely viewed as the first step in a move toward creation of a South American Free Trade Area (SAFTA). Eighteen Pacific Rim countries, including the NAFTA member states, Japan, and China, have been discussing the possible creation of a pan-Pacific free trade area under the auspices of the Asian Pacific Economic Cooperation forum (APEC). There are also active attempts at regional economic integration to be found in Central America, the Andean region of South America, Southeast Asia, and parts of Africa.

As the opening case demonstrates, the move toward regional economic integration is not without some dislocation and economic pain. As described in the case, Bernard Cornille found his traditional line of work threatened by a flood of imports from Italy and Spain after enactment of the EU's single market. His income fell and he had to lay off employees. At the same time, however, regional economic integration can create new opportunities. This was the case for Mr. Cornille, who took advantage of the opportunities created by the single market to establish a new wine merchant business. But even here, Mr. Cornille's gain was someone else's loss, in this case, wine merchants in Britain who have seen their business decline as a result of an increase in direct purchases from France by British consumers.

Despite the fact that there are winners and losers in this kind of situation, in general, as predicted by the theory of comparative advantage (see Chapter 4), there should be a substantial net gain from regional free trade agreements such as that implemented by the EU. This argument, however, is of little help to those who suffer from regional free trade agreements, and as a result, many regional agreements have aroused substantial opposition from those whose interests are threatened. In addition, there are fears that the world is moving toward a situation in which a number of regional trading blocs compete against each other. In this scenario, free trade would exist within each bloc, but each bloc would protect its market from outside competition with high tariffs. The specter of the EU and NAFTA turning into "economic fortresses" that shut out foreign producers with high tariff barriers is particularly worrisome to those who believe in the value of unrestricted free trade. If such a scenario were to materialize, the resulting decline in trade between blocs could more than offset the gains from free trade within blocs.

Against this backdrop, the main objectives of this chapter are as follows:

1 To explore the economic and political debate surrounding regional economic integration, paying particular attention to the economic and political benefits and costs of integration.

2 To review progress toward regional economic integration around the world.

3 To map the important implications of regional economic integration for the practice of international business.

Before tackling these objectives, however, we first need to examine the levels of integration that are theoretically possible.

Levels of Economic Integration

Several levels of economic integration are possible in theory (see Figure 7.2). From least integrated to most integrated, they are a free trade area, a customs union, a common market, an economic union, and, finally, a full political union.

Free Trade Area

In a free trade area all barriers to the trade of goods and services among member countries are removed. In the theoretically ideal free trade area, no discriminatory tariffs, quotas, subsidies, or administrative impediments are allowed to distort trade between member countries. Each country, however, is allowed to determine its own trade policies with regard to nonmembers. Thus, for example, the tariffs placed on the products of nonmember countries may vary among members.

The most enduring free trade area in the world is the European Free Trade Association (EFTA). Established in January 1960, EFTA currently joins three countries—Norway, Iceland, and Switzerland—down from six in 1995 (on

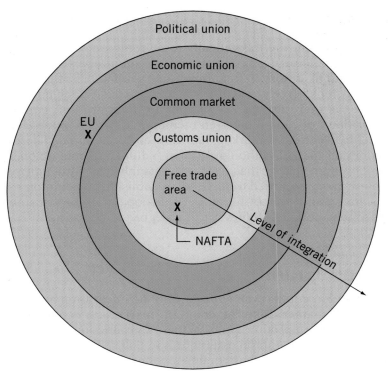

FIGURE 7.2

Levels of Economic Integration

January 1, 1996, three EFTA members, Austria, Finland, and Sweden, joined the EU). EFTA was founded by those Western European countries that initially decided not to be part of the European Community (the forerunner of the EU). Its original members included Austria, Britain, Denmark, Finland, and Sweden, all of which are now members of the EU. The emphasis of EFTA has been on free trade in industrial goods. Agriculture was left out of the arrangement, each member being allowed to determine its own level of support. Members were also left free to determine the level of protection applied to goods coming from outside EFTA. Other free trade areas include the North American Free Trade Agreement (NAFTA).

Customs Union

The customs union is one step further along the road to full economic and political integration. A customs union eliminates trade barriers between member countries and adopts a common external trade policy. A common external trade policy requires significant administrative machinery to oversee trade relations with nonmembers. Most countries that enter into a customs union desire even greater economic integration down the road. The EU began as a customs union and has moved beyond this stage. Other customs unions around the world include the current version of the Andean Pact (between Bolivia, Colombia, Ecuador, and Peru). The Andean Pact seeks to establish free trade between member countries and to impose a common tariff, of 5 to 20 percent, on products imported from outside.[3]

...on Market

...toms union, the theoretically ideal common market has no barri-
...e between member countries and a common external trade policy.
... a customs union, in a common market, factors of production also
...d to move freely between members. Thus, labor and capital are
...ve, as there are no restrictions on immigration, emigration, or
...er flows of capital between members. Hence, a much closer union
...d in a common market than in a customs union. The EU is cur-
...mmon market, although its goal is full economic union. No other
...common market has ever been established, although several re-
...pings have aspired to this goal. Establishing a common market de-
...gnificant degree of harmony and cooperation on fiscal, monetary,
and employment policies. Achieving this degree of cooperation has proven
very difficult.

Economic Union

An economic union entails even closer economic integration and cooperation
than a common market. Like the common market, an economic union involves the free flow of products and factors of production between members
and the adoption of a common external trade policy. Unlike a common market, a full economic union also requires a common currency, harmonization
of the member countries' tax rates, and a common monetary and fiscal policy. Such a high degree of integration demands a coordinating bureaucracy
and that members sacrifice significant amounts of their national sovereign-
ties to that bureaucracy. There are no true economic unions in the world today, but the EU aims to establish itself as one by the end of the century.

Political Union

The move toward economic union raises the issue of how to make a coordinating bureaucracy accountable to the citizens of member-nations. The answer is through political union. The EU is already on the road toward political union. The European Parliament, which is playing an ever more important
role in the EU, has been directly elected by citizens of the EU countries since
the late 1970s. In addition, the Council of Ministers (the controlling, decision-
making body of the EU) is composed of government ministers from each
EU member. Canada and the United States provide examples of even closer
degrees of political union; in each country independent states were combined into a single nation. Ultimately, the EU may move toward a similar federal structure.

The Case for Regional Integration

The case for regional integration is both economic and political. The case for
integration is typically not accepted by many groups within a country, which
explains why most attempts to achieve regional economic integration have

been contentious and halting. In this section we examine the economic and political cases for integration and two impediments to integration. In the next section we look at the case against integration.

The Economic Case for Integration

The economic case for regional integration is straightforward. We saw in Chapter 4 how economic theories of international trade predict that unrestricted free trade will allow countries to specialize in the production of goods and services that they can produce most efficiently. The result is greater world production than would be possible with trade restrictions. We also saw in that chapter how opening a country to free trade stimulates economic growth in the country, which in turn creates dynamic gains from trade. Further, we saw in Chapter 6 how foreign direct investment (FDI) can transfer technological, marketing, and managerial know-how to host nations. Given the central role of knowledge in stimulating economic growth, opening a country to FDI also is likely to stimulate economic growth. In sum, economic theories suggest that free trade and investment is a positive-sum game in which all participating countries gain.

Given this, the theoretical ideal is a total absence of barriers to the free flow of goods, services, and factors of production among nations. However, as we saw in Chapters 5 and 6, a case can be made for government intervention in international trade and FDI. Because many governments have accepted part or all of the case for intervention, unrestricted free trade and FDI have proved to be only an ideal. Although international institutions such as the WTO have been moving the world toward a free trade regime, success has been less than total. One problem is that in a world of many nations and many political ideologies, it is difficult to get all countries to agree to a common set of rules.

Against this background, regional economic integration can be seen as an attempt to achieve additional gains from the free flow of trade and investment between countries beyond those attainable under international agreements such as the WTO. Undoubtedly, it is easier to establish a free trade and investment regime among a limited number of adjacent countries than among the whole world community. Problems of coordination and policy harmonization are largely a function of the number of countries that seek agreement. The greater the number of countries involved, the greater the number of different perspectives that must be reconciled, and the harder it will be to reach agreement.

The Political Case for Integration

The political case for regional economic integration has also loomed large in most attempts to establish free trade areas, customs unions, and the like. Linking neighboring economies and making them increasingly dependent on each other creates incentives for political cooperation between neighboring states. Also, the potential for violent conflict between the states is reduced. In addition, by grouping their economies together, the countries can enhance their political weight in the world.

These considerations were behind the establishment of the European Community (EC) in 1957 (the EC was the forerunner of the EU). Europe had suffered two devastating wars in the first half of the century, both arising from the unbridled ambitions of nation-states. A united Europe is seen as one way to prevent another outbreak of war in Europe, to make it unthinkable. Many Europeans also believed that after World War II the European nation-states were no longer large enough to hold their own in world markets and world politics. The need for a united Europe to deal with the United States and the politically alien USSR loomed large in the minds of many of the EC's founders.[4]

Impediments to Integration

Despite the strong economic and political arguments for integration, it has never been easy to achieve or sustain. There are two main reasons for this. First, although economic integration benefits the majority, it has its costs. Although a nation as a whole may benefit significantly from a regional free trade agreement, certain groups may lose. Moving to a free trade regime involves painful adjustments. For example, as a result of the 1994 establishment of NAFTA some Canadian and U.S. workers in such industries as textiles, which employ low-cost, low-skilled labor, will lose their jobs as Canadian and U.S. firms move production to Mexico. The promise of significant net benefits to the Canadian and U.S. economies as a whole is little comfort to those who will lose as a result of NAFTA. Such groups were in the forefront of opposition to NAFTA and will continue to oppose any widening of the agreement.

A second impediment to integration arises from concerns over national sovereignty. For example, Mexico's concerns about maintaining control of its oil interests resulted in an agreement with Canada and the United States to exempt the Mexican oil industry from any liberalization of foreign investment regulations achieved under NAFTA. More generally, concerns about national sovereignty arise because close economic integration demands that countries give up some degree of their control over such key policy issues as monetary policy, fiscal policy (e.g., tax policy), and trade policy. This has been a major stumbling block in the EU. To achieve full economic union, the EU has been trying to reach agreement on a common currency to be controlled by a central EU bank. While most members agree in principle, Britain and Denmark remain important holdouts. A politically important segment of public opinion in both countries opposes a common currency on the grounds that it would require relinquishing control of their country's monetary policy to the EU, which many perceive as a bureaucracy run by foreigners. Accordingly, both countries have won the right to opt out of the agreement to establish a common EU currency in 2002.[5]

The Case Against Regional Integration

trade creation Occurs when high-cost domestic producers are replaced by low-cost producers within the free trade area.

Although the tide has been running strongly in favor of regional free trade agreements in recent years, some economists have expressed concern that the benefits of regional integration have been oversold, while the costs have often been ignored.[6] They point out that the benefits of regional integration to the participants are determined by the extent of trade creation, as opposed to trade diversion. **Trade creation** occurs when high-cost domestic producers are replaced by low-cost producers within the free trade area. **Trade diversion** occurs when lower-cost external suppliers are replaced by higher-cost suppliers within the free trade area. A regional free trade agreement will benefit the world only if the amount of trade it creates exceeds the amount it diverts.

trade diversion Occurs when lower-cost external suppliers are replaced by higher-cost suppliers within the free trade area.

Suppose the United States and Mexico imposed tariffs on imports from all countries, and then they set up a free trade area, scrapping all trade barriers between them but maintaining tariffs on imports from the rest of the world. If the United States began to import textiles from Mexico, would this change be for the better? If the United States previously produced all its own textiles at a higher cost than Mexico, then the free trade agreement has shifted production to the cheaper source. According to the theory of comparative advantage, trade has been created within the regional grouping, and there would be no decrease in trade with the rest of the world. Clearly, the change would be for the better. If, however, the United States previously imported textiles from South Korea, which produced them more cheaply than either Mexico or the United States, then trade has been diverted from a low-cost source—a change for the worse.

In theory, WTO rules should ensure that a free trade agreement does not result in trade diversion. These rules allow free trade areas to be formed only if the members set tariffs that are not higher or more restrictive to outsiders than the ones previously in effect. However, as we saw in Chapter 5, in recent years there has been a proliferation of nontariff barriers not covered by the GATT and WTO. As a result, fear is growing that regional trade blocs could emerge whose markets are protected from outside competition by high nontariff barriers. In such cases, the trade diversion effects might outweigh the trade creation effects. The only way to guard against this possibility, according to those concerned about this potential, is to increase the scope and power of the WTO so that it covers nontariff barriers to trade. There is no sign that this is going to occur anytime soon, however, so the risk remains that regional economic integration will result in trade diversion.

Regional Economic Integration in Europe

There are now two trade blocs in Europe: the European Union and the European Free Trade Association. Of the two, the EU is by far the more significant, not just in terms of membership (the EU has 15 members, and EFTA has 3), but also in terms of economic and political influence in the world economy. Many now see the EU as an emerging economic and political superpower of the same order as the United States and Japan. Accordingly, we will concentrate our attention on the EU.[7]

Evolution of the European Union

The EU is the product of two political factors: first, the devastation of two world wars on Western Europe and the desire for a lasting peace, and second, the European nations' desire to hold their own on the world's political and economic stage. In addition, many Europeans were aware of the potential economic benefits of closer economic integration of the countries.

The original forerunner of the EU, the European Coal and Steel Community, was formed in 1951 by Belgium, France, West Germany, Italy, Luxembourg, and the Netherlands. Its objective was to remove barriers to intragroup shipments of coal, iron, steel, and scrap metal. With the signing of the Treaty of Rome in 1957, the European Community (EC) was established. The name changed again in 1994 when the *European Community* became the *European Union* following the ratification of the Maastricht treaty (discussed later). The Treaty of Rome provided for the creation of a common market. It called for the elimination of internal trade barriers and the creation of a common external tariff and required member states to abolish obstacles to the free movement of factors of production among the members. To facilitate the free movement of goods, services, and factors of production, the treaty provided for any necessary harmonization of the members' laws. Furthermore, the treaty committed the EC to establish common policies in agriculture and transportation.

The first enlargement of the community occurred in 1973, when Great Britain, Ireland, and Denmark joined. These three were followed in 1981 by Greece, in 1986 by Spain and Portugal, and in 1996 by Austria, Finland, and Sweden (see Map 7.1), bringing the total membership to 15 (East Germany became part of the EC after the reunification of Germany in 1990). With a population of 350 million and a GDP greater than that of the United States, these enlargements made the EU a potential global superpower.

The Single European Act

Two revolutions occurred in Europe in the late 1980s. The first was the dramatic collapse of Communism in Eastern Europe. The second revolution was much quieter, but its impact on Europe and the world may have been just as profound as the first. It was the adoption of the Single European Act by the member nations of the EC in 1987. This act committed the EC countries to work toward establishment of a single market by December 31, 1992.

THE STIMULUS FOR THE SINGLE EUROPEAN ACT The Single European Act was born of a frustration among EC members that the community was not living up to its promise. By the early 1980s it was clear that the EC had fallen short of its objectives of removing barriers to the free flow of trade and investment between members and of harmonizing the wide range of technical and legal standards for doing business. At the end of 1982 the European Commission found itself inundated with 770 cases of intra-EC protectionism to investigate. In addition, some 20 EC directives setting common technical standards for a variety of products ranging from cars to thermometers were deadlocked.

For many companies, the main problem with the EC was the disharmony of the members' technical, legal, regulatory, and tax standards. The "rules of the game" differed substantially from country to country, which stalled creation of a true single internal market. Consider the European automobile industry. In the mid-1980s there was no single EC-wide automobile market similar to the U.S. automobile market. Instead, the EC market remained fragmented into 12 national markets. There were four main reasons for this:

- Different technical standards in different countries required cars to be customized to national requirements (e.g., the headlights and sidelights of cars sold in Great Britain must be wired in a significantly different way than

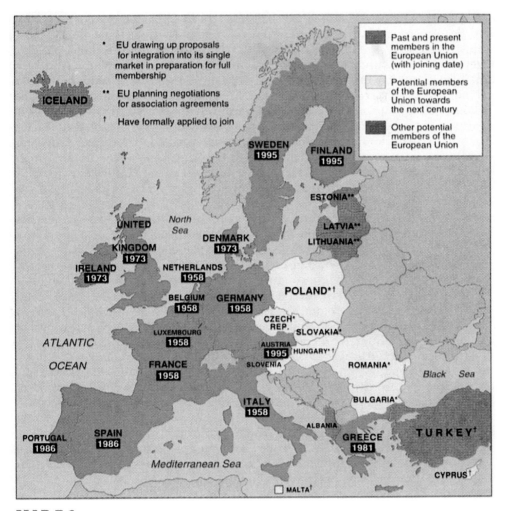

MAP 7.1

The European Union: Current Members and Applicants

those of cars sold in Italy, and the standards for car windshields in France are very different from those in Germany).

- Different tax regimes created price differentials across countries that would not be found in a single market.

- An agreement to allow automobile companies to sell cars through exclusive dealer networks allowed auto companies and their dealers to adapt their model ranges and prices on a country-by-country basis with little fear that these differences would be undermined by competing retailers.

- In violation of Article 3 of the Treaty of Rome, each country had adopted its own trade policy with regard to automobile imports (e.g., whereas Japanese imports were not restricted in Belgium, they were limited to 11 percent of the car market in Great Britain and to less than 2 percent in France and Italy). The net result of these divisions was substantial price differentials between countries. For example, in 1989 the prices of the same model of car were, on average, 31 percent higher in Great Britain and 11 percent higher in Germany than in Belgium.[8]

Numerous other administrative barriers to intra-EC trade and investment had become apparent by the mid-1980s. French buildings were uninsurable unless tiled with French-standard tiles. Government procurement policies often favored local companies. Local banking rules inhibited creation of a single EC banking industry. The French had persistently refused to abolish exchange controls, thereby limiting the ability of French companies to invest in other EC countries and companies from other EC countries to repatriate profits to their home countries. Truck drivers traveling between EC countries had to carry some 35 documents for import-export declarations and community transit forms. Simply dealing with the paperwork could make a journey take three to five times longer than it would have needed to take, and the costs of the paperwork accounted for more than 3 percent of the value of the sales involved.[9]

In addition to the profusion of barriers to intra-EC trade, many member countries were subsidizing national firms, thereby distorting competition. For example, in 1990 the French government decided to pump FFr 6 billion into Groupe Bull, a state-owned computer maker, and Thompson, a defense and electronics group. This brought protests from ICL, a British computer maker, on the grounds that such a subsidy would allow Groupe Bull to capture more of the EC computer market.[10]

Against this background, in the early 1980s many of the EC's prominent businesspeople mounted an energetic campaign to end the EC's economic divisions. Under the leadership of industrialists such as Wisse Dekker, CEO of the Dutch company Philips, the Roundtable of European Industrialists was established in 1983. Roundtable participants were chairmen, CEOs, and managing directors of large corporations with important manufacturing and technological commitments in the EC. Its principal objective was to foster creation of a single market by encouraging the EC to harmonize the rules of the game and by encouraging the member countries to remove their administrative barriers to trade within the EC. The Roundtable members believed that a single EC market was essential if European firms were to be competitive with their U.S. and Asian rivals.

The EC responded to this stimulus by creating a commission under the chairmanship of Jacques Delors, the former French finance minister and president of the EC Commission. The commission produced a discussion paper in 1985 that proposed that all impediments to the formation of a single market be eliminated by December 31, 1992. Two more years passed before the EC persuaded all members to accept the proposals contained in the discussion paper. The result was the Single European Act, which was independently ratified by the parliaments of each member country and became EC law in 1987.

THE OBJECTIVES OF THE ACT The purpose of the Single European Act was to have a single market in place by December 31, 1992. The changes the act proposed include the following.[11]

1 Frontier controls—remove all frontier controls between EC countries, thereby abolishing delays and reducing the resources required for complying with trade bureaucracy.

2 Mutual recognition of standards—apply the principle of "mutual recognition," which is that a standard developed in one EC country should be accepted in another, provided it meets basic requirements in such matters as health and safety. To harmonize the product standards of different EC members would have been a huge task. Germany has some 20,000 standards, France 8,000, and Great Britain 12,000.

3 Public procurement—open procurement to nonnational suppliers. This should reduce costs directly by allowing lower-cost suppliers into national economies and indirectly by forcing national suppliers to compete.

4 Financial services—lift barriers to competition in the retail banking and insurance businesses, which should drive down the costs of financial services, including borrowing, throughout the EC.

5 Exchange controls—remove all restrictions on foreign exchange transactions between members by the end of 1992.

6 Freight transport—abolish restrictions on cabotage, the right of foreign truckers to pick up and deliver goods within another member's borders, by the end of 1992. This could reduce the cost of haulage within the EC by 10 to 15 percent.

7 Supply-side effects—all those changes should lower the costs of doing business in the EC, but the single-market program is also expected to have more complicated supply-side effects. For example, the expanded market should give EC firms greater opportunities to exploit economies of scale. In addition, the increase in competition created by removing internal barriers to trade and investment should force EC firms to become more efficient.

To signify the importance of the Single European Act, the European Community also decided to change its name to the European Union once the act took effect.

IMPLICATIONS The implications of the Single European Act are potentially enormous. If the EU is successful in establishing a single market, member countries can expect significant gains from the free flow of trade and investment. These gains may be greater than those predicted by standard trade theory that accrue when regions specialize in producing those goods and services that they produce most efficiently. The lower costs of doing business implied by the Single European Act will benefit EU firms, as will the potential economies of scale inherent in serving a single market of 360 million consumers.

On the other hand, as a result of the Single European Act many EU firms are facing increased competitive pressure. Countries such as France and Italy have long used administrative trade barriers and subsidies to protect their home markets from foreign competition. Removal of these barriers has increased competition, and some firms may go out of business. Ultimately, however, both consumers and EU firms will benefit from this. Consumers will benefit from the lower prices implied by a more competitive market. EU firms will benefit if the increased competitive pressure forces them to become more efficient, thereby transforming them into more effective international competitors capable of going head-to-head with U.S. and Asian rivals in the world marketplace.

But the shift toward a single market has not been as rapid as many would like. Five years after the Single European Act became EU law, there have been a number of delays in applying the act to certain industries, often because countries have appealed to the Council of Ministers for more time. The insurance industry, for example, was exempt until July 1994, and even now is moving only slowly toward a single market (see the "Regional Focus" on page 244 for details). Investment services were not liberalized until January 1996, and there is no compulsion to liberalize basic telephone services until 1998 (and until 2003 in poorer countries such as

Greece to protect local telephone companies from being "crushed" by the likes of Britain's BT or America's AT&T).[12] Moreover, as the opening case illustrated, many European countries have found their dreams of a single market dashed by the realities of deep and enduring cultural and language barriers between countries, which still separate many national markets, although not as effectively as formal barriers to trade once did. Still, the long-run prognosis remains very strong, and despite all the short-term setbacks the EU will probably have a reasonably well-functioning single market by the early years of the next century.

The Treaty of Maastricht and Its Aftermath

In December 1991 leaders of the 12 EC member states met in Maastricht, the Netherlands, to discuss the next steps for the EC. The results of the Maastricht meeting surprised both Europe and the rest of the world. For months the EC countries had been fighting over the issue of a common currency. The British in particular had opposed any attempt to establish a common currency. Although many economists believed a common currency was required to cement a closer economic union, deadlock had been predicted. Instead, the member states signed a treaty that not only committed them to adopting a common EC currency, but also paved the way for closer political cooperation and the possible creation of a European superstate.

The treaty lays down the main elements of a future European government: a single currency, a common foreign and defense policy, a common citizenship, and an EU parliament with teeth. It is now just a matter of waiting, some believe, for history to take its course and a "United States of Europe" to emerge. Of more immediate interest are the implications for business of the plans to establish a single currency.

EUROPEAN MONETARY UNION As with many of the provisions of the Single European Act, the move to a single currency should significantly lower the costs of doing business in the EU. The gains come from reduced exchange costs and reduced risk.[14] Let us consider exchange costs first. The EU has calculated that EU businesses convert roughly $8 trillion from one EU currency to another every year, which necessitates about $12 billion in exchange costs. A single currency would avoid these costs and help firms in other ways, as fewer resources would be required for accounting, treasury management, and the like. As for reduced risk, a single currency would reduce the risks that arise from currency fluctuations. The values of currencies fluctuate against each other continually. As we will see in Chapter 8, this introduces risks into international transactions. For example, if a British firm builds a factory in Greece, and the value of the Greek currency subsequently declines against the British pound, the value of the British firm's Greek assets will also decline. A single currency would eliminate such risks. Eliminating these risks would reduce the cost of capital. Interest rates would fall, and investment and output would increase.

The drawback of a single currency is that national authorities would lose control over monetary policy. Thus, it is crucial to ensure that the EU's monetary policy is well managed. The Maastricht treaty calls for an independent EU central bank, similar to the U.S. Federal Reserve, with a clear mandate to manage monetary policy so as to ensure price stability. The British and Danes in particular are concerned about the effectiveness of such an arrangement and the implied loss of national sovereignty. Accordingly, Britain and Denmark have won the right from other members to stay out of the monetary union if they should so choose.

The treaty went into force on January 1, 1994. Skepticism remains, however, as to whether the timetable for closer economic and political union laid out in the treaty will be met. According to current agreements, monetary union will be achieved January 1, 1999, when the exchange rates of the currencies of the 13 participating states will be irrevocably locked against each other, and a common currency, the euro, will be introduced in 2002. To achieve monetary union by 1999 member countries must achieve low inflation rates and a stable exchange rate and limit public debt to 60 percent of a country's gross domestic product. No country at present meets all criteria, and skeptics question whether any will within the Maastricht timetable—in which case monetary union will not occur in 1999.[15]

Enlargement of the European Union

The other big issue that the EU must now grapple with is that of enlargement. After a bitter dispute in March 1994, the member states agreed to enlarge the EU to include Austria, Finland, Sweden, and Norway. Most of the opposition to enlargement came from Britain, which worried that enlargement, and a subsequent reduction in its voting power in the EU's top decision-making body, the Council of Ministers, would limit its ability to block EU developments that it did not like. Britain backed down in the face of strong opposition from other EU members and agreed to enlargement. Voters in the four countries went to the polls in late 1994. Austria, Finland, and Sweden all voted to join the EU, but Norway voted to stay out. Thus, the EU of 12 became the EU of 15 on January 1, 1996. Next the EU must deal with membership applications from Hungary, Poland, the Czech Republic, Malta, Cyprus, and Turkey.[16]

Fortress Europe?

U.S. and Asian countries are concerned that the EU at some point will impose new barriers on imports from outside the EU. The fear is that the EU might increase external protection as weaker members attempt to offset their loss of protection against other EU countries by arguing for limitations on outside competition.

In theory, given the free market philosophy that underpins the Single European Act, this should not occur. In October 1988, the European Commission debated external trading policy and published a detailed statement of the EC's trading intentions in the post-1992 era.[17] The commission stressed the EC's interests in vigorous external trade. It noted that exports by EC countries to non-EC countries are equivalent to 20 percent of total world exports, compared to 15 percent for the United States and 9 percent for Japan. These external exports are equivalent to 9 percent of its own GDP, compared to 6.7 percent for the United States and 9.7 percent for Japan. In short, it is not in the EU's interests to adopt a protectionist stance, given the EU's reliance on external trade. The commission has also promised loyalty to WTO rules on international trade. As

The Creation of a
Single European
Insurance Market

In early 1994 a simple 10-year life insurance policy in Portugal cost three times more than the same policy in France, while automobile insurance for an experienced driver cost twice as much in Ireland as in Italy and four times as much as in Britain. But such price discrepancies began to fade in July 1994 as new rules relaxing restrictions on cross-border trade in the European Union insurance market came into effect. These rules implement guidelines set down in the Single European Act, which became EU law January 1, 1993. It took 18 months to get to this point because many member states pleaded for more time to adjust to the coming deregulation. Only 5 EU countries implemented all the new rules in July 1994, although 10 had done so by January 1995.

The new rules do two main things. First, they make genuine cross-border trade possible by allowing insurance companies to sell their products anywhere in the EU on the basis of regulations in their home state, the so-called "single license." Second, insurers throughout the EU will be allowed to set their own rates for all classes of insurance policy. They will no longer need to submit policy wordings to local officials for approval, effectively dismantling the highly regulated protectionist regime behind which much of the industry has been sheltered.

Although some countries—such as France and Belgium—liberalized their insurance regulations well in advance of July

for the types of trade not covered by the WTO, the EU maintains that it will push for reciprocal access. The EU has stated that in certain cases it might replace individual national trade barriers with EU protection against imports, but it also has promised that the overall level of protection would not rise.

Despite such reassurances, there is no guarantee that the EU will not adopt a protectionist stance toward external trade, and there are indications that this has occurred in two industries, agriculture and automobiles. In agriculture, the EU has continued the Common Market Agricultural Policy, which limits many food imports. In autos, the EU has reached an agreement with the Japanese to limit the Japanese market share of the EU auto market. Those countries that have quotas on Japanese car imports agreed to lift them gradually between 1993 and the end of 1998, when they are scheduled to be abolished. Meanwhile, Japanese producers have committed themselves to voluntarily restraining sales so that by the end of the century they hold no more than 17 percent of the European market. Then all restrictions are to be abolished. These examples of protectionism, however, are not the norm, and in general the EU countries have adopted a liberal trade policy with regard to third parties, such as Japan and the United States. In a recently published report the WTO has stated that so far the growth of regional trade groups such as the EU has not impeded the growth of freer world trade, as some fear, and may have helped promote it.[18]

1994, many other countries had not. In the countries that have been slowest to move toward a deregulated environment, the new EU rules will unleash a sharp increase in competition. The overall effect will be to erode the cartel-like arrangements through which large national companies—such as Allianz of Germany and Generali of Italy—have long dominated their local markets. Consumers should benefit from the resulting lower prices.

However, despite the injection of greater competition, price differentials between countries are likely to exist for some time for a number of reasons. First, the incidence of claims varies widely across the EU. For example, when setting prices, motor insurers must consider varying degrees of road safety and different levels of court awards to accident victims across states. Second, the level of service offered by insurers, and expected by customers, varies from country to country, and this too can lead to price differentials. Belgium consumers, for example, expect insurance brokers to drive to their homes at all hours to settle claims. This drives up costs and hence prices. Third, variations in tax regimes across member states will inhibit the development of a single market. The tax advantages of life insurance policies, for example, vary from country to country, and until tax regimes are harmonized (which is still some way off) these differences will be reflected in pricing differences. Finally, cultural factors will also inhibit cross-border trade. Most continental insurers market home, life, and motor insurance through networks of exclusive local agents, who enjoy long-term and loyal relationships with customers. Many customers are unlikely to switch insurers on the basis of price alone.

Despite all these factors, the new rules do create the potential for insurance companies to penetrate each other's national markets. However, given existing distribution arrangements this may require setting up operations in other EU countries, rather than simple cross-border selling. In particular, control over retail outlets will be critical to successful market entry. Because of this, the volume of mergers and acquisitions in the European insurance industry has been growing by 20 percent a year in recent years as European companies purchase each other. In one such example, Union des Assurances de Paris, France's largest insurance company, acquired Germany's Colonia Insurance for about $3.9 billion.[13]

Regional Economic Integration in the Americas

No other attempt at regional economic integration comes close to the EU in its boldness or its potential implications for the world economy. But there are signs that attempts at regional economic integration are on the rise again, particularly in the Americas. The most significant attempt is the North American Free Trade Agreement (NAFTA). In addition to NAFTA, several other trade blocs are in the offing in the Americas (see Map 7.2), the most significant of which appear to be the Andean Group and MERCOSUR.

The North American Free Trade Agreement

In 1988 the governments of the United States and Canada agreed to enter into a free trade agreement, which went into effect January 1, 1989. The goal of the agreement was to eliminate all tariffs on bilateral trade between Canada and the United States by 1998. This was followed in 1991 by talks among the United States, Canada, and Mexico aimed at establishing a North American

MAP 7.2

Economic Integration in South America

Free Trade Agreement (NAFTA). The talks concluded in August 1992 with an agreement in principle.

For the free trade area to become a reality, each country had to ratify the agreement. Both Canada and Mexico committed themselves to NAFTA by the fall of 1993, leaving only the U.S. government to signal its intention to go forward with the agreement. The Clinton administration had already committed itself to NAFTA and passage by the U.S. Senate looked likely, but the agreement faced stiff opposition in the U.S. House of Representatives. The vote on NAFTA in the House of Representatives was scheduled for November 17, 1993. Hours before the vote the outcome was still in doubt, and then a last-minute round of lobbying by President Clinton led to a surge for NAFTA and the bill passed the House by a comfortable margin.

The agreement became law January 1, 1994.[19] It contains the following actions:

- Abolishes within 10 years tariffs on 99 percent of the goods traded between Mexico, Canada, and the United States.

- Removes most barriers on the cross-border flow of services, allowing financial institutions, for example, unrestricted access to the Mexican market by 2000.

- Protects intellectual property rights.

- Removes most restrictions on foreign direct investment between the three member countries, although special treatment (protection) will be given to Mexican energy and railway industries, American airline and radio communications industries, and Canadian culture.

- Allows each country to apply its own environmental standards, provided such standards have a scientific basis. Lowering of standards to lure investment is described as being inappropriate.

- Establishes two commissions with the power to impose fines and remove trade privileges when environmental standards or legislation involving health and safety, minimum wages, or child labor are ignored.

ARGUMENTS FOR NAFTA   Opinions remained divided as to the consequences of NAFTA. Proponents argue that NAFTA should be viewed as an opportunity to create an enlarged and more efficient productive base for the entire region. One likely short-term effect of NAFTA will be that many U.S. and Canadian firms will move some production to Mexico to take advantage of lower labor costs. In 1991 the average hourly labor costs in Mexico were $2.32, compared with $14.31 in the United States and $14.71 in Canada. Movement of production to Mexico is most likely to occur in low-skilled, labor-intensive manufacturing industries where Mexico might have a comparative advantage (e.g., textiles). Many will benefit from such a trend. Mexico benefits because it gets needed investment and employment. The United States and Canada should benefit because the increased incomes of the Mexicans will allow them to import more U.S. and Canadian goods, thereby increasing demand and making up for the jobs lost in industries that moved production to Mexico. U.S. and Canadian consumers will benefit from the lower costs, and hence prices, of products produced in Mexico. In addition, the international competitiveness of U.S. and Canadian firms that move production to Mexico to take advantage of lower labor costs will be enhanced, enabling them to better compete with Asian and European rivals.

ARGUMENTS AGAINST NAFTA   Those who opposed NAFTA claimed that ratification would be followed by a mass exodus of jobs from the United States and Canada into Mexico as employers sought to profit from Mexico's lower wages and less strict environmental and labor laws. According to one extreme opponent, Ross Perot, up to 5.9 million U.S. jobs would be lost to Mexico after NAFTA. Most economists, however, dismissed these numbers as being absurd and alarmist. They pointed out that Mexico would have to run a bilateral trade surplus with the United States of close to $300 billion for job loss on such a scale to occur—and $300 billion is about the size of Mexico's present GDP. In other words, such a scenario was implausible.

More sober estimates of the impact of NAFTA ranged from a net creation of 170,000 jobs in the United States (due to increased Mexican demand for U.S. goods and services) and an increase of $15 billion per year to the U.S. and Mexican GDP, to a net loss of 490,000 U.S. jobs. To put these numbers in perspective, employment in the U.S. economy is predicted to grow by 18 million over the next 10 years. As most economists repeatedly stress, in the grand scheme of things NAFTA will have a small impact on both Canada and the United States. It could hardly be any other way, since the Mexican economy is only 5 percent of the size of the U.S. economy. The country that really took the economic leap of faith by signing NAFTA is Mexico. Falling trade barriers will now expose Mexican firms to highly efficient U.S. and Canadian competitors that have far greater capital resources, access to highly educated and skilled workers, and much greater technological sophistication than the average Mexican firm. The short-run outcome is bound to be painful economic restructuring and unemployment in Mexico. But if economic theory is any guide, in the long run there should be dynamic gains in the efficiency of Mexican firms as they adjust to the rigors of a more competitive marketplace. To the extent that this happens, an acceleration of Mexico's long-run rate of economic growth will follow, and Mexico might yet become a major market for Canadian and U.S. firms.[20]

Environmentalists have also voiced concerns about NAFTA. They point to the sludge in the Rio Grande River and the smog in the air over Mexico City and warn that Mexico could degrade clean air and toxic-waste standards across the continent. Already, they claim, the lower Rio Grande is the most polluted river in the United States, increasing in chemical waste and sewage along its course from El Paso, Texas, to the Gulf of Mexico.

There is also continued opposition in Mexico to NAFTA from those who fear a loss of national sovereignty. Mexican critics argue that their entire country will be dominated by U.S. firms that will not really contribute to Mexico's economic growth, but instead will use Mexico as a low-cost assembly site, while keeping their high-paying, high-skilled jobs north of the border.

THE EARLY EXPERIENCE   The first year after NAFTA turned out to be a positive experience for all three countries. U.S. trade with Canada and Mexico expanded at about twice the rate of trade with non-NAFTA countries in the first nine months of 1994, compared with the same period in 1993. U.S. exports to Mexico grew by 22 percent, while Mexican exports to the United States grew by 23 percent. Anti-NAFTA campaigners had warned of doom for the U.S. auto industry, but exports of autos to Mexico from the United States increased by nearly 500 percent in the first nine months of 1993. The U.S. Commerce Department estimated that the surge in exports to Mexico secured about 130,000 U.S. jobs, while only 13,000 people applied for aid under a program designed to help workers displaced by the movement of jobs to Mexico, suggesting that job losses from NAFTA had been small.[21]

However, the early euphoria over NAFTA was snuffed out in December 1994 when the Mexican economy was shaken by a financial crisis. Through 1993 and 1994 Mexico's trade deficit with the rest of the world had grown sharply, while Mexico's inflation rate had started to accelerate. This put increasing pressure on the Mexican currency, the peso. Traders in the foreign exchange markets, betting that there would be a large decline in the value of the peso against the dollar, began to sell pesos and buy dollars. As a result, in December 1994 the Mexican government was forced to devalue the peso by about 35 percent against the U.S. dollar. This effectively increased the cost of imports from the United States by 35 percent. The devaluation of the peso was followed quickly by a collapse in the value of the Mexican stock market, and the country suddenly and unexpectedly appeared to be in the midst of a major economic crisis. Shortly afterward, the Mexican government introduced an austerity program designed to rebuild confidence in the country's financial institutions and rein in growth and inflation. The program was backed by a $20 billion loan guarantee from the U.S. government.[22]

One result of this turmoil was a sharp decline in Canadian and U.S. exports to Mexico. Many companies have also reduced or delayed their plans for expansion into Mexico. The U.S. retailer Wal-Mart, for example, put on hold plans to open another 24 stores in Mexico (for further details on Wal-Mart's post-NAFTA experience, see the accompanying "Management Focus"). As might be expected, critics of NAFTA seized on Mexico's financial crisis to crow that they had been right all along. But in reality, just as the celebrations of NAFTA's success were premature, so are claims of its sudden demise.

In late 1996 the first hard evidence started to come in as to the economic impact of the free trade area. It suggests that so far at least, the claims of both advocates and detractors appear to have been exaggerated. The most comprehensive study was undertaken by researchers at the University of California-Los Angeles and funded by various departments of the U.S. government.[24] Their findings are enlightening. First, they conclude that the growth in trade between Mexico and the United States began to change nearly a decade before implementation of NAFTA when Mexico unilaterally started to liberalize its own trade regime to conform with GATT standards. The period since NAFTA went into effect has had little impact on trends already in place. The study found that trade growth in those sectors that underwent tariff liberalization in the first two and a half years of NAFTA was only marginally higher than trade growth in sectors not yet liberalized. For example, between 1993 and 1996, U.S. exports to Mexico in sectors liberalized under NAFTA grew by 5.83 percent annually, while exports in sectors not liberalized under NAFTA grew by 5.35 percent. In short, the authors argue that NAFTA has so far had only a marginal impact on the level of trade between the United States and Mexico.

As for the much debated impact of NAFTA on jobs in the United States, the study concluded the impact was positive but very small. The study found that while NAFTA created 31,158 new jobs in the United States, 28,168 jobs were lost due to imports from Mexico, for a net job gain of about 3,000 in the first two years of NAFTA.

However, as the report authors point out, trade flows and employment in the 1995–96 period have been significantly affected by the economic crisis that gripped Mexico in early 1995. Given this, it is probably far too early to draw conclusions about the true impact of NAFTA on trade flows and employment. It will be a decade or more before any meaningful conclusions can be stated. The most that can be said at this juncture is that while the optimistic picture of job creation painted by NAFTA's advocates has not yet come to pass, neither has the apocalyptic vision of widespread job losses in the United States and Canada propagated by NAFTA's opponents.

ENLARGEMENT One big issue now confronting NAFTA is that of enlargement. After the U.S. Congress approved NAFTA, a number of other Latin American countries indicated their desire to eventually join the free trade area. Currently the governments of both Canada and the United States are adopting a wait-and-see attitude with regard to most countries. Getting NAFTA approved was such a bruising political experience that neither the Canadian nor U.S. government wants to repeat the process soon. Nevertheless, the Canadian, Mexican, and U.S. governments began negotiations in May 1995 with Chile regarding that country's possible entry into NAFTA.

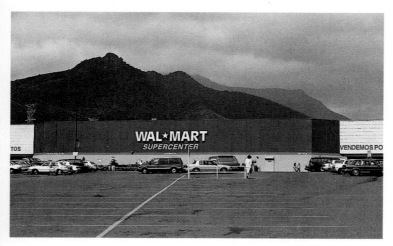

Courtesy Wal-Mart Stores, Inc.

Wal-Mart's Expansion Plans in Mexico Run into Red Tape

Wal-Mart, the major U.S. discount retail chain, saw the January 1, 1994, implementation of NAFTA as a chance to expand its operations into Mexico. Only five years before, Mexican regulations severely limited any direct investment by foreign companies into its market. Now managers at Wal-Mart thought they had received a green light for investment. The company responded by launching an ambitious expansion program in Mexico that involved opening 4 Wal-Mart stores in 1994 and 10 warehouse-style Sam's Clubs, with more to follow.

Reality struck home in the summer of 1994 when Mexican government inspectors made a surprise visit to Wal-Mart's new superstore in Mexico City. The green light was apparently wrapped in bureaucratic red tape. The inspectors found thousands of products that they claimed were improperly labeled or lacking instructions in Spanish. The store was ordered shut for 72 hours while the oversights were corrected. This brush with what they saw as overzealous inspectors has sobered Wal-Mart's managers. They note that the 200,000-square-foot super center that was raided carries around 80,000 products. Each now has to be labeled in Spanish indicating the country of origin, content, instructions, and in some cases an import permit number. The inspectors charged that some 11,700 pieces of merchandise lacked such labels. Wal-Mart's managers responded by pointing out that many of the targeted goods—some 40 percent or more—were purchased from a local Mexican distributor. Nevertheless, the regulators insisted that the retailer had ultimate responsibility for the labeling. Wal-Mart's managers see this kind of bureaucratic red tape as a deliberate attempt by government bureaucrats to raise their costs of doing business in Mexico, thereby frustrating their expansion plans.

To make matters worse, Mexico's financial crisis, which exploded unexpectedly in December 1994, stalled Wal-Mart's ambitious expansion plans. Wal-Mart saw the dollar value of its Mexican assets and earnings plunge as the peso fell by more than 35 percent against the dollar. At the same time, the sharp drop in Mexican business and consumer confidence that followed the peso's fall translated into a decline in sales at Wal-Mart stores in Mexico. The company responded by putting on hold plans to open 24 new stores in Mexico in 1995. Despite all the bureaucratic and currency problems, Wal-Mart has experienced in Mexico, the company insists it will remain in Mexico for the long haul, and it is still optimistic about the long-run potential of the Mexican economy and the benefits of NAFTA.[23]

The Andean Group

The Andean Group was formed in 1969 when Bolivia, Chile, Ecuador, Colombia, and Peru signed the Cartagena Agreement. The Andean Pact was largely based on the EC model, but it has been far less successful at achieving its stated goals. The integration steps begun in 1969 included an internal tariff reduction program, a common external tariff, a transportation policy, a common industrial policy, and special concessions for the smallest members, Bolivia and Ecuador.

By the mid-1980s the Andean Pact had all but collapsed. It had failed to achieve any of its stated objectives. There was no tariff-free trade between member countries, no common external tariff, and no harmonization of economic policies. The attempt to achieve cooperation between member countries seems to have been substantially hindered by political and economic problems. The countries of the Andean Pact have had to deal with low economic growth, hyperinflation, high unemployment, political unrest, and crushing debt. All these problems have made it extremely difficult to achieve cooperation. In addition, the dominant political ideology in many of the Andean countries during this period tended toward the radical/socialist end of the political spectrum. Since such an ideology is hostile to the free market economic principle on which the Andean Pact was based, progress toward closer integration could not be expected.

The tide began to turn in the late 1980s when, after years of economic decline, the governments of Latin America began to adopt free market economic policies. In 1990 the heads of the five current members of the Andean Group—Bolivia, Ecuador, Peru, Colombia, and Venezuela—met in the Galápagos Islands. The resulting Galápagos Declaration effectively relaunched the Andean Group. The declaration's objectives included establishment of a free trade area by 1992, a customs union by 1994, and a common market by 1995.

While a common market has not yet been achieved, there are some grounds for cautious optimism. For the first time, the controlling political ideology of the Andean countries is at least consistent with the free market principles underlying a common market. In addition, since the Galápagos Declaration, internal tariff levels have been reduced by all five members, and a customs union with a common external tariff was established in mid-1994, six months behind schedule. On the other hand, significant differences among members may make harmonization of policies and close integration difficult. For example, Venezuela's GDP per person is four times that of Bolivia's, and Ecuador's tiny production-line industries can hardly compete with Colombia's and Venezuela's more advanced industries. Such differences are a recipe for disagreement and suggest that many of the adjustments required to achieve a true common market will be painful—even though the net benefits will probably outweigh the costs.[25]

MERCOSUR

MERCOSUR originated in 1988 as a free trade pact between Brazil and Argentina. The modest reductions in tariffs and quotas accompanying this pact reportedly helped bring about an 80 percent increase in trade between the two countries in the late 1980s.[26] Encouraged by this success, the pact was expanded in March 1990 to include Paraguay and Uruguay. The aim of the MERCOSUR pact was to establish a full free trade area by the end of 1994 and a common market sometime thereafter. The four countries of MERCOSUR have a combined population of 200 million. With a market of this size, MERCOSUR could have a significant impact on the economic growth rate of the four economies.

In a transition period between 1991 and 1994, MERCOSUR's members sharply cut tariffs on trade with each other. Today most goods go tariff free within MERCOSUR, although there are some nontrivial exceptions to this policy, including cars and sugar. MERCOSUR is aiming to cut internal tariffs on most products to zero by 2000, by which time autos and sugar are supposed to be brought into the agreement. In December 1995 MERCOSUR's members also agreed to a five-year program under which it hopes to perfect its free trade area and move toward a full customs union, similar to the EU. MERCOSUR is also contemplating enlargement. In 1996 MERCOSUR entered into free trade agreements with Chile and Bolivia, and it started talks with the Andean Group regarding a possible South American free trade area.

MERCOSUR seems to be making a positive contribution to the economic growth rates of its member states. Trade among MERCOSUR's four core members grew from $4 billion in 1990 to $14.5 billion in 1995. Moreover, the combined GDP of the four member states grew at an annual average rate of 3.5 percent between 1990 and 1995, a performance significantly better than the four attained during the 1980s.

However, MERCOSUR has its critics, including most notably, Alexander Yeats, a senior economist at the World Bank, who wrote a stinging critique of MERCOSUR that was "leaked" to the press in October 1996.[27] According to Yeats, the trade diversion effects of MERCOSUR outweigh its trade creation effects. Yeats points out that the fastest-growing items in intra-MERCOSUR trade are cars, buses, agricultural equipment, and other capital-intensive goods that are produced relatively inefficiently in the four member countries. MERCOSUR countries, insulated from outside competition by external tariffs that run as high as 70 percent of value on motor vehicles, are investing in factories that build products that are too expensive to sell to anyone but themselves. The result, according to Yeats, is that MERCOSUR countries might not be able to compete globally once the group's external trade barriers come down. In the meantime, capital is being drawn away from more efficient enterprises. Moreover, in the near term, countries with more efficient manufacturing enterprises lose because MERCOSUR's external trade barriers keep them out of the market.

The leak of Yeats' report caused a storm at the World Bank, which typically does not release reports that are critical of member states (the MERCOSUR countries are members of the World Bank). It also drew strong protests from Brazil, which was one of the primary targets of Yeats' critique. Still, in tacit admission that some of Yeats' arguments have merit, a senior MERCOSUR diplomat let it be known that external trade barriers will gradually be reduced, forcing member countries to compete globally.[28] Already many external MERCOSUR tariffs, which average 14 percent, are lower than they were before the group's creation, and there are plans for a hemispheric Free Trade Area of the Americas to be established by 2005 (which will combine MERCOSUR, NAFTA, and other American countries). If that occurs, MERCOSUR will have no choice but to reduce its external tariffs further.

Other Latin American Trade Pacts

The countries of Central America are trying to revive their trade pact. In the early 1960s, Costa Rica, El Salvador, Guatemala, Honduras, and Nicaragua attempted to set up a Central American common market. It collapsed in 1969 when war broke out between Honduras and El Salvador after a riot at a soccer match between teams from the two countries. Now the five countries are trying to revive their agreement, although no real progress had been made by 1995.

A customs union was to have been created in 1991 between the English-speaking Caribbean countries under the auspices of the Caribbean Community. The Caribbean Community, referred to as CARICOM, was established in 1973. However, it has repeatedly failed to progress toward economic integration. A formal commitment to economic and monetary union was adopted by CARICOM's members in 1984, but since then little progress has been made. In October 1991 the CARICOM governments failed, for the third consecutive time, to meet a deadline for establishing a common external tariff.

Regional Economic Integration Elsewhere

Outside of Western Europe and the Americas, until recently there had been few significant attempts at regional economic integration. Although a number of regional trade groupings had existed for a long time throughout Asia and Africa, few existed in anything other than name. In the last few years, however, the pace of regional economic integration has increased, particularly in Asia. Perhaps the most significant group outside of Europe and the Americas today is the Association of Southeast Asian Nations (ASEAN). In addition, the Asia Pacific Economic Cooperation (APEC) forum has recently emerged as a potential free trade region.

Association of Southeast Asian Nations

Formed in 1967, ASEAN currently includes Brunei, Indonesia, Malaysia, the Philippines, Singapore, Thailand, and, most recently, Vietnam (see Map 7.3). The ASEAN countries are characterized by an abundance of natural resources (with the exception of the city-state of Singapore), large international trade sectors, and an emphasis on free market economic policies (with the partial exception of Vietnam). Singapore and Thailand are two of Southeast Asia's most successful economies, and Malaysia and Indonesia are now developing rapidly. The seven member states contain 420 million people. Thus, the potential exists for a vibrant free trade area.

The basic objectives of ASEAN are to foster freer trade between member countries and to achieve some cooperation in their industrial policies. Progress has been very limited, however. For example, although some progress has been made in tariff reduction between ASEAN countries, only

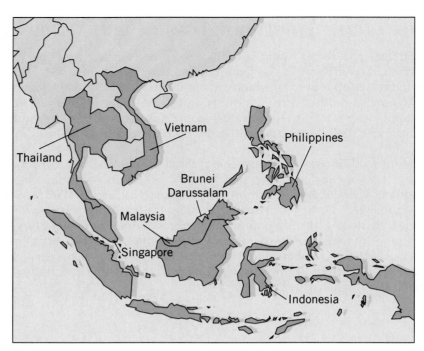

MAP 7.3

ASEAN Member Countries

5 percent of intra-ASEAN trade consists of goods whose tariffs have been reduced through the ASEAN preferential trade arrangement. Still, a recently revitalized ASEAN now aims to reduce tariffs on a wide range of intraregional trade to zero by 2003. Moreover, ASEAN is considering expanding its membership to include Cambodia, Laos, and Myanmar. If ASEAN can make significant progress on both of these fronts, it could become one of the world's more vibrant free trade areas by early in the next century.

Asia Pacific Economic Cooperation

Asia Pacific Economic Cooperation (APEC) was founded in 1990 at the suggestion of Australia. APEC currently has 18 members including such economic powerhouses as the United States, Japan, and China (see Map 7.4). The 18 member states account for half of the world's GDP, 46 percent of world trade, and most of the growth in the world economy. The stated aim of APEC is to increase multilateral cooperation in view of the economic rise of the Pacific nations and the growing interdependence within the region. U.S. support for APEC was also based on the belief that it might prove a viable strategy for heading off any moves to create Asian groupings from which it would be excluded.

Interest in APEC was heightened considerably in November 1993 when for the first time the heads of APEC member states met for a two-day conference in Seattle. Debate before the meeting focused on the likely future role of APEC. One view was that APEC should commit itself to the ultimate forma-

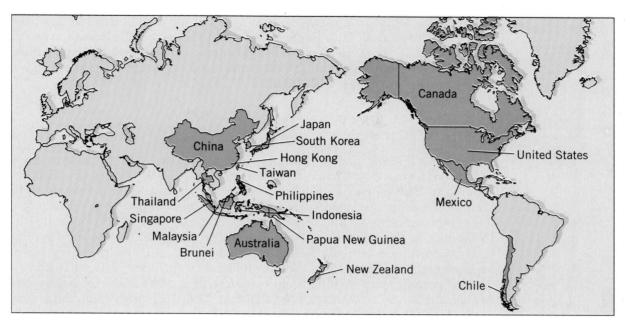

MAP 7.4

Asia Pacific Economic Cooperation

tion of a free trade area. Such a move would transform the Pacific Rim from a geographical expression into the world's largest free trade area. Another view was that APEC would produce no more than hot air and lots of photo opportunities for the leaders involved. In actuality, the APEC meeting produced little more than some vague commitments from member states to work closely together for greater economic integration and a general lowering of trade barriers. However, member states did not rule out the possibility of closer economic cooperation in the future.[29]

The heads of state met again in November 1994 in Jakarta, Indonesia. This time they agreed to take more concrete steps, and the joint statement at the end of the meeting formally committed APEC's industrialized members to remove their trade and investment barriers by 2010 and developing economies to do so by 2020. Subsequent meetings in 1995 and 1996 produced limited progress toward this ambitious goal in the form of a detailed blueprint specifying how the goal of removing barriers to free trade and investment might be achieved. However, member states have not had to take any tangible action, so the viability of APEC remains to be seen.[30] Although few observers expect much progress toward this lofty goal of a trans-Pacific free trade area anytime soon, if the goal is eventually attained, the result will be the world's largest free trade area. APEC is therefore worth watching closely.

Implications for Business

Currently the most significant developments in regional economic integration are occurring in Europe and North America. Although some Latin American trade blocs may have greater economic significance in the future, as ultimately may APEC, at present the events in Europe and North America have far more profound and immediate implications for business practice. Accordingly, in this section we will concentrate on the business implications of the EU and NAFTA. Similar conclusions, however, could be drawn for a single market anywhere in the world.

Opportunities

Creation of a single market offers significant opportunities because markets that were formerly protected from foreign competition are opened. For example, in Europe before 1992 the large French and Italian markets were among the most protected. These markets are now much more open to foreign competition in the form of both exports and direct investment. Nonetheless, the specter of "Fortress Europe" suggests that to fully exploit such opportunities, it will pay non-EU firms to set up EU subsidiaries. Many major U.S. firms have long had subsidiaries in Europe. Those that do not should consider establishing them now, lest they run the risk of being shut out of the EU by nontariff barriers. In fact, non-EU firms rapidly increased their direct investment in the EU in anticipation of the creation of a single market. During the 1983–88 period, for example, approximately 30 percent of the FDI inflows were directed at EU member states. By 1991 this figure had risen to 50, although it had slipped back to 30 percent by the mid-1990s.[31]

Additional opportunities arise from the inherent lower costs of doing business in a single market as opposed to 15 national markets in the case of the EU or 3 national markets in the case of NAFTA. Free movement of goods across borders, harmonized product standards, and simplified tax regimes make it possible for firms based in the EU and the NAFTA countries to realize potentially enormous cost economies by centralizing production where the mix of factor costs and skills is optimal. Rather than producing a product in each of the 15 EU countries or the 3 NAFTA countries, a firm may be able to serve the whole EU or North American market from a single carefully selected location.

For example, in response to the challenges created by the EU after 1992, the Minneapolis, Minnesota, company 3M has been consolidating its European manufacturing and distribution facilities to take advantage of economies of scale. Thus, a plant in Great Britain now produces 3M's printing products and a German factory its reflective traffic control materials for all of the EU. In each case, 3M chose a location for centralized production after carefully considering the likely production costs in alternative locations within the EU. The ultimate goal of 3M is to dispense with national distinctions, directing R&D, manufacturing, distribution, and marketing for each product group from an EU headquarters.[32] Similarly, Unilever, one of Europe's largest companies, was busy rationalizing its production in advance of 1992 to attain scale economies. Unilever concentrated its production of dishwashing powder for the EU in one plant, toilet soap in another, and so on.[33]

But even after the removal of barriers to trade and investment, enduring differences in culture and competitive practices often limit the ability of companies to realize cost economies by centralizing production in key locations and producing a standardized product for the single multicountry market. Thus, as we saw in the opening case, Atag, the Belgium-based producer of kitchen ware, thought it would be able to realize cost economies by supplying just two types of ceramic stove tops to consumers throughout the EU. The reality, however, was that consumers in different countries demanded different types. Atag was forced to respond by producing 11 different models, not 2. Similarly, the profile of the European insurance market (see the "Regional Focus") illustrated that the removal of barriers to trade and investment is by itself not enough to create a true single market. Cultural, historic, and institutional factors still get in the way. Dealing with these factors requires that insurance companies customize their pricing and selling practices on a country-by-country basis within the EU.

Threats

Just as the emergence of single markets in the EU and North America creates opportunities for business, so it also presents a number of threats. For one thing, the business environment within both groups will become more competitive. The lowering of barriers to trade and investment between countries is likely to lead to increased price competition throughout the EU and North America. For example, before 1992 a Volkswagen Golf cost 55 percent more in Great Britain than in Denmark and 29 percent more in Ireland than in Greece.[34] Such price differentials will vanish in a single market. This is a direct threat to any firm doing business in the EU or the NAFTA countries. To survive in the tougher single-market environment, firms must take advantage of the opportunities offered by the creation of a single market to rationalize their production and reduce their costs. Otherwise, they will be at a disadvantage.

A further threat to non-EU and/or non-North American firms arises from the likely long-term improvement in the competitive position of many European and North American companies. This is particularly relevant in the EU, where many firms are currently limited in their ability to compete globally with North American and Asian firms by a high cost structure. The creation of a single market and the resulting increased competition in the EU can be expected to result in serious attempts by many EU firms to reduce their cost structure by rationalizing production. This could transform many EU companies into efficient global competitors. The message for non-EU businesses is that they need to prepare for the emergence of more capable European competitors by reducing their own cost structures.

A final threat to non-EU and/or non-North American firms inherent in the creation of a single market has already been alluded to. This is the threat of being shut out of the single market by the creation of "Fortress Europe" or "Fortress North America." As noted earlier in the chapter, although the free trade philosophy underpinning the EU theoretically argues against the creation of any fortress in Europe, there are signs that the EU may raise barriers to imports and investment in certain areas, such as autos. Non-EU firms might be well advised, therefore, to establish their own EU operations as quickly as possible. This could also occur in the NAFTA countries, but it seems less likely.

Key Terms

regional economic integration,
p. 230

Summary

Three main objectives have been pursued in this chapter. They were to examine the economic and political debate surrounding regional economic integration; to review the progress toward regional economic integration in Europe, the Americas, and elsewhere; and to distinguish the important implications of regional economic integration for the practice of international business. The following points have been made.

1 A number of levels of economic integration are possible in theory. In order of increasing integration, they include a free trade area, a customs union, a common market, an economic union, and full political union.

2 In a free trade area, barriers to trade between member countries are removed, but each country determines its own external trade policy. In a customs union, internal barriers to trade are removed and a common external trade policy is adopted. A common market is similar to a customs union, except that in a common market factors of production also are allowed to move freely between countries. An economic union involves even closer integration, including the establishment of a common currency and the harmonization of tax rates. A political union is the logical culmination of attempts to achieve closer economic integration.

3 Regional economic integration is an attempt to achieve economic gains from the free flow of trade and investment between neighboring countries.

4 Integration is not easily achieved or sustained. Although integration brings benefits to the majority, it is never without costs for the minority. Concerns over national sovereignty often slow or stop integration attempts.

5 Regional integration will not increase economic welfare if the trade creation effects in the free trade area are outweighed by the trade diversion effects.

6 The Single European Act sought to create a true single market by abolishing administrative barriers to the free flow of trade and investment between EU countries.

7 The treaty of Maastricht aims to take the EU even further along the road to economic union by establishing a common currency. The economic gains from a common currency come from reduced exchange costs and reduced risk associated with currency fluctuations.

8 Although no other attempt at regional economic integration comes close to the EU in terms of potential economic and political significance, various other attempts are being made in the world. The most notable include NAFTA in North America, the Andean Pact and MERCOSUR in Latin America, ASEAN in Southeast Asia, and (perhaps) APEC.

9 The creation of single markets in the EU and North America means that many markets that were formerly protected from foreign competition are now more open. This creates major investment and export opportunities for firms within and outside these regions.

10 The free movement of goods across borders, the harmonization of product standards, and the simplification of tax regimes make it possible for firms based in the EU and North America to realize potentially enormous cost economies by centralizing production in those locations in the EU and NAFTA countries where the mix of factor costs and skills is optimal.

11 The lowering of barriers to trade and investment between countries will probably be followed by increased price competition throughout the EU and North America.

Critical Thinking and Discussion Questions

1 NAFTA is likely to produce net benefits for the U.S. economy. Discuss.

2 What are the economic and political arguments for regional economic integration? Given these arguments, why don't we see more integration in the world economy?

3 What is the likely effect of creation of a single market within the EU likely to be on competition within the EU? Why?

4 How should a U.S. firm that currently exports only to Western Europe respond to the creation of a single market?

5 How should a firm with self-sufficient production facilities in several EU countries respond to the creation of a single market? What are the constraints on its ability to respond in a manner that minimizes production costs?

Internet Exercise

As the global economy grows, so have sites discussing regional economic integration. European Union, the topic of this chapter's opening case, is widely reviewed at a variety of sites. From the provision of the treaty (http://europa.eu.int/en/record/mt/top.html; http://www.ph.kcl.ac.uk/local/maas/contents.html) to the sharing of educational information on issues common to the Member States (http://europa.eu.int/en/comm/dg22/euryen.html) to the legislative process in the European Union (http://cwis.kub.nl/~dbi/instruct/eue/legislat.htm), surfers can become informed on many facets of the agreement. Also, the viewpoints of the European Parliament (http://dylee.keel.econ.ship.edu/intntl/INTFIN/epsheets.htm) and treaty critics (http://www.eusceptic.org/welcome.html) provide insight of the citizens affected by the agreement.

Similar sites abound for the Andean Pact and for MERCOSUR. The Andean Pact is summarized and key issues are discussed at the Trade Ageement Summaries site (http://americas.fiu.edu/trade_agreements/andean.htm) as is criticism of the United State's influence on the agreement (http://pele.nando.net/newsroom/ntn/world/030996/world6_1989.html). Regarding MERCOSUR, the treaty and annexes are found at the InterAm Database site, which also provides links to supplemental materials discussing related agreements, the treaty's effectiveness, and the taxation framework. Also, the historical background, trade policies, and international jurisdiction regulations concerning contracts are posted (http://www.americasnet.com/mauritz/mercosur/english/) with a discussion of Latin America's efforts to achieve economic integration (http://www.area-development.com/NOV9610.HTM).

Global Surfing

What specific provisions of the European Union's Treaty of Maastricht promote economic integration? What information is promoted in educational systems and policies? Summarize the garbage dump case discussing the legislative process in the EU. What is the viewpoint of the European Parliament regarding the EU? What arguments are presented to oppose the EU, specifically regarding currency and Maastricht II? What key issues involving exporters, services, and manufacturing/production are described regarding the Andean Pact? Why are United States' actions criticized? How do the MERCOSUR annexes address dispute resolution and working groups? How does MERCOSUR provide guidance for resolving contractual disputes between countries? How have Latin American countries worked to attain economic integration?

Martin's Textiles

August 12, 1992, was a really bad day for John Martin. That was the day Canada, Mexico, and the United States announced in principle the North American Free Trade Agreement (NAFTA). Under the plan, all tariffs between the three countries would be eliminated within the next 10 to 15 years, with most being cut in 5. What disturbed John most was the plan's provision that all tariffs on trade of textiles among the three countries are to be removed within 10 years. Under the proposed agreement, Mexico and Canada would also be allowed to ship a specific amount of clothing and textiles made from foreign materials to the United States each year, and this quota would rise slightly over the first five years of the agreement. "My God!" thought John. "Now I'm going to have to decide about moving my plants to Mexico."

John is the CEO of a New York-based textile company, Martin's Textiles. The company has been in the Martin family for four generations, having been founded by his great-grandfather in 1910. The company employs 1,500 people in three New York plants that produce cotton-based clothes, primarily underwear. All production employees are union members, and the company has a long history of good labor relations. The company has never had a labor dispute, and John, like his father, grandfather, and great-grandfather before him, regards the work force as part of the "Martin family." John prides himself not only on knowing many of the employees by name, but also on knowing a great deal about the family circumstances of many of the longtime employees.

Over the past 20 years the company has experienced increasingly tough competition, both from overseas and at home. The mid-1980s was particularly difficult. The strength of the dollar on the foreign exchange market during that period enabled Asian producers to enter the U.S. market with very low prices. Since then, although the dollar has weakened against many major currencies, the Asian producers have not raised their prices in response to the falling dollar. In a low-skilled, labor-intensive business such as clothing manufacture, costs are driven by wage rates and labor productivity. Not surprisingly, most of John's competitors in the northeastern United States responded to the intense cost competition by moving production south, first to states such as South Carolina and Mississippi, where nonunion labor could be hired for significantly less than in the unionized Northeast, and then to Mexico, where labor costs for textile workers were less than $2 per hour. In contrast, wage rates are $12.50 per hour at John's New York plant and $8 to $10 per hour at nonunion textile plants in the southeastern United States.

The last three years have been particularly tough at Martin's Textiles. The company has regis-

tered a small loss each year, and John knows the company cannot go on like this. His major customers, while praising the quality of Martin's products, have warned him that his prices are getting too high and they may not be able to continue to do business with him. His longtime banker has told him that he must get his labor costs down. John agrees, but he knows of only one surefire way to do that, to move production south—way south, to Mexico. He has always been reluctant to do that, but now he seems to have little choice. He fears that in five years the U.S. market will be flooded with cheap imports from Asian, U.S., and Mexican companies, all producing in Mexico. It looks like the only way for Martin's Textiles to survive is to close the New York plants and move production to Mexico. All that would be left in the United States would be the sales force.

John's mind was spinning. How could something that throws good, honest people out of work be good for the country? The politicians said it would be good for trade, good for economic growth, good for the three countries. John could not see it that way. What about Mary Morgan, who has worked for Martin's for 30 years? She is now 54 years old. How will she and others like her find another job? What about his moral obligation to his workers? What about the loyalty his workers have shown his family over the years? Is this a good way to repay it? How would he break the news to his employees, many of whom have worked for the company 10 to 20 years? And what about the Mexican workers; could they be as loyal and productive as his present employees? From other U.S. textile companies that had set up production in Mexico he had heard stories of low productivity, poor workmanship, high turnover, and high absenteeism. Is this true? If so, how could he ever cope with that? John has always felt that the success of Martin's Textiles is partly due to the family atmosphere, which encourages worker loyalty, productivity, and attention to quality, an atmosphere that has been built up over four generations. How could he replicate that in Mexico with foreign workers who speak a language that he doesn't even understand?

Case Discussion Questions

1 What are the economic costs and benefits to Martin's Textiles of shifting production to Mexico?
2 What are the social costs and benefits to Martin's Textiles of shifting production to Mexico?

3 Are the economic and social costs and benefits of moving production to Mexico independent of each other?
4 What seems to be the most ethical action?

5 What would you do if you were John Martin?

Chapter 8
The Foreign Exchange Market

©PhotoDisc

Opening Case

JAL

One of the world's largest airlines, Japan Air Lines (JAL), is also one of the best customers of Boeing, the world's biggest manufacturer of commercial airplanes. Every year JAL needs to raise about $800 million to purchase aircraft from Boeing. Boeing aircraft are priced in U.S. dollars, with prices ranging from about $35 million for a 737 to $160 million for a top-of-the-line 747-400. JAL orders an aircraft two to six years before the plane is

Learning Objectives:

1 Be familiar with the form and function of the foreign exchange market.

2 Understand the difference between spot and forward exchange rates.

3 Understand how currency exchange rates are determined.

4 Appreciate the role of the foreign exchange market in insuring against foreign exchange risk.

5 Be familiar with the merits of different approaches toward exchange rate forecasting.

6 Appreciate why some currencies cannot always be converted into other currencies.

7 Understand how countertrade is used to mitigate problems associated with an inability to convert currencies.

needed. JAL normally pays Boeing a 10 percent deposit when ordering, and the bulk of the payment is made when the aircraft is delivered.

The long lag between placing an order and making a final payment presents a conundrum for JAL. Most of JAL's revenues are in Japanese yen, not U.S. dollars. When purchasing Boeing aircraft, JAL must change its yen into dollars to pay Boeing. In the interval between placing an order and

making final payment, the value of the Japanese yen against the U.S. dollar may change. This can increase or decrease the cost of an aircraft when calculated in yen. Consider an order placed in 1985 for a 747 aircraft that was to be delivered in 1990. In 1985 the dollar value of this order was $100 million. The prevailing exchange rate in 1985 was $1=¥240 (i.e., one dollar was worth 240 yen), so the price of the 747 in yen was ¥2.4 billion.

By 1990 when final payment was due, however, the dollar–yen exchange rate might have changed. One possibility is that the yen might have declined in value against the dollar. If in 1990 the dollar–yen exchange rate was $1=¥300, the price of the 747 in yen would have gone from 2.4 billion to 3.0 billion, an increase of 25 percent. Another (more favorable) scenario is that the yen might have risen in value against the dollar to $1=¥200. If this had occurred, the yen price of the 747 would have fallen 16.7 percent to ¥2.0 billion.

In 1985 JAL has no way of knowing what the value of the yen will be against the dollar by 1990. However, JAL can enter into a contract with foreign exchange traders in 1985 to purchase dollars in 1990 based on the assessment of those traders as to what they think the dollar/yen exchange rate will be in 1990. This is called entering into a *forward exchange contract*. The advantage of entering into a forward exchange contract is that JAL knows in 1985 what it will have to pay for the 747 in 1990. So, for example, if the value of the yen is expected to increase against the dollar between 1985 and 1990, foreign exchange traders might offer a forward exchange contract that allows JAL to purchase dollars at a rate of $1=¥185 in 1990, instead of the $1=¥240 rate that prevailed in 1985. At this forward exchange rate, the 747 would cost ¥1.85 billion, a 23 percent saving over the yen price implied by the 1985 exchange rate.

JAL was confronted with just this scenario in 1985. JAL entered into a 10-year forward exchange contract with a total value of about $3.6 billion. This contract gave JAL the right to buy U.S. dollars from a consortium of foreign exchange traders at various points during the next 10 years for an average exchange rate of $1=¥185. To JAL this looked like a great deal given the 1985 exchange rate of $1=¥240. However, by September 1994 when the bulk of the contract had been executed, it no longer looked like a good deal. To everyone's surprise, the value of the yen had surged against the dollar.

By 1992 the exchange rate stood at $1=¥120, and by 1994 it was $1=¥99. Unfortunately, JAL could not take advantage of this more favorable exchange rate. Instead, JAL was bound by the terms of the contract to purchase dollars at the contract rate of $1=¥185, a rate that by 1994 looked outrageously expensive. This misjudgment cost JAL dearly. In 1994 JAL was paying 86 percent more than it needed to for each Boeing aircraft bought with dollars purchased via the forward exchange contract! In October 1994 JAL admitted publicly that in its most recent financial year the loss from this misjudgment amounted to $450 million, or ¥45 billion. Foreign exchange traders speculated that JAL had probably lost ¥155 billion ($1.5 billion) on this contract since 1988.[1]

Introduction

This chapter has three main objectives. The first is to explain how the foreign exchange market works. The second is to examine the forces that determine exchange rates and to discuss the degree to which it is possible to predict exchange rate movements. The third objective is to map the implications for international business of exchange rate movements and the foreign exchange market. In the next chapter we will explore the institutional structure of the international monetary system. The institutional structure is the context within which the foreign exchange market functions. As we shall see, changes in the institutional structure of the international monetary system can exert a profound influence on the development of foreign exchange markets.

foreign exchange market
Market for converting the currency of one country into that of another country.

exchange rate Rate at which one currency is converted into another.

The **foreign exchange market** is a market for converting the currency of one country into that of another country. An **exchange rate** is simply the rate at which one currency is converted into another. We saw in the opening case how JAL used the foreign exchange market to convert Japanese yen into U.S. dollars. Without the foreign exchange market, international trade and international investment on the scale that we see today would be impossible; companies would have to resort to barter. The foreign exchange market is the lubricant that enables companies based in countries that use different currencies to trade with each other.

We know from earlier chapters that international trade and investment have their risks. As the opening case illustrates, some of these risks exist because future exchange rates cannot be perfectly predicted. The rate at which one currency is converted into another typically changes over time. One function of the foreign exchange market is to provide some insurance against the risks that arise from changes in exchange rates, commonly referred to as foreign exchange risk. But the foreign exchange market cannot provide complete insurance against foreign exchange risk. JAL's loss of $1.5 billion on foreign exchange transactions is an extreme example of what can happen, but it is not at all unusual for international businesses to suffer losses because of unpredicted changes in exchange rates. Currency fluctuations can make seemingly profitable trade and investment deals unprofitable, and vice versa. The opening case contains an example of this as it relates to trade. For an example that deals with investment, consider the case of Mexico. Between 1976 and 1987, the value of the Mexican peso dropped from 22 per U.S. dollar to 1,500 per U.S. dollar. As a result, a U.S. company with an investment in Mexico that yielded an income of 100 million pesos per year would have seen the dollar value of that income shrink from $4.55 million in 1976 to $66,666 by 1987!

In addition to altering the value of trade deals and foreign investments, currency movements can open or close export opportunities and alter the attractiveness of imports. In 1984, for example, the U.S. dollar was trading at an all-time high against most other currencies. At that time one dollar could buy one British pound or 250 Japanese yen, compared to 0.55 of a British pound and about 85 yen in early 1995. In the 1984 U.S. presidential campaign, President Reagan boasted about how good the strong dollar was for the United States. Many U.S. companies did not see it that way. Companies such as Caterpillar that earned their living by exporting to other countries were being priced out of foreign markets by the strong dollar. In 1980 when the dollar-to-pound exchange rate was $1 = £0.63, a $100,000 Caterpillar earthmover cost a British buyer £63,000. In 1984, with the exchange rate at $1 = £0.99, it cost close to £99,000—a 60 percent increase in four years! At that exchange rate Caterpillar's products were overpriced compared to those of its foreign competitors, such as Japan's Komatsu. At the same time, the strong dollar reduced the price of the earthmovers Komatsu imported into the United States, which allowed the Japanese company to take U.S. market share away from Caterpillar.

Thus, while the existence of foreign exchange markets is a necessary precondition for large-scale international trade and investment, the movement of exchange rates introduces many risks into international trade and investment. Some of these risks can be insured against by using instruments offered by the foreign exchange market, such as the forward exchange contracts discussed in the opening case; others cannot be.

In this chapter we will examine these issues. We begin by looking at the functions and the form of the foreign exchange market. This includes distinguishing between spot exchanges and forward exchanges. Then we will consider the factors that determine exchange rates. We will also look at how foreign trade is conducted when a country's currency cannot be exchanged for other currencies; that is, when its currency is not convertible. The chapter closes with a discussion of these things in terms of their implications for business.

The Functions of the Foreign Exchange Market

The foreign exchange market serves two main functions. The first is to convert the currency of one country into the currency of another. The second is to provide some insurance against **foreign exchange risk**, by which we mean the adverse consequences of unpredictable changes in exchange rates. We consider each function in turn.[2]

Currency Conversion

Each country has a currency in which the prices of goods and services are quoted. In the United States it is the dollar ($); in Great Britain, the pound (£); in France, the French franc (FFr); in Germany, the deutsche mark (DM); in Japan, the yen (¥); and so on. In general, within the borders of a particular country one must use the national currency. A U.S. tourist cannot walk into a store in Edinburgh, Scotland, and use U.S. dollars to buy a bottle of Scotch whisky. Dollars are not recognized as legal tender in Scotland; the tourist must use British pounds. Fortunately, the tourist can go to a bank and exchange her dollars for pounds. Then she can buy the whisky.

When a tourist exchanges one currency into another, she is participating in the foreign exchange market. The exchange rate is the rate at which the market converts one currency into another. For example, an exchange rate of $1 = ¥85 specifies that one U.S. dollar has the equivalent value of 85 Japanese yen. The exchange rate allows us to compare the relative prices of goods and services in different countries. Returning to our example of the U.S. tourist in Edinburgh, she may find that she must pay £25 for the bottle of whisky, and she knows that the same bottle costs $40 in the United States. Is this a good deal? Imagine the current dollar/pound exchange rate is $1 = £0.50. Our intrepid tourist takes out her calculator and converts £25 into dollars. (The calculation is 25/0.50.) She finds that the bottle of Scotch costs the equivalent of $50. She is surprised that a bottle of Scotch whisky could cost less in the United States than in Scotland. (This is true; alcohol is heavily taxed in Britain.)

Tourists are minor participants in the foreign exchange market; companies engaged in international trade and investment are major ones. There are four main uses of foreign exchange markets to international businesses. First, the payments a company receives for its exports, the income it receives from foreign investments, or the income it receives from licensing agreements with foreign firms may be in foreign currencies. To use those funds in its home country, the company must convert them to its home country's currency. Consider the Scotch distillery that exports its whisky to the United States. The distillery is paid in dollars, but since those dollars cannot be spent in Great Britain, they must be converted into British pounds.

Second, international businesses use foreign exchange markets when they must pay a foreign company for its products or services in its country's currency. For example, our friend Michael runs a company called NST, a large British travel service for school groups. Each year Michael's company arranges vacations for thousands of British schoolchildren and their teachers in France.

French hotel proprietors demand payment in francs, so Michael must convert large sums of money from pounds into francs to pay them.

Third, international businesses use foreign exchange markets when they have spare cash that they wish to invest for short terms in money markets. For example, consider a U.S. company that has $10 million it wants to invest for three months. The best interest rate it can earn on these funds in the United States may be 8 percent. Investing in a French money market account, however, it may be able to earn 12 percent. Thus, the company may change its $10 million into francs and invest it in France. Note, however, that the rate of return it earns on this investment depends not only on the French interest rate, but also on the changes in the value of the franc against the dollar in the intervening period.

Finally, currency speculation is another use of foreign exchange markets. **Currency speculation** typically involves the short-term movement of funds from one currency to another in the hopes of profiting from shifts in exchange rates. Consider again the U.S. company with $10 million to invest for three months. Suppose the company suspects that the U.S. dollar is overvalued against the French franc. That is, the company expects the value of the dollar to depreciate against that of the franc. Imagine the current dollar/franc exchange rate is $1 = FFr 6. The company exchanges its $10 million into francs, receiving FFr 60 million. Over the next three months the value of the dollar depreciates until $1 = FFr 5. Now the company exchanges its FFr 60 million back into dollars and finds that it has $12 million. The company has made a $2 million profit on currency speculation in three months on an initial investment of $10 million.

One of the most famous currency speculators is George Soros, whose Quantum Group of "hedge funds" controls about $12 billion in assets. The activities of Soros, who has been spectacularly successful, are profiled in the next "Management Focus." In general, however, companies should beware of speculation for it is by definition a very risky business. The company cannot know for sure what will happen to exchange rates. While a speculator may profit handsomely if his speculation about future currency movements is correct, he can also lose vast amounts of money if it is wrong. For example, in 1991 Clifford Hatch, the finance director of the British food and drink company Allied-Lyons, bet large amounts of the company's funds on the speculation that the British pound would rise in value against the U.S. dollar. Over the previous three years Hatch had made over $25 million for Allied-Lyons by placing similar currency bets. His 1991 bet, however, went spectacularly wrong when instead of increasing in value, the British pound plummeted in value against the U.S. dollar. In February 1991 one pound bought $2; by April it bought less than $1.75. The total loss to Allied-Lyons from this speculation was a staggering $269 million, more than the company was to earn from all its food and drink activities during 1991![3]

Insuring against Foreign Exchange Risk

A second function of the foreign exchange market is to provide insurance to protect against the possible adverse consequences of unpredictable changes in exchange rates (foreign exchange risk). To explain how the market performs this function, we must first distinguish between spot exchange rates and forward exchange rates.

George Soros—The Man Who Moves Markets

George Soros, a 65-year-old Hungarian-born financier, is the principal partner of the Quantum Group, which controls a series of hedge funds with assets of around $12 billion. **A hedge fund** is an investment fund that not only buys financial assets (such as stocks, bonds, and currencies) but also sells them short. **Short selling** occurs when an investor places a speculative bet that the value of a financial asset will decline and profits from that decline. A common variant of short selling occurs when an investor borrows stock from his broker and sells that stock. The short seller has to ultimately pay back that stock to his broker. However, he hopes that in the intervening period the value of the stock will decline so that the cost of repurchasing the stock to pay back the broker is significantly less than the income he received from the initial sale of the stock. For example, imagine that a short seller borrows 100 units of IBM stock and sells it in the market at $150 per share, yielding a total income of $15,000. In one year the short seller has to give the 100 units of IBM stock back to his broker. In the intervening period the value of the IBM stock falls to $50. Consequently, it now costs the short seller only $5,000 to repurchase the 100 units of IBM stock for his broker. The difference between the initial sales price ($150), and the repurchase price ($50) represents the short seller's profit, which in this case is $100 per unit of stock for a total profit of $10,000. Short selling was originally developed as a means of reducing risk (of hedging), but it is often used for speculation.

Along with other hedge funds, Soros' Quantum Fund often takes a short position in currencies that he expects to decline in value. For example, if Soros expects the British pound to decline against the U.S. dollar he may borrow one billion pounds from a currency trader and immediately sell those one billion for U.S. dollars. Soros will then hope that the value of the pound will decline against the dollar, so that when he has to repay the one billion pounds it will cost him considerably less (in U.S. dollars) than he received from the initial sale.

Since the 1970s Soros has consistently earned huge returns by making such speculative bets.

---

hedge fund Investment fund that buys financial assets and also sells them short.

short selling Speculating that the value of a financial asset will decline and profiting from that decline.

spot exchange rate Rate at which a foreign exchange dealer converts one currency into another currency on a particular day.

SPOT EXCHANGE RATES When two parties agree to exchange currency and execute the deal immediately, the transaction is referred to as a spot exchange. Exchange rates governing such "on the spot" trades are referred to as spot exchange rates. The **spot exchange rate** is the rate at which a foreign exchange dealer converts one currency into another currency on a particular day. Thus, when our U.S. tourist in Edinburgh goes to a bank to convert her dollars into pounds, the exchange rate is the spot rate for that day.

Although it is necessary to use a spot rate to execute a transaction immediately, it may not be the most attractive rate. Exchange rates can change constantly. The value of a currency is determined by the interaction between the demand and supply of that currency relative to the demand and supply of other currencies. For example, if lots of people want U.S. dollars and dollars are in short supply, and few people want French francs and francs are in plentiful supply, the spot exchange rate for converting dollars into francs will

His most spectacular triumph came in September 1992. At that time he believed that the British pound was likely to decline in value against major currencies, particularly the German deutsche mark. The prevailing exchange rate was £1=DM2.80. The British government was obliged by a European Union agreement on monetary policy to try to keep the pound above DM2.77. Soros doubted that the British could do this, so he shorted the pound, borrowing billions of pounds (using the $12 billion assets of the Quantum Fund as collateral) and immediately selling them for German deutsche marks. His simultaneous sale of pounds and purchase of marks was so large that it helped drive down the value of the pound against the mark. Other currency traders, seeing Soros' market moves and knowing his reputation for making successful currency bets, jumped on the bandwagon and started to sell pounds short and

Rates of Exchange

Against Sterling

Currency	We Sell	We Buy
	1 39	1 47
	1 95	2 07
	9 05	9 65
	2 78	2 94

N.B.

WE DO NOT BUY COIN
EXCEPT £ OR s

©Cameramann International, Ltd.

buy deutsche marks. The resulting *bandwagon effect* put enormous pressure on the pound. The British Central Bank, at the request of the British government, spent about 20 billion pounds on September 16 to try to prop up the value of the pound against the deutsche mark (by selling marks and buying pounds), but to no avail. The pound continued to fall and on September 17 the British government gave up on the attempt and let the pound

decline (it fell to £1=DM2.00). Soros made a $1 billion profit in four weeks!

Like all currency speculators, however, George Soros has had his losses. In February 1994 he bet that the Japanese yen would decline in value against the U.S. dollar and promptly shorted the yen. However, the yen defied the expectations of Soros and continued to rise, costing his Quantum Fund $600 million. Similarly, a series of incorrect bets in 1987 resulted in losses of over $800 million for Quantum. Despite such defeats, however, Quantum Fund has earned an average annual rate of return of over 40 percent since 1970. Meanwhile, Soros has gained a reputation for being able to move currency markets by his actions. This is the result not so much of the money that Soros puts into play, but of the bandwagon effect that results when other speculators follow his lead.[4]

change. The dollar is likely to appreciate against the franc (or, conversely, the franc will depreciate against the dollar). Imagine the spot exchange rate is $1 = FFr 5 when the market opens. As the day progresses, dealers demand more dollars and fewer francs. By the end of the day the spot exchange rate might be $1 = FFr 5.3. The dollar has appreciated, and the franc has depreciated.

FORWARD EXCHANGE RATES The fact that spot exchange rates change daily as determined by the relative demand and supply for different currencies can be problematic for an international business. One example was given in the opening case; here is another. A U.S. company that imports laptop computers from Japan knows that in 30 days it must pay yen to a Japanese supplier when a shipment arrives. The company will pay the Japanese supplier ¥200,000 for each laptop computer, and the current dollar/yen spot exchange rate is $1 = ¥120. At this rate, each computer costs the importer $1,667 (i.e., 1,667 = 200,000/120). The importer knows she can

TABLE 8.1

Foreign Exchange Quotations

CURRENCY TRADING

EXCHANGE RATES

Thursday, January 25, 1996

The New York foreign exchange selling rates below apply to trading among banks in amounts of $1 million and more, as quoted at 3 p.m. Eastern time by Dow Jones Telerate Inc. and other sources. Retail transactions provide fewer units of foreign currency per dollar.

Country	U.S. $ equiv. Thu	Wed	Currency per U.S. $ Thu	Wed
Argentina (Peso)	1.0007	1.0007	.9993	.9993
Australia (Dollar)	.7358	.7360	1.3591	1.3587
Austria (Schilling)	.09533	.09603	10.490	10.413
Bahrain (Dinar)	2.6532	2.6532	.3769	.3769
Belgium (Franc)	.03296	.03282	30.340	30.470
Brazil (Real)	1.0288	1.0288	.9720	.9720
Britain (Pound)	1.5080	1.5109	.6631	.6619
30-Day Forward	1.5070	1.5100	.6636	.6623
90-Day Forward	1.5051	1.5081	.6644	.6631
180-Day Forward	1.5023	1.5054	.6656	.6643
Canada (Dollar)	.7250	.7292	1.3793	1.3713
30-Day Forward	.7250	.7291	1.3793	1.3715
90-Day Forward	.7248	.7289	1.3797	1.3719
180-Day Forward	.7245	.7274	1.3803	1.3749
Chile (Peso)	.002430	.002436	411.45	410.45
China (Renminbi)	.1199	.1202	8.3380	8.3163
Colombia (Peso)	.0009744	.0009744	1026.30	1026.30
Czech. Rep. (Koruna)				
Commercial rate	.03674	.03664	27.219	27.291
Denmark (Krone)	.1751	.1744	5.7100	5.7325
Ecuador (Sucre)				
Floating rate	.0003410	.0003410	2932.50	2932.50
Finland (Markka)	.2189	.2204	4.5693	4.5370
France (Franc)	.1960	.1967	5.1025	5.0845
30-Day Forward	.1960	.1968	5.1024	5.0805
90-Day Forward	.1964	.1971	5.0923	5.0745
180-Day Forward	.1966	.1974	5.0852	5.0670
Germany (Mark)	.6715	.6733	1.4891	1.4852
30-Day Forward	.6715	.6744	1.4891	1.4828
90-Day Forward	.6749	.6767	1.4817	1.4778
180-Day Forward	.6715	.6800	1.4891	1.4706
Greece (Drachma)	.004069	.004083	245.76	244.91
Hong Kong (Dollar)	.1293	.1293	7.7342	7.7322
Hungary (Forint)	.006937	.006937	144.16	144.16
India (Rupee)	.02787	.02791	35.880	35.830
Indonesia (Rupiah)	.0004340	.0004340	2290.00	2290.00
Ireland (Punt)	1.5620	1.5649	.6402	.6390
Israel (Shekel)	.3194	.3194	3.1310	3.1310
Italy (Lira)	.0006256	.0006285	1598.50	1591.00
Japan (Yen)	.009354	.009339	106.91	107.08
30-Day Forward	.009395	.009380	106.45	106.62
90-Day Forward	.009472	.009456	105.57	105.75
180-Day Forward	.009582	.009565	104.36	104.55
Jordan (Dinar)	1.4104	1.4104	.7090	.7090
Kuwait (Dinar)	3.3372	3.3361	.2997	.2997
Lebanon (Pound)	.0006279	.0006279	1592.50	1592.50
Malaysia (Ringgit)	.3907	.3905	2.5598	2.5610
Malta (Lira)	2.7643	2.7567	.3618	.3627
Mexico (Peso)				
Floating rate	.1354	.1352	7.3850	7.3950
Netherland (Guilder)	.5995	.6019	1.6681	1.6615
New Zealand (Dollar)	.6673	.6649	1.4986	1.5040
Norway (Krone)	.1547	.1540	6.4637	6.4925
Pakistan (Rupee)	.02922	.02923	34.220	34.216
Peru (new Sol)	.4292	.4292	2.3300	2.3300
Philippines (Peso)	.03820	.03820	26.180	26.180
Poland (Zloty)	.3937	.3938	2.5400	2.5393
Portugal (Escudo)	.006461	.006502	154.77	153.81
Russia (Ruble) (a)	.0002120	.0002120	4718.00	4716.00
Saudi Arabia (Riyal)	.2667	.2666	3.7500	3.7503
Singapore (Dollar)	.7050	.7037	1.4185	1.4210
Slovak Rep. (Koruna)	.03322	.03322	30.098	30.098
South Africa (Rand)	.2742	.2739	3.6475	3.6512
South Korea (Won)	.001272	.001270	786.10	787.10
Spain (Peseta)	.007951	.007999	125.77	125.02
Sweden (Krona)	.1447	.1457	6.9113	6.8636
Switzerland (Franc)	.8351	.8382	1.1975	1.1931
30-Day Forward	.8378	.8406	1.1936	1.1893
90-Day Forward	.8428	.8460	1.1865	1.1821
180-Day Forward	.8501	.8534	1.1764	1.1718
Taiwan (Dollar)	.03643	.03643	27.450	27.450
Thailand (Baht)	.03948	.03948	25.330	25.330
Turkey (Lira)	.00001619	.00001624	61763.00	61594.50
United Arab (Dirham)	.2724	.2723	3.6710	3.6726
Uruguay (New Peso)				
Financial	.1387	.1387	7.2100	7.2100
Venezuela (Bolivar)	.003448	.003448	290.00	290.00
Brady Rate	.002762	.002762	362.00	362.00
SDR	1.4580	1.4557	.6859	.6870
ECU	1.2389	1.2389		

Special Drawing Rights (SDR) are based on exchange rates for the U.S., German, British, French, and Japanese currencies. Source: International Monetary Fund.

European Currency Unit (ECU) is based on a basket of community currencies.

a-fixing, Moscow Interbank Currency Exchange

Source: *The Wall Street Journal,* April 16, 1997.

sell the computers the day they arrive for $2,000 each, which yields a gross profit of $333 on each computer ($2,000 − $1,667). However, the importer will not have the funds to pay the Japanese supplier until the computers have been sold. If over the next 30 days the dollar unexpectedly depreciates against the yen, say to $1 = ¥95, the importer will still have to pay the Japanese company ¥200,000 per computer, but in dollar terms that would be equivalent to $2,105 per computer, which is more than she can sell the computers for. In other words, a depreciation in the value of the dollar against the yen from $1 = ¥120 to $1 = ¥95 would transform a profitable deal into an unprofitable one.

To avoid this risk, the U.S. importer might want to engage in a forward exchange. A **forward exchange** occurs when two parties agree to exchange currency and execute the deal at some specific date in the future. Exchange rates governing such future transactions are referred to as forward exchange rates. For most major currencies, **forward exchange rates** are quoted for 30, 90, and 180 days into the future. (An example of exchange rate quotations appears in Table 8.1.) In some cases, it is possible to get forward exchange rates for several years into the future. In the opening case, for example, we saw

forward exchange Two parties agree to exchange currency and execute the deal at some specific date in the future.

forward exchange rates Rates for currency exchange quoted for 30, 90, or 180 days into the future.

how JAL entered into a contract that predicted forward exchange rates up to 10 years in the future. Returning to our example, let us assume the 30-day forward exchange rate for converting dollars into yen is $1 = ¥110. The importer enters into a 30-day forward exchange transaction with a foreign exchange dealer at this rate and is guaranteed that she will have to pay no more than $1,818 for each computer (1,818 = 200,000/110). This guarantees her a profit of $182 per computer ($2,000 − $1,818). Moreover, she insures herself against the possibility that an unanticipated change in the dollar/yen exchange rate will turn a profitable deal into an unprofitable one.

In this example the spot exchange rate ($1 = ¥120) and the 30-day forward rate ($1 = ¥110) differ. Such differences are normal; they reflect the expectations of the foreign exchange market about future currency movements. In our example, the fact that $1 bought more yen with a spot exchange than with a 30-day forward exchange indicates that foreign exchange dealers expected the dollar to depreciate against the yen in the next 30 days. When this occurs we say the dollar is selling at a *discount* on the 30-day forward market (i.e., it is worth less than on the spot market). Of course, the opposite can also occur. If the 30-day forward exchange rate were $1 = ¥130, for example, $1 would buy more yen with a forward exchange than with a spot exchange. In such a case, we say the dollar is selling at a *premium* on the 30-day forward market. This reflects the foreign exchange dealers' expectations that the dollar will appreciate against the yen over the next 30 days.

The Nature of the Foreign Exchange Market

So far we have dealt with the foreign exchange market only as an abstract concept. Now we take a closer look at the nature of this market. The foreign exchange market is not located in any one place. Rather, it is a global network of banks, brokers, and foreign exchange dealers connected by electronic communications systems. When companies wish to convert currencies, they typically go through their own banks rather than entering the market directly themselves. In recent years the foreign exchange market has been growing at a rapid pace, reflecting a general growth in the volume of cross-border trade and investment (see Chapter 1). In March 1986, for example, the average total value of global foreign exchange trading was about $200 billion per day. By April 1989 it had soared to over $650 billion per day, by 1994 it was over $1,000 billion per day, and in 1995 it hit $1,200 billion per day.[5]

The most important trading centers are London, New York, and Tokyo. In April 1995 about 30 percent of global foreign exchange transactions were routed through London, more than for New York and Tokyo, the next biggest markets, combined. London, Singapore, and Hong Kong are the most global of the leading centers, with domestic currencies involved in less than 20 percent of deals. By contrast, in New York and Tokyo the domestic currency is involved in more than 80 percent of deals.[6]

London's dominance in the foreign exchange market is due to both history and geography. As the capital of the world's first major industrial trading nation, London had become the world's largest center for international banking by the end of the last century, a position it has retained. Today London also has an advantageous location; its central position between Tokyo to the east and New York to the west has made it the critical link between the Tokyo and New York markets. Because of time zone differences, London opens as Tokyo shuts down for the night and is still open for the first few hours of trading in New York.

Two features of the foreign exchange market are of particular note. The first is that the market never sleeps. There are only 3 hours out of every 24 that Tokyo, London, and New York are all shut down. During these three hours, trading continues in a number of minor centers, particularly San Francisco and Sydney, Australia.

The second feature of the market is the integration of the various trading centers. Direct telephone lines, fax, and computer linkages between trading centers around the globe have effectively created a single market. The integration of financial centers implies there can be no significant difference in exchange rates quoted in the trading centers. For example, if the dollar/franc exchange rate quoted in London at 3 P.M. is $1 = FFr 5.0, the dollar/franc exchange rate quoted in New York at the same time (9 A.M. New York time) will be identical. If the New York dollar/franc exchange rate were $1 = FFr 5.5, a dealer could make a profit through **arbitrage**, the process of buying a currency low and selling it high. For example, if the prices differed in London and New York as given, a dealer could purchase FFr 550,000 for $100,000 in New York and immediately sell them in London for $110,000, making a quick profit of $10,000. If all dealers tried to cash in on the opportunity, however, the demand for francs in New York would result in an appreciation of the franc against the dollar, while the increase in the supply of francs in London would result in their depreciation there. Very quickly, the discrepancy in the New York and London exchange rates would disappear. Since foreign exchange dealers are continually watching their computer screens for arbitrage opportunities, the few that arise tend to be small, and they disappear in minutes.

Another feature of the foreign exchange market is the important role played by the U.S. dollar. Although a foreign exchange transaction can involve any two currencies, most transactions involve dollars. This is true even when a dealer wants to sell one nondollar currency and buy another. A dealer wishing to sell Dutch guilders for Italian lire, for example, will usually sell the guilders for dollars and then use the dollars to buy lire. Although this may seem a roundabout way of doing things, it is cheaper than trying to find a holder of lire who wants to buy guilders. The advantage of trading through the dollar is a result of the United States' importance in the world economy. Because the volume of international transactions involving dollars is so great, it is not hard to find dealers who wish to trade dollars for guilders or lire. In contrast, relatively few transactions require a direct exchange of guilders for lira.

Due to its central role in so many foreign exchange deals, the dollar is a vehicle currency. After the dollar, the most important vehicle currencies are the German mark, the Japanese yen, and the British pound—reflecting the importance of these trading nations in the world economy. The British pound used to be second in importance to the dollar as a vehicle currency, but its importance has diminished in recent years.

arbitrage Process of buying a currency low and selling it high.

What Determines Exchange Rates?

At the most basic level, exchange rates are determined by the demand and supply of one currency relative to the demand and supply of another. For example, if the demand for dollars outstrips the supply of them and if the supply of German deutsche marks is greater than the demand for them, the dollar/mark exchange rate will change. The dollar will appreciate against the mark (or, alternatively, the mark will depreciate against the dollar). However, while differences in relative demand and supply explain the determination of exchange rates, they do so only in a superficial sense. This simple explanation does not tell us what factors underlie the demand for and supply of a currency. Nor does it tell us when the demand for dollars will exceed the supply (and vice versa) or when the supply of German marks will exceed demand for them (and vice versa). Neither does it tell us under what conditions a currency is in demand or under what conditions it is not demanded. In this section we will review economic theories' answers to these questions. This will give us a deeper understanding of how exchange rates are determined.

If we understand how exchange rates are determined, we may be able to forecast exchange rate movements. Since future exchange rate movements influence export opportunities, the profitability of international trade and investment deals, and the price competitiveness of foreign imports, this is valuable information for an international business. Unfortunately, there is no simple explanation. The forces that determine exchange rates are complex, and no theoretical consensus exists, even among academic economists who study the phenomenon every day. Nonetheless, most economic theories of exchange rate movements seem to agree that three factors have an important impact on future exchange rate movements in a country's currency: the country's price inflation, its interest rate, and market psychology.[7]

Prices and Exchange Rates

To understand how prices are related to exchange rate movements, we first need to discuss an economic proposition known as the law of one price. Then we will discuss the theory of purchasing power parity (PPP), which links changes in the exchange rate between two countries' currencies to changes in the countries' price levels.

THE LAW OF ONE PRICE The **law of one price** states that in competitive markets free of transportation costs and barriers to trade (such as tariffs), identical products sold in different countries must sell for the same price when their price is expressed in terms of the same currency.[8] For example, if the exchange rate between the dollar and the French franc is $1 = FFr 5, a jacket that retails for $50 in New York should retail for FFr 250 (50 × 5) in Paris. To see why this must be so, consider what would happen if the jacket cost FFr 300 in Paris ($60 in U.S. currency). At this price, it would pay a company to buy jackets in New York and sell them in Paris (an example of arbi-

law of one price
Identical products sold in different countries must sell for the same price when their price is expressed in the same currency in competitive markets free of transportation costs and barriers to trade.

trage). Initially the company could make a profit of $10 on each jacket by purchasing them for $50 in New York and selling them for FFr 300 in Paris. (Remember we are assuming away transportation costs and trade barriers.) However, the increased demand for jackets in New York would raise their price in New York, and the increased supply of jackets in Paris would lower their price there. This would continue until prices were equalized. Thus, prices might equalize when the jacket cost $55 in New York and FFr 275 in Paris (assuming no change in the exchange rate of $1 = FFr 5).

PURCHASING POWER PARITY If the law of one price were true for all goods and services, the purchasing power parity (PPP) exchange rate could be found from any individual set of prices. By comparing the prices of identical products in different currencies, it would be possible to determine the "real" or PPP exchange rate that would exist if markets were efficient. (An **efficient market** has no impediments to the free flow of goods and services, such as trade barriers.)

A less extreme version of the PPP theory states that given **relatively efficient markets**—that is, markets in which few impediments to international trade and investment exist—the price of a "basket of goods" should be roughly equivalent in each country. To express the PPP theory in symbols, let $P_\$$ be the U.S. dollar price of a basket of particular goods and P_{DM} be the price of the same basket of goods in German deutsche marks. The PPP theory predicts that the dollar/DM exchange rate should be equivalent to:

$$\$/DM \text{ exchange rate} = P_\$/P_{DM}$$

Thus, if a basket of goods costs $200 in the United States and DM 600 in Germany, PPP theory predicts that the dollar/DM exchange rate should be $200/DM600 or $0.33 per DM (i.e., $1 = DM 3).

The next step in the PPP theory is to argue that the exchange rate will change if relative prices change. For example, imagine there is no price inflation in the United States, while prices in Germany are increasing by 20 percent a year. At the beginning of the year, a basket of goods costs $200 in the United States and DM 600 in Germany, so the dollar/DM exchange rate, according to PPP theory, should be $0.33 = DM 1. At the end of the year, the basket of goods still costs $200 in the United States, but it costs DM 720 in Germany. PPP theory predicts that the exchange rate should change as a result. More precisely, by the end of the year, $0.27 = DM 1 (i.e., $1 = DM 3.6). Due to the effects of price inflation, the DM has depreciated against the dollar. One dollar should buy more marks at the end of the year than at the beginning.

MONEY SUPPLY AND PRICE INFLATION In essence, PPP theory predicts that changes in relative prices will result in a change in exchange rates. Theoretically, a country in which price inflation is running wild should expect to see its currency depreciate against that of countries in which inflation rates are lower. So by predicting the likely inflation rates of different countries, we can forecast exchange rate movements. The inflation rate can be predicted through its close correlation to the growth rate of a country's money supply.[9]

Inflation is a monetary phenomenon. Inflation occurs when the quantity of money in circulation rises faster than the stock of goods and services; that is, when the money supply increases faster than output increases. The reason

efficient market Market that has no impediments to the free flow of goods and services.

relatively efficient market Market in which few impediments to international trade and investment exist.

for this is relatively straightforward. Imagine what would happen if everyone in the country was suddenly given $10,000 by the government. Many people would rush out to spend their extra money on those things they had always wanted—new cars, new furniture, better clothes, and so on. There would be a surge in demand for goods and services. How would car dealers, department stores, and other providers of goods and services respond to this upsurge in demand? They would do what any sensible businessperson would do—raise prices. The result would be price inflation.

A government increasing the money supply is analogous to giving people more money. An increase in the money supply makes it easier for banks to borrow from the government and for individuals and companies to borrow from banks. The resulting increase in credit causes increases in demand for goods and services. Unless the output of goods and services is growing at a rate similar to that of the money supply, the result will be inflation. This relationship has been observed time after time in country after country.

So now we have a connection among the growth in a country's money supply, price inflation, and exchange rate movements. When the growth in a country's money supply is faster than the growth in its output, price inflation is fueled. In turn, the PPP theory tells us that a country with a high inflation rate will see a depreciation in its currency exchange rate. A detailed example of how this can occur is given in the accompanying "Country Focus," which describes Bolivia's experience.

Another way of looking at the same phenomenon is that an increase in a country's money supply—which increases the amount of currency available—changes the relative demand and supply conditions in the foreign exchange market. If the U.S. money supply is growing more rapidly than U.S. output, dollars will be relatively more plentiful than the currencies of countries where monetary growth is closer to output growth. As a result of this relative increase in supply of dollars, the dollar will depreciate on the foreign exchange market against the currencies of countries with slower monetary growth.

The only remaining question is, what determines whether the rate of growth in a country's money supply is greater than the rate of growth in output? The answer is government policy. Governments generally have significant control over the money supply. A government can increase the money supply simply by telling the country's central bank to print more money. Governments tend to do this to finance public expenditure (building roads, paying government workers, paying for defense, etc.). Of course, a government could finance public expenditure by raising taxes, but since nobody likes paying more taxes and since politicians do not like to be unpopular, they have a natural preference for printing money. Unfortunately, there is no magic money tree. The inevitable result of excessive growth in money supply is price inflation. However, this has not stopped governments around the world from printing money, with predictable results. In short, if an international business is attempting to predict future movements in the value of a country's currency on the foreign exchange market, it should examine that country's government's policy toward monetary growth. If the government seems committed to controlling the rate of growth in money supply, the country's future inflation rate may be low (even if the current rate is high) and its currency should not depreciate too much on the foreign exchange market. But if the country's government seems to lack the political will to control the rate of growth in the money supply, the future inflation rate may be high, which is likely to cause its currency to depreciate. Historically, many Latin American govern-

Money Supply Growth, Inflation, and Exchange Rates in Bolivia

In the mid-1980s Bolivia experienced hyper-inflation—an explosive and seemingly uncontrollable price inflation in which money loses value very rapidly. Table 8.2 presents data on Bolivia's money supply, its inflation rate, and its peso's exchange rate with the U.S. dollar during the period of hyperinflation. The exchange rate is actually the "black market" exchange rate because the Bolivian government prohibited converting the peso to other currencies during the period. The data show that the growth in money supply, the rate of price inflation, and the depreciation of the peso against the dollar all moved in step with each other. This is just what PPP theory and monetary economics predict. Between April 1984 and July 1985, Bolivia's money supply increased by 17,433 percent, prices increased by 22,908 percent, and the value of the peso against the dollar fell by 24,662 percent! In October 1985 the Bolivian government instituted a dramatic stabilization plan—which included the introduction of a new currency and tight control of the money supply—and by 1987 the country's inflation rate was down to 16 percent a year.[10]

---

ments have fallen into this latter category, including Argentina, Bolivia, and Brazil. More recently, there are signs that many of the newly democratic states of Eastern Europe might be making the same mistake.

EMPIRICAL TESTS OF PPP THEORY PPP theory predicts that changes in relative prices will result in a change in exchange rates. A country in which price inflation is running wild should expect to see its currency depreciate against that of countries with lower inflation rates. This is intuitively appealing, but is it true? There are certainly several good examples of the connection between a country's price inflation and exchange rate position (such as Bolivia; see the "Country Focus"). Some evidence of this connection can be seen in Figure 8.1 (page 278). This figure compares a country's *total* inflation rate between 1973 and 1993 relative to the U.S. inflation rate against

TABLE 8.2

Macroeconomic Data for Bolivia: April 1984–October 1985

Month	Money Supply (billions of pesos)	Price Level Relative to 1982 (average = 1)	Exchange Rate (pesos per dollar)
1984			
April	270	21.1	3,576
May	330	31.1	3,512
June	440	32.3	3,342
July	599	34.0	3,570
August	718	39.1	7,038
September	889	53.7	13,685
October	1,194	85.5	15,205
November	1,495	112.4	18,469
December	3,296	180.9	24,515
1985			
January	4,630	305.3	73,016
February	6,455	863.3	141,101
March	9,089	1,078.6	128,137
April	12,885	1,205.7	167,428
May	21,309	1,635.7	272,375
June	27,778	2,919.1	481,756
July	47,341	4,854.6	885,476
August	74,306	8,081.0	1,182,300
September	103,272	12,647.6	1,087,440
October	132,550	12,411.8	1,120,210

Source: Juan-Antino Morales, "Inflation Stabilization in Bolivia," in *Inflation Stabilization: The Experience of Israel, Argentina, Brazil, Bolivia, and Mexico*, ed. Michael Bruno et al. (Cambridge, MA: MIT Press, 1988).

the change in the foreign currency price of U.S. dollars between 1973 and 1993 (an increase in the foreign currency price means there has been a fall in the value of that currency against the dollar). The figure shows that currencies of countries with higher inflation rates than the United States (e.g., Italy and the United Kingdom) depreciated against the U.S. dollar (and vice versa). Price inflation in Italy, for example, was 160 percent greater than in the United States over the 1973–93 period. Consistent with the predications of PPP theory, the value of the Italian lira against the dollar declined by about 150 percent over the same period. Similarly, inflation in Germany was about 55 percent less than in the United States, and the value of the German deutsche mark against the U.S. dollar increased by about 55 percent over this period.

Extensive empirical testing of the PPP theory has not shown it to be completely accurate in estimating exchange rate changes.[11] While the PPP theory

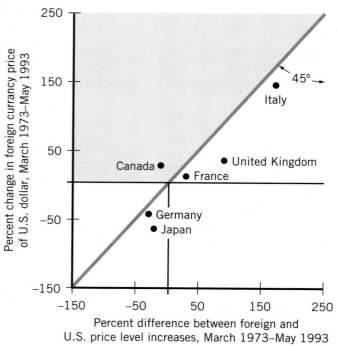

FIGURE 8.1

Exchange Rate Trends and Inflation Differentials, 1973–93
Source: OECD, *Main Economic Indicators.*

seems to yield relatively accurate predictions *in the long run*, such as the 20-year period illustrated in Figure 8.1, it does not appear to predict *short-run* movements in exchange rates. PPP theory does not seem to be a particularly good predictor of exchange rate movements for time spans of five years or less. In addition, the theory seems to best predict exchange rate changes for countries with very high rates of inflation and underdeveloped capital markets (e.g., Colombia, Poland, Mexico, and Russia). The theory is much less useful for predicting short-term exchange rate movements between the currencies of advanced industrialized nations that have relatively small differentials in inflation rates.

Several factors may explain the failure of PPP theory to predict exchange rates more accurately. PPP theory assumes away transportation costs and barriers to trade and investment. In practice, these factors are significant and they tend to create price differentials between countries. As we saw in Chapters 5 and 6, governments routinely intervene in international trade and investment. Such intervention, by violating the assumption of efficient markets, weakens the link between relative price changes and changes in exchange rates predicted by PPP theory.

Another factor is that governments also intervene in the foreign exchange market in attempting to influence the value of their currencies. We will look at why and how they do this in Chapter 9. For now, the important thing to note is that governments regularly intervene in the foreign exchange market, and this further weakens the link between price changes and changes in exchange rates.

Perhaps the most important factor explaining the failure of PPP theory to predict short-term movements in foreign exchange rates, however, is the impact of investor psychology on currency purchasing decisions and exchange rate movements. We will discuss this issue in more detail later in this chapter.

Interest Rates and Exchange Rates

Economic theory tells us that interest rates reflect expectations about likely future inflation rates. In countries where inflation is expected to be high, interest rates also will be high, because investors want compensation for the decline in the value of their money. This relationship was first formalized by economist Irvin Fisher and is thus referred to as the Fisher Effect. The Fisher Effect states that a country's "nominal" interest rate (i) is the sum of the required "real" rate of interest (r) and the expected rate of inflation over the period of time for which the funds are to be lent (I). More formally,

$$i = r + I$$

For example, if the real rate of interest in a country is 5 percent and annual inflation is expected to be 10 percent, the nominal interest rate will be 15 percent. As predicted by the Fisher Effect, a strong relationship does seem to exist between inflation rates and interest rates.[12]

We can take this one step further and consider how it applies in a world of many countries and unrestricted capital flows. When investors are free to transfer capital between countries, real interest rates will be the same in every country. If differences in real interest rates did emerge between countries, arbitrage would soon equalize them. For example, if the real interest rate in Germany was 10 percent and only 6 percent in the United States, it would pay investors to borrow money in the Unites States and invest it in Germany. The resulting increase in the demand for money in the United States would raise the real interest rate there, while the increase in the supply of foreign money in Germany would lower the real interest rate there. This would continue until the two sets of real interest rates were equalized. (In practice, differences in real interest rates may persist due to government controls on capital flows; investors are not always free to transfer capital between countries.)

It follows from the Fisher Effect that if the real interest rate is the same worldwide, any difference in interest rates between countries reflects differing expectations about inflation rates. Thus, if the expected rate of inflation in the United States is greater than that in Germany, U.S. nominal interest rates will be greater than German nominal interest rates.

Since we know from PPP theory that there is a link (in theory at least) between inflation and exchange rates, and since interest rates reflect expectations about inflation, it follows that there must also be a link between interest rates and exchange rates. This link is known as the International Fisher Effect (IFE). The **International Fisher Effect** states that for any two countries, the spot exchange rate should change in an equal amount but in the opposite direction to the difference in nominal interest rates between two countries. Stated more formally,

$$(S_1 - S_2)/S_2 \times 100 = i_\$ - i_{DM}$$

where $i_\$$ and i_{DM} are the respective nominal interest rates in the United States and Germany (for the sake of example), S_1 is the spot exchange rate at

International Fisher Effect For any two countries, the spot exchange rate should change in an equal amount but in the opposite direction to the difference in the nominal interest rates between the two countries.

the beginning of the period, and S_2 is the spot exchange rate at the end of the period.

In essence, if the U.S. nominal interest rate is higher than Germany's, reflecting greater expected inflation rates, the value of the dollar against the deutsche mark should fall by that interest rate differential in the future. So if the interest rate in the United States is 10 percent, and in Germany it is 6 percent, reflecting 4 percent higher expected inflation in the United States, we would expect the value of the dollar to depreciate by 4 percent against the mark.

So do interest rate differentials help predict future currency movements? The evidence is mixed; as in the case of PPP theory, in the long run there does seem to be a relationship between interest rate differentials and subsequent changes in spot exchange rates. However, considerable short-run deviations occur. Like PPP, the International Fisher Effect is not a good predictor of short-run changes in spot exchange rates.[13]

Investor Psychology and Bandwagon Effects

As we have noted, empirical evidence suggests that neither PPP theory nor the International Fisher Effect is particularly good at explaining *short-term* movements in exchange rates. One reason for this may be the impact of investor psychology on short-run exchange rate movements. There is increasing evidence that various psychological factors, as opposed to macroeconomic fundamentals, play an important role in determining the expectations of market traders as to likely future exchange rates.[14] In turn, expectations have a tendency to become self-fulfilling prophecies. We discussed a good example of this mechanism in the "Management Focus" on George Soros. When George Soros shorted the British pound in September 1992, many foreign exchange traders, fully aware of Soros' previous successes, jumped on the bandwagon and did likewise, selling British pounds and purchasing German marks. As the bandwagon effect built up, with more and more traders selling British pounds and purchasing deutsche marks in expectation of a decline in the pound, their expectations became a self-fulfilling prophecy with massive selling forcing down the value of the pound against the deutsche mark. The pound declined in value not because of any major shift in macroeconomic fundamentals, but because investors moved in a herd in response to a bet placed by a major speculator, George Soros. According to a number of recent studies, such bandwagon effects play a major role in determining short-run exchange rate movements.[15] However, by their very nature such bandwagon effects are hard to predict.

Summary

We have seen that relative monetary growth, relative inflation rates, and nominal interest rate differentials are all moderately good predictors of long-run changes in exchange rates. They are poor predictors of short-run changes in exchange rates, however, probably because of the impact of psychological factors, investor expectations, and bandwagon effects on short-term currency movements. This information is useful for an international business. Insofar as the long-term profitability of foreign investments, export opportunities, and the price competitiveness of foreign imports are all influenced by long-term movements in exchange rates, international businesses would be advised to pay attention to countries' differing monetary growth, inflation, and interest rates. International businesses that engage in foreign exchange transactions on a day-to-day basis could benefit by knowing some predictors of short-term foreign exchange rate movements. Unfortunately, short-term exchange rate movements are difficult to predict.

Exchange Rate Forecasting

A company's need to predict future exchange rate variations raises the issue of whether it is worthwhile for the company to invest in exchange rate forecasting services to aid decision making. Two schools of thought address this issue. The efficient market school argues that forward exchange rates do the best possible job of forecasting future spot exchange rates, so investing in forecasting services would be a waste of money. The other school of thought, the inefficient market school, argues that companies can improve the foreign exchange market's estimate of future exchange rates (as contained in the forward rate) by investing in forecasting services. In other words, this school of thought does not believe the forward exchange rates are the best possible predictors of future spot exchange rates.

The Efficient Market School

Forward exchange rates represent market participants' collective predictions of likely spot exchange rates at specified future dates. If forward exchange rates are the best possible predictor of future spot rates, it would make no sense for companies to spend money trying to forecast short-run exchange rate movements. Many economists believe the foreign exchange market is efficient at setting forward rates.[16] An efficient market is one in which prices reflect all available information. (If forward rates reflect all available information about likely future changes in exchange rates, there is no way a company can beat the market by investing in forecasting services.)

If the foreign exchange market is efficient, forward exchange rates should be unbiased predictors of future spot rates. This does not mean the predictions will be accurate in any specific situation; it means inaccuracies will not be consistently above or below future spot rates—that they will be random. There have been a large number of empirical tests of the efficient market hypothesis. Although most of the early work seems to confirm the hypothesis (suggesting that companies should not waste their money on forecasting services), more recent studies have challenged it.[17] There is increasing evidence that forward rates are not unbiased predictors of future spot rates, and that more accurate predictions of future spot rates can be calculated from publicly available information.[18]

The Inefficient Market School

Citing evidence against the efficient market hypothesis, some economists believe the foreign exchange market is inefficient. An **inefficient market** is one in which prices do not reflect all available information. In an inefficient mar-

inefficient market

Market in which prices do not reflect all available information.

ket, forward exchange rates will not be the best possible predictors of future spot exchange rates.

If this is true, it may be worthwhile for international businesses to invest in forecasting services (as many do). The belief is that professional exchange rate forecasts might provide better predictions of future spot rates than forward exchange rates do. However, the track record of professional forecasting services is not that good. An analysis of the forecasts of 12 major forecasting services over the 1978–82 period concluded the forecasters in general did not provide better forecasts than the forward exchange rates.[19]

Approaches to Forecasting

Assuming the inefficient market school is correct that the foreign exchange market's estimate of future spot rates can be improved, on what basis should forecasts be prepared? Here again, there are two schools of thought. One adheres to fundamental analysis, while the other uses technical analysis.

fundamental analysis Draws on economic theory to construct sophisticated econometric models for predicting exchange rate movements.

FUNDAMENTAL ANALYSIS **Fundamental analysis** draws on economic theory to construct sophisticated econometric models for predicting exchange rate movements. The variables contained in these models typically include those we have discussed, such as relative money supply growth rates, inflation rates, and interest rates. In addition, they may include variables related to countries' balance-of-payments positions.

The logic for including balance-of-payments data in exchange rate forecasts is that if a country is running a deficit on its balance-of-payments current account (it is importing more goods and services than it is exporting), pressures are created that result in the depreciation of its currency on the foreign exchange market. Consider what might happen if the United States was running a persistent current account balance-of-payments deficit. Since the United States would be importing more than it was exporting, people in other countries would be increasing their holdings of U.S. dollars. If these people were willing to hold their dollars, the dollar's exchange rate would not be influenced. However, if these people converted their dollars into other currencies, the supply of dollars in the foreign exchange market would increase (as would demand for the other currencies). This shift in demand and supply conditions would create pressures that could lead to the depreciation of the dollar against other currencies.

The problem with this argument is that it hinges on whether people in other countries are willing to hold dollars. This in turn depends on such factors as U.S. interest rates and inflation rates. So, in a sense, the balance-of-payments position is not a fundamental predictor of future exchange rate movements. For example, during the 1981–85 period, the U.S. dollar appreciated against most major currencies despite a growing balance-of-payments deficit. Relatively high real interest rates in the United States made the dollar very attractive to foreigners, so they did not convert their dollars into other currencies. Given this, we are back to the argument that the fundamental determinants of exchange rates are monetary growth, inflation rates, and interest rates.

Technical analysis uses price and volume data to determine past trends, which are expected to continue into the future. This approach does not rely on a consideration of economic fundamentals. Technical analysis is based on the premise that there are analyzable market trends and waves and that previous trends and waves can be used to predict future trends and waves. Since there is no theoretical rationale for this assumption of predictability, many economists compare technical analysis to fortune-telling. Despite this skepticism, technical analysis has gained favor in recent years.[20]

technical analysis Predicts exchange rate movements by using price and volume data to determine past trends, which are expected to continue into the future

Currency Convertibility

Until this point we have assumed that the currencies of various countries are freely convertible into other currencies. This assumption is invalid. Many countries restrict the ability of residents and nonresidents to convert the local currency into a foreign currency. This makes international trade and investment more difficult in those countries. Many international businesses have used "countertrade" practices to circumvent problems that arise when a currency is not freely convertible.

Convertibility and Government Policy

Due to government restrictions, a significant number of currencies are not freely convertible into other currencies. A country's currency is said to be **freely convertible** when the country's government allows both residents and nonresidents to purchase unlimited amounts of a foreign currency with it. A currency is said to be **externally convertible** when only nonresidents may convert it into a foreign currency without any limitations. A currency is **nonconvertible** when neither residents nor nonresidents are allowed to convert it into a foreign currency.

Free convertibility is the exception rather than the rule. Many countries place some restrictions on their residents' ability to convert the domestic currency into a foreign currency (a policy of external convertibility). Restrictions on convertibility for residents range from the relatively minor (such as restricting the amount of foreign currency they may take with them out of the country on trips) to the major (such as restricting domestic businesses' ability to take foreign currency out of the country). External convertibility restrictions can limit domestic companies' ability to invest abroad, but they present few problems for foreign companies wishing to do business in that country. For example, even if the German government placed tight controls on the ability of its residents to convert the mark into U.S. dollars, all U.S. businesses with deposits in German banks may at any time convert all of their marks into dollars and take them out of the country. Thus, a U.S. company with a subsidiary in Germany is assured it will be able to convert the profits from its German operation into dollars and take them out of the country.

Serious problems arise, however, when a policy of nonconvertibility exists. This was the practice of the former Soviet Union, and it continued to be the practice in Russia until recently. When strictly applied, nonconvertibility

freely convertible Currency able to be used by both residents and nonresidents to purchase foreign currency in unlimited amounts.

externally convertible Currency able to be used by nonresidents only to purchase foreign currency in unlimited amounts.

nonconvertible Currency that cannot be converted into a foreign currency.

means that although a U.S. company doing business in a country such as Russia may generate significant ruble profits, it may not convert those rubles into dollars and take them out of the country. Obviously this is not desirable for international business.

Governments limit convertibility to preserve their foreign exchange reserves. A country needs an adequate supply of these reserves to service its international debt commitments and to purchase imports. Governments typically impose convertibility restrictions on their currency when they fear that free convertibility will lead to a run on their foreign exchange reserves. This occurs when residents and nonresidents rush to convert their holdings of domestic currency into a foreign currency—a phenomenon generally referred to as capital flight. Capital flight is most likely to occur when the value of the domestic currency is depreciating rapidly because of hyperinflation or when a country's economic prospects are shaky in other respects. Under such circumstances, both residents and nonresidents believe their money is more likely to hold its value if it is converted into a foreign currency and invested abroad. Not only will a run on foreign exchange reserves limit the country's ability to service its international debt and pay for imports, but it will also lead to a precipitous depreciation in the exchange rate as residents and nonresidents alike unload their holdings of domestic currency on the foreign exchange markets (thereby increasing the market supply of the country's currency). Governments fear that the rise in import prices resulting from currency depreciation will lead to further increases in inflation. This fear provides another rationale for limiting convertibility.

Due to a combination of these reasons, in 1990 more than 80 countries had placed major restrictions on conversions of their currency. Another 32 countries had imposed minor restrictions, and only 31 countries' currencies were considered freely convertible. Countries with major restrictions on currency convertibility include many of the former Communist states of Eastern Europe, most of Africa, China, many of the Middle Eastern countries, and several Latin American nations.[21]

Countertrade

How can a company deal with the nonconvertibility problem? By engaging in countertrade. **Countertrade** refers to a range of barterlike agreements by which goods and services can be traded for other goods and services. Countertrade can make sense when a country's currency is nonconvertible. Consider the deal that General Electric struck with the Romanian government in 1984, when that country's currency was nonconvertible. When General Electric won a contract for a $150 million generator project in Romania, it agreed to take payment in the form of Romanian goods that could be sold for $150 million on international markets. In a similar case, the Venezuelan government negotiated a contract with Caterpillar in 1986 under which Venezuela would trade 350,000 tons of iron ore for Caterpillar heavy construction equipment. Caterpillar subsequently traded the iron ore to Romania in exchange for Romanian farm products, which it then sold on international markets for dollars.[22]

How important is countertrade? One estimate is that 20 to 30 percent of world trade in 1985 involved some form of countertrade agreements. Other estimates are that by 1990 more than 40 percent of world trade by volume involved countertrade.[23] Although these estimates might seem high—and they are difficult to verify because of the lack of hard data—they are plausible, given the large number of countries whose currencies remain nonconvertible.

Implications for Business

A number of clear implications for business are contained in this chapter. First, it is absolutely critical that international businesses understand the influence of exchange rates on the profitability of trade and investment deals. Adverse changes in exchange rates can make apparently profitable deals unprofitable. The risk introduced into international business transactions by changes in exchange rates is referred to as foreign exchange risk. Means of hedging against foreign exchange risk are available. Most significant, forward exchange rates and currency swaps allow companies to insure against this risk.

International businesses must also understand the forces that determine exchange rates. This is particularly true in light of the increasing evidence that forward exchange rates are not unbiased predictors. If a company wants to know how the value of a particular currency is likely to change over the long term on the foreign exchange market, it should take a close look at those economic fundamentals that appear to predict long-run exchange rate movements (i.e., the growth in a country's money supply, its inflation rate, and its nominal interest rates). For example, an international business should be very cautious about trading with or investing in a country with a recent history of rapid growth in its domestic money supply. The upsurge in inflation that is likely to follow such rapid monetary growth could lead to a sharp drop in the value of the country's currency on the foreign exchange market, which could transform a profitable deal into an unprofitable one. This is not to say that an international business should not trade with or invest in such a country. Rather, it means an international business should take some precautions before doing so, such as buying currency forward on the foreign exchange market or structuring the deal around a countertrade arrangement.

Complicating this picture is the issue of currency convertibility. The proclivity that many governments seem to have to restrict currency convertibility suggests that the foreign exchange market does not always provide the lubricant necessary to make international trade and investment possible. Given this, international businesses need to explore alternative mechanisms for facilitating international trade and investment that do not involve currency conversion. Countertrade seems the obvious mechanism.

Key Terms

Summary

The objectives of this chapter were to explain how the foreign exchange market works, to examine the forces that determine exchange rates, and then to discuss the implications of these factors for international business. Given that changes in exchange rates can dramatically alter the profitability of foreign trade and investment deals, this is an area of major interest to international business. These points have been made in the chapter:

1 One function of the foreign exchange market is to convert the currency of one country into the currency of another.

2 International businesses participate in the foreign exchange market to facilitate international trade and investment, to invest spare cash in short-term money market accounts abroad, and to engage in currency speculation.

3 A second function of the foreign exchange market is to provide insurance against foreign exchange risk.

4 The spot exchange rate is the exchange rate at which a dealer converts one currency into another currency on a particular day.

5 Foreign exchange risk can be reduced by using forward exchange rates. A forward exchange rate is an exchange rate governing future transactions.

6 The law of one price is that in competitive markets that are free of transportation costs and barriers to trade, identical products sold in different countries must sell for the same price when their price is expressed in the same currency.

7 Purchasing power parity (PPP) theory states the price of a basket of particular goods should be roughly equivalent in each country. PPP theory predicts that the exchange rate will change if relative prices change.

8 The rate of change in countries' relative prices depends on their relative inflation rates. A country's inflation rate seems to be a function of the growth in its money supply.

9 The PPP theory of exchange rate changes yields relatively accurate predictions of *long-term* trends in exchange rates, but not of *short-term* movements. The failure of PPP theory to predict exchange rate changes more ac-

curately may be due to the existence of transportation costs and barriers to trade and investment and the impact of psychological factors, such as bandwagon effects, on market movements and short-run exchange rates.

10 Interest rates reflect expectations about inflation. In countries where inflation is expected to be high, interest rates also will be high.

11 The International Fisher Effect (IFE) states that for any two countries, the spot exchange rate should change in an equal amount but in the opposite direction to the difference in nominal interest rates.

12 The most common approach to exchange rate forecasting is fundamental analysis. This relies on variables such as money supply growth, inflation rates, nominal interest rates, and balance-of-payments positions to predict future changes in exchange rates.

13 In many countries, government policy restricts the ability of residents and nonresidents to convert local currency into a foreign currency. A government restricts the convertibility of its currency to protect the country's foreign exchange reserves and to halt any capital flight.

14 Particularly bothersome for international business is a policy on nonconvertibility, which prohibits residents and nonresidents from exchanging local currency for foreign currency. A policy of nonconvertibility makes it very difficult to engage in international trade and investment in the country.

15 One way of coping with nonconvertibility is to engage in countertrade—to trade goods and services for other goods and services.

Critical Thinking and Discussion Questions

1 The interest rate on German government securities with one-year maturity is 4 percent, and the expected inflation rate for the coming year is 2 percent. The interest rate on U.S. government securities with one-year maturity is 7 percent, and the expected rate of inflation is 5 percent. The current spot exchange rate for German marks is $1 = DM 1.4. Forecast the spot exchange rate one year from today. Explain the logic of your answer.

2 Two countries, France and the United States, produce just one good: beef. Suppose the price of beef in the United States is $2.80 per pound and in France it is FFr 3.70 per pound.

a. According to PPP theory, what should the $/FFr spot exchange rate be?

b. Suppose the price of beef is expected to rise to $3.10 in the United States and to FFr 4.65 in France. What should the one-year forward $/FFr exchange rate be?

c. Given your answers to parts *a* and *b*, and given that the current interest rate in the United States is 10 percent, what would you expect the current interest rate to be in France?

3 You manufacture wine goblets. In mid-June you receive an order for 10,000 goblets from Germany. Payment of DM 400,000 is due in mid-December. You expect the deutsche mark to rise from its present rate of $1 = DM 1.5 to $1 = DM 1.4 by December. You can borrow marks at 6 percent annually. What should you do?

Internet Exercise

The foreign exchange market services businesses and investors worldwide, so the World Wide Web is an ideal instrument to assist them with gaining information about currency, converting money, and insuring against foreign exchange risk. The Policy Analysis Computing & Information Facility in Commerce (PACIFIC) at the University of British Columbia has an extensive Exchange Rate Service (http://pacific.commerce.ubc.ca/xr/) to access current and historic exchange rates in 65 countries. At the Yahoo Finance site (http://quote.yahoo.com/forex?u), surfers can convert currency from one country to that of another at an up-to-date exchange rate. The History of Money from Ancient Times to the Present Day site (http://www.ex.ac.uk/~RDavies/arian/llyfr.html) provides insight on the origin of currency and monetary conflicts.

Global Surfing

Using the PACIFIC site, what are today's current exchange rates for countries of your national origin? What are the historic exchange rates for the currency from these countries for the past year? Plot the data to show the positive and negative changes in these rates. What is the exchange rate forecast for the Canadian dollar vis-à-vis the U.S. dollar? Next, convert $1,000 of U.S. dollars to these three countries at the Yahoo Finance site. Finally, surf to the History of Money site and read about the conflicts regarding money. What historical developments have led to today's worldwide conflicts regarding the foreign exchange market?

The **Collapse** of the Russian **Ruble**

Between January 1992 and April 1995 the value of the ruble against the U.S. dollar fell from $1 = Rbs125 to $1 = Rbs5,130! This dramatic fall occurred at the same time Russia was implementing an economic reform program designed to transform the country's crumbling centrally planned economy into a dynamic market economy. The reform program involved a number of steps, including the removal of price controls on most goods and services, the gradual dismantling of much of the bureaucratic apparatus that had formerly controlled the economy, the privatization of many formerly state-owned enterprises, and the abolition of laws prohibiting private ownership.

One of the first steps to be implemented was the liberalization of price controls on January 1, 1992. Immediately after liberalization, prices surged and inflation was soon running at a *monthly* rate of about 30 percent. For the whole of 1992 the inflation rate in Russia was 3,000 percent. The annual rate for 1993 was approximately 900 percent. The inflation rate moderated during 1994, and by August it was running at a monthly rate of less than 5 percent. At this point price stabilization seemed possible. However, by January

1995 inflation had again surged to 17.8 percent.

Several factors contributed to Russia's high inflation rate. Prices had been held at artificially low levels by state planners during the Communist era. At the same time there was a shortage of many basic goods, so with nothing to spend their money on many Russians simply hoarded rubles. After the liberalization of price controls, the country was suddenly awash in rubles chasing a still limited supply of goods. The result was to rapidly bid up prices.

The inflationary fires that followed price liberalization were stoked by the Russian government itself. Unwilling to face the social consequences of the massive unemployment that would follow if many state-owned enterprises were quickly privatized, the government continued to subsidize the operations of many money-losing establishments. The result was a surge in the government's budget deficit. In the first quarter of 1992 the budget deficit amounted to 1.5 percent of the country's GDP. By the end of 1992 it had risen to 17 percent. Unable or unwilling to finance this deficit by raising taxes, the government settled on another solution—it printed money.

With inflation roaring ahead, the ruble tumbled. By the end of 1992 the exchange rate was $1 = Rbs480. By the end of 1993 it was $1 = Rbs1,500. However, the rate of decline in the ruble began to slow in early 1994. It looked as if the Russian government was starting to bring both the budget deficit and inflation under control. Unfortunately, as the year progressed it became evident that due to vigorous political opposition, the government would not be able to bring down its budget deficit as quickly as had been thought. By September the monthly inflation rate was rising again. October started badly with the ruble sliding more than 10 percent in value against the U.S. dollar in the first 10 days of the month. Then on October 11 the ruble plunged a staggering 21.5 percent against the dollar, reaching a value of $1 = Rbs3,926 by the time the foreign exchange market closed!

Many in the Russian government blamed the decline on currency speculation. Some officials even claimed that a cartel of 10 banks had been dumping rubles on the market in a deliberate attempt to drive down its price against the dollar and destabilize the economy. Despite the announcement of a tough budget plan with tight controls on the money supply, the ruble continued to slide and by April 1995 the exchange rate stood at $1 = Rbs5,120.

However, by mid-1995 inflation was again on the way down. In June 1995 the monthly inflation rate was at a yearly low of 6.7 percent. Moreover, the ruble had recovered to stand at $1 = Rbs4,559 by July 6. On that day the Russian government announced it would intervene in the currency market to keep the ruble in a trading range of Rbs4,300 to Rbs4,900 against the dollar. The Russian government believed that it was essential to maintain a relatively stable currency. Officials announced that the central bank would be able to draw on $10 billion in foreign exchange reserves to defend the ruble against any speculative selling in Russia's relatively small foreign exchange market.[24]

Case Discussion Questions

1 What was the root cause of the fall in the external value of the Russian ruble between 1992 and 1995?

2 What must the Russian government do to halt the decline in the value of the ruble?

3 Why do you think that it is important for a government to promote a stable currency?

4 Do you think the Russian central bank will be able to defend the ruble against speculative pressure and keep it in the trading range announced on July 6, 1995?

Chapter 9
The Global Monetary System

©PhotoDisc

Opening Case

The Tumbling Peso and the Auto Industry

In the euphoria that followed the January 1, 1994, implementation of the North American Free Trade Agreement (NAFTA) no industry looked set to gain more than the auto industry. Due to falling trade barriers and booming demand in Mexico, between January and October 1994 U.S. car exports to Mexico increased 500 percent. In 1994 Ford shipped 30,000 vehicles to Mexico, up from 6,000 in 1993. The company planned to ship 50,000 in 1995. General

Learning Objectives:

1 Understand the role played by the global monetary system in exchange rate determination.

2 Be familiar with the historical development of the modern global monetary system.

3 Appreciate the differences between a fixed and a floating exchange rate system.

4 Understand why the world's fixed exchange rate regime collapsed in the 1970s.

5 Understand the arguments for and against fixed and floating exchange systems.

6 Be familiar with the role played by the International Monetary Fund and World Bank in the global monetary system.

7 Understand the implications of the global monetary system for currency management and business strategy.

Motors and Chrysler also saw their shipments to Mexico surge in 1994 and were planning for even greater increases in 1995. Forecasts suggested that the number of vehicles sold in Mexico would rise to 1.2 million by 1999, up from 600,000 in 1994. With this growth in mind, auto companies had been investing in Mexican-based production capacity, both for serving the Mexican market and for exporting elsewhere. Among the biggest

foreign investors were Chrysler, Ford, General Motors, Nissan, Mercedes-Benz, and Volkswagen.

In the space of a few short days in December 1994, the euphoric bubble of the post-NAFTA boom was burst by an unexpected decision by the Mexican government to abandon a system of pegging the value of the peso at 3.5 to the dollar. Instead, the government decided to allow the peso to float freely against the dollar. In the weeks that followed

this decision, the peso plummeted 40 percent, and by mid-January 1995 it was trading at 5.6 to the dollar.

The peso had been pegged to the dollar since the early 1980s when the International Monetary Fund (IMF) had made it a condition for lending money to the Mexican government to help bail the country out of a 1982 financial crisis. Under the IMF-brokered arrangement, the peso had been allowed to trade within a tolerance band of plus or minus 3 percent against the dollar. The band was also permitted to "crawl" down daily, allowing for an annual peso depreciation of about 4 percent against the dollar. The IMF believed that the need to maintain the exchange rate within a fairly narrow trading band would force the Mexican government to adopt stringent financial policies to limit the growth in the money supply and contain inflation.

Until the early 1990s it looked as if the IMF policy had worked. However, by 1994 the strains were beginning to show. Since the mid-1980s Mexican producer prices had risen 45 percent more than prices in the United States, and yet there had not been a corresponding adjustment in the exchange rate. Moreover, by late 1994 Mexico was running a $17 billion trade deficit, which amounted to some 6 percent of the country's gross domestic product. Despite these strains, Mexican government officials had been stating publicly that they would support the value of the peso by adopting appropriate monetary policies and by intervening in the currency markets if necessary. Encouraged by such public statements, investment money poured into Mexico as corporations and mutual fund money

managers sought to take advantage of the booming economy.

However, many currency traders concluded that the peso would have to be devalued, and they began to dump pesos on the foreign exchange market. The government tried to hold the line by intervening in the market to buy pesos and sell dollars, but it soon found that it lacked the foreign currency reserves required to halt the speculative tide. In mid-December 1994 it abruptly changed course and announced a devaluation. Immediately, much of the short-term investment money that had flowed into Mexican stocks and bonds over the previous year reversed its course, as foreign investors bailed out of peso-denominated financial assets. This exacerbated the selling of the peso and contributed to the rapid 40 percent drop in its value.

As with many other industries, the impact on the auto industry was dramatic and immediate. By February 1995 the price of imported autos had risen by 40 percent. There had also been a substantial rise in the price of most autos assembled in Mexico, such as those coming out of Ford's Cuautitlan plant, because many of these operations depended on parts imported from the United States and Canada. Then in

March 1995 the Mexican government introduced an economic austerity plan. The plan tightened credit and forced up interest rates, which further depressed demand for autos.

For all of 1995 demand for autos was forecasted to come in between 30 percent and 50 percent below the levels attained in 1994. Volkswagen, Nissan, Mercedes-Benz, and Ford all temporarily closed their Mexican factories in January in expectation of the drop in demand. Fiat of Italy dropped plans to build a new auto factory in Mexico, and Nissan announced plans to cut its 1995 production in Mexico from 210,000 to 180,000 vehicles.

However, while the short-term outlook was grim, in the longer run many auto companies may benefit from the fall in the value of the peso. Although Volkswagen closed its Mexican plant for two weeks in January, it estimated it would ship 175,000 Mexican-made vehicles to the United States in 1995, 25,000 more than in 1994. Similarly, the big three U.S. automakers planned to keep their Mexican plants operating at full capacity in the second half of 1995 by boosting exports to the United States.[1]

Introduction

Although we discussed the workings of the foreign exchange market in some depth in Chapter 8, we did not mention the international monetary system's role in determining exchange rates. We simplified our explanation of how exchange rates are determined by assuming that currencies were free to "float" against each other. In reality, exchange rates are determined within the context of an international monetary system in which many currencies' ability to float against other currencies is limited by their respective governments or by intergovernmental arrangements.

In the opening case, for example, we saw that until December 1994 the value of the Mexican peso was pegged against that of the U.S. dollar. During the early 1990s only 25 of the world's 118 viable currencies were freely floating.[2] The exchange rates of 85 minor currencies were pegged to the exchange rates of particular major currencies, particularly the U.S. dollar and the French franc. Thus, the exchange rates of 25 currencies (including those of Angola, Barbados, Ethiopia, Panama, and Mexico) were pegged to the U.S. dollar's exchange rate. By this means, the value of the Mexican peso against major currencies, such as the Japanese yen, was determined by the value of the U.S. dollar against the yen. As the dollar appreciated against the yen in the early 1980s, so did the peso; and as the dollar depreciated against the yen in the 1990s, so did the peso.

The objective of this chapter is to explain how the international monetary system works and to point out its implications for international business. To understand how the international monetary system works, we must study the system's evolution. Accordingly, we will begin with a discussion of the gold standard and its breakup during the 1930s. Then we will discuss the 1944 Bretton Woods conference, which established the basic framework for the post-World War II international monetary system. The Bretton Woods system called for fixed exchange rates against the U.S. dollar. Under this **fixed exchange rate** system the value of most currencies in terms of the U.S. dollar was fixed for long periods and allowed to change only under a specific set of circumstances. The Bretton Woods conference also created two major international institutions: the International Monetary Fund (IMF) and the World Bank. The IMF, which we encountered in the opening case, was given the task of maintaining order in the international monetary system; the World Bank's goal was to promote development. Since both of these institutions continue to play a major role in the world economy, we discuss them in some detail.

The Bretton Woods system of fixed exchange rates collapsed in 1973. Since then the world has operated with a managed float system. Under a **managed float system**, some currencies are allowed to float freely, but the majority are either managed in some way by government intervention or pegged to another currency. We will explain the reasons for the failure of the Bretton Woods system as well as the nature of the present managed float system.

Two decades after the breakdown of the Bretton Woods system, the debate continues over what kind of exchange rate regime is best for the world. Some economists advocate a system in which major currencies are allowed to float against each other. Others argue for a return to a fixed exchange rate regime similar to the one established at Bretton Woods. This debate is intense and important, and we will examine the arguments of both sides.

Finally, we will discuss the implications of all this for international business. The opening case illustrates some implications of exchange rate policy for business practice. Mexico's December 1994 decision to let the peso float freely against the dollar resulted in a 40 percent depreciation in the dollar value of pesos, which undoubtedly hurt companies that were importing cars or car parts from the United States into Mexico. This shows how vulnerable international businesses are to a government's exchange rate policies. At the same time, the case also illustrates how government exchange rate policies can create business opportunities. In the long run a cheaper peso increases the competitiveness and export potential of Mexican-based auto manufacturing plants.

fixed exchange rate Value of most currencies in terms of U.S. dollars was fixed for long periods and allowed to change only under a specific set of circumstances.

managed float system Value of some currencies is allowed to float freely, but the majority are either managed in some way by government intervention or pegged to another currency.

The Gold Standard

The gold standard had its origin in the use of gold coins as a medium of exchange, unit of account, and store of value—a practice that stretches back to ancient times. In the days when international trade was limited in volume, payment for goods purchased from another country was typically made in gold or silver. However, as the volume of international trade expanded after the Industrial Revolution, a more convenient means of financing international trade was needed. Shipping large quantities of gold and silver around the world to finance international trade seemed impractical. The solution adopted was to arrange for payment in paper currency and for governments to agree to convert the paper currency into gold on demand at a fixed rate.

Nature of the Gold Standard

The practice of pegging currencies to gold and guaranteeing convertibility is known as the **gold standard**. By 1880 most of the world's major trading nations—including Great Britain, Germany, Japan, and the United States—had adopted the gold standard. Given a common gold standard, the value of any currency in units of any other currency (the exchange rate) was easy to determine.

For example, under the gold standard one U.S. dollar was defined as equivalent to 23.22 grains of "fine" (pure) gold. Thus, one could, in theory, demand that the U.S. government convert that one dollar into 23.22 grains of gold. Since there are 480 grains in an ounce, one ounce of gold cost $20.67 (480/23.22). The amount of a currency needed to purchase one ounce of gold was referred to as the gold par value. The British pound was defined as containing 113 grains of fine gold. In other words, one ounce of gold cost £4.25 (480/113). From the gold par values of pounds and dollars, we can calculate the exchange rate for converting pounds into dollars—£1 = $4.87 (i.e., $20.67/£4.25).

The Strength of the Gold Standard

The great strength claimed for the gold standard was that it contained a powerful mechanism for simultaneously achieving balance-of-trade equilibrium by all countries.[3] A country is said to be in balance-of-trade equilibrium when the income its residents earn from exports is equal to the money its residents pay to people in other countries for imports (i.e., the current account of its balance of payments is in balance).

Suppose there are only two countries in the world, Japan and the United States. Imagine Japan's trade balance is in surplus because it exports more to the United States than it imports from the United States. Japanese exporters are paid in U.S. dollars, which they exchange for Japanese yen at a Japanese bank. In turn, the Japanese bank submits the dollars to the U.S. government and demands payment of gold in return. (This is a simplification of what actually would occur.)

Under the gold standard, when Japan has a trade surplus there will be a net flow of gold from the United States to Japan. These gold flows automatically reduce the U.S. money supply and swell Japan's money supply. As we saw in Chapter 8, there is a close connection between money supply growth and price inflation. An increase in money supply will raise prices in Japan, while a decrease in the U.S. money supply will push U.S. prices downward. The rise in the price of Japanese goods will decrease demand for these goods, while the fall in the price of U.S. goods will increase demand for these goods. Thus, Japan will start to buy more from the United States, and the United States will buy less from Japan, until a balance-of-trade equilibrium is achieved.

This adjustment mechanism seems so simple and attractive that even today, more than half a century after the collapse of the gold standard, some people believe the world should return to a gold standard.

The Period between the Wars, 1918–39

The gold standard worked reasonably well from the 1870s until the start of World War I in 1914, when it was abandoned. During the war several governments financed their massive military expenditures by printing money. This resulted in inflation, and by the war's end in 1918, price levels were higher everywhere. The United States returned to the gold standard in 1919, Great Britain in 1925, and France in 1928.

Great Britain returned to the gold standard by pegging the pound to gold at the prewar gold parity level of £4.25 per ounce, despite substantial inflation between 1914 and 1925. This priced British goods out of foreign markets, which pushed the country into a deep depression. When foreign holders of pounds lost confidence in Great Britain's commitment to maintaining its currency's value, they began converting their holdings of pounds into gold. The British government saw that it could not satisfy the demand for gold without depleting its gold reserves, so it suspended convertibility in 1931.

The United States followed suit and left the gold standard in 1933 but returned to it in 1934, raising the dollar price of gold from $20.67 per ounce to $35 per ounce. Since more dollars were needed to buy an ounce of gold than before, the implication was that the dollar was worth less. This effectively amounted to a devaluation of the dollar relative to other currencies. Thus, whereas before the devaluation the pound/dollar exchange rate was £1 = $4.87, after the devaluation it was £1 = $8.24. By reducing the price of U.S. exports and increasing the price of U.S. imports, the government was trying to create employment in the United States by boosting output. However, a number of other countries adopted a similar tactic, and in the cycle of competitive devaluations that soon emerged, no country could win.

The net result was the shattering of any remaining confidence in the system. With countries devaluing their currencies at will, one could no longer be certain how much gold a currency could buy. Instead of holding onto another country's currency, people often tried to change it into gold immediately, lest the country devalue its currency in the intervening period. This put pressure on the gold reserves of various countries, forcing them to suspend gold convertibility. As a result, by the start of World War II in 1939, the gold standard was dead.

The Bretton Woods System

In 1944, at the height of World War II, representatives from 44 countries met at Bretton Woods, New Hampshire, to design a new international monetary system. With the collapse of the gold standard and the Great Depression of the 1930s fresh in their minds, these statesmen were determined to build an enduring economic order that would facilitate postwar economic growth. There was general consensus that fixed exchange rates were desirable. In addition, the conference participants wanted to avoid the senseless competitive devaluations of the 1930s, and they recognized that the gold standard would not assure this. The major problem with the gold standard as previously constituted was that there was no multinational institution that could stop countries from engaging in competitive devaluations.

The agreement reached at Bretton Woods established two multinational institutions—the International Monetary Fund and the World Bank. The task of the IMF would be to maintain order in the international monetary system, and that of the World Bank would be to promote general economic development. The Bretton Woods agreement also called for a system of fixed exchange rates that would be policed by the IMF. Under the agreement, all countries were to fix the value of their currency in terms of gold but were not required to exchange their currencies for gold. Only the dollar remained convertible into gold—at a price of $35 per ounce. Each other country decided what it wanted its exchange rate to be vis-à-vis the dollar and then calculated the gold par value of its currency based on that selected dollar exchange rate. All participating countries agreed to try to maintain the value of their currencies within 1 percent of the par value by buying or selling currencies (or gold) as needed. For example, if foreign exchange dealers were selling more of a country's currency than they demanded, the government of that country would intervene in the foreign exchange markets, buying its currency in an attempt to increase demand and maintain its gold par value.

Another aspect of the Bretton Woods agreement was a commitment not to use devaluation as a weapon of competitive trade policy. However, if a currency became too weak to defend, a devaluation of up to 10 percent would be allowed without any formal approval by the IMF. Larger devaluations required IMF approval.

The Role of the IMF

The IMF Articles of Agreement were heavily influenced by the worldwide financial collapse, competitive devaluations, trade wars, high unemployment, hyperinflation in Germany and elsewhere, and general economic disintegration experienced between the wars. The aim of the Bretton Woods agreement, of which the IMF was the main custodian, was to try to avoid a repetition of that chaos through a combination of discipline and flexibility.

DISCIPLINE   A fixed exchange rate regime imposes discipline in two ways. First, the need to maintain a fixed exchange rate puts a brake on competitive devaluations and brings stability to the world trade environment. Second, a fixed exchange rate regime imposes monetary discipline on countries, thereby curtailing price inflation. Consider what would happen under a fixed exchange rate regime if Great Britain rapidly increased its money supply by printing pounds. As explained in Chapter 8, the increase in money supply would lead to price inflation. In turn, given fixed exchange rates, inflation would make British goods uncompetitive in world markets, while the prices of imports would become more attractive in Great Britain. The result would be a widening trade deficit in Great Britain, with the country importing more than it exports. To correct this trade imbalance under a fixed exchange rate regime, Great Britain would be required to restrict the rate of growth in its money supply to bring price inflation back under control. Thus, fixed exchange rates are seen as a mechanism for controlling inflation and imposing economic discipline on countries.

FLEXIBILITY Although monetary discipline was a central objective of the Bretton Woods agreement, it was recognized that a rigid policy of fixed exchange rates would be too inflexible. It would probably break down just as the gold standard had. Moreover, in some cases a country's attempts to reduce its money supply growth and correct a balance-of-payments deficit could force the country into recession and create high unemployment. The architects of the Bretton Woods agreement wanted to avoid high unemployment, so they built some limited flexibility into the system. Two major features of the IMF Articles of Agreement fostered this flexibility: IMF lending facilities and adjustable parities.

The IMF stood ready to lend foreign currencies to members to tide them over during short periods of balance-of-payments deficit, when a rapid tightening of monetary or fiscal policy would hurt domestic employment. A pool of gold and currencies contributed by IMF members provided the resources for these lending operations. A persistent balance-of-payments deficit can lead to depletion of a country's reserves of foreign currency, forcing it to devalue its currency. By providing deficit countries with short-term foreign currency loans, IMF funds would buy countries time in which to bring down their inflation rates and reduce their balance-of-payments deficit. The belief was that such loans would reduce pressures for devaluation and allow for a more orderly and less painful adjustment.

Countries were to be allowed to borrow a limited amount from the IMF without adhering to any specific agreements. However, extensive drawings from IMF funds would require a country to agree to increasingly stringent IMF supervision of its macroeconomic policies. In other words, heavy borrowers from the IMF must agree to conditions concerning monetary and fiscal policy set down by the IMF, which typically include IMF-mandated targets on domestic money supply growth, exchange rate policy, tax policy, government spending, and so on.

The system of adjustable parities allows for the devaluation of a country's currency by more than 10 percent if the IMF agrees that the country's balance of payments is in "fundamental disequilibrium." The term *fundamental disequilibrium* was not defined in the IMF's Articles of Agreement, but it was intended to apply to countries that had suffered permanent adverse shifts in the demand for their products. Without a devaluation, such a country would experience high unemployment and a persistent trade deficit until the domestic price level had fallen far enough to restore a balance-of-payments equilibrium. The belief was that devaluation could help sidestep a painful adjustment process in such circumstances.

The Role of the World Bank

The official name for the World Bank is the International Bank for Reconstruction and Development (IBRD). When the Bretton Woods participants established the World Bank, the need to reconstruct the war-torn economies of Europe was foremost in their minds. The bank's initial mission was to help finance the building of Europe's economy by providing low-interest loans. As it turned out, the World Bank was overshadowed in this role by the Marshall Plan, under which the United States lent money directly to European nations to help them rebuild. So the bank soon turned its attention to development and began lending money to the less developed nations of the Third World. In the 1950s the bank concentrated its efforts on public-sector projects. Power station projects, road building, and other transportation investments were much in favor. During the 1960s the bank also began to lend heavily in support of agriculture, education, population control, and urban development.

The bank lends money under two schemes. Under the IBRD scheme, money is raised through bond sales in the international capital market. Borrowers pay what the bank calls a market rate of interest—the bank's cost of funds plus a margin for expenses. In fact, this "market" rate is lower than commercial banks' market rate. Essentially, under the IBRD scheme the bank offers low-interest loans to risky customers whose credit rating is often poor.

A second scheme is overseen by the International Development Agency (IDA), an arm of the bank created in 1960. Resources to fund IDA loans are raised through subscriptions from wealthy members such as the United States, Japan, and Germany. IDA loans go only to the poorest countries. (In 1991 those were defined as countries with annual incomes per capita of less than $580.) Borrowers have 50 years to repay at an interest rate of 1 percent a year.

The Collapse of the Fixed Exchange Rate System

The system of fixed exchange rates established at Bretton Woods worked well until the late 1960s, when it began to show signs of strain. The system finally collapsed in 1973, and since then we have had a managed float system. To understand why the system collapsed, one must appreciate the special role of the U.S. dollar in the system. As the only currency that could be converted into gold, and as the currency that served as the reference point for all others, the dollar occupied a central place in the system. Any pressure on the dollar to devalue could wreak havoc with the system, and that is what happened.

Most economists trace the breakup of the fixed exchange rate system to the U.S. macroeconomic policy package of 1965–68.[4] To finance both the Vietnam conflict and his welfare programs, President Johnson backed an increase in U.S. government spending that was not financed by an increase in taxes. Instead, it was financed by an increase in the money supply, which led to a rise in price inflation from less than 4 percent in 1966 to close to 9 percent by 1968 (see Figure 9.1). At the same time, the rise in government spending had stimulated the economy. With more money in their pockets, people spent

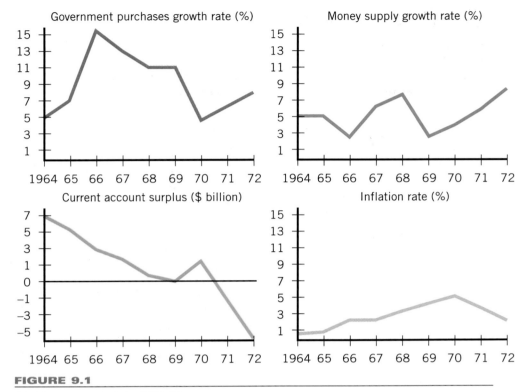

FIGURE 9.1

U.S. Macroeconomic Data, 1964–72
Source: *Economic Report of the President, 1985.*

more—particularly on imports—and the U.S. trade balance began to deteriorate rapidly.

The increase in inflation and the worsening of the U.S. foreign trade position gave rise to speculation in the foreign exchange market that the dollar
would be devalued. Things came to a head in spring 1971 when U.S. trade
figures were released. The figures showed that for the first time since 1945,
the United States was importing more than it was exporting. This set off massive purchases of deutsche marks in the foreign exchange market by speculators who guessed that the DM would be revalued against the dollar. On a
single day, May 4, 1971, the Bundesbank (Germany's central bank) had to buy
$1 billion to hold the dollar/DM exchange rate at its fixed exchange rate given
the great demand for DMs. On the morning of May 5, the Bundesbank purchased another $1 billion during the first hour of foreign exchange trading!
At that point, the Bundesbank allowed its currency to float.

In the weeks following the decision to float the DM, the foreign exchange
market became increasingly convinced that the dollar would have to be devalued. However, devaluation of the dollar was no easy matter. Under the
Bretton Woods provisions, any other country could change its exchange rates
against all currencies simply by fixing its dollar rate at a new level. But as the
key currency in the system, the dollar could be devalued only if all countries
agreed to simultaneously revalue against the dollar. And many countries did
not want this, since it would make their products more expensive relative to
U.S. products.

To force the issue, in August 1971 President Nixon announced that the dollar was no longer convertible into gold. He also announced that a new 10 percent tax on imports would remain in effect until U.S. trading partners agreed to revalue their currencies against the dollar. This brought the trading partners to the bargaining table, and in December 1971 an agreement was reached to devalue the dollar by about 8 percent against foreign currencies. The import tax was then removed.

The problem was not solved, however. The U.S. balance-of-payments position continued to deteriorate throughout 1972, while the U.S. money supply continued to expand at an inflationary rate (see Figure 9.1). Speculation continued to grow that the dollar was still overvalued and that a second devaluation would be necessary. In anticipation, foreign exchange dealers began converting dollars to deutsche marks and other currencies. After a massive wave of speculation in February, which culminated with European central banks spending $3.6 billion on March 1 to try to prevent their currencies from appreciating against the dollar, the foreign exchange market was closed. When the foreign exchange market reopened March 19, the currencies of Japan and most European countries were floating against the dollar, although many developing countries continued to peg their currency to the dollar, and many still do to this day. At that time, the switch to a floating system was viewed as a temporary response to unmanageable speculation in the foreign exchange market. But it is now 25 years since the Bretton Woods system of fixed exchange rates collapsed, and the temporary solution is beginning to look permanent.

It is clear that the Bretton Woods system had an Achilles' heel: the system could not work if its key currency, the U.S. dollar, was under speculative attack. The Bretton Woods system could work only as long as the U.S. inflation rate remained low and the United States did not run a balance-of-payments deficit. Once these things occurred, the system soon became strained to the breaking point.

The Floating Exchange Rate Regime

The floating exchange rate regime that followed the collapse of the fixed exchange rate system was formalized in January 1976 when IMF members met in Jamaica and agreed to the rules for the international monetary system that are in place today. We will discuss the Jamaica agreement before looking at how the floating exchange rate regime has operated in practice.

The Jamaica Agreement

The purpose of the Jamaica meeting was to revise the IMF's Articles of Agreement to reflect the new reality of floating exchange rates. The main elements of the Jamaica agreement include the following:

1 Floating rates were declared acceptable. IMF members were permitted to enter the foreign exchange market to even out "unwarranted" speculative fluctuations.

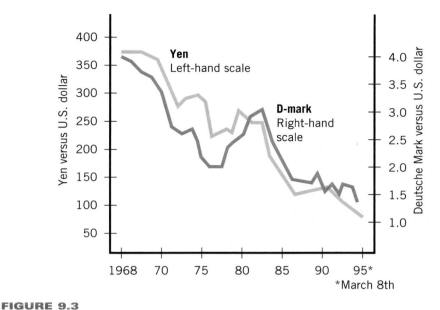

FIGURE 9.3

The U.S. Dollar against the Yen and Deutsche Mark, 1970–96
Source: Morgan Guaranty, *World Financial Markets*, various issues.

The dollar continued to decline until early 1987. The governments of the Group of Five began to worry that the dollar might decline too far. So in February 1987 the finance ministers of the Group of Five met in Paris and reached a new agreement known as the Louvre Accord. They agreed that exchange rates had been realigned sufficiently and pledged to support the stability of exchange rates around their current levels by intervening in the foreign exchange markets when necessary to buy and sell currency. Although the dollar continued to decline for a few months after the Louvre Accord, the rate of decline slowed, and by early 1988 the decline had ended. Except for a brief speculative flurry around the time of the Persian Gulf War in 1991, the dollar has been relatively stable since then against most major currencies. However, the dollar continued to slide against the Japanese yen and, to a lesser extent, the German deutsche mark until mid-1995, before rising again through 1996 and early 1997 (see Figure 9.3). According to many observers, the decline in the value of the dollar against these currencies during the early 1990s was less a reflection of any inherent weakness in the dollar than it was a confirmation of the unusual strength of these two currencies, particularly that of the yen.[6] The yen situation is discussed in more detail in the next "Country Focus."

Thus, we see that in recent history the value of the dollar has been determined by both market forces and government intervention. Under a floating exchange rate regime, market forces have produced a volatile dollar exchange rate. Governments have responded by intervening in the market—buying and selling dollars—in attempting to limit the market's volatility and to correct what they see as overvaluation (in 1985) or potential undervaluation (in 1987) of the dollar. The frequency of government intervention in the foreign exchange markets explains why the current system is variously referred to as a managed float system or a dirty float system.

Yen **Shock**

In 1971, before the collapse of the Bretton Woods system of fixed exchange rates, one U.S. dollar purchased 350 Japanese yen. In 1985 the exchange rate was $1=¥250; in 1990 it stood at $1=¥150; in 1993 it was $1=¥125; by March 1995 the exchange rate stood at $1=¥85.

Much of the decline in the value of the dollar against the yen between 1971 and 1995 can be explained by differences in relative inflation rates. Between 1983 and 1989, for example, inflation in Japan averaged 1.1 percent a year, whereas U.S. price inflation ran at an average annual rate of 3.6 percent. Similarly, between 1988 and 1993 inflation in Japan ran at an average annual rate of 2 percent, compared to 4.1 percent in the United States.

Between 1993 and early 1995 the yen appreciated by 50 percent against the dollar. On a purchasing power parity basis, by mid-1995 the yen looked to be overvalued against the dollar by about 30 percent. This overvaluation suggested that differences in U.S. and Japanese inflation rates were not sufficient to explain the rise of the yen during this period.

One explanation for the dramatic rise in the dollar value of the yen between 1993 and 1995 can be found in the recent behavior of Japanese investment institutions (particularly banks and insurance companies). Japan has long run a large balance-of-trade surplus with the United States. One consequence of this surplus is that many Japanese companies have found themselves holding lots of dollars (earned from the sale of products to U.S. consumers). During the 1980s Japanese financial institutions helped recycle these dollars by purchasing them from Japanese companies and reinvesting them in U.S. stocks and bonds.

As long as Japanese financial institutions reinvested dollars in the United States, as opposed to selling them for yen, the dollar/yen exchange rate was relatively stable. However, in the early 1990s Japan entered its worst recession since 1945. The severity of this recession was

Fixed versus Floating Exchange Rates

The breakdown of the Bretton Woods system has not stopped the debate about the relative merits of fixed versus floating exchange rate regimes. Disappointment with the system of floating rates in recent years has led to renewed debate about the merits of a fixed exchange rate system. In this section we review the arguments for fixed and floating exchange rate regimes.[8] In the next section we will discuss the European monetary system's exchange rate mechanism, which many see as a prototype for a future fixed exchange rate system. We will discuss the case for floating rates before discussing why many commentators are disappointed with the experience under floating exchange rates and yearn for a system of fixed rates.

The Case for Floating Exchange Rates

The case for floating exchange rates has two main elements: monetary policy autonomy and automatic trade balance adjustments.

compounded by a collapse in Japanese stock and property prices, both of which fell more than 50 percent. This deflation hit Japanese financial institutions hard. Most Japanese financial institutions held many of their assets in the form of Japanese stock and property investments. With stock and property prices plunging, Japanese financial institutions saw their balance sheets deteriorate. Their weak balance sheets reduced their appetite for risky investments, so they reduced their purchases of U.S. assets and increased their investments in Japanese government bonds. In short, the financial institutions stopped recycling dollars back to the United States. Beginning in 1993 they changed many of these dollars into yen and reinvested them in Japan. To make matters worse, many financial institutions started liquidating their holdings of U.S. stocks and bonds to increase the funds available for investment in low-risk Japanese government bonds. Thus, after having doubled the value of their U.S. investments in the two years before 1989, Japanese financial institutions reduced their foreign assets by 20 percent over the next four years.

The net effect of these developments was to reduce the demand for dollars and increase the demand for yen; hence the appreciation of the yen against the dollar. As the value of the yen accelerated in 1993, U.S. assets began to look even less attractive (their valuation in yen declined). This only increased the reluctance of Japanese institutions to invest in U.S. stocks and bonds. Thus, by 1995 a self-fulfilling bandwagon effect had led to a massive rise in the value of the yen as Japanese investors held back from investing in U.S. assets lest they see the value of those assets reduced by a subsequent appreciation in the value of the yen. The appreciation in the value of the yen was a major blow for export-oriented Japanese companies. In what was widely referred to in Japan as "yen shock," Japanese firms saw prices and profit margins on exports to the United States squeezed relentlessly as the yen climbed to new highs.

The extreme overvaluation of the yen persisted for about 18 months. The dollar/yen exchange returned to a more realistic level in 1996 as Japanese institutions once more started to invest heavily in U.S. assets, such as stocks and bonds. By April 1997 the exchange rate had climbed back to around $1=¥120, up substantially from the 1995 low of $1=¥85.[7]

MONETARY POLICY AUTONOMY It is argued that a floating exchange rate regime gives countries monetary policy autonomy. Under a fixed system, a country's ability to expand or contract its money supply as it sees fit is limited by the need to maintain exchange rate parity. Monetary expansion can lead to inflation, which puts downward pressure on a fixed exchange rate (as predicted by PPP theory; see Chapter 8). Similarly, monetary contraction requires high interest rates (to reduce the demand for money). Higher interest rates lead to an inflow of money from abroad, which puts upward pressure on a fixed exchange rate. Thus, to maintain exchange rate parity under a fixed system, countries were limited in their ability to use monetary policy to expand or contract their economies.

Advocates of a floating exchange rate regime argue that removal of the obligation to maintain exchange rate parity restores monetary control to a government. If a government faced with unemployment wanted to increase its money supply to stimulate domestic demand and reduce unemployment, it could do so unencumbered by the need to maintain its exchange rate. While monetary expansion might lead to inflation, this in turn would lead to a depreciation in the country's currency. If PPP theory is correct, the resulting currency depreciation on the foreign exchange markets should offset the effects of inflation. Put another way, although under a floating exchange rate regime domestic inflation would have an impact on the exchange rate, it should have no impact on the country's businesses' international cost competitiveness due to exchange rate depreciation. The rise in domestic costs should be exactly offset by the fall in the value of the country's currency on the foreign exchange markets. Similarly, a government could use monetary policy to contract the economy without worrying about the need to maintain parity.

TRADE BALANCE ADJUSTMENTS Under the Bretton Woods system, if a country developed a permanent deficit in its balance of trade (importing more than it exported) that could not be corrected by domestic policy, the IMF would agree to a currency devaluation. Critics of this system argue that the adjustment mechanism works much more smoothly under a floating exchange rate regime. They argue that if a country is running a trade deficit, the imbalance between the supply and demand of that country's currency in the foreign exchange markets (supply exceeding demand) will lead to depreciation in its exchange rate. An exchange rate depreciation should correct the trade deficit by making the country's exports cheaper and its imports more expensive.

The Case for Fixed Exchange Rates

The case for fixed exchange rates rests on arguments about monetary discipline, speculation, uncertainty, and the lack of connection between the trade balance and exchange rates.

MONETARY DISCIPLINE We discussed the monetary discipline inherent in a fixed exchange rate system when we discussed the Bretton Woods system. The need to maintain a fixed exchange rate parity ensures that governments do not expand their money supplies at inflationary rates. While advocates of floating rates argue that each country should be allowed to choose its own inflation rate (the monetary autonomy argument), advocates of fixed rates argue that governments too often give in to political pressures and expand the monetary supply far too rapidly, causing unacceptably high price inflation. A fixed exchange rate regime will ensure that this does not occur.

SPECULATION Critics of a floating exchange rate regime also argue that speculation can cause fluctuations in exchange rates. They point to the dollar's rapid rise and fall during the 1980s, which they claim had nothing to do with comparative inflation rates and the U.S. trade deficit, but everything to do with speculation. They argue that if foreign exchange dealers see a currency depreciating, they tend to sell the currency in the expectation of future depreciation regardless of the currency's longer-term prospects. As more traders jump on the bandwagon, the expectations of depreciation are realized. Such destabilizing speculation accentuates the fluctuations around the exchange rate's long-run value. It can be very damaging to a country's economy by distorting export and import prices. (For example, in 1985 U.S. exports may have been overpriced and imported goods underpriced due to the very high value of the dollar.) Thus, advocates of a fixed exchange rate regime argue that such a system will limit the destabilizing effects of speculation.

UNCERTAINTY Speculation also adds to the uncertainty surrounding future currency movements that characterizes floating exchange rate regimes. The unpredictability of exchange rate movements in the post-Bretton Woods era has made business planning difficult and it makes exporting, importing, and foreign investment risky activities. Given a volatile exchange rate, international businesses do not know how to react to the changes—and often they do not react. Why change plans for exporting, importing, or foreign investment after a 6 percent fall in the dollar this month, when the dollar may rise 6 percent next month? This uncertainty, according to the critics, hinders the growth of international trade and investment. They argue that a fixed exchange rate, by eliminating such uncertainty, promotes the growth of international trade and investment. Advocates of a floating system reply that the forward exchange market does a good job of insuring against the risks associated with exchange rate fluctuations (see Chapter 8). Accordingly, the adverse impact of uncertainty on the growth of international trade and investment has been overstated.

TRADE BALANCE ADJUSTMENTS Those in favor of floating exchange rates argue that floating rates help adjust trade imbalances. Critics question the closeness of the link between the exchange rate and the trade balance. They claim trade deficits are determined by the balance between savings and investment in a country, not by the external value of its currency.[9] Moreover, they argue that a depreciation in a currency will lead to inflation (due to the resulting increase in import prices). This inflation will wipe out any apparent gains in cost competitiveness that come from currency depreciation. In other words, a depreciating exchange rate will not boost exports and reduce imports, as advocates of floating rates claim; it will simply boost price inflation. In support of this argument, those who favor fixed rates point out that the 40 percent drop in the value of the dollar between 1985 and 1988 did not seem to correct the U.S. trade deficit. In reply, advocates of a floating exchange rate regime argue that between 1985 and 1992, the U.S. trade deficit fell from over $160 billion to about $70 billion, and they attribute this in part to the decline in the value of the dollar.

Who Is Right?

We see today a vigorous debate between those who favor a fixed exchange rate regime and those who favor a floating exchange rate regime. Which side is right? We don't know. From a business perspective, this is unfortunate, since as a major player on the international trade and investment scene, business has a large stake in the resolution of the debate. Would international business be better off under a fixed regime or are flexible rates better? The evidence is not yet in.

We do, however, know that a fixed exchange rate regime modeled along the lines of the Bretton Woods system will not work. It is telling that speculation ultimately broke the system—a phenomenon that advocates of fixed rate regimes claim is associated with floating exchange rates! Nevertheless, a different kind of fixed exchange rate system might be more enduring and might foster the kind of stability that would facilitate more rapid growth in international trade and investment.

The IMF and World Bank after Bretton Woods

The collapse of the Bretton Woods system left the IMF with a diminished role in the international monetary system. The IMF's original function was to provide a pool of money from which members could borrow, short term, to adjust their balance-of-payments position and maintain their exchange rate. Under a floating exchange rate regime, the demand for short-term loans was diminished. A trade deficit would presumably lead to a decline in a country's exchange rate, which in turn would help reduce imports and boost exports. No temporary IMF adjustment loan would be needed. Consistent with this, most industrialized countries tended to let the foreign exchange market determine exchange rates in response to demand and supply. No major industrial country has borrowed funds from the IMF since the mid-1970s, when Great Britain and Italy did. Since the early 1970s the rapid development of global capital markets has allowed developed countries such as Great Britain and the United States to finance their deficits by borrowing private money, as opposed to drawing on IMF funds.

In response to these changes, the IMF has done what any bureaucracy interested in self-preservation might do: it found a new mission. This new mission was inspired by the OPEC oil price hikes of 1973 and 1979 and the resulting debt crisis in the developing world.[10]

IMF and the Developing World Debt

The OPEC oil price increases in 1973 and 1979 resulted in massive flows of funds from the major oil-importing nations (e.g., Germany, Japan, and the United States) to the oil-producing nations of OPEC. Never slow to spot a profit opportunity, commercial banks quickly stepped in to recycle this money—borrowing from OPEC countries and lending to governments and businesses around the world. Much of the recycled money—too much, as it turned out—ended up in the form of loans to the governments of various Latin American and African nations. These loans were made on the basis of optimistic assessments about these nations' short- and medium-term growth prospects, which did not materialize. Rather, economic growth in the developing world was choked off in the early 1980s by a combination of factors, including:

- Rising short-term interest rates worldwide (which increased the costs of debt).
- Poor macroeconomic management in a number of developing countries—in particular, inflationary growth policies.
- Poor use of the funds borrowed by the governments of developing nations (too often used to finance consumption rather than investment).
- A slowdown in the growth rate of the industrialized West, the main markets for the products of developing nations.

The consequence was a debt crisis of massive proportions. At one point it was calculated that commercial banks had over $1 trillion of bad debts on their books, debts that the debtor nations had no hope of paying off. If any major country had defaulted at this time, the shock waves would have shaken the world financial system. Many feared that if this were to occur, the resulting bank failures in the advanced nations would turn the widespread recession of the 1980s into a deep depression.

Against this background, Mexico, long thought to be the most creditworthy of the major debtor countries in the developing world, announced in 1982 that it could no longer service its $80 billion in international debt without an immediate new loan of $3 billion. Brazil quickly followed, revealing that it could not meet the required payments on its borrowed $87 billion. Then Argentina and several dozen other countries of lesser credit standings followed suit. The international monetary system was facing a crisis of enormous dimensions.

From the IMF Solution to the Brady Plan

Into the breach stepped the IMF. Together with several Western governments, particularly that of the United States, the IMF emerged as the key player in resolving the debt crisis. The deal with Mexico involved three elements:

1 Rescheduling of Mexico's old debt.

2 New loans to Mexico from the IMF, the World Bank, and commercial banks.

3 The Mexican government's agreement to abide by a set of IMF-dictated macroeconomic prescriptions for its economy, including tight control over the growth of the money supply and major cuts in government spending.

Orchestrating this agreement required the IMF to persuade approximately 1,600 commercial banks that had already lent money to Mexico to increase the amount of their loans by 8 percent. The IMF's success in pulling this off, first for Mexico and later for other debt-ridden countries, was no small achievement.

However, the IMF's solution to the debt crisis contained a major weakness: it depended on the rapid resumption of growth in the debtor nations. If this occurred, their capacity to repay debt would grow faster than their debt itself, and the crisis would be resolved. By the mid-1980s, it was clear this was not going to happen. The IMF-imposed macroeconomic policies did succeed in bringing the trade deficits and inflation rates of many debtor nations under control, but it was at the price of sharp contractions in their economic growth rates.

By 1989 it was clear that the debt problem was not going to be solved merely by rescheduling debt. In April of that year, the IMF endorsed a new approach that had first been proposed by Nicholas Brady, the U.S. Treasury secretary. The Brady Plan, as it became known, stated that debt reduction—as distinguished from debt rescheduling—was a necessary part of the solution and that the IMF and World Bank would assume roles in financing it. The essence of the plan was that the IMF, the World Bank, and the Japanese government would each contribute $10 billion to the task of debt reduction. To gain access to these funds, a debtor nation would once again have to submit to a set of imposed conditions for macroeconomic policy management and debt repayment. The first application of the Brady Plan was the Mexican debt reduction of 1989. The deal, which reduced Mexico's 1989 debt of $107 billion by about $15 billion, has been widely regarded as a success, and by the mid-1990s the debt crisis was over.[11]

The Future of the IMF and the World Bank[12]

One consequence of the IMF's involvement in resolving the developing world debt crisis has been the blurring of the line between it and the World Bank. Under the original Bretton Woods agreement, the IMF was to provide short-term loans, and the World Bank was to provide long-term loans. Since the 1970s, however, the IMF has been increasingly involved in providing long-term loans to debt-ridden nations. According to one estimate, 20 of these countries have been continuous users of IMF credit for more than 12 years.

The evolution of the IMF into a long-term lending and development agency looks likely to continue. The collapse of Communism in Eastern Europe and the subsequent breakup of the Soviet Union resulted in a flood of applications for IMF membership from the newly democratic nations there, including Russia. Given the problems associated with transforming their centrally planned economies into market economies, many of these potential new members will be calling on the IMF for long-term loans. As of 1997 both Russia and the Ukraine had become major recipients of IMF loans. The IMF is playing a major role in both countries, helping them to transform from state planning to a market economic system.

Not only is the IMF moving closer to the World Bank, but the World Bank also has been moving closer to the IMF since the 1970s. During the 1970s the bank noticed that many of its specific loan projects—such as those for irrigation, energy, and transportation projects—were failing to produce the kind of long-term economic gains for the borrowing countries that the bank's officials had predicted. On closer examination, the bank found that many of its specific projects were undermined not by defects in their design but by the broader policy environment of the particular country. The bank found that the returns on its loan projects were much lower in countries where growth was limited by a poor macroeconomic policy. A good project in a bad economy was likely to be a bad project. It was obvious that loan conditions needed to extend beyond the project to the economy as a whole.

In response, the World Bank has devised a new type of loan. In addition to providing funds to support specific projects, the bank will now also provide loans for the government of a nation to use as it sees fit in return for promises on macroeconomic policy. This is essentially the same approach used by the IMF in recent years. As we have seen, the IMF has lent money to debtor nations in return for promises about macroeconomic policy. Now the World Bank is doing the same thing.

The convergence between the World Bank and the IMF points to the possibility of a merger between the IMF and the bank sometime in the future. Since these two institutions are now doing each other's jobs, the argument for merging them is compelling. But not now. Both institutions currently are so busy with their new commitments in Eastern Europe that they would not have the time to effect a merger. As one commentator put it, "This is not the time to sap the institutions' energies with grandiose schemes of reform. But a merger makes sense, and in time it will happen."[13]

The evolution of global capital markets has also raised questions about the role of the IMF and the World Bank. In 1944 the global capital market hardly existed. By the mid-1990s it was channeling immense flows of money around the world every day. Before the emergence of a global capital market there was arguably a strong need for lending institutions such as the World Bank and the IMF to channel funds to poorer nations. Now critics argue that with the exception of emergencies such as a debt crisis, the capital market should perhaps decide which governments are worth lending to and which are not. Do we need the IMF and the World Bank? At this time, there is significant debate over this issue.

Implications for Business

The implications for international businesses of the material discussed in this chapter fall into three main areas: currency management, business strategy, and corporate–government relations.

Currency Management

An obvious implication with regard to currency management is that companies must recognize that the foreign exchange market does not work quite as depicted in Chapter 8. The current system is a managed float system in which government intervention can help drive the foreign exchange market (e.g., as in the cases of the Plaza Accord and the Louvre Accord). Companies engaged in significant foreign exchange activities need to be aware of this and to adjust their foreign exchange transactions accordingly. For example, the currency management unit of Caterpillar claims it made millions of dollars in the hours following the announcement of the Plaza Accord by selling dollars and buying currencies that it expected to appreciate on the foreign exchange market following government intervention.

A second message contained in this chapter is that under the present system, speculative buying and selling of currencies can create very volatile movements in exchange rates (as exhibited by the rise and fall of the dollar during the 1980s). Moreover, contrary to the predictions of the purchasing power parity theory (see Chapter 8), exchange rate movements during the 1980s, at least with regard to the dollar, did not seem to be strongly influenced by relative inflation rates. Insofar as volatile exchange rates increase foreign exchange risk, this is not good news for business. On the other hand, as we saw in Chapter 8, the foreign exchange market has developed a number of instruments, such as the forward market and swaps, that can help to insure against foreign exchange risk. Not surprisingly, use of these instruments has increased markedly since the breakdown of the Bretton Woods system in 1973.

Business Strategy

The volatility of the present floating exchange rate regime presents a conundrum for international businesses. Exchange rate movements are difficult to predict, and yet their movement can have a major impact on the competitive position of a business. An example is given in the accompanying "Management Focus," which details how exchange rate movements have affected the profitability of the German auto and aerospace concern Daimler-Benz. An increase in the value of the German mark against other major currencies (except the yen) has made Daimler-Benz's German-based production increasingly uncompetitive in world markets.

One response to the uncertainty that arises from a floating exchange rate regime might be to build strategic flexibility. Faced with uncertainty about the future value of currencies, firms can utilize the forward exchange market. However, the forward market is far from perfect as a predictor of future exchange rates (see Chapter 8). Moreover, it is difficult if not impossible to get adequate insurance coverage for exchange rate changes that might occur several years in the future. The forward market tends to offer coverage for exchange rate changes a few months—not years—ahead. Given this, it makes sense to pursue strategies that will increase the company's strategic flexibility in the face of unpredictable exchange rate movements.

Maintaining strategic flexibility can take the form of dispersing production to different locations around the globe as a hedge against currency fluctuations (as Daimler-Benz is now trying to do; see the "Management Focus"). Ingersoll-Rand has taken this approach, increasing its overseas capacity and reducing its dependence on U.S. exports in an attempt to protect itself against any future speculative upsurges in the value of the dollar. Similarly, the move by Japanese automobile companies to expand their productive capacity in the United States and Europe can be seen as a hedge against continued appreciation of the yen (as well as against trade barriers).

Another way to build strategic flexibility involves contracting out manufacturing. This allows a company to shift suppliers from country to country in response to shifts in relative costs brought about by exchange rate movements. However, this strategy works only for low-value-added manufacturing (e.g., textiles), in which the individual manufacturers have few, if any, firm-specific skills that contribute to the value of the product. It is inappropriate in the case of high-value-added manufacturing, in which firm-specific technology and skills add significant value to the product (e.g., the heavy equipment industry) and in which switching costs are correspondingly high. In high-value-added manufacturing, switching suppliers will lead to a reduction in the value that is added, which may offset any cost gains arising from exchange rate fluctuations.

The role of the IMF and the World Bank in the present international monetary system also has implications for business strategy. Increasingly, the IMF and World Bank are acting as macroeconomic police, insisting that countries coming to them for significant borrowings adopt IMF- or World Bank-mandated macroeconomic policies. These policies typically include anti-inflationary monetary policy and reductions in government spending. In the short run, such policies usually result in a sharp contraction of demand. International businesses selling or producing in such countries need to be aware of this and plan accordingly. But in the long run, the kind of policies imposed by the IMF and World Bank can promote economic growth and an expansion of demand, which create opportunities for international business.

Corporate–Government Relations

As major players in the international trade and investment environment, businesses can influence government policy toward the international monetary system. For example, intense government lobbying by U.S. exporters helped convince the U.S. government that intervention in the foreign exchange market was necessary. Business can and should use its influence to promote an international monetary system that facilitates the growth of international trade and investment. Whether a fixed or floating regime is optimal is a sub-

Daimler-Benz Suffers from a Strong Mark

H. Armstrong Roberts, ©M. Barrett

In June 1995 the German auto and aerospace company Daimler-Benz stunned the German business community when it announced that it expected to post a severe loss in 1995 of about $720 million. The cause was Germany's strong currency, which had appreciated by 4 percent against a basket of major currencies since the beginning of 1995 and had risen by over 30 percent against the U.S. dollar since late 1994. By mid-1995 the exchange rate against the dollar stood at $1=DM1.38. Daimler's management figures it cannot make money with an exchange rate under $1=DM1.60.

The main problem seemed to be in Daimler's aerospace division, DASA, which accounted for about 20 percent of the group's total sales, although its Mercedes-Benz automobile division was feeling some pain too. DASA receives 74 percent of its income in dollars (airplanes are priced in U.S. dollars), but only 27 percent of its costs are in dollars. This means that an appreciation of the mark against the dollar hits DASA particularly hard. The primary reason for DASA's high cost structure is that the bulk of its production is still concentrated in Germany. The Mercedes-Benz division is also suffering from a lack of foreign production. Currently Mercedes-Benz produces only 2 percent of its cars outside of Germany, and yet exports, particularly to the United States, account for 15 percent of Mercedes sales. The strong mark pushed up the price of these exports and made them increasingly uncompetitive.

Daimler's senior managers have concluded that the appreciation of the mark against the dollar is probably permanent. Their strategy for dealing with this problem is to move substantial production outside of Germany and to increase purchasing of foreign components. This will reduce the vulnerability of the company to future exchange rate movements. The Mercedes-Benz division has already made plans for such a move. Mercedes intends to be producing 10 percent of its cars outside of Germany by 2000, mostly in the United States. As for DASA, industry analysts calculate that to become competitive this division will have to cut employment by 20,000 and move substantial productive activities to lower-cost locations outside of Germany.[14]

---

ject for debate. What does seem probable, however, is that exchange rate volatility such as the world experienced during the 1980s creates an environment less conducive to international trade and investment than one with more stable exchange rates. Therefore, it would seem to be in the interests of international business to promote an international monetary system that minimizes volatile exchange rate movements, particularly when those movements are unrelated to long-run economic fundamentals.

Key Terms

fixed exchange rate, p. 293   gold standard, p. 294   managed float system, p. 293

Summary

The objectives of this chapter were to explain the workings of the international monetary system and to point out its implications for international business. Specific points we have made include the following:

1 The gold standard is a monetary standard that pegs currencies to gold and guarantees convertibility to gold.

2 It was thought that the gold standard contained an automatic mechanism that contributed to the simultaneous achievement of a balance-of-payments equilibrium by all countries.

3 The gold standard broke down during the 1930s as countries engaged in competitive devaluations.

4 The Bretton Woods system of fixed exchange rates was established in 1944. The U.S. dollar was the central currency of this system; the value of every other currency was pegged to its value. Significant exchange rate devaluations were allowed only with the permission of the IMF.

5 The role of the IMF was to maintain order in the international monetary system (i) to avoid a repetition of the competitive devaluations of the 1930s and (ii) to control price inflation by imposing monetary discipline on countries.

6 To build flexibility into the system, the IMF stood ready to lend countries funds to help protect their currency on the foreign exchange market in the face of speculative pressure and to assist countries in correcting a fundamental disequilibrium in their balance-of-payments position.

7 The fixed exchange rate system collapsed in 1973, primarily due to speculative pressure on the dollar following a rise in U.S. inflation and a growing U.S. balance-of-trade deficit.

8 Since 1973 the world has operated with a floating exchange rate regime, and exchange rates have become more volatile and far less predictable. Volatile exchange rate movements have helped reopen the debate over the merits of fixed and floating systems.

9 The case for a floating exchange rate regime claims: (i) such a system gives countries autonomy regarding their monetary policy and (ii) floating exchange rates facilitate smooth adjustment of trade imbalances.

10 The case for a fixed exchange rate regime claims: (i) the need to maintain a fixed exchange rate imposes monetary discipline on a country, (ii) floating exchange rate regimes are vulnerable to speculative pres-

sure, (iii) the uncertainty that accompanies floating exchange rates hinders the growth of international trade and investment, and (iv) far from correcting trade imbalances, depreciating a currency on the foreign exchange market tends to cause price inflation.

11 The collapse of the Bretton Woods system left the IMF and World Bank with diminished roles in the international monetary system. In response, both the IMF and the World Bank have developed into global macroeconomic police. Today they lend money to countries with balance-of-payments, debt, or development problems, extracting promises to adopt specific macroeconomic policies as a condition.

12 The present managed float system of exchange rate determination has increased the importance of currency management in international businesses.

13 The volatility of exchange rates under the present managed float system creates both opportunities and threats. One way of responding to this volatility is for companies to build strategic flexibility by dispersing production to different locations around the globe by contracting out manufacturing (in the case of low-value-added manufacturing) and other means.

Critical Thinking and Discussion Questions

1 Why did the gold standard collapse? Is there a case for returning to some type of gold standard? What is it?

2 What opportunities might IMF lending policies to developing nations create for international businesses? What threats might they create?

3 Do you think it is in the best interests of Western international businesses to have the IMF lend money to the former Communist states of Eastern Europe to help them transform their economies? Why?

4 Debate the relative merits of fixed and floating exchange rate regimes. From the perspective of an international business, what are the most important criteria in a choice between the systems? Which system is the more desirable for an international business?

Internet Exercise

The origin and development of the International Monetary Fund and the World Bank are explored extensively in this chapter. Although their roles have diminished to "global macroeconomic policemen," they have developed extensive sites on the World Wide Web. Both the IMF (http://www.imf.org/) and World Bank Group (http://www.worldbank.org) sites describe the latest developments, publications, annual meetings, and organization structure. The IMF site also gives details on the joint World Bank-IMF Library and the IMF Institute, while the World Bank site adds public service announcement movies, weekly summaries of approved new projects, speeches, and topics in development.

Global Surfing

Visit both sites and describe the latest news on each. What information do they provide on their historic roles in the global monetary system? What is on their agendas at their next annual meetings? What are some of their latest publications? What is available in the joint World Bank-IMF Library? What is the purpose of the IMF Institute? What topics are covered in the World Bank public service announcements and speeches? What new projects have been approved by the World Bank? What topics are being developed in the financial, human resources and poverty, and infrastructure and urban development areas?

Closing Case

The **Fall** and **Rise** of Caterpillar Tractor

Caterpillar Tractor Company (Cat) is the world's largest manufacturer of heavy earthmoving equipment. Earthmoving equipment typically represents about 70 percent of the annual dollar sales of construction equipment worldwide. In 1980 Cat held 53.3 percent of the global market for earthmoving equipment. Its closest competitor was Komatsu of Japan, with 60 percent of the Japanese market but only 15.2 percent worldwide.

In 1980 Caterpillar was widely considered one of the premier manufacturing and exporting companies in the United States. The company had enjoyed 50 consecutive years of profits and returns on shareholders' equity as high as 27 percent. In 1981, 57 percent of its sales were outside the United States, and roughly two-thirds of these orders were filled by exports. Cat was the third largest U.S. exporter. Reflecting this underlying strength, in 1981 Cat recorded record pretax profits of $579 million. However, the next three years were disastrous. Caterpillar lost $1 billion and saw its market share slip to as low as 40 percent in 1985, while Komatsu increased its share to 25 percent. Three factors explain this startling turn of events: the higher productivity of Komatsu, the rise in the value of the dollar, and the debt crisis in the developing world.

In retrospect, Komatsu had been creeping up on Cat for a long time. In the 1960s the company had a minuscule presence outside of Japan. By 1974 it had managed to increase its global market share of heavy earthmoving equipment to 9 percent, and by 1980 it was over 15 percent. Part of Komatsu's growth was due to its superior labor productivity; throughout the 1970s it had been able to price its machines 10 to 15 percent below Caterpillar's. However, Komatsu lacked an extensive dealer network outside of Japan, and Cat's worldwide dealer network and superior after-sale service and support functions were seen as justifying a price premium for Cat machines. For these reasons, many industry observers believed Komatsu would not increase its share much beyond its 1980 level.

An unprecedented rise in the value of the dollar against most major world currencies changed the picture. Between 1980 and 1987, the dollar rose an average of 87 percent against the currencies of 10 other industrialized countries. The dollar was driven up by strong economic growth in the United States, which attracted heavy inflows of capital from foreign investors seeking high returns on capital assets. At the same time, political turmoil in other parts of the world and relatively slow economic growth in Europe helped create the view that the United States was a good place in which to invest.

These inflows of capital increased the demand for dollars in the foreign exchange market, which pushed the value of the dollar upward against other currencies.

Obviously the strong dollar substantially increased the dollar price of Cat's machines. At the same time, the dollar price of Komatsu products imported into the United States fell. Due to the shift in the relative values of the dollar and the yen, by 1985 Komatsu was able to price its machines as much as 40 percent below Caterpillar's prices. In light of this enormous price difference, many consumers chose to forgo Caterpillar's superior after-sale service and support and bought Komatsu machines.

The third factor, the developing world debt crisis, became apparent in 1982. During the early 1970s the oil-exporting nations of OPEC quadrupled the price of oil, which resulted in a massive flow of funds into these nations. Commercial banks borrowed this money from the OPEC countries and lent it to the governments of many developing nations to finance massive construction projects, which led to a global boom in demand for heavy earthmoving equipment. Caterpillar benefited richly from this development. By 1982, however, it became apparent that the commercial banks had lent far too much money to risky and unproductive investments, and the governments of several countries (including Mexico, Brazil, and Argentina) threatened to suspend debt payments. At this point the International Monetary Fund stepped in and arranged for new loans to indebted developing nations, but on the condition that they adopt deflationary macroeconomic policies. For Cat, the party

was over; orders for heavy earthmoving equipment dried up almost overnight, and those that were placed went to the lowest bidder—which all too often was Komatsu.

As a result of these factors, Caterpillar was in deep trouble by late 1982. The company responded quickly and between 1982 and 1985 cut costs by more than 20 percent. This was achieved by reducing the work force 40 percent, closing 9 plants, and investing $1.8 billion in flexible manufacturing technologies designed to boost quality and lower cost. At the same time the company launched a campaign of pressing the government to lower the value of the dollar on foreign exchange markets. By 1984 Cat was a leading voice among U.S. exporters in their efforts to get the Reagan administration to intervene in the foreign exchange market.

In early 1985 things began to go Caterpillar's way. Prompted by Cat and other exporters, representatives of the U.S. government met with representatives of Japan, Germany, France, and Great Britain at the Plaza Hotel in New York. In the resulting communiqué—known as the Plaza Accord—the five governments acknowledged that the dollar was overvalued and pledged to take actions that would drive down its price on the foreign exchange market. The dollar had already begun to fall in early 1985 in response to a string of record U.S. trade deficits. The Plaza Accord accelerated this trend, and over the next three years the dollar fell back to its 1980 level.

The effect for Caterpillar was almost immediate. Like any major exporter, Caterpillar had its own foreign exchange unit. Suspecting that an adjustment in the dollar would come soon, Cat had increased its holdings of foreign currencies in early 1985, using the strong dollar to purchase them. As the dollar fell, the company was able to convert these currencies back into dollars for a healthy profit. In 1985 Cat had pretax profits of $32 million; without foreign exchange gains of $89 million, it would have lost money. In 1986, foreign exchange gains of $100 million accounted for nearly two-thirds of its pretax profits of $159 million.

More significant for Cat's long-term position, by 1988 the fall in the dollar against the yen and Caterpillar's cost-cutting efforts had helped to eradicate the 40 percent cost advantage that Komatsu had enjoyed over Caterpillar four years earlier. After trying to hold its prices down, Komatsu had to raise its prices that year by 18 percent, while Cat was able to hold its price increase to 3 percent. With the terms of trade no longer handicapping Caterpillar, the company regained some of its lost market share. By 1989 it reportedly held 47 percent of the world market for heavy earthmoving equipment, up from a low of 40 percent three years earlier, while Komatsu's share had slipped to below 20 percent.[15]

Case Discussion Questions

1 To what extent is the competitive position of Caterpillar against Komatsu dependent on the dollar/yen exchange rate?

2 If you were the CEO of Caterpillar Tractor, what actions would you take now to make sure there is no repeat of the early 1980s experience?

3 What potential impact can the actions of the IMF and World Bank have on Caterpillar's business? Is there anything that Cat can do to influence the actions of the IMF and World Bank?

4 As the CEO of Caterpillar, would you prefer a fixed exchange rate regime or a continuation of the current managed float regime? Why?

I'm a Gamblin' Man

If you are willing to take a chance and have the ability to bluff, an opportunity to start your own business may lie in the most unlikely situation. For Danny Wong, self-acclaimed gambler and risk taker, it arose during a game of mah jong. Mah jong is a Chinese gambling game played with tiles resembling dominoes bearing various designs. Tiles are drawn and discarded until one player wins with a hand of four combinations of three tiles each and a pair of matching tiles.

A year ago Danny, 20, was playing mah jong with his aunt, uncle, and best friend Harry Lee, 23. During their casual conversation, Danny's uncle, knowing that the young men were interested in computers, asked if they were aware of any sources for recordable compact disks (CDRs). He had a friend in Germany who needed to purchase 200,000 CDRs.

Danny and Harry recognized that this could be their golden opportunity to start their own international business. It did not matter that Danny was still in

Danny Wong

college and that neither had any experience in running a business. It did not matter that at that moment they did not know of a likely source. They sprang into action.

The next day Danny contacted his girlfriend, who was working in Taiwan for the summer. He knew that her mother operated an international trading company and thought she could provide the necessary lead. However, the mother's help wasn't necessary. His girlfriend had her own contacts through the computer store where she was employed.

Danny then set out to convince both manufacturer and buyer that he was a credible businessman. Doing so presented some challenges particularly since all his contacts were over the telephone. For example, when asked which company he was working for, Danny spontaneously replied LD Trading. When pressed about what the letters stood for, Danny apologetically said he did not know since he was only an employee. After consulting with Harry, LD expanded into LEDA Trading Inc. Coincidently LEDA was the combination of his first name and his partner's surname. Le and Da also sounded like two Chinese characters, which now appear on their business cards, and loosely translated into "We are at your disposal."

Both Danny and Harry represented themselves as sales/project managers. "You never see a president or CEO handing out business cards to buyers. A viable company needs employees," Danny reasoned.

Danny took a crash course in international business terms like

FOB, L/C, and CIF. He learned quickly from friends and from Harry, who had recently graduated with a business degree. He never showed his lack of knowledge to his clients.

Since he had limited access to capital, Danny did not wish to pay for a transferable letter of credit, which middlemen use to prevent being cut out of a deal. A letter of credit is issued from the buyer's to the seller's bank. It is an agreement whereby payment is issued upon performance. A transferable L/C is used to transfer credit to a second beneficiary but it costs a hefty percentage. Danny therefore convinced the German client to issue an L/C directly to the Taiwanese factory's bank. He assured the German client that he would be paid since he was the factory's official representative. Only after he obtained the purchase order did Danny's partner fly to Taiwan to secure in writing the factory's promise to compensate them.

After a month of dealings, Danny trusted his instincts and came out a winner. Danny and Harry netted 30 cents on each of the pieces that were sold.

Danny may have been so willing to take chances partly because he has relied on himself for a number of years. Danny came to the United States from Taiwan alone at 13 to attend high school. He lived with family friends until he turned 15, when he moved into a house purchased by his father. His father was a Chinese businessman who traveled constantly. When Danny first arrived, he spoke no English and was one of three Asians at his high school

Danny's goal now is to become the exclusive distributor for the Taiwanese CDR manufacturer. He must therefore increase his sales volume. To accomplish this objective, Danny has reinvested the proceeds from the first deal and purchased some additional recordable compact discs on spec.

While looking for the next big deal, he has landed two smaller contracts to supply CDRs to local businesses. These contracts yield about $2,000 a month, which he uses to expand the business. He has moved the operation into a corner of his uncle's office and has hired two part time employees. Both employees are his friends and like Danny are college students. One answers the phone and the other combs the Internet looking for leads for buyers.

Danny spends about five hours a day following up on leads, sending out samples, and negotiating prices. His work usually begins around 10 PM since he contacts people by fax or phone all over the world. During the day he is earning his degree in international business. Harry, who works full time in hotel management, still handles some of the paperwork, and is developing LEDA's homepage on the Internet.

The business remains a gamble. The CDR market has been flooded with cheap products of inferior quality and Danny has lost some money as prices have fallen. He is wagering, however, that prices will turn around in the future as companies merge and unprofitable ones exit. He has also been wooed by competitive manufacturers offering him lower prices. However, he has decided to bet on the company which had faith in him originally.

Chances are good that Danny will succeed. He possesses the strategy, skill, and luck that in the past have helped him win the game—whether it be mah jong or international business.

Helena Czepiec
California State Polytechnic University, Pomona

Chapter 10
Global Strategy

Registered trademarks of the Coca-Cola Company

Opening Case

It's a Mac World

Established in 1955, by the early 1980s McDonald's faced a problem: after three decades of rapid growth, the U.S. fast food market was beginning to show signs of market saturation. McDonald's response to the slowdown was to expand abroad rapidly. In 1980, 28 percent of the chain's new restaurant openings were abroad; in 1986 the figure was 40 percent; in 1990 it was close to 60 percent; and in 1994 it hit 66 percent. Since the early 1980s the firm's foreign revenues and profits have grown at 22 percent per year. By 1994 the firm had

Learning Objectives:

1 Be conversant with the concept of strategy.
2 Understand how firms can profit from expanding their activities globally.

3 Be familiar with the different strategies for competing globally.
4 Understand how cost pressures influence a firm's choice of global strategy.

5 Understand how country differences can influence a firm's choice of global strategy.
6 Understand how firms can use strategic alliances to support their global strategy.

4,700 restaurants in 72 countries outside of the United States. Together they generated $3.4 billion (46 percent) of the firm's $7.4 billion in revenues.

McDonald's shows no signs of slowing down. Management notes there is still only one McDonald's restaurant for every 600,000 people in the 72 foreign countries in which it currently does business. This compares to one McDonald's restaurant for every 25,000 people in the United States. The firm's plans call for this foreign expansion to continue at a rapid

rate. In England, France, and Germany combined, the firm planned to open 500 more restaurants between 1995 and 1997 for a total gain of 37 percent. During the same period McDonald's expected to double to 800 the number of its restaurants in the Caribbean, Mexico, Central America, and South America. The firm also plans to enter another 25 to 30 countries by the end of the century.

One key to the firm's successful foreign expansion is detailed planning. When McDonald's enters a foreign country, it does so

only after careful preparation. Before McDonald's opened its first Polish restaurant in 1992 the firm spent 18 months establishing essential contacts and getting to know the local culture. Locations, real estate, construction, supply, personnel, legal requirements, and government relations were all worked out in advance. In June 1992 a team of 50 employees from the United States, Russia, Germany, and Britain went to Poland to help with the opening of the first four restaurants. A primary objective was to hire and train local personnel. By mid-1994 all of these employees except one had returned to their home country. They were replaced by Polish nationals who had now been brought up to the skill level required to run a McDonald's operation.

Another key to the firm's international strategy is the export of the management skills that spurred its growth in the United States. McDonald's U.S. success was built on a formula of close relations with suppliers, nationwide marketing, tight control over store-level operating procedures, and a franchising system that encourages entrepreneurial individual franchisees. Although this system has worked flawlessly in the United States, some modifications must be made in other countries. One of the firm's biggest challenges has been to infuse each store with the same gung-ho culture and standardized operating procedures that have been the hallmark of its success in the United States. To aid in this task, in many countries McDonald's has enlisted the help of large partners through joint-venture arrangements. The partners play a key role in learning and transplanting the organization's values to local employees.

Foreign partners have also played a key role in helping McDonald's adapt its marketing methods and menu to local conditions. Although U.S.-style fast food remains the staple fare on the menu, local products have been added. In Brazil, for example, McDonald's sells a soft drink made from the guarana, an Amazonian berry. Patrons of McDonald's in Malaysia, Singapore, and Thailand savor shakes flavored with durian, a foul-smelling (to U.S. tastes, at least) fruit considered an aphrodisiac by the locals. In addition to their help in product adaptation, these partners can steer the firm away from potentially expensive marketing pitfalls. In Japan, for example, Den Fujita, president of McDonald's in Japan, avoided the suburban locations typical in the United States and stressed urban sites that consumers could walk to.

McDonald's biggest problem, however, has been to replicate its U.S. supply chain in other countries. U.S. suppliers are fiercely loyal to McDonald's; their fortunes are closely linked to those of McDonald's. McDonald's maintains very rigorous specifications for all the raw ingredients it uses; this is the key to its consistency and quality control. Outside of the United States, however, McDonald's has found suppliers far less willing to make the investments required to meet its specifications. In Great Britain, for example, McDonald's had problems getting local bakeries to produce the hamburger bun. After experiencing quality problems with two local bakeries, McDonald's built its own bakery to supply its stores there. In a more extreme case, when McDonald's decided to open a store in Russia, it found that local suppliers lacked the capability to produce goods of the quality it demanded. The firm was forced to vertically integrate through the local food industry on a heroic scale, importing potato seeds and bull semen and indirectly managing dairy farms, cattle ranches, and vegetable plots. It also had to construct the world's largest food-processing plant, at a cost of $40 million. The restaurant itself cost only $4.5 million.

Now that it has a successful foreign operation, McDonald's is experiencing benefits that go beyond the immediate financial ones. The firm's foreign franchisees are a source for valuable new ideas. The Dutch operation created a prefabricated modular store that can be moved over a weekend and is now widely used to set up temporary restaurants at big outdoor events. The Swedes came up with an enhanced meat freezer that is now used firmwide. And satellite stores, or low overhead mini-McDonald's, which are now appearing in hospitals and sports arenas in the United States, were invented in Singapore.[1]

Introduction

Our primary concern so far in this book has been with aspects of the larger environment in which international businesses compete. This environment has included the different political, economic, and cultural institutions found in different nations, the global trade and investment framework, and the global monetary system. Now our focus shifts from the environment to the firm itself and, in particular, to the actions managers can take to compete more effectively as an international business. In this chapter we look at how firms can increase their profitability by expanding their operations in foreign markets, we discuss the different strategies that firms pursue when competing internationally, we consider the pros and cons of these strategies, and we discuss the various factors that affect a firm's choice of strategy.

McDonald's, which was profiled in the opening case, gives us a preview of some issues we'll be dealing with in the current chapter. McDonald's started to expand internationally in order to continue growing in the face of an increasingly mature and saturated U.S. fast food market. The pursuit of greater profit opportunities has driven many other firms to expand internationally. McDonald's has generated a high profit from its international operations primarily because it has figured out how to transfer the management skills that made it so successful in the United States to other countries where indigenous competitors lack those skills. Before McDonald's arrived, many countries lacked U.S.-style fast food outlets. Thus, in country after country McDonald's has been the pioneer in the introduction of the fast food concept, and it has reaped enormous gains from this first-mover position. At the same time, the case describes how another cornerstone of McDonald's success is its willingness to customize the menu so it appeals to national differences in tastes and preferences. Thus, McDonald's success is built both on a successful management formula that is applied worldwide and on a willingness to customize aspects of the product offering when it is necessary. As we shall see, while it is not always required, this combination of a clear central strategic vision and a willingness to customize the firm's product offering on a country-by-country basis is a hallmark of many successful international businesses.

Strategy and the Firm

The fundamental purpose of any business firm is to make a profit. A firm makes a profit if the price it can charge for its output is greater than its costs of producing that output. To do this, a firm must produce a product that is valued by consumers. Thus, we say that business firms engage in value creation. The price consumers are prepared to pay for a product indicates the value of the product to consumers.

Firms can increase their profits in two ways: by adding value to a product so consumers are willing to pay more for it and by lowering the costs of value creation (i.e., the costs of production). A firm adds value to a product when it improves the product's quality, provides a service to the consumer, or customizes the product to consumer needs in such a way that consumers will pay more for it; that is, when the firm *differentiates* the product from that offered by competitors. For example, consumers will pay more for a Mercedes-Benz car than a Hyundai because they value the superior quality of the Mercedes. Firms lower the costs of value creation when they find ways to perform value creation activities more efficiently. Thus, there are two basic strategies for improving a firm's profitability—a *differentiation strategy* and a *low cost strategy*.[2]

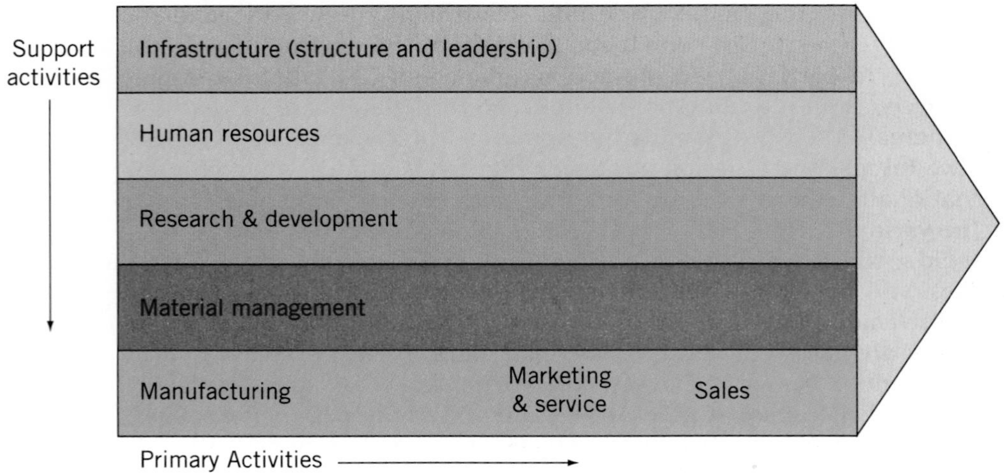

FIGURE 10.1

The Firm as a Value Chain

The Firm as a Value Chain

It is useful to think of the firm as a value chain composed of a series of distinct value creation activities, including production, marketing, materials management, R&D, human resources, information systems, and the firm infrastructure. We can categorize these value creation activities as primary activities and support activities (see Figure 10.1).[3]

PRIMARY ACTIVITIES The primary activities of a firm have to do with creating the product, marketing and delivering the product to buyers, and providing support and after-sale service to the buyers of the product. Here we consider the activities involved in the physical creation of the product as production and those involved in marketing, delivery, and after-sale service as marketing. Efficient production can reduce the costs of creating value (e.g., by realizing scale economies) and can add value by increasing product quality (e.g., by reducing the number of defective products), which facilitates premium pricing. Efficient marketing also can help the firm reduce its costs creating value (e.g., by generating the volume of sales necessary to realize scale economies) and can add value by helping the firm customize its product to consumer needs and differentiate its product from competitors' products—both of which facilitate premium pricing.

SUPPORT ACTIVITIES Support activities provide the inputs that allow the primary activities of production and marketing to occur. The materials management function controls the transmission of physical materials through the value chain—from procurement through production and into distribution. The efficiency with which this is carried out can significantly reduce the cost of creating value. In addition, an effective materials management function can monitor the quality of inputs into the production process. This results in improved quality of the firm's outputs, which adds value and facilitates premium pricing.

The R&D function develops new product and process technologies. Technological developments can reduce production costs and can result in the creation of more useful and more attractive products that can demand a premium price. Thus, R&D can affect primary production and marketing activities and, through them, value creation.

An effective human resource function ensures that the firm has an optimal mix of people to perform its primary production and marketing activities, that the staffing requirements of the support activities are met, and that employees are well trained for their tasks and compensated accordingly. The information systems function makes certain management has the information it needs to maximize the efficiency of its value chain and to exploit information-based competitive advantages in the marketplace. Firm infrastructure—consisting of such factors as organizational structure, general management, planning, finance, and legal and government affairs—embraces all other activities of the firm and establishes the context for them. An efficient infrastructure helps both to create value and to reduce the costs of creating value.

The Role of Strategy

A firm's **strategy** can be defined as the actions that managers take to attain the goals of the firm. For most firms a principal goal is to be highly profitable. Markets are now extremely competitive due to the liberalization of the world trade and investment environment. In industry after industry, many capable competitors confront each other around the globe. To be profitable in such an environment, a firm must pay continual attention to both reducing the costs of value creation and to differentiating its product offering in such a manner that consumers are willing to pay more for the product than it costs to produce it. Thus, strategy is often concerned with identifying and taking actions that will *lower the costs* of value creation and/or will *differentiate* the firm's product offering through superior design, quality, service, functionality, and the like.

To fully understand this, consider the case of Swan Optical, which is profiled in the accompanying "Management Focus." A U.S.-based manufacturer of eyeglasses, Swan found its survival threatened by low-cost foreign competitors. To deal with this threat, Swan adopted a strategy intended to lower its cost structure: It shifted production from a high-cost location, the United States, to a low-cost location, Hong Kong. Later Swan adopted a strategy intended to differentiate its basic product so it could charge a premium price. Reasoning that premium pricing in eyewear depended on superior design, its strategy involved investing capital in French, Italian, and Japanese factories that had reputations for superior design. In sum, Swan's strategies included some actions intended to reduce its costs of creating value and other actions intended to add value to its product through differentiation.

strategy Actions that managers take to attain the firm's goals.

Profiting from Global Expansion

Expanding globally allows companies to increase their profitability in ways not available to purely domestic enterprises. Firms that operate internationally are able to:

Strategy at Swan Optical

Swan Optical is a manufacturer and distributor of eyewear. Started in the 1960s by Alan Glassman, the firm today generates annual gross revenues of more than $30 million. Not exactly small, but no corporate giant either, Swan Optical is also a multinational firm with production facilities on three continents and customers around the world. Swan began its move toward becoming a multinational in the 1970s. The strong dollar at that time made U.S.-based manufacturing very expensive. Low-priced imports were taking a larger share of the U.S. eyewear market, and Swan realized it could not survive unless it also began to import. Initially the firm bought from independent overseas manufacturers, primarily in Hong Kong. However, the firm became dissatisfied with

these suppliers' quality and delivery. As Swan's volume of imports increased, Glassman decided the best way to guarantee quality and delivery was to set up Swan's own manufacturing operation overseas. Accordingly, Swan found a Chinese partner, and together they opened a manufacturing facility in Hong Kong, with Swan being the majority shareholder.

The choice of the Hong Kong location was influenced by its combination of low labor costs, a skilled work force, and tax breaks given by the Hong Kong government. By 1986, however, the increasing industrialization of Hong Kong and a growing labor shortage had pushed up wage rates to the extent that it was no longer a "low-cost" location. In response, Glassman and his Chinese partner moved part of their manufacturing to a plant in mainland China to take advantage of the lower wage rates there. The parts for eyewear

frames manufactured at this plant are shipped to the Hong Kong factory for final assembly and then distributed to markets in North and South America. The Hong Kong factory now employs 80 people and the China plant between 300 and 400.

At the same time Swan began to look for opportunities to invest in foreign eyewear firms with reputations for fashionable design and high quality. Its objective in this case was not to reduce manufacturing costs but to launch a line of high-quality, "designer" eyewear. Swan did not have the design capability in-house to support such a line, but Glassman knew that certain foreign manufacturers had the capability. As a result, Swan invested in factories in Japan, France, and Italy, taking a minority shareholding in each case. These factories now supply eyewear for Swan's Status Eye division, which markets high-priced designer eyewear.[4]

---

1 Earn a greater return from their distinctive skills, or core competencies.

2 Realize location economies by dispersing particular value creation activities to locations where they can be performed most efficiently.

3 Realize greater experience curve economies, which reduce the costs of value creation.

As we will see, however, a firm's ability to increase its profitability by pursuing these strategies is constrained by the need to customize its product offering, marketing strategy, and business strategy to differing national conditions.

Transferring Core Competencies

core competence Skills within the firm that competitors cannot easily match or imitate.

The term **core competence** refers to skills within the firm that competitors cannot easily match or imitate.[5] These skills may exist in any of the firm's value creation activities—production, marketing, R&D, human resources, general management, and so on. Such skills are typically expressed in product offerings that other firms find difficult to match or imitate, and thus the core competencies are the bedrock of a firm's competitive advantage. They enable a firm to reduce the costs of value creation and/or to create value in such a way that premium pricing is possible. For example, Toyota has a core competence in the production of cars. It can produce high-quality, well-designed cars at a lower delivered cost than any other firm in the world. The skills that enable Toyota to do this seem to reside primarily in the firm's production and materials management functions.[6] Similarly, McDonald's has a core competence in managing fast food operations; Toys R Us has a core competence in managing high-volume, discount toy stores; Procter & Gamble has a core competence in developing and marketing name brand consumer products; and so on.

For such firms, global expansion is a way of further exploiting the value creation potential of their skills and product offerings by applying those skills and products in a larger market. The potential for creating value from such a strategy is greatest when the skills and products of the firm are most unique, when the value placed on them by consumers is great, and when there are very few capable competitors with similar skills and/or products in foreign markets. Firms with unique and valuable skills can often realize enormous returns by applying those skills, and the products they produce, to foreign markets where indigenous competitors lack similar skills and products.

For example, as we saw in the opening case, McDonald's has expanded rapidly overseas in recent years. Its skills in managing fast food operations have proven to be just as valuable in countries as diverse as France, Russia, China, Germany, and Brazil as they have been in the United States. Before McDonald's entry, none of these countries had American-style fast food chains, so McDonald's brought a unique product as well as unique skills to each country. The lack of indigenous competitors with similar skills and products, and the implied lack of competition, has greatly enhanced the profitability of this strategy for McDonald's.

In earlier eras U.S. firms such as Kellogg, Coca-Cola, H. J. Heinz, and Procter & Gamble expanded overseas to exploit their skills in developing and marketing consumer products. These skills and the resulting products—which were developed in the U.S. market during the 1950s and 60s—yielded enormous returns when applied to European markets, where most indigenous competitors lacked similar marketing skills and products. Their near-monopoly on consumer marketing skills allowed these U.S. firms to dominate many European consumer product markets during the 1960s and 70s. Similarly, in the 1970s and 1980s many Japanese firms expanded globally to exploit their skills in production, materials management, and new product development—skills that many of their indigenous North American and European competitors seemed to lack at the time.

Realizing Location Economies

We know from earlier chapters that countries differ along a whole range of dimensions—economic, political, legal, and cultural—and that these differences can either raise or lower the costs of doing business. We also know from the theory of international trade that due to differences in factor costs, certain countries have a comparative advantage in the production of particular products. For example, Japan excels in the production of automobiles and consumer electronics. The United States excels in the production of chemicals, pharmaceuticals, biotechnology products, and financial services. Switzerland excels in the production of precision instruments and pharmaceuticals.[7]

What does all this mean for a firm that is trying to survive in a competitive global market? It means that, trade barriers and transportation costs permitting, the firm will benefit by basing each value creation activity it performs at that location where economic, political, and cultural conditions, including relative factor costs, are most conducive to the performance of that activity. Thus, if the best designers for a product live in France, a firm should base its design operations in France. If the most productive labor force for assembly operations is in Mexico, assembly operations should be based in Mexico. If the best marketers are in the United States, the marketing strategy should be formulated in the United States. And so on.

Firms that pursue such a strategy can realize what we refer to as location economies. We can define **location economies** as the economies that arise from performing a value creation activity in the optimal location for that activity, wherever in the world that might be (transportation costs and trade barriers permitting). Locating a value creation activity in the optimal location for that activity can have one of two effects. *Either it can lower the costs of value creation and help the firm to achieve a low cost position, or it can enable a firm to differentiate its product offering from the offerings of competitors.* Both of these considerations were at work in the case of Swan Optical, which was profiled in the "Management Focus." Swan Optical moved its manufacturing operations out of the United States, first to Hong Kong and then to mainland China, to take advantage of low labor costs, thereby lowering the costs of value creation. At the same time, Swan shifted some of its design operations from the United States to France and Italy. Swan reasoned that skilled Italian and French designers could probably help the firm better differentiate its product. In other words, Swan thinks that the optimal location for performing manufacturing operations is China, whereas the optimal locations for performing design operations are France and Italy. The firm has configured its value chain accordingly. By doing so, Swan hopes to be able to *simultaneously* lower its cost structure and differentiate its product offering. In turn, differentiation should allow Swan to charge a premium price for its product offering.

CREATING A GLOBAL WEB One result of the kind of thinking exhibited in the Swan example is the creation of a **global web** of value creation activities, with different stages of the value chain being dispersed to those locations around the globe where the value added is maximized or where the costs of value creation are minimized. Consider the case of General Motor's (GM) Pontiac Le Mans, cited in Robert Reich's *The Work of Nations*.[8] Marketed primarily in the United States, the car was designed in Germany; key components were manufactured in Japan, Taiwan, and Singapore; the assembly operation was performed in South Korea; and the advertising strategy was formulated in Great Britain. The car was designed in Germany, because GM believed the designers in its German subsidiary had the skills most suited to the job at hand. (They were the most capable of producing a design that added value.) Components were manufactured in Japan, Taiwan, and

Singapore because favorable factor conditions there—relatively low-cost, skilled labor—suggested those locations had a comparative advantage in the production of components (which helped reduce the costs of value creation). The car was assembled in South Korea because GM believed that due to its low labor costs, the costs of assembly could be minimized there (also helping to minimize the costs of value creation). Finally, the advertising strategy was formulated in Great Britain because GM believed a particular advertising agency there was the most able to produce an advertising campaign that would help sell the car. (This decision was consistent with GM's desire to maximize the value added.)

In theory, a firm that realizes location economies by dispersing each of its value creation activities to its optimal location should have a competitive advantage vis-à-vis a firm that bases all of its value creation activities at a single location. It should be able to better differentiate its product offering and lower its cost structure than its single-location competitor. In a world where competitive pressures are increasing, such a strategy may become an imperative for survival.

SOME CAVEATS   Introducing transportation costs and trade barriers complicates this picture. Due to favorable factor endowments, New Zealand may have a comparative advantage for automobile assembly operations, but high transportation costs would make it an uneconomical location for them. A consideration of transportation costs and trade barriers helps explain why many U.S. firms are now shifting their production from Asia to Mexico. Mexico has three distinct advantages over many Asian countries as a location for value creation activities. First, low labor costs make it a good location for labor-intensive production processes. In recent years wage rates have increased significantly in Japan, Taiwan, and Hong Kong, but they have remained low in Mexico. Second, Mexico's proximity to the large U.S. market reduces transportation costs. This is particularly important in the case of products with high weight-to-value ratios (e.g., automobiles). And third, the North American Free Trade Agreement (see Chapter 7) has removed many trade barriers among Mexico, the United States, and Canada, increasing Mexico's attractiveness as a production site for the North American market. Although value added and the costs of value creation are important, transportation costs and trade barriers also must be considered in location decisions.

Another caveat concerns the importance of assessing political risks when making location decisions. Even if a country looks very attractive as a production location when measured against all the standard criteria, if its government is unstable or totalitarian, the firm might be advised not to base production there. (Political risk is discussed in Chapter 2.)

Realizing Experience Curve Economies

The **experience curve** refers to the systematic reductions in production costs that have been observed to occur over the life of a product.[9] A number of studies have observed that a product's production costs decline by some characteristic about each time accumulated output doubles. The relationship was first observed in the aircraft industry, where each time accumulated output of airframes was doubled, unit costs typically declined to 80 percent of their

experience curve
Systematic reductions in production costs that occur over the life of a product.

previous level.[10] Thus, production cost for the fourth airframe would be 80 percent of production cost for the second airframe, the eighth airframe's production costs 80 percent of the fourth's, the sixteenth's 80 percent of the eighth's, and so on. This experience curve relationship between production costs and output is illustrated in Figure 10.2. Two things explain this: learning effects and economies of scale.

LEARNING EFFECTS **Learning effects** refer to cost savings that come from learning by doing. Labor, for example, learns by repetition how to carry out a task, such as assembling airframes, most efficiently. Labor productivity increases over time as individuals learn the most efficient ways to perform particular tasks. In new production facilities, management typically learns how to manage the new operation more efficiently over time. Hence, production costs eventually decline due to increasing labor productivity and management efficiency.

Learning effects tend to be more significant when a technologically complex task is repeated, since there is more that can be learned about the task. Thus, learning effects will be more significant in an assembly process involving 1,000 complex steps than in one of only 100 simple steps. No matter how complex the task, however, learning effects typically die out after awhile. It has been suggested that they are important only during the start-up period of a new process and that they cease after two or three years.[11] Any decline in the experience curve after such a point is due to economies of scale.

ECONOMIES OF SCALE The term **economies of scale** refers to the reduction in unit cost achieved by producing a large volume of a product. Economies of scale have a number of sources, the most important of which seems to be the ability to spread fixed costs over a large volume. Fixed costs are the costs required to set up a production facility, develop a new product, and the like, and they can be substantial. For example, establishing a new production line to manufacture semiconductor chips costs about $1 billion. According to one estimate, developing a new drug costs about $250 million and takes about 12 years.[12] The only way to recoup such high fixed costs is to sell the product worldwide, which reduces unit costs by spreading them over a larger volume. Moreover, the more rapidly cumulative sales volume is built up, the more rapidly fixed costs can be amortized, and the more rapidly unit costs fall. Hence, in addition to learning effects, economies of scale underlie the experience curve.

STRATEGIC SIGNIFICANCE The strategic significance of the experience curve is clear. Moving down the experience curve allows a firm to reduce its cost of creating value. The firm that moves down the experience curve most rapidly will have a cost advantage vis-à-vis its competitors. Thus, firm A in Figure 10.2, because it is further down the experience curve, has a cost advantage over firm B.

Many of the underlying sources of experience-based cost economies are plant based. This is true for most learning effects as well as for the economies of scale derived by spreading the fixed costs of building productive capacity over a large output. Thus, the key to progressing downward on the experience curve as rapidly as possible is to increase the volume produced by a single plant as rapidly as possible. Since global markets are larger than domestic markets, a firm that serves a global market from a single location is likely to

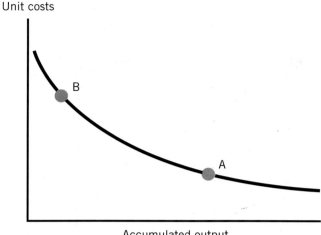

Unit costs

B

A

Accumulated output

FIGURE 10.2

The Experience Curve

build up accumulated volume more quickly than a firm that serves only its home market or that serves multiple markets from multiple production locations. Thus, serving a global market from a single location is consistent with moving down the experience curve and establishing a low-cost position. In addition, to get down the experience curve rapidly, a firm must price and market very aggressively so demand will expand rapidly. It will also need to build sufficient production capacity for serving a global market. The cost advantages of serving the world market from a single location will be all the more significant if that location is the optimal one for performing the particular value creation activity.

Once a firm has established a low-cost position, it can act as a barrier to new competition. An established firm that is well down the experience curve, such as firm A in Figure 10.2, can price so that it is still making a profit while new entrants that are further up the curve, such as firm B in the figure, are suffering losses.

Matsushita has excelled in the pursuit of such a strategy. Along with Sony and Philips, Matsushita was in the race to develop a commercially viable VCR in the 1970s. Although Matsushita initially lagged behind Philips and Sony, it was able to get its VHS format accepted as the world standard and to reap enormous experience-curve-based cost economies in the process. This cost advantage subsequently constituted a formidable barrier to new competition. Matsushita's strategy was to build global volume as rapidly as possible. To ensure it could accommodate worldwide demand, the firm increased its production capacity 33-fold from 205,000 units in 1977 to 6.8 million units by 1984. By serving the world market from a single location in Japan, Matsushita realized significant learning effects and economies of scale. These allowed Matsushita to drop its prices 50 percent within five years of selling its first VHS-formatted VCR. As a result, Matsushita was the world's major VCR producer by 1983, accounting for approximately 45 percent of world production and enjoying a significant cost advantage over its competitors. The next largest firm, Hitachi, accounted for only 11.1 percent of world production in 1983.[13]

Pressures for Cost Reductions and Local Responsiveness

Firms that compete in the global marketplace typically face two types of competitive pressure. They face *pressures for cost reductions* and *pressures to be locally responsive* (see Figure 10.3). These pressures place conflicting demands on a firm. Responding to pressures for cost reductions requires that a firm try to minimize its unit costs. Attaining such a goal may necessitate that a firm base its productive activities at the most favorable low-cost location, wherever in the world that might be. It may also necessitate that a firm offer a standardized product to the global marketplace in order to ride down the experience curve as quickly as possible. In contrast, responding to pressures to be locally responsive requires that a firm differentiate its product offering and marketing strategy from country to country in an attempt to accommodate the diverse demands that arise from national differences in consumer tastes and preferences, business practices, distribution channels, competitive conditions, and government policies. Because customizing product offerings to different national requirements can involve duplication and a lack of product standardization, it may raise costs.

While some firms, such as firm A in Figure 10.3, face high pressures for cost reductions and low pressures for local responsiveness, and others, such as firm B, face low pressures for cost reductions and high pressures for local responsiveness, many firms are in the position of firm C. They face high pressures for cost reductions and high pressures for local responsiveness. Dealing with these conflicting and contradictory pressures is a difficult strategic challenge for a firm, primarily because being locally responsive tends to raise costs. In the rest of this section we will look at the source of pressures for cost reductions and local responsiveness. In the next section we look at the strategies that firms adopt to deal with these pressures.

Pressures for Cost Reductions

Increasingly international businesses are facing pressures for cost reductions. Responding to pressures for cost reduction requires a firm to try to lower the costs of value creation by mass producing a standardized product at the optimal location in the world, wherever that might be, to realize location and experience curve economies. Cost reduction pressures can be particularly intense in industries producing commodity-type products where meaningful differentiation on nonprice factors is difficult and price is the main competitive weapon. This tends to be the case for products that serve universal needs. Universal needs exist when the tastes and preferences of consumers in different nations are similar if not identical. This is the case for conventional commodity products such as bulk chemicals, petroleum, steel, sugar, and the like. It also tends to be the case for many industrial and consumer products (for example, handheld calculators, semiconductor chips, and personal computers). Pressures for cost reductions are also intense in industries where major competitors are based in low-cost locations, where there is persistent excess capacity, and where consumers are powerful and face low switching costs. Many commentators have also argued that the liberalization of the

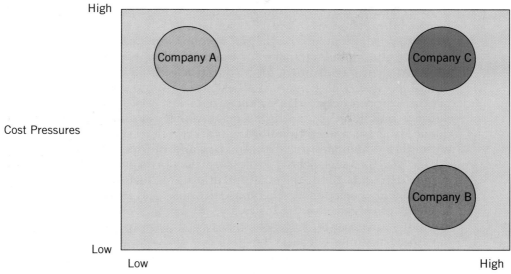

FIGURE 10.3

Pressures for Cost Reduction and Local Responsiveness

world trade and investment environment in recent decades, by facilitating greater international competition, has increased cost pressures.[14]

Cost reduction pressures have been intense in the global tire industry in recent years. Tires are essentially a commodity product where meaningful differentiation is difficult and price is the main competitive weapon. The major buyers of tires, automobile firms, are powerful and face low switching costs, so they have been playing tire firms against each other in an attempt to get lower prices. And the decline in global demand for automobiles in the early 1990s created serious excess capacity in the tire industry, with as much as 25 percent of world capacity standing idle. The result was a worldwide price war with almost all tire firms suffering heavy losses in the early 1990s. In response to the resulting cost pressures, most tire firms are now trying to attain a low cost position. This includes moving production facilities to low-cost facilities and offering globally standardized products to try to realize experience curve economies.[15]

Pressures for Local Responsiveness

Pressures for local responsiveness arise from a number of sources, including:

- Differences in consumer tastes and preferences.
- Differences in infrastructure and traditional practices.
- Differences in distribution channels.
- Host government demands.

DIFFERENCES IN CONSUMER TASTES AND PREFERENCES Strong pressures for local responsiveness emerge when consumer tastes and preferences differ significantly between countries. In such cases, product and/or marketing messages have to be customized to appeal to the tastes and preferences of local consumers. This typically creates pressures to delegate production and marketing functions to national subsidiaries.

In the automobile industry, for example, there is a strong demand among North American consumers for pickup trucks. This is particularly true in the South and West where many families have a pickup truck as a second or third car. In European countries pickup trucks are seen purely as utility vehicles and are purchased primarily by firms rather than individuals. As a consequence, there is a need to tailor the marketing message to address the different nature of demand in North America and Europe.

Harvard Business School Professor Theodore Levitt has argued that consumer demands for local customization are on the decline worldwide.[16] According to Levitt, modern communications and transport technologies allow the convergence of the tastes and preferences of consumers from different nations. The result is the emergence of enormous global markets for standardized consumer products. Levitt cites worldwide acceptance of McDonald's hamburgers, Coca-Cola, Levi Strauss blue jeans, and Sony television sets, all of which are sold as standardized products, as evidence of the increasing homogeneity of the global marketplace.

Levitt's argument, however, has been characterized as extreme by many commentators. For example, Christopher Bartlett and Sumantra Ghoshal have observed that in the consumer electronics industry, consumers reacted to an overdose of standardized global products by showing a renewed preference for products that are differentiated to local conditions.[17] They note that Amstrad, the fast-growing British computer and electronics firm, got its start by recognizing and responding to local consumer needs. Amstrad captured a major share of the British audio player market by moving away from the standardized inexpensive music centers marketed by global firms such as Sony and Matsushita. Amstrad's product was encased in teak rather than metal cabinets with a control panel designed to appeal to British consumers' preferences. In response, Matsushita had to reverse its earlier bias toward standardized global design and place more emphasis on local customization.

DIFFERENCES IN INFRASTRUCTURE AND TRADITIONAL PRACTICES Pressures for local responsiveness emerge when there are differences in infrastructure and/or traditional practices between countries. Customizing a product to meet the needs of the distinctive infrastructure and practices of different nations may necessitate the delegation of manufacturing and production functions to foreign subsidiaries. For example, in North America consumer electrical systems are based on 110 volts, while in some European countries 240-volt systems are standard. Thus, domestic electrical appliances have to be customized to take this difference in infrastructure into account. Traditional practices also often vary across nations. In Britain people drive on the left side of the road, creating a demand for right-hand drive cars, but in neighboring France, people drive on the right side of the road, creating a demand for left-hand drive cars. Obviously automobiles have to be customized to address this difference in traditional practices.

DIFFERENCES IN DISTRIBUTION CHANNELS A firm's marketing strategies may have to be responsive to differences in distribution channels between countries. This may necessitate delegating marketing functions to national subsidiaries. In laundry detergents, for example, five retail chains control 65 percent of the market in Germany, but no chain controls more than 2 percent of the market in neighboring Italy. Thus, retail chains have considerable buying power in Germany but relatively little in Italy. Dealing with these differences requires different marketing approaches. Similarly, in the pharmaceutical industry the British and Japanese distribution system is radically different from the U.S. system. British and Japanese doctors will not accept or respond favorably to an American-style high-pressure sales force. Thus, pharmaceutical firms have to adopt different marketing practices in Britain and Japan compared to the United States (soft sell versus hard sell).

HOST GOVERNMENT DEMANDS Economic and political demands imposed by host country governments may necessitate a degree of local responsiveness. For example, the politics of health care around the world requires that pharmaceutical firms manufacture in multiple locations. Pharmaceutical firms are subject to local clinical testing, registration procedures, and pricing restrictions, all of which require that the manufacturing and marketing of a drug should meet local requirements. Since governments and government agencies control a significant proportion of the health care budget in most countries, they are in a powerful position and can demand a high level of local responsiveness. Threats of protectionism, economic nationalism, and local content rules (which require that a certain percentage of a product should be manufactured locally) all dictate that international businesses manufacture locally. Part of the motivation for Japanese auto firms setting up U.S. production, for example, is to counter the threat of protectionism that is being increasingly voiced by members of the U.S. Congress.

IMPLICATIONS Pressures for local responsiveness imply that it may not be possible for a firm to realize the full benefits from experience curve and location economies. It may not be possible to serve the global marketplace from a single low-cost location, producing a globally standardized product and marketing it worldwide to achieve experience curve cost economies. The need to customize the product offering to local conditions may work against such a strategy. Automobile firms, for example, have found that Japanese, American, and European consumers demand different kinds of cars, and this necessitates producing products that are customized for local markets. In response, Honda, Ford, and Toyota are pursuing a strategy of establishing top-to-bottom design and production facilities in each of these regions so they can better serve local demands. While such customization brings benefits, it also limits the ability of a firm to realize significant experience curve cost economies and location economies.

In addition, pressures for local responsiveness imply that it may not be possible to transfer the skills and products associated with a firm's core competencies wholesale from one nation to another. Concessions often have to be made to local conditions. You will recall from the opening case, for example, that McDonald's does customize its product offering (i.e., its menu) to account for national differences in tastes and preferences.

Strategic Choice

Firms use four basic strategies to compete in the international environment: an international strategy, a multidomestic strategy, a global strategy, and a transnational strategy.[18] Each of these strategies has its advantages and dis-

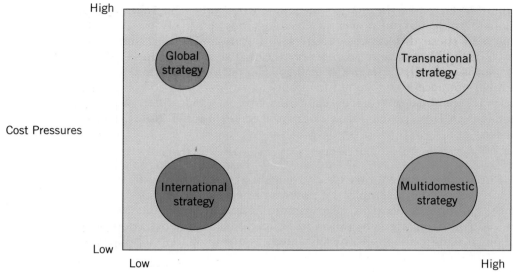

High

Cost Pressures

Low

Low — Pressures for local responsiveness — High

Global strategy

Transnational strategy

International strategy

Multidomestic strategy

FIGURE 10.4

Four Basic Strategies

advantages. The appropriateness of each strategy varies with the extent of pressures for cost reductions and local responsiveness. Figure 10.4 illustrates when each of these strategies is most appropriate. In this section we describe each strategy, identify when it is appropriate, and discuss the pros and cons of each strategy.

International Strategy

Firms that pursue an international strategy try to create value by transferring valuable skills and products to foreign markets where indigenous competitors lack those skills and products. Most international firms have created value by transferring differentiated product offerings developed at home to new markets overseas. Accordingly, they tend to centralize product development functions at home (e.g., R&D). However, they also tend to establish manufacturing and marketing functions in each major country in which they do business. But while they may undertake some local customization of product offering and marketing strategy, this tends to be limited. Ultimately, in most international firms the head office retains tight control over marketing and product strategy.

International firms include the likes of Toys R Us, McDonald's, IBM, Kellogg, and Procter & Gamble. Most U.S. firms that expanded abroad in the 1950s and 1960s fall into this category. Procter & Gamble, which is profiled in the accompanying "Management Focus," has traditionally had production facilities in all its major markets, including Britain, Germany, and Japan. These facilities, however, manufactured differentiated products that had been developed by the U.S. parent firm and were often marketed using the marketing message developed in the United States. Historically, local responsiveness at P&G has been rather limited.

An international strategy makes sense if a firm has a valuable core competence that indigenous competitors in foreign markets lack and if the firm faces relatively weak pressures for local responsiveness and cost reductions. In such circumstances, an international strategy can be very profitable. However, when pressures for local responsiveness are high, firms pursuing this strategy lose out to firms that place a greater emphasis on customizing the product offering and market strategy to local conditions. Moreover, due to the duplication of manufacturing facilities, firms that pursue an international strategy tend to suffer from high operating costs. This makes the strategy inappropriate in those industries where cost pressures are high.

Multidomestic Strategy

Firms pursuing a multidomestic strategy orient themselves toward achieving maximum local responsiveness. Like firms pursuing an international strategy, firms pursuing a multidomestic strategy also tend to transfer skills and products developed at home to foreign markets. However, unlike international firms, multidomestic firms extensively customize both their product offering and their marketing strategy to different national conditions. Consistent with this, they also have a tendency to establish a complete set of value creation activities—including production, marketing, and R&D—in each major national market in which they do business. As a consequence, they are generally unable to realize value from experience curve effects and location economies. Accordingly, many multidomestic firms have a high cost structure.

A multidomestic strategy makes most sense when there are high pressures for local responsiveness and low pressures for cost reductions. The high cost structure associated with the duplication of production facilities makes this strategy inappropriate in industries where cost pressures are intense. Another weakness associated with this strategy is that many multidomestic firms have developed into decentralized federations in which each national subsidiary functions in a largely autonomous manner. As a result, after a time they begin to lack the ability to transfer the skills and products derived from core competencies to their various national subsidiaries around the world. In a famous case that illustrates the problems this can cause, the ability of Philips NV to establish its V2000 VCR format as the dominant design in the VCR industry during the late 1970s, as opposed to Matsushita's VHS format, was effectively killed by the refusal of its U.S. subsidiary firm to adopt the V2000 format. Instead, the subsidiary bought VCRs produced by Matsushita and put its own label on them!

Global Strategy

Firms that pursue a global strategy focus upon increasing profitability by reaping the cost reductions that come from experience curve effects and location economies. That is, they are pursuing a low cost strategy. The production, marketing, and R&D activities of firms pursuing a global strategy are concentrated in a few favorable locations. Global firms tend not to customize their product offering and marketing strategy to local conditions, the reason being that customization raises costs (because it involves shorter

Procter & Gamble's
International Strategy

Procter & Gamble (P&G), the large U.S. consumer products company, has a well-earned reputation as one of the world's best marketers. With over 80 major brands P&G generates more than $20 billion in revenues worldwide. Together with Unilever, P&G is a dominant global force in laundry detergents, cleaning products, and personal care products. P&G expanded abroad after World War II by pursuing an international strategy— transferring brands and marketing policies developed in the United States to Western Europe, initially with considerable success. Over the next 30 years this policy resulted in the development of a classic international firm in which new-product development and marketing strategies were pioneered in the United States and then transferred to other countries. Although some

adaptation of marketing policies to accommodate country differences was pursued, this adaptation was minimal.

The first signs that this strategy was flawed began to emerge in the 1970s when P&G suffered a number of major setbacks in Japan. By 1985, after 13 years in Japan, P&G was still losing $40 million a year there. After introducing disposable diapers into Japan and at one time commanding an 80 percent share of the market, by the early 1980s P&G had seen its share slip to a miserable 8 percent. Three major Japanese consumer products firms dominated the market. P&G's diapers, developed in America, were too bulky for Japanese consumers. The Japanese consumer products firm Kao developed a line of trim-fit diapers that appealed more to Japanese consumers. Kao supported the product introduction with a marketing blitz. The company was quickly rewarded with a 30 percent share of the market.

As for P&G, only belatedly did it realize it had to modify its diapers to accommodate the tastes of Japanese consumers. Now the company has increased its share of the Japanese market to 30 percent. And in an example of global learning, P&G's trim-fit diapers, originally developed for the Japanese market, have now become a best-seller in the United States.

P&G's experience with disposable diapers in Japan prompted the company to rethink its new-product development and marketing philosophy. The company has now admitted that its U.S.-centered way of doing business will no longer work. Since the late 1980s P&G has been attempting to delegate more responsibility for new-product development and marketing strategy to its major subsidiary firms in Japan and Europe. The result has been a company that is more responsive to local differences in consumer tastes and preferences and more willing to admit that

production runs and the duplication of functions). Instead, global firms prefer to market a standardized product worldwide so that they can reap the maximum benefits from the economies of scale that underlie the experience curve. They also tend to use their cost advantage to support aggressive pricing in world markets.

This strategy makes most sense in those cases where there are strong pressures for cost reductions, and where demands for local responsiveness are minimal. Increasingly, these conditions prevail in many industrial goods industries. In the semiconductor industry, for example, global standards have emerged which have created enormous demands for standardized global products. Accordingly, firms such as Intel, Texas Instruments, and Motorola good new products can be developed outside the United States.

But P&G's venture into the Polish shampoo market illustrates that the company still has some way to go in altering its long-established practices. In the summer of 1991 P&G entered the Polish market with its Vidal Sasson Wash & Go, an all-in-one shampoo and conditioner that is a best-seller in America and Europe. The product launch was supported by an American-style marketing blitz on a scale never before seen in Poland. At first the campaign seemed to be working as P&G captured more than 30 percent of the market for shampoos in Poland, but in early 1992 sales suddenly plummeted. Then came the rumors—Wash & Go caused dandruff and hair loss—allegations that P&G strenuously denied. Next came the jokes. One doing the rounds in Poland runs as follows: "I washed my car with Wash & Go and the tires went bald." And when President Lech Walesa proposed earlier this year that he also become prime minister, critics derided the idea as a "two in one solution, just like Wash & Go."

Where did P&G go wrong? The most common theory is that it promoted Wash & Go too hard in a country which has little enthu-

SuperStock, ©Dale Brown

siasm for brash American style advertising. A poll by Pentor, a private market research company in Warsaw, found that almost three times more Poles disliked P&G's commercials than liked them. Pentor also argues that the high profile marketing campaign backfired because years of Communist Party propaganda have led Polish consumers to suspect that advertising is simply a way to shift goods that nobody wants. Some also believe that Wash & Go, which was developed

for U.S. consumers who shampoo daily, was far too sophisticated for Polish consumers who are less obsessed with personal hygiene. Underlying all of these criticisms seems to be the idea that P&G was once again stumbling because it had transferred a product and marketing strategy wholesale from the U.S. to another country without modification to accommodate the tastes and preferences of local consumers.[19]

all pursue a global strategy. However, as we noted earlier, these conditions are not found in many consumer goods markets, where demands for local responsiveness remain high (e.g., audio players, automobiles, processed food). The strategy is inappropriate when demands for local responsiveness are high.

Transnational Strategy

Christopher Bartlett and Sumantra Ghoshal have argued that in today's environment, competitive conditions are so intense that to survive in the global marketplace firms *must exploit experience-based cost economies and location*

339

economies, *they must transfer distinctive competencies within the firm, and they must do all of this while paying attention to pressures for local responsiveness.*[20] Moreover, they note that in the modern multinational enterprise, distinctive competencies do not just reside in the home country. They can develop in any of the firm's worldwide operations. Thus, they maintain that the flow of skills and product offerings should not be all one way, from home firm to foreign subsidiary, as in the case of firms pursuing an international strategy. Rather, the flow should also be from foreign subsidiary to home country, and from foreign subsidiary to foreign subsidiary—a process they refer to as **global learning** (for an example of such knowledge flows, see the opening case on McDonald's). Bartlett and Ghoshal refer to the strategy pursued by firms that are trying to achieve all these objectives simultaneously as a **transnational strategy**.

A transnational strategy makes sense when a firm faces high pressures for cost reductions and high pressures for local responsiveness. Firms that pursue a transnational strategy are trying to simultaneously achieve low cost and differentiation advantages. The strategy is not an easy one to pursue. Earlier we noted that pressures for local responsiveness and cost reductions place conflicting demands on a firm. Being locally responsive raises costs, which obviously makes cost reductions difficult to achieve. How, then, can a firm effectively pursue a transnational strategy?

Some clues can be derived from the case of Caterpillar Tractor. The need to compete with low-cost competitors such as Komatsu of Japan has forced Caterpillar to look for greater cost economies. At the same time, variations in construction practices and government regulations mean Caterpillar has to be responsive to local demands. Therefore, as illustrated in Figure 10.5, Caterpillar confronts significant pressures for cost reductions and for local responsiveness.

To deal with cost pressures, Caterpillar redesigned its products to use many identical components and invested in a few large-scale component manufacturing facilities at favorable locations to fill global demand and realize scale economies. The firm augments the centralized manufacturing of components with assembly plants in each of its major global markets. At these plants, Caterpillar adds local product features, tailoring the finished product to local needs. Thus, Caterpillar realizes many of the benefits of global manufacturing while responding to pressures for local responsiveness by differentiating its product among national markets.[21]

For another example, consider Unilever. Once a classic multidomestic firm, in recent years Unilever has had to shift toward more of a transnational strategy. A rise in low-cost competition, which increased cost pressures, forced Unilever to look for ways of rationalizing its detergent business. During the 1980s Unilever had 17 different and largely self-contained detergent operations in Europe. The duplication, in terms of assets and marketing, was enormous. And because Unilever was so fragmented, it could take as long as four years for the firm to introduce a new product across Europe. Now Unilever is trying to weld its European operation into a single entity, with detergents being manufactured in a handful of cost-efficient plants and standard packaging and advertising being used across Europe. According to firm estimates, the result could be an annual cost saving of over $200 million. At the same time, however, due to national differences in distribution channels and brand awareness, Unilever recognizes that it must still remain locally responsive, even while it tries to realize economies from consolidating production and marketing at the optimal locations.[22]

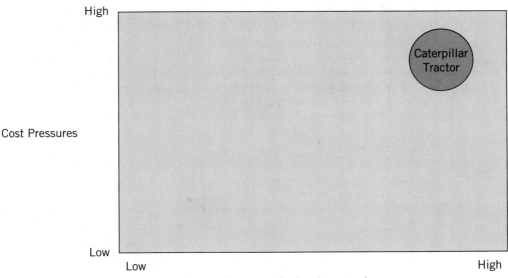

FIGURE 10.5

Cost Pressures and Pressures for Local Responsiveness Facing Caterpillar

Bartlett and Ghoshal admit that building an organization that is capable of supporting a transnational strategic posture is complex and difficult. The core of the problem is that simultaneously trying to achieve cost efficiencies, global learning, and local responsiveness places contradictory demands on an organization. The organizational problems associated with pursuing conflicting objectives constitute a major impediment to the pursuit of a transnational strategy. Firms that attempt to pursue a transnational strategy can become bogged down in an organizational morass that only leads to inefficiencies.

Fortunately, Bartlett and Ghoshal may be overstating the case for the transnational strategy. Bartlett and Ghoshal present the transnational strategy as the only viable strategy. While no one doubts that in some industries the firm that can adopt a transnational strategy will have a competitive advantage, in other industries global, multidomestic, and international strategies remain viable. In the global semiconductor industry, for example, pressures for local customization are minimal and competition is purely a cost game, in which case a global strategy, not a transnational strategy, is optimal. This is true in many industrial goods markets where the product serves universal needs. But the argument can be made that to compete in certain consumer goods markets, such as the consumer electronics industry, a firm has to try to adopt a transnational strategy.

Summary

The advantages and disadvantages of each of the four strategies discussed above are summarized in Figure 10.6. While a transnational strategy appears to offer the most advantages, implementing a transnational strategy raises difficult organizational issues. As shown in Figure 10.3, the appropriateness of each strategy depends on the relative strength of pressures for cost reductions and pressures for local responsiveness.

Strategy	Advantages	Disadvantages
Global	• Exploit experience curve effects • Exploit location economies	• Lack of local responsiveness
International	• Transfer distinctive competencies to foreign markets	• Lack of local responsiveness • Inability to realize location economies • Failure to exploit experience curve effects
Multidomestic	• Customize product offerings and marketing in accordance with local responsiveness	• Inability to realize location economies • Failure to exploit experience curve effects • Failure to transfer distinctive competencies to foreign markets
Transnational	• Exploit experience curve effects • Exploit location economies • Customize product offerings and marketing in accordance with local responsiveness • Reap benefits of global learning	• Difficult to implement due to organizational problems

FIGURE 10.6

The Advantages and Disadvantages of the Four Strategies

Strategic Alliances

Many firms that compete globally see strategic alliances as an important component of their strategy. In this context, the term **strategic alliances** refers to cooperative agreements between potential or actual competitors. In this section we are concerned specifically with strategic alliances between firms from different countries. Strategic alliances run the range from formal joint ventures, in which two or more firms have equity stakes (e.g., Fuji–Xerox), to short-term contractual agreements in which two companies agree to cooperate on a particular task (such as developing a new product). Collaboration between competitors is fashionable; the 1980s and early 1990s have seen an explosion in the number of strategic alliances. Examples include:

strategic alliances Cooperative agreements between potential or actual competitors.

- A cooperative arrangement between Boeing and a consortium of Japanese companies to produce the 767 wide-bodied commercial jet.
- An alliance between General Electric and Snecma of France to build a family of low-thrust commercial aircraft engines.
- An agreement between Siemens and Philips to develop new semiconductor technology.
- An agreement between ICL, the British computer company, and Fujitsu of Japan to develop a new generation of mainframe computers capable of competing with IBM's products.

- An alliance between Eastman Kodak and Canon of Japan under which Canon manufactures a line of medium-volume copiers for sale under Kodak's name.
- An agreement between Texas Instruments and Kobe Steel, Inc., of Japan to make logic semiconductors in Japan.
- An agreement between Motorola and Toshiba to pool their technological know-how in the manufacture of microprocessors.

The Advantages of Strategic Alliances

Firms ally themselves with actual or potential competitors for various strategic purposes.[23] First, strategic alliances may facilitate entry into a foreign market. For example, Motorola initially found it very difficult to gain access to the Japanese cellular telephone market. In the mid-1980s the firm complained loudly about formal and informal Japanese trade barriers. The turning point for Motorola came in 1987 when it allied itself with Toshiba to build microprocessors. As part of the deal, Toshiba provided Motorola with marketing help—including some of its best managers. This helped Motorola in the political game of securing government approval to enter the Japanese market and getting radio frequencies assigned for its mobile communications systems. Motorola no longer complains about Japan's trade barriers. Although privately the company admits such barriers still exist, with Toshiba's help Motorola has become skilled at getting around them.[24]

Another reason firms make strategic alliances is that it allows them to share the fixed costs (and associated risks) of developing new products or processes. Motorola's alliance with Toshiba also was partly motivated by a desire to share the high fixed costs of setting up an operation to manufacture microprocessors. The microprocessor business is so capital intensive—Motorola and Toshiba each contributed close to $1 billion to set up their facility—that few firms can afford the costs and risks by themselves. Similarly, the alliance between Boeing and a number of Japanese companies to build the 767 was motivated by Boeing's desire to share the estimated $2 billion investment required to develop the aircraft.

Third, an alliance is a way to bring together complementary skills and assets that neither company could easily develop on its own. An example is the alliance between France's Thompson and Japan's JVC to manufacture videocassette recorders. JVC and Thompson are trading core competencies; Thompson needs product technology and manufacturing skills, while JVC needs to learn how to succeed in the fragmented European market. Both sides believe there is an equitable chance for gain. Similarly, in 1990 AT&T struck a deal with NEC Corporation of Japan to trade technological skills. AT&T will give NEC some of its computer-aided design technology and NEC will give AT&T access to the technology underlying its advanced logic computer chips. Such trading of core competencies seems to underlie many of the most successful strategic alliances.

Fourth, it can make sense to form an alliance that will help the firm establish technological standards for the industry that will benefit the firm. For example, in 1992 Philips NV allied with its global competitor, Matsushita, to manufacture and market the digital compact cassette (DCC) system Philips had developed. Philips' motive was that this linking with Matsushita would help it establish the DCC system as a new technological standard in the recording and consumer electronics industries. The issue is important, because Sony has developed a competing "mini-compact disc" technology that it hopes to establish as the new technical standard. Since the two technologies do very similar things, there is probably room for only one new standard. The technology that becomes the new standard will be the one that succeeds. The loser will probably have to write off investments in the billions of dollars. Philips sees its alliance with Matsushita as a tactic for winning the race.[25]

The Disadvantages of Strategic Alliances

The advantages we have discussed can be very significant. Despite this, some commentators have criticized strategic alliances on the grounds that they give competitors a low-cost route to new technology and markets. For example, Robert Reich and Eric Mankin have argued that strategic alliances between U.S. and Japanese firms are part of an implicit Japanese strategy to keep higher-paying, higher value-added jobs in Japan while gaining the project engineering and production process skills that underlie the competitive success of many U.S. companies.[26] They argue that Japanese successes in the machine tool and semiconductor industries were largely built on U.S. technology acquired through various strategic alliances. And they argue that, increasingly, U.S. managers are aiding the Japanese in achieving their goals by entering alliances that channel new inventions to Japan and provide a U.S. sales and distribution network for the resulting products. Although such deals may generate short-term profits, Reich and Mankin argue, in the long run the result is to "hollow out" U.S. firms, leaving them with no competitive advantage in the global marketplace.

Reich and Mankin have a point. Alliances do have risks. Unless a firm is careful, it can give away more than it receives. But there are so many examples of apparently successful alliances between firms—including alliances between U.S. and Japanese firms—that their position seems extreme. For example, it is difficult to see how the Motorola–Toshiba alliance fits Reich and Mankin's thesis since both partners seem to have gained from the alliance. Nevertheless, since Reich and Mankin do have a point, the question becomes, Why do some alliances benefit both firms while others benefit one firm and hurt the other? The next section provides an answer.

Making Alliances Work

The failure rate for international strategic alliances seems to be quite high. For example, one recent study of 49 international strategic alliances found that two-thirds run into serious managerial and financial troubles within two years of their formation, and that although many of these problems are ultimately solved, 33 percent are rated as failures by the parties involved.[27] The accompanying "Management Focus" provides us with a detailed look at one strategic alliance that failed—that between General Motors and the Korean Daewoo Group to build cars (the Daewoo Motor Company). Below we argue that the success of an alliance seems to be a function of three main factors: partner selection, alliance structure, and the manner in which the alliance is managed. We will look at each of these issues in turn.

Partner Selection

A key to making a strategic alliance work is to select the right ally. A good ally, or partner, has three principal characteristics. First, a good partner helps the firm achieve its strategic goals—whether they be market access, sharing the costs and risks of new-product development, or gaining access to critical core competencies. The partner must have capabilities that the firm lacks and that it values. Second, a good partner shares the firm's vision for the purpose of the alliance. If two firms approach an alliance with radically different agendas, the chances are great that the relationship will not be harmonious, will not flourish, and will end in divorce. This seems to have been the case with the alliance between GM and Daewoo (see the "Management Focus"). GM's agenda was to use Daewoo Motor as a source of cheap labor to produce cars for the Korean and U.S. markets, whereas Daewoo wanted to use GM's know-how and distribution systems to expand Daewoo's business not just in Korea and the United States, but also in Europe. Different perceptions over the strategic role of the venture ultimately helped contribute to the dissolution of the alliance.

Third, a good partner is unlikely to try to opportunistically exploit the alliance for its own ends; that is, to expropriate the firm's technological know-how while giving away little in return. In this respect, firms with good reputations to maintain probably make the best allies. For example, IBM is involved in so many strategic alliances that it would not pay the company to trample over individual alliance partners. Such action would tarnish IBM's hard-won reputation of being a good ally and would make it more difficult for IBM to attract alliance partners in the future. Since IBM attaches great importance to its alliances, it is unlikely to engage in the kind of opportunistic behavior that Reich and Mankin highlight. Similarly, their reputations make it less likely (but by no means impossible) that such Japanese firms as Sony, Toshiba, and Fuji, which have histories of alliances with non-Japanese firms, would opportunistically exploit an alliance partner.

To select a partner with these three characteristics, a firm needs to research potential alliance candidates. To increase the probability of selecting a good partner, the firm should:

1 Collect as much pertinent, publicly available information on potential allies as possible.

2 Collect data from informed third parties. These include firms that have had alliances with the potential partners, investment bankers who have had dealings with them, and some of their former employees.

3 Get to know the potential partner as well as possible before committing to an alliance. This should include face-to-face meetings between senior managers (and perhaps middle-level managers) to ensure that the chemistry is right.

Alliance Structure

Having selected a partner, the alliance should be structured so that the firm's risks of giving too much away to the partner are reduced to an acceptable level. Figure 10.7 depicts the four safeguards against opportunism by alliance partners that we discuss here. (Opportunism includes the "theft" of technol-

Anatomy of a Failed Alliance—General Motors and the Daewoo Group

In June 1984 General Motors and the Daewoo Group of South Korea signed an agreement that called for each to invest $100 million in a Korean-based 50/50 joint venture, Daewoo Motor Company, that would manufacture a subcompact car, the Pontiac LeMans, based on GM's popular German-designed Opel Kadett (Opel is a wholly owned German subsidiary of GM). Much of the day-to-day management of the alliance was to be placed in the hands of Daewoo executives, with managerial and technical advice being provided by a limited number of GM executives. At the time many hailed the alliance as a smart move for both companies. GM doubted that a small car could be built profitably in the United States because of high labor costs, and it saw enormous advantages in this marriage of German technology and Korean cheap labor. Roger Smith, GM's chairman, told Korean reporters that GM's North American operation would probably import 80,000 to 100,000 cars a year from Daewoo Motor. As for the Daewoo Group, it expected to get access to the superior engineering skills of GM and an entrée into the world's largest car market—the United States.

Eight years of financial losses later the joint venture collapsed in a blizzard of mutual recriminations between Daewoo and General Motors. From the perspective of GM, things started to go seriously wrong in 1987, just as the first LeMans was rolling off Daewoo's production line. South Korea had lurched toward democracy, and workers throughout the country demanded better wages.

ogy and/or markets that Reich and Mankin describe.) First, alliances can be designed to make it difficult (if not impossible) to transfer technology not meant to be transferred. The design, development, manufacture, and service of a product manufactured by an alliance can be structured so as to "wall off" sensitive technologies to prevent their leakage to the other participant. In the alliance between General Electric and Snecma to build commercial aircraft engines, for example, GE reduced the risk of "excess transfer" by walling off certain sections of the production process. The modularization effectively cut off the transfer of what GE regarded as key competitive technology, while permitting Snecma access to final assembly. Similarly, in the alliance between Boeing and the Japanese to build the 767, Boeing walled off research, design, and marketing functions considered central to its competitive position, while allowing the Japanese to share in production technology. Boeing also walled off new technologies not required for 767 production.[29]

Second, contractual safeguards can be written into an alliance agreement to guard against the risk of opportunism by a partner. For example, TRW, Inc., has three strategic alliances with large Japanese auto component suppliers to produce seat belts, engine valves, and steering gears for sale to Japanese-owned auto assembly plants in the United States. TRW has clauses in each of its alliance contracts that bar the Japanese firms from competing

346

Daewoo Motor was hit by a series of bitter strikes that repeatedly halted LeMans production. To calm the labor troubles, Daewoo Motor more than doubled workers' wages. Suddenly it was cheaper to build Opels in Germany than Korea (German wages were still higher, but German productivity was also much higher, which translated into lower labor costs).

Equally problematic was the poor quality of the cars rolling off the Daewoo production line. Electrical systems often crashed on the LeMans, and the braking system had a tendency to fail after just a few thousand miles. The LeMans soon gained a reputation for poor quality, and U.S. sales plummeted to 37,000 vehicles in 1991, down 86 percent from their 1988 high. Hurt by the car's reputation as a lemon, Daewoo's share of the rapidly growing Korean car market also slumped from a high of 21.4 percent in 1987 to 12.3 percent in 1991.

But if General Motors was disappointed in Daewoo, that was nothing compared to Daewoo's frustration with GM. Daewoo Group Chairman Kim WooChoong complained publicly that GM executives were arrogant and treated him shabbily. Mr. Kim was angry that GM tried to prohibit him from expanding the market for Daewoo's cars. In late 1988 Mr. Kim negotiated a deal to sell 7,000 of Daewoo Motor's cars in Eastern Europe. GM executives immediately tried to kill the deal, telling Mr. Kim that Europe was the territory of GM's German subsidiary, Opel. Daewoo ultimately agreed to limit the sale to 3,000 cars and never sell again in Eastern Europe. To make matters worse, when Daewoo developed a new sedan and asked GM to sell it in the United States, GM said no. Also, Daewoo management believed that the poor sales of the LeMans in the United States were not due to quality problems, but to the poor marketing efforts of GM.

Things came to a head in 1991 when Daewoo asked GM to agree to expand the manufacturing facilities of the joint venture. The plan called for each partner to put in another $100 million, and for Daewoo Motor to double its output. GM management refused on the grounds that increasing output would not help Daewoo Motor unless the venture could first improve its product quality. The matter festered until late 1991 when GM management delivered a blunt proposal to Daewoo—either GM would buy out Daewoo's stake, or Daewoo would buy out GM's stake in the joint venture. Much to GM's surprise, Daewoo agreed to buy out GM's stake. The divorce was completed in November 1992 with an agreement by Daewoo to pay GM $170 million over three years for its 50 percent stake in Daewoo Motor Company.[28]

with TRW to supply U.S.-owned auto companies with component parts. By doing this, TRW protects itself against the possibility that the Japanese companies are entering into the alliances merely as a means of gaining access to North America to compete with TRW in its home market.

Third, both parties to an alliance can agree in advance to swap skills and technologies that the other covets, thereby ensuring a chance for equitable gain. Cross-licensing agreements are one way to achieve this goal. For example, in the alliance between Motorola and Toshiba, Motorola has licensed some of its microprocessor technology to Toshiba, and in return Toshiba has licensed some of its memory chip technology to Motorola.

Fourth, the risk of opportunism by an alliance partner can be reduced if the firm extracts a significant credible commitment from its partner in advance. The long-term alliance between Xerox and Fuji to build photocopiers for the Asian market perhaps best illustrates this. Rather than enter into an informal agreement or some kind of licensing arrangement (which Fuji Photo initially wanted), Xerox insisted that Fuji invest in a 50/50 joint venture to serve Japan and East Asia. This venture constituted such a significant investment in people, equipment, and facilities that Fuji Photo was committed from the outset to making the alliance work in order to earn a return on its investment. By agreeing to the joint venture, Fuji essentially made a credible

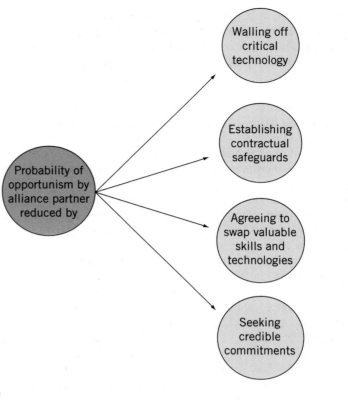

FIGURE 10.7

Structuring Alliances to Reduce Opportunism

commitment to the alliance. Given this, Xerox felt secure in transferring its photocopier technology to Fuji.[30]

Managing the Alliance

Once a partner has been selected and an appropriate alliance structure has been agreed on, the task facing the firm is to maximize its benefits from the alliance. As in all international business deals, an important factor is sensitivity to cultural differences (see Chapter 3). Many differences in management style are attributable to cultural differences, and managers need to make allowances for these in dealing with their partner. Beyond this, maximizing the benefits from an alliance seems to involve building trust between partners and learning from partners.

BUILDING TRUST. Part of the trick of managing an alliance successfully seems to be to build interpersonal relationships between the firms' managers. This is one lesson that can be drawn from the successful strategic alliance between Ford and Mazda. Ford and Mazda have set up a framework of meetings that not only allow their managers to discuss matters pertaining to the alliance but also provide sufficient "nonwork" time for the managers to get to know each other better. The belief is that the resulting friendships help build trust and facilitate harmonious relations between the two firms. Personal relationships foster an informal management network between the two firms. This network can then be used to help solve problems arising in more formal contexts (such as in joint committee meetings between personnel from the two firms).

LEARNING FROM PARTNERS. After a five-year study of 15 strategic alliances between major multinationals, Gary Hamel, Yves Doz, and C. K. Prahalad concluded that a major determinant of how much a company gains from an alliance is its ability to learn from its alliance partner.[31] They focused on a number of alliances between Japanese companies and Western (European or American) partners. In every case in which a Japanese company emerged from an alliance stronger than its Western partner, the Japanese company had made a greater effort to learn. Few Western companies studied seemed to want to learn from their Japanese partners. They tended to regard the alliance purely as a cost-sharing or risk-sharing device, rather than as an opportunity to learn how a potential competitor does business.

Consider the alliance between General Motors and Toyota to build the Chevrolet Nova constituted in 1985 and still operating today. This alliance is structured as a formal joint venture, called New United Motor Manufacturing, Inc., and each party has a 50 percent equity stake. The venture owns an auto plant in Fremont, California. According to one of the Japanese managers, Toyota quickly achieved most of its objectives from the alliance: "We learned about U.S. supply and transportation. And we got the confidence to manage U.S. workers."[32] All that knowledge was then quickly transferred to Georgetown, Kentucky, where Toyota opened a plant of its own in 1988. It may be that all GM got was a new product, the Chevrolet Nova. Some GM managers complained that the knowledge they gained through the alliance with Toyota has never been put to good use inside GM. They believe they should have been kept together as a team to educate GM's engineers and workers about the Japanese system. Instead, they have been dispersed to various GM subsidiaries.

To maximize the learning benefits of an alliance, a firm must try to learn from its partner and then apply the knowledge within its own organization. It has been suggested that all operating employees should be well briefed on the partner's strengths and weaknesses and should understand how acquiring particular skills will bolster their firm's competitive position. Hamel, Doz, and Prahalad note that this is already standard practice among Japanese companies. For example, they made this observation:

> We accompanied a Japanese development engineer on a tour through a partner's factory. This engineer dutifully took notes on plant layout, the number of production stages, the rate at which the line was running, and the number of employees. He recorded all this despite the fact that he had no manufacturing responsibility in his own company, and that the alliance did not encompass joint manufacturing. Such dedication greatly enhances learning.[33]

For such learning to be of value, it must be diffused throughout the organization (as was seemingly not the case at GM following the GM–Toyota joint venture). To achieve this, the managers involved in the alliance should be explicitly used to educate their colleagues in the firm about the skills of the alliance partner.

Key Terms

core competence, p. 326
economies of scale, p. 330
experience curve, p. 329
global learning, p. 340

global web, p. 328
learning effects, p. 330
location economies, p. 328
strategic alliances, p. 342

strategy, p. 325
transnational strategy, p. 340

Summary

In this chapter we reviewed the various ways in which firms can profit from global expansion, we reviewed the strategies firms that compete globally can adopt, we discussed the optimal choice of entry mode to serve a foreign market, and we looked at the issue of strategic alliances. The following points have been made:

1 For some firms international expansion represents a way of earning greater returns by transferring the skills and product offerings derived from their core competencies to markets where indigenous competitors lack those skills.

2 Due to national differences, it pays a firm to base each value creation activity where factor conditions are most conducive to the performance of that activity. We refer to this strategy as focusing on location economies.

3 By building sales volume more rapidly, international expansion can help a firm move down the experience curve.

4 The best strategy for a firm to pursue may depend on a consideration of the pressures for cost reductions and the pressures for local responsiveness.

5 Pressures for cost reductions are greatest in industries producing commodity-type products where price is the main competitive weapon.

6 Pressures for local responsiveness arise from differences in consumer tastes and preferences, national infrastructure and traditional practices, distribution channels, and from host government demands.

7 Firms pursuing an international strategy transfer the skills and products derived from distinctive competencies to foreign markets, while undertaking some limited local customization.

8 Firms pursuing a multidomestic strategy customize their product offering, marketing strategy, and business strategy to national conditions.

9 Firms pursuing a global strategy focus on reaping the cost reductions that come from experience curve effects and location economies.

10 Many industries are now so competitive that firms must adopt a transnational strategy. This involves a simultaneous focus on reducing costs, transferring skills and products, and creating local responsiveness. Implementing such a strategy, however, may not be easy.

11 Strategic alliances are cooperative agreements between actual or potential competitors.

12 The advantages of alliances are that they facilitate entry into foreign markets, enable partners to share the fixed costs and risks associated with new products and processes, facilitate the transfer of complementary skills between companies, and can help firms establish technical standards.

13 The disadvantage of a strategic alliance is that the firm risks giving away technological know-how and market access to its alliance partner in return for very little.

14 The disadvantages associated with alliances can be reduced if the firm selects partners carefully, paying close attention to the issue of reputation, and structures the alliance so as to avoid unintended transfers of knowledge.

Critical Thinking and Discussion Questions

1 In a world of zero transportation costs, no trade barriers, and nontrivial differences between nations with regard to factor conditions, firms must expand internationally if they are to survive. Discuss.

2 Plot the position of the following firms on Figure 10.3—Procter & Gamble, IBM, Coca-Cola, Dow Chemical, US Steel, McDonald's. In each case justify your answer.

3 Are the following global industries or multidomestic industries: bulk chemicals, pharmaceuticals, branded food products, moviemaking, television manufacture, personal computers, airline travel?

4 Discuss how the need for control over foreign operations varies with the strategy and core competencies of a firm. What are the implications of this for the choice of entry mode?

5 What are the main organizational problems likely in implementation of a transnational strategy?

6 What kinds of companies stand to gain the most from entering into strategic alliances with potential competitors? Why?

Internet Exercise

Managers use global strategy to compete effectively in today's international markets, as you learned in this chapter. One of the most competitive and dynamic markets is the computer field, and Digital has devoted part of its web site (http://www.alliance.digital.com/index.htm) to explain its strategic alliances with several computer companies: Computer Associates, MCI, Microsoft, Oracle, and SAP. The Digital-CA Alliance for Enterprise Management (http://www.alliance.digital.com/alliances/ca/index.htm) uses CA's enterprise management software with the goal of improving the client-server environment. The Digital-Microsoft Alliance for Intranet Computing (http://www.alliance.digital.com/alliances/mci/index.htm) combines the resources of Digital, MCI, and Microsoft to create a productive corporate intranet. The Alliance for Enterprise Computing (http://www.alliance.digital.com/alliances/microsoft/index.htm) between Digital and Microsoft delivers open client-server computing solutions. The Digital-Oracle Alliance for Networked Applications (http://www.alliance.digital.com/alliances/oracle/index.htm) provides on-line transaction processing solutions.

Global Surfing

Surf to the Digital site to learn about the company's alliances. What are the goals of the strategic alliances? What news updates are listed? What events are listed for today? What are the advantages of the alliances? How should the alliances help the six companies compete globally? What cost reductions are described? How do the alliances address the pressures for local responsiveness?

Sweden's IKEA

Originally established in the 1940s in Sweden by Ingvar Kamprad, IKEA has grown rapidly in recent years to become one of the world's largest retailers of home furnishings. In its initial push to expand globally, IKEA largely ignored the retailing rule that international success involves tailoring product lines closely to national tastes and preferences. Instead, IKEA stuck with the vision, articulated by founder Kamprad, that the company should sell a basic product range that is "typically Swedish" wherever it ventures in the world. The company also remained primarily production-oriented; that is, the Swedish management and design group decided what it was going to sell and then presented it to the worldwide public—often with little research as to what the public actually wanted. Moreover, the company emphasized its Swedish roots in its international advertising, even insisting on a "Swedish" blue-and-yellow color scheme for its stores.

Despite breaking some key rules of international retailing, the formula of selling Swedish-designed products in the same manner everywhere seemed to work. Between 1974 and 1994 IKEA expanded from a company with 10 stores, only one of which was outside Scandinavia, and annual revenues of $210 million to a group with 125 stores in 26 countries and sales of close to $5 billion. In 1994 only 11 percent of its sales were generated in Sweden. Of the balance, 29.6 percent of sales came from Germany, 42.5 percent from the rest of Western Europe, and 14.2 percent from North America. IKEA's expansion in North America was its most recent international venture.

The foundation of IKEA's success has been to offer consumers good value for money. IKEA's approach starts with a global network of suppliers, which now numbers 2,700 firms in 67 countries. An IKEA supplier gains long-term contracts, technical advice, and leased equipment from the company. In return, IKEA demands an exclusive contract and low prices. IKEA's designers work closely with suppliers to build savings into the products from the outset by designing products that can be produced at a low cost. IKEA displays its enormous range of more than 10,000 products in cheap out-of-town stores. It sells most of its furniture as kits for customers to take home and assemble themselves. The firm reaps huge economies of scale from the size of each store and the big production runs made possible by selling the same products all over the world. This strategy allows IKEA to match its rivals on quality, while undercutting them by up to 30 percent on price and still maintaining a healthy aftertax return on sales of around 7 percent.

This strategy worked well until 1985 when IKEA decided to enter the North American market. Between 1985 and 1990 IKEA opened six stores in North America, but unlike the company's experience across Europe, the stores did not quickly become profitable. Instead, by 1990 it was clear that IKEA's North American operations were in trouble. Part of the problem was an adverse movement in exchange rates. In 1985 the exchange rate was $1 = 8.6 Swedish kronar; by 1990 it was $1 = SKr5.8. At this exchange rate many products imported from Sweden did not look inexpensive to American consumers.

But there was more to IKEA's problems than adverse exchange rates. IKEA's unapologetically Swedish products, which had sold so well across Europe, jarred with American tastes and sometimes physiques. Swedish beds were narrow and measured in centimeters. IKEA did not sell the matching bedroom suites that Americans liked. Its kitchen cupboards were too narrow for large dinner plates. Its glasses were too small for a nation that adds ice to everything. And the drawers in IKEA's bedroom chests were too shallow for American consumers, who tend to store sweaters in them.

In 1990 the company's top management realized that if it was going to succeed in North America, it would have to customize its product offering to North American tastes. The company redesigned its product range. The drawers on bedroom chests were designed to be two inches deeper—and sales immediately increased by 30 to 40 percent. IKEA now sells American-style king- and queen-sized beds, measured in inches, and it sells them as part of complete bedroom suites. It is redesigning its kitchen furniture and kitchen ware to better appeal to American tastes. The company also boosted the amount of products being sourced locally from 15 percent in 1990 to 45 percent in 1994, a move that makes the company far less vulnerable to adverse movements in exchange rates.

This break with IKEA's traditional strategy has paid off. Between 1990 and 1994 IKEA's North American sales tripled to $480 million, and the company claims it has been making a profit in North America since early 1993. By 1994 the company had also expanded the number of North American stores to 13, and it planned to have 15 open by the end of 1995.[34]

Case Discussion Questions

1 What strategy was IKEA pursuing as it expanded throughout Europe during the 1970s and early 1980s—a multidomestic strategy, a global strategy, or an international strategy?

2 Why do you think this strategy did not work as well in North America as it did in Europe?

3 As of 1995 what strategy is IKEA pursuing? Does this strategy make sense? Can you see any drawbacks with this strategy?

Have Fax Will Travel

At the age of 23 while majoring in marketing at a state university in California, Heather Kinney started the export arm of Gold Source Computers, Inc., a reseller of computer hardware, peripherals, and software. When she started at the firm, her recommendations that the company expand into exporting were met with a great deal of resistance. The firm took the risk only when Heather agreed to sell exclusively to the foreign markets on commission.

If Heather had read the traditional textbooks, she might have been totally demoralized. She was young, spoke no foreign language, had not visited the countries she would be selling to, and had no foreign contacts or connections. On the plus side, she was energetic, enthusiastic, and confident. She was also knowledgeable about her product and a credible spokesperson. She said that if you are going to succeed in marketing globally you have "to learn to think outside

Heather Kinney

the box." You have to take a chance.

She targeted two countries, Germany and Ireland—Germany because of its robust economy and because she had a cousin who worked for Hewlett-Packard there. She thought the contact might be useful. She selected Ireland because her last name is Irish and she could communicate in English. The Irish connection turned out to be a real ice-breaker; in the course of most

telephone conversations prospective clients would remark that Kinney was one of the oldest clans in Ireland.

She generated her leads from a variety of sources: the yellow pages from the large cities in these countries, subscriptions to personal computer magazines in the foreign countries, Frost and Sullivan Reports. From the *Export Interest Directory*, a listing of U.S. companies that are interested in exporting their products and/or services internationally, she learned about the competition, what they were exporting and where. The Irish Trade Board developed a promotional packet which contained information about a company that turned out to be one of her best customers. She attended Comdex, the largest electronics and computer tradeshow in the United States According to Heather, "Comdex is a magnet for international dealers and distributors, and I felt like the foreigner." At the trade show she collected literature that foreign companies had developed to market themselves and used it as a source of telephone, fax, and other information about potential customers.

Having compiled a list of contacts, she faxed a form to 500 prospects. The sales did not come overnight. First she had to build trust electronically, which she identified as one of the most critical determinants of her success. To build this trust she telephoned her prospects to establish a rapport. She was pleasant and personable and took a real interest in the people on the other end of the line. Her approach was to first ask about the company and then to ask about the people. Heather believes that "people enjoy talking about themselves." She has made many friends electronically.

Frequent contact and follow-up were also important for building trust electronically. She would send the customers new product information, information on specials, and lots of promotional material. She would then immediately follow up on their requests for information.

She always treated the customer as part of her selling team rather than the object of her selling efforts. "You can't sell without them." Heather would often provide her customers with information about U.S. market trends. For example, if the price of memory chips dropped she passed along the information. More often than not, within a couple of weeks the same thing happened abroad. The customers were grateful for the insight and came to trust Heather more readily.

Within three months, Heather received her first wire transfer of $20,000 for a shipment of 300 CD-ROMs from Ireland from someone she had never seen for a product that had not yet been shipped. Heather had succeeded in building trust electronically.

The firm now sells its products to Ireland, Germany, the United Kingdom, and Norway, still using the techniques Heather introduced.

Helena Czepiec
California State Polytechnic University, Pomona

Chapter 11
Entering Foreign Markets

©PhotoDisc

Opening Case

Artais Weather Check

Artais Weather Check, Inc., is a small Ohio company with 1994 sales of just $5.5 million. It is also a company that is riding the back of a boom in exports for its main product—an automated weather observation system, or AWOS, for small airports. Artais' AWOS system records runway conditions such as wind speed, direction, and temperature and converts the data into a voice message that pilots can listen to. Only three other companies besides Artais have been certified by the U.S. Federal Aviation

Learning Objectives:

1 Identify the different modes that firms use to enter a foreign market.
2 Understand the advantages and disadvantages of each entry mode.

3 Appreciate the relationship between strategy and a firm's choice of entry mode.
4 Appreciate some pitfalls of exporting.

5 Be familiar with the steps a firm can take to improve its export performance.
6 Have a good grasp of the mechanics of export and import financing.

Administration to produce the equipment, and Artais dominates the market with a share of over 80 percent.

Unfortunately for Artais, the U.S. market for automated weather observation systems is extremely small. Although there are 18,000 public and private airports in the country, the largest have round-the-clock human weather watchers, while most of the smaller airports cannot afford the $45,000 to $60,000 required to install an AWOS system. Thus, by 1993

only 400 U.S. airports had purchased automatic weather observation systems, and the prospects for growth in the United States seemed to be limited to sales of about 75 systems per year nationwide.

To continue to grow the company's revenues, Artais has increasingly looked toward export sales. From slow beginnings in the late 1980s, Artais' exports have surged to account for close to two-thirds of the company's total revenues. However, to get foreign orders Artais has had to deal

with frustrations it never encountered at home. The first problem it came up against was one of name recognition. Although Artais is well known within the United States, the company found that its name recognition was close to zero overseas. Another problem involves subsidized competition; according to Artais, in some foreign markets its main competitors are subsidized by their government in an attempt to protect jobs. Artais has also found that it needs to customize its products for foreign markets. To sell its systems in Egypt, for example, its system had to be reprogrammed to relay weather information in Arabic as well as English. Customers also require that a cache of spare parts be located close by and that Artais employees install the equipment and provide on-site training, all of which raises Artais' costs of doing business.

Political factors have also had a major impact on the outcome of some deals. For example, after working hard to secure a deal in Romania, Artais unexpectedly saw the deal fall through at the last moment. Instead, the deal went to a German competitor. According to some locals, the Romanian government, eager to improve trading relations with the European Union, gave the job to the German company in an attempt to curry favor with the trading bloc's most powerful member.

Despite problems such as these, Artais has sold systems to airports in Taiwan, China, Ecuador, Saudi Arabia, and Egypt. Moreover, Artais has found that such overseas contracts can be more lucrative than its domestic sales because of all the extras such as spare parts, installation fees, and training. The value of the foreign contracts has ranged from $200,000 to $2 million, compared with $45,000 to $60,000 in the United States. Artais can now see the day when almost all its revenues will be generated by sales outside of the United States.[1]

Introduction

As suggested by the opening case, this chapter is about entering foreign markets. Artais' foreign market entry strategy involves exporting. However, exporting is not the only way of entering foreign markets. Other entry modes include licensing or franchising to a host country firm, entering into a joint venture with a host country firm, and establishing a wholly owned subsidiary in a host country to serve that market. Each option has different advantages and disadvantages associated with it. In this chapter we look at how the advantages and disadvantages associated with each entry mode are determined by a number of factors, including transport costs, trade barriers, political risks, economic risks, and firm strategy. As we will discover, the best entry mode to adopt varies from situation to situation depending on these various factors.

Although we review a variety of entry modes in this chapter, we shall discuss exporting in more depth than we discuss the other entry modes. We will review the "nuts and bolts" of exporting because most firms start as exporters, and only later switch to other entry modes. As we can see from the opening case, exporting is not an activity just for large multinational enterprises; many small firms such as Artais have benefited significantly from exporting. Artais is merely part of a much wider story of the money-making opportunities of exporting discovered by small and medium-sized enterprises. In the United States, for example, 49 percent of companies with annual revenues of less than $100 million said they exported products in 1993, up from 36 percent of such companies in 1990.[2] However, the United States is still behind a number of other countries in this regard. In Germany, for example, companies with less than 500 employees account for about 30 percent of that nation's exports. The comparable figure in the United States is 10 percent.[3]

Evidence suggests the volume of export activity in the world economy, by firms of all sizes, is likely to increase in the foreseeable future. One reason for this is that exporting has become easier over the years. The gradual decline in trade barriers under the umbrella of GATT and now the WTO along with regional economic agreements such as the European Union and the

North American Free Trade Agreement have significantly increased export opportunities. At the same time, modern communications and transportation technologies have alleviated the logistical problems associated with exporting. Firms are increasingly using fax machines, international 800 numbers, and international air express services to reduce the costs of exporting. As a consequence, it is no longer unusual to find small companies such as Artais that are thriving as exporters.

Nevertheless, exporting remains a difficult challenge for many firms. While large multinational enterprises have long been conversant with the steps to exporting successfully, smaller enterprises can find the process intimidating. The firm wishing to export must identify foreign market opportunities, avoid a host of unanticipated problems that are often associated with doing business in a foreign market, familiarize itself with the mechanics of export and import financing, learn where it can get financing and export credit insurance, and learn how it should deal with foreign exchange risk. The whole process is made all the more problematic by nonconvertible currencies. As a result, firms must arrange payment for exports to countries with weak currencies.

Entry Modes

A firm considering entering a foreign market must decide the best means of doing so. There are basically six different ways to enter a foreign market:

- Exporting.
- Turnkey projects.
- Licensing.
- Franchising.
- Establishing a joint venture with a host country firm.
- Setting up a wholly owned subsidiary in the host country.

Each entry mode has advantages and disadvantages. Managers need to consider these carefully when deciding which entry mode to use.[4]

Exporting

Most manufacturing firms begin their global expansion as exporters and only later switch to another mode for serving a foreign market. We take a close look at the mechanics and processing of exporting later in this chapter. Here we focus on the advantages and disadvantages of exporting as an entry mode.

ADVANTAGES Exporting has two distinct advantages. The first is that it avoids the often substantial cost of establishing manufacturing operations in the host country. Second, exporting may help a firm achieve experience curve and location economies (see Chapter 10). By manufacturing the product in a centralized location and exporting it to other national markets, the firm may be able to realize substantial scale economies from its global sales volume. This is how Sony came to dominate the global TV market, how

Matsushita came to dominate the VCR market, and how many Japanese auto firms made inroads into the U.S. auto market.

DISADVANTAGES   On the other hand, exporting has a number of drawbacks. First, exporting from the firm's home base may not be appropriate if there are lower-cost locations for manufacturing the product abroad (i.e., if the firm can realize location economies by moving production elsewhere). Thus, particularly for firms pursuing global or transnational strategies, it may be preferable to manufacture in a location where the mix of factor conditions is most favorable from a value creation perspective and to export to the rest of the world from that location. This is not so much an argument against exporting as an argument against exporting from the firm's home country. Many U.S. electronics firms have moved some of their manufacturing to the Far East due to the availability of low-cost, highly skilled labor there. They then export from that location to the rest of the world, including the United States.

A second drawback to exporting is that high transport costs can make exporting uneconomical, particularly for bulk products. One way to get around this is to manufacture bulk products regionally. This strategy enables the firm to realize some economies from large-scale production and at the same time to limit its transport costs. For example, many multinational chemical firms manufacture their products regionally, serving several countries from one facility.

Another drawback to exporting is that tariff barriers can make it uneconomical. Similarly, the threat of tariff barriers by the host country government can make it very risky. It was an implicit threat of the U.S. Congress to impose tariffs on imported Japanese autos that led to many Japanese auto firms' decisions to set up manufacturing plants in the United States. As a consequence, by 1990 almost 50 percent of all Japanese cars sold in the United States were manufactured locally—up from 0 percent in 1985.

A fourth drawback to exporting arises when a firm delegates its marketing in each country where it does business to a local agent. (This is common for firms that are just beginning to export.) Foreign agents often carry the products of competing firms and, as a result, have divided loyalties. In such cases, the foreign agent may not do as good a job as the firm would if it managed its marketing itself. There are ways around this problem, however. One way is to set up a wholly owned subsidiary in the country to handle local marketing. By doing this, the firm can exercise tight control over marketing in the country while reaping the cost advantages of manufacturing the product in a single location.

Turnkey Projects

turnkey project
Contractor handles every detail of the project for a foreign client, including the training of operating personnel, and then hands the foreign client the key to a plant that is ready for operation.

Firms that specialize in the design, construction, and start-up of turnkey plants are common in some industries. In a **turnkey project**, the contractor agrees to handle every detail of the project for a foreign client, including the training of operating personnel. At completion of the contract, the foreign client is handed the "key" to a plant that is ready for full operation—hence the term *turnkey*. This is actually a means of exporting process technology to other countries. In a sense it is just a very specialized kind of exporting. Turnkey projects are most common in the chemical, pharmaceutical, petroleum refining, and metal refining industries, all of which use complex, expensive production-process technologies.

ADVANTAGES The know-how required to assemble and run a technologically complex process, such as refining petroleum or steel, is a valuable asset. The main advantage of turnkey projects is that they are a way of earning great economic returns from that asset. The strategy is particularly useful in cases where foreign direct investment (FDI) is limited by host government regulations. For example, the governments of many oil-rich countries have set out to build their own petroleum refining industries and, as a step toward that goal, have restricted FDI in their oil and refining sectors. Because many of these countries lacked petroleum refining technology, however, they had to gain it by entering into turnkey projects with foreign firms that had the technology. Such deals are often attractive to the selling firm, since without them, they would probably have no way to earn a return on their valuable know-how in that country.

Also, a turnkey strategy, as opposed to a more conventional type of FDI, may make sense in a country where the political and economic environment is such that a longer-term investment might expose the firm to unacceptable political and/or economic risks (e.g., the risk of nationalization or of economic collapse).

DISADVANTAGES Three main drawbacks are associated with a turnkey strategy. First, by definition, the firm that enters into a turnkey deal will have no long-term interest in the foreign country. This can be a disadvantage if that country subsequently proves to be a major market for the output of the process that has been exported. One way around this is to take a minority equity interest in the operation set up by the turnkey project.

Second, the firm that enters into a turnkey project with a foreign enterprise may create a competitor. For example, many of the Western firms that sold oil refining technology to firms in Saudi Arabia, Kuwait, and other Gulf states now find themselves competing head to head with these firms in the world oil market. Third, and related to the second point, if the firm's process technology is a source of competitive advantage, then selling this technology through a turnkey project is also selling competitive advantage to potential and/or actual competitors.

Licensing

A **licensing agreement** is an arrangement whereby a licensor grants the rights to intangible property to another entity (the licensee) for a specified time period, and in return, the licensor receives a royalty fee from the licensee.[5] Intangible property includes patents, inventions, formulas, processes, designs, copyrights, and trademarks.

licensing agreement Arrangement whereby a licensor grants the rights to intangible property to the licensee for a specified time period in exchange for royalties.

ADVANTAGES In the typical international licensing deal, the licensee puts up most of the capital necessary to get the overseas operation going. Thus, a primary advantage of licensing is that the firm does not have to bear the development costs and risks associated with opening a foreign market. Licensing is a very attractive option for firms lacking the capital to develop operations overseas. In addition, licensing can be attractive when a firm is unwilling to commit substantial financial resources to an unfamiliar or politically volatile foreign market. Licensing is also often used when a firm wishes to participate in a foreign market, but is prohibited from doing so by barriers to investment. Finally, licensing is frequently used when a firm possesses some intangible property that might have business applications, but it does not want to develop those applications itself. For example, Bell Laboratories at AT&T originally invented the transistor circuit in the 1950s, but AT&T decided it did not want to produce transistors, so it licensed the technology to a number of other companies, such as Texas Instruments. Similarly, Coca-Cola has licensed its famous trademark to clothing manufacturers, which have incorporated the design into their clothing.

DISADVANTAGES Licensing has three serious drawbacks. First, it does not give a firm the tight control over manufacturing, marketing, and strategy that is required for realizing experience curve and location economies (as global and transnational firms must do; see Chapter 10). Licensing typically involves each licensee setting up its own manufacturing operations. This severely limits the firm's ability to realize experience curve and location economies by manufacturing its product in a centralized location. Thus, when these economies are important, licensing may not be the best way to expand overseas.

Second, competing in a global market may require a firm to coordinate strategic moves across countries by using profits earned in one country to support competitive attacks in another (again, see Chapter 10). Licensing severely limits a firm's ability to do this. A licensee is unlikely to allow a multinational firm to use its profits (beyond those due in the form of royalty payments) to support a different licensee operating in another country.

A third problem with licensing is one that we first encountered in Chapter 6 when we reviewed the economic theory of FDI. This is the risk associated with licensing technological know-how to foreign companies. Technological know-how constitutes the competitive advantage of many multinational firms. Most firms wish to maintain control over how their know-how is used, and a firm can quickly lose control over its technology by licensing it. Many firms have made the mistake of thinking they could maintain control over their know-how within the framework of a licensing agreement. RCA Corporation, for example, once licensed its color TV technology to a number of Japanese firms, including Matsushita and Sony. The Japanese firms quickly assimilated the technology, improved on it, and used it to enter the U.S. market. Now the Japanese firms have a bigger share of the U.S. market than the RCA brand. Similar concerns surfaced over the 1989 decision by Congress to allow Japanese firms to produce the advanced FSX fighter plane under license from McDonnell-Douglas. Critics of the decision fear the Japanese will use the FSX technology to support the development of a commercial airline industry that will compete with Boeing and McDonnell-Douglas in the global marketplace.

But there are ways of reducing the risks of this occurring. One way is by entering into a cross-licensing agreement with a foreign firm. Under a **cross-licensing agreement**, a firm might license some valuable intangible property to a foreign partner, but in addition to a royalty payment, the firm might also request that the foreign partner license some of its valuable know-how to the firm. Such agreements are reckoned to reduce the risks associated with licensing technological know-how, since the licensee realizes that if it violates the spirit of a licensing contract (by using the knowledge obtained to com-

cross-licensing agreement Arrangement whereby a company grants the rights to intangible property to another firm for a specified time period in exchange for royalties and a license from the foreign partners for some of its technological know-how.

pete directly with the licensor), the licensor can do the same to it. Cross-licensing agreements enable firms to hold each other "hostage," thereby reducing the probability that they will behave opportunistically toward each other.[6] Such cross-licensing agreements are increasingly common in high-technology industries. For example, the U.S. biotechnology firm Amgen has licensed one of its key drugs, Nuprogene, to Kirin, the Japanese pharmaceutical company. The license gives Kirin the right to sell Nuprogene in Japan. In return, Amgen receives a royalty payment and the right to sell certain Kirin products in the United States.

Another way of reducing the risk associated with licensing is to link an agreement to license know-how with the formation of a joint venture in which the licensor and licensee take an important equity stake. Such an approach aligns the interests of licensor and licensee, since both have a stake in ensuring that the venture is successful. The highly successful joint venture between Fuji Photo and Xerox Corp., Fuji–Xerox, is structured in this manner. Xerox licensed its photocopier technology to Fuji–Xerox, which produces photocopiers for the Asian market. The risk that Fuji Photo might appropriate Xerox's technological know-how, and then compete directly against Xerox in the global photocopier market, was reduced by the establishment of a joint venture in which both Xerox and Fuji Photo had an important stake (for further details, see the accompanying "Management Focus").

Franchising

Franchising is basically a specialized form of licensing in which the franchisor not only sells intangible property to the franchisee (normally a trademark), but also insists that the franchisee agree to abide by strict rules as to how it does business. The franchisor will also often assist the franchisee to run the business on an ongoing basis. As with licensing, the franchisor typically receives a royalty payment that amounts to some percentage of the franchisee's revenues. Whereas licensing is pursued primarily by manufacturing firms, franchising is employed primarily by service firms.[8] McDonald's has grown by using a franchising strategy. McDonald's has set down strict rules as to how franchisees should operate a restaurant. These rules extend to control over the menu, cooking methods, staffing policies, and the design and location of a restaurant. McDonald's also organizes the supply chain for its franchisees and provides management training and financial assistance for franchisees.[9]

franchising
Specialized form of licensing in which the franchisor sells intangible property to the franchisee and insists that the franchisee agree to follow strict rules in operating the business.

ADVANTAGES   The advantages of franchising as an entry mode are very similar to those of licensing. Specifically, the firm is relieved of many of the costs and risks of opening a foreign market on its own. Instead, the franchisee typically assumes those costs and risks. This creates a good incentive for the franchisee to build a profitable operation as quickly as possible. Thus, using a franchising strategy, a service firm can build up a global presence quickly and at a relatively low cost and risk, as McDonald's has.

DISADVANTAGES   The disadvantages are less pronounced than in the case of licensing. Since franchising is often used by service companies, there is no reason to consider the need for coordination of manufacturing to achieve experience curve and location economies. On the other hand, franchising

Fuji–Xerox is one of the most enduring and reportedly successful joint ventures between two companies from different countries. Established in 1962, today Fuji–Xerox is structured as a 50/50 joint venture between the Xerox Group, the U.S. maker of photocopiers, and Fuji Photo Film, Japan's largest manufacturer of film products. With 1994 sales of close to $8 billion, Fuji–Xerox provides Xerox with over 20 percent of its worldwide revenues.

A prime motivation for establishment of the joint venture was

revised to give Fuji–Xerox manufacturing rights. Day-to-day management of the venture was placed in the hands of a Japanese management team who were given considerable autonomy to develop their own operations and strategy, subject to oversight by a board of directors that contained representatives from both Xerox and Fuji Photo.

Initially, Fuji–Xerox followed the lead of Xerox in manufacturing and selling the large, high-volume copiers developed by Xerox in the United States. These

its own against a blizzard of new competition in Japan that followed the expiration of many of Xerox's key patents.

Around the same time, Fuji–Xerox also embarked on a total quality control (TQC) program. The aims of the program were to speed up development of new products, reduce waste, improve quality, and lower manufacturing costs. The first fruit of this program was the FX3500. Introduced in 1977, by 1979 the FX3500 had broken the Japanese record for the number of copiers

Fuji-Xerox

that in the early 1960s the Japanese government did not allow foreign companies to set up wholly owned subsidiaries in Japan. The joint venture was conceived of as a marketing organization to sell xerographic products that would be manufactured by Fuji Photo under license from Xerox. However, when the Japanese government refused to approve establishment of a joint venture intended solely as a sales company, the joint-venture agreement was

machines were sold at a premium price to the high end of the market. However, Fuji–Xerox noticed that in the Japanese market new competitors, such as Canon and Ricoh, were making significant inroads by building small, low-volume copiers and focusing on the mid- and low-priced segments of the market. This led to Fuji–Xerox's development of its first "homegrown" copier, the FX2200, which at the time was billed as the world's smallest copier. Introduced in 1973, the FX2200 hit the market just in time to allow Fuji–Xerox to hold

sold in one year. Partly because of the success of the FX3500, in 1980 the company won Japan's prestigious Demming Prize. The success of the FX3500 was all the more notable because at the same time Xerox was canceling a series of programs to develop low- to mid-level copiers and reaffirming its commitment to serving the high end of the market. Because of these cancellations, Tony Kobayashi, the CEO of Fuji–Xerox, was initially told to stop work on development of the FX3500. He refused, arguing that the FX3500 was crucial for the

may inhibit the firm's ability to take profits out of one country to support competitive attacks in another.

A more significant disadvantage of franchising is quality control. The foundation of franchising arrangements is that the firm's brand name conveys a message to consumers about the quality of the firm's product. Thus, a business traveler checking in at a Hilton International hotel in Hong Kong can reasonably expect the same quality of room, food, and service that she would receive in New York. The Hilton name is supposed to guarantee consistent survival of Fuji–Xerox in the Japanese market. Given the arm's-length relationship between Xerox and Fuji–Xerox, Kobayashi prevailed.

By the early 1980s Fuji–Xerox was number two in the Japanese copier market with a share in the 20 to 22 percent range, just behind that of market leader Canon. In contrast, Xerox was running into all sorts of problems in the U.S. market. As Xerox's patents expired, a number of companies, including Canon, Ricoh, Kodak, and IBM, began to take market share from Xerox. Canon and Ricoh were particularly successful by focusing on that segment of the market that Xerox had ignored—the low end. As a result, Xerox's market share in the Americas fell from 35 percent in 1975 to 25 percent in 1980, while its profitability slumped.

To recapture share, Xerox began to sell Fuji–Xerox's FX3500 copier in the United States. Not only did the FX3500 help Xerox to halt the rapid decline in its share of the U.S. market, but it also opened Xerox's eyes to the benefits of Fuji–Xerox's TQC program. Xerox found that the reject rate for Fuji–Xerox parts was only a fraction of the reject rate for American-produced parts. Visits to Fuji–Xerox revealed another important truth: quality in manufacturing doesn't increase real costs—it reduces costs by reducing defective products and service costs.

These developments forced Xerox to rethink the way it did business. From being the main provider of products, technology, and management know-how to Fuji–Xerox, Xerox became the willing pupil of Fuji–Xerox in the 1980s. In 1983 Xerox introduced its Leadership Through Quality program, which was based on Fuji–Xerox's TQC program. As part of this effort, Xerox launched a quality training effort with its suppliers and was rewarded when the number of defective parts from suppliers fell from 25,000 per million in 1983 to 300 per million by 1992.

In 1985 and 1986 Xerox began to focus on its new-product development process. One goal was to design products that while customized to market conditions in different countries also contained a large number of globally standardized parts. Another goal was to reduce the time it took to design new products and bring them to market. To achieve these goals Xerox set up joint product development teams with Fuji–Xerox. Each team managed the design, component sources, manufacturing, distribution, and follow-up customer service on a worldwide basis. The use of design teams cut as much as one year from the overall product development cycle and saved millions of dollars.

One consequence of the new approach to product development was the 5100 copier. This was the first product designed jointly by Xerox and Fuji–Xerox for the worldwide market. The 5100 is manufactured in U.S. plants. It was launched in Japan in November 1990 and the United States the following February. The 5100's global design reportedly reduced the overall time to market and saved the company more than $10 million in development costs.

As a result of the skills and products acquired from Fuji–Xerox, Xerox's position improved markedly during the 1980s. Due to its improved quality, lower costs, shorter product development time, and more appealing product range, Xerox was able to gain market share back from its competitors and to boost its profits and revenues. Xerox's share of the U.S. copier market increased from a low of 10 percent in 1985 to 18 percent in 1991.[7]

---

product quality. This presents a problem in that foreign franchisees may not be as concerned about quality as they are supposed to be, and the result of poor quality can extend beyond lost sales in a particular foreign market to a decline in the firm's worldwide reputation. For example, if the business traveler has a bad experience at the Hilton in Hong Kong, she may never go to another Hilton hotel and may urge her colleagues to do likewise. The geographical distance of the firm from its foreign franchisees, however, can make poor quality difficult for the franchisor to detect. In addition, the sheer number of franchisees—in the case of McDonald's, tens of thousands—can make quality control difficult. Due to these factors, quality problems may persist.

One way around this disadvantage is to set up a subsidiary in each country or region in which the firm expands. The subsidiary might be wholly owned by the company or a joint venture with a foreign company. In either case, the subsidiary assumes the rights and obligations to establish franchises throughout the particular country or region. McDonald's, for example, establishes a master franchisee in many countries. Typically, this master franchisee is a joint venture between McDonald's and a local firm. The combination of proximity and the smaller number of franchises to oversee reduces the quality control challenge. In addition, because the subsidiary (or master franchisee) is at least partly owned by the firm, the firm can place its own managers in the subsidiary to help ensure it is monitoring the franchises in that country or region. This organizational arrangement has proven very satisfactory in practice, and it also has been used by Kentucky Fried Chicken, Hilton International, and others to expand their international operations.

Joint Ventures

joint venture
Establishment of a firm that is jointly owned by two or more otherwise independent firms.

A **joint venture** entails establishment of a firm that is jointly owned by two or more otherwise independent firms. Fuji–Xerox, for example, was set up as a joint venture between Xerox and Fuji Photo. Establishing a joint venture with a foreign firm has long been a popular mode for entering a new market. The most typical joint venture is a 50/50 venture, in which there are two parties, each of which holds a 50 percent ownership stake (as is the case with Fuji–Xerox) and contributes a team of managers to share operating control. Some firms, however, have sought joint ventures in which they have a majority share and thus tighter control.[10]

ADVANTAGES   Joint ventures have a number of advantages. First, a firm can benefit from a local partner's knowledge of the host country's competitive conditions, culture, language, political systems, and business systems. For many U.S. firms, joint ventures have involved the U.S. company providing technological know-how and products and the local partner providing the marketing expertise and the local knowledge necessary for competing in that country. This was the case with the Fuji–Xerox joint venture profiled in the "Management Focus." Second, when the development costs and/or risks of opening a foreign market are high, a firm might gain by sharing these costs and/or risks with a local partner. Third, in many countries, political considerations make joint ventures the only feasible entry mode. Again, this was a consideration in establishment of the Fuji–Xerox venture. Furthermore, research suggests that joint ventures with local partners face a low risk of being subject to nationalization or other forms of government interference.[11] This appears to be because local equity partners, who may have some influence on host government policy, have a vested interest in speaking out against nationalization or government interference.

DISADVANTAGES   Despite these advantages, there are two major disadvantages with joint ventures. First, just as with licensing, a firm that enters into a joint venture risks giving control of its technology to its partner. The joint venture between Boeing and a consortium of Japanese firms to build the 767 airliner raised fears that Boeing was unwittingly giving away its commercial airline technology to the Japanese. However, joint-venture agreements can be constructed to minimize this risk. One option is to hold majority ownership in the venture. This allows the dominant partner to exercise greater control over its technology. The drawback with this is that it can be difficult to find a foreign partner who is willing to settle for minority ownership.

A second disadvantage is that a joint venture does not give a firm the tight control over subsidiaries that it might need to realize experience curve or location economies. Nor does it give a firm the tight control over a foreign subsidiary that it might need for engaging in coordinated global attacks against its rivals. Consider the entry of Texas Instruments (TI) into the Japanese semiconductor market. When TI established semiconductor facilities in Japan, it did so for the dual purpose of checking Japanese manufacturers' market share and limiting their cash available for invading TI's global market. In other words, TI was engaging in global strategic coordination. To implement this strategy, TI's subsidiary in Japan had to be prepared to take instructions from corporate headquarters regarding competitive strategy. The strategy also required the Japanese subsidiary to run at a loss if necessary. Few if any potential joint-venture partners would have been willing to accept such conditions, since it would have necessitated a willingness to accept a negative return on their investment. Thus, to implement this strategy, TI set up a wholly owned subsidiary in Japan.

A third disadvantage with joint ventures is that the shared ownership arrangement can lead to conflicts and battles for control between the investing firms if their goals and objectives change over time, or if they take different views as to what the venture's strategy should be. This has apparently not been a problem with the Fuji–Xerox joint venture. According to Tony Kobayashi, the CEO of Fuji–Xerox, a primary reason for this is that both Xerox and Fuji Photo adopted a very arm's-length relationship with Fuji–Xerox, giving the venture's managers considerable freedom to determine their own strategy.[12] However, conflicts of interest that can ultimately result in the dissolution of a venture have apparently been a serious problem in many other joint ventures.[13]

Wholly Owned Subsidiaries

In a **wholly owned subsidiary**, the firm owns 100 percent of the stock. Establishing a wholly owned subsidiary in a foreign market can be done two ways. The firm can either set up a new operation in that country or it can acquire an established firm and use that firm to promote its products in the country's market.

wholly owned subsidiary Company in which the parent firm owns 100 percent of the stock.

ADVANTAGES There are three clear advantages of wholly owned subsidiaries. First, when a firm's competitive advantage is based on technological competence, a wholly owned subsidiary will often be the preferred entry mode, since it reduces the risk of losing control over that competence. (See Chapter 6 for more details.) For this reason, many high-tech firms prefer this entry mode for overseas expansion (e.g., firms in the semiconductor, electronics, and pharmaceutical industries). Second, a wholly owned subsidiary gives a firm the tight control over operations in different countries that is necessary for engaging in global strategic coordination (i.e., using profits from one country to support competitive attacks in another). Third, a wholly owned subsidiary may be required if a firm is trying to realize location and experience curve economies (as firms pursuing global and transnational strategies try to do). As we saw in Chapter 10, when cost pressures are intense, it may pay a firm to configure its value chain in such a way that the value added at each stage is maximized. Thus, a national subsidiary may specialize in manufacturing only part of the product line or certain components of the end product, exchanging parts and products with other subsidiaries in the firm's global system. Establishing such a global production system requires a high degree of control over the operations of each affiliate. The various operations must be prepared to accept centrally determined decisions as to how they will produce, how much they will produce, and how their output will be priced for transfer to the next operation. Since licensees or joint-venture partners are unlikely to accept such a subservient role, wholly owned subsidiaries may be necessary.

DISADVANTAGES   On the other hand, establishing a wholly owned subsidiary is generally the most costly method of serving a foreign market. Firms doing this must bear the full costs and risks of setting up overseas operations. The risks associated with learning to do business in a new culture are less if the firm acquires an established host country enterprise. However, acquisitions raise a whole set of additional problems, including those associated with trying to marry divergent corporate cultures. These problems may more than offset any benefits derived by acquiring an established operation.[14]

Selecting an Entry Mode

As the preceding discussion demonstrated, there are advantages and disadvantages associated with all the entry modes; they are summarized in Table 11.1. Due to these advantages and disadvantages, trade-offs are inevitable when selecting an entry mode. For example, when considering entry into an unfamiliar country with a track record for nationalizing foreign-owned enterprises, a firm might favor a joint venture with a local enterprise. Its rationale might be that the local partner will help it establish operations in an unfamiliar environment and will speak out against nationalization should the possibility arise. However, if the firm's core competency is based on proprietary technology, entering a joint venture might risk losing control of that technology to the venture partner—in which case the strategy may seem very unattractive. Despite the existence of such trade-offs, it is possible to generalize about the optimal choice of entry mode. That is what we do in this section.[15]

Core Competencies and Entry Mode

We saw in Chapter 10 that firms often expand internationally to earn greater returns from their core competencies—transferring the skills and products derived from their core competencies to foreign markets where indigenous competitors lack those skills. We say that such firms are pursuing an international strategy. The best entry mode for these firms depends to some de-

TABLE 11.1

Advantages and Disadvantages of Entry Modes

Entry Mode	Advantage	Disadvantage
Exporting	Ability to realize location and experience curve economies	High transport costs Trade barriers Problems with local marketing agents
Turnkey contracts	Ability to earn returns from process technology skills in countries where FDI is restricted	Creating efficient competitors Lack of long-term market presence
Licensing	Low development costs and risks	Lack of control over technology Inability to realize location and experience curve economies Inability to engage in global strategic coordination
Franchising	Low development costs and risks	Lack of control over quality Inability to engage in global strategic coordination
Joint ventures	Access to local partner's knowledge Sharing development costs and risks Politically acceptable	Lack of control over technology Inability to engage in global strategic coordination Inability to realize location and experience economies
Wholly owned subsidiaries	Protection of technology Ability to engage in global strategic coordination Ability to realize location and experience economies	High costs and risks

gree on the nature of their core competencies. A distinction can be drawn between firms whose core competency is in technological know-how and those whose core competency is in management know-how.

TECHNOLOGICAL KNOW-HOW As was initially observed in Chapter 6, if a firm's competitive advantage (its core competency) is based on control over proprietary technological know-how, licensing and joint-venture arrangements should be avoided so the risk of losing control over that technology is minimized. Thus, if a high-tech firm sets up operations in a foreign country to profit from a core competency in technological know-how, it will probably do so through a wholly owned subsidiary.

This rule should not be viewed as hard and fast, however. One exception is when a licensing or joint-venture arrangement can be structured so as to reduce the risks of a firm's technological know-how being expropriated by licensees or joint-venture partners. We will see how this might be achieved later in the chapter when we examine the structuring of strategic alliances. Another exception exists when a firm perceives its technological advantage to be only transitory—when it expects rapid imitation of its core technology by competitors. In such cases, the firm might want to license its technology as rapidly as possible to foreign firms to gain global acceptance for its technology before the imitation occurs.[16] Such a strategy has some advantages. By licensing its technology to competitors, the firm may deter them from developing their own, possibly superior, technology. Further, by licensing its technology, the firm may be able to establish its technology as the dominant design in the industry (as Matsushita did with its VHS format for VCRs). In turn, this may ensure a steady stream of royalty payments. Such situations apart, however, the attractions of licensing are probably outweighed by the risks of losing control over technology, and thus licensing should be avoided.

MANAGEMENT KNOW-HOW   The competitive advantage of many service firms is based on management know-how (e.g., McDonald's, Hilton International). For such firms, the risk of losing control over their management skills to franchisees or joint-venture partners is not that great. These firms' valuable asset is their brand name, and brand names are generally well protected by international laws pertaining to trademarks. Given this, many of the issues arising in the case of technological know-how are of less concern here. As a result, many service firms favor a combination of franchising and subsidiaries to control the franchises within particular countries or regions. The subsidiaries may be wholly owned or joint ventures, but most service firms have found that joint ventures with local partners work best for the controlling subsidiaries. This is because a joint venture is often politically more acceptable and brings a degree of local knowledge to the subsidiary.

Pressures for Cost Reductions and Entry Mode

The greater the pressures for cost reductions, the more likely a firm will want to pursue some combination of exporting and wholly owned subsidiaries. By manufacturing in those locations where factor conditions are optimal and then exporting to the rest of the world, a firm may be able to realize substantial location and experience curve economies. The firm might then want to export the finished product to marketing subsidiaries based in various countries. These subsidiaries will typically be wholly owned and have the responsibility for overseeing distribution in their particular countries. Setting up wholly owned marketing subsidiaries is preferable to joint-venture arrangements and to using foreign marketing agents because it gives the firm the tight control over marketing that might be required for coordinating a globally dispersed value chain. It also gives the firm the ability to use the profits generated in one market to improve its competitive position in another market. In other words, firms pursuing global or transnational strategies tend to prefer establishing wholly owned subsidiaries.

The Promise and Pitfalls of Exporting

As noted earlier, most firms initially start their international expansion by exporting. For most firms in most industries there are huge revenue and profit opportunities to be found in foreign markets. The case of Artais is instructive here. Artais is a company with a very solid competitive position in the United States, including an 80 percent share of the U.S. market for automated weather observing systems, but that alone was insufficient to guarantee continued strong growth in revenues and profits. The company found, however, that the opportunities for growth in foreign markets can more than make up for any lack of opportunities in the United States. What is true for Artais is also true for a large number of other enterprises of all sizes based in many other countries. The international market is normally so much larger than the firm's domestic market that exporting is nearly always a way of increasing the revenue and profit base of a company.

Despite the opportunities, studies have shown that while many large firms tend to be *proactive* about seeking out opportunities for profitable exporting, systematically scanning foreign markets to see where the opportunities lie for leveraging their technology, products, and marketing skills in foreign countries, many medium-sized and small firms are very *reactive*.[17] Typically such reactive firms do not even consider exporting until their domestic market is saturated and excess productive capacity at home forces them to look for growth opportunities in foreign markets. Also, many small and medium-sized firms tend to wait for the world to come to them, rather than going out into the world to seek opportunities. And even when the world does comes to them, they may not respond. An example is MMO Music Group, which makes sing-along tapes for karaoke machines. Foreign sales accounted for about 15 percent of MMO's 1993 revenues of $8 million, but the firm's CEO admits that this figure would probably have been much higher had he paid attention to building international sales during the 1980s. At that time unanswered faxes and phone messages from Asia and Europe piled up while he was trying to manage the burgeoning domestic side of the business. By the time MMO did turn its attention to foreign markets, other competitors had stepped into the breach and MMO found it tough going to build export volume.[18]

MMO's experience is common, and it suggests a need for firms to become more proactive about seeking export opportunities. One reason more firms are not proactive is that they are very unfamiliar with foreign market opportunities; they simply do not know how big the opportunities actually are, or where they might lie. Ignorance of the potential opportunities is a huge barrier to exporting.[19] Moreover, many would-be exporters are often intimidated by the complexities and mechanics of exporting to countries where business practices, language, culture, legal systems, and currency are all very different from those that managers are used to in their home market.

To make matters worse, many neophyte exporters have run into significant problems when first trying to do business abroad, and this has soured them on future exporting ventures. Common pitfalls include poor market analysis, a poor understanding of competitive conditions in the foreign market, a failure to customize the product offering to the needs of foreign customers, lack of an effective distribution program, and a poorly executed promotional campaign in the foreign market.[20] Neophyte exporters also tend to underestimate the time and expertise needed to cultivate business in foreign countries.[21] Few realize the amount of management resources that have to be dedicated to this activity. Many foreign customers require face-to-face negotiations on their home turf. An exporter may have to spend months learning about a country's trade regulations, business practices, and mores before a deal can be closed.

Moreover, exporters often face voluminous paperwork, complex formalities, and many potential delays and errors. According to a recent United

Nations report on trade and development, a typical international trade transaction may involve 30 different parties, 60 original documents, and 360 document copies, all of which have to be checked, transmitted, re-entered into various information systems, processed, and filed. The United Nations has calculated that the time involved in preparing documentation, along with the costs of common errors in paperwork, often amounts to 10 percent of the final value of goods exported.[22]

Improving Export Performance

There are a number of ways in which inexperienced exporters can gain information about foreign market opportunities and avoid some common pitfalls that tend to discourage and frustrate neophyte exporters. In this section we look at information sources that exporters can use to increase their knowledge of foreign market opportunities, we consider the pros and cons of utilizing export management companies (EMCs) to assist in the export process, and we review various exporting strategies that can be adopted to increase the probability of successful exporting.

Government Information Sources

Most national governments maintain departments that can help firms establish exporting opportunities. In the United States, the most comprehensive source of information is probably the U.S. Department of Commerce and its district offices all over the country. Within that department are two organizations dedicated to providing businesses with intelligence and assistance for attacking foreign markets: the International Trade Administration and its sister, the United States and Foreign Commercial Service Agency. Similar agencies can be found in many other countries.

These agencies provide the potential exporter with a "best prospects" list, which lists the names and addresses of potential distributors in foreign markets along with businesses they are in, the products they handle, and their contact person. In addition, the Department of Commerce has assembled a "comparison shopping service" for 14 countries that are major markets for U.S. exports. For a small fee, a firm can receive a customized market research survey on a product of its choice. This survey provides information on marketability, the competition, comparative prices, distribution channels, and names of potential sales representatives. Each study is conducted on-site by an officer of the U.S. Department of Commerce.

The Department of Commerce also organizes trade events that help potential exporters make foreign contacts and explore export opportunities. The department organizes exhibitions at international trade fairs, which are held regularly in major cities worldwide. The department also has a matchmaker program, in which department representatives accompany groups of U.S. businesspeople abroad to meet with qualified agents, distributors, and customers.

In addition to the Department of Commerce, nearly every state and many large cities maintain active trade commissions whose purpose is to promote exports. Most of these provide business counseling services, information-gathering service, technical assistance, and financing service. Unfortunately, many have fallen victim to budget cuts or to turf battles for political and financial support with other export agencies.

A number of private organizations are also beginning to gear up to provide more assistance to would-be exporters. Commercial banks and major accounting firms are more willing to assist small firms in starting export operations than they were a decade ago. In addition, large multinationals that have been successful in the global arena are typically more than willing to discuss opportunities overseas with the owners or managers of small firms.[23]

Utilizing Export Management Companies

First-time exporters can identify the opportunities associated with exporting and avoid many of the associated pitfalls by hiring an **export management company** (EMC). EMCs are export specialists that act as the export marketing department or international department for their client firms. EMCs normally accept two types of export assignments. They can start exporting operations for a firm with the understanding that the firm will take over operations after they are well established. Or they can perform start-up with the understanding that the EMC will have continuing responsibility for selling the firm's products. Many EMCs specialize in serving firms in particular industries and in particular areas of the world. Thus, one EMC may specialize in selling agricultural products in the Asian market, while another may focus on exporting electronics products to Eastern Europe.

In theory, the advantage of EMCs is that they are experienced specialists who can help the neophyte exporter identify opportunities and avoid common pitfalls. A good EMC will have a network of contacts in potential markets, will have multilingual employees, will have a good knowledge of different business mores, and will be fully conversant with the ins and outs of the exporting process and with local business regulations. However, studies have revealed a large variation in the quality of EMCs.[24] While some perform their functions very well, others appear to add little value to the exporting company. Therefore, an exporter should carefully review a number of EMCs, and check references from an EMC's past clients, before deciding on a particular EMC. Moreover, one drawback of overrelying on EMCs is that the company fails to develop its own exporting capabilities in-house.

export management company Export specialist that acts as the export marketing department or international department for client firms.

373

Chapter 11 Entering Foreign Markets

Exporting Strategy

In addition to utilizing EMCs, a firm can reduce the risks associated with exporting if it is careful about its choice of exporting strategy. Here a few guidelines can help firms to improve their odds of success. For example, 3M, one of the most successful exporting firms in the world, has built its export success on three main principles: enter on a small scale to reduce risks, add additional product lines once the exporting operation starts to become successful, and hire locals to promote the firm's products (3M's export strategy is profiled in the next "Management Focus").

The probability of exporting successfully can be increased dramatically by taking a handful of simple strategic steps. First, particularly for the neophyte exporter, it helps to hire an EMC, or at least an experienced export consul-

Export Strategy at 3M

The Minnesota Mining and Manufacturing Company (3M) is one of the world's great multinational corporations. In 1994 almost half the firm's $15 billion in revenues were generated outside the United States. Although the bulk of these revenues came from foreign-based operations, 3M is a major exporter with $1.5 billion of exports in 1994. Moreover, 3M often uses its exports to establish an initial presence in a foreign market, only building foreign production facilities once sales volume rises to a level where local production is justified.

The export strategy of 3M is built around some very simple principles. One is known as "FIDO," which stands for First In (to a new market) Defeats Others. The essence of FIDO is to gain an advantage over other exporters by getting into a market first and learning about that country, and how to sell there, before others do. A second principle is "make a little, sell a little"—which is the idea of entering on a small scale with a very modest investment and pushing one basic

3M Corporation

product, such as reflective sheeting for traffic signs in the Soviet Union or scouring pads in Hungary. Once 3M believes it has learned enough about the market to reduce the risks of failure to reasonable levels, it adds additional products.

A third principle at 3M is to hire local employees to sell the firm's products. The company normally sets up a local sales subsidiary to handle its export activities in a country. It then staffs this subsidiary with local hires. Its reasoning is that foreign nationals are likely to have a much better idea of how to sell in their own country than

American expatriates. As a result of the implementation of this principle, just 160 of 3M's 39,500 foreign employees are U.S. expatriates.

Another common practice at 3M is to formulate global strategic plans for the export—and eventual overseas production—of its products. Within the context of these plans, 3M gives local managers considerable autonomy to find the best way to sell the product within their particular country. Thus, when 3M first exported its Post-it™ notes in 1981 it planned to "sample the daylights" out of the product, but it also told local managers to find the best way of doing this. Local managers hired office cleaning crews to pass out samples in Britain and Germany. In Italy office products distributors were used to pass out free samples, while in Malaysia local managers employed young women to go from office to office handing out samples of the product. In typical 3M fashion, when the volume of Post-it notes was sufficient to justify it, exports from the United States were replaced by local production. Thus, by 1984 3M found it worthwhile to set up production facilities in France to produce Post-it notes for the European market.

tant, to help with the identification of opportunities and navigate through the tangled web of paperwork and regulations often involved in exporting. Second, it often makes sense to initially focus on one or a few markets. The idea here is to learn about what is required to succeed in those markets before moving on to other markets. In contrast, the firm that enters many different markets at once runs the risk of spreading its limited management resources too thin. The result of such a "shotgun approach" to exporting may be a failure to become established in any one market. Third, as with 3M, it often makes sense to enter a foreign market on a fairly small scale to reduce the costs of any subsequent failure. Most importantly, entering on a small scale gives the firm the time and opportunity to learn about the foreign country before making significant capital commitments to that market. Fourth, the exporter needs to recognize the time and managerial commitment involved in building export sales and should hire additional personnel to oversee this activity lest the existing management of the firm be stretched too thin. Fifth, in many countries it is important to devote a lot of attention to building strong and enduring relationships with local distributors and/or customers. Sixth, as 3M often does, it is important to hire local personnel to help the firm establish itself in a foreign market. After all, local people are likely to have a much greater sense of how to do business in a given country than a manager from an exporting firm that has previously never set foot in that country.

Finally, it is important for the exporter to keep the option of local production in mind. Once exports build up to a sufficient volume to justify cost-efficient local production, the exporting firm should consider establishing production facilities in the foreign market. Such localization helps foster good relations with the foreign country and can lead to greater market acceptance. Exporting is often not an end in itself, but merely a step on the road toward establishment of foreign production (again, 3M provides us with an example of this philosophy).

Export (and Import) Financing

Mechanisms for financing exports and imports have evolved over the centuries in response to a problem that can be particularly acute in international trade: the lack of trust that exists when one must put faith in a stranger. Here we examine the financial devices that have evolved to cope with this problem in the context of international trade: the letter of credit, the draft (or bill of exchange), and the bill of lading. Then we will trace the 14 steps of a typical export–import transaction.

Lack of Trust

Firms engaged in international trade have to trust someone they may have never seen, who lives in a different country, who speaks a different language, who abides by (or does not abide by) a different legal system, and who could be very difficult to track down if he or she defaults on an obligation. Consider, for example, a U.S. firm exporting to a distributor in France. The U.S. businessman might be concerned that if he ships the products to France before he receives payment for them from the French businesswoman, she might take delivery of the products and not pay him for them. Conversely, the French importer might worry that if she pays for the products before they are shipped, the U.S. firm might keep the money and never ship the products— or might ship defective products. In short, neither party to the exchange com-

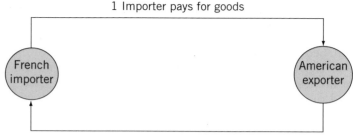

1 Importer pays for goods

French importer

American exporter

2 Exporter ships the goods after being paid

FIGURE 11.1

Preference of the U.S. Exporter

pletely trusts the other. This lack of trust is exacerbated by the distance between the two parties—in space, language, and culture—and by the problems of using an underdeveloped international legal system to enforce contractual obligations.

Due to the (quite reasonable) lack of trust between the two parties, each has his or her own preferences as to how the transaction should be configured. To make sure he is paid, the manager of the U.S. firm would prefer the French distributor to pay for the products before he ships them (see Figure 11.1). Alternatively, to ensure she receives the products, the French distributor would prefer not to pay for them until they arrive (see Figure 11.2). Thus, each party has a different set of preferences. Unless there is some way of establishing trust between the parties, the transaction might never occur.

The problem is solved by using a third party trusted by both—normally a reputable bank—to act as an intermediary. What happens can be summarized as follows (see Figure 11.3). First, the French importer obtains the bank's promise to pay on her behalf, knowing the U.S. exporter will trust the bank. This promise is known as a letter of credit. Having seen the letter of credit, the U.S. exporter now ships the products to France. Title to the products is given, in due course, to the bank in the form of a document called a bill of lading. In return, the U.S. exporter tells the bank to pay for the products, which the bank does. The document for requesting this payment is referred to as a draft. The bank, having paid for the products, now passes the title on to the French importer, whom the bank trusts. At that time or later, depending on their agreement, the importer reimburses the bank. In the remainder of this section, we will examine how this system works in more detail.

Letter of Credit

A letter of credit, abbreviated as L/C, stands at the center of international commercial transactions. Issued by a bank at the request of an importer, the letter of credit states the bank will pay a specified sum of money to a beneficiary, normally the exporter, on presentation of particular, specified documents.

Consider once again the example of the U.S. exporter and the French importer. The French importer applies to her local bank, let's say the Bank of Paris, for the issuance of a letter of credit. The Bank of Paris then undertakes a credit check of the importer. If the Bank of Paris is satisfied with her

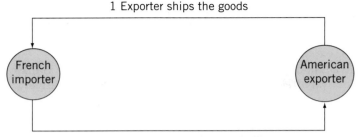

FIGURE 11.2

Preference of the French Importer

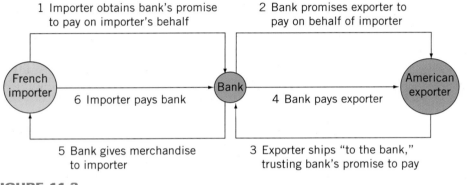

FIGURE 11.3

The Use of a Third Party

creditworthiness, it will issue a letter of credit. However, the Bank of Paris might require a cash deposit or some other form of collateral from her first. In addition, the Bank of Paris will charge the importer a fee for this service. Typically this amounts to between 0.5 percent and 2 percent of the value of the letter of credit, depending on the importer's creditworthiness and the size of the transaction. (As a rule, the larger the transaction, the lower the percentage.)

Assume the Bank of Paris is satisfied with the French importer's creditworthiness and agrees to issue a letter of credit. The letter states that the Bank of Paris will pay the U.S. exporter for the merchandise as long as it is shipped in accordance with certain specified instructions and conditions. At this point the letter of credit becomes a financial contract between the Bank of Paris and the U.S. exporter. The Bank of Paris then sends the letter of credit to the U.S. exporter's bank, let's say the Bank of New York. The Bank of New York tells the exporter it has received a letter of credit and he can ship the merchandise. After the exporter has shipped the merchandise, he draws a draft against the Bank of Paris in accordance with the terms of the letter of credit, attaches the required documents, and presents the draft to his own bank, the Bank of New York, for payment. The Bank of New York then forwards the letter of credit and associated documents to the Bank of Paris. If all the terms and conditions contained in the letter of credit have been complied with, the Bank of Paris will honor the draft and will send payment to the Bank of New York. When the Bank of New York receives the funds, it will pay the U.S. exporter.

Once the Bank of Paris has transferred the funds to the Bank of New York, it will collect payment from the French importer. Alternatively, the Bank of Paris may allow the importer some time to resell the merchandise before requiring payment. This is not unusual, particularly when the importer is a distributor and not the final consumer of the merchandise, since it helps the importer's cash flow. Of course, the Bank of Paris will treat such an extension of the payment period as a loan to the importer and will charge an appropriate rate of interest.

The great advantage of this system is that both the French importer and the U.S. exporter are likely to trust reputable banks, even if they do not trust each other. Once the U.S. exporter has seen a letter of credit, he knows he is guaranteed payment and will ship the merchandise. An exporter may find that having a letter of credit will facilitate obtaining pre-export financing. For example, having seen the letter of credit, the Bank of New York might be willing to lend the exporter funds to process and prepare the merchandise for shipping to France. This loan may not have to be repaid until the exporter has received his payment for the merchandise. As for the French importer, the great advantage of the letter of credit arrangement is that she does not have to pay out funds for the merchandise until the documents have arrived and unless all conditions stated in the letter of credit have been satisfied. The drawback for the importer is the fee she must pay the Bank of Paris for the letter of credit. In addition, since the letter of credit is a financial liability against her, it may reduce her ability to borrow funds for other purposes.

Draft

A draft, sometimes referred to as a bill of exchange, is the instrument normally used in international commerce for payment. A draft is simply an order written by an exporter instructing an importer, or an importer's agent, to pay a specified amount of money at a specified time. In the example of the U.S. exporter and the French importer, the exporter writes a draft that instructs the Bank of Paris, the French importer's agent, to pay for the merchandise shipped to France. The person or business initiating the draft is known as the maker (in this case, the U.S. exporter). The party to whom the draft is presented is known as the drawee (in this case, the Bank of Paris).

International practice is to use drafts to settle trade transactions. This differs from domestic practice in which a seller usually ships merchandise on an open account, followed by a commercial invoice that specifies the amount due and the terms of payment. In domestic transactions the buyer can often obtain possession of the merchandise without signing a formal document acknowledging his or her obligation to pay. In contrast, due to the lack of trust in international transactions, payment or a formal promise to pay is required before the buyer can obtain the merchandise.

Drafts fall into two categories, sight drafts and time drafts. A sight draft is payable on presentation to the drawee. A time draft allows for a delay in payment—normally 30, 60, 90, or 120 days. It is presented to the drawee, who signifies acceptance of it by writing or stamping a notice of acceptance on its face. Once accepted, the time draft becomes a promise to pay by the accepting party. When a time draft is drawn on and accepted by a bank, it is called a banker's acceptance. When it is drawn on and accepted by a business firm, it is called a trade acceptance.

Time drafts are negotiable instruments; that is, once the draft is stamped with an acceptance, the maker can sell the draft to an investor at a discount from its face value. Going back to our example, imagine the agreement between the U.S. exporter and the French importer calls for the exporter to present the Bank of Paris (through the Bank of New York) with a time draft requiring payment 120 days after presentation. The Bank of Paris stamps the time draft with an acceptance. Imagine further that the draft is for $100,000.

The exporter can either hold onto the accepted time draft and receive $100,000 in 120 days or he can sell it to an investor, let's say the Bank of New York, for a discount from the face value. If the prevailing discount rate is 7 percent, the exporter could receive $96,500 by selling it immediately (7 percent per year discount rate for 120 days for $100,000 equals $3,500; $100,000 − $3,500 = $96,500). The Bank of New York would then collect the full $100,000 from the Bank of Paris in 120 days. The exporter might choose to sell the accepted time draft immediately if he needed the funds to finance merchandise in transit and/or to cover cash flow shortfalls.

Bill of Lading

The third key document for financing international trade is the bill of lading. The bill of lading is issued to the exporter by the common carrier transporting the merchandise. It serves three purposes: it is a receipt, a contract, and a document of title. As a receipt, the bill of lading indicates the carrier has received the merchandise described on the face of the document. As a contract, it specifies that the carrier is obligated to provide a transportation service in return for a certain charge. As a document of title, it can be used to obtain payment or a written promise of payment before the merchandise is released to the importer. The bill of lading can also function as collateral against which funds may be advanced to the exporter by its local bank before or during shipment and before final payment by the importer.

Summary: A Typical International Trade Transaction

Now that we have reviewed all the elements of an international trade transaction, let us see how the whole process works in a typical case, sticking with the example of the U.S. exporter and the French importer. The typical transaction involves 14 distinct steps (see Figure 11.4).

Step 1: The French importer places an order with the U.S. exporter and asks the American if he would be willing to ship under a letter of credit.

Step 2: The U.S. exporter agrees to ship under a letter of credit and specifies relevant information such as prices and delivery terms.

Step 3: The French importer applies to the Bank of Paris for a letter of credit to be issued in favor of the U.S. exporter for the merchandise the importer wishes to buy.

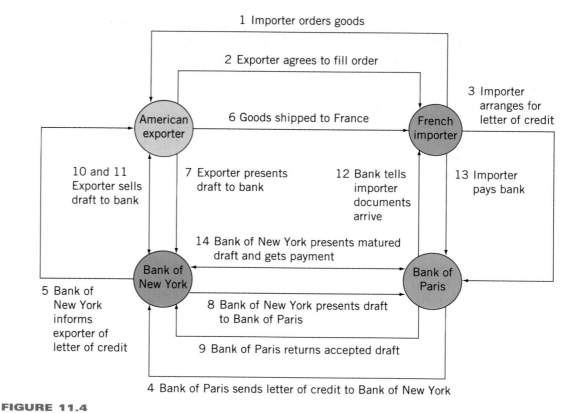

1 Importer orders goods

2 Exporter agrees to fill order

3 Importer arranges for letter of credit

6 Goods shipped to France

10 and 11 Exporter sells draft to bank

7 Exporter presents draft to bank

12 Bank tells importer documents arrive

13 Importer pays bank

14 Bank of New York presents matured draft and gets payment

5 Bank of New York informs exporter of letter of credit

8 Bank of New York presents draft to Bank of Paris

9 Bank of Paris returns accepted draft

4 Bank of Paris sends letter of credit to Bank of New York

American exporter

French importer

Bank of New York

Bank of Paris

FIGURE 11.4

A Typical International Trade Transaction

Step 4: The Bank of Paris issues a letter of credit in the French importer's favor and sends it to the U.S. exporter's bank, the Bank of New York.

Step 5: The Bank of New York advises the U.S. exporter of the opening of a letter of credit in his favor.

Step 6: The U.S. exporter ships the goods to the French importer on a common carrier. An official of the carrier gives the exporter a bill of lading.

Step 7: The U.S. exporter presents a 90-day time draft drawn on the Bank of Paris in accordance with its letter of credit and the bill of lading to the Bank of New York. The U.S. exporter endorses the bill of lading so title to the goods is transferred to the Bank of New York.

Step 8: The Bank of New York sends the draft and bill of lading to the Bank of Paris. The Bank of Paris accepts the draft, taking possession of the documents and promising to pay the now-accepted draft in 90 days.

Step 9: The Bank of Paris returns the accepted draft to the Bank of New York.

Step 10: The Bank of New York tells the U.S. exporter that it has received the accepted bank draft, which is payable in 90 days.

Step 11: The exporter sells the draft to the Bank of New York at a discount from its face value and receives the discounted cash value of the draft in return.

Step 12: The Bank of Paris notifies the French importer of the arrival of the documents. She agrees to pay the Bank of Paris in 90 days. The Bank of Paris releases the documents so the importer can take possession of the shipment.

Step 13: In 90 days the Bank of Paris receives the importer's payment, so it has funds to pay the maturing draft.

Step 14: In 90 days the holder of the matured acceptance (in this case, the Bank of New York) presents it to the Bank of Paris for payment. The Bank of Paris pays.

Key Terms

Summary

In this chapter we have reviewed different entry modes and we have examined the steps that firms must take in exporting. The following points have been made in this chapter:

1 There are six ways of entering a foreign market: exporting, turnkey projects, licensing, franchising, establishing a joint venture, and setting up a wholly owned subsidiary.

2 Exporting has the advantages of facilitating the realization of experience curve economies and of avoiding the costs of setting up manufacturing operations in another country. Disadvantages include high transport costs and trade barriers and problems with local marketing agents. The latter can be overcome if the firm sets up a wholly owned marketing subsidiary in the host country.

3 Turnkey projects allow firms to export their process know-how to countries where FDI might be prohibited, thereby enabling the firm to earn a greater return from this asset. The disadvantage is that the firm may create efficient global competitors in the process.

4 The main advantage of licensing is that the licensee bears the costs and risks of opening a foreign market. Disadvantages include the risk of losing technological know-how to the licensee and a lack of tight control over licensees.

5 The main advantage of franchising is that the franchisee bears the costs and risks of opening a foreign market. Disadvantages center on problems of quality control of distant franchisees.

6 Joint ventures have the advantages of sharing the costs and risks of opening a foreign market and of gaining local knowledge and political influence. Disadvantages include the risk of losing control over technology and a lack of tight control.

7 The advantages of wholly owned subsidiaries include tight control over operations and tight control over technological know-how. The main disadvantage is that the firm must bear all the costs and risks of opening a foreign market.

8 The optimal choice of entry mode depends on the firm's strategy. When technological know-how constitutes a firm's core competency, wholly owned subsidiaries are preferred. When management know-how constitutes a firm's core competency, foreign franchises controlled by joint ventures seem to be optimal. When the firm is pursuing a global or transnational strategy, the need for tight control over operations in order to realize location and experience curve economies suggests wholly owned

subsidiaries are the preferred entry mode.

9 One big impediment to exporting is ignorance of foreign market opportunities. Moreover, neophyte exporters often become discouraged or frustrated with the exporting process because they encounter many problems, delays, and pitfalls.

10 The way to overcome ignorance is to gather information. Government agencies and export management companies can also help an exporter to identify export opportunities.

11 Many of the pitfalls associated with exporting can be avoided if a company hires an experienced export management company, or export consultant, and if it adopts the appropriate export strategy.

12 Firms engaged in international trade must do business with people they cannot trust, people who may be very difficult to track down if they default on an obligation. Due to the lack of trust, each party to an international transaction has a different set of preferences regarding the configuration of the transaction.

13 The problems arising from lack of trust between exporters and importers can be solved by using a third party that is trusted by both—normally a reputable bank.

14 A letter of credit is issued by a bank at the request of an importer. It states that the bank promises to pay a beneficiary, normally the exporter, on presentation of documents specified in the letter.

15 A draft is the instrument normally used in international commerce to effect payment. It is an order written by an exporter instructing an importer, or an importer's agent, to pay a specified amount of money at a specified time. Drafts are either sight drafts or time drafts. Time drafts are negotiable instruments.

16 A bill of lading is issued to the exporter by the common carrier transporting the merchandise. It serves as a receipt, a contract, and a document of title.

Critical Thinking and Discussion Questions

1 Licensing proprietary technology to foreign competitors is the best way to give up a firm's competitive advantage. Discuss.

2 Discuss how the need for control over foreign operations varies with firms' strategies and core competencies. What are the implications for the choice of entry mode?

3 A small Canadian firm that has developed some valuable new medical products using its unique biotechnology know-how is trying to decide how best to serve the European Union. Its choices are

a. Manufacture the product at home and let foreign sales agents handle marketing.

b. Manufacture the products at home and set up a wholly owned subsidiary in Europe to handle marketing.

c. Enter into a strategic alliance with a large European pharmaceutical firm. The product would be manufactured in Europe by the 50/50 joint venture and marketed by the European firm.

The cost of investment in manufacturing facilities will be a major one for the Canadian firm, but it is not outside its reach. If these are the firm's only options, which one would you advise it to choose? Why?

4 You are the assistant to the CEO of a small textile firm that manufactures high-quality, premium-priced, stylish clothing. The CEO has decided to see what the opportunities are for exporting and has asked you for advice as to the steps the company should take. What advice would you give to the CEO?

Internet Exercise

Firms undertaking exporting might find two sites on the World Wide Web to be of interest. Trade Compass (http://www.tradecompass.com/) promotes itself as the "Gateway to International Commerce" and includes a daily briefing of trade news and regulatory issues, a library, featured companies, and trade statistics. The second site, which is run by the International Franchise Association (http://www.franchise.org/resources/links.html), is a resource for "current and prospective franchisees and franchisors, the media, and the government," according to its mission statement. Its extensive list of links includes publications, associations, the U.S. government, and franchise research.

Global Surfing
Visit the Trade Compass site and summarize the Daily Brief articles concerning exporting. Search the Table of Contents for links to exporting information and summarize three topics. Explore three Featured Companies and describe their exporting activities. Jump to the International Franchise Association and summarize the articles in its News area. In the Resource Center, select two links, such as those to the U.S. government's Export-Import Bank and The Export Hotline and TradeBank, and summarize the contents of those sites. Jump to the What's Hot area and choose three featured companies. Write an abstract profiling these companies.

Downey's Soup

Downey's is an Irish tavern in Philadelphia created over 20 years ago by Jack Downey. Over the years, the restaurant's fortunes have wavered, but the strength of some favorite menu items has helped it survive economic downturns. In particular, the lobster bisque soup was met with increasing popularity, but Downey's efforts to market it have been very sporadic. Never did Downey imagine that his lobster bisque would someday be the cause of an international trade dispute.

Unbeknown to Downey, the Japanese have a strong penchant for lobster. When the Philadelphia office of the Japanese External Trade Organization (Jetro) asked Downey to serve his lobster bisque at a mini trade show in 1991, he began to think about mass production of his soups. The Japanese loved the lobster bisque. They gave Downey a strong impression that the soup would sell very well in Japan. At that time, Downey did not have a formal product line but that seemed to be only a minor obstacle.

After the trade show, Michael Fisher, executive vice president for the newly formed Downey Foods Inc., was sent on an all-expenses-paid 10-day marketing trip to Japan by Jetro. (Jetro sponsors approximately 60 Americans for similar trips each year.) Although interest expressed by the food brokers and buyers he met seemed to be more polite than enthusiastic, he did get an initial order of 1,000 cases of the lobster bisque. The only condition placed by the buyer was to have the salt content reduced to comply with local Japanese tastes. Both Jetro and Fisher considered this initial order the beginning of a rich export relationship with Japan.

Fisher contracted with a food processor in Virginia, adapted the recipe for the new salt content, and shipped the soup to Japan in short order. Visions of expanded sales in Japan were quickly dashed as the cases of soup were detained at customs. Samples were sent to a government laboratory and eventually denied entry for containing polysorbate, an emulsifying and anti-foaming agent used by food processors. Though it is considered harmless in the United States, polysorbate is not on Jetro's list of 347 approved food additives.

Fisher and Downey did not give up. They reformulated the soup to improve the taste and comply with Jetro's additive regulations. They had the soup tested and certified by a Japanese-approved lab, the Oregon Department of Agriculture's Export Service Center, to meet all Japanese standards. Then, in the fall of 1993, they sent another 1,000 cases to Japan.

But the soup was denied entry again. Japanese officials said the expiration date on the Oregon tests had passed, so they retested the cans. Traces of polysorbate were found. A sample from that shipment was sent back to Oregon, and it passed. Two identical cans of soup were sent back to Japan and tested. They failed. Back in Oregon, a sample of the same shipment was tested again and no traces of polysorbate were found.

Japanese officials refused to allow the soup into Japan anyway. By this time, Downey's had been paid $20,000 that it could not afford to give back. "It stunned the customer," says Fisher. "But it stunned me a lot more. I was counting on dozens of reorders."

Fisher filed appeals with the U.S. Embassy in Tokyo to no avail. "It became a bureaucratic/political issue," says Fisher. "There was a face-saving problem. The Japanese had rejected the soup twice. There was no way they could reverse the decision."

The final irony came when a New York-based Japanese trader sent a few cases of Downey's regular (no reduced salt content) lobster bisque to Japan. This shipment sailed through customs without a problem.

Where was Jetro when Downey's soups were stalled in customs? Fisher thought he had everything covered. He followed the advice of Jetro, adjusted the soups to meet Japanese palates, and had them tested to meet Japanese food standards. Apparently, Jetro failed to inform Fisher of the apparent need for a local partner to sell and distribute in Japan. Most food companies have trouble getting into Japan, whether large or small. Agricultural products are one of the most difficult things to get into the Japanese market.

Jetro's agricultural specialist, Tatsuya Kajishima, contradicts this claim that Japan is hostile to food imports by stating the following statistic, 30 percent of Japan's food imports come from the United States. Further, Japan is the fourth largest importer of America's soups to the tune of $6.5 million worth of soup purchased in 1993. Most of these sales came from Campbell's.

Although this venture was not particularly profitable for Downey Foods, Inc., the company has been able to redirect its research and development efforts to build its domestic product line. Through its local broker, Santucci Associates, Downey Foods attracted the attention of Liberty Richter Inc., a national distributor of gourmet and imported food items.[25]

Case Discussion Questions

1 Did Downey Foods' export opportunity occur as a result of proactive action by Downey, or was its strategy reactive?

2 Why did Downey experience frustrations when trying to export to Japan? What actions might Downey take to improve its prospects of succeeding in the Japanese market?

3 You have been hired by Downey Foods to develop an exporting strategy for the firm. What steps do you think Downey should take to increase the volume of its exports?

Chapter 12
Global Marketing and Product Development

©1996 MTV Networks, Division of Viacom International

Opening Case

MTV and the Globalization of Teen Culture

In a world where there are still major differences in the tastes, preferences, and purchasing habits of consumers in different countries, no one group is more homogeneous than those in their teens and early 20s. Whether they live in Los Angeles or London, Tokyo or Prague, Rio de Janeiro or Sydney, young adults the world over wear Levi's and Doc Martens, dance to the Red Hot Chili Peppers, drink Coke or Pepsi, and eat at McDonald's. Increasingly, they also watch MTV, the music video channel owned by Viacom.

Learning Objectives:

1 Understand why and how it may make sense to vary the attributes of a product across countries.

2 Appreciate why and how a firm's distribution strategy might vary across countries.

3 Understand why and how advertising and promotional strategies might vary across countries.

4 Understand why and how a firm's pricing strategy might vary across countries.

5 Understand how the globalization of the world economy is affecting new-product development within international businesses.

MTV has been singled out by many observers as a major cause of the global homogenization of teen culture and also as a major beneficiary. Both charges are probably true. Introduced in the United States in 1981, MTV is now a global marketing phenomenon broadcasting in over 80 countries. By February 1997 the channel reached an impressive 66.4 million households in the United States, but it is outside of North America that most of the recent growth has occurred. MTV Europe, which was established in

1987, was received by over 56.5 million households across the continent by February 1997. In Asia, over 24 million households receive MTV Asia, and the number is growing exponentially. And in Central and South America, where MTV launched its service in 1990, 22.8 million households received the channel by February 1997 (see Figure 12.1).

MTV is keenly aware of the concerns and interest of those in their teens and early 20s, and its global program strategy reflects this. Its international services,

like its U.S. operation, broadcast news and socially conscious programming of interest to the target audience, such as features on global warming, the destruction of the rain forests, and AIDS. The guts of MTV, however, is its music programming. Initially, MTV's music programming was dominated by U.S. and British artists. It was thanks to MTV that grunge rock became a global phenomenon, and teens from Italy to Japan came to know Seattle not as the home of Boeing or Microsoft, but as the

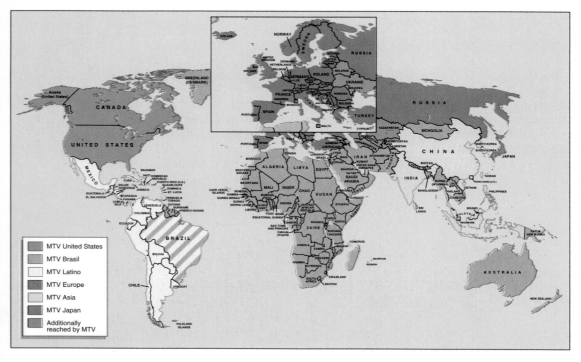

FIGURE 12.1

MTV: Rocking All over the World
Source: Viacom

birthplace of grunge. Increasingly, however, MTV is championing little-known artists from other parts of the world, and it has shown that it has the power to make them international stars. MTV Europe helped discover the Swedish pop group Ace of Base in 1992. Its global programming of the group's single and video, "All That She Wants," gave it a top 10 hit in Britain, Germany, Italy, and the United States. Thanks to MTV Asia, one of the best-selling albums of 1993 in India was by Cheb Khaled singing in his native Algerian. In Japan, the Swedish "gothic rock" guitarist Yngwie Malmsteen has become a huge star, in part due to promotion by MTV Japan. And for heavily anticipated new albums by big international stars, MTV stages what it calls "plane-

tary premieres", airing a new video in 24 hours in all 80-plus countries that it covers.

This worldwide marketing reach has made MTV a premier conduit for many companies hoping to profit from the globalization of teen culture. MTV's roster of 200 major advertisers includes Levi Strauss, Procter & Gamble, Johnson & Johnson, Apple Computer, and Pepsi-Cola. According to Donald Holdsworth, head of sales and marketing for Pepsi-Cola International, "MTV not only has broad global coverage, it's also targeted exactly at that segment we want to reach: teenagers." MTV Networks Chairman and CEO Tom Freston argues that marketing to those in their teens and early 20s through global communications media such as MTV is becoming in-

creasingly important for many global consumer products companies. He sees music as the most global of communications media. "You could argue that this is a business even more global than movies, because music is more pervasive than any other form of culture." Due to this pervasiveness, MTV is a natural communications conduit for advertisers trying to build a global brand. Today it is still difficult to sell the same products to 35-year-olds in different countries. They prefer traditional food and fashion. In part that's because they never bonded with international brands as teenagers. But MTV's Freston believes that due to media such as MTV this generation is different; they are becoming more homogenized in their tastes and preferences.[1]

Introduction

In this chapter our focus is on how an international business can perform marketing and R&D activities so it will reduce the costs of value creation and add value by better serving customer needs. In Chapter 10 we spoke of the tension existing in most international businesses between the need to reduce costs and the need to customize product offerings and strategy to local conditions, which tends to raise costs. This tension continues to be a major theme in this chapter. A global marketing strategy, which views the world's consumers as similar in their tastes and preferences, is consistent with the mass production of a standardized output. By mass producing a standardized output, the firm can realize substantial unit cost reductions from experience curve and other scale economies. But ignoring country differences in consumer tastes and preferences can lead to failure. Thus, an international business's marketing function needs to determine when product standardization is appropriate and when it is not. Similarly, the firm's R&D function needs to be able to develop globally standardized products when appropriate as well as products customized to local requirements when they are needed.

We consider marketing and R&D within the same chapter because of their close relationship. A critical aspect of the marketing function is identifying gaps in the market so that new products can be developed to fill those gaps. Developing new products requires R&D; thus, the linkage between marketing and R&D. New products should be developed with market needs in mind, and only marketing can define those needs for R&D personnel. Moreover, only marketing can tell R&D whether to produce globally standardized or locally customized products. Consistent with this, academic research has long maintained that a major factor of success for new-product introductions is the closeness of the relationship between marketing and R&D. The closer the linkage, the greater the success rate.[2]

The opening case illustrates some issues we will be debating in this chapter. The international success of MTV is a testament to the global convergence of tastes and preferences among those in their teens and early 20s in different countries. As the case notes, MTV may be able to further this trend through its ability to promote a global teen culture. However, it is easy to overstate the importance of such globalization. Although there is no doubt that music is, as MTV Chairman Freston notes, the most pervasive and global form of culture, the case also alludes to the fact that important differences still exist between the tastes and preferences of teens in different nations. MTV may have helped to turn Yngwie Malmsteen into a big star in Japan, but there is no sign that this Swedish master of "gothic rock" is going to break into the U.S. market anytime soon, to say nothing of India's favorite Algerian rock star, Cheb Khaled. In other words, even in one of the most global of industries—the music industry—and even among the most homogeneous group in the world—teenagers—product standardization has its limits and national differences in tastes and preferences are still of major importance.

We begin this chapter by reviewing the debate on the globalization of markets. Then we discuss the four elements that constitute a firm's marketing mix: product attributes, distribution strategy, communication strategy, and pricing strategy. The marketing mix is the set of choices the firm offers to its targeted markets. Many firms vary their marketing mix from country to country depending on differences in national culture, economic development, product standards, distribution channels, and so on. We close the chapter by looking at the issue of new-product development and considering the role R&D and marketing can play in this process in an international business.

The Globalization of Markets?

In a now-famous *Harvard Business Review* article, Theodore Levitt waxed lyrically about the globalization of world markets.[3] Levitt's arguments are worth quoting at some length, since they have become a lightning rod for the debate about the extent of globalization. According to Levitt:

> A powerful force drives the world toward a converging commonalty, and that force is technology. It has proletarianized communication, transport, and travel. The result is a new commercial reality—the emergence of global markets for standardized consumer products on a previously unimagined scale of magnitude.
>
> Gone are accustomed differences in national or regional preferences . . . The globalization of markets is at hand. With that, the multinational commercial world nears its end, and so does the multinational corporation. The multinational corporation operates in a number of countries and adjusts its products and practices to each—at high relative costs. The global corporation operates with resolute consistency—at low relative cost—as if the entire world were a single entity; it sells the same thing in the same way everywhere.
>
> Commercially, nothing confirms this as much as the success of McDonald's from the Champs Elysees to the Ginza, of Coca-Cola in Bahrain and Pepsi-Cola in Moscow, and of rock music, Greek salad, Hollywood movies, Revlon cosmetics, Sony television, and Levi's jeans everywhere.
>
> Ancient differences in national tastes or modes of doing business disappear. The commonalty of preference leads inescapably to the standardization of products, manufacturing, and the institutions of trade and commerce.

This is eloquent and evocative writing, but is Levitt correct? Certainly, the rise of global media such as MTV (see the opening case) and CNN, and the ability of such media to help shape a global culture, would seem to lend weight to Levitt's argument. If Levitt is correct, his argument has major implications for the marketing strategies pursued by international business. However, the current consensus among academics seems to be that Levitt overstates his case.[4] Although Levitt may have a point when it comes to many basic industrial products—such as steel, bulk chemicals, and semiconductor chips—globalization seems to be the exception rather than the rule in most consumer goods markets and many industrial markets. Even a firm such as McDonald's, which Levitt holds up as the perfect example of a consumer products firm that sells a standardized product worldwide, modifies its menu from country to country in light of local consumer preferences.[5] And as we saw in the opening case, although MTV may help to sell teen music across borders, there are still important differences in the tastes and preferences of teens in different nations, which is why the music of Algerian Cheb Khaled sells in India, but not in Britain or the United States.

On the other hand, Levitt is probably correct to assert that modern transportation and communications technologies, such as MTV, are facilitating a convergence of the tastes and preferences of consumers in the more advanced countries of the world. The popularity of sushi in Los Angeles, hamburgers in Tokyo, and grunge rock almost everywhere certainly support this. In the long run, such technological forces may lead to the evolution of a global culture. At present, however, the continuing persistence of cultural and economic differences among nations acts as a major brake on any trend toward global consumer tastes and preferences. In addition, trade barriers and differences in product and technical standards also constrain a firm's ability to sell a standardized product to a global market. We discuss the sources of these differences in the next section when we look at how products must be altered from country to country. For now, note that these differences are so substantial that Levitt's globally standardized markets seem a long way off in many industries.

Product Attributes

A product can be viewed as a bundle of attributes.[6] For example, the attributes that make up a car include power, design, quality, performance, fuel consumption, and comfort; the attributes of a hamburger include taste, texture, and size; a hotel's attributes include atmosphere, quality, comfort, and service. Products sell well when their attributes match consumer needs (and when their prices are appropriate). BMW cars sell well to people who have high needs for luxury, quality, and performance, precisely because BMW builds those attributes into its cars. If consumer needs were the same the world over, a firm could simply sell the same product worldwide. But consumer needs vary from country to country depending on culture and the level of economic development. In addition, a firm's ability to sell the same product worldwide is further constrained by countries' differing product standards. In this section we review each of these issues and discuss how they influence product attributes.

Cultural Differences

We discussed countries' cultural differences in Chapter 3. There we pointed out that countries differ along a whole range of dimensions, including social structure, language, religion, and education. And as mentioned in Chapter 2, these differences have important implications for marketing strategy. The most important aspect of countries' cultural differences is probably the impact of tradition. Tradition is particularly important in foodstuffs and beverages. For example, reflecting differences in traditional eating habits, the Findus frozen food division of Nestlé, the Swiss food giant, markets fish cakes and fish fingers in Great Britain, but beef bourguignon and coq au vin in France and vitèllo con funghi and braviola in Italy. Similarly, in addition to its normal range of products, Coca-Cola in Japan markets "Georgia," a cold coffee in a can, and "Aquarius," a tonic drink, products that appeal to traditional Japanese tastes.

For historic and idiosyncratic reasons, a whole range of other cultural differences exist among countries. For example, scent preferences differ from one country to another. S. C. Johnson & Son, a manufacturer of waxes and polishes, encountered resistance to its lemon-scented Pledge furniture polish among older consumers in Japan. Careful market research revealed that the polish smelled similar to latrine disinfectant used widely in Japan in the 1940s. Sales rose sharply after the scent was adjusted.[7]

At the same time, there is some evidence of the trends Levitt talked about. Tastes and preferences are becoming more cosmopolitan. Coffee is gaining ground against tea in Japan and Great Britain, while American-style frozen dinners have become popular in Europe (with some fine-tuning to local tastes). Taking advantage of these trends, Nestlé has found that it can market its instant coffee, spaghetti bolognese, and Lean Cuisine frozen dinners in essentially the same manner in both North America and Western Europe. However, there is no market for Lean Cuisine dinners in most of the rest of the world, and there may never be. The diet-conscious Asian is difficult to find. Although some cultural convergence has occurred, particularly among the advanced industrial nations of North America and Western Europe, Levitt's global culture is still a long way off.

Economic Differences

Just as important as differences in culture are differences in the level of economic development. We discussed the extent of country differences in economic development in Chapter 2. Consumer behavior is influenced by the level of economic development of a country. Firms based in highly developed countries such as the United States tend to build a lot of extra performance attributes into their products. These extra attributes are not usually demanded by consumers in less developed nations, where the preference is for more basic products. Thus, cars sold in less developed nations typically lack many of the features found in the West, such as air-conditioning, power steering, power windows, radios, and cassette players. For most consumer durables, product reliability may be a more important attribute in less developed nations, where such a purchase may account for a major proportion of a consumer's income, than it is in advanced nations.

The other side of the coin is that, contrary to Levitt's suggestions, consumers in the most developed countries are often not willing to sacrifice their preferred attributes for lower prices. Consumers in the most advanced countries often shun globally standardized products that have been developed with the lowest common denominator in mind. They are willing to pay more for products that have additional features and attributes customized to their tastes and preferences. For example, demand for top-of-the-line four-wheel-drive sport utility vehicles—such as Chrysler's Jeep, Ford's Explorer, and Toyota's Land Cruiser—is almost totally restricted to the United States. This is due to a combination of factors, including the high income level of U.S. consumers, the country's vast distances, the relatively low cost of gasoline, and the culturally grounded "outdoor" theme of American life.

Product and Technical Standards

Notwithstanding the forces that are creating some convergence of consumer tastes and preferences (at least among advanced industrialized nations), Levitt's vision of global markets may still be a long way off due to national differences in product and technological standards.

Differing product standards mandated by governments can rule out mass production and marketing of a standardized product. For example, Caterpillar, the U.S. construction equipment firm, manufactures backhoe-loaders for all of Europe in Great Britain. These tractor-type machines have a bucket in front and a digger at the back. Several special parts must be built into backhoe-loaders that will be sold in Germany: a separate brake attached to the rear axle, a special locking mechanism on the backhoe operating valve, specially positioned valves in the steering system, and a lock on the bucket for traveling. These extras account for 5 percent of the total cost of the product in Germany.[8] The European Union (EU) is trying to harmonize such divergent product standards among its member nations. If the EU is successful, the need to customize products will be reduced, at least within the boundaries of the EU.

Differences in technical standards also constrain the globalization of markets. Some of these differences result from idiosyncratic decisions, rather than government actions. Their long-term effects are nonetheless profound. For example, video equipment manufactured for sale in the United States will not play videotapes recorded on equipment manufactured for sale in Great Britain, Germany, and France (and vice versa). Different technical standards for frequency of television signals emerged in the 1950s that require television and video equipment to be customized to countries' prevailing standards. RCA stumbled in the 1970s when it failed to account for this in its marketing of TVs in Asia. Although several Asian countries had adopted the U.S. standard, Singapore, Hong Kong, and Malaysia had adopted the British standard. People who bought RCA TVs in those countries could receive a picture but no sound![9]

Distribution Strategy

A critical element of a firm's marketing mix is its distribution strategy, the means it chooses for delivering the product to the consumer. The way the product is delivered is determined by the firm's entry strategy, which we discussed in Chapter 11. Here we examine a typical distribution system, discuss how its structure varies among countries, and look at how appropriate distribution strategies vary from country to country.

A Typical Distribution System

Figure 12.2 illustrates a typical distribution system consisting of a channel that includes a wholesale distributor and a retailer. If the firm manufactures its product in the particular country, it can sell directly to the consumer, to the retailer, or to the wholesaler. The same options are available to a firm that manufactures outside the country. Alternatively, this firm may decide to sell to an import agent, who then deals with the wholesale distributor, the retailer, or the consumer. The factors that determine the firm's choice of channel are considered later in this section.

Differences among Countries

The main differences among countries' distribution systems are threefold: retail concentration, channel length, and channel exclusivity.

RETAIL CONCENTRATION In some countries the retail system is very concentrated, whereas in other countries it is fragmented. In a concentrated system, a few retailers supply most of the market. A fragmented sys-

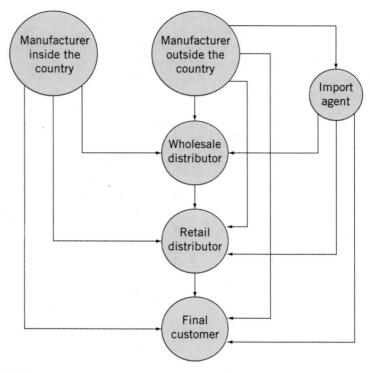

FIGURE 12.2

A Typical Distribution System

tem is one in which there are many retailers, no one of which has a major share of the market. In Germany, for example, four retail chains control 65 percent of the market for food products. In neighboring Italy, retail distribution is fragmented, with no chain controlling more than 2 percent of the market.

Many of the differences in concentration are rooted in history and tradition. In the United States the importance of the automobile and the relative youth of many urban settlements have resulted in a retail system centered around large stores or shopping malls to which people can drive. This has facilitated concentration of the system. Japan's much greater population density, together with the large number of urban centers that grew up before the advent of the automobile, has resulted in a more fragmented retail system of many small stores that serve local neighborhoods and to which people frequently walk. In addition, the Japanese legal system protects small retailers. By law, small retailers can block establishment of a large retail outlet by petitioning their local government.

Developed countries tend to have greater retail concentration. Three factors contribute to this:

- Increases in car ownership.
- Number of households with refrigerators and freezers.
- Number of two-income households that accompany development.

All these factors have changed shopping habits and facilitated the growth of large retail establishments away from traditional shopping areas.

CHANNEL LENGTH Channel length refers to the number of intermediaries between the producer (or manufacturer) and the consumer. If the producer sells directly to the consumer, the channel is very short. If the producer sells through an import agent, a wholesaler, and a retailer, a long channel exists. The choice of a short or long channel is primarily a strategic decision for the producing firm. Some countries have longer distribution channels than others. The most important determinant of channel length is the degree to which the retail system is fragmented. Fragmented retail systems tend to promote the growth of wholesalers to serve retailers, which lengthens channels.

The reason for this is simple economics. Basically, the more fragmented the retail system, the more expensive it is for a firm to make contact with each individual retailer. Imagine, for example, a firm that sells toothpaste in a country where there are 50,000 small retailers. To sell directly to the retailers, the firm would have to build a huge sales force. This would be very expensive, particularly since each sales call would yield a very small order. Imagine, however, that there are 50 wholesalers in the country that supply retailers not only with toothpaste but also with all other personal care and household products. Since these wholesalers carry a wide range of products, they get bigger orders with each sales call. Thus, it becomes worthwhile for them to deal directly with the retailers. Accordingly, it makes economic sense for the firm to sell to the wholesalers and the wholesalers to deal with the retailers.

As a result of such factors, countries with fragmented retail systems also tend to have long channels of distribution. The classic example is Japan, where there are often two or three layers of wholesalers between the firm and retail outlets. In contrast, in countries such as Great Britain, Germany, and the United States where the retail system is far more concentrated, channels are much shorter. When the retail sector is very concentrated, it makes sense for the firm to deal directly with retailers, cutting out wholesalers. This is because a relatively small sales force is required to deal with a concentrated retail sector, and the orders generated from each sales call can be large. Such circumstances tend to prevail in the United States, where large food companies sell directly to supermarkets rather than going through wholesale distributors.

CHANNEL EXCLUSIVITY An exclusive distribution channel is one that is difficult for outsiders to access. For example, it is often difficult for a new firm to get access to shelf space in U.S. supermarkets because retailers tend to prefer to carry the products of long-established manufacturers with national reputations, rather than gamble on the products of unknown firms. How exclusive a distribution system is varies among countries. Japan's system is often held up as an example of a very exclusive system. In Japan, relationships between manufacturers, wholesalers, and retailers often go back decades. Many of these relationships are based on the understanding that distributors will not carry the products of competing firms. In return, the distributors are guaranteed an attractive markup by the manufacturer. As many U.S. and European manufacturers have learned, the close ties that result from this arrangement can make access to the Japanese market very difficult.

Choosing a Distribution Strategy

A choice of distribution strategy determines which channel the firm will use to reach potential consumers. Should the firm try to sell directly to the consumer or should it go through retailers; should it go through a wholesaler; should it use an import agent? The optimal strategy is determined by the relative costs and benefits of each alternative. In turn, the relative costs and benefits of each alternative vary from country to country depending on the three factors we have just discussed: retail concentration, channel length, and channel exclusivity.

Since each intermediary in a channel adds its own markup to the products, there is generally a critical link between channel length and the firm's profit margin. The longer a channel, the greater is the aggregate markup, and the higher the price that consumers are charged for the final product. To ensure that prices do not get too high due to markups by multiple intermediaries, a firm might be forced to operate with lower profit margins. Thus, if price is an important competitive weapon, and if the firm does not want to see its profit margins squeezed, other things being equal, the firm would prefer to use a shorter channel.

However, the benefits of using a longer channel often outweigh these drawbacks. As we have seen, one benefit of using a longer channel is that it economizes on selling costs when the retail sector is very fragmented. Thus, it makes sense for an international business to use longer channels in countries where the retail sector is fragmented and shorter channels in countries where the retail sector is concentrated.

Another benefit of using a longer channel is market access—the ability to enter an exclusive channel. Import agents may have long-term relationships with wholesalers, retailers, and/or important consumers and thus be better able to win orders and get access to a distribution system than the firm on its own. Similarly, wholesalers may have long-standing relationships with retailers and, therefore, be better able to persuade them to carry the firm's product than the firm itself would.

Import agents are not limited to independent trading houses; any firm with a strong local reputation could serve just as well. For example, to break down channel exclusivity and gain greater access to the Japanese market, in 1991 and 1992 Apple Computer signed distribution agreements with five large Japanese firms—business equipment giant Brother Industries, stationery leader Kokuyo, Mitsubishi, Sharp, and Minolta. These firms use their own long-established distribution relationships with consumers, retailers, and wholesalers to push Apple Macintosh computers through the Japanese distribution system. As a result, Apple's share of the Japanese market increased from less than 1 percent in 1988 to 6 percent in 1991, and it was projected to reach 13 percent by 1994.[10]

If such an arrangement is not possible, the firm might want to consider other, less traditional alternatives to gaining market access. Frustrated by channel exclusivity in Japan, some foreign manufacturers of consumer goods have attempted to sell directly to Japanese consumers using direct mail and catalogs. REI, a Northwest U.S. retailer of outdoor clothing and equipment, had trouble persuading Japanese wholesalers and retailers to carry its products. So it began a direct-mail campaign in Japan that is proving very successful.

Communication Strategy

Another critical element in the marketing mix is communicating the attributes of the product to prospective customers. A number of communication channels are available to a firm; they include direct selling, sales promotion, direct marketing, and advertising. A firm's communication strategy is partly defined by its choice of channel. Some firms rely primarily on direct selling, others on point-of-sale promotions or direct marketing, others on mass advertising; still others use several channels simultaneously to communicate their message to prospective customers. In this section we will look first at the barriers to international communication. Then we will survey the various factors that determine which communication strategy is most appropriate in a particular country. After that we discuss global advertising.

Barriers to International Communication

International communication occurs whenever a firm uses a marketing message to sell its products in another country. The effectiveness of a firm's international communication can be jeopardized by three potentially critical variables: cultural barriers, source effects, and noise levels.

CULTURAL BARRIERS Cultural barriers can make it difficult to communicate messages across cultures. We have discussed some sources and consequences of cultural differences among nations in Chapter 3 and in the previous section of this chapter. Due to cultural differences, a message that means one thing in one country may mean something quite different in another. For example, when Procter & Gamble promoted its Camay soap in Japan in 1983 it ran into unexpected trouble. In a TV commercial, a Japanese man walked into the bathroom while his wife was bathing. The woman began telling her husband all about her new beauty soap, but the husband, stroking her shoulder, hinted that suds were not on his mind. This ad had been very popular in Europe, but it flopped in Japan because it is considered very bad manners there for a man to intrude on his wife.[11] Benetton, the Italian clothing manufacturer and retailer, is another firm that has run into cultural problems with its advertising. The company launched a worldwide advertising campaign in 1989 with the theme "United Colors of Benetton" that had won awards in France. One of its ads featured a black woman breastfeeding a white baby, and another one showed a black man and a white man handcuffed together. Benetton was surprised when the ads were attacked by U.S. civil rights groups for promoting white racial domination. Benetton had to withdraw its ads and it fired its advertising agency, Eldorado of France.

The best way for a firm to overcome cultural barriers is to develop cross-cultural literacy (see Chapter 3). In addition, it should employ some local input in developing its marketing message; for example, it could use a local advertising agency. Alternatively, if the firm uses direct selling rather than advertising to communicate its message, it would be advisable to develop a local sales force whenever possible. Cultural differences limit a firm's ability to use the same marketing message the world over. What works well in one country may be offensive in another.

SOURCE EFFECTS Source effects occur when the receiver of the message (the potential consumer in this case) evaluates the message based on the status or image of the sender. Source effects can be damaging for an international business when potential consumers in a target country have a bias against "foreign firms." For example, a wave of "Japan bashing" swept the

United States in 1992. Worried that U.S. consumers might view their advertisements negatively, Honda responded by creating advertisements that emphasized the U.S.-made content of its cars to show how "American" the company had become. Many international businesses try to counter negative source effects by deemphasizing their foreign origins. When British Petroleum acquired Mobil Oil's extensive network of U.S. gas stations, it changed its name to BP, thereby diverting attention away from the fact that one of the biggest operators of gas stations in the United States is a British firm.

Source effects are not always negative; they can be positive. French wine, Italian clothes, and German luxury cars benefit from nearly universal positive source effects. In such cases it may pay a firm to emphasize its foreign origins. In Japan, for example, there is currently a boom in demand for high-quality foreign goods, particularly those from Europe. It has become chic to carry a Gucci handbag, sport a Rolex watch, drink expensive French wine, and drive a BMW.

NOISE LEVELS Noise tends to reduce the probability of effective communication. In this context, noise refers to the number of other messages competing for a potential consumer's attention, and this too varies across countries. In highly developed countries such as the United States, noise from firms competing for the attention of target consumers is extremely high. In contrast, fewer firms vie for the attention of prospective customers in developing countries, and the noise level is lower.

Push versus Pull Strategies

The main decision with regard to communications strategy is the choice between a push strategy and a pull strategy. A push strategy emphasizes personal selling rather than mass media advertising in the promotional mix. Although very effective as a promotional tool, personal selling requires intensive use of a sales force and is relatively costly. A pull strategy depends more on mass media advertising to communicate the marketing message to potential consumers.

Although some firms employ only a pull strategy and others only a push strategy, still other firms combine direct selling with mass advertising to maximize communication effectiveness. Factors that determine the relative attractiveness of push and pull strategies include product type relative to consumer sophistication, channel length, and media availability.

PRODUCT TYPE AND CONSUMER SOPHISTICATION A pull strategy is generally favored by firms in consumer goods industries that are trying to sell to a large segment of the market. For such firms, mass communication has cost advantages, and direct selling is rarely used. In contrast, a push strategy is favored by firms that sell industrial products or other complex products. One of the great strengths of direct selling is that it allows the firm to educate potential consumers about the features of the product. This may not be necessary in advanced nations where a complex product has been in use for some time, where the product's attributes are well understood, and where consumers are sophisticated. However, customer education may be very important when consumers have less sophistication toward the product, which can be the case in developing nations, or in more advanced nations when a complex product is being introduced.

Part 5 Competing in a Global Marketplace

CHANNEL LENGTH The longer the distribution channel, the more intermediaries there are that must be persuaded to carry the product for it to reach the consumer. This can lead to inertia in the channel, which can make entry very difficult. Moreover, using direct selling to push a product through many layers of a distribution channel can be very expensive. In such circumstances, a firm may try to pull its product through the channels by using mass advertising to create consumer demand—the theory being that once demand is created, intermediaries will feel obliged to carry the product.

While U.S. distribution channels are relatively short, in other countries they can be quite long. As discussed earlier, in Japan products often pass through two, three, or even four wholesalers before they reach the final retail outlet. This can make it difficult for foreign firms to break into the Japanese market. Not only must the foreigner persuade a Japanese retailer to carry her product, but she may also have to persuade every intermediary in the chain to carry the product. Mass advertising may be one way to break down channel resistance in such circumstances.

MEDIA AVAILABILITY A pull strategy relies on access to advertising media. In the United States, a large number of media are available, including print media (newspapers and magazines) and electronic media (television and radio). Moreover, the rise of cable television in the United States has facilitated extremely focused advertising targeted at particular segments of the market (e.g., MTV for teens and young adults, Lifetime for women, ESPN for sports enthusiasts). With a few exceptions such as Canada and Japan, this level of media sophistication is not found outside the United States. Even many advanced nations have far fewer electronic media available for advertising. In Scandinavia, for example, no commercial television or radio stations existed in 1987; all electronic media were state owned and carried no commercials. In many developing nations the situation is even more restrictive, since mass media of all types are typically more limited. Obviously, a firm's ability to use a pull strategy is limited in some countries by media availability. In such circumstances, a push strategy is more attractive.

Media availability is limited by law in some cases. Few countries allow advertisements for tobacco and alcohol products on television and radio, though they are usually permitted in print media. When the leading Japanese whiskey distiller, Suntory, entered the U.S. market, it had to do so without television, its preferred medium.

THE PUSH-PULL MIX In sum, the optimal mix between push and pull strategies depends on product type and consumer sophistication, channel length, and media sophistication. Push strategies tend to be emphasized:

- For industrial products and/or complex new products.
- When distribution channels are short.
- When few print or electronic media are available.

Pull strategies tend to be emphasized:

- For consumer goods.
- When distribution channels are long.
- When sufficient print and electronic media are available to carry the marketing message.

Global Advertising

In recent years, largely inspired by the work of visionaries such as Theodore Levitt, there has been much discussion about the pros and cons of standardizing advertising worldwide. One of the most successful standardized campaigns has been Philip Morris's promotion of Marlboro cigarettes. The campaign was instituted in the 1950s, when the brand was repositioned, to assure smokers that the flavor would be unchanged by the addition of a filter. The campaign theme of "Come to where the flavor is. Come to Marlboro country." was a worldwide success. Marlboro built on this when it introduced "the Marlboro man," a rugged cowboy smoking his Marlboro while riding his horse through the great outdoors. This ad proved successful in almost every major market around the world, and it helped propel Marlboro to the top of the world market share table.

FOR STANDARDIZED ADVERTISING The support for global advertising is threefold. First, it has significant economic advantages. Standardized advertising lowers the costs of value creation by spreading the fixed costs of developing the advertisements over a large number of countries. For example, in the early 1980s Levi Strauss paid an advertising agency $550,000 to produce a series of TV commercials. By reusing this series in many countries, rather than developing a series for each country, the company enjoyed significant cost savings. Similarly, over a 20-year period Coca-Cola's advertising agency, McCann-Erickson, claims to have saved Coca-Cola $90 million by using certain elements of its campaign globally.

Second, there is the concern that creative talent is scarce and that one large effort to develop a campaign will produce better results than 40 or 50 smaller efforts.

A third justification for a standardized approach is that many brand names are global. With the substantial amount of international travel today and the considerable overlap in media across national borders, many international firms want to project a single image to avoid confusion caused by local campaigns that conflict with each other. This is particularly important in regions such as Western Europe, where travel across borders is as common as travel across state lines in the United States.

AGAINST STANDARDIZED ADVERTISING There are two main arguments against globally standardized advertising. First, as we have seen repeatedly in this chapter and in Chapter 3, cultural differences among nations are such that a message that works in one nation can fail miserably in another. For a detailed example of this phenomenon, see the case of Polaroid, which is reviewed in the accompanying "Management Focus." Due to cultural diversity, it is extremely difficult to develop a single advertising theme that is effective worldwide. Messages directed at the culture of a given country may be more effective than global messages.

Second, country differences in advertising regulations may block implementation of standardized advertising. For example, Kellogg could not use a television commercial it produced in Great Britain to promote its cornflakes in many other European countries. A reference to the iron and vitamin content of its cornflakes was not permissible in the Netherlands, where claims relating to health and medical benefits are outlawed. A child wearing a Kellogg T-shirt had to be edited out of the commercial before it could be used in

France, since French law forbids the use of children in product endorsements. Furthermore, the key line, "Kellogg's makes their cornflakes the best they have ever been," was disallowed in Germany because of a prohibition against competitive claims.[12] Similarly, American Express recently ran afoul of regulatory authorities in Germany when it launched a promotional scheme that had proved very successful in other countries. The scheme advertised the offer of "bonus points" every time an American Express cardholder used his or her card. According to the advertisements, these "bonus points" could be used toward air travel with three airlines and hotel accommodations. American Express soon found itself charged with breaking Germany's competition law, which prevents an offer of free gifts in connection with the sale of goods, and the firm had to withdraw the advertisements at considerable cost.[13]

DEALING WITH COUNTRY DIFFERENCES Given the arguments for and against the feasibility of globally standardized advertising, the question arises as to whether it might be possible to capture some of the benefits of global standardization while recognizing differences in countries' cultural and legal environments. As it turns out, some firms have been experimenting with this. A firm may select some features for all of its advertising campaigns and localize other features. By doing so, it may save on some costs and build international brand recognition and yet customize its advertisements to different cultures.

This is what Polaroid did with the "Learn to Speak Polaroid" campaign (see the "Management Focus" for details). Pepsi-Cola used a similar approach in its 1986 advertising campaign. The company wanted to use modern music to connect its products with local markets. Pepsi hired popular U.S. singer Tina Turner and rock stars from six countries to team up in singing and performing the Pepsi-Cola theme song in a big rock concert. In the commercials the local rock stars appear with Tina Turner. Except for the footage of the local stars which is spliced into the finished product, all the commercials are identical. By shooting the commercials all at once, Pepsi saved on production costs. The campaign was extended to 30 countries, which relieved the local subsidiaries or bottlers of having to develop their own campaigns.[14]

Pricing Strategy

International pricing strategy is an important component of the overall international marketing mix. In this section we look at three aspects of international pricing strategy. First, we examine the case for pursuing price discrimination, charging different prices for the same product in different countries. Second, we look at what might be called strategic pricing. Third, we briefly review some regulatory factors, such as government-mandated price controls and antidumping regulations, that limit a firm's ability to charge the prices it would prefer.

Price Discrimination

In an international context, price discrimination exists whenever consumers in different countries are charged different prices for the same product. In

Global Advertising at
Polaroid

Polaroid introduced its SX-70 instant camera in Europe in the mid-1970s with the same marketing strategy, TV commercials, and print ads it had used in North America. Polaroid's headquarters believed the camera served a universal need—the pleasure of instant photography—and that the communication strategy should be the same the world over.

The television commercials featured testimonials of personalities well known in the United States. Few of these personalities were known in Europe, however, and managers of Polaroid's European operations pointed this out to headquarters. Unperturbed by these concerns, headquarters management set strict guidelines to discourage deviation from the global plan. Nonetheless, the European personnel were proved correct. The testimonials by "unknown" personalities left consumers cold. The commercials never achieved much impact in raising awareness of Polaroid's instant camera. Even though the camera later became successful in Europe, local management believes the misguided introductory campaign in no way helped its performance.

The lesson was remembered a decade later when Polaroid's European management launched a pan-European program to reposition Polaroid's instant photography from the "party camera" platform to a serious, "utilitarian" platform. This time headquarters did not assume it had the answers. Instead, it looked for inspiration in the various advertising practices of its European subsidiaries, and it found it in the strategy of one of its smallest subsidiaries in Switzerland. With considerable success, the Swiss subsidiary had promoted the functional uses of instant photography as a means of communicating with family and friends. A task force was set up to test this concept in other markets. The tests showed that the Swiss strategy was transferable and that it produced the desired impact. Thus was born Europe's "Learn to

essence, price discrimination involves charging whatever the market will bear; in a competitive market, prices may have to be lower than in a market where the firm has a monopoly. Price discrimination can help a company maximize its profits. It makes economic sense to charge different prices in different countries.

Two conditions are necessary for profitable price discrimination. First, the firm must be able to keep its national markets separate. If it cannot do this, individuals or businesses may undercut its attempt at price discrimination by engaging in arbitrage. Arbitrage occurs when an individual or business capitalizes on a price differential between two countries by purchasing the product in the country where prices are lower and reselling it in the country where prices are higher. For example, many automobile firms have long practiced price discrimination in Europe. At one point a Ford Escort cost $2,000 more in Germany than it did in Belgium. This policy broke down when car dealers bought Escorts in Belgium and drove them to Germany, where they sold them at a profit for slightly less than Ford was selling Escorts in Germany. To protect the market share of its German auto dealers, Ford had to bring its German prices into line with those being charged in Belgium. In other words, Ford could not keep these markets separate.

Speak Polaroid" campaign, one of the firm's most successful advertising efforts. Ultimately, non-European subsidiaries, including those in Japan and Australia, liked the strategy so much they adopted it.

What made this campaign different from the SX-70 campaign a decade earlier was the decentralized decision making. Instead of headquarters imposing on Europe an advertising campaign developed in the United States, the European subsidiaries were able to develop their own campaign. Equally important, even after the pan-European program was adopted, European managers had the freedom to adapt the campaign to local tastes and needs. For example, where tests showed that the "Learn to Speak Polaroid" tag did not convey the intended meaning in the local language, the subsidiary was free to change it. By adopting this approach, Polaroid reaped some of the benefits of standardized advertisements, while at the same time customizing its message to local conditions when that proved necessary.[15]

In its latest European ad campaign, dubbed the "Live for the Moment" series, Polaroid continues to use local resources like London-based Bartle Bogle Hegarty (BBH) to create more regionally appropriate messages. In one commercial from the series, which first aired in London in April of 1995, an attractive young female fan at a rock concert takes a picture of herself and then tosses it on stage, where it lands at the singer's feet. But when the singer looks up to search for her face, she has mysteriously vanished into the crowd.

Courtesy Polaroid Corporation

However, Ford still practices price discrimination between Great Britain and Belgium. A Ford car can cost up to $3,000 more in Great Britain than in Belgium. In this case, arbitrage has not been able to equalize the price because right-hand-drive cars are sold in Great Britain and left-hand-drive cars in the rest of Europe. Because there is no market for left-hand-drive cars in Great Britain, Ford has been able to keep the markets separate.

The second necessary condition for profitable price discrimination is different price elasticities of demand in different countries. The price elasticity of demand is a measure of the responsiveness of demand for a product to changes in price. Demand is said to be elastic when a small change in price produces a large change in demand; it is said to be inelastic when a large change in price produces only a small change in demand. Elastic and inelastic demand curves are illustrated in Figure 12.3. As a rule, a firm can charge a higher price in a country where demand is inelastic.

THE DETERMINANTS OF DEMAND ELASTICITY The elasticity of demand for a product in a given country is determined by a number of factors, of which income level and competitive conditions are perhaps the two most important. Price elasticity tends to be greater (more elastic) in

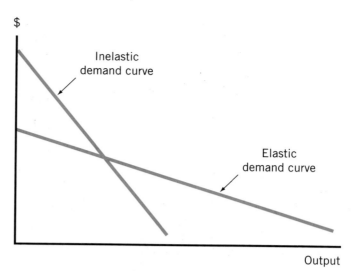

$

Inelastic
demand curve

Elastic
demand curve

Output

FIGURE 12.3

Elastic and Inelastic Demand Curves

countries with low income levels. Consumers with limited incomes tend to be very price conscious; they have less to spend, so they look much more closely at price. Thus, price elasticities for products such as television sets are greater in countries such as India, where a television set is still a luxury item, than in the United States, where it is considered a necessity.

With regard to competitive conditions, in general, the more competitors there are, the greater consumers' bargaining power will be and the more likely consumers will be to buy from the firm that charges the lowest price. Thus, a large number of competitors causes high elasticity of demand. In such circumstances, if a firm raises its prices above those of its competitors, consumers will switch to the competitors' products. The opposite is true when a firm faces few competitors. When competitors are limited, consumers' bargaining power is weaker and price is less important as a competitive weapon. Thus, a firm may charge a higher price for its product in a country where competition is limited than in a country where competition is intense.

PROFIT MAXIMIZING UNDER PRICE DISCRIMINATION

For those readers with some grasp of economic logic, we can offer a more formal presentation of the above argument. (Readers unfamiliar with basic economic terminology may want to skip this subsection.) Figure 12.4 shows the situation facing a firm that sells the same product in only two countries, Japan and the United States. The Japanese market is very competitive, so the firm faces an elastic demand curve (D_J) and marginal revenue curve (MR_J). The U.S. market is not competitive, so there the firm faces an inelastic demand curve (D_U) and marginal revenue curve (MR_U). Also shown in the figure are the firm's total demand curve (D_{J+U}), total marginal revenue curve (MR_{J+U}), and marginal cost curve (MC). The total demand curve is simply the summation of the demand facing the firm in Japan and the United States, as is the total marginal revenue curve.

To maximize profits, the firm must produce at the output where MR = MC. In Figure 12.4 this implies an output of 55 units. If the firm does not prac-

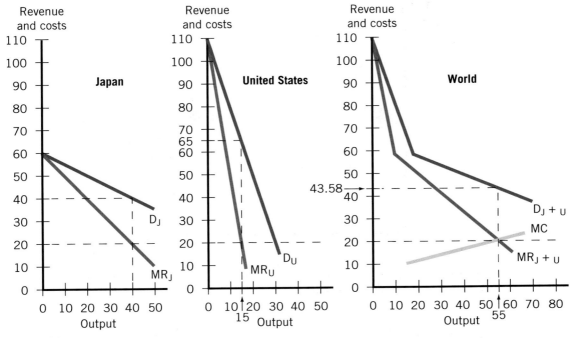

FIGURE 12.4

Price Discrimination

tice price discrimination, it will charge a price of $43.58 to sell an output of 55 units. Thus, without price discrimination the firm's total revenues are

$$\$43.58 \times 55 = \$2,396.90$$

Now look what happens when the firm decides to engage in price discrimination. It will still produce 55 units, since that is where MR = MC. However, the firm must now allocate this output between the two countries to take advantage of the difference in demand elasticity. Proper allocation of output between Japan and the United States can be determined graphically by drawing a line through their respective graphs at $20 to indicate that $20 is the marginal cost in each country (see Figure 12.4). To maximize profits in each country, prices are now set in each country at that level where the marginal revenue for that country equals marginal costs. In Japan this is a price of $40, and the firm sells 40 units. In the United States the optimal price is $65, and it sells 15 units. Thus, reflecting the different competitive conditions, the price charged in the United States is over 50 percent more than the price charged in Japan. More important, look at what happens to total revenues. With price discrimination, the firm earns revenues of

$$\$40 \times 40 \text{ units} = \$1,600$$

in Japan and

$$\$65 \times 15 \text{ units} = \$975$$

in the United States. By engaging in price discrimination, the firm can earn total revenues of

$$\$1,600 + \$975 = \$2,575,$$

which is $178.10 more than the $2,396.90 it earned before. Price discrimination pays!

Strategic Pricing

The concept of strategic pricing has two aspects, which we will refer to as predatory pricing and experience curve pricing. Both predatory pricing and experience curve pricing can result in problems with antidumping regulations. Accordingly, once we have reviewed predatory and experience curve pricing, we will look at antidumping rules and other regulatory policies.

PREDATORY PRICING Predatory pricing is the use of price as a competitive weapon to drive weaker competitors out of a national market. Once the competitors have left the market, the firm can raise prices and enjoy high profits. For such a pricing strategy to work, the firm must normally have a profitable position in another national market, which it can use to subsidize aggressive pricing in the market it is trying to monopolize. Many Japanese firms have been accused of pursuing this strategy. The argument runs similarly to this: Because the Japanese market is protected from foreign competition by high informal trade barriers, Japanese firms can charge high prices and earn high profits at home. They then use these profits to subsidize aggressive pricing overseas, the aim of which is to drive competitors out of those markets. Once this has occurred, so it is claimed, the Japanese firms then raise prices. For example, Matsushita has been accused of using this strategy to enter the U.S. TV market. As one of the major TV producers in Japan, Matsushita earned high profits at home. It then used these profits to subsidize the losses it made in the United States during its early years there, when it priced low to increase its market penetration. Ultimately, Matsushita became the world's largest manufacturer of TVs.[16]

EXPERIENCE CURVE PRICING We encountered the experience curve in Chapter 10. There we saw that as a firm builds its accumulated production volume over time, unit costs fall due to "experience effects." Learning effects and economies of scale underlie the experience curve. Price comes into the picture, because aggressive pricing (along with aggressive promotion and advertising) is a way to build accumulated sales volume rapidly and thus move down the experience curve. And firms further down the experience curve have a cost advantage vis-à-vis firms further up the curve.

Many firms pursuing an experience curve pricing strategy on an international scale price low worldwide in attempting to build global sales volume as rapidly as possible, even if this means taking large losses initially. Such a firm believes that several years in the future, when it has moved down the experience curve, it will be making substantial profits and, moreover, have a cost advantage over its less aggressive competitors.

Regulatory Influences on Prices

Firms' abilities to engage in either price discrimination or strategic pricing may be limited by national or international regulations. Most important, a firm's freedom to set its own prices is constrained by antidumping regulations and competition policy.

ANTIDUMPING REGULATIONS   Both predatory pricing and experience curve pricing can run afoul of antidumping regulations. Technically, dumping occurs whenever a firm sells a product for a price that is less than the cost of producing it. Most regulations, however, define dumping more vaguely. For example, a country is allowed to bring antidumping actions against an importer under Article 6 of GATT as long as two criteria are met: sales at "less than fair value" and "material injury to a domestic industry." The problem with this terminology is that it does not indicate what is a fair value. The ambiguity has led some to argue that selling abroad at prices below those in the country of origin, as opposed to below cost, is dumping.

It was such logic that led the Bush administration to place a 25 percent duty on imports of Japanese light trucks in 1988. The Japanese manufacturers protested that they were not selling below cost. Admitting that their prices were lower in the United States than in Japan, they argued that this simply reflected the intensely competitive nature of the U.S. market (i.e., different price elasticities). In a similar example, the European Commission found Japanese exporters of dot matrix printers to be in violation of dumping regulations. To correct what they saw as dumping, the EU placed a 47 percent import duty on imports of dot matrix printers from Japan. According to EU rules, this import duty must be passed on to European consumers as a price increase.[17]

From the perspective of an international business, the important point is that antidumping rules set a floor under export prices and limit a firm's ability to pursue strategic pricing. The rather vague terminology used in most antidumping actions suggests that a firm's ability to engage in price discrimination also may be challenged under antidumping legislation.

COMPETITION POLICY   Most industrialized nations have regulations designed to promote competition and to restrict monopoly practices. These regulations can be used to limit the prices a firm can charge in a given country. For example, during the 1960s and 1970s the Swiss pharmaceutical manufacturer Hoffmann-LaRoche had a monopoly on the supply of Valium and Librium tranquilizers. In 1973 the company was investigated by the British Monopolies and Mergers Commission, which is responsible for promoting fair competition in Great Britain. The commission found that Hoffmann-LaRoche was overcharging for its tranquilizers and ordered the company to reduce its prices 35 to 40 percent. Hoffmann-LaRoche maintained unsuccessfully that it was merely engaging in price discrimination. Similar actions were later brought against Hoffmann-LaRoche by the German cartel office and by the Dutch and Danish governments.[18]

Configuring the Marketing Mix

A firm might vary aspects of its marketing mix from country to country to take into account local differences in culture, economic conditions, competitive conditions, product and technical standards, distribution systems, government regulations, and the like. Such differences may require some variation in product attributes, distribution strategy, communications strategy, and pricing strategy. As a result of the cumulative effect of these factors, it is rare to find a firm operating in an industry where it can adopt the same marketing mix worldwide.

For example, financial services is often thought of as an industry where global standardization of the marketing mix is the norm. However, while a financial services company such as American Express may sell the same basic charge card service worldwide, utilize the same basic fee structure for that product, and adopt the same basic global advertising message ("never leave home without it"), differences in national regulations still mean it has to vary aspects of its communications strategy from country to country (as pointed out earlier, the promotional strategy it had developed in the United States was illegal in Germany). Similarly, while McDonald's is often thought of as the quintessential example of a firm that sells the same basic standardized product worldwide, in reality it varies one important aspect of its marketing mix—its menu—from country to country. McDonald's also varies its distribution strategy from country to country. In Canada and the United States most McDonald's are located in areas that are easily accessible by car, whereas in more densely populated societies—such as Japan and Great Britain—location decisions are driven by the accessibility of a restaurant to pedestrian traffic, not cars. Because countries typically still do differ along one or more of the dimensions discussed above, some customization of the marketing mix is normal.

By the same token, however, there are often significant opportunities for standardization in one or more elements of the marketing mix. Firms may find that it is possible and desirable to standardize their global advertising message and/or core product attributes in order to realize substantial cost economies. They may find it desirable to customize their distribution and pricing strategy to take advantage of local differences. In reality, the "customization versus standardization" debate is not an all or nothing issue; it frequently makes sense to standardize some aspects of the marketing mix and customize others, depending on conditions prevailing in various national marketplaces. An example, that of Castrol Oil, is given in the accompanying "Management Focus." Castrol sells a standardized product worldwide—lubricating oil—and yet it varies other aspects of its marketing mix from country to country, depending on economic conditions, competitive conditions, and distribution systems. Decisions about what to customize, and what to standardize, should be driven by a detailed examination of the costs and benefits of doing so for each element in the marketing mix.

New-Product Development

Firms that successfully develop and market new products can earn enormous returns. Some examples are:

- Xerox's 20-year domination of the photocopier market.
- Du Pont's steady stream of inventions such as cellophane, nylon, Freon (used in all air-conditioners), and Teflon.
- Sony's development of the Walkman and compact disc.
- Bausch & Lomb's development of contact lenses.
- Matsushita's development of the videocassette recorder.
- Intel's pioneering work with microprocessors.

Castrol Oil is the lubricants division of the British chemical, oil, and gas concern Burmah Castrol. In Europe and in the United States where Castrol now has a 15 percent share of the do-it-yourself lubricants market, Castrol targets motorists who want to cosset their engine by paying a bit more for the liquid engineering of Castrol's high-margin GTX brand, rather than a standard lubricant. This differentiated positioning strategy is supported by sponsoring Formula One racing and the Indy car se-

Castrol Oil

ries in the United States and by heavy spending on television and in automobile magazines in both Europe and the United States.

Some of Castrol's most notable successes in recent years, however, have not been in Europe or the United States; rather, they have been in the developing nations of Asia where Castrol reaps only one-sixth of its sales but over one-fourth of its operating profits. In Vietnam, where automobiles are still relatively rare, Castrol has targeted the vast army of motorcycle owners. Castrol's strategy is to target people who want to take care of their new motorcycles. The long-term

goal is to build brand loyalty, so that when automobile ownership becomes common in Vietnam, as Castrol believes it ultimately will, former motorcycle owners will stick with Castrol when they trade up to cars. This strategy has already worked in Thailand. Castrol has held the leading share of the motorcycle market in Thailand since the early 1980s, and it now holds the leading share in that country's rapidly growing automobile market.

Unlike its practice in more developed countries, in Vietnam

Castrol's communications strategy does not focus on television and glossy print media (since there is relatively little of either in Vietnam). Rather, Castrol focuses on building consumer awareness through extensive use of billboards, car stickers, and above all, some 4,000 signboards at Vietnam's ubiquitous roadside garages and motorcycle cleaning shops. Castrol also developed a unique slogan that has a rhythmic quality in Vietnamese—"*Dau nhot tot nhat*" ("best quality lubricants"). This rhythmic slogan sticks in consumers' minds. Castrol's own researchers say the slogan is now recognized by

99 percent of people in Ho Chi Minh City.

As elsewhere, Castrol has adopted a premium pricing strategy in Vietnam, which is consistent with the company's attempt to build a global brand image of high quality. Castrol Oil costs about $1.50 per liter in Vietnam, about three times as much as the price of cheaper oil imported from countries such as Taiwan and Thailand. Despite the high price, Castrol claims it is gaining share in Vietnam as its branding strategy wins converts.

Castrol has had to tailor its distribution strategy to Vietnam's unique conditions. In most countries where it operates, Castrol divides the country into regions and has a single distributor in each region. In Vietnam, however, Castrol will often have two distinct distributors in a region—one to deal with state-owned customers, of which there are still many in this still nominally Communist country, and one to deal with private customers. Castrol acknowledges that the system is costly, but says it is the only way to operate in a country where there is still some tension between state- and privately-owned entities.[20]

In the late 20th century, competition is as much about technological innovation as anything else. The pace of technological change has accelerated since the Industrial Revolution in the 18th century, and it continues to do so today. The result has been a dramatic shortening of product life cycles. Technological innovation is both creative and destructive.[19] An innovation can make established products obsolete overnight. At the same time, an innovation can make a host of new products possible. Witness recent changes in the electronics industry. For 40 years before the early 1950s, vacuum valves were a major component in radios and then in record players and early computers. The advent of transistors destroyed the market for vacuum valves, but at the same time it created new opportunities connected with transistors. Transistors took up far less space than vacuum valves, creating a trend toward miniaturization that continues today. The transistor held its position as the major component in the electronics industry for just a decade. In the 1970s microprocessors were developed, and the market for transistors declined rapidly. However, the microprocessor created yet another set of new product opportunities—handheld calculators (which destroyed the market for slide rules), compact disc players (which destroyed the market for analog record players), personal computers (which destroyed the market for typewriters), to name a few.

This process of "creative destruction" unleashed by technological change makes it critical that a firm stay on the leading edge of technology, lest it lose out to a competitor's innovations. As we explain in the next subsection, this not only creates a need for the firm to invest in R&D, but it also requires the firm to establish R&D activities at those locations around the globe where expertise is concentrated. Moreover, as we shall see, leading-edge technology on its own is not enough to guarantee a firm's survival. The firm must also apply that technology in developing products that satisfy consumer needs. To do that, the firm needs to build close links between marketing and R&D. This is difficult enough for the domestic firm, but it is even more problematic for the international business competing in an industry where consumer tastes and preferences differ from country to country.

The Location of R&D

Ideas for new products are stimulated by the interactions of scientific research, demand conditions, and competitive conditions. Other things being equal, the rate of new-product development seems to be greater in countries where:

- More money is spent on basic and applied research and development.
- Demand is strong.
- Consumers are affluent.
- Competition is intense.[21]

Basic and applied R&D discovers new technologies and then commercializes them. Strong demand and affluent consumers create a potential market for new products. Intense competition between firms stimulates innovation as the firms try to beat out their competitors and reap potentially enormous first-mover advantages that result from successful innovation.

For most of the post-World War II period, the country that ranked highest in these criteria was the United States. The United States devoted a greater proportion of its GDP to R&D than any other country did. Its scientific establishment was the largest and most active in the world. U.S. consumers were the most affluent in the world, the market was large, and competition among U.S. firms was brisk. Due to these factors, the United States was the lead market—the market where most new products were developed and introduced. Accordingly, it was the best location for R&D activities; it was where the action was.

Since the late 1970s things have been changing. The U.S. monopoly on new-product development has disappeared. Although U.S. firms are still at the leading edge of many new technologies, Japanese and European firms are also strong players. When the Japanese government's Economic Planning Agency surveyed 110 critical leading-edge technologies in 1991, it concluded that U.S. firms dominated 43 of them; Japanese firms, 33; and European firms, the remaining 34.[22] Both Japan and Germany are now devoting a greater proportion of their GDP to nondefense R&D than is the United States. In 1990 Japan spent 3 percent of its GDP on nondefense R&D ; Germany, 2.7 percent; and the United States, 1.8 percent.[23] In addition, both Japan and the European Union are large, affluent markets, and the wealth gap between them and the United States is closing.

It is no longer appropriate to consider the United States the lead market. Indeed, it is questionable if any country is. To succeed today, it is often necessary to simultaneously introduce new products in all major industrialized markets. Moreover, since leading-edge research is now carried out in many locations around the world, the argument for centralizing R&D activity in the United States is now much weaker than it was two decades ago. (It used to be argued that centralized R&D eliminated duplication.) Much leading-edge research is now occurring in Japan and Europe, and it makes sense for many firms to disperse their R&D activities to those locations. Such dispersion allows a firm to stay close to the center of leading-edge activity to gather scientific and competitive information and to draw on local scientific resources. This may result in some duplication of R&D activities, but the cost disadvantages of duplication are outweighed by the advantages of dispersion.

For example, to expose themselves to the research and new-product development work now being done in Japan, many U.S. firms have recently set up satellite R&D centers in Japan. Kodak's $65 million R&D center in Japan employs approximately 200 people. The company hired about 100 professional Japanese researchers and directed the lab to concentrate on electronic imaging technology. A few U.S. firms that have established R&D facilities in Japan are Corning, Texas Instruments, IBM, Digital Equipment, Procter & Gamble, Upjohn, Pfizer, Du Pont, and Monsanto.[24] The National Science Foundation (NSF) has documented a sharp increase in the proportion of total R&D spending by U.S. firms that is now sent abroad. According to NSF data, between 1985 and 1993 the amount of funds committed to foreign R&D soared ninefold, while R&D spending in the United States remained essentially flat.[25] At the same time, to internationalize their own research and gain access to U.S. research talent, the NSF reports that many European and Japanese firms have begun to make heavy investments in U.S.-based research facilities.

Linking R&D and Marketing

Although a firm that is successful at developing new products may earn enormous returns, new-product development is a very risky business with a high failure rate. One estimate suggests that 80 to 88 percent of all research and development projects either fail to produce a marketable product or produce a product that fails to earn an economic return in the marketplace.[26] Another study found that 45 percent of new products that were introduced did not meet their profitability goals.[27] Despite this high failure rate, some firms seem consistently better than others at successfully introducing new products. Firms such as 3M, Sony, and Matsushita have well-earned reputations for successful innovation. One reason for these firms' success seems to be that they build close links between their R&D activities and their marketing function to ensure new products are tailored to consumer needs.[28] Many new products fail because they are not adequately commercialized. For example, many of the early personal computers failed to sell because the user needed to be a computer programmer; their technology had not been commercialized. Steve Jobs of Apple Computer realized that if the technology could be made "user friendly," the market for it would be enormous.

The need to adequately commercialize new technologies poses special problems in the international business, since commercialization may require different versions of a new product to be produced for different countries. To do this, the firm must build close links between its R&D centers and its various country operations. This may require R&D centers in North America, Asia, and Europe that are closely linked by formal and informal integrating mechanisms with marketing operations in each country in their regions. The imperative of linking R&D and local marketing has been identified by the NSF as one of the main factors leading U.S. firms to shift R&D activities overseas. The NSF has found that as U.S. firms moved their manufacturing overseas in the 1980s and early 1990s, their R&D activities followed.[29]

Summary

This chapter has discussed the marketing and R&D functions in international business. A persistent theme of the chapter is the tension that exists between the need to reduce costs and the need to be responsive to local conditions, which raises costs. Specifically, the following points have been made.

1 Levitt has argued that, due to the advent of modern communications and transport technologies, consumer tastes and preferences are becoming global, which is creating global markets for standardized consumer products. However, this position is regarded as extreme by many commentators, who argue that substantial differences still exist between countries.

2 A product can be viewed as a bundle of attributes. Product attributes need to be varied from country to country to satisfy different consumer tastes and preferences.

3 Country differences in consumer tastes and preferences are due to differences in culture and economic development. In addition, differences in product and technical standards may require the firm to customize product attributes from country to country.

4 A distribution strategy decision is an attempt to define the optimal channel for delivering a product to the consumer.

5 Significant country differences exist in distribution systems. In some countries the retail system is concentrated; in others it is fragmented. In some countries channel length is short; in others it is long. Access to some countries' distribution channels is difficult to achieve.

6 A critical element in the marketing mix is communication strategy, which defines the process the firm will use in communicating the attributes of its product to prospective customers.

7 Barriers to international communication include cultural differences, source effects, and noise levels.

8 A communication strategy is either a push strategy or a pull strategy. A push strategy emphasizes personal selling, whereas a pull strategy emphasizes mass media advertising. Whether a push strategy or a pull strategy is optimal depends on the type of product, consumer sophistication, channel length, and media availability.

9 A globally standardized advertising campaign, which uses the same marketing message all over the world, has economic advantages, but it fails to account for differences in culture and the various governments' advertising regulations.

10 Price discrimination exists when consumers in different countries are charged different prices for the same product. Price discrimination can help a firm maximize its profits. For price discrimination to be effective, the national markets must be separate and their price elasticities of demand must differ.

11 Predatory pricing is the use of profit gained in one market to support aggressive pricing in another market to drive competitors out of that market.

12 Experience curve pricing is the use of aggressive pricing to build accumulated volume as rapidly as possible to move the firm down the experience curve.

13 New-product development is a high-risk, potentially high-return activity. To build up a competency in new-product development, an international business must do two things: (*i*) disperse R&D activities to those countries where new products are being pioneered and (*ii*) integrate R&D with marketing.

Critical Thinking and Discussion Questions

1 Imagine you are the marketing manager for a U.S. manufacturer of disposable diapers. Your firm is considering entering the European market, concentrating on the major EU countries. Your CEO believes the advertising message that has been effective in the United States will suffice in Europe. Outline some possible objections to this.

2 By the end of this century we will have seen the emergence of enormous global markets for standardized consumer products. Do you agree with this statement? Justify your answer.

3 You are the marketing manager of a food products company that is considering entering the South Korean market. The retail system in South Korea tends to be very fragmented. Moreover, retailers and wholesalers tend to have long-term ties with South Korean food companies, which makes access to distribution channels difficult. What distribution strategy would you advise the company to pursue? Why?

4 Price discrimination is indistinguishable from dumping. Discuss the accuracy of this statement.

Internet Exercise

Astute managers in today's global marketplace need to keep abreast of market trends. One tool to help them in undertaking their marketing and R&D activities is an online magazine. For example, *Marketing Tools* magazine (http://www.demographics.com/Publications/MT/index.htm), *Forecast* (http://www.demographics.com/Publications/FC/index.htm), and *American Demographics Magazine* (http://www.demographics.com/Publications/AD/index.htm) are U.S.-based electronic magazines that analyze consumer and market trends. *Marketing Week* (http://www.marketing-week.co.uk/mw0001/) provides weekly reports and analyses of the United Kingdom marketing industry.

Global Surfing

Explore the four electronic magazines and describe the featured articles in their latest editions. Search their back issues to find three articles analyzing teen culture. How does this information compare with the global marketing strategies discussed in this chapter's Opening Case? Summarize two articles discussing product attributes. Compare and contrast one article discussing push strategy and another discussing pull strategy. Summarize one article describing integrating R&D with marketing.

Closing Case

Procter & Gamble

Procter & Gamble (P&G), the large U.S. consumer products company, has a well-earned reputation as one of the world's best marketers. With its 80-plus major brands, P&G generates more than $20 billion in annual revenues worldwide. Along with Unilever, P&G is a dominant global force in laundry detergents, cleaning products, and personal care products. P&G expanded abroad in the post-World War II years by exporting its brands and marketing policies to Western Europe, initially with considerable success. Over the next 30 years this policy of developing new products and marketing strategies in the United States and then transferring them to other countries became well entrenched. Although some adaptation of marketing policies to accommodate country differences was pursued, this adaptation was fairly minimal.

The first signs that this policy was no longer effective emerged in the 1970s, when P&G suffered a number of major setbacks in Japan. By 1985, after 13 years in Japan, P&G was still losing $40 million a year there. It had introduced disposable diapers in Japan and at one time had commanded an 80 percent share of the market, but yet by the early 1980s it held a miserable 8 percent. Three large Japanese consumer products companies were dominating the market. P&G's problem was that its diapers, developed in the United States, were too bulky for the tastes of Japanese consumers. With this in mind, Kao, a Japanese company, had developed a line of trim-fit diapers that appealed more to Japanese tastes. Kao introduced its product with a marketing blitz and was quickly rewarded with a 30 percent share of the market. As for P&G, it realized it would have to modify its diapers if it were to compete in Japan. So it did, and the company now has a 30 percent share of the Japanese market. Moreover, ironically, P&G's trim-fit diapers have become a best-seller in the United States.

P&G had a similar experience in marketing education in the Japanese laundry detergent market. In the early 1980s P&G introduced its Cheer laundry detergent in Japan. Developed in the United States, Cheer was promoted in Japan with the U.S. marketing message—that Cheer works in all temperatures and produces lots of rich suds. The problem was that many Japanese consumers wash their clothes in cold water, which made the claim of working in all temperatures irrelevant. Moreover, many Japanese add fabric softeners to their water, which reduces detergents' sudsing action, so Cheer did not suds up as advertised. After a disastrous launch, P&G knew it had to adapt its marketing message. Cheer is now promoted as a product that works effectively in cold water with fabric softeners added, and it is one of P&G's best-selling products in Japan.

P&G's experience with disposable diapers and laundry detergents in Japan forced the company to rethink its product development and marketing phi-losophy. The company now admits that its U.S.-centered way of doing business no longer works. Since the late 1980s P&G has been delegating more responsibility for new-product development and marketing to its major subsidiaries in Japan and Europe. The company is more responsive to local differences in consumer tastes and preferences and more willing to admit that good new products can be developed outside the United States.

Despite the apparent changes at P&G, P&G may not have achieved the revolution in thinking required to alter its long-standing practices. Its venture into the Polish shampoo market seems to illustrate the company still has a way to go. In the summer of 1991 P&G entered the Polish market with its Vidal Sasson Wash & Go, an "all-in-one" shampoo and conditioner that is a best-seller in the United States and Europe. The product launch was supported by a U.S.-style marketing blitz on a scale never before seen in Poland. At first the campaign seemed to be effective as P&G captured more than 30 percent of the shampoo market, but early in 1992 sales suddenly plummeted. Then came the rumors—Wash & Go causes dandruff and hair loss—allegations P&G has strenuously denied. Next came the jokes. One doing the rounds in Poland is, "I washed my car with Wash & Go, and the tires went bald." And when President Lech Walesa proposed about that time that he also be named prime minister, critics derided the idea as a "two-in-one solution, just like Wash & Go."

Where did P&G go wrong? The most common theory is that it promoted Wash & Go too hard in a country that has little enthusiasm for brash U.S.-style advertising. A poll by Pentor, a private market research company in Warsaw, found that almost three times more Poles disliked P&G's commercials than liked them. Pentor also argues that the high-profile marketing campaign backfired because years of Communist party propaganda have led Polish consumers to suspect that advertising is simply a way to move goods nobody wants. Some also believe Wash & Go, which was developed for U.S. consumers who shampoo daily, was far too sophisticated for Polish consumers who are less obsessed with personal hygiene. Underlying all these criticisms is the idea that P&G once again stumbled because it transferred a product and marketing strategy wholesale from the United States to another country without modifying it to the tastes and preferences of local consumers.[30]

Case Discussion Questions

1 What was the root cause of P&G's marketing failures in Japan and Poland?

2 What strategic and organizational actions do you think P&G should take to increase its sensitivity to national differences and their impact on the marketing mix?

3 How might P&G improve its ability to leverage products and marketing strategies developed in one part of the world and apply them to markets elsewhere?

Exporting by the Seat of Your Pants

The more limited your resources, the more resourceful you should be. Sometimes it is necessary to export "by the seat of your pants." Take, for example, Nick Zumbiehl, a 20-year-old college student with dual French and American citizenship who began his exporting career three years ago. Working as a paragliding instructor in France during summer vacation, someone approached him and asked if he could buy the palazzo pants Nick was wearing. Palazzo pants are colorful, fluorescent, and loose-fitting. They were quite common and inexpensive in the United States but virtually unknown in France at the time. Nick liked their appearance, and their color matched the fluorescent paragliding equipment that he used.

Nick not only sold that pair of pants for a 600% profit but enough other pants (about $2,500 per year) to finance other European vacations. Although at first he had no idea how popular his pants would become, he was able to spot a trend (opportunity) and capitalize on it.

The next time, he returned to France with a box full of pants and sold them direct to his paragliding buddies. Sometimes his brother and his friends would accompany him and also take along boxes of pants.

Nick Zumbiehl

Nick recognized that paragliders were the right market for this product. They were innovative, flamboyant, trendy, and risk takers and they were coming to him. He realized, however, that it would not be very long before he saturated the small market where he was giving instruction. Without any money for marketing and without any established retail channels of distribution, Nick decided to hit the road. He began visiting friends and acquaintances at other European paragliding schools, which all operated stores that sold equipment, accessories, and clothing. He asked if they would sell the pants. If they didn't buy his inventory outright, he left the pants on consignment. The stores would then take a 10 percent commission. When exporting on a shoestring budget, trust is very important, but so is taking a risk. "I trusted these people," Nick said. "They were all my friends. Of course, I counted too just to make sure."

In order to succeed it is necessary to spot hot U.S. trends which will eventually find their way abroad. Nick was able to ride such a trend. However, it is also important to recognize when the trend has peaked. For example, Nick is now looking for other products (e.g., surfer sandals) to export, since palazzo pants are now widely available and less expensive throughout Europe.

Successful exporters must be highly motivated. This motivation is strongest when it originates from another of the individual's passions. Nick discovered a product to export as a result of his love of paragliding. He turned it into a business to finance his other desire to travel and soar beyond the mountain peaks. "I was already able to fly," Nick explained. "However, I wanted the chance to explore."

Helena Czepiec
California State Polytechnic University, Pomona

Chapter 13
Global Operations Management

©PhotoDisc

Opening Case

Global Manufacturing and Logistics at Timberland

Timberland, a New Hampshire-based manufacturer of rugged, high-quality shoes, is one of the world's fastest-growing companies. From small beginnings in the late 1970s, Timberland has grown into a global business with sales of over $450 million. The company's global expansion began in 1979 when an Italian distributor walked into the then small U.S. outfit and expressed an interest in shoe #100-81, a hand-sewn moccasin with a lug sole. The Italian thought the shoe would sell well in Italy—the land

Learning Objectives:

1 Be familiar with the important influence that operations management can have on the competitive position of an international business.

2 Understand how country differences, manufacturing technology, and product features all affect the choice of where to locate production operations.

3 Appreciate the factors that influence a firm's decision of whether to source component parts from within the company or purchase them from a foreign supplier.

4 Understand what is required to efficiently coordinate a globally dispersed manufacturing system.

of high-style Gucci shoes. He was right; Timberland quickly became a phenomenon in Italy where Timberland shoes often sold for a 60 percent premium over prices in the United States. Other countries followed, and by the mid-1990s Timberland was generating 50 percent of its sales from 50 foreign countries, including Italy, Germany, France, Britain, and Japan.

Ignored during this rapid growth phase, however, was any attempt to build a tightly managed and coordinated global

manufacturing and logistics system. As a result, by the early 1990s Timberland found itself confronted with an extremely complex global manufacturing and logistics network. To take advantage of lower wage costs outside the United States, the company had established manufacturing facilities in Singapore and Spain as well as the United States. Moreover, Timberland had also found it cost efficient to source footwear and apparel from independent suppliers based in dozens of other low-wage coun-

tries in Asia, Europe, and Latin America. At the same time, Timberland's distribution network had grown to serve consumers in over 50 countries. To complicate things further, the average shipment of footwear to retailers was for less than 12 pairs of each type of shoe, which made for an enormous volume of individual shipments to keep track of.

By the early 1990s Timberland's logistics system was breaking down under the strains imposed by rapid volume growth, a globally dispersed supply and distribution chain, and a large volume of individual shipments. The company simply lacked the information systems required to coordinate and control its dispersed production and distribution network. The consequences included high costs, poor delivery, and inaccurate billing. There were no common information systems linking suppliers, Timberland, and retailers. Nor was there any attempt to consolidate shipments from different regions of the world in order to realize shipping economies. So, for example, products were shipped from six countries in Southeast Asia to the United States and Europe, as opposed to being consolidated at one location and then shipped.

In 1993 Timberland decided to reorganize its global logistics system. The plan was to streamline its logistics information pipeline first and then its cargo pipeline. The information challenge was to come up with a system that would enable Timberland to track a product from the factory to its final destination. The various links in the supply chain—which included manufacturers, warehouses, shippers, and retailers—did not share common data links and as a consequence were not sharing any information. As Timberland's director of distribution explains it: "At every link in the chain, you can make a decision about cargo that would make it flow better, but only if you have the information about the product and the ability to communicate with that location in real time to direct the product." For example, when a product leaves the factory, Timberland can in theory direct a freight forwarder to send the product by air or by ocean carrier, depending on the urgency of the shipment. Moreover, when a shipment lands in, say, Los Angeles, it can be shipped to a distribution center or shipped directly to a customer, again depending on need. These kinds of choices, however, can be made only if Timberland has the requisite information systems. Until 1994 the company lacked such systems.

The company is developing the required information systems in conjunction with ACS, a freight forwarder, and The Rockport Group, a software house. To simplify its physical distribution system and to make implementation of its information systems easier, Timberland is also moving rapidly toward consolidated regional warehousing. Timberland currently has separate warehouses in a dozen Asian countries, several in the United States, and three in Europe. Under the new system being developed sources in Asia will feed into one warehouse. The company will also have single continental distribution centers in North America and Europe. By centralizing its warehousing at three locations, the company will be able to better track where the product is located so it can be routed quickly and flexibly to where it is needed. The result should be a dramatic improvement in Timberland's ability to deliver products to customers exactly when they need them, as opposed to delivering products too late or too soon. Moreover, by consolidating warehousing, Timberland should be able to realize cost savings from reduced warehousing costs and from shipping economies. Timberland will now have the ability to consolidate shipments from a region into one single transoceanic shipment, which should enable the company to negotiate much better shipping rates.[1]

Introduction

In the opening case Timberland is described as having to deal with a number of operational issues that many other firms competing in today's global economy have also had to address. Over the years Timberland has had to decide where in the world to locate its manufacturing activities, how much manufacturing to perform in-house and how much to outsource to foreign suppliers, and how best to organize and control the resulting supply chain to minimize costs and increase its ability to serve its customers in a timely and cost-effective manner. In Timberland's case, the company's decisions regarding global manufacturing and outsourcing have resulted in creation of a globally dispersed supply chain. Timberland is now faced with coordinating and controlling this global web of activities to deliver its product to customers who are dispersed across 50 nations.

In this chapter we take a detailed look at the issues that Timberland and firms like it are facing in the operations area. By **operations**, we mean the activities involved in the procurement of inputs into the production process, the creation of a product, and its delivery to customers. These activities include manufacturing and materials management activities. Managers in an international business have to make a number of critical decisions in the operations arena. They have to decide where in the world to locate productive activities, how much production to outsource to foreign suppliers, and how best to coordinate globally dispersed supply and distribution chains. The Timberland case points toward some answers to these questions. For example, Timberland's decision to establish foreign manufacturing establishments and to outsource significant amounts of manufacturing to independent producers in foreign countries was based on a consideration of relative wage costs. Manufacturing shoes is a labor-intensive activity, and Timberland can save substantial amounts of money by manufacturing in low-wage countries. In this regard Timberland is no different from other large shoe firms, such as the athletic shoe companies Nike and Reebok, which also outsource most of their manufacturing activities to independent suppliers based in low-wage countries.[2] We also learn from the case that coordinating a globally dispersed supply chain required Timberland to develop sophisticated electronic information systems that tied together the different links in the chain. As we shall see later in this chapter, Timberland is again no different from many other global enterprises, which have also found they need to develop sophisticated information systems to manage their global logistics.

To further explore these issues, in this chapter we shall examine each of the three questions posed. We begin, however, by reviewing how the information covered in this chapter fits into the big picture of global strategy that we introduced in Chapter 10.

Strategy, Manufacturing, and Materials Management

In Chapter 10 we introduced the concept of the value chain and discussed a number of value creation activities, including production, marketing, materials management, R&D, human resources, and information systems. In this chapter we are going to focus on two of these activities—production and materials management—and attempt to clarify how they might be performed internationally to (1) lower the costs of value creation and (2) add value by better serving customer needs. We will discuss the contributions of information technology to these activities. In the chapter that follows we will look at human resource management.

In Chapter 10 we defined **production** as the activities involved in creating a product. We used the term *production* to denote both service and manufacturing activities, since one can produce a service or produce a physical product. In this chapter we focus more on manufacturing than on service activities, so we will use the term *manufacturing* rather than production. **Materials management** is the activity that controls the transmission of phys-

operations Activities involved in the procurement of inputs into the production process, the creation of a product, and its delivery to customers.

production Activities involved in creating a product.

materials management Activity that controls the transmission of physical materials through the value chain, from procurement through production and into distribution.

logistics The procurement and physical transmission of material through the supply chain, from suppliers to customers.

ical materials through the value chain, from procurement through production and into distribution. Materials management includes **logistics**, which refers to the procurement and physical transmission of material through the supply chain, from suppliers to customers. Manufacturing and materials management are closely linked, since a firm's ability to perform its manufacturing function efficiently depends on a continuous supply of high-quality material inputs, for which materials management is responsible.

The manufacturing and materials management functions of an international firm have a number of important strategic objectives.[3] Two important objectives that are shared by both manufacturing and materials management are to *lower costs* and to *simultaneously increase product quality* by eliminating defective products from both the supply chain and the manufacturing process.[4] These objectives are not independent of each other. As shown in Figure 13.1, the firm that improves its quality control will also reduce its costs of value creation. Improved quality control reduces costs in three ways:

1 Productivity increases because time is not wasted manufacturing poor-quality products that cannot be sold. This saving leads to a direct reduction in unit costs.

2 Increased product quality means lower rework and scrap costs.

3 Greater product quality means lower warranty and rework costs.

The effect is to lower the costs of value creation by reducing manufacturing *and* service costs.

total quality management Management technique that focuses on the need to improve the quality of a company's products and services.

The main management technique that companies are utilizing to boost their product quality is **total quality management** (TQM). TQM takes as its central focus the need to improve the quality of a company's products and services. The TQM concept was developed by a number of American consultants such as W. Edwards Deming, Joseph Juran, and A.V. Feigenbaum.[5] Deming has identified a number of steps that should be part of any TQM program. Deming argues that management should embrace the philosophy that mistakes, defects, and poor-quality materials are not acceptable and should be eliminated. He suggests that the quality of supervision should be improved by allowing more time for supervisors to work with employees and by providing them with the tools they need to do the job. He recommends that management should create an environment in which employees will not fear reporting problems or recommending improvements. He believes that work standards should be defined not only as numbers or quotas, but also should include some notion of quality to promote the production of defect-free output. He argues that management has the responsibility to train employees in new skills to keep pace with changes in the workplace. And he believes that achieving better quality requires the commitment of everyone in the company.

The growth of international standards has focused greater attention on the importance of product quality. In Europe, for example, the European Union requires that the quality of a firm's manufacturing processes and products be certified under a quality standard known as **ISO 9000** before the firm is allowed access to the European Union marketplace. Although the ISO 9000 certification process has proved to be somewhat bureaucratic and costly for many firms, it does focus management attention on the need to improve the quality of products and processes.[6]

ISO 9000 Standard designed to assure the quality of products and processes.

In addition to lowering costs and improving quality, two other objectives have particular importance in international businesses. First, manufacturing

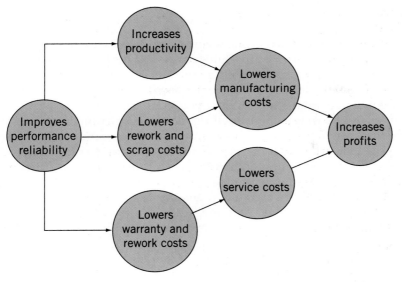

FIGURE 13.1

The Relationship between Quality and Costs
Source: Adapted from David A. Garvin, "What Does Product Quality Really Mean?" *Sloan Management Review* 26 (Fall 1984), Figure 1, p. 37.

and materials management must be able to accommodate demands for local responsiveness. As we saw in Chapter 10, demands for local responsiveness arise from national differences in consumer tastes and preferences, infrastructure, distribution channels, and host government demands. Demands for local responsiveness create pressures to decentralize manufacturing activities to the major national or regional markets in which the firm does business.

Second, manufacturing and materials management must be able to respond quickly to shifts in customer demand. In recent years time-based competition has grown more important.[7] In other words, when consumer demand is prone to large and unpredictable shifts, the firm that can adapt most quickly to these shifts will gain an advantage. As we shall see, both manufacturing and materials management play critical roles here. This issue surfaced in the opening case. One feature of Timberland's new logistics information system is that it should enable Timberland to respond to consumer needs in a more timely manner by ensuring that products arrive at retailers just when they are needed, and not too late or too soon (which would mean the retailer would have to bear the costs of storing the inventory until it was needed).

Where to Manufacture

A key decision facing an international firm is *where to locate its manufacturing activities* to achieve the twin goals of minimizing costs and improving product quality. For the firm that considers international production to be a feasible option, a number of factors must be considered. These factors can be grouped under three broad headings: country factors, technological factors, and product factors.[8]

Country Factors

We reviewed country-specific factors in some detail earlier in the book and we will not dwell on them here. Suffice it to say that political economy, culture, and relative factor costs differ from country to country. In Chapter 4, for example, we saw that due to differences in factor costs, certain countries have a comparative advantage for producing certain products. In Chapters 2 and 3 we saw how differences in political economy and national culture influence the benefits, costs, and risks of doing business in a country. It follows that, other things being equal, a firm should locate its various manufacturing activities where the economic, political, and cultural conditions, including relative factor costs, are more conducive to the performance of those activities. In Chapter 10 we referred to the benefits derived from such a strategy as location economies. We argued that one result of the strategy is the creation of a global web of value creation activities.

Of course, other things are not equal. Other country factors that impinge on location decisions include formal and informal trade barriers and rules and regulations regarding foreign direct investment. Thus, for example, although relative factor costs may make a country look attractive as a location for performing a manufacturing activity, regulations prohibiting foreign direct investment may eliminate this option. Similarly, factor costs might suggest that a firm should source production of a certain component from a particular country, but trade barriers could make this uneconomical.

Another country factor is expected future movements in currency exchange rates. Adverse changes in exchange rates can quickly alter a country's attractiveness as a manufacturing base. Currency appreciation can transform a low-cost location into a high-cost location. Many Japanese corporations have grappled with this problem in recent years. The relatively low value of the yen on foreign exchange markets between 1950 and 1980 helped strengthen Japan's position as a low-cost location for manufacturing. Since the early 1980s, however, the yen's appreciation against the dollar has increased the dollar cost of products exported from Japan, making Japan less attractive as a manufacturing location. In response, many Japanese firms have been moving their manufacturing offshore to lower-cost locations in East Asia.

Technological Factors

The technology we are concerned with in this subsection is manufacturing technology—the technology that performs specific manufacturing activities. The type of technology a firm uses in its manufacturing can be pivotal in location decisions. For example, due to technological constraints, in some cases it is feasible to perform certain manufacturing activities in only one location and serve the world market from there. In other cases, the technology may make it feasible to perform an activity in multiple locations. Three characteristics of a manufacturing technology are of interest here: the level of its fixed costs, its minimum efficient scale, and its flexibility.

FIXED COSTS As we noted in Chapter 10, in some cases the fixed costs of setting up a manufacturing plant are so high that a firm must serve the world market from a single location or from a very few locations. For example, it can cost as much as $1 billion to set up a plant to manufacture semiconductor chips. Given this, serving the world market from a single plant sited at a single (optimal) location makes sense.

On the other hand, a relatively low level of fixed costs can make it economical to perform a particular activity in several locations at once. This allows the firm to better accommodate demands for local responsiveness. Manufacturing in multiple locations may also help the firm avoid the risk of becoming too dependent on one location. Being too dependent on one location is particularly risky in a world of floating exchange rates.

MINIMUM EFFICIENT SCALE The concept of economies of scale tells us that as plant output expands, unit costs decrease. The reasons for this relationship include the greater utilization of capital equipment and the productivity gains that come with greater specialization of employees within the plant.[9] In general, however, beyond a certain level of output, few additional scale economies are available. Thus, the "unit cost curve" declines with output until a certain output level is reached, at which point further increases in output realize little reduction in unit costs. The level of output at which most plant-level scale economies are exhausted is referred to as the minimum efficient scale of output. This is the scale of output a plant must operate at to realize all major plant-level scale economies (see Figure 13.2).

This concept implies that the larger the minimum efficient scale of a plant, the greater the argument for centralizing production in a single location or a limited number of locations. Alternatively, when the minimum efficient scale of production is low it may be economical to manufacture a product at several locations. As in the case of low fixed costs, the advantages are allowing the firm to better accommodate demands for local responsiveness or to hedge against currency risk by manufacturing the same product in several locations.

FLEXIBLE MANUFACTURING (LEAN PRODUCTION) Central to the concept of economies of scale is the idea that the best way to achieve high efficiency, and hence low unit costs, is through the mass production of a standardized output. The trade-off implicit in this idea is one between unit costs and product variety. Producing greater product variety from a factory implies shorter production runs, which in turn implies an inability to realize economies of scale. So increasing product variety makes it difficult for a company to increase its manufacturing efficiency, and thus reduce its unit costs. According to this logic, the way to increase efficiency and drive down unit costs is to limit product variety and produce a standardized product in large volumes.

This view of manufacturing efficiency has been challenged by the recent rise of flexible manufacturing technologies. The term *flexible manufacturing technology*—or **lean production** as it is often called—covers a range of manufacturing technologies that are designed to (1) reduce setup times for complex equipment, (2) increase the utilization of individual machines through better scheduling, and (3) improve quality control at all stages of the manufacturing process.[10] Flexible manufacturing technologies allow the company to produce a wider variety of end products at a unit cost that at one time could be achieved only through the mass production of a standardized output. Recent research suggests that the adoption of flexible manufacturing technologies may actually increase efficiency and lower unit costs relative to what can be achieved by the mass production of a standardized output.[11]

lean production
Manufacturing technologies designed to reduce setup times, increase use of individual machines through better scheduling, and improve quality control at all stages of manufacturing.

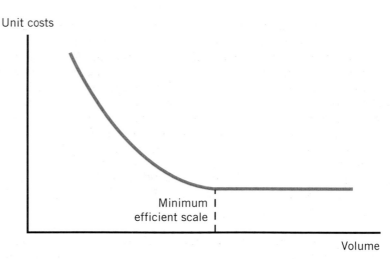

Unit costs

Minimum
efficient scale

Volume

FIGURE 13.2

A Typical Unit Cost Curve

One of the most famous examples of a flexible manufacturing technology was pioneered at Toyota and has been credited with making Toyota the most efficient auto company in the global industry. Toyota's flexible manufacturing system was developed by Ohno Taiichi, a company engineer. After working at Toyota for five years and visiting Ford's U.S. plants, Taiichi became convinced that the mass production philosophy for making cars was flawed. He saw numerous problems with the mass production system. First, long production runs created massive inventories that had to be stored in large warehouses. This was expensive, both because of the cost of warehousing and because inventories tied up capital in unproductive uses. Second, if the initial machine settings were wrong, long production runs resulted in the production of a large number of defects (i.e., waste). And third, the mass production system was unable to accommodate consumer preferences for product diversity.

Taiichi looked for ways to make shorter production runs economical. He developed a number of techniques designed to reduce setup times for production equipment (a major source of fixed costs). By using a system of levers and pulleys he was able to reduce the time required to change dies on stamping equipment from a full day in 1950 to three minutes by 1971! This made small production runs economical, which in turn allowed Toyota to respond better to consumer demands for product diversity. Small production runs also eliminated the need to hold large inventories, thereby reducing warehousing costs. Furthermore, small product runs and the lack of inventory meant that defective parts were produced only in small numbers and entered the assembly process immediately. This reduced waste and helped in tracing defects back to their source and fixing the problem. In sum, Taiichi's innovations enabled Toyota to produce a more diverse product range at a lower unit cost than was possible with conventional mass production.[12]

As the Toyota example makes clear, flexible manufacturing technologies can help improve the efficiency of a company. Not only do flexible manufacturing technologies allow companies to lower costs, but they also enable companies to customize products to the unique demands of small consumer groups—and to do so at a cost that at one time could be achieved only by mass producing a standardized output. Thus, they help a company to increase its customer responsiveness. Most important for an international business, flexible manufacturing technologies can help the firm customize products for different national markets. The importance of this cannot be overstated. When flexible manufacturing technologies are available, a firm can manufacture products customized to various national markets at a single factory at the optimal location. Moreover, it can do this without absorbing a significant cost penalty. Thus, the idea that manufacturing facilities must be established in each major national market in which the firm does business to provide products that satisfy the specific consumer tastes and preferences (part of the rationale for a multidomestic strategy) is becoming outdated (see Chapter 10).

SUMMARY A number of technological factors support the economic arguments for concentrating manufacturing facilities in a few choice locations, or even in a single location. Most important, other things being equal, the arguments for concentrating production at a few choice locations are strong when

- Fixed costs are substantial.
- The minimum efficient scale of production is high.
- Flexible manufacturing technologies are available.

This is true even when substantial differences in consumer tastes and preferences exist between national markets, since flexible manufacturing technologies allow the firm to customize products to national differences at a single facility. Alternatively, the arguments for concentrating production at one or a few locations are not as compelling when

- Fixed costs are low,
- The minimum efficient scale of production is low,
- Flexible manufacturing technologies are not available.

In such cases, it may make more sense to manufacture in each major market in which the firm is active if this helps the firm better respond to local demands. However, this holds only if the increased local responsiveness more than offsets the cost disadvantages of not concentrating manufacturing. With the advent of flexible manufacturing technologies, such a strategy is becoming less attractive. In sum, technological factors are making it feasible, and indeed necessary, for firms to concentrate their manufacturing facilities at optimal locations. Trade barriers and transportation costs are probably the major brakes on this trend.

Product Factors

Two product features impact location decisions. The first is the product's *value-to-weight* ratio because of its influence on transportation costs. Many electronic components have high value-to-weight ratios; they are expensive and they do not weigh very much. Thus, even if they are shipped halfway around the world, their transportation costs account for a very small percentage of total costs. Given this, other things being equal, there is great pressure to manufacture these products in the optimal location and to serve the world market from there. The opposite holds for products with low value-to-weight ratios. Refined sugar, certain bulk chemicals, paints, and petroleum products all have low value-to-weight ratios; they are relatively inexpensive products that weigh a lot. Accordingly, when they are shipped long distances, transportation costs account for a large percentage of total costs. Thus, other things being equal, there is great pressure to manufacture these products in multiple locations close to major markets to reduce transportation costs.

The other product feature that can influence location decisions is whether the product serves **universal needs**, needs that are the same all over the world. Examples include many industrial products (e.g., industrial electronics, steel, bulk chemicals) and modern consumer products (e.g., handheld calculators and personal computers). Since there are few national differences in consumer taste and preference for such products, the need for local responsiveness is reduced. This increases the attractiveness of concentrating manufacturing at an optimal location.

428

Part 5 Competing in a Global Market

universal needs Needs that are the same all over the world.

Locating Manufacturing Facilities

There are two basic strategies for locating manufacturing facilities: concentrating them in the optimal location and serving the world market from there, and decentralizing them in various regional or national locations that are close to major markets. The appropriate strategic choice is determined by the various country, technological, and product factors we have discussed in this section. They are summarized in Table 13.1. Concentration of manufacturing makes most sense when:

- Differences in factor costs, political economy, and culture have a substantial impact on the costs of manufacturing in various countries.
- Trade barriers are low.
- Important exchange rates are expected to remain relatively stable.
- The production technology has high fixed costs or a high minimum efficient scale or a flexible manufacturing technology exists.
- The product's value-to-weight ratio is high.
- The product serves universal needs.

Alternatively, decentralization of manufacturing is appropriate when:

- Differences between countries in factor costs, political economy, and culture do not have a substantial impact on the costs of manufacturing in various countries.
- Trade barriers are high.
- Volatility in important exchange rates is expected.
- The production technology has low fixed costs, low minimum efficient scale, and flexible manufacturing technology is not available.
- The product's value-to-weight ratio is low.
- The product does not serve universal needs (that is, significant differences in consumer tastes and preferences exist among nations).

In practice, location decisions are seldom clear cut. It is not unusual for differences in factor costs, technological factors, and product factors to point

TABLE 13.1

Location Strategy and Manufacturing

	Favored Manufacturing Strategy	
	Concentrated	Decentralized
Country factors		
Differences in political economy	Substantial	Few
Differences in culture	Substantial	Few
Differences in factor costs	Substantial	Few
Trade barriers	Few	Many
Technological factors		
Fixed costs	High	Low
Minimum efficient scale	High	Low
Flexible manufacturing technology	Available	Not available
Product factors		
Value-to-weight ratio	High	Low
Serves universal needs	Yes	No

toward concentrated manufacturing while a combination of trade barriers and volatile exchange rates points toward decentralized manufacturing. This is probably the case in the world automobile industry. Although the availability of flexible manufacturing and cars' relatively high value-to-weight ratios suggest concentrated manufacturing, the combination of formal and informal trade barriers and the uncertainties of the world's current floating exchange rate regime have inhibited firms' ability to pursue this strategy.

For these reasons, Honda is establishing "top-to-bottom" manufacturing operations in its three major markets: Japan, North America, and Western Europe. Honda can treat Western Europe as a single market because of the European Union's success in removing trade barriers and stabilizing exchange rates in the member countries.

Make-or-Buy Decisions

International businesses face **sourcing decisions**, decisions about whether they should make or buy the component parts that go into their final product. That is, should the firm vertically integrate to manufacture its own component parts or should it outsource them—buy them from independent suppliers? Make-or-buy decisions are important factors in many firms' manufacturing strategies. In the automobile industry, for example, the typical car contains more than 10,000 components, so automobile firms constantly face make-or-buy decisions. Ford of Europe, for example, produces only about 45 percent of the value of the Fiesta in its own plants. The remaining 55 percent, mainly accounted for by component parts, comes from independent suppliers. In the athletic shoe industry the make-or-buy issue has been taken to an extreme with companies such as Nike and Reebok hav-

sourcing decisions
Decisions about whether a firm should make or buy the component parts that go into the final product.

ing no involvement in manufacturing—all production has been outsourced, primarily to manufacturers based in low-wage countries.

Make-or-buy decisions pose plenty of problems for purely domestic businesses but even more for international businesses. These decisions in the international arena are complicated by the volatility of countries' political economies, exchange rate movements, changes in relative factor costs, and the like. In this section we examine the arguments for making components and for buying them, and we consider the trade-offs involved in these decisions. We also discuss alliances as an alternative to manufacturing component parts within the company.

The Advantages of Make

The arguments that support making component parts in-house—vertical integration—are fourfold. Specifically, vertical integration may be associated with lower costs, facilitate investments in highly specialized assets, protect proprietary product technology, and facilitate the scheduling of adjacent processes.

LOWER COSTS It may pay a firm to continue manufacturing a product or component part in-house, as opposed to outsourcing it to an independent manufacturer, if the firm is more efficient at that production activity than any other enterprise. Boeing, for example, recently undertook a very detailed review of its make-or-buy decisions with regard to commercial jet aircraft (for details see the next "Management Focus"). As part of that review process, it decided that although it would outsource the production of some component parts to other enterprises, it would keep the production of aircraft wings in-house. Its rationale was that Boeing has a core competence in the production of wings, and that it is more efficient at this activity than any other comparable enterprise in the world. Therefore, it makes little sense for Boeing to outsource this particular activity.

FACILITATING SPECIALIZED INVESTMENTS Imagine Ford of Europe has developed a new, high-performance, high-quality, and uniquely designed carburetor. The carburetor's increased fuel efficiency will help sell Ford cars. Ford must decide whether to make the carburetor in-house or to contract out the manufacturing to an independent supplier. Manufacturing these uniquely designed carburetors requires investments in equipment that can be used only for this purpose; it cannot be used to make carburetors for any other auto firm. In such cases, we say that the investment in this equipment constitutes an investment in **specialized assets**.

Consider this scenario from the perspective of an independent supplier that has been asked by Ford to make this investment. The supplier might reason that once it has made the investment it will become dependent on Ford for business since Ford is the only possible customer for the output of this equipment. The supplier perceives this as putting Ford in a strong bargaining position and worries that once the specialized investment has been made, Ford might use this fact to squeeze down prices for the carburetors. Given this risk, the supplier declines to make the investment in specialized equipment.

specialized assets
Equipment that can be used for only one purpose.

Ford might reason that if it contracts out production of these carburetors to an independent supplier, it might become too dependent on that supplier for a vital input. Since specialized equipment is required to produce the carburetors, Ford cannot easily switch its orders to other suppliers that lack that equipment. (It would face high switching costs.) Ford perceives this as increasing the bargaining power of the supplier and worries that the supplier might use its bargaining strength to demand higher prices.

Thus, the mutual dependency that outsourcing would create in this case makes Ford nervous and scares away potential suppliers. The problem here is lack of trust. Neither party completely trusts the other to play fair. As a result, Ford might reason that the only safe way to get the new carburetors is to manufacture them itself. Indeed, it may be unable to persuade any independent supplier to manufacture them. Thus, Ford decides to make rather than buy.

Thus, in general, we can predict that when substantial investments in specialized assets are required to manufacture a component, the firm will prefer to make the component internally rather than contract it out to a supplier.[13]

PROPRIETARY PRODUCT TECHNOLOGY PROTECTION

Proprietary product technology is technology unique to a firm. If it enables the firm to produce a product containing superior features, proprietary technology can give the firm competitive advantage. Obviously the firm would not want this technology to fall into the hands of competitors. If the firm contracts out the manufacture of components containing proprietary technology, it runs the risk that those suppliers will expropriate the technology for their own use or that they will sell it to the firm's competitors. Thus, to maintain control over its technology, the firm might prefer to make such component parts in-house. An example of a firm that has made such decisions is given in the accompanying "Management Focus," which looks at make-or-buy decisions at Boeing. While Boeing has decided to outsource a number of important components in the production of an aircraft, it has decided not to outsource the manufacture of wings and cockpits, primarily because it believes that doing so would give away key technology to potential competitors.

IMPROVED SCHEDULING The weakest argument for vertical integration is that production cost savings result from it because it makes planning, coordination, and scheduling of adjacent processes easier.[14] This is particularly important in firms with just-in-time inventory systems (which we discuss later in the chapter). In the 1920s, for example, Ford profited from tight coordination and scheduling made possible by backward vertical integration into steel foundries, iron ore shipping, and mining. Deliveries at Ford's foundries on the Great Lakes were coordinated so well that ore was turned into engine blocks within 24 hours. This substantially reduced Ford's production costs by eliminating the need to hold excessive ore inventories.

For international businesses that source worldwide, scheduling problems can be exacerbated by the time and distance between the firm and its suppliers. This is true whether the firms use their own subunits as suppliers or use independent suppliers. Ownership is not the issue here. As we saw in the opening case, Timberland may be able to achieve tight scheduling with its globally dispersed parts suppliers without vertical integration. Thus, although this argument for vertical integration is often made, it is not compelling.

Make-or-Buy Decisions at Boeing

The Boeing Company is the world's largest manufacturer of commercial jet aircraft with a 60 percent share of the global market. Despite its large market share, in recent years Boeing has found it tough going competitively. The company's problems are twofold. First, Boeing faces a very aggressive competitor in Europe's Airbus Industrie. The dogfight between Boeing and Airbus for market share has enabled major airlines to play the two companies off against each other in an attempt to bargain down the price for commercial jet aircraft. Second, as if this weren't bad enough, the world's major airlines have been through some very rough years recently, with many airlines racking up massive financial losses. As a result, many now lack the financial resources required to purchase new aircraft. Instead, they are holding onto their used aircraft for much longer than has typically been the case. Thus, while the typical service life of a Boeing 737 was once reckoned to be about 15 years, many airlines are now making the aircraft last as long as 25 years. This translates into lower orders for new aircraft. In 1994 Boeing and Airbus gained orders for only 150 new aircraft, down from nearly 700 orders in 1989 at the peak of the last order boom. Confronted with this new reality, Boeing has concluded that the only way it can persuade cash-starved airlines to replace their used aircraft with new is if it prices very aggressively.

If prices are going to come under pressure, the only way Boeing can continue to make a profit is if it also drives down its cost structure. With this in mind, in 1993 Boeing reviewed its make-or-buy decisions. The objective was to identify activities

The Advantages of Buy

The advantages of buying component parts from independent suppliers are that it gives the firm greater flexibility, it can help drive down the firm's cost structure, and it may help the firm to capture orders from international customers.

STRATEGIC FLEXIBILITY The great advantage of buying component parts from independent suppliers is that the firm can maintain its flexibility, switching orders between suppliers as circumstances dictate. This is particularly important in the international context, where changes in exchange rates and trade barriers can alter the attractiveness of supply sources over time. One year Hong Kong might be the lowest-cost source for a particular component, and the next year Mexico may be.

Sourcing component parts from independent suppliers can also be advantageous when the optimal location for manufacturing a product is beset by political risks. Under such circumstances, foreign direct investment to establish a component manufacturing operation in that country would expose the firm to political risks. The firm can avoid many of these risks by buying from an independent supplier in that country, thereby maintaining the flexibility to switch sourcing to another country if a war, revolution, or other political change alters that country's attractiveness as a supply source.

that could be outsourced to subcontractors, both in the United States and abroad, in order to drive down production costs.

When making these decisions, Boeing applied a number of criteria. First, Boeing looked at the *basic economics* of the outsourcing decision. The central issue here was whether an activity could be performed more cost effectively by an outside manufacturer or by Boeing. Second, Boeing considered the *strategic risk* associated with outsourcing an activity. Boeing decided it would not outsource any activity that it deemed to be part of its long-term competitive advantage. For example, the company decided not to outsource the production of wings because it believed that doing so might give away valuable technology to potential competitors. Third, Boeing looked at the *operational risk* associated with outsourcing an activity. The basic objective here was to make sure Boeing did not become too dependent on a single outside supplier for critical components. Boeing's philosophy is to hedge operational risk by purchasing from two or more suppliers. Finally, Boeing considered whether it made sense to outsource certain activities to a supplier in a given country in order to help secure orders for commercial jet aircraft from that country. This practice is known as *offsetting*, and it is common in many industries. For example, Boeing decided to outsource the production of certain components to China. This decision was influenced by the fact that current forecasts suggest the Chinese will purchase over $100 billion worth of commercial jets over the next 20 years. Boeing's hope is that pushing some subcontracting work China's way will help it gain a larger share of this market than its global competitor, Airbus.

One of the first decisions to come out of this process was a decision to outsource the production of insulation blankets for 737 and 757 aircraft to suppliers in Mexico. Insulation blankets are wrapped around the inside of the fuselage of an aircraft to keep the interior warm at high altitudes. Boeing has traditionally made these blankets in-house, but it found it could save $50 million per year by outsourcing production to a Mexican supplier. In total, Boeing reckoned that outsourcing would cut its cost structure by $600 million per year between 1994 and 1997. By the time the outsourcing is complete, the amount of an aircraft that Boeing builds will have been reduced from 52 percent to 48 percent.

However, maintaining strategic flexibility has its downside. If a supplier perceives the firm will change suppliers in response to changes in exchange rates, trade barriers, or general political circumstances, that supplier might not be willing to make specialized investments in plant and equipment that would ultimately benefit the firm.

LOWER COSTS Although vertical integration is often undertaken to lower costs, it may end up having the opposite effect and raise costs. When this is the case, outsourcing may be associated with lowering the firm's cost structure. How might vertical integration raise a firm's costs? One potential source of higher costs arises because vertical integration into the manufacture of component parts increases an organization's scope, and the resulting increase in organizational complexity can raise a firm's cost structure. There are three reasons for this.

First, the greater the number of subunits in an organization, the greater are the problems of coordinating and controlling those units. Coordinating and controlling subunits requires top management to effectively process large amounts of information about subunit activities. The greater the number of subunits, the more information top management must process and the harder it is to do this well. Theoretically, when the firm becomes involved in too many activities, headquarters management will be unable to effectively control all of them, and the resulting inefficiencies will more than offset any advantages derived from vertical integration.[15] This problem can be particularly serious in an international business, where the problem of controlling subunits is exacerbated by distance and differences in time, language, and culture.

Second, the firm that vertically integrates into component part manufacture may find that because its internal suppliers have a captive customer in the firm, they will lack an incentive to reduce costs. The fact that they do not have to compete for orders with other suppliers may result in high operating costs. The managers of the supply operation may be tempted to pass on any cost increases to other parts of the firm in the form of higher transfer prices, rather than looking for ways to reduce those costs.

Third, vertically integrated firms have to determine appropriate prices for goods transferred to subunits within the firm. This is a challenge in any firm, but it is even more complex in international businesses. Different tax regimes, exchange rate movements, and headquarters' ignorance about local conditions all increase the complexity of transfer pricing decisions in the international business. This complexity enhances internal suppliers' ability to manipulate transfer prices to their advantage, passing cost increases downstream rather than looking for ways to reduce costs.

The firm that buys its components from independent suppliers can avoid all these problems and the associated costs. The firm that sources from independent suppliers has fewer subunits to control. The incentive problems that occur with internal suppliers do not arise when independent suppliers are used. Independent suppliers know they must continue to be efficient if they are to win business from the firm. Moreover, since independent suppliers' prices are set by market forces, the transfer pricing problem does not exist. In sum, the bureaucratic inefficiencies and resulting costs that can arise when firms vertically integrate backward and manufacture their own components are avoided by buying component parts from independent suppliers.

OFFSETS Another reason for outsourcing some manufacturing to independent suppliers based in other countries is that it may help the firm capture more orders from that country. As noted in the "Management Focus" on Boeing, the practice of offsets is common in the commercial aerospace industry. For example, before Air India places a large order with Boeing, the Indian government might ask Boeing to push some subcontracting work the way of Indian manufacturers. This kind of quid pro quo is not unusual in international business, and it affects far more than just the aerospace industry. In another example, representatives of the U.S. government have repeatedly urged Japanese automobile companies to purchase more component parts from U.S. suppliers in order to partially *offset* the large volume of automobile exports from Japan to the United States.

Trade-offs

It is clear that trade-offs are involved in make-or-buy decisions. The benefits of manufacturing components in-house seem to be greatest when highly specialized assets are involved, when vertical integration is necessary for protecting proprietary technology, or when the firm is simply more efficient than external suppliers at performing a particular activity.

When these conditions are not present, the risk of strategic inflexibility and organizational problems suggests that it may be better to contract out component part manufacturing to independent suppliers. Since issues of strategic flexibility and organizational control loom even larger for international businesses than purely domestic ones, it follows that an international business should be particularly wary of vertical integration into component part manufacture. In addition, we should not forget that some outsourcing in the form of *offsets* may help a firm to gain larger orders in the future.

Strategic Alliances with Suppliers

Several international businesses have tried to reap some of the benefits of vertical integration without the associated organizational problems by entering into strategic alliances with key suppliers. For example, in recent years we have seen an alliance between Kodak and Canon, under which Canon builds photocopiers for sale by Kodak; an alliance between Apple and Sony, under which Sony builds laptop computers for Apple; and an alliance between IBM and Epson, under which Epson provides key component parts for IBM's PRO-PRINTER. By these alliances, Kodak, Apple, and IBM have committed themselves to long-term relationships with these suppliers, which have, no doubt, encouraged the suppliers to undertake specialized investments. Recall from our earlier discussion that a lack of trust inhibits suppliers from making specialized investments to supply a firm with inputs. Strategic alliances are a way to build trust between the firm and its suppliers. Trust is built when a firm makes a credible commitment to continue purchasing from a supplier on reasonable terms. For example, the firm may invest money in a supplier—perhaps by taking a minority shareholding—to signal its intention to build a productive, mutually beneficial long-term relationship.

This kind of arrangement between the firm and its parts suppliers was pioneered in Japan by large auto companies such as Toyota. Many Japanese automakers have cooperative relationships with their suppliers that go back for decades. The auto companies and their suppliers collaborate on ways to increase value added by, for example, implementing just-in-time inventory systems or cooperating in the design of component parts to improve quality and reduce assembly costs. These relationships have been formalized when the auto firms acquired minority shareholdings in many of their key suppliers to symbolize their desire for long-term cooperative relationships with them. At the same time, the relationship between the firm and each key supplier remains market mediated and terminable if the supplier fails to perform up to standard. By pursuing such a strategy, the Japanese automakers have captured many of the benefits of vertical integration—particularly those arising from investments in specialized assets—without suffering the organizational problems that come with formal vertical integration. The parts suppliers also benefit from these relationships since they grow with the firm they supply and they share in its success. As a result of these strategies, Toyota manufactures only 27 percent of its component parts in-house, compared to 48 percent at Ford and 68 percent at GM. Of these three firms, Toyota appears to spend the least on component parts, suggesting it has captured many of the benefits that induced Ford and GM to vertically integrate while it has avoided organizational inefficiencies. For example, in 1985 U.S. manufacturers spent an average of $3,350 on parts, materials, and services for small cars, whereas the average Japanese company spent $2,750—a cost saving of $600 that was achieved mainly through more efficient vendor relations.[16]

In general, the trends toward just-in-time systems (JIT), computer-aided design (CAD), and computer-aided manufacturing (CAM) seem to have increased pressures for firms to establish long-term relationships with their suppliers. JIT, CAD, and CAM systems all rely on close links between firms and their suppliers supported by substantial specialized investment in equipment and information systems hardware. To get a supplier to agree to adopt such systems, a firm must make a credible commitment to an enduring relationship with the supplier. In other words, it must build trust with the supplier. It can do this within the framework of a strategic alliance.

Coordinating a Global Manufacturing System

Until this point in the chapter we have been discussing manufacturing strategy. Now it is time to turn our attention to materials management. Materials management, which encompasses *logistics*, embraces the activities necessary to get materials to a manufacturing facility, through the manufacturing process, and out through a distribution system to the end user.[17] The twin objectives of materials management are to achieve this at the lowest possible cost and in a way that best serves customer needs, thereby lowering the costs of value creation and helping the firm establish a competitive advantage through superior customer service.

The potential for reducing costs through more efficient materials management is enormous. For the typical manufacturing enterprise, material costs account for between 50 and 70 percent of revenues depending on the industry. Even a small reduction in these costs can have a substantial impact on profitability. According to one estimate, for a firm with revenues of $1 million, a return on investment rate of 5 percent, and materials costs that are 50 percent of sales revenues, a $15,000 increase in total profits could be achieved either by increasing sales revenues 30 percent or by reducing materials costs 3 percent.[18] In a saturated market it would be much easier to reduce materials costs by 3 percent than to increase sales revenues by 30 percent.

The materials management task is a major undertaking in a firm with a globally dispersed manufacturing system and global markets. Consider the example of Bose Corporation, which is presented in the accompanying "Management Focus." Bose purchases component parts from suppliers scattered over North America, Europe, and the Far East. It assembles its high-fidelity speakers in Massachusetts and ships them to customers the world over. Bose's materials management function must coordinate the flow of component parts so they arrive at the assembly plant just in time to enter the production system. Then it must oversee the timely distribution of finished speakers to customers around the globe. These tasks are complicated by the vast distances involved and by the fact that component parts and finished products are shipped across national borders, where they must pass customs. Moreover, as explained in the "Management Focus," from time to time Bose must be able to interrupt the normal supply chain to accelerate the delivery of key components to respond to sudden upsurges in demand for Bose's products.

In the remainder of this section we will see how firms such as Bose can manage materials efficiently. First, we will look at the just-in-time inventory system's role in influencing the performance of the materials management function. Then we discuss the role of information technology in facilitating an efficient materials management function.

The Power of Just-in-Time

Pioneered by Japanese firms during the 1950s and 60s, just-in-time inventory systems now play a major role in most manufacturing firms. The basic philosophy behind just-in-time (JIT) systems is to economize on inventory holding costs by having materials arrive at a manufacturing plant just in time to enter the production process, and not before. The major cost saving comes from speeding up inventory turnover; this reduces inventory holding costs, such as warehousing and storage costs. For example, Ford's switch to JIT systems in the early 1980s reportedly brought the firm a huge onetime savings of $3 billion. Minimal inventory now turns over nine times a year at Ford instead of the former six, which reduced carrying costs by a third almost immediately.

In addition to the cost benefits, JIT systems can also help firms improve product quality. Under a JIT system, parts enter the manufacturing process immediately; they are not warehoused. This allows defective inputs to be spotted right away. The problem can then be traced to the supply source and fixed before more defective parts are produced. Under a more traditional system, the practice of warehousing parts for months before they are used allows a large number of defective parts to be produced by a supplier before a problem is recognized.

The drawback of a JIT system is that it leaves a firm without a buffer stock of inventory. Although buffer stocks are expensive to store, they can help tide a firm over shortages brought about by disruption among suppliers (such as a labor dispute in a key supplier). Buffer stocks can also help a firm respond quickly to increases in demand. However, there are ways around these limitations. To reduce the risks associated with depending on one supplier for an important input, some firms source these inputs from several suppliers. As for responding quickly to increases in consumer demand, the experience of Bose Corporation shows that it is possible to do this while maintaining a JIT system—even if it involves shipping component parts by air express rather than overland or by ship (see "Management Focus").

The Role of Information Technology

As we saw in the "Management Focus" on Bose and the opening case on Timberland, information systems play a crucial role in modern materials management. By tracking component parts as they make their way across the globe toward an assembly plant, information systems enable a firm to opti-

Materials Management at **Bose**

Bose Corporation manufactures some of the world's best high-fidelity speakers. The Massachusetts corporation annually generates about $300 million in revenues. Its worldwide esteem is evidenced by the fact that Bose speakers are best-sellers in Japan, the world leader in consumer electronics. Bose's core competence is its electronic engineering skills, but the company attributes much of its business success to tightly coordinated materials management.

Bose purchases most of its electronic and nonelectronic components from independent suppliers scattered around North America, the Far East, and Europe. Roughly 50 percent of its purchases are from foreign suppliers, the majority of them in the Far East. Bose attempts to coordinate this globally dispersed supply chain so that material holding and transportation costs are minimized. In general, this requires component parts to arrive at Bose's Massachusetts assembly plant just in time to enter the production process. All the same, Bose must remain responsive to customer demands, which requires the company to respond quickly to increases in customer demand for certain speakers. If it does not, it can lose a big order to competitors. Since Bose does not want to hold extensive inventories at its Massachusetts plant, this need for responsiveness requires Bose's globally dispersed supply chain to respond rapidly to increased demand for component parts.

Responsibility for coordinating the supply chain to meet both objectives—minimizing transportation and inventory holding costs and yet responding quickly to customer demands—falls on Bose's materials management function. This function coordinates everything through a sophisticated logistics operation. Most of Bose's imports from the Far East come via ships to the West Coast and then across North America to its Massachusetts plant via train. Most of the company's exports also move by ocean freight, but Bose does not hesitate to use airfreight when goods are needed in a hurry. To control this supply chain, Bose has a long-standing relationship

mize its production scheduling according to when components are expected to arrive. By locating component parts in the supply chain precisely, good information systems allow the firm to accelerate production when needed by pulling key components out of the regular supply chain and having them air expressed to the manufacturing plant.

Firms are increasingly using electronic data interchange (EDI) to help coordinate the flow of materials into manufacturing, through manufacturing, and out to customers. At a minimum, EDI systems require computer linkages among a firm, its suppliers, and its shippers. Sometimes customers also are integrated into the system. These electronic linkages are then used to place orders with suppliers, to register parts leaving a supplier, to track them as they travel toward a manufacturing plant, and to register their arrival. Suppliers typically use an EDI link to send invoices to the purchasing firm. One consequence of an EDI system is that suppliers, shippers, and the purchasing firm are able to communicate with each other in "real time" (with no time delay), which vastly increases the flexibility and responsiveness of the with W. N. Procter, a Boston-based freight forwarder and customs broker. Procter handles customs clearance and shipping from suppliers to Bose. Procter provides Bose up-to-the-minute electronic data interchange (EDI) capabilities, which gives it the ability to track parts as they move through its global supply chain. Whenever a shipment leaves a supplier, it is entered in this "ProcterLink" system. Bose is then able to fine-tune its production scheduling so supplies enter the production process just in time. ProcterLink is more than a simple tracking system, however. The EDI system also allows Bose to run simulations that allow its logistics managers to examine a variety of factors, such as the effect of duties on the cost of goods sold.

Procter provides several other services to Bose, such as selecting overseas agents who can help

Courtesy Bose

move goods out of the Far East. Procter's well-established network of overseas contacts is especially useful when shipments must be expedited through foreign customs. Moreover, Procter is elec-

tronically linked into the U.S. customs system, which allows it to clear freight electronically as much as five days before a ship arrives at a U.S. port or hours before an international air freight shipment arrives. This can get goods to Bose's manufacturing plant several days sooner.

Just how well this system can work was demonstrated recently when a Japanese customer doubled its order for Bose speakers. Bose needed to gear up its manufacturing immediately, but many of the essential components were far from Massachusetts. Using ProcterLink, Bose located the needed parts in its supply chain, pulled them out of the normal delivery chain, and airfreighted them to the manufacturing line to satisfy the accelerated schedule. As a result, Bose was able to fill the doubled order for its Japanese customer.[19]

whole supply system. The second consequence is that much of the paperwork between suppliers, shippers, and the purchasing firm is eliminated. Furthermore, good EDI systems can help a firm decentralize materials management decisions to the plant level. It does this by giving corporate-level managers the information they need for coordinating and controlling decentralized materials management groups.

Key Terms

Summary

This chapter has explained how efficient manufacturing and materials management functions can improve an international business's competitive position by lowering the costs of value creation and by performing value creation activities in such ways that customer service is enhanced and value added is maximized. We looked closely at three issues central to international manufacturing and materials management: where to manufacture, what to make and what to buy, and how to coordinate a globally dispersed manufacturing and supply system. The following points were made in the chapter:

1 The choice of an optimal manufacturing location must consider country factors, technological factors, and product factors.

2 Country factors include the influence of factor costs, political economy, and national culture on manufacturing costs.

3 Technological factors include the fixed costs of setting up manufacturing facilities, the minimum efficient scale of production, and the availability of flexible manufacturing technologies.

4 Product factors include the value-to-weight ratio of the product and whether the product serves universal needs.

5 Location strategies either concentrate or decentralize manufacturing. The choice should be made in light of country, technological, and product factors. All location decisions involve trade-offs.

6 A key issue in many international businesses is determining which component parts should be manufactured in-house and which should be outsourced to independent suppliers.

7 The advantages of making components in-house are that it facilitates investments in specialized assets and helps the firm protect its proprietary technology. It may also improve scheduling between adjacent stages in the value chain. In-house production also makes sense if the firm is an efficient, low-cost producer of a technology.

8 The advantages of buying components from independent suppliers are that it facilitates strategic flexibility and helps the firm avoid the organizational problems associated with extensive vertical integration. Outsourcing might also be employed as part of an "offset" policy, which is designed to win more orders for the firm from a country by pushing some subcontracting work in that country.

9 Several firms have tried to attain the benefits of vertical integration and avoid its associated organizational problems by entering into long-term strategic alliances with key suppliers.

10 Although alliances with suppliers can give a firm the benefits of vertical integration without dispensing entirely with the benefits of a market relationship, alliances have drawbacks. The firm that enters into a strategic alliance may find its strategic flexibility limited by commitments to alliance partners.

11 Materials management encompasses all the activities that move materials to a manufacturing facility, through the manufacturing process, and out through a distribution system to the end user. The materials management function is complicated in an international business by distance, time, exchange rates, custom barriers, and other things.

12 Just-in-time systems generate major cost savings from reduced warehousing and inventory holding costs. In addition, JIT systems help the firm spot defective parts and remove them from the manufacturing process, thereby improving product quality.

13 Information technology, particularly electronic data interchange, plays a major role in materials management. EDI facilitates the tracking of inputs, allows the firm to optimize its production schedule, allows the firm and its suppliers to communicate in real time, and eliminates the flow of paperwork between a firm and its suppliers.

Critical Thinking and Discussion Questions

1 An electronics firm is considering how best to supply the world market for microprocessors used in consumer and industrial electronic products. A manufacturing plant costs approximately $500 million to construct and requires a highly skilled work force. The total value of the world market for this product over the next 10 years is estimated to be between $10 and $15 billion. The tariffs prevailing in this industry are currently low. What kind of manufacturing strategy do you think the firm should adopt—concentrated or decentralized? What kind of location(s) should the firm favor for its plant(s)?

2 A chemical firm is considering how best to supply the world market for sulfuric acid. A manufacturing plant costs approximately $20 million to construct and requires a moderately skilled work force. The total value of the world market for this product over the next 10 years is estimated to be between $20 and $30 billion. The tariffs prevailing in this industry are moderate. Should the firm favor concentrated manufacturing or decentralized manufacturing? What kind of location(s) should the firm seek for its plant(s)?

3 A firm must decide whether to make a component part in-house or to contract it out to an independent supplier. Manufacturing the part requires a nonrecoverable investment in specialized assets. The most efficient suppliers are located in countries with currencies that many foreign exchange analysts expect to appreciate substantially over the next decade. What are the pros and cons of (a) manufacturing the component in-house and (b) outsourcing manufacture to an independent supplier? Which option would you recommend? Why?

4 Explain how an efficient materials management function can help an international business compete more effectively in the global marketplace.

Internet Exercise

International manufacturing issues revolve around effective manufacturing techniques and materials management. Global corporations can benefit from Internet resources, such as the web site of the National Center for Manufacturing Sciences (http://www.ncms.org/home.html). The NCMS is a consortium of companies based in the United States and Canada with the goal of "making North American manufacturing globally competitive through development and implementation of next-generation manufacturing technologies." The site lists NCMS research areas, collaborative projects, strategic initiative groups, and special programs (http://www.ncms.org/research/projects.html). Also included are resources from the NCMS' Manufacturing Information Resource Center (http://www.ncms.org/mirc/), including data to assist industry leaders in keeping abreast of current technology, predicting trends, and becoming aware of strategic opportunities.

Global Surfing
Explore the NCMS site and read the Center's corporate and subsidiary information, including the mission statement. What specific technological and product resources does it offer to members to help them compete globally? Describe the functions of the strategic initiative groups, particularly in the area of manufacturing processes and materials. What research and library resources and Industry Connect databases in the Manufacturing Information Resource Center would assist corporation officials in their manufacturing efforts?

The **Global Supply Chain** at Digital Equipment

Digital Equipment Corporation (DEC), one of the world's largest computer companies, made its name in the 1970s and early 1980s by pioneering the global market for midrange computers (between mainframes and desktop computers). Like IBM, the company was highly vertically integrated, making almost every major component that went into a DEC computer. This vertical integration strategy was driven by DEC's desire to keep its proprietary computer technology in-house. Physically, this in-house supply chain included 33 plants in 13 countries, with service, repair, and distribution supplied by 30 facilities around the globe. By 1991 DEC served more than 250,000 customer sites, with over half of its $14 billion revenues coming from 81 countries outside of the United States. By this time DEC was also a company in deep financial trouble. From having been one of the most profitable companies in America during much of the 1970s and 1980s, DEC found itself looking at a $3 billion loss for 1991.

DEC's problem was that the computer market had moved rapidly away from it. Demand for midrange computers was slumping as customers switched to companywide networks of computer workstations and personal computers linked by central computer servers. Moreover, the new computer industry of the 1990s was based on an *open standards* philosophy, in which computer companies such as Compaq and Dell Computer purchased component parts "off the shelf" from independent manufacturers and assembled and marketed the final product. The key feature of the new open standards environment was that, unlike the *closed standards* environment once championed by DEC and IBM, technical standards were published, allowing any company to build a product that matched the standard—whether that be a component part or a complete computer. In this new world, DEC's massive vertical integration, once viewed as a way of keeping proprietary technology in-house, was now seen as a high-cost albatross around the company's neck. DEC realized it needed to move to an open standards model, and it needed to get into the personal computer, workstation, and computer networking business if it was to have any hope of stemming its huge losses.

The announcement of this strategic shift by DEC CEO Robert Palmer in 1991 was followed by a top-to-bottom review of DEC's global manufacturing and logistics network. DEC's systems had been designed to consolidate and deliver a moderate number of complex orders for large computer systems. Now it needed to reengineer its systems to deliver a huge number of desktop personal computers and workstations rapidly and reliably. DEC also needed to drive down its cost structure and recognized that this would involve substantial outsourcing of activities that had historically been performed in-house.

As part of this review, DEC looked closely at its global manufacturing supply chain. The study recommended an 18-month plan to restructure its manufacturing and logistics capabilities. The objectives were to reduce costs, reduce assets, and improve customer services. The number of plants was to be reduced from 33 to 12, partly due to the consolidation of certain activities in fewer plants and partly due to much greater outsourcing of component manufacturing to independent suppliers. Moreover, following an evaluation of relative labor costs, tax rates, export and import duties, and currency risk, some manufacturing was moved to new locations. For example, a semiconductor facility in Germany was closed while production was transferred to Queensferry in Scotland, primarily because labor costs were significantly lower at the Queensferry site

The plan also called for three major customer regions—Pacific Rim, Americas, and Europe—to be served by plants within their own regions. Each region, in other words, was set up as a relatively self-contained entity. These changes allowed the company to streamline its global logistics network. There were now far fewer points to ship between, which drove down shipping costs, and the volume of shipping between regions was reduced significantly by the policy that each region become a self-contained entity.

By the spring of 1994 some of the early results were becoming apparent. DEC's annual manufacturing costs had fallen by $167 million and were expected to fall by another $160 million by mid-1995. Similarly, annual logistics costs had been reduced by $200 million relative to their 1991 level. By the time the plan is fully implemented, annual manufacturing costs should have fallen by $500 million, annual logistics costs by $300 million, and DEC will have reduced its asset base—largely due to plant closures—by over $400 million.[20]

Case Discussion Questions

1 What change occurred in DEC's operating environment during the 1980s that transformed its high level of vertical integration from a source of competitive strength into a source of high costs?

2 Why does it make sense for DEC to outsource more activities in the computer industry of the 1990s?

3 How was DEC able to reduce its annual logistics costs? What was the main source of cost saving?

Family Ties & Tobacco Roots

How do you decide to develop and market your own cigar label, a global business which will span at least three continents, at age 21? If your family roots are intertwined with tobacco in Spain, the Philippines, the United States, and Indonesia, perhaps it seems less daunting.

Henry Slonsky, while earning his undergraduate degree in international business, is parlaying his unique heritage into a profitable business opportunity which will capitalize on the cigar craze that is sweeping the United States. Henry and his mother have formed Tropical Import/Export Company to import cigars into the United States from Indonesia and the Philippines. The business requires very little capital investment, since they will act only as middlemen arranging the shipments between the producers and the distributors.

Cigars are very popular in the United States, but premium ones are in short supply. According to the Cigar Association of America, Americans smoked 3.5 billion cigars in 1996, more than any other nationality except the

Henry Slonsky

Chinese. Presently, there are six million cigar smokers in the United States, of which some one million are premium cigar smokers. Premium cigar imports rose from 107 million in 1993 to 166 million in 1995. Imports of foreign cigars rose significantly in 1996 in the United States, by 32% in volume and 45% in dollar value. Their popularity is attributed in part to celebrities who have glamorized cigar smoking. There has also been an increase of invitation-only smoker nights at restaurants, microbreweries, and coffee shops.

The biggest problem cigar companies have is getting enough product to sell. The industry expects to sell more than 2.3 billion cigars in 1997 and back orders for quality smokes are estimated at 20 million. The shortage is due to the cigar makers' failure to anticipate the smoking boom. Furthermore, it takes years to train someone to properly roll cigars, so production cannot be increased overnight.

Henry's maternal grandfather has strong connections with numerous Indonesian and Filipino tobacco growers. He moved to the Philippines from Spain over 30 years ago to work in the tobacco industry. He is now owner of a cigar warehouse in Indonesia. He has extensive experience buying and selling tobacco leaves and has developed his own blend. He has always dreamed of starting his own cigar label, and calling it "Veguerous," Spanish for "view of the plantation". However, until now, he feared that starting his own plantation could jeopardize the steady income he needed to support his family.

Henry's mother, born in Spain but raised in the Philippines, moved to the United States with her husband and children 17 years ago. She inherited both her father's sense of family duty and his desire for independence. All these years she has helped support her family by working in a number of jobs, but always for someone else. Now after completing her bachelor's degree in business administration, she is ready to make her and her father's dream a reality. She now owns Coffee Bazaar in San Dimas, and recently added a cigar lounge to the café.

Henry, the eldest of three sons, and the first grandson, is leading the family at long last into a cigar business of their own. Henry shares the family's strong work ethic, but has always been much more risk-tolerant. He has already obtained a pilot's license, and has earned his master scuba diver certificate.

This is not Henry's first attempt at international business. In the past, Henry tried to arrange a deal to ship fertilizer from Mexico to Spain for a client of his uncle. Henry's uncle operates his own import/export company in Spain which handles everything from tobacco to plywood. Henry's fertilizer deal failed to materialize when the family friend upon whom he was relying to locate a source fell through. In international trade, buyers contact multiple sources looking for the best deal. Henry learned that if one does not seize the moment, the buyer will disappear.

Henry also tried unsuccessfully to ship compact discs from the United States to Spain for another of his uncle's clients. In the compact disc deal, Henry did locate a U.S. supplier, but the deal fell through when his uncle delayed in providing him accurate customer requirements. According to Henry, "There is always a time limit on such deals. Any miscommunication can be very costly."

Henry and his mother are teaming up to sell and distribute a variety of cigars in the United States. Their flagship brand will be his grandfather's brand. It will be positioned as a high-quality cigar that will stand the test of time. However, it will not be ready for distribution for several more months. The family is in the process of hiring experienced cigar rollers to train rollers in Indonesia. Also, tobacco used in premium cigars is aged 18 to 24 months before it can be rolled. Some manufacturers even age the cigars for an additional year before shipping them to market. In the meantime Henry is designing a label, obtaining copyrights, and contacting distributors and retailers about carrying the brand.

The family has also negotiated the exclusive right to import cigars produced by a small Indonesian company. These cigars will be positioned as hand-rolled, earthy cigars and sold under the "Wild Javaneros," label, which Henry designed. The cigars look rugged and should appeal to smokers with a more adventuresome, machismo self-image.

Henry can also import cigars from the Philippines, the supply of which his grandfather can guarantee. However, they are of lower quality and he is concerned that they will not fit into his premium line.

Henry is committed to participating in every aspect of the business. He intends to design the cigar labels himself, negotiate with the distributors and retailers as well as participate in other strategic decisions, learn how to roll the cigars, and improve his Spanish. This is an ambitious agenda for someone so young, but perhaps not impossible for someone like Henry who has already learned to fly.

Helena Czepiec
California State Polytechnic University, Pomona

Chapter 14
Global Human Resource Management

©PhotoDisc

Opening Case

Global Human Resource Management at Coca-Cola

Coca-Cola Company is perhaps one of the most successful multinational enterprises of our times. With operations in close to 200 countries and nearly 80 percent of its operating income being derived from businesses outside the United States, Coca-Cola is typically perceived as the quintessential global corporation. Coca-Cola, however, likes to think of itself as a "multi-local" company that just happens to be headquartered in Atlanta but could be headquartered anywhere and that presents the Coca-Cola brand with a "local

Learning Objectives:

1 Be familiar with pros and cons of different approaches to staffing policy in international businesses.
2 Understand why managers may fail to thrive in foreign postings.

3 Understand what can be done to increase an executive's chance of succeeding in a foreign posting.

4 Appreciate the role that training, management development, and compensation practices can play in effectively managing human resources within an international business.

face" in every country where it does business. The philosophy is perhaps best summarized by the phrase "think globally, act locally," which captures the essence of Coca-Cola's cross-border management mentality. A dominant theme at Coca-Cola is to grant different national businesses the freedom to conduct operations in a manner that is appropriate to the market in which they are competing. At the same time, the company tries to establish a common mind-set that all its employees share.

Coca-Cola manages its global operations through 25 operating divisions that are organized under six regional groups: North America, the European Union, the Pacific Region, the North East Europe/Middle East Group, Africa, and Latin America. Coca-Cola's corporate human resources management (HRM) function is charged with providing the glue that binds these various divisions and groups into the Coca-Cola family. The corporate HRM function achieves this in two main ways: first, by propagating a com-

mon human resources philosophy within the company, and second, by developing a group of internationally minded midlevel executives for future senior management responsibility.

The corporate HRM group sees its mission as one of developing and providing the underlying philosophy around which local businesses can develop their own human resource practices. For example, rather than have a standard salary *policy* for all its national operations, Coca-Cola has a common salary *philosophy*—its total compensation package will be competitive with the best companies in their local market. Twice a year the corporate HRM group also conducts two-week HRM orientation sessions for the human resource staff from each of its 25 operating divisions. One purpose of these sessions is to give an overview of the company's HRM philosophy and to talk about how different local businesses can translate that philosophy into human resource policies in their area. Coca-Cola has found that information sharing is one of the great benefits of bringing HRM professionals together. For example, tools that have been developed in Brazil to deal with a specific HRM problem might also be useful in Australia. The sessions provide a medium through which HRM professionals can communicate and learn from each other, facilitating the rapid transfer of innovative and valuable HRM tools from region to region.

With regard to international staffing policies, as much as possible Coca-Cola tries to staff its local operations with local personnel. To quote one senior executive: "We strive to have a limited number of international people in the field because generally local people are better equipped to do business at their home locations." However, there's still a need for expatriates in the system for two main reasons. One is to fill a need for a specific set of skills that might not exist at a particular location. For example, when Coca-Cola started operations in Eastern Europe it had to bring in an expatriate from Chicago, who was of Polish descent, to fill the position of finance manager. The second reason for utilizing expatriates is to improve the employee's own skill base. Coca-Cola believes that because it is a global company, anyone assuming serious senior management responsibility should have international exposure.

Currently the corporate HRM group has about 500 high-level managers that are involved in what it calls its "global service program." Coca-Cola characterizes these managers as people who have knowledge of their particular field, plus knowledge of the company, and who can do two things in an international location—add value by the expertise they bring to each assignment and enhance their contribution to the company by having international experience. Of the 500 participants in the program, about 200 move each year. To ease the costs of transfer for these employees, Coca-Cola gives those in its global service program a U.S.-based compensation package. In other words, they are paid according to U.S. benchmarks, as opposed to the benchmark prevailing in whatever country they are currently located in. Thus, an Indian manager in this program who is currently working in Britain will be paid according to U.S. salary benchmarks—and not those prevailing in either India or Britain. One of the ultimate goals of this program is to build a cadre of internationally minded high-level managers from which the future senior managers of Coca-Cola will be drawn.[1]

Introduction

human resource management Activities an organization carries out to use its human resources effectively.

Human resource management refers to the activities an organization carries out to utilize its human resources effectively.[2] These activities include determining the firm's human resource strategy, staffing, performance evaluation, management development, compensation, and labor relations. As the opening case on Coca-Cola makes clear, none of these activities is performed in a vacuum; all are related to the strategy of the firm. Human resource management has an important strategic component.[3] Through its influence on the character, development, quality, and productivity of the firm's human resources, the HRM function can help the firm achieve its primary strategic goals of reducing the costs of value creation and adding value by better serving customer needs.

The role of HRM is complex enough in a purely domestic firm, but it is more complex in an international business, where staffing, management development, performance evaluation, and compensation activities are complicated by profound differences between countries in labor markets, culture, legal systems, economic systems, and the like (see Chapters 2 and 3). For example,

- Compensation practices may have to vary from country to country depending on prevailing management customs.
- Labor laws may prohibit union organization in one country and mandate it in another.
- Equal employment legislation may be strongly pursued in one country and not in another.

Moreover, if it is to build a cadre of international managers, the HRM function must deal with a host of issues related to expatriate managers. (An **expatriate manager** is a citizen of one country who is working abroad in one of the firm's subsidiaries.)

In the opening case we saw how Coca-Cola deals with some of these issues. Coca-Cola copes with differences by articulating a common HRM *philosophy*, but by letting each national operation translate this philosophy into specific *policies* that are best suited to their particular operating environment. Coca-Cola also tries to build a cadre of internationally minded executives through its global service program, which involves the HRM function identifying and managing the career development of a key group of executives from which future senior management will be selected. Finally, and perhaps most importantly, Coca-Cola sees the HRM function as a vital link in the implementation of its strategic goal of thinking globally and acting locally.

In this chapter we will look closely at the role of HRM in an international business. We shall review the four major tasks of the HRM function—staffing policy, management training and development, performance appraisal, and compensation policy. Throughout these sections we will point out the strategic implications of each of these tasks. We relate HRM policy back to the different strategies that we first discussed in Chapter 10.

Staffing Policy

Staffing policy is concerned with the selection of employees for particular jobs. At one level, this involves selecting individuals who have the skills required to do particular jobs. At another level, staffing policy can be a tool for developing and promoting corporate culture.[4] By corporate culture we mean the organization's norms and value systems. A strong corporate culture can help a firm pursue its strategy. General Electric, for example, is not just concerned with hiring people who have the skills required for performing particular jobs; it wants to hire individuals whose behavioral styles, beliefs, and value systems are consistent with those of GE. This is true whether an American is being hired, an Italian, a German, or an Australian and whether the hiring is for a U.S. operation or a foreign operation. The belief is that if employees are predisposed toward the organization's norms and value systems by their personality type, the firm will be able to attain higher performance.

Research has identified three types of staffing policies in international businesses: the ethnocentric approach, the polycentric approach, and the geocentric approach.[5] We will review each policy and link it to the strategy pursued by the firm. As we will see, the most attractive staffing policy is probably the geocentric approach, although there are several impediments to adopting it.

The Ethnocentric Approach

ethnocentric Type of staffing policy in which all key management positions are filled by citizens from the parent firm's home country.

An **ethnocentric** staffing policy is one in which all key management positions are filled by parent country nationals. This practice was very widespread at one time. Firms such as Procter & Gamble, Philips NV, and Matsushita originally followed it. In the Dutch firm Philips, for example, all important positions in most foreign subsidiaries were at one time held by Dutch nationals who were referred to by their non-Dutch colleagues as the Dutch Mafia. In many Japanese firms today, such as Toyota and Matsushita, key positions in international operations are still often held by Japanese nationals.

Firms pursue an ethnocentric staffing policy for three reasons. First, the firm may believe there is a lack of qualified individuals in the host country to fill senior management positions. This argument is heard most often when the firm has operations in less developed countries. Second, the firm may see an ethnocentric staffing policy as the best way to maintain a unified corporate culture. Many Japanese firms, for example, prefer their foreign operations to be headed by expatriate Japanese managers because these managers will have been socialized into the firm's culture while employed in Japan.[6] Similarly, until recently Procter & Gamble preferred to staff important management positions in its foreign subsidiaries with U.S. nationals who had been socialized into P&G's corporate culture by years of employment in its U.S. operations. Such reasoning tends to predominate when a firm places a high value on its corporate culture.

Third, if the firm is trying to create value by transferring core competencies to a foreign operation, as firms pursuing an international strategy are, it may believe that the best way to do this is to transfer parent country nationals who have knowledge of that competency to the foreign operation. Imagine what might occur if a firm tried to transfer a core competency in marketing to a foreign subsidiary without supporting the transfer with a corresponding transfer of home country marketing management personnel. The transfer would probably fail to produce the anticipated benefits because the knowledge underlying a core competency cannot easily be articulated and written down. Such knowledge often has a significant tacit dimension; it is acquired through experience over time. Just like the great tennis player who cannot instruct others how to become great tennis players simply by writing a handbook, the firm that has a core competency in marketing, or anything else, cannot just write a handbook that tells a foreign subsidiary how to build the firm's core competency anew in a foreign setting. It must also transfer management personnel to the foreign operation so they can show foreign managers how to become good marketers, for example. The need to transfer managers overseas arises because the knowledge that underlies the firm's core competency resides in the heads of its domestic managers. In turn, they have acquired this knowledge through years of experience, not by reading a handbook. Thus, if a firm is to transfer a core competency to a foreign subsidiary, it must also transfer the appropriate managers.

Despite this rationale for pursuing an ethnocentric staffing policy, the policy is now on the wane in most international businesses. There are two reasons for this. First, an ethnocentric staffing policy limits advancement opportunities for host country nationals. This can lead to resentment, lower productivity, and increased turnover among that group. Resentment can be greater still if, as often occurs, expatriate managers are paid significantly more than home country nationals.

Second, an ethnocentric policy can lead to "cultural myopia," the firm's failure to understand host country cultural differences that require different approaches to marketing and management. The adaptation of expatriate managers can take a long time, during which they may make major mistakes. For example, expatriate managers may fail to appreciate how product attributes, distribution strategy, communications strategy, and pricing strategy should be adapted. The result may be some costly blunders. The closing case to Chapter 12 described how this occurred at Procter & Gamble on a number of occasions. In response, P&G is now hiring more host country nationals to senior management positions in its foreign operations.

The Polycentric Approach

A **polycentric** staffing policy requires host country nationals to be recruited to manage subsidiaries, while parent country nationals occupy key positions at corporate headquarters. In many respects a polycentric approach is a response to the shortcomings of an ethnocentric approach. One advantage of adopting a polycentric approach is that the firm is less likely to suffer from cultural myopia. Host country managers are unlikely to make the mistakes arising from cultural misunderstandings that expatriate managers are vulnerable to. A second advantage is that a polycentric approach may be less expensive to implement. Expatriate managers can be very expensive to maintain.

However, a polycentric approach also has its drawbacks. Host country nationals have limited opportunities to gain experience outside their own country and thus cannot progress beyond senior positions in their own subsidiary. As in the case of an ethnocentric policy, this may cause resentment. Perhaps the major drawback with a polycentric approach, however, is the gap that can form between host country managers and parent country managers. Language barriers, national loyalties, and a range of cultural differences may isolate the corporate headquarters staff from the various foreign subsidiaries. The lack of management transfers from home to host countries, and vice versa, can exacerbate this isolation and lead to a lack of integration between corporate headquarters and foreign subsidiaries. The result can be a "federation" of largely independent national units with only nominal links to the corporate headquarters. Within such a federation, the coordination required to transfer core competencies or to pursue experience curve and location economies may be difficult to achieve. Thus, although a polycentric approach may be effective for firms pursuing a multidomestic strategy, it is inappropriate for other strategies.

Moreover, the federation that may result from a polycentric approach can be a force for inertia within the firm. For example, after decades of pursuing a polycentric staffing policy, food and detergents giant Unilever found that shifting from a multidomestic strategic posture to a transnational posture was very difficult. Unilever's foreign subsidiaries had evolved into quasi-autonomous operations, each with its own strong national identity. These "lit-

polycentric Type of staffing policy in which citizens of the host country are recruited to manage subsidiaries while key management positions at headquarters are filled by citizens from the parent firm's home country.

tle kingdoms" objected strenuously to corporate headquarters' attempts to limit their autonomy and to rationalize global manufacturing.[7]

The Geocentric Approach

A **geocentric** staffing policy seeks the best people for key jobs throughout the organization, regardless of nationality. There are a number of advantages to this policy. First, it enables the firm to make the best use of its human resources. Second, and perhaps more important, a geocentric policy enables the firm to build a cadre of international executives who feel at home working in a number of different cultures. Creation of such a cadre may be a critical first step toward building a strong unifying corporate culture and an informal management network, both of which are required to implement global and transnational strategies.[8] Firms using a geocentric staffing policy may be better able to create value from the pursuit of experience curve and location economies and from the multidirectional transfer of core competencies than firms using other staffing policies. In addition, the multinational composition of the management team that results from geocentric staffing tends to reduce cultural myopia and to enhance local responsiveness. Thus, other things being equal, a geocentric staffing policy seems the most attractive.

Despite this, a number of problems limit the firm's ability to pursue a geocentric policy. Many countries want foreign subsidiaries to employ their citizens. To achieve this goal, they use immigration laws to require the employment of host country nationals if they are available in adequate numbers and have the necessary skills. Most countries (including the United States) require firms to provide extensive documentation if they wish to hire a foreign national instead of a local national. This documentation can be time-consuming, expensive, and at times futile. A further problem is that a geocentric staffing policy can be very expensive to implement. There are increased training costs, relocation costs involved in transferring managers from country to country, and the need for a compensation structure with a standardized international base pay level that may be higher than national levels in many countries. In addition, the higher pay enjoyed by managers placed on an international "fast track" may be a source of resentment within a firm.

Summary

The advantages and disadvantages of the three approaches to staffing policy are summarized in Table 14.1. Broadly speaking, an ethnocentric approach is compatible with an international strategy, a polycentric approach is compatible with a multidomestic strategy, and a geocentric approach is compatible with both global and transnational strategies. (See Chapter 10 for details of the strategies.)

While the staffing policy typology described here is well known and widely used among both practitioners and scholars of international businesses, recently some critics have claimed the typology is too simplistic and it may obscure the internal differentiation of management practices within international businesses. The critics claim that within some international businesses, staffing policies vary significantly from national subsidiary to national subsidiary so that while some are managed on an ethnocentric basis, others are

TABLE 14.1

Comparison of Staffing Approaches

Staffing Approach	Strategic Appropriateness	Advantages	Disadvantages
Ethnocentric	International	Overcomes lack of qualified managers in host nation Unified culture Helps transfer core competencies	Produces resentment in host country Can lead to cultural myopia
Polycentric	Multidomestic	Alleviates cultural myopia Inexpensive to implement	Limits career mobility Isolates headquarters from foreign subsidiaries
Geocentric	Global and transnational	Uses human resources efficiently Helps build strong culture and informal management network	National immigration policies may limit implementation Expensive

managed in a polycentric or geocentric manner.[9] Other critics note that the staffing policy adopted by a firm is primarily driven by its geographic scope, as opposed to its strategic orientation, with firms that have a very broad geographic scope being the most likely to have a geocentric mind-set.[10] Thus, Coca-Cola, which is involved in about 200 countries, is by this argument more likely to have a geocentric mind-set than a firm that is involved in only three countries.

The Expatriate Problem

Two of the three staffing policies we have discussed—the ethnocentric and the geocentric—rely on extensive use of expatriate managers. With an ethnocentric policy, the expatriates are all home country nationals who are transferred abroad. With a geocentric approach, the expatriates need not be home country nationals; the firm does not base transfer decisions on nationality. A prominent issue in the international staffing literature is **expatriate failure**—the premature return of an expatriate manager to his or her home country.[11] Here we briefly review the evidence on expatriate failure before discussing a number of ways in which the expatriate failure rate can be minimized.

expatriate failure
Premature return of an expatriate manager to his or her home country.

Expatriate Failure Rates

Expatriate failure represents a failure of the firm's selection policies to identify individuals who will not thrive abroad. The costs of expatriate failure are high. One estimate is that the average cost per failure to the parent firms can be as high as three times the expatriate's annual domestic salary plus the cost of relocation (which is affected by currency exchange rates and location of assignment).[12] Other research suggests that between 16 and 40 percent of all

American employees sent abroad return from their assignments early, and each premature return costs over $100,000. In addition, approximately 30 to 50 percent of American expatriates, whose average compensation package runs to $250,000 per year, stay at their international assignments but are considered ineffective or marginally effective by their firms.[13] In one study, R. L. Tung surveyed a number of U.S., European, and Japanese multinationals.[14] Her results, summarized in Table 14.2, suggest that 76 percent of U.S. multinationals experience expatriate failure rates of 10 percent or more, with 7 percent of U.S. multinationals experiencing a failure rate of more than 20 percent. Tung's work also suggests that U.S.-based multinationals experience a much higher expatriate failure rate than either European or Japanese multinationals.

Tung asked her sample of multinational managers to indicate reasons for expatriate failure. For U.S. multinationals, the reasons, in descending order of importance, were

1 Inability of spouse to adjust.
2 Manager's inability to adjust.
3 Other family problems.
4 Manager's personal or emotional maturity.
5 Inability to cope with larger overseas responsibility.

Managers of European firms gave only one reason consistently to explain expatriate failure: the inability of the manager's spouse to adjust to a new environment. For the Japanese firms, the reasons for failure, in descending order of importance, were

1 Inability to cope with larger overseas responsibility.
2 Difficulties with new environment.
3 Personal or emotional problems.
4 Lack of technical competence.
5 Inability of spouse to adjust.

TABLE 14.2

Expatriate Failure Rates

Recall Rate Percent	Percent of Companies
U.S. multinationals	
20–40%	7%
10–20	69
<10	24
European multinationals	
11–15%	3%
6–10	38
<5	59
Japanese multinationals	
11–19%	14%
6–10	10
<5	76

Source: R. L. Tung, "Selection and Training Procedures of U.S., European, and Japanese Multinationals," *California Management Review* 25 (1982), pp. 57–71.

Perhaps the most striking difference between these lists is that "inability of spouse to adjust" was the number one reason for expatriate failure among U.S. and European multinationals but only the number five reason among Japanese multinationals. Tung comments that this difference is not surprising, given the role and status to which Japanese society traditionally relegates the wife and the fact that most of the Japanese expatriate managers in the study were men.

Since Tung's study a number of other studies have confirmed that the inability of a spouse to adjust, the inability of the manager to adjust, or other family problems remain major reasons for continuing high levels of expatriate failure. One recent study by International Orientation Resources, an HRM consulting firm, found that 60 percent of expatriate failures occur due to these three reasons.[15] The inability of expatriate managers to adjust to foreign postings seems to be caused by a lack of cultural skills on the part of the manager being transferred. According to one HRM management consulting firm, this is because the expatriate selection process at many firms is fundamentally flawed.

> Expatriate assignments rarely fail because the person cannot accommodate to the technical demands of the job. Typically, the expatriate selections are made by line managers based on technical competence. They fail because of family and personal issues and lack of cultural skills that haven't been part of the selection process.[16]

The failure of spouses to adjust to a foreign posting seems to be related to a number of factors. Often spouses find themselves in a foreign country without the familiar network of family and friends. Language differences make it difficult for them to make new friends. While this may not be too great a problem for the manager, who can make friends at work, it can be difficult for the spouse who might feel trapped at home. The problem is often exacerbated by immigration regulations prohibiting the spouse from taking employment.

Expatriate Selection

One way of reducing expatriate failure rates is through improved selection procedures. In a review of the research on this issue, Mendenhall and Oddou state that a major problem in many firms is that HRM managers tend to fall into the trap of equating domestic performance with overseas performance potential, selecting candidates for foreign postings accordingly.[17] Domestic performance and overseas performance potential are not the same thing. An executive who performs well in a domestic setting may not be able to adapt to managing in a different cultural setting. From their review of the research, Mendenhall and Oddou identified four dimensions that seem to predict success in a foreign posting: self-orientation, others-orientation, perceptual ability, and cultural toughness.

1 *Self-orientation.* The attributes of this dimension strengthen the expatriate's self-esteem, self-confidence, and mental well-being. Expatriates with high self-esteem, self-confidence, and mental well-being were more likely to succeed in foreign postings. Mendenhall and Oddou concluded that such individuals were able to adapt their interests in food, sport, and music; had interests outside of work that could be pursued (e.g., hobbies); and were technically competent.

2 *Others-orientation*. The attributes of this dimension enhance the expatriate's ability to interact effectively with host country nationals. The more effectively the expatriate interacts with host country nationals, the more likely he or she is to succeed. Two factors seem to be particularly important here: relationship development and willingness to communicate. Relationship development refers to the ability to develop long-lasting friendships with host country nationals. Willingness to communicate refers to the expatriate's willingness to use the host country language. Although language fluency helps here, an expatriate need not be fluent to show willingness to communicate. Making the effort to use the language is what is important. Such gestures tend to be rewarded with greater cooperation by host country nationals.

3 *Perceptual ability*. This is the ability to understand why people of other countries behave the way they do; that is, the ability to empathize with them. This dimension seems critical for managing host country nationals. Expatriate managers who lack this ability tend to treat foreign nationals as if they were home country nationals. As a result, they may experience significant management problems and considerable frustration. As one expatriate executive from Hewlett-Packard observed, "It took me six months to accept the fact that my staff meetings would start 30 minutes late, and that it would bother no one but me." According to Mendenhall and Oddou, well-adjusted expatriates tend to be nonjudgmental and nonevaluative in interpreting the behavior of host country nationals and willing to be flexible in their management style, adjusting it as cultural conditions warrant.

4 *Cultural toughness*. This dimension refers to the fact that how well an expatriate adjusts to a particular posting tends to be related to the country of assignment. Some countries are much tougher postings than others because their cultures are more unfamiliar and uncomfortable. For example, many Americans regard Great Britain as a relatively easy foreign posting, and for good reason—U.S. and British cultures have much in common. On the other hand, many Americans find postings in non-Western cultures—such as India, Southeast Asia, and the Middle East—to be much tougher.[18] The reasons are many, including poor health care and housing standards, inhospitable climate, a lack of Western entertainment, and language difficulties. It is also important to stress that many cultures are extremely male dominated and thus may be particularly difficult postings for female Western managers.

Mendenhall and Oddou note that standard psychological tests can be used to assess the first three of these dimensions, whereas a comparison of cultures can give managers a feeling for the fourth dimension. Their basic point is that in addition to domestic performance, these four dimensions should be given weight when selecting a manager for foreign posting. However, current practice does not conform to Mendenhall and Oddou's recommendations. Tung's research, for example, showed that only 5 percent of the firms in her sample used formal procedures and psychological tests to assess the personality traits and relational abilities of potential expatriates.[19] Similarly, recent work by International Orientation Resources suggests that when selecting employees for foreign assignments, only 10 percent of the 50 Fortune 500 firms they surveyed tested for important psychological traits such as cultural sensitivity, interpersonal skills, adaptability, and flexibility. Instead, 90 percent of the time employees were selected on the basis of their technical expertise, not their cross-cultural fluency.[20]

One factor that Mendenhall and Oddou do not address is the problem of expatriate failure due to a spouse's inability to adjust. According to a number of other researchers, a review of the family situation should be a part of the expatriate selection process.[21] Yet a recent survey by Windam International, another international HRM management consulting firm, found that spouses were included in preselection interviews for foreign postings only 21 percent of the time, and that only half of them ever receive any cross-cultural training.[22]

Training and Management Development

Selection is just the first step in matching a manager with a job. The next step is training the manager to do the specific job. For example, an intensive training program might be used to give expatriate managers the skills required for success in a foreign posting. In contrast, management development is a much broader concept. It is intended to develop the manager's skills over his or her career with the firm. Thus, as part of a management development program, over a number of years a manager might be sent on several foreign postings to build up her cross-cultural sensitivity and experience. At the same time, along with a group of other managers in the firm, she might attend management education programs at regular intervals.

Historically, most international businesses have been more concerned with training than with management development. They tended to focus their training efforts on preparing home country nationals for foreign postings. Recently, however, the shift toward greater global competition and the rise of transnational firms have changed this. It is increasingly common for firms to provide general management development programs in addition to training for particular posts. In many international businesses, the explicit purpose of these management development programs is strategic. The belief is management development is a tool that can be used to help the firm achieve its strategic goals.

With this distinction between training and management development in mind, in this section we first examine the types of training managers receive for foreign postings. Then we discuss the connection between management development and strategy in the international business.

Training for Expatriate Managers

Earlier in the chapter we saw that the two most common reasons for expatriate failure were the inability of a manager's spouse to adjust to a foreign environment and the manager's own inability to adjust to a foreign environment. Training can help the manager and his or her spouse cope with both of these problems. Cultural training, language training, and practical training all seem to reduce expatriate failure. We discuss each of these kinds of training here.[23] However, we should note that despite the usefulness of these kinds of training, evidence suggests that many managers receive no training before they are sent on foreign postings. One study found that only about 30 percent of managers sent on one- to five-year expatriate assignments received training before their departure.[24]

CULTURAL TRAINING Cultural training seeks to foster an appreciation for the host country's culture. The belief is that understanding a host country's culture will help the manager empathize with the culture, which will enhance her effectiveness in dealing with host country nationals. It has been suggested that expatriates should receive training in the host country's culture, history, politics, economy, religion, and social and business practices.[25] If possible, it is also advisable to arrange for a familiarization trip to the host country before the formal transfer, since this seems to ease culture shock. Given the problems related to spouse adaptation, it is important that the spouse, and perhaps the whole family, be included in cultural training programs.

LANGUAGE TRAINING English is the language of world business; it is possible to conduct business all over the world using only English. For example, at ABB, a Swiss electrical equipment giant, the company's top 13 managers hold frequent meetings in different countries. Since they share no common first language, they speak only English, a foreign tongue to all but one.[26] Despite the prevalence of English, however, an exclusive reliance on English diminishes an expatriate manager's ability to interact with host country nationals. As noted earlier in the chapter, a willingness to communicate in the language of the host country, even if the expatriate is far from fluent, can help build rapport with local employees and improve the manager's effectiveness. Despite this, J. C. Baker's study of 74 executives of U.S. multinationals found that only 23 believed knowledge of foreign languages was necessary for conducting business abroad.[27] Those firms that did offer foreign language training for expatriates believed it improved their employees' effectiveness and enabled them to relate more easily to a foreign culture, which fostered a better image of the firm in the host country.

PRACTICAL TRAINING Practical training is aimed at helping the expatriate manager and her family ease themselves into day-to-day life in the host country. The sooner a day-to-day routine is established, the better are the prospects that the expatriate and her family will adapt successfully. One of the most critical needs is for a support network of friends for the expatriate. Where an expatriate community exists, firms often devote considerable effort to ensuring the new expatriate family is quickly integrated into that group. The expatriate community can be a useful source of support and information and can be invaluable in helping the family adapt to a foreign culture.

Repatriation of Expatriates

A largely overlooked but critically important issue in the training and development of expatriate managers is to prepare them for reentry into their home country organization. Repatriation should be seen as the final link in an integrated, circular process that connects good selection and cross-cultural training of expatriate managers with completion of their term abroad and reintegration into their national organization. However, instead of having employees come home to share their knowledge and encourage other high-performing managers to take the same international career track, expatriates often face a different scenario.[28]

Often when they return home after a stint abroad—during which they have typically been autonomous, well compensated, and celebrated as a big fish in a little pond—they face an organization that doesn't know what they have done for the last few years, doesn't know how to use their new knowledge, and, worse still, doesn't particularly care. In the worst cases, reentering employees have to scrounge for jobs, or firms will create standby positions that don't use the expatriates' skills and capabilities and fail to make the most of the business investment the firm has made in that individual.

Recent research illustrates the extent of this problem. According to one study of repatriated employees, 60 percent to 70 percent didn't know what their position would be when they returned home. Moreover, 60 percent said their organizations were vague about repatriation, about their new roles, and about their future career progression within the company, while 77 percent of those surveyed actually took jobs at a lower level in their home organization than in their international assignments.[29] It is small wonder then that 10 percent of returning expatriates leave their firm within a year of arriving home, while 14 percent leave within three years.[30]

The key to solving this problem is again good human resource planning. Just as the HRM function needs to develop good selection and training programs for its expatriates, so it also needs to develop good programs for reintegrating expatriates back into work life within their home country organization once their foreign assignment is over and for utilizing the knowledge they acquired while abroad. For an example of the kind of program that might be used, read the accompanying "Management Focus," which looks at the repatriation program at Monsanto.

Management Development and Strategy

Management development programs are designed to increase the overall skill levels of managers through a mix of ongoing management education and rotations of managers through a number of jobs within the firm to give them varied experiences. Management development programs are attempts to improve the overall productivity and quality of the firm's management resources.

Increasingly, international businesses are using management development as a strategic tool. Management development programs help build a unifying corporate culture by socializing new managers into the norms and value systems of the firm. In-house company training programs and intense interaction during off-site training can foster esprit de corps—shared experiences, informal networks, perhaps a company language or jargon—as well as develop technical competencies. These training events often include songs, picnics, and sporting events that promote feelings of togetherness. These rites of integration may include "initiation rites" wherein personal culture is stripped, company uniforms are donned (e.g., T-shirts bearing the company logo), and humiliation is inflicted (e.g., a pie in the face). The aim of all these activities is to strengthen a manager's identification with the company.[32]

Bringing managers together in one location for extended periods and rotating them through different jobs in several countries help the firm build an informal management network. Consider the Swedish telecommunications company L. M. Ericsson. Interunit cooperation is extremely important in Ericsson, particularly for transferring know-how and core competencies from the parent to foreign subsidiaries, from foreign subsidiaries to the parent, and

Monsanto's Repatriation Program

Monsanto is a global agricultural, chemical, and pharmaceutical company with revenues in excess of $10 billion and 30,000 employees. At any one time the company will have 100 mid- and higher-level managers who are on extended postings abroad. Two-thirds of these are Americans who are being posted overseas, while the remainder are foreign nationals being employed in the United States.

At Monsanto the process of managing expatriates and their repatriation begins with a rigorous selection process and intensive cross-cultural training, both for the managers and for their families. As at many other global companies, the idea is to build an internationally minded cadre of highly capable managers who will lead the organization in the future.

One of the strongest features of this program is that employees and their sending and receiving managers, or sponsors, develop an agreement about their understanding of this assignment and how it will fit into the firm's business objectives. The focus is on why they are sending assignees abroad to do the job, and what their contribution to Monsanto will be when they return home. As part of this process, sponsoring managers are expected to be explicit about the kind of job opportunities the expatriate will have once she returns home.

Once they do arrive back in their home country, expatriate managers meet with cross-cultural trainers during debriefing sessions. They are also given the opportunity to showcase their experience to their peers, subordinates, and superiors, in special information exchanges.

However, Monsanto's repatriation program focuses on more than just business—it also attends to the family's reentry. Monsanto has found that difficulties with repatriation often have more to do with personal and family-related issues than with work-related issues. But the personal matters obviously affect an employee's work performance, so it is important for the company to pay attention to such issues.

This is why Monsanto offers returning employees an opportunity to work through personal difficulties. About three months after they return home, expatriates meet for three hours at work with several colleagues of their choice. The debriefing session is a conversation aided by a trained facilitator who has an outline to help the expatriate cover all the important aspects of the repatriation. The debriefing allows the employee to share important experiences and enlightens managers, colleagues, and friends about his or her expertise so others within the organization can use some of the global knowledge.

According to one participant, "It sounds silly, but it's such a hectic time in the family's life, you don't have time to sit down and take stock of what's happening. You're going through the move, transitioning to a new job, a new house, the children may be going to a new school. This is a kind of oasis; a time to talk and put your feelings on the table." And apparently it works, for since the program was introduced in 1992 the attrition rate among returning expatriates has dropped sharply.[31]

---

between foreign subsidiaries. To facilitate cooperation, Ericsson has a long-standing policy of transferring large numbers of people back and forth between headquarters and subsidiaries. Ericsson sends a team of 50 to 100 engineers and managers from one unit to another for a year or two. This process establishes a network of interpersonal contacts. This policy is effective for both solidifying a common culture in the company and coordinating the company's globally dispersed operations.[33]

Performance Appraisal

A particularly thorny issue in many international businesses is how best to evaluate expatriate managers' performance.[34] In this section we look at this issue and consider some guidelines for appraising expatriate performance.

Performance Appraisal Problems

Unintentional bias makes it difficult to evaluate the performance of expatriate managers objectively. In most cases, two groups evaluate the performance of expatriate managers—host nation managers and home office managers—and both are subject to bias. The host nation managers may be biased by their own cultural frame of reference and set of expectations. For example, Oddou and Mendenhall report the case of a U.S. manager who introduced participative decision making while working in an Indian subsidiary.[35] The manager subsequently received a negative evaluation from host country managers. Due to the strong social stratification that exists in India, managers are seen as experts who should not have to ask subordinates for details. The local employees apparently viewed the U.S. manager's attempt at participatory management as an indication that he was incompetent and did not know his job. His host country manager's evaluation of his performance was negative.

Home country managers' appraisals may be biased by distance and, in some cases, by their own lack of experience working abroad. Home office management is often not aware of what is going on in a foreign operation. Accordingly, they tend to rely on "hard" data in evaluating an expatriate's performance—data such as the subunit's productivity, profitability, or market share. The problem with using such criteria is that they may reflect factors outside the expatriate manager's control (e.g., adverse changes in exchange rates, economic downturns). Moreover, hard data do not take into account many less visible "soft" variables that are also important, such as an expatriate's ability to develop cross-cultural awareness and to work productively with local managers.

Due to such biases, many expatriate managers appear to believe that headquarters management evaluates them unfairly and does not fully appreciate the value of their skills and experience. This could be one reason many expatriates believe a foreign posting does not benefit their careers. In one study of personnel managers in U.S. multinationals, 56 percent of the managers surveyed stated that a foreign assignment is either detrimental or immaterial to one's career.[36]

Guidelines for Performance Appraisal

Several things can reduce bias in the performance appraisal.[37] First, most expatriates appear to believe more weight should be given to an on-site manager's appraisal than to an off-site manager's appraisal. Due to proximity, an on-site manager is more likely to be able to evaluate the soft variables that are important aspects of an expatriate's performance. The evaluation may be especially valid when the on-site manager is of the same nationality as the expatriate, since cultural bias should be alleviated.

In practice, however, home office managers often write performance evaluations after receiving input from on-site managers. When this is the case, most experts recommend that a former expatriate who served in the same location should be involved in the appraisal process to help reduce bias. Finally, when the policy is for foreign on-site managers to write performance evaluations, home office managers should probably be consulted before an on-site manager completes a formal termination evaluation. This makes sense because it gives the home office manager the opportunity to balance what could be a very hostile evaluation based on a cultural misunderstanding.

Compensation

Two issues are raised in every discussion of compensation practices in an international business. One is how compensation should be adjusted to reflect national differences in economic circumstances and compensation practices. The other issue is how expatriate managers should be paid. In this section we consider each issue in turn.

National Differences in Compensation

Substantial differences exist in the compensation of executives at the same level in various countries. Figure 14.1 compares the gross pay of general managers of $30 million companies in the United States and nine European countries. As can be seen, U.S. executives are paid significantly more than executives in most other countries except for Switzerland. The average U.S. executive is paid twice as much as his or her British counterpart. For example, in 1994 the average European CEO of firms with sales in excess of $250 million was paid $398,7121, while the average U.S. CEO was paid $819,428.[38] However, much of the difference between U.S. CEOs and the other CEOs is that the U.S. CEOs receive a substantial proportion of their pay in the form of long-term incentives such as stock options. This reflects the belief—which has gained wider currency in the United States than elsewhere—that performance-related bonuses motivate managers to do a better job.

These differences in compensation practices raise a perplexing question for an international business: should the firm pay executives in different countries according to the prevailing standards in each country, or should it equalize pay on a global basis? The problem does not really arise in firms pursuing ethnocentric or polycentric staffing policies. In ethnocentric firms the issue can be reduced to that of how much home country expatriates should be paid (which we will consider later). As for polycentric firms, the lack of managers' mobility among national operations implies that pay can and should be kept country-specific. There would seem to be no point in paying executives in Great Britain the same as U.S. executives if they never work side by side.

However, this problem is very real in firms with geocentric staffing policies. Recall that a geocentric staffing policy is consistent with a transnational strategy. One aspect of this policy, from the HRM perspective, is the need for

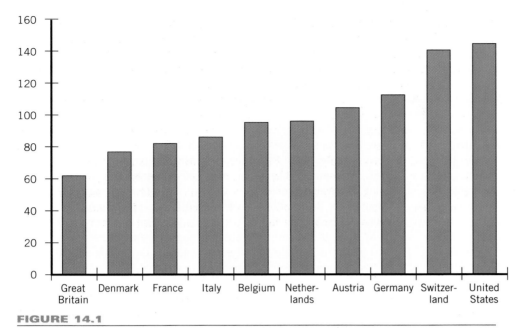

FIGURE 14.1

Compensation of General Managers of $30 Million Firms in Selected Countries
Source: G. Oddou and M. Mendenhall, "Expatriate Performance Appraisal: Problems and Solutions," in *International Human Resource Management*, ed. M. Mendenhall and G. Oddou (Boston: PSW-Kent, 1991).

a cadre of international managers. By definition, this cadre may comprise managers of many different nationalities. Should all members of such a cadre be paid the same salary and the same incentive pay? For a U.S.-based firm this would mean raising the compensation of foreign nationals to U.S. levels, which, given the high pay rates prevailing in the United States, could be very expensive. On the other hand, if the firm does not equalize pay, it could cause considerable resentment among foreign nationals who are members of the international cadre and work side by side with U.S. nationals. In general, if a firm is serious about building an international cadre, it may have to pay its international executives the same basic salary irrespective of their country of origin or assignment. The accompanying "Management Focus" contains several examples of how some international businesses have tried to deal with this problem.

Expatriate Pay

The most common approach to expatriate pay is the balance sheet approach. This approach equalizes purchasing power across countries so employees can enjoy the same living standard in their foreign posting that they enjoyed at home. In addition, the approach provides financial incentives to offset qualitative differences between assignment locations.[40] Figure 14.2 (page 466) shows a typical balance sheet. Note that home country outlays for the employee are designated as income taxes, housing expenses, expenditures for goods and services (food, clothing, entertainment, etc.), and reserves (savings, pension contributions, etc.) The balance sheet approach attempts to provide expatriates with the same standard of living in their host countries as they

Executive Pay Policies for Global Managers

A recent survey of human resource professionals in 45 large U.S. multinational companies undertaken by Organizational Resources Consulting, an international HRM consulting firm, found that all 45 companies viewed differing pay levels and perks as their biggest problem when trying to develop an international work force. In contrast, only 60 percent of these companies stated that cultural differences and repatriation processes were a serious problem. The root of the problem is cost; expatriate pay packages that are based on American salaries and needs are increasingly seen as too expensive. In an attempt to deal with this issue, many international businesses are trying to develop special pay schemes for their cadre of internationally mobile managers.

At Hewlett-Packard (HP) about 600 people a year are transferred across national borders. Although most of these transferees are on short-term (one-to-two-year) assignments, up to 25 percent are on indefinite assignments. HP ties the pay of short-term transferees to pay scales in their home country, but longer-term HP transferees are quickly switched to the pay scale of their host country and paid according to prevailing local standards. For employees moving from high-pay countries such as Germany to lower-pay countries, such as Britain, HP offers temporary bridging payments to ease the adjustment.

On the other hand, 3M has a different type of program for longer-term expatriates. The company developed the program because it drastically altered its international organization. In Europe, for example, 3M used to organize its operations on a country-by-country basis. Now, however, 3M has established Europeanwide divisions. As a result many 3M executives who might have spent their entire career in one country are now being asked to move, perhaps permanently, to another country.

The 3M program compares net salaries in both the old and new country by subtracting the major costs, such as taxes and housing,

---

enjoy at home plus a financial inducement (i.e., premium, incentive) for accepting an overseas assignment.

The components of the typical expatriate compensation package are a base salary, a foreign service premium, allowances of various types, tax differentials, and benefits. We shall briefly review each of these components.[41] An expatriate's total compensation package may amount to three times what he or she would cost the firm in a home country posting. Because of the high cost of expatriates, many firms have reduced their use of them in recent years. However, their ability to do so is often limited by their desire to build a cadre of international managers. Thus, a firm's ability to reduce its use of expatriates may be limited, particularly if it is pursuing an ethnocentric or geocentric staffing policy.

BASE SALARY An expatriate's base salary is normally in the same range as the base salary for a similar position in the home country. The base salary is normally paid in either the home country currency or in the local currency.

did. Any housing subsidy that resulted could last for the rest of an executive's career following a transfer—and this would be a very expensive proposition.

Phillips Petroleum has adopted yet another policy. At Phillips the policy used to be that when a third country national, such as a British citizen, was transferred abroad (for example, from Britain to Kuwait), he would be paid in U.S. dollars and his salary would be raised to a level equivalent to that of someone in the United States doing a similar job. This, however, turned out to be very expensive given the generally high level of pay prevailing in the United States. Thus, now Phillips has a "third country nationals program." Under this program, the transferred employee is given generous housing allowances and educational assistance for his children. However, his salary is now pegged to the level prevailing in his home country or the country to which the employee is being transferred.[39]

from gross pay. The transferred executive then gets whichever pay packet is highest. Thus, when 3M transfers a German executive to France, the German remains on her home country pay scale. But a British employee transferred to Germany, where salaries are higher, can expect to be switched to the German pay scale. However, although the policy considers local housing costs, it doesn't compensate for higher housing costs through a special payment scheme, the way many traditional expatriate pay policies

FOREIGN SERVICE PREMIUM A foreign service premium is extra pay the expatriate receives for working outside his or her country of origin. It is offered as an inducement to accept foreign postings. It compensates the expatriate for having to live in an unfamiliar country isolated from family and friends, having to deal with a new culture and language, and having to adapt to new work habits and practices. Many firms pay foreign service premiums as a percentage of base salary ranging from 10 to 30 percent after tax.

ALLOWANCES Four types of allowances are often included in an expatriate's compensation package: hardship allowances, housing allowances, cost-of-living allowances, and education allowances. A hardship allowance is paid when the expatriate is being sent to a difficult location. A difficult location is usually defined as one where such basic amenities as health care, schools, and retail stores are grossly deficient by the standards of the expatriate's home country. A housing allowance is normally given to ensure that the expatriate can afford the same quality of housing in the foreign country

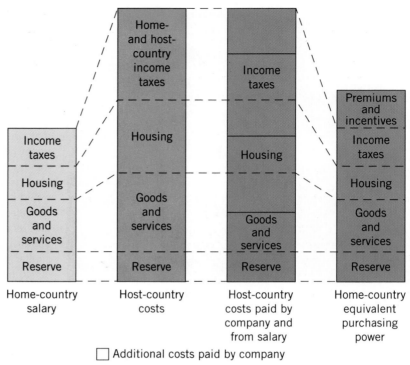

Income taxes	Home- and host-country income taxes	Income taxes	Premiums and incentives
Housing	Housing		Income taxes
Goods and services	Goods and services	Housing	Housing
Reserve	Reserve	Goods and services	Goods and services
		Reserve	Reserve

Home-country salary Host-country costs Host-country costs paid by company and from salary Home-country equivalent purchasing power

☐ Additional costs paid by company

FIGURE 14.2

A Typical Balance Sheet

Source: C. Reynolds, "Compensation of Overseas Personnel," in *Handbook of Human Resource Administration*, 2nd ed., ed. J. J. Famularo (New York: McGraw-Hill, 1986), p. 51.

as at home. In locations where housing is very expensive (e.g., London, Tokyo), this allowance can be substantial—as much as 10 to 30 percent of the expatriate's total compensation package. A cost-of-living allowance ensures that the expatriate will enjoy the same standard of living in the foreign posting as at home. An education allowance ensures that an expatriate's children receive adequate schooling (by home country standards). Host country public schools are sometimes not suitable for an expatriate's children, in which case they must attend a private school.

TAXATION   Unless a host country has a reciprocal tax treaty with the expatriate's home country, the expatriate may have to pay income tax to both the home and host country governments. When a reciprocal tax treaty is not in force, the firm typically pays the expatriate's income tax in the host country. In addition, firms normally make up the difference when a higher income tax rate in a host country reduces an expatriate's take-home pay.

BENEFITS   Many firms also ensure that their expatriates receive the same level of medical and pension benefits abroad that they received at home. This can be very costly for the firm, since many benefits that are tax deductible for the firm in the home country (e.g., medical and pension benefits) may not be deductible out of the country.

Key Terms

ethnocentric, p. 450

expatriate failure, p. 453

expatriate manager, p. 449

geocentric, p. 452

human resource management, p. 448

polycentric, p. 451

staffing policy, p. 449

Summary

This chapter has focused on human resource management in international businesses. HRM activities include human resource strategy, staffing, performance evaluation, management development, and compensation. None of these activities is performed in a vacuum; all must be appropriate to the firm's strategy. The following points were made in the chapter:

1 Staffing policy is concerned with selecting employees who have the skills required to perform particular jobs. Staffing policy can be a tool for developing and promoting a corporate culture.

2 An ethnocentric approach to staffing policy fills all key management positions in an international business with parent country nationals. The policy is congruent with an international strategy. A drawback is that ethnocentric staffing can result in cultural myopia.

3 A polycentric staffing policy uses host country nationals to manage foreign subsidiaries and parent country nationals for the key positions at corporate headquarters. This approach can minimize the dangers of cultural myopia, but it can create a gap between home and host country operations. The policy

is best suited to a multidomestic strategy.

4 A geocentric staffing policy seeks the best people for key jobs throughout the organization, regardless of their nationality. This approach is consistent with building a strong unifying culture and informal management network and is thus well suited to both global and transnational strategies. Immigration policies of national governments may limit a firm's ability to pursue this policy.

5 A prominent issue in the international staffing literature is expatriate failure, defined as the premature return of an expatriate manager to his or her home country. The costs of expatriate failure can be substantial.

6 Expatriate failure can be reduced by selection procedures that screen out inappropriate candidates. The most successful expatriates seem to be those who have high self-esteem and self-confidence, get along well with others, are willing to attempt to communicate in a foreign language, and can empathize with people of other cultures.

7 Training can lower the probability of expatriate failure. It should include cultural training, language training, and practical training, and it should be pro-

vided to both the expatriate manager and the spouse.

8 Management development programs attempt to increase the overall skill levels of managers through a mix of ongoing management education and rotation of managers through different jobs within the firm to give them varied experiences. Management development is often used as a strategic tool to build a strong unifying culture and informal management network, both of which support transnational and global strategies.

9 It can be difficult to evaluate the performance of expatriate managers objectively due to the intrusion of unintentional bias. A number of steps can be taken to reduce this bias.

10 Country differences in compensation practices raise a difficult question for an international business: Should the firm pay executives in different countries according to the standards in each country or equalize pay on a global basis?

11 The most common approach to expatriate pay is the balance sheet approach. This approach aims to equalize purchasing power so employees can enjoy the same living standard in their foreign posting that they had at home.

Critical Thinking and Discussion Questions

1 What are the main advantages and disadvantages of the ethnocentric, polycentric, and geocentric approaches to staffing policy? When is each approach appropriate?

2 Research suggests that many expatriate employees encounter problems that limit both their effectiveness in a foreign posting and their contribution to the company when they return home. What are the main causes and consequences of these problems, and how might a firm reduce the occurrence of such problems?

3 What is the link between an international business's strategy and its human resource management policies, particularly with regard to the use of expatriate employees and their pay scale?

Internet Exercise

The strategic component of effective human resource management guides a corporation in reducing the costs of manufacturing while increasing customer relations. Three human resource organizations have a presence on the World Wide Web, and their sites offer diverse information to corporations worldwide. The International Association for Human Resource Information Management (IHRIM) has 6,000 members, and the site (http://www.ihrim. org/) contains a Management Resources Center, a HR Education Center, and forums for special interest groups. Likewise, the Society for Human Resource Management (SHRM), which serves 85,000 members worldwide, has an extensive site (http://www.shrm.org/text.htm) filled with HRM news, information on the Institute for International HR, government affairs, and seminars. Created in 1919, the International Labour Organization (ILO) is a specialized agency of the United Nations and is the only major remnant of the Treaty of Versailles. The ILO sets labor standards and promotes social justice, and its site (http://www.ilo.org/public/english/index.htm) explains its policies, has the full text of reports and speeches, and lists employment standards and guidelines for a full spectrum of work-related issues.

Global Surfing

Visit the three sites and discuss how they address staffing policies. What publications do they distribute to help managers deal with expatriate employees and compensation practices? What current topics are discussed at their seminars and conferences? What information is available in the IHRIM Management Resources Center? What is the function of the SHRM Institute for International HR? Using the ILO site, what topics have been addressed by which world leaders within the past six months?

Closing Case

Global HRM at Colgate-Palmolive, Inc.

Colgate-Palmolive, the $6 billion a year personal products giant, earns nearly two-thirds of its revenues outside the United States.

For years Colgate succeeded, as many U.S. multinationals have, by developing products at home and then "throwing them over the wall" to foreign subsidiaries. Each major foreign subsidiary was responsible for local manufacturing and marketing. Senior management positions in these subsidiaries were typically held by Americans, and practically all of the company's U.S.-based managers were U.S. citizens.

In the early 1980s Colgate realized that if it was going to succeed in the rapidly changing international business environment, it would have to develop more of a transnational orientation. Its competitors, such as Procter & Gamble, Unilever, and Kao, were trying to become transnational companies, and Colgate needed to follow suit. One important aspect of becoming a transnational is developing an international cadre of executive managers who are as at home working in one culture as in another and who have the ability to rise above their ethnocentric perspectives.

As a first step toward building such a cadre, Colgate began recruiting college graduates in 1987 and putting them through an intensive international training program. The typical recruit holds an M.B.A. from a U.S. university, speaks at least one foreign language, has lived outside the United States, and has strong computer skills and business experience. Over one-quarter of the participants are foreign nationals.

The trainees spend 24 months in a U.S. program. During three-month stints, they learn global business development secrets of, for example, Colgate toothpaste, compiling a guide for introducing a new product or revamping an existing one in various national markets. Participants also receive additional language instruction and take international business trips. When they have completed the program, the participants become associate product managers in the United States or abroad. Unlike most U.S. companies, Colgate does not send foreign-born trainees to their native countries for their initial jobs. Instead, it is more likely that a French national will remain in the United States, a U.S. national will be sent to Germany, and a British national will go to Spain. The foreigners receive the same generous expatriate compensation packages the

Americans do, even if they are assigned to their home country. One problem that has emerged is that this extra pay can create resentment among locally hired managers of foreign subsidiaries. Colgate is trying to resolve this problem by urging its foreign subsidiaries to send their brightest young managers to the training program.

In addition to the management training program, Colgate has taken a number of other steps to develop its international cadre of managers. In Europe, for example, the company is trying to develop "Euromanagers," managers who have experience working in several European countries. This is a departure from the established practice of having managers spend most (if not all) of their working careers in their home country. Also, Colgate now tries to ensure that project teams contain managers from several countries.[42]

Case Discussion Questions

1 What is the relationship between HRM and strategy at Colgate-Palmolive?

2 How do you think Colgate-Palmolive's international training program might improve its economic performance?

3 What potential problem and pitfalls do you see with Colgate-Palmolive's international training program?

Endnotes

Chapter 1

1 C. J. Loomis, "Citicorp: John Reed's Second Act," *Fortune*, April 29, 1996, pp. 89–98. K. Klee, "Brand Builders," *Institutional Investor*, March 1997, pp. 89–101.

2 T. Levitt, "The Globalization of Markets," *Harvard Business Review*, May–June 1983, pp. 92–102.

3 P. Abrahams, "Getting Hooked on Fish and Chips in Japan," *Financial Times*, May 17, 1994.

4 See: F. T. Knickerbocker, *Oligopolistic Reaction and Multinational Enterprise* (Boston: Harvard Business School Press, 1973), and R. E. Caves, "Japanese Investment in the U.S.: Lessons for the Economic Analysis of Foreign Investment," *The World Economy* 16 (1993), pp. 279–300.

5 I. Metthee, "Playing a Large Part," *Seattle Post-Intelligencer*, April 9, 1994, p. 13.

6 C. S. Tranger, "Enter the Mini-Multinational," *Northeast International Business*, March 1989, pp. 13–14.

7 R. B. Reich, *The Work of Nations* (New York: Alfred A. Knopf, 1991).

8 J. Bhagwati, *Protectionism* (Cambridge, MA: MIT Press, 1989).

9 F. Williams, "Trade Round Like This May Never Be Seen Again," *Financial Times*, April 15, 1994, p. 8.

10 "Another World," *The Economist*, September 19, 1992, pp. 15–18.

11 World Trade Organization, *International Trade Trends and Statistics, 1996*.

12 World Trade Organization, "Beyond Borders: Managing a World of Free Trade and Deep Interdependence," press release 55, September 10, 1996.

13 United Nations, *World Investment Report 1996* (New York: United Nations, 1996).

14 World Trade Organization, "Beyond Borders."

15 Moore's Law is named after Intel founder Gorden Moore.

16 A. Adonis, "Lines Open for the Global Village," *Financial Times*, September 17, 1994, p. 8.

17 A. Cane, "Competition Down the Line," *Financial Times*, January 19, 1995, p. 11.

18 P. Taylor, "Revenues of $10 Billion," *Financial Times*, June 15, 1995, p. 4.

19 P. Dicken, *Global Shift* (New York: Guilford Press, 1992).

20 Interviews with Hewlett-Packard personnel by the author.

21 See "War of the Worlds," *The Economist: A Survey of the Global Economy*, October 1, 1994, pp. 3–4.

22 Ibid.

23 One of the classics being J. J. Servan-Schreiber, *The American Challenge* (New York: Atheneum Publishers, 1968).

24 United Nations Press Release, TAD/1835.

25 L. Nakarmi, "A Flying Leap toward the 21st Century," *Business Week*, March 20, 1995, pp. 78–80; J. Burton, "Samsung Drives on towards Globalization," *Financial Times*, October 25, 1994, p. 21; and G. de Jonquieres and J. Burton, "Big Gamble on a European Thrust," *Financial Times*, October 2, 1995, p. 13.

26 R. A. Mosbacher, "Opening Up Export Doors for Smaller Firms," *Seattle Times*, July 24, 1991, p. A7.

27 "Small Companies Learn How to Sell to the Japanese," *Seattle Times*, March 19, 1992.

28 W. J. Holstein, "Why Johann Can Export but Johnny Can't," *Business Week*, November 4, 1991, pp. 64–65.

29 P. Engardio and L. Curry, "The Fifth Tiger Is on China's Coast," *Business Week*, April 6, 1992, pp. 42–43.

30 See, for example, Ravi Batra, *The Myth of Free Trade* (New York: Touchstone Books, 1993).

31 James Goldsmith, "The Winners and the Losers," in *The Case Against the Global Economy*, ed. J. Mander and E. Goldsmith (San Francisco: The Sierra Book Club, 1996).

32 D. L. Bartlett and J. B. Steele, "America: Who Stole the Dream," *Philadelphia Inquirer*, September 9, 1996.

33 For example, see Paul Krugman, *Pop Internationalism* (Cambridge, MA: MIT Press, 1996).

34 Organization for Economic Cooperation and Development, "Income Distribution in OECD Countries," OECD Policy Studies, no. 18 (October 1995).

35 See Krugman, *Pop Internationalism*, and D. Belman and T. M. Lee, "International Trade and the Performance of U.S. Labor Markets," in *U.S. Trade Policy and Global Growth*, ed. R. A. Blecker (New York: Economic Policy Institute, 1996).

36 E. Goldsmith, "Global Trade and the Environment," in: *The Case Against the Global Economy*.

37 Batra, *The Myth of Free Trade*.

38 P. Choate, *Jobs at Risk: Vulnerable U.S. Industries and Jobs under NAFTA* (Washington, DC: Manufacturing Policy Project, 1993).

39 Krugman, *Pop Internationalism*.

40 R. Kuttner, "Managed Trade and Economic Sovereignty," in *U.S. Trade Policy and Global Growth*.

41 Ralph Nader and Lori Wallach, "GATT, NAFTA, and the Subversion of the Democratic Process," in *U.S. Trade Policy and Global Growth*, pp. 93–94.

42 "Perestroika in Soapland," *The Economist*, June 10, 1989, pp. 69–71, and C. Bartlett and S. Ghoshal, *Managing Across Borders: The Transnational Solution* (Boston: Harvard Business School Press, 1989).

43 E. Norton, "Kodak to Slash Price for Film It Sells in Japan," *The Wall Street Journal*, August 24, 1995, p. A2; "The Revenge of Big Yellow," *The Economist*, November 10, 1990, pp. 77–78; D. P. Hamilton and V. Reitman, "Fuji Hoping to Derail U.S. Probe," *The Wall Street Journal*, August 1, 1995, p. A11; W. Bounds, "Fuji Accused by Kodak of Hogging Markets," *The Wall Street Journal*, July 31, 1995, p. A1; and S. Latham, "Kodak's Self-Inflicted Wounds," *The Wall Street Journal*, August 14, 1995, p. A10.

Chapter 2

1 J. Perlez, "GE Finds Tough Going in Hungary," *New York Times*, July 25, 1994, pp. C1, C3, and C. R. Whitney, "East Europe's Hard Path to New Day," *New York Times*, September 30, 1994, pp. A1, A4.

2 As we shall see, there is not a strict one-to-one correspondence between political systems and economic systems. A. O. Hirschman, "The On-and-Off Again Connection between Political and Economic Progress," *American Economic Review* 84, no. 2 (1994), pp. 343–48.

3 For a discussion of the roots of collectivism and individualism, see H. W. Spiegel, *The Growth of Economic Thought* (Durham, NC: Duke University Press, 1991). An easily assessable discussion of collectivism and individualism can be found in M. Friedman, and R. Friedman, *Free to Choose* (London: Penguin Books, 1980).

4 For a classic summary of the tenets of Marxism details, see A. Giddens, *Capitalism and Modern Social Theory* (Cambridge: Cambridge University Press, 1971).

5 For details see "A Survey of China," *The Economist*, March 18, 1995.

6 J. S. Mill, *On Liberty* (London: Longman's, 1865), p. 6.

7 A. Smith, *The Wealth of Nations*, Vol. 1 (London: Penguin Books), p. 325.

8 R. Wesson, *Modern Government—Democracy and Authoritarism*, 2nd ed. (Englewood Cliffs, NJ: Prentice Hall, 1990).

9 For a detailed but accessible elaboration of this argument, see Friedman and Friedman, *Free to Choose*. Also see P. M. Romer, "The Origins of Endogenous Growth," *Journal of Economic Perspectives* 8, no. 1 (1994), pp. 2–32.

10 D. North, *Institutions, Institutional Change, and Economic Performance* (Cambridge: Cambridge University Press, 1991).

11 P. Klebnikov, "Russia's Robber Barons," *Forbes*, November 21, 1994, pp. 74–84, and C. Mellow, "Russia: Making Cash from Chaos," *Fortune*, April 17, 1995, pp. 145–51.

12 K. van Wolferen, *The Enigma of Japanese Power* (New York: Vintage Books, 1990), pp. 100–05.

13 K. M. Murphy, A. Shleifer, and R. Vishny, "Why Is Rent Seeking so Costly to Growth," *American Economic Review* 83, no. 2, (1993), pp. 409–14.

14 Keiran Cooke, "Honeypot of as Much as $4 Billion down the Drain," *Financial Times*, February 26, 1994, p. 4.

15 Douglass North has argued that the correct specification of intellectual property rights is one factor that lowers the costs of doing business and, thereby, stimulates economic growth and development. See North, *Institutions, Institutional Change, and Economic Performance*.

16 M. Magnier, "U.S. Gains in Effort to Protect Intellectual Property in Asia," *Journal of Commerce*, February 3, 1992, pp. 1A, 3A.

17 **Business Software Alliance**, "Global Software Piracy," press release, June 21, 1996.

18 "Making war on china's pirates," *The Economist*, February 11, 1995, pp. 33–34.

19 "Trade Tripwires," *The Economist*. August 27, 1994, p. 61.

20 **Business Software Alliance**, "Software Piracy in China," Press release, November 18, 1996.

21 S. Bilello, "U.S. Wages War on China's Pirates," *Newsday*, February 7, 1995, p. A41; C. S. Smith, "Microsoft May Get Help in China from its Uncle Sam," *The Wall Street Journal*, November 21, 1994, p. B4; *The Economist*, "Making War on China's Pirates," and interviews with Microsoft officials.

22 "A Survey of the Legal Profession," *The Economist*, July 18, 1992, pp. 1–18.

23 *The Economist, Pocket World In Figures* (London: Penguin Books, 1995).

24 G. M. Grossman and E. Helpman, "Endogenous Innovation in the Theory of Growth," *Journal of Economic Perspectives* 8, no. 1, (1994), pp. 23–44, and Romer, "The Origins of Endogenous Growth," pp. 3–22.

25 F. A. Hayek, *The Fatal Conceit: Errors of Socialism* (Chicago: University of Chicago Press, 1989).

26 James Gwartney, Robert Lawson, and Walter Block, *Economic Freedom of the World: 1975–1995* (London: Institute of Economic Affairs, 1996).

27 North, *Institutions, Institutional Change, and Economic Performance*. See also Murphy, Shleifer, and Vishny, "Why Is Rent Seeking so Costly to Growth?"

28 Hirschman, "The On-and-Off Again Connection between Political and Economic Progress," and A. Przeworski, and F. Limongi, "Political Regimes and Economic Growth," *Journal of Economic Perspectives* 7, no. 3, (1993), pp. 51–59.

29 As an example see "Why Voting is Good for You," *The Economist*, August 27, 1994, pp. 15–17.

30 Ibid.

31 For details of this argument, see M. Olson, "Dictatorship, Democracy, and Development," *American Political Science Review*, September 1993.

32 M. Bleaney, "Economic Liberalization in Eastern Europe: Problems and Prospects," *The World Economy* 17, no. 4, (1994), pp. 497–507.

33 M. Wolf and C. Freeland, "The Long Day's Journey to Market," *Financial Times*, March 7, 1995, p. 15.

34 "Lessons of Transition," *The Economist*, June 29, 1996, p. 81.

35 T. Jackson, "State Run Groups Get Used to New Identity," *Financial Times*, January 24, 1994, pp. 13, 15.

36 S. Moshavi and P. Endarido, "India Shakes off Its Shackles," *Business Week*, January 30, 1995, pp. 48–49; "A Survey of India: The Tiger Steps Out," *The Economist*, January 21, 1995; and J. F. Burns, "India Now Winning U.S. Investment," *New York Times*, February 3, 1995, pp. C1, C5.

37 D. Perkins, "Completing China's Move to the Market," *Journal of Economic Perspectives* 8, no. 2 (1994), pp. 23–46.

38 "A Survey of China," *The Economist*, March 8, 1995.

39 "A Flicker of Light," *The Economist*, March 5, 1994, pp 21–23, and "Continent of Hazard and Opportunity," *Financial Times*, February 7, 1994, p. 14.

40 For a discussion of first-mover advantages, see M. Liberman and D. Montgomery, "First Mover Advantages," *Strategic Management Journal* 9 (Summer Special Issue, 1988), pp. 41–58.

41 "Of Liberty and Prosperity," *The Economist*, January 13, 1996, pp. 21–23.

42 S.H. Robock, "Political Risk: Identification and Assessment," *Columbia Journal of World Business*, July/August 1971, pp. 6–20.

43 Steven L. Myers, "Report Says Business Interests Overshadow Rights," *New York Times*, December 5, 1996, p. A8.

44 A. Ignatius, "GM Dealer Hits Rough Road in Russia," *The Wall Street Journal*, June 28, 1994, pp. A1, 15; and M. Goldman, "In Russia the Mafia Seizes the Commanding Heights of the Economy," *Washington Post*, February 12, 1995, p. C2.

Chapter 3

1 R. J. Barnet and J. Cavanagh. *Global Dreams*, (New York: Touchstone Books, 1994) p. 33.

2 (i) P. Gumble and R. Turner. "Mouse trap: fans like Euro Disney but its parent's goofs weigh the park down," *Wall Street Journal*, March 10, 1994, p. A1. (ii) R. J. Barnet and J. Cavanagh. *Global Dreams*, (New York: Touchstone Books, 1994) pp. 33-34. (iii) J. Huey. "Eisner Explains Everything," *Fortune*, April 17, 1995, pp. 45-68. (iv) R. Anthony. "Euro: Disney: The First 100 Days," Harvard Business School Case # 9-693-013.

3 See R. Dore. *Taking Japan Seriously*, (Stanford, CA: Stanford University Press, 1987).

4 E. B. Tylor. *Primitive Culture*, (London: Murray, 1871).

5 G. Hofstede. *Culture's Consequences: International Differences in Work Related Values*, (Beverley Hills, CA: Sage, 1984) p. 21.

6 J. Z. Namenwirth and R. B. Weber. *Dynamics of Culture*, (Boston: Allen & Unwin, 1987) p. 8.

7 R. Mead. *International Management: Cross Cultural Dimensions*. (Oxford: Blackwell Business, 1994) p. 7.

8 *The Economist*. Iraq: Down but not out. April 8, 1995, pp. 21-23.

9 M. Thompson, R. Ellis, and A. Wildavsky. *Cultural Theory*, (Boulder, CO: Westview Press, 1990).

10 M. Douglas. Cultural bias. *In the Active Voice*, (London: Routledge, 1982) pp. 183-254.

11 M. L. Dertouzos, R. K. Lester, and R. M. Solow. 1989. *Made in America*, (Cambridge, MA: MIT Press).

12 C. Nakane. 1970. *Japanese Society*, (Berkeley: University of California Press).

13 C. Nakane. 1970. *Japanese Society*, (Berkeley: University of California Press).

14 For details see: M. Aoki. 1988. *Information, incentives, and bargaining in the Japanese economy*, (Cambridge: Cambridge University Press). M. L. Dertouzos, R. K. Lester and R. M. Solow. 1989. *Made in America*. (Cambridge, MA: MIT Press).

15 For an excellent historical treatment of the evolution of the English class system see E. P. Thompson. *The Making of the English Working Class*, (London: Vintage Books, 1966). See also R. Miliband. *The*

State in Capitalist Society, (New York: Basic Books, 1969), especially chapter 2.

16 N. Goodman. 1991. *An Introduction to Sociology*, (New York: Harper Collins).

17 M. Weber. 1958 (original 1904-1905). *The Protestant Ethic and the Spirit of Capitalism*, (New York: Scribner's Sons). For an excellent review of Weber's work see A. Giddens, 1971. *Capitalism and Modern Social Theory*, (Cambridge: Cambridge University Press).

18 M. Weber. 1958 (original 1904-1905). *The Protestant Ethic and the Spirit of Capitalism*, (New York: Scribner's Sons) p. 35.

19 See (i) S. M. Abbasi, K. W. Hollman, and J. H. Murrey, 1990. Islamic Economics: Foundations and Practices. *International Journal of Social Economics*, 16(5): 5-17. (ii) R. H. Dekmejian, *Islam in Revolution: Fundamentalism in the Arab World*, (Syracuse, NY: Syracuse University Press, 1995).

20 R. H. Dekmejian. *Islam in Revolution: Fundamentalism in the Arab World*, (Syracuse, NY: Syracuse University Press, 1995).

21 M. K. Nydell. *Understanding Arabs*, (Yarmouth, ME: Intercultural Press, 1987).

22 *The Economist*, The cracks in the kingdom. March 18, 1995 pp. 21-25.

23 The material in this section is based largely upon S. M. Abbasi, K. W. Hollman and J. H. Murrey. 1990. Islamic Economics: Foundations and Practices. *International Journal of Social Economics*, 16(5): pp. 5-17.

24 *The Economist*, Islam's interest. January 18, 1992 33-34.

25 For details of Weber's work and views see A. Giddens. 1971. *Capitalism and Modern Social Theory*, (Cambridge: Cambridge University Press).

26 See for example the views expressed in *The Economist*, A Survey of India: The Tiger steps out. January 21, 1995.

27 See (i) R. Dore. *Taking Japan Seriously*, (Stanford, CA: Stanford University Press, 1987). (ii) C. W. L. Hill. 1995. Transaction cost economizing as a source of compara-tive advantage: The case of Japan. *Organization Science*, 6, in press.

28 See (i) M. Aoki. 1988. *Information, incentives, and bargaining in the Japanese economy*, (Cambridge University Press: Cambridge). (ii) J. P. Womack, D. T. Jones, and D. Roos. 1990. *The machine that changed the world*, (New York: Rawson Associates).

29 This hypothesis dates back to two anthropologists, Edward Sapir and Benjamin Lee Whorf. See (i) E. Sapir. 1929. The status of linguistics as a science. *Language*, 5: 207-214. (ii) B. L. Whorf. 1956. *Language, Thought, and Reality*, (Cambridge, MA: MIT Press).

30 D. A. Ricks. *Big Business Blunders: Mistakes in Multinational Marketing*, (Homewood, IL: Dow Jones Irwin, 1983).

31 N. Goodman. 1991. *An Introduction to Sociology*, (New York: Harper Collins).

32 M. E. Porter. 1990. *The competitive advantage of nations*, (New York: Free Press).

33 M. E. Porter. 1990. *The competitive advantage of nations*, (New York: Free Press) pp. 395-397.

34 G. Hofstede. The Cultural Relativity of Organizational Practices and Theories. *Journal of International Business* Studies, Fall, 1983, pp. 75-89.

35 For more a detailed critique see R. Mead. *International Management: Cross-Cultural Dimensions*, (Oxford: Blackwell, 1994) pp. 73-75.

36 R. Mead, *International Management: Cross-Cultural Dimensions*, (Oxford: Blackwell, 1994), chapter 17.

37 *The Economist*, Free, young, and Japanese. December 21, 1991.

38 *The Economist*, The long march from harmony. In: A survey of Japan, July 9, 1994, pp. 6-10.

39 J. Z. Namerwirth and R. P. Weber, *Dynamics of Culture*, (Boston: Allen & Unwin, 1987).

40 G. Hofstede, National cultures in four dimensions. *International Studies of Management and Organization*, 13(1), pp. 46-74.

41 R. J. Barnet and J. Cavanagh, *Global Dreams: Imperial Corporations and the New World Order*, (New York: Touchstone, 1994).

42 See: M. Aoki. 1988. *Information, incentives, and bargaining in the Japanese economy*, (Cambridge: Cambridge University Press). M. L. Dertouzos, R. K. Lester, and R. M. Solow. 1989. *Made in America*. (Cambridge, MA: MIT Press). M. E. Porter, 1990. *The competitive advantage of nations*, (New York: Free Press), pp. 395-397.

43 W. Taylor, "The Logic of Global Business: An Interview with ABB's Percy Barnevik," *Harvard Business Review*, March-April 1991, pp. 91-105.

Chapter 4

1 "Poor Man's Burden: A Survey of the Third World," *The Economist*, September 23, 1989, and World Bank, *World Development Report, 1944* (Oxford: Oxford University Press, 1944).

2 H. W. Spiegel, *The Growth of Economic Thought* (Durham, NC: Duke University Press, 1991.)

3 G. de Jonquieres, "Mercantilists Are Treading on Thin Ice," *Financial Times*, July 3, 1994, p. 16.

4 Jarl Hagelstam, "Mercantilism Still Influences Practical Trade Policy at the End of the Twentieth Century," *Journal of World Trade*, 1991, pp. 95–105.

5 Y. Sazanami, S. Urata, and H. Kawai, *Measuring the Costs of Protection in Japan* (Washington, DC: Institute for International Economics, 1994); M. Nakamoto, "All Action and No Talk," *Financial Times*, March 17, 1995, p. 5; and N. Dunne, "U.S. Threatens WTO Complaint against Japan," *Financial Times*, March 29, 1995, p. 6.

6 S. Hollander, *The Economics of David Ricardo* (Buffalo, NY: The University of Toronto Press, 1979).

7 D. Ricardo, *The Principles of Political Economy and Taxation* (Homewood, IL: Richard D. Irwin, 1967) (first published in 1817).

8 For example, R. Dornbusch, S. Fischer, and P. Samuelson, "Comparative Advantage: Trade and Payments in a Ricardian Model with a Continuum of Goods," *American Economic Review* 67 (December 1977), pp. 823–39.

9 B. Balassa, "An Empirical Demonstration of Classic Comparative Cost Theory," *Review of Economics and Statistics*, 1963, pp. 231–38.

10 See P. R. Krugman, "Is Free Trade Passé?" *Journal of Economic Perspectives* 1 (Fall 1987), pp. 131–44.

11 P. Samuelson, "The Gains from International Trade Once Again," *Economic Journal* 72 (1962), pp. 820–829.

12 For a summary, see "The gains from trade", *The Economist*, September 23, 1989, pp. 25–26.

13 B. Ohlin, *Interregional and International Trade* (Cambridge, MA: Harvard University Press, 1933). For a summary see R. W. Jones and J. P. Neary, "The Positive Theory of International Trade," in *Handbook of International Economics*, ed. R. W. Jones and P. B. Kenen, (Amsterdam: North Holland, 1984.)

14 W. Leontief, "Domestic Production and Foreign Trade: The American Capital Position Re-Examined," *Proceedings of the American Philosophical Society* 97 (1953), pp. 331–49.

15 R. M. Stern and K. Maskus, "Determinants of the Structure of U.S. Foreign Trade," *Journal of International Economics* 11 (1981), pp. 207–44.

16 See H. P. Bowen, E. E. Leamer, and L. Sveikayskas, "Multicountry, Multifactor Tests of the Factor Abundance Theory," *American Economic Review* 77 (1987), pp. 791–809.

17 R. Vernon, "International Investments and International Trade in the Product Life Cycle," Quarterly Journal of Economics, May 1966, pp. 190–207, and R. Vernon and L. T. Wells, *The Economic Environment of International Business*, 4th ed. (Englewood Cliffs, NJ: Prentice Hall, 1986).

18 For a good summary of this literature, see E. Helpman and P. Krugman, *Market Structure and Foreign Trade: Increasing*

Returns, Imperfect Competition, and the International Economy (Cambridge, MA: MIT Press, 1985). Also see P. Krugman, "Does the New Trade Theory Require a New Trade Policy?" *World Economy* 15, no. 4, (1992), pp. 423–41.

19 M. B. Lieberman and D. B. Montgomery, "First-Mover Advantages," *Strategic Management Journal* 9 (Special issue, Summer 1988), pp. 41–58.

20 A. D. Chandler, *Scale and Scope* (New York: Free Press, 1990).

21 Krugman, "Does the New Trade Theory Require a New Trade Policy?"

22 M. E. Porter, *The Competitive Advantage of Nations* (New York: Free Press, 1990). For a good review of this book, see R. M. Grant, "Porter's Competitive Advantage of Nations: An Assessment," *Strategic Management Journal* 12 (1991), pp. 535–48.

23 Porter, *Competitive Advantage of Nations*, p. 121.

24 "Lessons from the Frozen North", *The Economist*, October 8, 1994, pp. 76-77, and G. Edmondson, "Grabbing Markets from the Giants," *Business Week, Special Issue: 21st Century Capitalism*, 1995, p. 156.

25 Lieberman and Montgomery, "First-Mover Advantages."

26 C. A. Hamilton, "Building Better Machine Tools," *Journal of Commerce*, October 30, 1991, p. 8, and "Manufacturing Trouble", *The Economist*, October 12, 1991, p. 71.

27 This case is based on a case prepared by M. J. Enright and P. Tenti, "The Italian Ceramic Tile Industry," which is reported in Porter, *The Competitive Advantage of Nations*.

Chapter 5

1 Thomas Friedman, "U.S. Hoping to Use Fears of Trade War to Pressure Japan," *New York Times*, February 16, 1994, pp. C1, C4; Michiyo Nakamoto, "Japan Trapped by Chip Import Deal," *Financial Times*, March 23, 1994, p. 4; and Emiko Terazono, "Japan Trade Package Yields to U.S. Demands on Imports," *Financial Times*, April 30, 1994, pp. 1, 4.

2 For a detailed welfare analysis of the effect of a tariff, see P. R. Krugman and M. Obstfeld, *International Economics: Theory and Policy* (New York: Harper Collins, 1994), chap. 9.

3 Y. Sazanami, S. Urata, and H. Kawai, *Measuring the Costs of Protection in Japan* (Washington, DC: Institute for International Economics, 1994).

4 See J. Bhagwati, *Protectionism* (Cambridge, MA: MIT Press, 1988), and "Costs of Protection," *Journal of Commerce*, September 25, 1991, p. 8A.

5 C. Hufbauer and K. A. Elliott, *Measuring the Costs of Protectionism in the United States* (Washington, DC: Institute for International Economics, 1993), and S. Nasar, "The High Costs of Protectionism," *New York Times*, November 12, 1993, pp. C1, C2.

6 "From the Sublime to the Subsidy," *The Economist*, February 24, 1990, p. 71

7 "Aid Addicts," *The Economist*, August 8, 1992, p. 61.

8 R.W.Crandall, *Regulating the Automobile* (Washington, DC: Brookings Institute, 1986).

9 Krugman and Obstfeld, *International Economics*.

10 Bhagwati, Protectionism, and "Japan to Curb VCR Exports," *New York Times*, November 21, 1983, p. D5.

11 N. Dunne and R. Waters, "U.S. Waves a Big Stick at Chinese Pirates," *Financial Times*, January 6, 1995, p. 4.

12 "Brazil's Auto Industry Struggles to Boost Global Competitiveness," *Journal of Commerce*, October 10, 1991, p. 6A.

13 For reviews see J. A. Brander, "Rationales for Strategic Trade and Industrial Policy," in *Strategic Trade Policy and the New International Economics*, ed. P. R. Krugman (Cambridge, MA: MIT Press, 1986); P. R. Krugman, "Is Free Trade Passé?" *Journal of Economic Perspectives 1*

(1987), pp. 131–44; and P. R. Krugman, "Does the New Trade Theory Require a New Trade Policy?" *World Economy* 15, no. 4 (1992), pp. 423–41.

14 "Airbus and Boeing: The Jumbo War," *The Economist*, June 15, 1991, p. 65–66.

15 For details, see Krugman, "Is Free Trade Passé?" and Brander, "Rationales for Strategic Trade and Industrial Policy."

16 Krugman, "Is Free Trade Passé?"

17 This dilemma is a variant of the famous prisoner's dilemma, which has become a classic metaphor for the difficulty of achieving cooperation between self-interested and mutually suspicious entities. For a good general introduction, see A. Dixit and B. Nalebuff, *Thinking Strategically: The Competitive Edge in Business, Politics, and Everyday Life* (New York: W.W. Norton & Co., 1991).

18 Note that the Smoot-Hawley Act did not cause the Great Depression. However, the beggar-thy-neighbor trade policies that it ushered in made things worse. See Bhagwati, *Protectionism*.

19 Bhagwati, *Protectionism*.

20 World Bank, *World Development Report* (New York: Oxford University Press, 1987).

21 World Trade Organization, *International Trade Trends and Statistics* (Geneva: WTO, 1995).

22 Frances Williams, "WTO—New Name Heralds New Powers," *Financial Times*, December 16, 1993, p. 5, and Frances Williams, "Gatt's Successor to Be Given Real Clout," *Financial Times*, April 4, 1994, p. 6.

23 The studies are OECD and the World Bank, *Trade Liberalization: The Global Economic Implications* (Paris and Washington, 1993); OECD, *Assessing the Effects of the Uruguay Round* (Paris, 1993); and GATT Secretariat, *Background Paper: The Uruguay Round* (Geneva, 1993).

24 Martin Wolf, "Doing Good Despite Themselves," *Financial Times*, December 16, 1993, p. 15.

25 Brent Bowers, "For Small Firms, Big Gains Are Seen in the Fine Print," *The Wall Street Journal*, December 16, 1993, p. A12, and "U.S. Business Likes Trade Pact as a Whole: But Not Some Parts," *The Wall Street Journal*, December 16, 1993, pp. A3, A13.

26 World Trade Organization, *Focus*, August–September 1996.

27 "A Disquieting New Agenda for Trade," *The Economist*, July 16, 1994, pp. 55–56, and Frances Williams, "Trade Round Like This May Never Be Seen Again," *Financial Times*, December 16, 1993, p. 7.

28 Edward Goldsmith, "Global Trade and the Environment," in *The Case Against the Global Economy*. ed. J. Mander and E. Goldsmith (San Francisco: Sierra Book Club, 1996).

29 United Nations, *World Investment Report* (New York: United Nations, 1995).

30 "All Free Traders Now?" *The Economist*, December 7, 1996.

31 C. W. L. Hill, "The Toyota Corporation in 1994," in *Strategic Management: An Integrated Approach*, ed. C. W. L. Hill and G. R. Jones (Boston: Houghton Mifflin, 1995).

32 Keiran Cooke, "Honeypot of As Much As 4 Billion Sterling Down the Drain," *Financial Times*, February 26, 1994, p. 4.

33 Keiran Cooke, "Arrogance of the West Riles a Maverick," *Financial Times*, February 26, 1994, p. 4, and Robert Peston, "Malaysia PM Says Die Is Cast over UK Ban," *Financial Times*, March 17, 1994, p. 1.

Chapter 6

1 C. Brown-Humes, "Electrolux Plugs into Households All over Asia," *Financial Times*, April 27, 1995, p. 15.

2 World Trade Organization, *Trade and Foreign Direct Investment* (Geneva: WTO Secretariat, October 9, 1996), issued as Press Release No. 57.

3 The data are taken from World Trade Organization, *Trade and Foreign Direct Investment*, and United Nations Conference on Trade and Development, *World*

Investment Report, 1996 (New York and Geneva: United Nations, 1996).

4 M. Kidron and R. Segal, *The New State of the World Atlas* (New York: Simon & Schuster, 1987).

5 United Nations Conference on Trade and Development, *World Investment Report, 1996.*

6 E. S. Browning, "British Firms' Outlays in U.S. Top Japanese," *The Wall Street Journal*, October 28, 1994, p. 2.

7 United Nations Conference on Trade and Development, *World Investment Report*, 1994.

8 For an example of this viewpoint, see M. Tolchin and S. Tolchin, *Buying into America* (New York: Times Books, 1988).

9 "Foreign Investment in the U.S.," *New York Times*, July 17, 1990, p. D2.

10 R. E. Caves, "Japanese Investment in the U.S.: Lessons for the Economic Analysis of Foreign Investment," *The World Economy* 16 (1993), pp. 279–300.

11 United Nations, *World Investment Report*, 1994, pp. 196–97; Nissan Motor Manufacturing Company (United Kingdom) Ltd.; and "A Survey of the Car Industry," *The Economist*, October 17, 1992, pp. 13–15.

12 "Crowded Road Leads to Vietnam Car Market," *Financial Times*, October 21, 1994, p. 5.

13 A. Barret, "It's a Small (Business) World," *Business Week*, April 17, 1995, pp. 96–101; R. A. Mosbacher, "Opening Export Doors for Smaller Firms," *Seattle Times*, July 24, 1991, p. A7; and R. A. King, "You Don't Have to Be a Giant to Score Big Overseas," *Business Week*, April 13, 1987, pp. 62–63.

14 For example, see S. H. Hymer, *The International Operations of National Firms: A Study of Direct Foreign Investment* (Cambridge, MA: MIT Press, 1976); A. M. Rugman, *Inside the Multinationals: The Economics of Internal Markets* (New York: Columbia University Press, 1981); D. J. Teece, "Multinational Enterprise, Internal Governance, and Industrial Organization," *American Economic Review* 75 (May 1983), pp. 233–38; and C. W. L. Hill and W. C. Kim, "Searching for a Dynamic Theory of the Multinational Enterprise: A Transaction Cost Model," *Strategic Management Journal* (special issue) 9 (1988), pp. 93–104.

15 J. P. Womack, D. T. Jones, and D. Roos, *The Machine that Changed the World* (New York: Rawson Associates, 1990).

16 The argument is most often associated with F. T. Knickerbocker, *Oligopolistic Reaction and Multinational Enterprise* (Boston: Harvard Business School Press, 1973).

17 R. E. Caves, *Multinational Enterprise and Economic Analysis* (Cambridge, England: Cambridge University Press, 1982).

18 R. E. Caves, "Japanese Investment in the U.S.: Lessons for the Economic Analysis of Foreign Investment," *The World Economy* 16 (1993), pp. 279–300.

19 For the use of Vernon's theory to explain Japanese direct investment in the United States and Europe, see S. Thomsen, "Japanese Direct Investment in the European Community," *The World Economy* 16 (1993), pp. 301–15.

20 J. H. Dunning, *Explaining International Production* (London: Unwin Hyman, 1988).

21 P. Krugman, "Increasing Returns and Economic Geography," *Journal of Political Economy* 99, no. 3 (1991), pp. 483–99.

22 J. H. Dunning and R. Narula, "Transpacific Foreign Direct Investment and the Investment Development Path," *South Carolina Essays in International Business* no. 10 (May 1995).

23 For elaboration, see S. Hood and S. Young, *The Economics of the Multinational Enterprise* (London: Longman, 1979), and P. M. Sweezy and H. Magdoff, "The Dynamics of U.S. Capitalism," *New York: Monthly Review Press*, 1972.

24 M. Itoh and K. Kiyono, "Foreign Trade and Direct Investment," in *Industrial Policy of Japan*, ed. R. Komiya, M. Okuno, and K. Suzumura (Tokyo: Academic Press, 1988).

25 P. M. Romer, "The Origins of Endogenous Growth," *Journal of Economic Perspectives* 8 no. 1 (1994), pp. 3–22.

26 J. Mann, "A Little Help from Their Friends," *Financial Times*, November 10, 1993, p. 28, and "Venezuela: A Survey," *The Economist*, October 14, 1994.

27 P. R. Krugman and M. Obstfeld, *International Economics: Theory and Policy* (New York: Harper Collins, 1994), chap. 9. Also see P. Krugman, *The Age of Diminished Expectations* (Cambridge, MA: MIT Press, 1990).

28 Robert B. Reich, *The Work of Nations: Preparing Ourselves for the 21st Century* (New York: Alfred A. Knopf, 1991).

29 For a recent review, see John H. Dunning, "Re-evaluating the Benefits of Foreign Direct Investment," *Transnational Corporations*, 3 no. 1 (February 1994), pp. 23–51.

30 This idea has recently been articulated, although not quite in this form, by C. A. Bartlett and S. Ghoshal, *Managing across Borders: The Transnational Solution* (Boston: Harvard Business School Press, 1989).

31 P. Magnusson, "The Mexico Pact: Worth the Price?" *Business Week*, May 27, 1991, pp. 32–35.

32 C. Johnston, "Political Risk Insurance," in *Assessing Corporate Political Risk*, ed. D. M. Raddock (Totowa, NJ: Rowan & Littlefield, 1986).

33 Martin Tolchin and Susan Tolchin, *Buying into America: How Foreign Money Is Changing the Face of Our Nation* (New York: Times Books, 1988).

34 J. Behrman and R. E. Grosse, *International Business and Government: Issues and Institutions* (Columbia, SC: University of South Carolina Press, 1990).

35 See Caves, *Multinational Enterprise and Economic Analysis*.

36 For a good general introduction to negotiation strategy, see M. H. Bazerman, *Negotiating Rationally* (New York: Free Press, 1995), A. Dixit and B. Nalebuff, *Thinking Strategically: The Competitive Edge in Business, Politics, and Everyday Life* (New York: W. W. Norton, 1991), and H. Raiffa, *The Art and Science of Negotiation* (Cambridge, MA: Harvard University Press, 1982).

37 C. S. Nicandros, "The Russian Investment Dilemma," *Harvard Business Review*, May–June 1994, p. 40; T. Carrington, "World Bank President Says Economists Were Too Optimistic on Soviet Block," *The Wall Street Journal*, October 14, 1994, p. 13; and R. Holman, "Russia to Lift Oil Restrictions," *The Wall Street Journal*, December 6, 1994, p. 24A.

Chapter 7

1 T. Horwitz, "Europe's Borders Fade," *The Wall Street Journal*, May 18, 1993, pp. A1, A12; "A Singular Market." *The Economist*, The European Union: A Survey, October 22, 1994, pp. 10–16; "Something Dodgy in Europe's Single Market," *The Economist*, May 21, 1994, pp. 69–70.

2 See World Trade Organization, *Regionalism and the World Trading System* (Geneva: World Trade Organization, 1995), and "All Free Traders Now?" *The Economist*, December 7, 1996.

3 The Andean Pact has been through a number of changes since its inception. The latest version was established in 1991. See "Free-Trade Free for All," *The Economist*, January 4, 1991, p. 63.

4 D. Swann, *The Economics of the Common Market*, 6th ed. (London: Penguin Books, 1990).

5 "And What Alice Found There," *The Economist*, December 14, 1996, pp. 23–25.

6 See J. Bhagwati, "Regionalism and Multilateralism: An Overview," Columbia University Discussion Paper 603, Department of Economics, Columbia University, New York; Augusto de la Torre and Margaret Kelly, "Regional Trade Arrangements," Occasional Paper 93 (Washington, DC: International Monetary Fund, March 1992), and J. Bhagwati, "The High Cost of Free Trade Areas," *Financial Times*, May, 1995, p. 13.

7 Sources for the material in this section: N. Colchester and D. Buchan, *Europower: The Essential Guide to Europe's Economic Transformation in 1992* (London: The Economist Books, 1990), and Swann, *The Economics of the Common Market*.

8 Colchester and Buchan, *Europower*.

9 Nan Stone, "The Globalization of Europe: An Interview with Wisse Dekker," *Harvard Business Review*, May–June 1989, pp. 90–95.

10 "The Aid Plague: Business in Europe, A Survey," *The Economist*, June 8, 1991, pp. 12–18.

11 "One Europe, One Economy," *The Economist*, November 30, 1991, pp. 53–54, and "Market Failure: A Survey of Business in Europe," *The Economist*, June 8, 1991, pp. 6–10.

12 "A Singular Market. In The European Union: A Survey," *The Economist*.

13 R. Lapper, "Hard Work to Be Free and Single," *Financial Times*, July 1, 1994, p. 19, and "A Singular Market," *The Economist*.

14 "One Europe, One Economy," *The Economist*.

15 "And What Alice Found There," *The Economist*.

16 "From the Arctic to the Mediterranean," *The Economist*, March 5, 1994, pp. 52, 57; Lionel Barber, "More Does Not Mean Merrier," *Financial Times*, March 14, 1994, p. 13; and L. Barber. "Hopes of Wider Union Turn to Fear of No Union," *Financial Times*, December 9, 1994, p. 2.

17 "What Are They Building? Survey of Europe's Internal Market," *The Economist*, July 8, 1989, pp. 5–7, and Colchester and Buchan, *Europower*.

18 World Trade Organization, *Regionalism and the World Trading System*.

19 "What Is NAFTA?" *Financial Times*, November 17, 1993, p. 6, and Susan Garland, "Sweet Victory," *Business Week*, November 29, 1993, pp. 30–31.

20 "NAFTA: The Showdown," *The Economist*, November 13, 1993, pp. 23–36.

21 "Happy Ever NAFTA?" *The Economist*, December 10, 1994, pp. 23–24, and Douglas Harbrecht, "What Has NAFTA Wrought? Plenty of Trade?" *Business Week*, November 21, 1994, pp. 48–49.

22 P. B. Carroll and C. Torres. "Mexico Unveils Program of Harsh Fiscal Medicine," *The Wall Street Journal*, March 3, 1995, pp. A1, A6.

23 G. Smith, "NAFTA: A Green Light for Red Tape," *Business Week*, July 25, 1994, p. 48, and A. DePalma, "Big Companies in Mexico among the Peso's Worst Victims," *New York Times*, January 30, 1995, p. D4.

24 Raúl Hinojosa Ojeda, Curt Dowds, Robert McCleery, Sherman Robinson, David Runsten, Craig Wolff, Goetz Wolff, "NAFTA—How Has it Done? North American Integration Three Years after NAFTA," *North American Integration and Development Center at UCLA*, December 1996.

25 "NAFTA Is Not Alone," *The Economist*, June 18, 1994, pp. 47–48; Sweeney, "First Latin American Customs Union Looms over Venezuela," *Journal of Commerce*, September 26, 1991, p. 5A; and "The Business of the American Hemisphere," *The Economist*, August 24, 1991, pp. 37–38.

26 "Business of the American Hemisphere," *The Economist*.

27 See Michael Philips, "South American Trade Pact under Fire," *The Wall Street Journal*, October 23, 1996, p. A2, and Alexander J. Yeats, *Does Mercosur's Trade Performance Justify Concerns about the Global Welfare-Reducing Effects of Free Trade Arrangements? Yes!* (Washington, DC: World Bank, 1996).

28 Mary Anastasia O'Grady, "Brazil Wants World Bank Critic of MERCOSUR Silenced." *The Wall Street Journal*, November 22, 1996, p. A15.

29 "Aimless in Seattle," *The Economist*, November 13, 1993, pp. 35–36.

30 Guy de Jonquieres, "Different Aims, Common Cause," *Financial Times*, November 18, 1995, p. 14.

31 United Nations, *World Investment Report*, 1995 (Geneva: United Nations, 1995).

32 P. Davis, "A European Campaign: Local Companies Rush for a Share of EC Market while Barriers Are Down," *Minneapolis-St. Paul City Business*, January 8, 1990, p. 1.

33 "The Business of Europe," *The Economist*, December 7, 1991, pp. 63–64.

34 E. G. Friberg, "1992: Moves Europeans Are Making," *Harvard Business Review*, May–June 1989, pp. 85–89.

Chapter 8

1 W. Dawkins, "JAL to Disclose Huge Currency Hedge Loss," *Financial Times*, October 4, 1994, p. 19, and W. Dawkins, "Tokyo to Lift Veil on Currency Risks," *Financial Times*, October 5, 1994, p. 23.

2 For a good general introduction to the foreign exchange market, see R. Weisweiller, *How the Foreign Exchange Market Works* (New York: New York Institute of Finance, 1990). A detailed description of the economics of foreign exchange markets can be found in P. R. Krugman and M. Obstfeld, *International Economics: Theory and Policy* (New York: Harper Collins, 1994).

3 C. Forman, "Allied-Lyons to Post $269 Million Loss from Foreign Exchange as Dollar Soars," *The Wall Street Journal*, March 20, 1991, p. A17.

4 P. Harverson, "Billion Dollar Man the Money Markets Fear," *Financial Times*, September 30, 1994, p. 10; "A Quantum Dive," *The Economist*, March 15, 1994, pp. 83–84; B. J. Javetski, "Europe's Money Mess," *Business Week*, September 28, 1992, pp. 30–31; and "Meltdown," *The Economist*, September 19, 1992, p. 69.

5 Federal Reserve Bank of New York, *Summary of Results of U.S. Foreign Exchange Market Turnover Survey Conducted April 1989* (New York: Federal Reserve Bank of New York, 1989); A. Meyerson, "Currency Markets Resisting Power of Central Banks," *New York Times*, September 25, 1992, pp. Al, C15; W. Glasgall, "Hot Money," *Business Week*, March 20, 1995, pp. 46–50; and Richard Lapper, "Forex Market Growth Slowing Says BIS," *Financial Times*, May 31, 1996, p. 6.

6 Lapper, "Forex Market Growth Slowing."

7 For a recent comprehensive review see M. Taylor, "The Economics of Exchange Rates," *Journal of Economic Literature* (1995), pp. 13–47.

8 Krugman and Obstfeld, *International Economics: Theory and Policy*.

9 M. Friedman, *Studies in the Quantity Theory of Money* (Chicago: University of Chicago Press, 1956). For an accessible explanation, see M. Friedman and R. Friedman, *Free to Choose* (London: Penguin Books, 1979), chap. 9.

10 Juan-Antino Morales, "Inflation Stabilization in Bolivia," in *Inflation Stabilization: The Experience of Israel, Argentina, Brazil, Bolivia, and Mexico*, ed. Michael Bruno et al. (Cambridge, MA: MIT Press, 1988), and The Economist, *World Book of Vital Statistics* (New York: Random House, 1990).

11 For reviews, see L. H. Officer, "The Purchasing Parity Theory of Exchange Rates: A Review Article," *International Monetary Fund Staff Papers*, March 1976, pp. 1–60, and Taylor, "The Economics of Exchange Rates."

12 For a summary of the evidence, see the survey by Taylor, "The Economics of Exchange Rates."

13 R. E. Cumby and M. Obstfeld, "A Note on Exchange Rate Expectations and Nominal Interest Differentials: A Test of the Fisher Hypothesis," *Journal of Finance*, June 1981, pp. 697–703.

14 Taylor, "The Economics of Exchange Rates."

15 See H. L. Allen and M. P. Taylor, "Charts, Noise, and Fundamentals in the Foreign Exchange Market," *Economic Journal* 100 (1990), pp. 49–59, and T. Ito, "Foreign Exchange Rate Expectations: Micro Survey Data," *American Economic Review* 80 (1990), pp. 434–49.

16 For example, see E. Fama, "Forward Rates as Predictors of Future Spot Rates,"

Journal of Financial Economics, October 1976, pp. 361–77.

17 R. M. Levich, "The Efficiency of Markets for Foreign Exchange," in *International Finance*, ed. G. D. Gay and R. W. Kold (Richmond, VA: Robert F. Dane, Inc., 1983).

18 J. Williamson, *The Exchange Rate System* (Washington, DC: Institute for International Economics, 1983).

19 R. M. Levich, "Currency Forecasters Lose Their Way," *Euromoney*, August 1983, p. 140.

20 C. Engel and J. D. Hamilton, "Long Swings in the Dollar: Are They in the Data and Do Markets Know It?" *American Economic Review*, September 1990, pp. 689–713.

21 *Exchange Agreements and Exchange Restrictions* (Washington, DC: International Monetary Fund, 1990).

22 J. R. Carter and J. Gagne, "The Do's and Don'ts of International Countertrade," *Sloan Management Review*, Spring 1988, pp. 31–37.

23 L. W. Tuller, *Going Global: New Opportunities for Growing Companies to Compete in World Markets* (Homewood, IL: Business One Irwin, 1991).

24 S. Erlanger, "Russia Will Test a Trading Band for the Ruble," *New York Times*, July 7, 1995, p. 1; C. Freeland, "Russia to Introduce a Trading Band for Ruble against Dollar," *Financial Times*, July 7, 1995, p. 1; and J. Thornhill, "Russians Bemused by 'Black Tuesday'," *Financial Times*, October 12, 1994, p. 4; and R. Sikorski, "Mirage of Numbers," *The Wall Street Journal*, May 18, 1994, p. 14.

Chapter 9

1 J. Darling and D. Nauss, "Stall in the Fast Lane," *Los Angeles Times*, February 19, 1995, p. 1; "Mexico Drops Efforts to Prop up Peso," *The Wall Street Journal*, December 23, 1994, p. A3; R. Dornbusch, "We Have Salinas to Thank for the Peso Debacle," *Business Week*, January 16, 1995, p. 20; and P. Carroll and C. Torres, "Mexico Unveils Program of Harsh Fiscal Medicine," *The Wall Street Journal*, March 10, 1995, pp. A1, A6.

2 International Monetary Fund, *International Financial Statistics*, March 1991, p. 22.

3 The argument goes back to 18th century philosopher David Hume. See D. Hume, "On the Balance of Trade," reprinted in *The Gold Standard in Theory and in History*, ed. B. Eichengreen (London: Methuen, 1985).

4 R. Solomon, *The International Monetary System, 1945–1981*. (New York: Harper & Row, 1982).

5 For an extended discussion of the dollar exchange rate in the 1980s, see B. D. Pauls, "U.S. Exchange Rate Policy: Bretton Woods to the Present," *Federal Reserve Bulletin*, November 1990, pp. 891–908.

6 S. Hansell, "A Currency Dragged Down by Twin Deficits," *New York Times*, June 23, 1994, p. C3, and "The Dollar's Slide Show," *The Economist*, July 16, 1994, p. 74.

7 S. Brittan, "Tragi-comedy of the Rising Yen," *Financial Times*, March 3, 1994, p. 16; G. Baker, "Stay at Home Investors Drive the Yen's Rise," *Financial Times*, April 21, 1995, p. 5; and "Dial C for Chaos," *The Economist*, March 11, 1995, pp. 69–70.

8 For a feel for the issues contained in this debate, see P. Krugman, *Has the Adjustment Process Worked?* (Institute for International Economics, 1991); "Time to Tether Currencies," *The Economist*, January 6, 1990, pp. 15–16; P. R. Krugman and M. Obstfeld, *International Economics: Theory and Policy* (New York: Harper Collins, 1994); and J. Shelton, *Money Meltdown* (New York: Free Press, 1994).

9 The argument is made by several prominent economists, particularly Stanford's Robert McKinnon. See R. McKinnon, "An International Standard for Monetary Stabilization," in *Policy Analyses in International Economics* (Washington, DC: Institute for International Economics, 1984). The details of this argument are beyond the scope of this book. For a relatively accessible exposition, see P. Krugman, *The Age of Diminished Expectations* (Cambridge, MA: MIT Press, 1990).

10 For details, see A. J. Schwartz, "International Debt: What's Fact and What's Fiction," *Economic Inquiry* 27 (January 1989), pp. 1–19; and "What Happens to the IMF when a Whole Nation Calls on It?" *The Economist*, December 11, 1982, pp. 69–80.

11 For a summary of the arguments for debt reductions, see "And Forgive Us Our Debts: A Survey of the IMF and the World Bank," *The Economist*, October 12, 1991, pp. 23–33; and Krugman, *Diminished Expectations*.

12 See J. Sachs, "Beyond Bretton Woods: A New Blueprint," *The Economist*, October 1944, pp. 23–27; and M. Wolf, "Bretton Twins at an Awkward Age," *Financial Times*, October 7, 1994, p. 17.

13 "Prelude to Testing Time: A Survey of the IMF and the World Bank," *The Economist*, October 12, 1991, p. 48.

14 P. Gumbel and B. Coleman, "Daimler Warns of Severe 95 Loss Due to Strong Mark," *New York Times*, June 29, 1995, pp. 1, 10, and M. Wolf, "Daimler-Benz Announces Major Losses," *Financial Times*, June 29, 1995, p. 1.

15 R. S. Eckley, "Caterpillar's Ordeal: Foreign Competition in Capital Goods," *Business Horizons*, March–April, 1989, pp. 80–86; H. S. Byrne, "Track of the Cat: Caterpillar Is Bulldozing Its Way Back to Higher Profits," *Barron's*, April 6, 1987, pp. 13, 70–71; R. Henkoff, "This Cat Is Acting like a Tiger," *Fortune*, December 19, 1988, pp. 71–76; and "Caterpillar and Komatsu," in *Transnational Management: Text, Cases, and Readings in Cross-Border Management*, ed. C. A. Bartlett and S. Ghoshal (Burr Ridge, IL: Richard D. Irwin, Inc., 1992).

Chapter 10

1 Kathleen Deveny et al., "McWorld?" *Business Week*, October 13, 1986, pp. 78–86; "Slow Food," *The Economist*, February 3, 1990, p. 64; Harlan S. Byrne, "Welcome to McWorld," *Barron's*, August 29, 1994, pp. 25–28; and Andrew E. Serwer, "McDonald's Conquers the World," *Fortune*, October 17, 1994, pp. 103–16.

2 M. E. Porter, *Competitive Strategy* (New York: Free Press, 1980).

3 M. E. Porter, *Competitive Advantage* (New York: Free Press, 1985).

4 C. S. Trager, "Enter the Mini-Multinational," *Northeast International Business*, March 1989, pp. 13–14.

5 G. Hamel and C. K. Prahalad, *Competing for the Future* (Boston: Harvard Business School Press, 1996).

6 J. P. Woomack, D. T. Jones, and D. Roos, *The Machine that Changed the World* (New York: Rawson Associates, 1990).

7 M. E. Porter, *The Competitive Advantage of Nations* (New York: Free Press, 1990).

8 R. B. Reich, *The Work of Nations* (New York: Alfred A. Knopf, 1991).

9 G. Hall and S. Howell, "The Experience Curve from an Economist's Perspective," *Strategic Management Journal* 6, (1985), pp. 197–212.

10 A. A. Alchain, "Reliability of Progress Curves in Airframe Production," *Econometrica* 31 (1963), pp. 697–93.

11 Hall and Howell, "Experience Curve from an Economist's Perspective."

12 J. Main, "How to Go Global—and Why," *Fortune*, August 28, 1989, pp. 70–76.

13 "Matsushita Electrical Industrial in 1987," in *Transnational Management*, ed C. A. Bartlett and S. Ghoshal (Burr Ridge, IL: Richard D. Irwin, Inc. 1992).

14 C. K. Prahalad and Yves L. Doz, *The Multinational Mission: Balancing Local Demands and Global Vision* (New York: Free Press, 1987). Prahalad and Doz actually talk about local responsiveness rather than local customization.

15 "The Tire Industry's Costly Obsession with Size," *The Economist*, June 8, 1993, pp. 65–66.

16 T. Levitt, "The Globalization of Markets," *Harvard Business Review*, May–June, 1983, pp. 92–102.

17 C. A. Bartlett and S. Ghoshal, *Managing across Borders* (Boston: Harvard Business School Press, 1989).

18 This section is based on Bartlett and Ghoshal, *Managing across Borders*.

19 Guy de Jonquieres and C. Bobinski, "Wash and Get into a Lather in Poland," *Financial Times*, May 28, 1989, p. 2; "Perestroika in Soapland," *The Economist*, June 10, 1989, pp. 69–71; "After Early Stumbles P&G Is Making Inroads Overseas," *The Wall Street Journal*, February 6, 1989, p. B1; and Bartlett and Ghoshal, *Managing across Borders*.

20 Bartlett and Ghoshal, *Managing across Borders*.

21 T. Hout, M. E. Porter and E. Rudden, "How Global Firms Win Out," *Harvard Business Review*, September–October 1982, pp. 98–108.

22 Guy de Jonquieres, "Unilever Adopts a Clean Sheet Approach," *Financial Times*, October 21, 1991, p. 13.

23 See K. Ohmae, "The Global Logic of Strategic Alliances," *Harvard Business Review*, March–April 1989, pp. 143–54; G. Hamel, Y. L. Doz, and C. K. Prahalad, "Collaborate with Your Competitors and Win!" *Harvard Business Review*, January–February 1989, pp. 133–39; and W. Burgers, C. W. L. Hill, and W. C. Kim, "Alliances in the Global Auto Industry," *Strategic Management Journal* 14 (1993), pp. 419–32.

24 "Asia Beckons," *The Economist*, May 30, 1992, pp. 63–64.

25 P. M. Reilly, "Sony's Digital Audio Format Pulls ahead of Philips's," *The Wall Street Journal*, August 6, 1993, p. B1.

26 R. B. Reich and E. D. Mankin, "Joint Ventures with Japan Give Away Our Future," *Harvard Business Review*, March–April 1986, pp. 78–90.

27 J. Bleeke and D. Ernst, "The Way to Win in Cross-Border Alliances," *Harvard Business Review*, November–December 1991, pp. 127–35.

28 D. Darlin, "Daewoo Will Pay GM $170 Million for Venture Stake," *The Wall Street Journal*, November 11, 1992, p. A6; and D. Darlin and J. B. White, "Failed Marriage," *The Wall Street Journal*, January 16, 1992, p. A1.

29 W. Roehl and J. F. Truitt, "Stormy Open Marriages Are Better," *Columbia Journal of World Business*, Summer 1987, pp. 87–95.

30 K. McQuade and B. Gomes-Casseres, "Xerox and Fuji-Xerox," **Harvard Business School Case #9-391-156**. 1994.

31 Hamel, Doz, and Prahalad, "Collaborate with Your Competitors."

32 B. Wysocki, "Cross-Border Alliances Become Favorite Way to Crack New Markets," *The Wall Street Journal*, March 4, 1990, p. A1.

33 Hamel, Doz, and Prahalad, "Collaborate with Your Competitors," p. 138.

34 *The Economist*, "Furnishing the World," November 19, 1994, pp. 79–80; and H. Carnegy, "Struggle to Save the Soul of IKEA," *Financial Times*, March 27, 1995, p. 12.

Chapter 11

1 S. N. Mehta, "Enterprise: Artais Finds that Smallness Isn't a Handicap in Global Market," *The Wall Street Journal*, June 23, 1994, p. B2.

2 Data from the consulting firm BDO Seidman; reported in S. N. Mehta. "Enterprise: Small Companies Look to Cultivate Foreign Business," *The Wall Street Journal*, July 7, 1994, p. B2.

3 W. J. Holstein, "Why Johann Can Export, but Johnny Can't," *Business Week*, November 4, 1991, pp. 64–65.

4 This section draws on two studies: C. W. L. Hill, P. Hwang, and W. C. Kim, "An Eclectic Theory of the Choice of International Entry Mode," *Strategic Management Journal* 11 (1990), pp. 117–28; and C. W. L. Hill and W. C. Kim, "Searching for a Dynamic Theory of the Multinational Enterprise: A Transaction Cost Model,"

Strategic Management Journal 9 (Special Issue on Strategy Content; 1988), pp. 93–104. See also E. Anderson and H. Gatignon, "Modes of Foreign Entry: A Transaction Cost Analysis and Propositions," *Journal of International Business Studies* 17 (1986), pp. 1–26; and F. R. Root, *Entry Strategies for International Markets* (Lexington, MA: D. C. Heath, 1980).

5 For a general discussion of licensing, see F. J. Contractor, "The Role of Licensing in International Strategy," *Columbia Journal of World Business*, Winter 1982, pp. 73–83.

6 O. E. Williamson, *The Economic Institutions of Capitalism* (New York: Free Press, 1985).

7 R. Howard, "The CEO as Organizational Architect," *Harvard Business Review*, September–October 1992, pp. 106–23; D. Kearns, "Leadership through Quality," *Academy of Management Executive* 4 (1990), pp. 86–89; K. McQuade and B. Gomes-Casseres, "Xerox and Fuji-Xerox," **Harvard Business School Case #9-391-156**; and E. Terazono and C. Lorenz, "An Angry Young Warrior," *Financial Times*, September 19, 1994, p. 11.

8 J. H. Dunning and M. McQueen, "The Eclectic Theory of International Production: A Case Study of the International Hotel Industry," *Managerial and Decision Economics* 2 (1981), pp. 197–210.

9 Andrew E. Serwer, "McDonald's Conquers the World," *Fortune*, October 17, 1994, pp. 103–16.

10 For an excellent review of the literature of joint ventures, see B. Kogut, "Joint Ventures: Theoretical and Empirical Perspectives," *Strategic Management Journal* 9 (1988), pp. 319–32.

11 D. G. Bradley, "Managing Against Expropriation," *Harvard Business Review*, July–August 1977, pp. 78–90.

12 Speech given by Tony Kobayashi at the University of Washington Business School, October 1992.

13 H. W. Lane and P. W. Beamish, "Cross-Cultural Cooperative Behavior in Joint Ventures in LDCs," *Management International Review* 30 (1990), pp. 87–102.

14 For a review of the kinds of problems encountered when making acquisitions, see Chapter 9 in C. W. L. Hill and G. R. Jones, *Strategic Management Theory* (Boston: Houghton-Mifflin, 1995).

15 This section draws on Hill, Hwang, and Kim, "Eclectic Theory of the Choice of International Entry Mode."

16 C. W. L. Hill, "Strategies for Exploiting Technological Innovations: When and When Not to License," *Organization Science* 3 (1992), pp. 428–41.

17 S. T. Cavusgil, "Global Dimensions of Marketing," in P. E. Murphy and B. M. Enis, *Marketing* (Glenview, IL: Scott, Foresman, 1985), pp. 577–99.

18 Mehta, "Enterprise: Small Companies Look to Cultivate Foreign Business."

19 W. Pavord and R. Bogart, "The Dynamics of the Decision to Export," *Akron Business and Economic Review*, 1975, pp. 6–11.

20 A. O. Ogbuehi and T. A. Longfellow, "Perceptions of U.S. Manufacturing Companies Concerning Exporting," *Journal of Small Business Management*, October 1994, pp. 37–59.

21 R. W. Haigh, "Thinking of Exporting?" *Columbia Journal of World Business*, 29 (December 1994), pp. 66–86.

22 F. Williams, "The Quest for More Efficient Commerce," *Financial Times*, October 13, 1994, p. 7.

23 L. W. Tuller, *Going Global* (Homewood, IL: Business One Irwin, 1991).

24 Haigh, "Thinking of Exporting?"

25 Case written by Mureen Kibelsted and Charles Hill from original research by Mureen Kibelsted.

Chapter 12

1 S. Tully, "Teens: The Most Global Market of All," *Fortune*, May 16, 1994, pp. 90–97; M. Robichaux, "Leave it to Beavis," *The Wall Street Journal*, February 8, 1995, p. A1;

A. Rawsthorn, "MTV Makes the Big Record Groups Dance to Its Tune," *Financial Times*, July 7, 1995, p. 17; and M. Cox, "Global Entertainment: We Are the World," *The Wall Street Journal*, March 26, 1993, p. 17.

2 See R. W. Ruekert and O. C. Walker, "Interactions between Marketing and R&D Departments in Implementing Different Business-Level Strategies," *Strategic Management Journal* 8 (1987), pp. 233–48, and K. B. Clark and S. C. Wheelwright, *Managing New Product and Process Development* (New York: Free Press, 1993).

3 T. Levitt, "The Globalization of Markets", *Harvard Business Review*, May–June 1983, pp. 92–102.

4 For example, see S. P. Douglas and Y. Wind, "The Myth of Globalization," *Columbia Journal of World Business*, Winter 1987, pp. 19–29; and C. A. Bartlett and S. Ghoshal, *Managing across Borders: The Transnational Solution* (Boston: Harvard Business School Press, 1989).

5 "Slow Food," *The Economist*, February 3, 1990, p. 64.

6 This approach was originally developed in K. Lancaster, "A New Approach to Demand Theory," *Journal of Political Economy* 74 (1965), pp. 132–57.

7 V. R. Alden, "Who Says You Can't Crack Japanese Markets?" *Harvard Business Review*, January–February 1987, pp. 52–56.

8 A. Rawthorn, "A Bumpy Ride over Europe's Traditions," *Financial Times*, October 31, 1988, p. 5.

9 "RCA's New Vista: The Bottom Line," *Business Week*, July 4, 1987, p. 44.

10 N. Gross and K. Rebello, "Apple? Japan Can't Say No," *Business Week*, June 29, 1992, pp. 32–33.

11 "After Early Stumbles P&G Is Making Inroads Overseas," *The Wall Street Journal*, February 6, 1989, p. B1.

12 "Advertising in a Single Market," *The Economist*, March 24, 1990, p. 64.

13 D. Waller. "Charged up over Competition Law," *Financial Times*, June 23, 1994, p. 14.

14 J. Lumbin, "Advertising: Tina Turner Helps Pepsi's Global Effort," *New York Times*, March 10, 1986, p. D13.

15 Kamran Kashani, "Beware the Pitfalls of Global Marketing," *Harvard Business Review*, September–October 1989, pp. 91–98.

16 These allegations were made on a PBS "Frontline" documentary telecast in the United States in May 1992.

17 "Printers Reflect Pattern of Trade Rows," *Financial Times*, December 20, 1988, p. 3.

18 J. F. Pickering, *Industrial Structure and Market Conduct*. (London: Martin Robertson, 1974).

19 V. Mallet, "Climbing the Slippery Slope," *Financial Times*, July 28, 1994, p. 7, and A. Bolger, "Growth by Successful Targeting," *Financial Times*, June 21, 1994, p. 27.

20 The phrase was first used by economist Joseph Schumpeter in *Capitalism, Socialism, and Democracy* (New York: Harper Brothers, 1942).

21 See D. C. Mowery and N. Rosenberg, *Technology and the Pursuit of Economic Growth* (Cambridge, UK: Cambridge University Press, 1989); and M. E. Porter, *The Competitive Advantage of Nations* (New York: The Free Press, 1990).

22 "Can America Compete?" *The Economist*, January 18, 1992, pp. 65–66.

23 C. Farrell, "Industrial Policy," *Business Week*, April 6, 1992, pp. 70–75.

24 "When the Corporate Lab Goes to Japan," *New York Times*, April 28, 1991, sec. 3, p. 1.

25 D. Shapley, "Globalization Prompts Exodus," *Financial Times*, March 17, 1994, p. 10.

26 E. Mansfield, "How Economists See R&D," *Harvard Business Review*, November–December 1981, pp. 98–106.

27 A. L. Page, "New Product Development Practices Survey: Performance and Best Practices," PDMA 15th Annual International Conference, Boston, MA, October 16, 1991.

28 Clark and Wheelwright, *Managing New Product and Process Development*.

29 Shapley, "Globalization Prompts Exodus."

30 Guy de Jonquieres and C. Bobinski, "Wash and Get into a Lather in Poland," *Financial Times*, May 28, 1992, p. 2; "Perestroika in Soapland," *The Economist*, June 10, 1989, pp. 69–71; "After Early Stumbles P&G Is Making Inroads Overseas," *The Wall Street Journal*, February 6, 1989, p. B1; and Bartlett and Ghoshal, *Managing across Borders*.

Chapter 13

1 P. Buxbaum, "Timberland's New Spin on Global Logistics," *Distribution*, May 1994, pp. 33–36; A. E. Serwer, "Will Timberland Grow Up?" *Fortune*, May 29, 1995, p. 24; and M. Tedeschi, "Timberland Vows to Get on the Ball," *Footwear News*, May 22, 1995, p. 2.

2 "Nike to Make Shoes in Mexico," *The Wall Street Journal*, January 6, 1995, p. A6.

3 B. C. Arntzen, G. G. Brown, T. P. Harrison, and L. L. Trafton, "Global Supply Chain Management at Digital Equipment Corporation," *Interfaces* 25 (1995), pp. 69–93.

4 D. A. Garvin, "What Does Product Quality Really Mean," *Sloan Management Review* 26 (Fall 1984), pp. 25–44.

5 For general background information, see "How to Build Quality," *The Economist*, September 23, 1989, pp. 91–92; A. Gabor, *The Man Who Discovered Quality* (New York: Penguin, 1990); and P. B. Crosby, *Quality is Free* (New York: Mentor, 1980).

6 M. Saunders, "U.S. Firms Doing Business in Europe Have Options in Registering for ISO 9000 Quality Standards," *Business America*, June 14, 1993, p. 7.

7 G. Stalk and T. M. Hout, "Competing Against Time" (New York: Free Press, 1990).

8 M. A. Cohen and H. L. Lee, "Resource Deployment Analysis of Global Manufacturing and Distrubution Networks," *Journal of Manufacturing and Operations Management* 2 (1989), pp. 81–104.

9 For a review of the technical arguments, see D. A. Hay and D. J. Morris, *Industrial Economics: Theory and Evidence* (Oxford: Oxford University Press, 1979). See also C. W. L. Hill and G. R. Jones, *Strategic Management: An Integrated Approach* (Boston: Houghton Mifflin, 1995).

10 See P. Nemetz and L. Fry, "Flexible Manufacturing Organizations: Implications for Strategy Formulation," *Academy of Management Review* 13 (1988), pp. 627–38; N. Greenwood, *Implementing Flexible Manufacturing Systems* (New York: Halstead Press, 1986); and J. P. Womack, D. T. Jones, and D. Roos, *The Machine That Changed the World* (New York: Rawson Associates, 1990).

11 Womack, Jones, and Roos, *The Machine That Changed the World*.

12 M. A. Cusumano, *The Japanese Automobile Industry* (Cambridge, MA: Harvard University Press, 1989); Taiichi Ohno, *Toyota Production System* (Cambridge, MA: Productivity Press, 1987); and Womack, Jones, and Roos, *The Machine That Changed the World*.

13 For a review of the evidence, see O. E. Williamson, *The Economic Institutions of Capitalism* (New York: The Free Press, 1985).

14 A. D. Chandler, *The Visible Hand* (Cambridge, MA: Harvard University Press, 1977).

15 For a review of these arguments, see C. W. L. Hill and R. E. Hoskisson, "Strategy and Structure in the Multiproduct Firm," *Academy of Management Review* 12 (1987), pp. 331–41.

16 C. W. L. Hill, "Cooperation, Opportunism, and the Invisible Hand," *Academy of Management Review* 15 (1990), pp. 500–13.

17 See R. Narasimhan and J. R. Carter, "Organization, Communication and Coordination of International Sourcing," *International Marketing Review* 7 (1990), pp. 6–20, and B. C. Arntzen, G. G. Brown, T. P. Harrison, and L. L. Trafton, "Global Supply Chain Management at Digital Equipment Corporation," *Interfaces* 25 (1995), pp. 69–93.

18 H. F. Busch, "Integrated Materials Management," *IJPD & MM* 18 (1990), pp. 28–39.

19 P. Bradley. "Global Sourcing Takes Split Second Timing," *Purchasing*, July 20, 1989, pp 52–58, and S. Greenblat, "Continuous Improvement in Supply Chain Management," *Chief Executive* 86 (June 1993), pp. 40–44.

20 Arntzen, Brown, Harrison, and Trafton, "Global Supply Chain Management at Digital Equipment Corporation."

Chapter 14

1 D. A. Amfuso, "HR Unites the World of Coca-Cola," *Personnel Journal*, November 1994, pp. 112–20, and S. Foley, "Internationalizing the Cola Wars," *Harvard Business School Case* #9-794-146.

2 P. J. Dowling and R. S. Schuler, *International Dimensions of Human Resource Management* (Boston: PSW-Kent, 1990).

3 J. Millman, M. A. von Glinow, and M. Nathan, "Organizational Life Cycles and Strategic International Human Resource Management in Multinational Companies," *Academy of Management Review* 16 (1991), pp. 318–39.

4 E. H. Schein, *Organizational Culture and Leadership* (San Francisco: Jossey-Bass, 1985).

5 H. V. Perlmutter, "The Tortuous Evolution of the Multinational Corporation," *Columbia Journal of World Business* 4 (1969), pp. 9–18; D. A. Heenan and H. V. Perlmutter, *Multinational Organizational Development* (Reading, MA: Addison-Wesley, 1979); and D. A. Ondrack, "International Human Resources Management in European and North American Firms," *International Studies of Management and Organization* 15 (1985), pp. 6–32.

6 S. Beechler and J. Z. Yang, "The Transfer of Japanese Style Management to American Subsidiaries," *Journal of International Business Studies* 25 (1994), pp. 467–91.

7 C. A. Bartlett, and S. Ghoshal, *Managing Across Borders: The Transnational Solution* (Boston: Harvard Business School Press, 1989).

8 S. J. Kobrin, "Geocentric Mind-set and Multinational Strategy," *Journal of International Business Studies* 25 (1994), pp. 493–511.

9 P. M. Rosenzweig and N. Nohria, "Influences on Human Resource Management Practices in Multinational Corporations," *Journal of International Business Studies* 25 (1994), pp. 229–51.

10 Kobrin, "Geocentric Mind-set and Multinational Strategy."

11 J. S. Black, M. Mendenhall, and G. Oddou, "Towards a Comprehensive Model of International Adjustment," *Academy of Management Review* 16 (1991), pp. 291–317.

12 M. G. Harvey, "The Multinational Corporation's Expatriate Problem: An Application of Murphy's Law," *Business Horizons* 26 (1983), pp. 71–78.

13 Black, Mendenhall, and Oddou, "Towards a Comprehensive Model of International Adjustment."

14 R. L. Tung, "Selection and Training Procedures of U.S., European, and Japanese Multinationals," *California Management Review* 25 (1982), pp. 57–71.

15 C. M. Salomon, "Success Abroad Depends upon More Than Job Skills," *Personnel Journal*, April 1994, pp. 51–58.

16 Ibid.

17 M. Mendenhall and G. Oddou, "The Dimensions of Expatriate Acculturation: A Review," *Academy of Management Review* 10 (1985), pp. 39–47.

18 I. Torbiorin, *Living Abroad: Personal Adjustment and Personnel Policy in the Overseas Setting* (New York: John Wiley, 1982).

19 R. L. Tung, "Selection and Training of Personnel for Overseas Assignments," *Columbia Journal of World Business* 16 (1981), pp. 68–78.

20 Salomon, "Success Abroad Depends upon More Than Job Skills."

21 S. Ronen, "Training and International Assignee," in *Training and Career Develop-*

ment, ed. I. Goldstein (San Francisco: Jossey-Bass, 1985), and Tung, "Selection and Training of Personnel for Overseas Assignments."

22 Salomon, "Success Abroad Depends upon More Than Job Skills."

23 Dowling and Schuler, *International Dimensions of Human Resource Management*.

24 Ibid.

25 G. Baliga and J. C. Baker, "Multinational Corporate Policies for Expatriate Managers: Selection, Training, and Evaluation," *Advanced Management Journal*, Autumn 1985, pp. 31–38.

26 C. Rapoport, "A Tough Swede Invades the U.S.," *Fortune*, June 20, 1992, pp. 67–70.

27 J. C. Baker, "Foreign Language and Departure Training in U.S. Multinational Firms," *Personnel Administrator*, July 1984, pp. 68–70.

28 J. S. Black and M. E. Mendenhall, *Global Assignments: Successfully Expatriating and Repatriating International Managers* (San Francisco: Jossey-Bass, 1992).

29 Ibid.

30 Figures from Global Reallocation Trend Survey undertaken by the National Foreign Trade Council. Cited in Salomon, "Success Abroad Depends upon More Than Job Skills."

31 C. M. Salomon, "Repatriation: Up, Down, or Out?" *Personnel Journal*, January 1995, pp. 28–34.

32 S. C. Schneider, "National v. Corporate Culture: Implications for Human Resource Management," *Human Resource Management* 27 (Summer 1988), pp. 231–46.

33 Bartlett and Ghoshal, *Managing across Borders*.

34 G. Oddou and M. Mendenhall, "Expatriate Performance Appraisal: Problems and Solutions," in *International Human Resource Management*, ed. Mendenhall and Oddou (Boston: PWS-Kent, 1991), Dowling and Schuler, *International Dimensions*; and R. S. Schuler and G. W. Florkowski, "International Human Resource Management," in *Handbook for International Management Research*, ed. B. J. Punnett and O. Shenkar (Oxford: Blackwell, 1996).

35 Oddou and Mendenhall, "Expatriate Performance Appraisal."

36 "Expatriates Often See Little Benefit to Careers in Foreign Stints, Indifference at Home," *The Wall Street Journal*, December 11, 1989, p. B1

37 Oddou and Mendenhall, "Expatriate Performance Appraisal," and Schuler and Florkowski, "International Human Resource Management."

38 Data from Towers Perrin. Cited in J. Flynn, "Continental Divide over Executive Pay," *Business Week*, July 3, 1995, pp. 40–41.

39 A. Bennett, "Executive Pay: What's an Expatriate?" *The Wall Street Journal*, April 21, 1994, p. A5, and J. Flynn, "Continental Divide over Executive Pay," *Business Week*, July 3, 1995, pp. 40–41.

40 C. Reynolds, "Compensation of Overseas Personnel," in *Handbook of Human Resource Administration*, ed. J. J. Famularo (New York: McGraw-Hill, 1986).

41 M. Helms, "International Executive Compensation Practices," in *International Human Resource Management*, ed. M. Mendenhall and G. Oddou (Boston: PWS-Kent, 1991).

42 J. S. Lublin, "Managing Globally: Younger Managers Learn Global Skills," *The Wall Street Journal*, March 31, 1992, p. B1; B. Hagerty, "Companies in Europe Seeking Executives Who Can Cross Borders in a Single Bound," *The Wall Street Journal*, January 25, 1991, p. B1; and C. M. Salomon, "Global Operations Demand that HR Rethink Diversity," *Personnel Journal*, 73, 1994, pp. 40–50.

Glossary

absolute advantage Situation in which one country is more efficient at producing a product than any other country.

administrative trade policies Bureaucratic rules that are designed to make it difficult for imports to enter a country.

ad valorem tariffs Taxes levied as a proportion of the value of the imported good.

arbitrage Process of buying a currency low and selling it high.

balance-of-payments account Record of a country's payments to and receipts from other countries.

capital account Record of transactions involving the purchase and sale of assets.

caste system Closed system of stratification in which social position is determined by the family into which a person is born, and change in that position is usually not possible during an individual's lifetime.

civil law system Legal system based on a detailed set of laws, organized into codes, that is used in more than 80 countries, including Germany, France, Japan, and Russia.

class consciousness Condition where people perceive themselves in terms of their class background, and this shapes their relationships with members of other classes.

Class system Form of open social stratification in which the position a person has by birth can be changed through his or her achievements or luck.

collectivism Political system that stresses the primacy of collective goals over individual goals.

command economy Economic system in which the goods and services produced, the quantity in which they are produced, and the prices at which they are sold are all planned by the government.

common law system Legal system based on tradition, precedent, and custom that evolved in England over hundreds of years and is now found in Britain's former colonies, including the United States.

Communists Followers of socialist ideology who believe that socialism can be achieved only through violent revolution and totalitarian dictatorship.

communist totalitarianism Form of totalitarianism that advocates achieving socialism through totalitarian dictatorship.

comparative advantage Situation in which a country specializes in producing the goods it produces most efficiently and buys the product it produces less efficiently from other countries, even if it could produce the goods more efficiently than that country itself.

copyrights Exclusive legal rights of authors, composers, playwrights, artists, and publishers to publish and dispose of their work as they see fit.

core competence Skills within the firm that competitors cannot easily match or imitate.

countertrade Barterlike agreements by which goods and services can be traded for other goods and services; used in international trade when a country's currency is nonconvertible.

cross-licensing agreement Arrangement whereby a company grants the rights to intangible property to another firm for a specified time period in exchange for royalties and a license from the foreign partner for some of its technological know-how.

culture System of values and norms that are shared among a group of people and that when taken together constitute a design for living.

current account Record of a country's export and import of goods and services.

491

currency speculation Short-term movement of funds from one currency to another in the hopes of profiting from shifts in exchange rates.

democracy Political system in which government is by the people, exercised either directly or through elected representatives.

eclectic paradigm Theory of foreign direct investment that combines two other perspectives into a single holistic explanation of FDI.

economies of scale Reduction in unit cost achieved by producing a large volume of a product.

efficient market Market that has no impediments to the free flow of goods and services.

ethnocentric Type of staffing policy in which all key management positions are filled by citizens from the parent firm's home country.

ethnocentric behavior Acting on the belief in the superiority of one's own ethnic group or culture.

exchange rate Rate at which one currency is converted into another.

expatriate failure Premature return of an expatriate manager to his or her home country.

expatriate manager Citizen of one country who is working abroad in one of the firm's subsidiaries.

experience curve Systematic reductions in production costs that occur over the life of a product.

exporting Producing goods at home and shipping them to the receiving country for sale.

export management company Export specialist that acts as the export marketing department or international department for client firms.

externally convertible Currency able to be used by nonresidents only to purchase foreign currency in unlimited amounts.

externalities Knowledge spillovers that occur when companies in the same industry locate in the same area.

first-mover advantages Economic and strategic advantages that accrue to early entrants into an industry.

fixed exchange rate Value of most currencies in terms of U.S. dollars was fixed for long periods and allowed to change only under a specific set of circumstances.

Flow of foreign direct investment The amount of money invested across national borders.

folkways Routine conventions of everyday life.

Foreign Corrupt Practices Act U.S. law enacted in 1977 that prohibits U.S. companies from making "corrupt" payments to foreign officials for the purpose of obtaining or retaining business.

Foreign direct investment The investing of resources in business activities outside a firm's home country.

foreign exchange market Market for converting the currency of one country into that of another country.

foreign exchange risk Adverse consequences of unpredictable changes in exchange rates.

forward exchange Two parties agree to exchange currency and execute the deal at some specific date in the future.

forward exchange rates Rates for currency exchange quoted for 30, 90, or 180 days into the future.

franchising Specialized form of licensing in which the franchisor sells intangible property to the franchisee and insists that the franchisee agree to follow strict rules in operating the business.

freely convertible Currency able to be used by both residents and nonresidents to purchase foreign currency in unlimited amounts.

free trade Situation where a government does not attempt to influence through quotas or duties what its citizens can buy from another country or what they can produce and sell to another country.

fundamental analysis Draws on economic theory to construct sophisticated econometric models for predicting exchange rate movements.

General Agreement on Tariffs and Trade Treaty designed to remove barriers to the free flow of goods, services, and capital between nations; often referred to as GATT.

geocentric Type of staffing policy in which the best people, regardless of nationality, are sought for key jobs throughout the company.

Globalization The trend toward a more integrated global economic system.

Globalization of markets The merging of historically distinct and separate national markets into one huge global marketplace.

Globalization of production The sourcing of goods and services from different locations around the globe to take advantage of national differences in the cost and quality of factors of production.

global learning Flow of skills and product offerings from home firm to foreign subsidiary and from foreign subsidiary to home firm and from foreign subsidiary to foreign subsidiary.

global web Dispersal of stages of a firm's value chain to those locations around the globe where the value added is maximized or where the costs of value creation are minimized.

gold standard Practice of pegging currencies to gold and guaranteeing convertibility.

group Association of two or more individuals who have a shared sense of identity and who interact with each other in structured ways on the basis of a common set of expectations about each other's behavior.

hedge fund Investment fund that buys financial assets and also sells them short.

home country Country that is the source of foreign direct investment.

host country Country that is on the receiving end of foreign direct investment.

Human Development Index United Nations-developed index based on life expectancy, literacy rates, and whether average incomes are sufficient to meet the basic needs of life in a country.

human resource management Activities an organization carries out to use its human resource effectively.

import quota Direct restrictions on the quantity of some good that may be imported into a country.

individualism Political philosophy that an individual should have freedom over his or her economic and political pursuits.

inefficient market Market in which prices do not reflect all available information.

inflows of foreign direct investment Flow of FDI into a country.

innovation Process through which people create new products, new processes, new organizations, new management practices, and new strategies.

intellectual property Property, such as computer software, screenplays, musical scores, or chemical formulas for new drugs, that is the product of intellectual activity.

internalization theory Explains why firms prefer foreign direct investment over licensing when entering foreign markets.

International business Any business that engages in international trade or investment.

International Fisher Effect For any two countries, the spot exchange rate should change in an equal amount but in the opposite direction to the difference in the nominal interest rates between the two countries.

International trade The exporting of goods or services to consumers in another country.

ISO 9000 Standard designed to assure the quality of products and processes.

joint venture Establishment of a firm that is jointly owned by two or more otherwise independent firms.

late-mover disadvantages Handicap suffered by late entrants into a business market.

law of one price Identical products sold in different countries must sell for the same price when their price is expressed in the same currency in competitive markets free of transportation costs and barriers to trade.

lean production Manufacturing technologies designed to reduce setup times, increase use of individual machines through better scheduling, and improve quality control at all stages of manufacturing.

learning effects Cost savings that come from learning by doing.

legal risk Likelihood that a trading partner will opportunistically break a contract or expropriate property rights.

legal system The rules, or laws, that regulate behavior and the processes by which the laws of a country are enforced and through which redress of grievances is obtained.

licensing Granting a foreign entity the right to produce and sell a firm's product in return for a royalty fee on every unit sold.

licensing agreement Arrangement whereby a licensor grants the rights to intangible property to the licensee for a specified time period in exchange for royalties.

local content requirement Government order that some specific fraction of a good be produced domestically.

location economies Economies that arise from performing a value creation activity in the optimal location for that activity.

location-specific advantages Advantages that arise from using resource endowments or assets that are tied to a particular location and that a firm finds valuable to combine with its own unique assets.

managed float system Value of some currencies is allowed to float freely, but the majority are either managed in some way by government intervention or pegged to another currency.

market economy Economic system in which the interaction of supply and demand determines the quantity in which goods and services are produced.

materials management Activity that controls the transmission of physical materials through the value chain, from procurement through production and into distribution.

mercantilism Theory of international trade that believes it is in a country's best interests to export more than it imports.

Moore's Law Prediction that the power of microprocessor technology doubles and its cost of production falls in half every 18 months.

mores Norms that are seen as central to the functioning of a society and to its social life.

Multinational enterprise Any business that has productive activities in two or more countries.

nonconvertible Currency that cannot be converted into a foreign currency.

norms Social rules and guidelines that prescribe appropriate behavior in particular situations.

oligopoly Industry composed of a limited number of large firms.

operations Activities involved in the procurement of inputs into the production process, the creation of a product, and its delivery to customers.

outflows of foreign direct investment Flows of FDI out of a country.

Paris Convention for the Protection of Industrial Property International agreement signed by 96 countries to protect intellectual property rights.

patent Document giving the inventor of a new product or process exclusive rights to the manufacture, use, or sale of that invention.

political economy Political, economic, and legal systems of a country.

political system System of government in a nation.

polycentric Type of staffing policy in which citizens of the host country are recruited to manage subsidiaries while key management positions at headquarters are filled by citizens from the parent firm's home country.

positive-sum game Situation in which all countries can benefit, even if some benefit more than others.

privatization Process of selling state-owned enterprises to private investors.

privatized Sold to private investors.

production Activities involved in creating a product.

property rights The bundle of legal rights addressing the use to which a resource is put and the use made of any income that may be derived from that resource.

regional economic integration Agreement between countries in a geographic region to reduce tariff and nontariff barriers to the free flow of goods, services, and factors of production between each other.

relatively efficient market Market in which few impediments to international trade and investment exist.

religion System of shared beliefs and rituals that are concerned with the realm of the sacred.

representative democracy Political system in which citizens periodically elect individuals to represent them.

right-wing totalitarianism Form of totalitarianism in which individual economic freedom is allowed but individual political freedom is restricted in the belief that it could lead to communism.

short selling Speculating that the value of a financial asset will decline and profiting from that decline.

Social Democrats Followers of socialist ideology who commit themselves to achieving socialism through democratic means.

social mobility Extent to which individuals can move out of the strata into which they are born.

social strata Social categories in a society defined on the basis of characteristics such as family background, occupation, and income.

society Group of people who share a common set of values and norms.

sourcing decisions Decisions about whether a firm should make or buy the component parts that go into the final product.

specialized assets Equipment that can be used for only one purpose.

specific tariffs Taxes levied as a fixed charge for each unit of a good imported.

spot exchange rate Rate at which a foreign exchange dealer converts one currency into another currency on a particular day.

staffing policy Policy concerned with the selection of employees for particular jobs; three types exist in international business.

Stock of foreign direct investment The total cumulative value of foreign investments in a country.

strategic alliances Cooperative agreements between potential or actual competitors.

strategy Actions that managers take to attain the firm's goals.

subsidy Government payment to a domestic producer.

tariff Tax levied on imports.

technical analysis Predicts exchange rate movements by using price and volume data to determine past trends, which are expected to continue into the future.

theocratic totalitarianism Form of totalitarianism in which political power is monopolized by a party, group, or individual that governs according to religious principles.

totalitarianism Form of government in which one person or political party exercises absolute control over all spheres of human life and in which opposing political parties are prohibited.

total quality management Management technique that focuses on the need to improve the quality of a company's products and services.

trade creation Occurs when high-cost domestic producers are replaced by low-cost producers within the free trade area.

trade diversion Occurs when lower-cost external suppliers are replaced by higher-cost suppliers within the free trade area.

trademarks Designs and names, often officially registered, by which merchants or manufacturers designate and differentiate their products.

transnational strategy Business strategy that seeks experience-based cost economies and location economies, transfers distinctive competencies within the firm, and pays attention to pressures for local responsiveness.

Tribal totalitarianism Form of totalitarianism found mainly in Africa in which a political party that represents the interests of a particular tribe monopolizes power.

turnkey project Contractor handles every detail of the project for a foreign client, including the training of operating personnel, and then hands the foreign client the key to a plant that is ready for operation.

universal needs Needs that are the same all over the world.

values Abstract ideas about what a group believes to be good, right, and desirable.

voluntary export restraint Quota on trade imposed by the exporting country, typically at the request of the importing country.

wholly owned subsidiary Company in which parent firm owns 100 percent of the stock.

World Trade Organization Agency established at the Uruguay Round in 1993 to police the international trading system.

zero-sum game Situation in which a gain by one country results in a loss by another.

Index

497